MW01010891

The New York Times

THE TIMES OF THE EIGHTIES

The New York Times

THE TIMES OF THE EIGHTIES

The Culture, Politics and Personalities that Shaped the Decade

Edited by William Grimes

Black Dog & Leventhal Publishers
New York

Published by
Black Dog & Leventhal Publishers, Inc.
151 West 19th Street
New York, NY 10011

Distributed by
Workman Publishing Company
225 Varick Street
New York, NY 10014

Manufactured in Singapore

Cover design by Evan Gaffney Design

Interior design by Pauline Neuwirth, Neuwirth & Associates, Inc.

Cover and interior images courtesy of Getty Images.

ISBN-13: 978-1-57912-933-0

h g f e d c b a

Library of Congress Cataloging-in-Publication Data on file.

Contents

Introduction

Every decade seems momentous to the people who are living through it. In that sense, all decades are created equal, but some are more equal than others. The 1980's can rightly claim to be one of the most equal of the 20th century.

There were no world wars, the defining cataclysms of the teens and the 40's. But the signal events of the 1980's transformed lives across the globe and continue to reverberate today.

The cold war ended as the Soviet Empire fell apart. The Internet came into being. AIDS, an utterly mysterious disease afflicting mostly young gay men, ravaged an entire generation and created a powerful new movement to advance the political rights of gay people. Cable television rewrote the script for news and entertainment. The baby boomers, dubbed the Me Generation by Tom Wolfe in the 1970's, morphed into the acquisitive, high-achieving tribe known as yuppies.

At the sharper edge of this movement, the predatory capitalists Wolfe satirized as "masters of the universe" in his 1987 novel "The Bonfire of the Vanities" helped jump-start the decade's wild financial ride. One after another, giant companies swallowed each other whole in a wave of leveraged buyouts and acquisitions. This was the era of the junk bobd and Gordon Gekko, the sharklike trader at the center of the film "Wall Street." His mantra, "greed is good," seemed to encapsulate the spirit of the times.

In an essay for The New York Times published on New Year's Day 1987, the novelist James Michener surveyed the decade thus far and pronounced judgment: "It begins to look as if the 1980's will have to be remembered as The Ugly Decade, because so many distasteful things have surfaced in the first six years and may continue into the last four."

Michener cited the growing gap between rich and poor in the United States, mounting government deficits, the deification of wealth and the worship of financial freebooters like Ivan F. Boesky. He noted with alarm the growing political influence of religious conservatism and a new spirit of adventurism in American foreign policy typified by the covert sale of arms to Iran to fund the right-wing "contras" in Nicaragua. The list included terrorism and the lethal advance of AIDS.

He might have written a different essay three years later. He most certainly would have marveled at the events of the previous two months.

For two generations national interests, domestic agendas and private fears had been shaped by the standoff between two glowering nuclear powers, each with the ability to annihilate the other and take a good portion of the globe with it.

The postwar division seemed permanent, with Eastern Europe in thrall to the Soviet Union and the West bound, often nervously, to the United States. The election of Ronald Reagan, a strident anti-Communist, as president of the United States seemed to guarantee an escalation of tensions, especially after he unveiled plans for the antimissile defense system known as "Star Wars" and, standing near the Berlin Wall in 1987, provocatively challenged the new Soviet premier, Mikhail Gorbachev, to "tear down this wall."

And then the unthinkable happened. On Nov. 9, 1989, astonished television viewers watched as thousand of jubilant East Germans poured through a gap in the Berlin Wall. Then, one by one, the regimes fell. Formerly omnipotent party bosses slunk away, rejected by the people they once lorded over. In Romania, Nicolae Ceausescu and his wife, Elena, were hunted down and executed on Christmas Day.

The opening of the Berlin Wall and the cascading events in Eastern Europe made for an unforgettable moment, the cold war's answer to Armistice Day in 1918 or V-E Day in 1945.

At the same time, an entirely different sort of revolution, quiet but equally powerful, was gathering strength. Largely unobserved, communications technologies were making advances unseen since the invention of the telegraph, the telephone and the radio.

In the early 1980's, the groundwork was being laid for a system that made it possible for users all over the world to communicate via personal computer. The terms "Internet" and "World Wide Web" would not appear until late in the decade, but private companies and consumers were already reaping the benefits of the giant government computer networks created in the United States and Europe for defense and scientific research. A new vocabulary entered the lexicon. Some were old words with new applications, like mouse, crash and virus. Others were strange hybrids, like e-mail and emoticon. All became common currency, reflecting a radical change in the way that offices were run and ordinary people exchanged information.

Cable television ended the three-network cartel that had defined television viewing in the United States. When Walter Cronkite, the longtime anchorman of "The CBS Evening News," announced his retirement in 1981, newspaper stories declared the end of an era. And so it was.

By the end of the decade, 57 percent of Americans had cable television, giving them access to hundreds of channels and a bewildering variety of programs. The news, thanks to fledgling channels like CNN, was delivered continuously, rather than in carefully edited 30-minute packages at 7 p.m. No longer did anchors like Cronkite and his NBC counterparts, David Brinkley and Chet Huntley, wield the power and influence of national political leaders. While reporting on these changes, few newspapers had any inkling that the combination of cable television and the Internet would revolutionize their own industry, forcing print journalism onto a bumpy road of perpetual crisis.

Musical styles changed, as they always do. But in the 1980's, the format did too. The compact disc, little more than a curiosity at the beginning of the decade, became universal, replacing the vinyl record. At the same time, pop music fans began watching their favorite songs as well as listening to them, thanks to a new television channel, MTV, which broadcast the hybrid form of entertainment called music videos round the clock.

It was a decade of heroes and villains. It belonged equally to Michael Milken, the disgraced junk-bond king, and Sally Ride, the first woman to go into space. Sometimes hero and villain were the same person: Pete Rose broke Ty Cobb's record for most lifetime hits but was later banned for life from major league baseball for betting on baseball games while he was a player and a manager with the Cincinnati Reds.

It was a decade of triumphs and tragedies. John Lennon was killed by a crazed young fan. Indira Gandhi and Anwar Sadat were assassinated. Ronald Reagan and Pope John Paul II were shot. A faction of the PLO hijacked a cruise ship, the Achille Lauro, and pushed a wheelchair-bound Jewish man overboard. Libyan operatives put a bomb aboard a Pan Am jet, causing it to crash into the little Scottish town of Lockerbie, killing 270 people. For pessimists, the decade offered abundant raw material.

But optimists could feast. The Voyager spacecrafts reached Saturn. Sandra Day O'Connor became the first woman to serve on the Supreme Court, and Geraldine Ferraro became the first woman to be selected as the vice-presidential nominee of a major party. The cause of AIDS was discovered, and the first drugs to treat the disease were developed.

No one experienced the 1980's as a ceaseless pageant of world-changing events, of course. NFL football carried on even as the Berlin Wall came down. And small events often linger longest in the memory. Under hypnosis, anyone who lived through the 1980's would speak not only of historic changes but also of "Dynasty" and "The Cosby Show," of Michael Jackson's "Thriller," of the Tylenol scare and Cabbage Patch dolls.

And who could forget Doug Flutie's Hail Mary pass, the one that lifted Boston College over the University of Miami, the defending national champions, in 1984? It was a once-in-a-lifetime moment, just as exciting as the return of Halley's Comet after 76 years. That too, was the 1980's. A memorable decade, by any reckoning.

National

The decade belonged to Ronald Reagan who took office in January 1981 and over the next eight years, to the shock and dismay of liberals, put an indelible stamp on American politics.

President Ronald Reagan at his desk in the Oval Office of the White House.

In an early signal of the Reagan approach, he responded to a strike by federal air traffic controllers by firing the workers and breaking their union. Pursuing an agenda of lower taxes, more spending on defense and less spending on social programs, he preached an antigovernment, pro-business economic gospel that came to be known as Reaganomics. Free enterprise was the order of the day, and "supply-side economics," "trickle-down theory" and "the Laffer curve" entered the American lexicon.

A centerpiece of Reaganomics was the Tax Reform Act of 1986. Reagan, a lifelong enemy of federal taxation, signed a bill that reduced the number of tax brackets, lowered the rates on top earners, closed loopholes and raised the deductions on home mortgages in a effort to promote home ownership. He also stood behind Paul Volcker, the chairman of the Federal Reserve, as he imposed stringent monetary policies to wring inflation out of the economy, even when the country plunged into recession in 1982.

Reagan's affable manner disarmed critics and took the edge off his more radical policies. When a deranged gunman shot him in 1981, his political opponents had no choice but to go easy on him, and his nonchalant response to the attack—"I should have ducked," he told his wife when she visited him in the hospital—further endeared him to the public.

With interest rates and unemployment falling, inflation in check and the economy growing, Reagan declared that it was "morning again in America" and went on to defeat Walter Mondale by a wide margin in the 1984 election.

President Reagan applauded by Rep. Jack Kemp, aides James Baker and Donald Regan, Sen. Bob Dole, and Rep. Daniel Rostenkowski during the 1986 Tax Reform Bill signing ceremony at the White House.

President Ronald Reagan addresses supporters a few days before the 1984 presidential election.

Geraldine Ferraro and Walter Mondale on the campaign trail in 1984.

The push for social tolerance and civil rights gained ground. Although the Equal Rights Amendment went down to defeat, dealing a blow to feminist aspirations, the Supreme Court welcomed its first female justice, Sandra Day O'Connor, and Geraldine Ferraro became the first female vice-presidential candidate on a major party's ticket. The Rev. Dr. Martin Luther King Jr.'s birthday was recognized as a federal holiday. The spread of AIDS stirred gay Americans to take political action, and groups like Act Up were formed to put pressure on elected officials. Just as important, writers and playwrights brought the tragedy of AIDS to the stage and screen, and expanded the boundaries of acceptance for a marginalized group.

The natural world served up spectacular disasters that killed dozens of Americans. The decade was bookended by the Mount St. Helens eruption and the Loma Prieta earthquake, which struck the San Francisco Bay area on the night the San Francisco Giants were getting ready to play the Oakland A's at

The crowds in Candlestick Park after the 1989 earthquake hit during game three of the World Series.

Candlestick Park. It was the first earthquake whose tremors were captured live on national television.

Technology transformed the workplace and leisure time, allowing the industry to deliver nonstop diversion. Americans enthusiastically explored an ever-expanding universe of entertainment choices: multichannel cable television, video games, portable cassette players, chat lines, online virtual communities. Suddenly the world was a much smaller but much more interesting place.

FEBRUARY 3, 1980

ABSCAM: High Officials Are Termed Subjects of a Bribery Investigation by the F.B.I.

Leslie Maitland

High public officials, including a United States Senator and seven Representatives, have been subjects of a two-year undercover operation in which agents posed as businessmen and Arab sheiks willing to pay bribes, according to law-enforcement authorities.

In the course of the operation, in which most meetings between undercover agents and public officials were surreptitiously videotaped and recorded, authorities said the agents paid out hundreds of thousands of dollars in cash to the officials. In exchange, the officials reportedly agreed to help the sheiks and their financial ventures.

The public officials include Senator Harrison A. Williams of New Jersey, Representative John M. Murphy of Staten Island, Representative Frank Thompson Jr. of Trenton, Representatives Michael O. Myers and Raymond F. Lederer of Philadelphia, and Representative John W. Jenrette Jr. of South Carolina.

The operation began in February 1978 with information from a man convicted of fraud who introduced agents to public officials he said he knew to be corrupt. The agents, claiming to be a wealthy Arab sheik and in some instances posing as Arab sheiks, met with officials throughout 1979. It was during those meetings that undercover agents pretending to work for the sheik's business, called Abdul Enterprises, Ltd., paid hundreds of dollars to the officials.

Law enforcement officials said the investigation was the sweeping inquiry into suspected political corruption by the F.B.I. in at least 25 years. Code name Abscam—short for "Arab Scam"—it was described as unusual in its use of undercover agents to attempt to identify corrupt officials. ■

MAY 18, 1980

AT LEAST 8 DEAD AS PEAK ERUPTS; WORST BLAST YET

MOUNT ST. HELENS THROWS MUD AND COLUMN OF ASH

Mount St. Helens on May 22, 1980, four days after an earthquake caused a landslide on Mount St. Helens' north face triggering an eruption that killed 57 people, wiped out river valleys and destroyed enough trees to build 300,000 homes.

Wallace Turner

VANCOUVER, Wash., May 18 — Mount St. Helens exploded at 8:39 A.M. today with a thud felt 100 miles away and with a drifting column of steam and pumice that turned day into night. At least eight people lost their lives fleeing flood waters, fires and mudslides that hit the Toutle River valley shortly after the volcano's eruption.

David Hubert, a spokesman for the Washington Department of Emergency Services, said that police officers working from helicopters had found some of the dead. "We have many overturned vehicles in the Toutle River valley," he said, "and our communication with the helicopters is so fragile that all I can tell you is that we have found five bodies." Two of them, found at a Weyerhaeuser Company logging camp near the mountain were flown to Kelso, Wash., by a helicopter of the Air Force reserve.

Minutes before the top of the 9,677-foot peak exploded with a shower of ash, two earthquakes registering about 5.0 on the Richter scale were recorded. Their impact was felt as far away as Port Angeles at the entrance of Puget Sound.

Within hours after the pillar of ash rose to a height measured by radar at 60,000 feet, wind had pushed it 160 miles east to Walla Walla, Wash., where automatic equipment turned on street lights as if dusk had come.

The eruption came from the old summit crater on the north side of the peak. It made a roar "like a truck," according to Greg Meyer, who was fishing at Mosquito Lakes about 40 miles east of Mount St. Helens.

The black cloud, carried by the high-level winds that blow from west to east at this time of year, was carried over the lake with pumice falling from it, he said. His visibility was cut to between 6 and 10 feet. Mr. Meyer abandoned his fishing equipment and canoe.

Mount St. Helens had been quiet from 1857 until earlier this year, when its slopes began to shake with localized earthquakes that geologists said indicated the inactive volcano's reservoir was filling with molten material.

On March 27, with an explosion, the peak began to spew steam and ash that drifted across into eastern Washington.

Jack Folliott, 25 years old, said that he thought "this will be the end" when the mountain shook with the earthquake that preceded the eruption. "My whole life is tied up in those five acres," he said of his home near the Toutle River. "I don't know what I'll have when this is over."

NOVEMBER 5, 1980

Reagan Easily Beats Carter; Republicans Gain in Congress

Hedrick Smith

Ronald Wilson Reagan, riding a tide of economic discontent against Jimmy Carter and promising "to put America back to work again," was elected the nation's 40th President yesterday with a sweep of surprising victories in the East, South and the crucial battlegrounds of the Middle West.

At 69 years of age, the former California Governor became the oldest person ever elected to the White House. He built a stunning electoral landslide by taking away Mr. Carter's Southern base, smashing his expected strength in the East, and taking command of the Middle West, which both sides had designated as the main testing ground. The entire West was his, as expected.

Mr. Carter, who labored hard for a comeback re-election victory similar to that of Harry S. Truman in 1948, instead became the first elected incumbent President since Herbert Hoover in 1932 to go down to defeat at the polls. ■

SEPTEMBER 26, 1981

JUSTICE O'CONNOR SEATED ON NATION'S HIGH COURT

Linda Greenhouse

WASHINGTON, September 25—Sandra Day O'Connor took her seat today as the 102d Justice and the first woman to serve on the United States Supreme Court.

President Reagan, who fulfilled a campaign promise to name a woman to the Court by nominating the 51-year-old Arizona judge, attended the brief ceremony in the courtroom. It was the first time a President had visited the Supreme Court since President Ford attended Associate Justice John Paul Steven's swearing-in ceremony in 1975.

President Reagan and Judge O'Connor entered the courtroom simultaneously but from opposite sides a few minutes past 2 o'clock. Judge O'Connor was escorted to a ceremonial chair, in the well of the courtroom below the bench, that was used in the Court's early years by Chief Justice John Marshall. The eight members of the Court took their seats on the bench moments later.

After swearing in the Court's new member, Chief Justice Warren E. Burger said: "Justice O'Connor, welcome to the Court. I wish you a very long life and a long and happy career in our common calling."

Justice O'Connor's work begins almost immediately. On Monday, the Justices will begin a weeklong conference to decide the disposition of about 1,000 cases that have come into the Court since June. The term opens the next Monday, Oct. 5. ■

Sandra Day O'Connor being sworn in before the Senate Judiciary committee during confirmation hearings in 1981.

justice

REAGAN WOUNDED IN CHEST BY GUNMAN;

Outlook 'Good' After 2-Hour Surgery; Aide and 2 Guards Shot; Suspect Held

Howell Raines

WASHINGTON, March 30—President Reagan was shot in the chest today by a gunman, apparently acting alone, as Mr. Reagan walked to his limousine after addressing a labor meeting at the Washington Hilton Hotel. The White House press secretary and two law-enforcement officers were also wounded by a burst of shots.

The President was reported in "good" and "stable" condition tonight at George Washington University Hospital after undergoing two hours of surgery. "The prognosis is excellent," said Dr. Dennis S. O'Leary, dean of clinical affairs at the university. "He is alert and should be able to make decisions by tomorrow."

The hospital spokesman said surgeons removed a .22-caliber bullet that struck Mr. Reagan's seventh rib, penetrating the left lung three inches and collapsing it.

A rapid series of five or six shots rang out at about 2:30 P.M. as Mr. Reagan left the hotel. A look of stunned disbelief swept across the President's face when the shots were fired just after he raised his left arm to wave to the crowd. Nearby, his press secretary, James S. Brady, fell to the sidewalk, critically wounded.

Eyewitnesses said six shots were fired at the Presidential entourage from a distance of about 10 feet. The assailant had positioned himself among the television camera crews and reporters assembled outside a hotel exit.

The authorities arrested a 25-year-old Colorado man, John W. Hinckley Jr., at the scene of the attack. He was later booked on Federal charges of attempting to assassinate the President and assault on a Federal officer.

Within minutes, Americans were witnessing for the second time in a generation television pictures of a chief executive being struck by gunfire during what appeared to be a routine public appearance. For the second time in less than 20 years, too, they watched as the nation's leaders scrambled to meet one of the sternest tests of the democratic system.

Mr. Reagan, apparently at first unaware that he had been wounded, was shoved forcefully by a Secret Service agent into the Presidential limousine, which sped away with the President in a sitting position in the backseat.

Behind him lay a scene of turmoil. A Secret Service agent writhed in pain on the rain-slick sidewalk. Nearby a District of Columbia plainclothesman had fallen alongside Mr. Brady. The press secretary lay face down, blood from a gushing head wound dripping into a steel grate. A pistol, apparently dropped by one of the security aides, lay near his head.

At the sixth shot, uniformed and plainclothes agents had piled on a blond-haired man in a raincoat, pinning him against a stone wall. "Get him out," a gun-waving officer yelled as the President's limousine sped off. At first, it raced down Connecticut Avenue toward the White House.

Only then, according to some reports, was it discovered that Mr. Reagan was bleeding. The vehicle turned west toward the hospital. Upon learning of the shooting, Vice President Bush returned to the capital from Austin, Tex., where he was to address the Texas Legislature. In Washington, Secretary of State Alexander M. Haig Jr. and other Cabinet officers began gathering in the White House situation room as soon as they learned of the assassination attempt.

At 4:14 P.M, Mr. Haig, in a voice shaking with emotion, told reporters that the Administration's "crisis management" plan was in effect, and citing provisions for Presidential succession, Mr. Haig asserted that he was in charge.

Mr. Reagan's wife, Nancy, and senior White House advisers rushed to the hospital and talked to Mr. Reagan before he entered surgery at about 3:24 P.M. Despite his wound, the 70-year-old President walked into the hospital and seemed determined to assure his wife and colleagues that he would survive.

"Honey, I forgot to duck," Mr. Reagan was quoted as telling his wife. As he was wheeled down a corridor on a hospital cart, he told Senator Paul Laxalt, a political associate, "Don't worry about me." According to Lyn Nofziger, the White House political director, Mr. Reagan winked at James A. Baker 3d, his chief of staff. Then, spying Edwin Meese 3d, the White House counselor, Mr. Reagan quipped, "Who's minding the store?" ■

U.S. president Ronald Reagan, moments before his assassination attempt.

JUNE 25, 1982

LEADERS CONCEDE LOSS ON EQUAL RIGHTS

Marjorie Hunter

WASHINGTON, June 24—Leaders of the fight for an equal rights amendment officially conceded defeat today. But they vowed to continue the struggle for equality of women by electing their backers to state legislatures and by suing corporations that practice sexual discrimination.

"We've just begun to fight," said Eleanor Smeal, the president of the National Organization for Women, the group that spearheaded the Equal Rights Amendment Countdown Campaign, which has now ended in defeat.

In the 10 years since Congress passed the proposed constitutional amendment to forbid discrimination on the basis of sex, it has been ratified by 35 states, three short of the three-fourths it needed to become part of the Constitution.

"We've just begun to fight"

Hopes for ratification before the deadline next Wednesday were dashed this week when the amendment was rejected by the Illinois House and the Florida Senate, two states in which supporters felt they had a fighting chance.

In 1972, the proposed amendment passed the House by the wide margin of 354 to 24, and the Senate by an equally top-heavy vote, 84 to 8. It was a one-sentence amendment: "Equality of rights under the law shall not be abridged or denied by the United States or any state on account of sex." ■

OCTOBER 3, 1982

100 AGENTS HUNT FOR KILLER IN 7 TYLENOL DEATHS

By Andrew H. Malcolm

CHICAGO, Oct. 2—The death of a seventh victim from Tylenol capsules laced with deadly cyanide was confirmed today by the local authorities. Officials also reported finding, for the first time, contaminated capsules in an unsold bottle of Tylenol from a store shelf at a suburban shopping center.

The announcements came as more than 100 state and Federal agents fanned out across the Chicago metropolitan area in a painstaking attempt to reconstruct the route of poisoned capsules of Tylenol, the nation's largest selling over-the-counter pain reliever.

So far, all confirmed cases of poisoning from the Tylenol capsules have been in the Chicago area. Investigators independently examining some unexplained deaths Wednesday in two adjacent suburbs here were alerted to the Tylenol threat by two firemen who noted that the separate ambulance reports said all the victims had recently taken that pain medicine.

The seventh victim was identified as Paula Prince, a 35-year-old flight attendant for United Airlines. She returned from a flight Wednesday night and, according to a receipt found near her body, had purchased a bottle of Extra-Strength Tylenol capsules at a Walgreen's drugstore on Chicago's Near North Side just before all the containers were removed from the store.

Investigators might then be able to trace the original contaminated capsules back to a precise point of time in their distribution. But they also note that given the amount of undetected shoplifting these days, someone could remove the bottles, replace the Tylenol medicine in a few capsules with cyanide and then surreptitiously return the contaminated bottles to a store shelf. ■

OCTOBER 11, 1983

MRS. REAGAN TAKES HER ANTI-DRUG CAMPAIGN TO TELEVISION

Sally Bedell Smith

First Lady Nancy Reagan speaking at a Just Say No anti-drug rally on the Mall.

OCTOBER 7, 1982

VIETNAM MEMORIAL:

QUESTIONS OF ARCHITECTURE; AN APPRAISAL

Paul Goldberger

When a plan by Maya Yang Lin, a 21-year-old Yale architecture student, was selected last year as the winner of a nationwide competition to find a design for the Vietnam Veterans Memorial on the Mall near the Lincoln Memorial in Washington, it was hailed by the architectural press with words such as "stunning," "dignified" and "eminently right." The reaction was less enthusiastic from Vietnam veterans themselves, some of whom found the proposed memorial rather more cool and abstract than they would have liked. Nonetheless, Miss Lin's scheme, which is neither a building nor a sculpture but, rather, a pair of 200-foot-long black granite walls that join to form a V and embrace a gently sloping plot of ground between them, was approved rapidly by the Department of the Interior, the Fine Arts Commission and other public agencies that have jurisdiction over what is built in official Washington.

Construction began last March. Next week, however, the Fine Arts Commission will hold a public hearing to consider a revised design for the memorial, despite the fact that by now the granite walls—on which are carved the names of all 57,692 Americans who were killed in Vietnam from 1963 to 1973—are nearly complete. Opposition to the scheme from Vietnam veterans, which was muted when Miss Lin's design was first announced, later grew so intense as to lead to the unusual step of a proposed design change in mid-construction.

To many of the Vietnam veterans, Miss Lin's scheme was too abstract to reflect the emotion that the Vietnam War symbolized to them, and too lacking in the symbols of heroism that more conventional monuments contain. They saw in the simple granite walls on which the names of the dead are inscribed not merely a means of honoring the dead, but a way of declaring that the Vietnam War was in some way different from past wars—from wars such as World War II, whose heroism could be symbolized in such a vibrant and active memorial as the Iwo Jima Monument just across the Potomac River, which contains a statue of marines struggling to raise the American flag.

It is a subtle design, like every great memorial capable of being given different meanings by each of us. The anguish of the Vietnam War is present here, but not in a way that does any dishonor to veterans. To call this memorial a "black gash of shame," as Tom Carhart, a Vietnam veteran who a losing entrant in the competition, has said, is to miss its point entirely, and to fail to see that this design gives every indication of being a place of extreme dignity that honors the veterans who served in Vietnam with more poignancy, surely, than any ordinary monument ever could.

The Vietnam Veterans Memorial, as it now nears completion, could be one of the most important works of contemporary architecture in official Washington—and perhaps the only one that will provide a contemplative space of the equal of any in the past. The insertion of statues and a flagpole not only destroys the abstract beauty of that mystical, inside-outside kind of space that Maya Yang Lin has created; it also tries to shift this memorial away from its focus on the dead, and toward a kind of literal interpretation of heroism and patriotism that ultimately treats the war dead in only the most simplistic of terms.

For in the original design, the dead are remembered as individuals through the moving list of their names carved against the granite. It is the presence of the names, one after the other, that speaks. But if the statues are added, they will overpower the space and change the mood altogether. A symbol of loss, which Miss Lin's design is, will become instead a symbol of war. The names of the dead and the hushed granite wall will become merely a background for something else, and the chance for a very special kind of honor—and for a very special kind of architecture—will be lost.

Crowd gathered at dedication ceremony of Vietnam Memorial on November 13, 1982.

OCTOBER 24, 1982

COCAINE TRAFFICKING AND ITS HUGE PROFITS LURING MIDDLE CLASS

Robert Lindsey

LOS ANGELES, Oct. 23—The huge profits to be found in cocaine trafficking are luring more and more middle-class and upper-income Americans to the cocaine trade, law-enforcement officials say, and relatively few of them are being caught.

Although no one knows how much money is involved, the United States Drug Enforcement Administration estimates that more than $30 billion is spent annually by cocaine users in this country.

The smuggling and distribution of the drug, officials say, are largely controlled by Colombians and other Latin Americans, as well as organized crime in this country.

But they say the trade is so lucrative, the chances of being caught are so small and the use of the drug has become so acceptable in some segments of American society that it is increasingly attracting dealers from middle-class professional and business life.

"It's greed," said Charles Palmer, a senior Drug Enforcement Administration agent in San Francisco. "Cocaine is a multibillion dollar industry, and it's polluting all levels of society, from the lower classes to the very affluent. The affluent are going into it because there are such incredible amounts of money."

Federal officials said last month that businessmen, physicians, lawyers and bank officials were among the leaders of a ring that smuggled into the country 3,748 pounds of cocaine confiscated in March in Florida in the largest cocaine seizure made in this country.

In another case, the officials in Georgia last month accused a once-prominent local businessman and a former Mayor of Clarkesville, Ga., of smuggling 300 pounds of cocaine into the state.

Investigators say many of the new white-collar drug dealers are more sophisticated than conventional street criminals and are more difficult to catch. Investigators say they tend to devise elaborate schemes to conceal the movement of their money through ostensibly legitimate companies, often in collaboration with bribed bank officials.

"They make so much money that they can buy the best planes, the best radios," Mr. Palmer, the agent in San Francisco, said. "They have fleets of airplanes, fleets of boats, and all kinds of other resources that are better than those we have."

Users of the drug say it induces intense euphoria and self-confidence that lasts for perhaps 15 minutes. Drug experts say cocaine, most often ingested by being inhaled into a nostril through a straw or from a small spoon, is now being taken increasingly by direct injection or, in a method called "freebasing," by smoking a cigarette that has been treated with a purified form of the drug. Both methods are said to provide faster, more intense "highs." ■

"Cocaine is a multi-billion dollar industry"

MARCH 27, 1983

Would a Space-Age Defense Ease Tensions or Create Them?

By Hedrick Smith

WASHINGTON—In the 1980 campaign, Ronald Reagan scored points by attacking Jimmy Carter for zigzags in dealing with the Soviet Union. As President, Mr. Reagan himself has oscillated at times between hardline and more moderate positions. But lately, in his crusade for a $239 billion defense budget, he has given vent to his natural inclination for tough talk, sounding echoes of the Cold War.

Last week on television, he used charts and declassified intelligence photos to draw a stark and menacing picture of growing Soviet offensive weaponry and the threat facing the United States. But he also urged a shift in scientific thinking from offensive arms to devising an esoteric system of lasers or particle beams that, by the next century, could render attacking nuclear missiles impotent. This was his "vision of the future which offers hope."

The President's push for exotic new weapons was partly a response to the jittery feelings in the United States and Europe about growing atomic arsenals. But the tactic could backfire. In Europe, the prospect of more American weapons makes some people feel less, rather than more, secure. And some critics contend that his portrayal of Soviet power may indirectly feed the nuclear freeze movement by increasing fears of nuclear war.

Mr. Reagan, more than most recent Presidents, has turned up the rhetoric. With evangelical fervor in Orlando, Fla., this month, he summoned Americans to resist "the aggressive impulses of an evil empire." He derided a nuclear weapons freeze as "a very dangerous fraud" (though not a Soviet-dominated movement, the F.B.I said last week). Later, he pictured Soviet proxies on the march in Central America. El Salvador, he said, "will join Cuba and Nicaragua as a base for spreading fresh violence to Guatemala, Honduras, Costa Rica" and beyond. The predatory Soviet design, he said, is "to tie down our forces on our southern border and so limit our capacity to act in more distant places such as Europe, the Persian Gulf, Indian Ocean, Sea of Japan."' ■

APRIL 14, 1983

DEMOCRAT ELECTED MAYOR OF CHICAGO BY NARROW MARGIN

WASHINGTON EDGES PAST EPTON AFTER A DIVISIVE RACE TO BECOME TO BE FIRST BLACK IN THE POST

Andrew H. Malcolm

Harold Washington on the campaign trail.

CHICAGO, April 13—Representative Harold Washington, the 60-year-old son of a Democratic precinct captain, won a narrow victory over his Republican opponent, Bernard E. Epton, this morning to become the first black mayor in the history of Chicago.

"Tonight we are here to celebrate a resounding victory," Mr. Washington said as he appeared before television cameras trained on a crowd of about 20,000 cheering campaign workers and supporters at Donnelly Hall. "We have finished our course and kept the faith."

Mr. Washington, who trailed Mr. Epston in early returns, built the lead early this morning, with totals from a few black wards yet to be included. True to expectations, the vote of this radically divided city was adhering closely to racial lines, fueled by a record voter turnout of 82 percent of 1.6 million registered voters in the nation's second largest city.

It was a low-key end to one of Chicago's most bitter and strange campaigns. Two months ago neither candidate had any realistic hopes of victory in a city long controlled by a powerful political machine that flew the banner of the Democratic Party but was basically a nonideological coalition of conservative neighborhood clan chiefs.

In the Democratic primary Feb. 22, Mr. Washington ran on a reform platform vowing to destroy the machine, and faced Mayor Jane M. Byrne and Richard M. Daley, the Country Prosecutor who is the son of Mayor Richard J. Daley, who died in 1976. Mrs. Byrne and Mr. Daley, who were reflections of long rivalries between two Irish factions here, divided the city's white and ethnic vote. Mr. Washington, who relied on solid black support from wards once the most obedient to the same machine, won a narrow victory.

But fear of his color and plans to eliminate patronage and install new party leaders prompted a surge of white support to Mr. Epton, a liberal Republican whose party has not controlled Chicago since 1931.

"In a way, my vote was based on color," said Harry Birnhaum, a retired postal worker who voted Republican. "I think blacks would take away jobs from whites."

There has been considerable concern expressed publicly here that such strong feelings about the election, whatever its outcome, could lead to social unrest. Chicago's police have quietly drawn up contingency plans, and a number of businesses are said to have postponed major investment decisions pending the election results.

JULY 13, 1984

GERALDINE FERRARO IS CHOSEN BY MONDALE AS RUNNING MATE, FIRST WOMEN ON MAJOR TICKET

Walter Mondale and Geraldine Ferraro in 1984.

Bernard Weinraub

ST. PAUL, July 12—Walter F. Mondale today named Representative Geraldine A. Ferraro of Queens as his running mate, the first woman selected to run for Vice President on a major party ticket.

Mr. Mondale, the probable Democratic Presidential nominee, announced his historic step before an ebullient crowd at the State Capitol. He introduced Mrs. Ferraro by saying: "I looked for the best Vice President and I found her in Gerry Ferraro."

"This is an exciting choice," he said, with Mrs. Ferraro by his side.

The 48-year-old former teacher and assistant prosecutor from Queens broke into a wide grin as Mr. Mondale said, "I'm delighted to announce that I will ask the Democratic convention" to ratify her.

Mr. Mondale said the decision to choose a woman was a "difficult" one, but added: "Gerry has excelled in everything she's tried, from law school at night to being a tough prosecutor to winning a difficult election, to winning positions of leadership and respect in the Congress."

Mr. Mondale said her political rise was "really the story of a classic American dream."

Mrs. Ferraro, who was first elected to Congress in 1978, has received the endorsements for the Vice Presidency of Thomas P. O'Neill Jr., the Speaker of the House, Governor Cuomo of New York and a wide range of Democrats as well as feminists.

Mrs. Ferraro, who taught elementary school in Queens while attending Fordham Law School at night, noted that her father came from Marcianise, a small town in Italy.

"Like millions of other immigrants he loved our country passionately but what he loved most about it was that in America anything is possible if you work for it," she said.

As Mr. Mondale listened intently, she said: "I grew up among working people, straightforward solid Americans trying to make ends meet, trying to bring up their families and leave their country a little bit better off than when they moved here and found it. Those are my values, too.

"I have a strong, loving family. And our neighborhood and our faith are important parts of our lives. So is our work."

Mrs. Ferraro said that her friend, Representative Charles B. Rangel, Democrat of Manhattan, phoned her earlier and said, "Gerry, my heart is full."

Mrs. Ferraro said quietly, "So is mine."

MARCH 24, 1983

REAGAN PROPOSES U.S. SEEK NEW WAY TO BLOCK MISSILES

Steven R. Weisman

WASHINGTON, March 23—President Reagan, defending his military program, proposed tonight to exploit advances in technology in coming decades so the United States can develop an effective defense against missiles launched by others.

In effect, Mr. Reagan proposed to make obsolete the current United States policy of relying on massive retaliation by its ballistic missiles to counter the threat of a Soviet nuclear attack.

In a television address from the White House, he coupled his proposal with his strongest appeal yet for his Administration's program to increase military spending.

Mr. Reagan declared that a new missile defense program presented "a vision of the future which offers hope," even though the necessary technological breakthroughs "may not be accomplished before the end of this century."

White House officials said the new program might involve lasers, microwave devices, particle beams and projectile beams. These devices, most of which are in a very early stage of development, in theory could be directed from satellites, airplanes or land-based installations to shoot down missiles in the air.

Scientists have felt the beam defenses could revolutionize the concept of nuclear strategy because, up to now, the idea of shooting missiles down after they were launched has been deemed impractical.

Mr. Reagan also used his speech to defend his Administration's arms reduction proposals to the Soviet Union, but for the first time he hinted publicly that he might be ready to modify his "zero-zero" proposal for banning all Soviet and American medium-range nuclear missiles from Europe.

Using charts, graphs and photographs—some of them recently declassified for tonight's speech—Mr. Reagan reviewed in detail what he said was the buildup of Soviet military forces in recent years, especially in Central America. His Administration's program, he said, is needed because of "our neglect in the 1970's."

On air reconaissance photographs, Mr. Reagan pointed to Soviet installations in Cuba, Nicaragua and Grenada to show how the Russians had tried to project power in the Caribbean. The photographs, however, did not show anything new beyond what the Administration had previously said existed in the region.

The speech tonight was aimed at defending his proposal to increase military spending by 10 percent in 1984. The proposal is under attack from Democrats and Republicans in both the House of Representatives and the Senate. ■

NOVEMBER 7, 1984

REAGAN WINS BY A LANDSLIDE, SWEEPING AT LEAST 48 STATES; G.O.P. GAINS STRENGTH IN HOUSE

Martin Tolchin

President Ronald Reagan shortly before the 1984 Presidential Election.

NOVEMBER 8, 1984

Reagan Faces Difficult Task in Leading Divided Congress

Hedrick Smith

Despite his overwhelming electoral victory Tuesday, President Reagan faces a much more complicated task in leading a divided Government in his second term than when he entered the White House four years ago.

The Republican failure to gain effective working control of the House of Representatives, leaders in both parties say, will bring greater pressure on Mr. Reagan to strike political compromises on major issues than he faced at the start of his first term.

Even before the President sets out an agenda to Congress and the country for the next four years, he faces conflicting pressures from moderates and conservatives within his own party and a Democratic majority of roughly 70 seats in the House that is in a position to block his initiatives. Democrats have already challenged the scope of his mandate.

What remains most important and still uncertain, Reagan aides and other politicians say, are the President's own priorities, whether he will side mainly with militant conservatives or favor a more flexible strategy, and how hard he intends to press his initiatives both with the Congress and the Russians.

On foreign policy, Mr. Reagan signaled recently that he would take a more conciliatory approach toward the Soviet Union and has declared several times that arms control will be a priority of his second term. Close political associates such as the retiring Senate majority leader, Howard H. Baker Jr., have come away from private sessions with Mr. Reagan convinced that he wants a place in history as a leader who has moved forward the cause of arms reduction.

Internally, however, his Administration is divided between Pentagon conservatives who are wary of Moscow's intentions, worried about the problems of verifying any arms agreement and eager to set tough terms for Moscow, and moderates in the State Department and White House who see those problems but advocate flexible diplomacy to bring about arms reduction. A question of some debate in Washington is how hard the President will work to break these bottlenecks.

In the immediate aftermath of his election triumph, the President has given no sign of compromise on his four-year effort to curb the role of the Federal Government and cut the size of its programs, a strategy that has produced repeated confrontations with House Speaker Thomas P. O'Neill Jr.

But voters who split their tickets by supporting both Mr. Reagan and local Democrats, which gave Republicans a net gain of about 14 seats in the House and cost them two seats in the Senate, signaled problems for Mr. Reagan on his economic formula of large increases in military spending, cuts in domestic programs and no tax increases.

But on the deficit and issues like taxes, abortion, school prayer and a constitutional amendment to balance the budget, the election results are likely to tug House and Senate Republicans in opposite directions. ■

NOVEMBER 16, 1986

The Iran Connection; Skirting Credibility's Border in Search of a Mideast Deal

David K. Shipler

President Ronald Reagan at his desk after making a speech on the Iran arms deal, with aides Patrick J. Buchanan Jr. and Donald T. Regan in rear.

WASHINGTON—In the soothing tones that have lubricated his entire Presidency, Ronald Reagan sidestepped the carping politicians, columnists and diplomats last week and took his case on Iran directly to the American people. In 12 minutes on television, he offered his version of a remarkable 18 months of secret diplomacy and arms sales to a country that his Administration had denounced as a font of terrorism and anti-American fanaticism.

The President's talk contained internal contradictions that seemed to neutralize his denials that arms had been traded for American hostages. He had "authorized the transfer of small amounts of defensive weapons and spare parts for defensive systems to Iran," he said, "for the simplest and best of reasons," namely, to woo that country back into a relationship with the United States that would spell the end of its support for terrorism.

"We did not—repeat, did no—trade weapons or anything else for hostages—nor will we," he added, just minutes after explaining: "The most significant step which Iran could take, we indicated, would be to use its influence in Lebanon to secure the release of all hostages held there." He did not mention arms deliveries by Israel to Iran, reportedly made at American request and timed to the release of three hostages who were held by a pro-Iranian group in Lebanon.

The Administration's credibility problems predated the Iran controversy. They began earlier this fall with reports that the White House had mapped a disinformation campaign last summer to plant false stories in the press that Colonel Muammar el-Qaddafi of Libya was planning new terrorist attacks; the leaks hinted at further American military action.

Then in September, officials contended that no swap had occured when an accused Soviet spy was released in New York as an American journalist was set free in Moscow. And when a weapons-laden plane with an American crew was shot down over Nicaragua, the Administration denied any involvement, although such aid to the Administration-backed Nicaraguan rebels had long been coordinated from the White House by Lieut. Col. Oliver L. North, a National Security Council official.

Colonel North was also reportedly involved in the surreptitious Iran connection, which the National Security Council apparently undertook without consulting the Middle East experts in the State Department and the Pentagon. President Reagan confirmed that his former national security adviser, Robert C. McFarlane, had gone secretly to Teheran to meet with Iranian factions in an operation overseen by the present national security adviser, Vice Adm. John M. Poindexter.

At least some of them doubted that the President's tactics would work. Nobody denied Iran's strategic importance, both because of its oil deposits and its "critical geography," in the President's words, between the Soviet Union and the Indian Ocean. The question is how to restore American influence. Mr. Reagan evidently accepted the Israeli argument that Washington could bolster pro-Western Iranians through arms sales. But there is no guarantee that such factions can be identified and trusted, or that weaponry can be an effective instrument for addressing the subtleties of a Middle Eastern country's internal politics. ■

MAY 26, 1986

MILLIONS JOIN HANDS ACROSS U.S. TO AID THE HOMELESS AND HUNGRY

Peter Kerr

The line twisted through 4,150 miles of America, through city streets, across bridges, through deserts and mountain passes.

Its links included the rich, the poor and the homeless, movie stars and public officials, a flotilla of hot air balloons, cowboys in covered wagons, a chain of paper dolls and, at times, a bit of Hollywood hokum.

And for 15 minutes, organizers of the Hands Across America event said, it connected millions of Americans from Battery Park in New York City to the Pacific Ocean in a singing, hand-holding statement of support for the nation's hungry and homeless.

President Ronald Reagan, wife Nancy, daughter Maureen and James Brady participating in Hands Across America outside the White House.

NOVEMBER 26, 1986

CONTRA SUPPLIES: MYSTERY UNRAVELS

Joel Brinkley

WASHINGTON, Nov. 25—The disclosure that millions of dollars paid for United States arms sent to Iran were channeled through Swiss bank accounts to the Nicaraguan rebels may explain much of the mystery behind the covert program to supply the rebels, Congressional investigators and Reagan Administration officials said today.

When a C-123 cargo plane crashed inside Nicaragua last month and one of its American crew members, Eugene Hasenfus, was captured by the Sandinistas, investigations showed that a vast supply operation had been delivering arms to the rebels for the last two years, the period during which Congress banned direct military aid to them.

Numerous Administration officials said the supply operation had been coordinated and directed by Lieut. Col. Oliver L. North of the National Security Council staff. But as a Congressional investigator said today, "We were never able to figure out the funding."

Rebel officers and Administration officials, including Colonel North, repeatedly asserted that the many millions of dollars needed to keep the supplies flowing had come from anonymous private donors in the United States and other countries.

Elliott Abrams, Assistant Secretary of State for Inter-American Affairs, said today: "There were a thousand rumors, Texas millionaires and so forth, and we didn't know."

At a news conference today, Attorney General Edwin Meese 3d said that "somewhere between $10 and $30 million" in what amounted to profits on the sale of arms going to Iran had been deposited in Swiss bank accounts for the contras, as the rebels are generally known. The man directing all that, Mr. Meese said, again was Colonel North.

Today President Reagan said Colonel North "has been relieved of his duties on the National Security Council staff." ■

NOVEMBER 3, 1983

PRESIDENT, SIGNING BILL, PRAISES DR. KING

Robert Pear

WASHINGTON, Nov. 2—Black and white Americans, Republicans and Democrats, liberals and conservatives joined today in an act of unity as President Reagan signed a bill to establish a Federal holiday in honor of the Rev. Dr. Martin Luther King Jr.

A crowd of several hundred began singing "We Shall Overcome" after Mr. Reagan signed the bill in the Rose Garden of the White House.

The President paid warm tribute to Dr. King, saying his words and deeds had "stirred our nation to the very depths of its soul."

The new law establishes the third Monday in January as a Federal holiday, starting in 1986. On such holidays, Federal offices are closed throughout the country. Many states observe Federal holidays, but state and local governments decide whether to close other places such as schools and banks.

Dr. King was born in Atlanta on Jan. 15, 1929. He was assassinated on April 4, 1968, in Memphis, Tenn. In his remarks today, Mr. Reagan said that those 39 years "changed America forever," and he accorded much of the credit to Dr. King.

Today's ceremony gave Mr. Reagan an opportunity to attempt to improve his political standing among blacks, who have repeatedly criticized his record on civil rights. Representative Charles B. Rangel, a Manhattan Democrat, one of many blacks in the audience, said: "The President was eloquent. If we could only get his policies to catch up with his speech, the country would be in great shape." ■

We shall overcome

JANUARY 21, 1986

Nation Pauses To Remember King

American civil rights campaigner, and widow of Dr. Martin Luther King Jr., Coretta Scott King and her son, Martin Luther King III.

William E. Schmidt

ATLANTA, Jan. 20— Singing the ballads of the civil rights movement, thousands of people marched slowly through Atlanta today as this city and the nation marked the first Federal holiday honoring the Rev. Dr. Martin Luther King Jr. In Atlanta, where Dr. King was born and where he is buried, and in cities across the country, church bells tolled, choirs sang and citizens paused to remember the slain civil rights leader, eulogized in speeches and services as nation's "drum major for justice and peace."

The day's stirring oratory, like the ranks of marchers moving in deliberate steps through downtown streets, was sharply evocative of another time, when Dr. King led similar marches through the streets of Selma, Montgomery and dozens of other cities.

In Atlanta, speakers at a service said that the best way that people could honor Dr. King was to live his dream. "Go out into the hedges and the highways and lift up those who are oppressed, and then Martin will have a gift," said the Rev. Joseph L. Roberts Jr., pastor of the Ebenezer Baptist Church, where Dr. King was once co-pastor.

In Memphis, there was a vigil in the parking lot of the Lorraine Motel, where Dr. King was killed by a sniper's bullet on April 4, 1968. "This is the site of the crucifixion," D'Army Bailey, a Memphis lawyer, said from the balcony of the motel.

Later, Coretta Scott King, Dr. King's widow, and other leaders of the civil rights movement led a huge march and parade through downtown Atlanta. At times, the number of marchers passing slowly in the street seemed to outnumber the spectators who crowded five and six deep along the curb.

There was a festive atmosphere to the day. Vendors sold balloons and pennants, and children sat on their parents' shoulders for a better view. The Atlanta police estimated that 500,000 people clogged downtown, where state and Federal offices, and many busineses, were closed.

There were other parades and observances in Washington, Chicago, Los Angeles and Philadelphia. And in the evening, more than a dozen stars, including Stevie Wonder, Harry Belafonte and Bill Cosby, were scheduled to be join a two-hour nationally televised program honoring Dr. King, to be broadcast from Atlanta, New York City and Washington.

Amid sharp debate over the holiday, and early opposition to a Federal declaration from President Reagan, who said the nation could not afford to honor all its heroes, Congress voted in 1983 to set aside the third Monday in January to commemorate Dr. King's birthday. Mrs. King and other leaders of the civil rights movement had lobbied for this for more than 15 years.

Had Dr. King lived, he would have been 57 years old on Jan. 15. He was slain by a sniper as he stood on the balcony of the Memphis motel. A white ex-convict, James Earl Ray, pleaded guilty and is serving a 99-year term in Brushy Mountain State Penitentiary in Tennessee. ■

lift up those who are oppressed

U.S. space shuttle Challenger lifts off from a launch pad at Kennedy Space Center, 72 seconds before its explosion killing it crew of seven.

THE SHUTTLE EXPLODES:

6 IN CREW AND HIGH-SCHOOL TEACHER ARE KILLED 74 SECONDS AFTER LIFTOFF

William J. Broad

CAPE CANAVERAL, Fla., Jan. 28—The space shuttle Challenger exploded in a ball of fire shortly after it left the launching pad today, and all seven astronauts on board were lost.

The worst accident in the history of the American space program, it was witnessed by thousands of spectators who watched in wonder, then horror, as the ship blew apart high in the air.

Flaming debris rained down on the Atlantic Ocean for an hour after the explosion, which occurred just after 11:39 A.M. It kept rescue teams from reaching the area where the craft would have fallen into the sea, about 18 miles offshore.

Americans who had grown used to the idea of men and women soaring into space reacted with shock to the disaster, the first time United States astronauts had died in flight. President Reagan canceled the State of the Union Message that had been scheduled for tonight, expressing sympathy for the families of the crew but vowing that the nation's exploration of space would continue.

Killed in the explosion were the mission commander, Francis R. (Dick) Scobee; the pilot, Comdr. Michael J. Smith of the Navy; Dr. Judith A. Resnik; Dr. Ronald E. McNair; Lieut. Col. Ellison S. Onizuka of the Air Force; Gregory B. Jarvis, and Christa McAuliffe.

Mrs. McAuliffe, a high-school teacher from Concord, N.H., was to have been the first ordinary citizen in space.

The Challenger lifted off flawlessly this morning, after three days of delays, for what was to have been the 25th mission of the reusable shuttle fleet that was intended to make space travel commonplace. The ship rose for about a minute on a column of smoke and fire from its five engines.

Suddenly, without warning, it erupted in a ball of flame.

The eerie beauty of the orange fireball and billowing white trails against the blue confused many onlookers, many of whom did not at first seem aware that the aerial display was a sign that something had gone terribly wrong.

There were few sobs, moans or shouts among the thousands of tourists, reporters and space agency officials gathered on an unusually cold Florida day to celebrate the liftoff, just a stunned silence as they began to realize that the Challenger had vanished.

As the explosion occured, Stephen A. Nesbitt of Mission Control in Houston, apparently looking at his notes and not the explosion on his television monitor, noted that the shuttle's velocity was "2,900 feet per second, altitude 9 nautical miles, downrange distance 7 nautical miles." That is a speed of about 1,977 miles an hour, a height of about 10 statute miles and a distance down range of about 8 miles.

JUNE 18, 1986

The Supreme Court: Dedicated Conservative Jurist: William Hubbs Rehnquist

Stephen Engelberg

WASHINGTON, June 17—Justice William H. Rehnquist, nominated to be Chief Justice of the United States by President Reagan today, is a conservative jurist whose polished opinions have won grudging respect even from those who oppose his views.

Justice Rehnquist, 61 years old, was named to the Court by President Nixon in 1971 after serving for two years in the Justice Department as head of the Office of Legal Counsel. As one of the Government's chief legal strategists, he articulated that Administration's policies on such issues as obscenity, wiretapping and defendants' rights. ■

OCTOBER 26, 1986

Tax Bill Is Signed, and Its Revision Gets Under Way

Caroline Rand Herron and Martha A. Miles

The Tax Reform Act of 1986, declared President Reagan as he signed the most sweeping overhaul of the Federal income tax in 40 years, is "less a reform than a revolution." The celebratory signing ceremony, before an audience of more than 1,000 on the White House South Lawn, marked less an end than a beginning.

The new volume of law will produce volumes of regulations on which the Internal Revenue Service has just begun, and, if history is any guide, yet another tax law, perhaps two.

One reason the legislators will go at it again is drafting errors and the need for "technical corrections," such as giving the proper address for Carnegie Hall in Manhattan, one of a number of beneficiaries of specially tailored tax breaks. Another is a lack of Congressional agreement on the last few such "transition rules."

A third reason could be the new law's design. Intended to be "revenue neutral"—it is written to raise business taxes by $120 billion over the next five years while cutting taxes for individuals by the same amount—many economists think it will cost the Government $20 billion a year, and pressure to raise taxes to cut the deficit is growing. The Reagan tax cuts of 1981 were followed by tax increases, in the form of adjustments, in 1982, 1983 and 1984. ■

taxes

OCTOBER 24, 1987

BORK'S NOMINATION IS REJECTED, 58-42; REAGAN 'SADDENED'

Linda Greenhouse

WASHINGTON, Oct. 23—One of the fiercest battles ever waged over a Supreme Court nominee ended today as the Senate decisively rejected the nomination of Judge Robert H. Bork.

The vote was 58 against confirmation and 42 in favor, the biggest margin by which the Senate has ever rejected a Supreme Court nomination. Judge Bork's was the 27th Supreme Court nomination to fail in the country's history, the sixth in this century, and the first since 1970, when the Senate rejected President Nixon's nomination of G. Harrold Carswell by a vote of 51 to 45. There have been 104 Supreme Court justices in the nation's history.

People carrying signs and attending rally for the rejection of Robert H. Bork as a Supreme Court Justice.

The vote came two weeks after Judge Bork, in the face of expected defeat, said he would not withdraw his name and wanted the full Senate to vote on his nomination. In a statement issued from his chambers at the Federal courthouse here, where he still serves on the United States Court of Appeals for the District of Columbia Circuit, Judge Bork said he was "glad the debate took place."

President Reagan, in a statement released by the White House, said, "I am saddened and disappointed that the Senate has bowed today to a campaign of political pressure."

The President has publicly vowed to find a nominee who will upset Judge Bork's opponents "just as much" as Judge Bork himself. Mr. Reagan said today, "My next nominee for the Court will share Judge Bork's belief in judicial restraint—that a judge is bound by the Constitution to interpret laws, not make them."

"If we receive a nominee who thinks like Judge Bork, who acts like Judge Bork, who opposes civil rights and civil liberties like Judge Bork, he will be rejected like Judge Bork, just like that," Senator Edward M. Kennedy of Massachusetts said on the Senate floor.

MAY 9, 1987

HART DROPS RACE FOR WHITE HOUSE IN A DEFIANT MOOD

Robin Toner

Gary Hart, saying he was "angry and defiant" but finally overwhelmed by controversy, withdrew from the race for the Democratic Presidential nomination today, ending a four-year drive for the White House just five days after a public storm began over his private life.

In a short speech that sealed an extraordinary political collapse that began last Sunday, the Colorado Democrat, who had led all his party rivals in public opinion polls, said the press and the political system had become far more concerned with a candidate's personal life than with his public agenda.

"Too much of it is just a mockery, and if it continues to destroy people's integrity and honor, then that system will eventually destroy itself," Mr. Hart told reporters and campaign staff members in a nine-minute speech at the Executive Tower Inn in downtown Denver. Mr. Hart, his campaign besieged since The Miami Herald reported last Sunday that he spent part of the weekend with Donna Rice, of Miami, asserted: "I believe I would have been a successful candidate. And I know I could have been a very good President, particularly for these times."

Mr. Hart's departure from the contest left the Democratic Party facing a drawn-out battle among a large field of candidates, most of whom lack national stature. Party officials said the campaign might not take a firm shape until the Iowa caucuses next February.

Mr. Hart, a former two-term Senator who came close to capturing the Democratic nomination in 1984 and who had been planning his 1988 campaign ever since, said at his new conference:

"Clearly, under the present circumstances, this campaign cannot go on. I refuse to submit my family and my friends and innocent people and myself to further rumors and gossip. It's simply an intolerable situation."

Mr. Hart and his wife, Lee, then returned to seclusion at their home near Denver, aides said. His staff members, stunned and often tearful, made plans to close down a campaign that had ended with shattering speed. "The campaign is over and the national headquarters is being closed," said William P. Dixon, who had served as campaign manager.

To Mr. Hart's believers, the withdrawal was the stuff of tragedy. "He could have been an incredible President," said Ms. Casey, whose face was taut with sadness. She noted later that Thomas Jefferson and Abraham Lincoln and Franklin Roosevelt had all had questions raised about their personal lives.

Ms. Casey added, "We've had Presidents who had personal lives that were beyond question, and we don't even remember their names." ■

American politician Gary Hart sits on a dock with Donna Rice on his lap in 1987.

President-elect George Bush and his family celebrate his victory during Bush's acceptance speech in 1988.

NOVEMBER 9, 1988

The 1988 Elections; Bush Is Elected By a 6-5 Margin with Solid G.O.P. Base In South; Democrats Hold Both

E. J. Dionne Jr.

George Herbert Walker Bush of Texas was elected the 41st President of the United States yesterday.

The Vice President fashioned a solid, 6-to-5 victory in the popular vote over Gov. Michael S. Dukakis of Massachusetts with a sweep of the once Democratic South. He captured enough major states in other regions to win a commanding majority in the Electoral College.

Of the total of 538 electoral votes, Mr. Bush appeared likely to get from 350 to 415.

His solid victory notwithstanding, Mr. Bush did little to help Republican candidates for the Senate. In states like Florida, New Jersey and Ohio, all carried by him and all with Senate races the Republicans had hoped to win, the Republican senatorial nominees went down to defeat.

As a result, the Democrats maintained control of not only the House of Representatives but also the Senate, as voters split their tickets in contest after contest. ■

MAY 05, 1989

NORTH GUILTY ON 3 OF 12 COUNTS; VOWS TO FIGHT TILL 'VINDICATED'

Stephen Engelberg

Oliver L. North, the cocky marine who became the Reagan Administration's covert guardian of the Nicaraguan rebels, was convicted today of shredding documents and two other crimes but was acquitted of nine other charges stemming from his role in the Iran-contra affair.

Federal District Judge Gerhard A. Gesell read the verdict in a tense, locked courtroom as Mr. North sat erect and taut, wearing the same blue suit he wore through much of trial, having retired as a lieutenant colonel after his indictment. The defendant bent his head before the 12 verdicts were read, but stared straight ahead as the counts were enumerated. His face hardened to a blank mask as the judge announced the three guilty verdicts.

Indicating his intention to appeal the guilty verdicts, Mr. North later said, "We will be fully vindicated."

The verdict seemed to reject important parts of the Government's case. Mr. North, who was an aide to the National Security Council, was found not guilty of accusations that he lied to Congress in 1985, spent contra traveler's checks on himself and defrauded the Internal Revenue Service in his efforts to raise funds to arm the rebels fighting the Sandinista government.

But the guilty verdict salvaged some of the Government's main charges. The jury held Mr. North accountable for personal acts: failing to pay for the $13,800 security system at his home, destroying and falsifying records and aiding and abetting the obstruction of Congress.

But it excused his participation in efforts to mislead Congress about his actions to aid the contras in violation of existing laws, and it showed leniency even about his direct lies to lawmakers in a White House meeting in August 1986.

The charges on which Mr. North was found guilty carry a maximum penalty of 10 years in prison and fines totaling $750,000. His conviction of destroying documents was significant because, if the verdict survives appeal, Mr. North would be barred from holding public office and would lose his Marine pension.

The conviction is the first guilty verdict to result from a criminal trial in the Iran-contra affair, although other people, like Robert C. McFarlane, the former national security adviser, and two private fund-raisers, have pleaded guilty to lesser offenses. ■

Lieutenant-Colonel Oliver North being sworn in before the House Foreign Affairs Committee hearing on the Iran-contra affair in 1986.

JUNE 22, 1989

SUPREME COURT, BACKS RIGHT TO BURN THE FLAG

Linda Greenhouse

In a decision virtually certain to be a First Amendment landmark, the Supreme Court ruled today that no laws could prohibit political protesters from burning the American flag.

In his majority opinion today, Justice William J. Brennan Jr. said, "We do not consecrate the flag by punishing its desecration, for in doing so we dilute the freedom that this cherished emblem represents."

The case began with a protest against the 1984 Republican National Convention in Dallas. In front of the City Hall, a demonstrator doused an American flag with kerosene and set it on fire as several dozen others chanted, "America, the red, white and blue, we spit on you."

The demonstrator, Gregory L. Johnson, was convicted of violating the Texas flag desecration law and was originally fined $2,000 and sentenced to one year in prison. He was represented at the Supreme Court by the Center for Constitutional Rights, a public-interest law firm in New York that represents liberal causes. William M. Kunstler, who argued the case for Mr. Johnson, said today that the decision "forbids the state from making the American flag a religious icon."

The case drew enormous attention and briefs from many outside groups. Jasper Johns, Robert Rauschenberg and a number of other artists filed an unusual brief on Mr. Johnson's behalf that included color prints of works of theirs that used the American flag as an image. ■

freedom for all

AUGUST 10, 1989

Bush Plans to Name Colin Powell to Head Joint Chiefs

Richard Halloran

President Bush will name Gen. Colin L. Powell of the Army to be the new Chairman of the Joint Chiefs of Staff, an appointment that would make him the first black officer to hold the nation's highest military post, Administration officials said today.

The choice is expected to meet little opposition in the Senate, whose approval is needed for the appointment. General Powell is considered a forceful leader, is highly respected in the diplomatic community and, like the man he would replace, Adm. William Crowe Jr. of the Navy, is a considered a military intellectual.

At the age of 52, General Powell is among the youngest four-star generals in American peacetime history. He was promoted to that rank in April.

As Chairman of the Joint Chiefs, General Powell will be the principal military adviser to the President, the National Security Council and the Secretary of Defense and a member of a new Pentagon executive committee that was established by Defense Secretary Dick Cheney as a means of advising the Secretary on everything from military budgets to military strategy. ■

OCTOBER 18, 1989

VIOLENT QUAKE HITS NORTHERN CALIFORNIA; HUNDREDS DEAD; DISASTER SCOPE UNCLEAR; HIGHWAY AND BAY BRIDGE'S DECK COLLAPSE

Firefighters extinguish fire in the Marina District in San Francisco on October 21, 1989, after a quake erupted killing an estimated 273 people and doing $1 billion worth of damage.

continued . . .

VIOLENT QUAKE HITS NORTHERN CALIFORNIA *continued*

James Barron

A devastating earthquake rocked the San Francisco Bay area at rush hour last night, killing at least 200 people, collapsing a mile-long span of an Interstate highway and wrecking part the Bay Bridge to Oakland.

The earthquake, which rumbled along the San Andreas Fault, was the second deadliest in United States history after the 1906 San Francisco earthquake and fire that killed more than 700 people. It started fires throughout San Francisco, Oakland and Berkeley and in the mountain areas near Santa Cruz.

It also forced the cancellation of the third game of the World Series and the evacuation of thousands of spectators from Candlestick Park.

Water, electricity, communication and transportation were knocked out in the nation's fourth largest metropolitan area, leaving officials to guess at the scope of the damage and residents to wander darkened streets, aware that they were in the middle of one of the worst catastrophes of their lives but unable to judge its extent. With little information except sketchy reports from transistor radios, they gathered in ones and twos on their porches and in larger numbers outside bars and hotels. There was a sense that they were surrounded by great damage, yet their isolation from the outside world made it impossible to know that so much had been destroyed in such a short time.

"This is just a devastating, terrible, terrible situation beyond everybody's imagination," said Marty Boyer, the public information officer for Alameda County.

Lieut. Gov. Leo McCarthy said the most extensive damage appeared to be south and east of San Francisco. He said he expected that states of emergency would be declared in Santa Clara, Alameda and Contra Costa counties.

The greatest loss of life appeared to have occurred on Interstate Highway 880 in Oakland, when a section of an upper roadway collapsed onto the lower section, crushing at least 200 people in their cars.

The earthquake rumbled through the area at 5:04 P.M., (8:04 P.M. Eastern time) and registered 6.9 on the Richter scale. It was centered near Hollister, 80 miles southeast of San Francisco in San Benito County, and shook buildings as far as 200 miles away.

Some people escaped from buildings seconds before the structures shook and collapsed in a hail of rubble. "It was like a movie, happening behind us," said Robert Northrup, who was leaving a meeting in Santa Cruz when the building fell. "It was absolutley like a Spielberg movie, like "Indiana Jones.'"

John F. Melvin, a guest at the Four Seasons Clift Hotel in San Francisco, said he had been on the telephone to New York when the room started to shudder. "It was like riding on a New York City subway car," he said. He tried to dive under the bed but ended up under a table, where he stayed until the swaying subsided.

Mike Krukow, a pitcher for the San Francisco Giants, said, "It was an unbelieveable thing." He was on the field awaiting the start of the World Series game when vibrations began. "The light towers were shaking," he said. "I was stunned, stunned."

The game was scheduled to begin in 16 minutes when the earthquake struck. ABC News and the Cable News Network reported that some of the 58,000 fans were injured as they rushed to the exits. Fans said they saw pieces of cracked concrete on the walkways outside the Candlestick Park, but the stadium itself did not appear to have been seriously damaged.

Baseball Commissioner Fay Vincent is to meet with other officials this morning to decide on when to reschedule the game between the San Francisco Giants and Oakland Athletics.

A 30-foot section of the upper deck of the San Francisco-Oakland Bay Bridge caved in. Witnesses said that at least two cars were dangling between the upper and lower levels.

In Oakland, where the Interstate highway collapsed, witnesses said the concrete and steel supports of the double-decked, elevated road crumpled.

"The freeway was fairly crowded when it collapsed," said Rick Andreotti, an Oakland police spokesman at a makeshift rescue center beneath the collapsed roadway. "It's not a matter of just getting to the cars, it's a matter of cutting the cars open."

He said rescuers believed that some of the the people in cars sandwiched between the two tiers were still alive. Television cameras zoomed in on two firefighters trying to rescue a 7-year-old boy trapped in the back seat of his parents' car. Witnesses said his 9-year-old sister had been pulled from the vehicle and taken to a hospital. Their parents were killed, witnesses said.

Five other freeways in the region were closed because of damage, including the curving overpasses leading into downtown San Francisco from the airport.

The hardest hit section of San Francisco seemed to be the Marina district, a fashionable area that was built on landfill brought in to make space for the Pan-American Pacific Exposition of 1905. Several apartment buildings there wobbled and collapsed onto parked cars. There were also a number of small fires that burned unattended while firefighters struggled to contain the biggest blazes. Some of the firefighters arrived by boat, squeezing past yachts docked near the fallen, burning buildings.

Everywhere people seemed in a state of shock. A steady stream of people came in to the Central Police Station on Vallejo Street near Stockton Street in the North Beach section. Most of them were neither distraught nor injured. The majority were from the East Bay and wanted to know there was any way to get home because they had heard the bridges and freeways were closed. They were told that there was no way, at least not before dawn today.

International

The world seemed not only a dangerous but also a dispiriting place as the presidency of Jimmy Carter wound to its conclusion. Iran held American hostages, and a daring rescue raid authorized by Carter failed miserably. Détente, the cornerstone of American policy toward the Soviet Union since the days of Nixon, was in tatters after the Soviet Union invaded Afghanistan in 1979 and exiled dissidents like Andrei Sakharov. Carter proposed an international boycott of the Summer Olympics, to be held in Moscow in 1980.

Afghan refugees and anti-Soviet resistance fighters in a camp in Pakistan

Ronald Reagan, taking office in January 1981, nevertheless held out the sunny promise that it was "morning again in America," although many of his listeners wondered how a politician who had spent a lifetime denouncing Communism could sit down at the same table across from the Russians to work out a livable nuclear policy.

Amazingly enough, he did, despite the rhetoric reflected in mottos like "peace through strength" and "trust but verify." In Britain, he had a like-minded ally in Prime Minister Margaret Thatcher, a "conviction politician," in her own words, keen to challenge the Soviet Union with the same iron will that she displayed in taking on the power of the British labor unions. Israel invaded Lebanon and expelled the Palestine Liberation organization from Beirut.

The nuclear-freeze movement gathered momentum when it was announced that the United States intended to base cruise missiles in Europe. In the United States, proponents of accommodation with the U.S.S.R. were aghast at the implications of Reagan's pet project, the Strategic Defense Initiative, a futuristic-sounding missile shield popularly known as "Star Wars."

British Prime Minister Margaret Thatcher with German Federal Chancellor Helmut Schmidt in 1982.

U.S. solders near St George's, the capital of the Grenada Island. U.S. troops invaded the island on October 27, 1983, ousting the Marxist government.

Relations between the two superpowers were chilly, but a genuine crisis never materialized. Instead of nuclear war, the 1980's experienced a series of nasty small-scale conflicts. The United States invaded the Caribbean island of Grenada and overthrew its new Marxist government. Britain declared war on Argentina over the Falkland Islands. The antigovernment forces known as "contras" waged a guerrilla war against the Sandinista regime in Nicaragua, secretly funded by the United States with money gained from the sale of arms to its bitter enemy Iran. When the secret dealings became public, the scandal badly damaged Reagan's presidency.

Fissures in the Eastern bloc widened, the Soviet economy weakened and a succession of aged, infirm Soviet leaders resisted change until, mid-decade, the relatively young, reform-minded Mikhail Gorbachev took over. Under the watchwords glasnost (openness) and perestroika (reform), he hoped to craft a more humane, efficient version of Leninism, but he too was at the mercy of powerful, historic changes beyond his power to direct.

In Poland, a prolonged strike by shipyard workers led to the creation of an independent trade union, directed by Lech Walesa, and the imposition of martial law. A long standoff ensued, and the future of the Soviet Empire hung in the balance. On their side, Poland's dissidents had a mighty ally, Pope John Paul II, a Pole whose forthright opposition to Communism and Soviet domination made him, in a sense, the spiritual leader of a movement that would spread throughout Eastern Europe.

Mikhail S. Gorbachev in 1985.

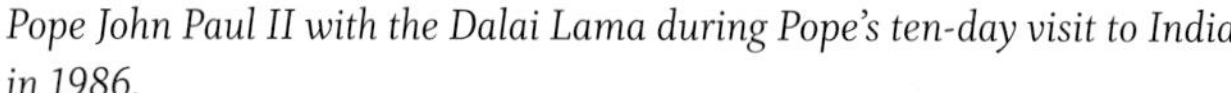

Pope John Paul II with the Dalai Lama during Pope's ten-day visit to India in 1986.

West Berliners crowd in front of the Berlin Wall early on November 11, 1989 as they watch East German border guards demolishing a section of the it.

By the end of the decade, the postwar order decided at the Yalta Conference in 1945 had unraveled with startling rapidity. Hungary, with Moscow's blessing, opened its borders and allowed East German tourists to reach the West. As the trickle became a flood, Erich Honecker, the longtime Communist leader, resigned, and his successor allowed East Germans to move freely through the gates in the Berlin Wall. In a wild night of jubilation, East Germans walked without restriction to greet their counterparts in West Berlin. Some began shattering the wall with hammers. It was a moment that millions had dreamed of but never expected to see.

There was more to come. The dismantling of the wall signaled the end of the Soviet empire. One by one, communist dictatorships collapsed. In the Soviet Union itself, Gorbachev discovered that he had unleashed forces far more powerful than he had envisioned. Instead of reforming the Soviet Union, he presided over its demise.

In China, events took a different course. Economic reform proceeded apace as the ideological grip of Maoism loosened and the Chinese heeded, with gusto, Deng Xiaoping's memorable injunction, "Enrich yourselves." It became clear that political freedom was not part of the equation when, in 1989, the government crushed, with startling brutality, a demonstration calling for civil liberties and political reform.

Chairman. Deng Xiaoping with PLO Chairman Yasser Arafat, in Beijing, China, in 1989.

It was a bitter conclusion to a period of exhilarating change. Once again the world learned that in history, happy endings are rare.

SEPTEMBER 24, 1980

OIL SITES IN IRAN AND IRAQ BOMBED AS BAGHDAD TROOPS CROSS BORDER

John Kifner

BAGHDAD, Iraq, Wednesday, Sept. 24—Iraq attacked Iran's huge oil refinery at Abadan yesterday, setting oil and gas tanks on fire, and Iran struck both Baghdad and Iraqi oil installations as hostilities between the two Persian Gulf nations widened.

The Iraqi military command said last night that its troops, crossing into Iran at several points, had surrounded Abadan and the neighboring port of Khurramshahr and were besieging the refinery itself.

Despite Iraqi raids on Iranian airfields Monday, Iranian planes struck three times at Baghdad yesterday, bombing the civil and military airports and firing rockets into the center of the city. The northern centers of Kirkuk and Mosul and a petrochemical complex near Basra in the south also came under Iranian air attack. Iraqi officials estimate that 50 people had been killed.

Twenty-nine of these were said to have died in the raid on the petrochemical complex, at Zubair, among them four Americans and four Britons working there, according to a British Foreign Office announcement in London.

The Iraqi command said yesterday that the latest advance had been decided upon in response to an announcement from Iran on Monday that is was in control of the Strait of Hormuz and that it would not allow any ships to carry cargo to Iraq. It said the cross-border attacks were also necessary to force Iran to accept Iraq's claim to sovereignty over the entire Shatt al Arab and to 90 square miles of territory in the Musian area. ■

A power plant of Baghdad after being bombarded by the Iranians in October 1980.

JULY 31, 1980

Israel Enacts a Law Making all of Jerusalem The Capital

Christopher S. Wren

JERUSALEM, July 30—In a final hectic session before its summer recess, the Parliament overwhelmingly enacted into law a bill affirming Jerusalem as the capital of Israel.

The legislation, which was approved by a vote of 69 to 15, with 3 abstentions, does nothing to change the city's defacto status.

Israel annexed the eastern, Arab part shortly after capturing it from Jordan in the 1967 was and has regarded the entire city as its capital for 13 years.

The bill, which was introduced in May by Geula Cohen, an ultranationalist who opposed the peace treaty with Egypt, has been criticized by Washington and Cairo, and many Israeli legislators admitted to having reservations about its value. Its enactment follows an announcement by Prime Minister Menachem Begin that he intends to move his office to East Jerusalem.

The developments together could make it harder to resuscitate the deadlocked negotiations between Israel and Egypt on the issue of self-rule for Palestinians in the occupied West Bank and Gaza. After a suspension of three months, a session of the talks had been scheduled for next week in Alexandria. ■

MAY 14, 1981

POPE IS SHOT IN CAR IN VATICAN SQUARE

Henry Tanner

ROME, Thursday, May 14—Pope John Paul II was shot and seriously wounded yesterday as he was standing in an open car moving slowly among more than 10,000 worshipers in St. Peter's Square.

The police arrested a gunman who was later identified as an escaped Turkish murderer who had previously threatened the Pope's life in the name of Islam.

Pope John Paul II being helped by his bodyguards after being shot by Mehmet Ali Agca at St Peter's Square in Rome on May 13, 1981.

The Pontiff, who was struck by two pistol bullets and wounded in the abdomen, right arm and left hand, underwent 5 hours and 25 minutes of surgery in which parts of his intestine were removed. A hospital bulletin at midnight said he was in "guarded" condition, but the director of surgery expressed confidence that "the Pontiff will recover soon."

The attack occurred as the Pope, dressed in white, was shaking hands and lifting small children in his arms while being driven around the square. Suddenly, as he reached a point just outside the Vatican's bronze gate, there was a burst of gunfire.

One hand rising to his face and blood staining his garments, the Pope faltered and fell into the arms of his Polish secretary, the Rev. Stanislaw Dziwisz, and his personal servant, Angelo Gugel, who were in the car with him.

The gunman, who the police said was armed with a 9-millimeter Browning automatic, was set upon in the square by bystanders, who knocked the pistol out of his hand. He was then arrested, taken away by police car and later identified as Mehmet Ali Agca, 23. Despite reports that another man had been seen fleeing from the square, the police said they were convinced that the gunman had acted alone.

The police quoted Mr. Agca as having told them, "My life is not important." He was said to have arrived in Italy last Saturday, landing at the Milan airport, and to have come to Rome on Monday. The police said that he had in his pocket several notes in handwritten Turkish, one of them saying, "I am killing the Pope as a protest against the imperialism of the Soviet Union and the United States and against the genocide that is being carried out in El Salvador and Afghanistan."

The Turkish news agency Anatolia reported that Mr. Agca had been convicted of murdering Abdi Ipekci, the editor of the Turkish newspaper Milliyet, in February 1979 but escaped from prison later that year. Anatolia said he wrote a letter to the newspaper on Nov. 26, 1979, saying that he had fled from prison with the intention of killing the Pope, who was just then due in Ankara and Istanbul. ■

JULY 30, 1981

AMID SPLENDOR, CHARLES WEDS DIANA

R.W. Apple Jr.

LONDON, July 29—In a blaze of martial and spiritual pageantry on a glorious summer morning, the Prince of Wales took as his wife today a shy and charming member of one of the kingdom's greatest families.

The 2,500 guests inside Christopher Wren's Baroque masterpiece, St. Paul's Cathedral, the hundreds of thousands who watched the wedding party ride in magnificent horse-drawn carriages from Buckingham Palace to the cathedral and back and the 700 million television viewers around the world witnessed a fairy tale come to life: the handsome Prince Charles in naval uniform marrying the lovely 20-year-old Diana Spencer, daughter of an earl, amid the sort of splendor the modern world has all but forgotten.

All the panoply of monarchy was deployed on this, one of the great days in the history of the House of Windsor: the stirring music of Handel and Purcell and Elgar; the Household Cavalry, in their burnished breastplates and helmets with red plumes; the stately royal horses, caparisoned in silver; almost all of the reigning sovereigns of Europe, come in their finery to share in the happy occasion, and the royal bride herself, resplendent in a gown of pale ivory, with puffy sleeves and a train 25 feet long.

It was a day that symbolized for the British people the continuity of the monarchy and thus of the nation itself, a day that many will recall as a punctuation mark in their own lives, a day that afforded surcease from a summer of joblessness, urban unrest and intractable problems in Ireland. It was a day that provided "a flash of color on the hard road we have to travel," as Sir Winston Churchill described the marriage of Prince Charles's mother, now Queen Elizabeth II.

As the bell in the tower above struck the first note of 11 o'clock, the organist sounded the first chord of the "Trumpet Voluntary" composed by Jeremiah Clarke, who was himself the organist of St. Paul's from 1699 to 1707. Down the aisle came Lady Diana in her gown of frills and flounces, pearls and crinolines. Sewn into the gown for luck was a tiny golden horseshoe, studded with diamonds. It took her four minutes to reach her fiance.

The ceremony, which lasted just over an hour, was the musical and emotional experience that the Prince said yesterday that he wanted. He said "I will" huskily but firmly; she said "I will" in a little girl's tentative voice. The stillness was broken first by the sound of a falling camera in the press stand. When Dr. Runcie said, "I pronounce that they be man and wife together," the joyous shouts of the crowd listening on loudspeakers outside was clearly audible.

Diana, Princess of Wales and Prince Charles, Prince of Wales, on their wedding day at St Paul's Cathedral. Sarah Armstrong-Jones is the bridesmaid behind them.

OCTOBER 7, 1981

Sadat Assassinated at Army Parade as Men Amid Ranks Fire into Stands

William E. Farrell

Egyptian president Anwar el-Sadat (left) and Ronald Reagan during a White House state arrival ceremony two months before his assassination.

President Anwar el-Sadat of Egypt was shot and killed today by a group of men in military uniforms who hurled hand grenades and fired rifles at him as he watched a military parade commemorating the 1973 war against Israel.

Vice President Hosni Mubarak, in announcing Mr. Sadat's death, said Mubarak. Egypt's treaties and international commitments would be respected. He said the Speaker of Parliament, Sufi Abu Taleb, would serve as interim President pending an election in 60 days.

The assassins' bullets ended the life of a man who earned a reputation for making bold decisions in foreign affairs, a reputation based in large part on his decision in 1977 to journey to the camp of Egypt's foe, Israel, to make peace.

Regarded as an interim ruler when he came to power in 1970 on the death of Gamal Abdel Nasser, Mr. Sadat forged his own regime and ran Egypt single-handedly. He was bent on moving this impoverished country into the late 20th century, a drive that led him to abandon an alliance with the Soviet Union and embrace the West.

That rule ended abruptly and violently today.

Information gathered from a number of sources indicated that eight persons had been killed and 27 wounded in the attack. Later reports, all unconfirmed, put the toll at 11 dead and 38 wounded.

The authorities did not disclose the identity of the assassins. They were being interrogated, and there were no clear indications whether the attack was to have been part of a coup attempt.

The assassination followed a recent crackdown by Mr. Sadat against religious extremists and other political opponents. There were unverifiable reports that some members of the armed forces had also been detained. ■

OBITUARY

SEPTEMBER 15, 1982

PRINCESS GRACE IS DEAD AFTER RIVIERA CAR CRASH

Clyde Haberman

Princess Grace of Monaco, whose stately beauty and reserve gave her enduring Hollywood stardom even long after she ended her film career, died yesterday in Monte Carlo of injuries suffered when her car plunged off a mountain road Monday. She was 52 years old.

The Princess, the former Grace Kelly, died of a cerebral hemorrhage, a palace spokesman said in Monaco. Princess Grace was driving her British Rover 3500 on a snaking road at Cap-d'Ail in the Cote d'Azur region when she lost control and plunged down a 45-foot embankment. The car burst into flames, and the Princess suffered multiple fractures, including a broken thighbone, collarbone and ribs.

Initial reports gave no sense that her life was in jeopardy. But a Monaco Government announcement yesterday said that her health had "deteriorated during the night."

"At the end of the day all therapeutic possibilities had been exceeded," the announcement said. With her in the car was Stephanie, 17, her youngest child by Prince Rainier III of Monaco. Stephanie was under observation at a hospital where she had been treated for shock and bruises.

Princess Grace's death brought expressions of grief from former Hollywood colleagues and from residents of her hometown, Philadelphia. President Reagan called her "a compassionate and gentle lady." In Philadelphia, a spokesman for John Cardinal Krol said the Cardinal, who was a close friend, would offer a memorial mass for her at noon Friday.

Alfred Hitchcock, who directed Grace Kelly in three films and was certainly in a position to judge, once said she had "sexual elegance." And it was that very elegance that probably made its most lasting impression on movie audiences of the 1950's.

Whether playing the heiress in "To Catch a Thief" or the Quaker pacifist in "High Noon" or the amusedly detached career girl—a term still in vogue when "Rear Window" was made—Grace Kelly carried herself with straight back and clipped-voice self-assurance. Yet just beneath the frosty exterior lay a sensuality and warmth that cracked the formidable reserve.

It was this delicate balance of contrasts that helped give her legendary status—a remarkable achievement for an actress whose career encompassed only 11 films. She made more of that small portfolio than actors who lasted in Hollywood many more decades. Twice she was nominated for an Academy Award, and once she won it, for her 1954 performance in "The Country Girl." There was a certain irony in the fact that the Oscar came, not for her portrayal of yet another detached beauty but of a frumpy harridan, desperate in her unhappy marriage.

The year before she was in Cannes filming "To Catch a Thief" with Cary Grant and it was at the film festival there that she met the Prince, a member of the Grimaldis, Europe's oldest royal family.

On April 18, 1956, shortly after she completed the movie "High Society," they were married in the Cathedral of St. Nicholas in Monaco. It was a media event of such staggering proportion that Miss Kelly, now Princess Grace, later suggested that she and the Prince should have been awarded battle ribbons for all the fighting that was required for them to push through the crowds.

SEPTEMBER 26, 1982

THE BEIRUT MASSACRE: THE FOUR DAYS

Thomas L. Friedman

BEIRUT, Lebanon, Sept. 25—The massacre of more than 300 Palestinian and Lebanese men, women and children at the Shatila refugee camp by Christian militiamen has left many unanswered questions.

The slayings, which began Wednesday, Sept. 15, and continued until Saturday, Sept. 18, raise questions that focus particularly on the role played by the Israeli Army in what is certain to be regarded as one of the most important events in the modern history of the Middle East.

Much is at stake in the answers to these questions. The relations between the Israeli people and their Government, the relations between world Jewry and Israel, the relations between Washington and Jerusalem and the relations between Israelis and Palestinians will all be affected by the truth of what happened in Shatila.

The full truth may never be known. Too many people have already fled the scene. Too many people were killed on the spot. Too many people are now under pressure to hide their deeds.

There has been no announcement of any investigation in Lebanon of the militiamen who actually did the killing. In Israel, Prime Minister Menachem Begin rejected the idea of an independent judicial commission of inquiry into the Israeli involvement in the massacre. On Friday, he proposed an investigation of lesser scope, but it was unclear whether the Chief Justice of Israel's Supreme Court will accept the invitation to head it. ■

Surviving families return to the refugee camps of Sabra and Shatila near Beirut after the 1982 massacre.

With marriage, she abandoned acting. The effect, as time passed, was to burnish her film career in public memory. Early on in her marriage she received many offers of movie roles but she kept turning them down.

Periodically, there would be reports that she was indeed about to resume her career but nothing ever came of them. "Here I have my obligations and duties as a princess and mother," she said. "One cannot do everything."

Her life as Princess of Monaco was obviously enhanced by privilege but also circumscribed by duty. She became a supporter of charities and cultural events. Much of her time was devoted to her three children, the oldest of whom, Princess Caroline, was born in 1957. In recent years, Princess Caroline outranked her mother as a source of fascination for curiosity-seekers, mostly as a result of her marriage to and then divorce from Phillipe Junot, a French businessman whom some people liked to describe as "the playboy next door."

A lot of people would have said the same thing about her. Always, she had a beauty that came perilously close to iciness but managed to stop safely short. Scratch that coating of ice—and most of her directors did—and exposed just beneath the surface was, variously, warmth, intelligence and sexuality. She could even be whimsical, in a detached fashion, a quality that she showed to advantage in "Rear Window," in which she was the girlfriend of James Stewart, a photographer with a broken leg who witnesses a murder across the courtyard from his apartment.

For herself, Miss Kelly was never comfortable with her popular image as an ice queen. "I'm not an extrovert—but I'm not unfriendly either," she told an interviewer early in 1955. "I'm not the exuberant type, but I don't like to read that I'm cold and distant. I don't think I am." ■

Princess Grace's car accident in Monaco, 1982.

NOVEMBER 12, 1982

BREZHNEV TRIED TO ADVANCE MOSCOW'S GOALS THROUGH DETENTE SOVIET LEADER

Soviet President Leonid Brezhev in 1981.

As the leader of the Soviet Union, Leonid Ilyich Brezhnev was a canny and careful Communist Party functionary who sought to make his country the military equal of the United States and promote its political influence around the world through the policy of detente.

In domestic affairs, as General Secretary of the Communist Party, Mr. Brezhnev ruled as first among his equals on the Politburo, not as an autocrat, and professed to want economic development of his country of 265 million people spread over a sixth of the globe's land area.

Both his policy and his health faltered in these tasks in the last years of his life. Detente, which had seemed a necessity to many Western leaders after Soviet tanks moved into Czechoslovakia in 1968 to crush the liberalization of the "Prague Spring," lost much of its appeal in the United States after the Soviet invasion of Afghanistan in 1979, and President Carter imposed an embargo on grain sales and other trade curbs.

After the Polish military authorities ceded to pressure from Moscow and declared martial law in December 1981, President Reagan imposed further economic and political sanctions on the Soviet Union, though not an embargo on grain sales. The Western European allies remained more reluctant to cut back their important industrial trade with the Russians, and insisted on going ahead with the deal, creating a political rift within the NATO alliance that Mr. Brezhnev obviously sought to exploit.

But domestic economic stagnation had become an acute domestic problem by the end of the Brezhnev years. In this area, despite their recognition of the crisis, the aging Soviet leaders made no effective attempt to reform the rigidities of centralized economic planning. And as the standard of living declined, political repression increased. Dissidents, who had emerged openly in the mid-1970's to criticize violations of human rights, were later harassed until most had either left the country or were in prison camps by the early 1980's. Soviet Jews, who had been permitted to emigrate by the thousands a month in 1977 and 1978, found that by 1982 permission to emigrate was virtually impossible to get.

In his last years, Mr. Brezhnev's speech became labored and his features pale and bloated, apparently as a result of medical treatments for a disability that was never publicly revealed. At the height of his powers in the early 1970's, in contacts with Presidents Nixon, Ford and Carter and Secretary of State Henry A. Kissinger, he was a burly, gray-haired, black-browed figure of 5 feet 10 inches, gregarious and talkative, but powerful and very much aware of his power over associates and adversaries alike.

Then he had a reputation as a lover of good food and drink, fast cars—which he collected—and hunting. Mr. Brezhnev talked extensively about his weight, which he sought vainly to keep under control, and often joked about his excessive cigarette smoking, which was thought to have aggravated his health problems.

His smoking (Philip Morris Multifilters) was such a vexation that he used a box with a time lock to slow his pace. But he conceded to one visitor, "I keep a reserve pack in the other pocket." Ultimately he had to give up smoking altogether. ■

APRIL 25, 1983

SKEPTICISM GROWING OVER THE 'HITLER DIARIES'

Robert D. McFadden

Skepticism over the authenticity of Hitler's purported diaries widened yesterday among historians, former aides of the dictator and handwriting experts in Britain, West Germany and the United States as the first excerpts were published.

Disbelief was expressed by David Irving and Lord Bullock, British historians and experts on Hitler; Werner Maser, a West German historian; two of Hitler's former personal aides; and Charles Hamilton Jr., an American expert on handwriting who has just completed an 800-page, two-volume study called "Autographs of the Third Reich."

"I'm sure it's a hoax," Mr. Hamilton said in an interview in New York yesterday after seeing three photostatic sheets from the purported diaries, including two bearing Hitler signatures. "The whole story is a misbegotten prevarication. The forgers are probably luxuriating right now in the south of France."

Some protagonists said the diaries, supposedly found in an East German hayloft in 1981 and bought by the West German news magazine Stern, were a major historical discovery and would contribute to the world's understanding of Hitler, the Third Reich and the events of the Nazi period.

Referring to the story of the loss and rediscovery of the documents, Mr. Hamilton said: "It's something Wilhelm and Jacob Grimm could have written. Stern said they have not got some parts of the diary ready for release yet. The only thing I can suggest is to tell the forger to hurry up and get them ready—and to make sure the ink is dry before he delivers them."

OCTOBER 31, 1984

INDIRA GANDHI ASSASSINATED BY GUNMEN

William K. Stevens

NEW DELHI, Wednesday, Oct. 31—Prime Minister Indira Gandhi was assassinated today by two gunmen who opened fire on her near her home.

Mrs. Gandhi, the dominant figure in Indian politics for nearly two decades, died less than four hours after undergoing emergency surgery at the All-India Institute of Medical Sciences for between 8 and 16 bullet wounds in the abdomen and thigh. She was 66 years old.

The Press Trust of India reported that the Prime Minister was gunned down by two members of her own security guard armed with a revolver and submachine gun as she walked from her residence to her office at 9:40 A.M. (11:10 P.M., Tuesday, Eastern standard time). The Press Trust report said the two assailants were members of the Sikh religion and had been captured.

Reports from news agencies and witnesses said Mrs. Gandhi fell to the ground with a cry and that members of her household and other security guards raced to her. She was admitted to the hospital and underwent surgery about 40 minutes after the shooting, according to hospital sources.

The Press Trust of India reported that the two gunmen were members of the Sikh religion, but this could not be independently confirmed. Mrs. Gandhi has been the target of Sikh anger since she ordered Government troops to raid the Golden Temple in Amritsar earlier this year to drive out Sikh militants who have been agitating for greater autonomy in the northwestern state of Punjab. ■

Mrs. Gandhi fell to the ground with a cry

The body of Indira Gandhi during the funeral procession on November 3, 1984.

SEPTEMBER 5, 1985

MANDELA: MAN, LEGEND AND SYMBOL OF RESISTANCE

Alan Cowell

JOHANNESBURG, Sept. 4—Percy Qoboza remembers the days fondly. One of them goes like this: In the early 1960's the man was on the run from the police, and Mr. Qoboza, a young black reporter, was following the story.

"He would disappear and then turn up, somewhere, at a public telephone, and call in with a statement. Of course the police would trace the call, but by that time, he was long gone. We had our own pimpernel."

Mr. Qoboza is now a prominent newspaper editor. The man he was talking about is Nelson Mandela, the imprisoned leader of the African National Congress, whose days as the pimpernel ran out in August 1962, when he was arrested for sabotage because of his role in the militant wing of the congress. He has been in prison ever since and has become, through incarceration and steadfast defiance from within the prison walls, South Africa's leading black hero, the man, according to a recent newspaper survey, whom 90 percent of the nation's black people want unconditionally freed.

"I think," Mr. Qoboza said in an interview today, "that he symbolizes black determination to be free."

The symbolism, from a black nationalist point of view, is evident. Pollsmoor prison, outside Cape Town, where Mr. Mandela is held, represents the system against which he rebels. His rebellion, from within, is the ambiguous emblem of defiance in a society where the rulers seem to call the shots.

The enigma, however, seems to be that, invisible and unheard, removed by white authority from black political activism, Mr. Mandela has captured the spirit and devotion not only of those who knew him at the time of his incarceration, but also of those who have, in the last year of upheaval, assumed the custodianship of black resistance—the teen-agers who were not yet born when he was jailed.

If Mr. Mandela, 67 years old, was released tomorrow, said Michael Morake, 18, in an interview in Soweto, Johannesburg's sprawling black satellite, "I will probably pass him by because I would not recognize him."

"All his life has been dedicated to the struggle," Mr. Qoboza said, "and I bet that the first thing he would do if he was released would be to organize a rally in Soweto and re-dedicate himself to the struggle." ■

APRIL 16, 1985

APARTHEID LAWS ON MIXED-RACE SEX TO BE ABOLISHED

Richard Bernstein

CAPE TOWN, April 15—The South African Government said today that it had decided to abolish the laws forbidding marriage and sex across racial lines.

Officials said they would accept a recommendation from a special committee of South Africa's new three-chamber Parliament to remove longstanding legal barriers to marriages and sexual relations between whites and and nonwhites.

The abolition of the marriage and sex laws is most likely to affect couples of different races whose marriages, contracted abroad or performed in South African churches, are not legally recognized by the Government. The parliamentary committee recommended that such marriages be legalized.

remove longstanding barriers

There are estimated to be thousands of such couples living in the legal shadows here, unable to travel on trains together or to get Government schooling for their children. They are forced to live in "gray" areas, places generally on the borders between white and nonwhite residential districts where they are less likely to attract attention.

Some legislators and Western diplomats said last month that they believed repeal of the laws relating to sexual behavior would be the main accomplishment of the first sitting of the new Parliament.

In the last five years, 918 people have been prosecuted for violating Article 16 of the Morality Act, 160 of them last year.

The proposed repeal of this feature of apartheid seems to be part of a Government effort to remove some parts of the system of racial separation. ■

Bishop Desmond M. Tutu attending a funeral in 1985.

APRIL 19, 1986

PRETORIA RESCINDS PASS-LAW CONTROL ON BLACKS' MOVES

Edward A. Garga

JOHANNESBURG, April 18—President P. W. Botha announced today that the pass laws controlling where black people can live and work would no longer be enforced. For blacks, the pass laws are among the most hated aspects of apartheid.

Blacks who have been convicted of violating pass laws, and those who are in jail awaiting trial, will be freed immediately, the President said in a speech to Parliament.

Mr. Botha said that the passes carried by black people would be abolished and that a standard identity card would be issued for all races beginning in July. Government officials have not said whether the new ones would contain racial information or restrictions.

Bishop Desmond M. Tutu, who was elected Archbishop of Cape Town this week, gave conditional praise to Mr. Botha's announcement.

"The moratorium and release of pass offenders can only be welcomed," Bishop Tutu said. "However, I hope there is not a sting in the tail. One has to be very careful that they are not going to find another way of harassing blacks."

Other anti-apartheid activists said they doubted whether the President's statement meant blacks would be free to live and work where they wanted.

Hundreds of thousands of blacks are arrested each year for violating various provisions of the pass laws, including failure to carry the pass book, an identity document, and for illegally being in restricted white urban and residential areas.

Figures are not precise, but arrests are thought to have averaged 200,000 to 300,000 a year in recent years. Amnesty International, the human rights organization, reported that 238,000 black people were arrested in 1984 for pass-law violations.

Scholars have calculated that 18 million blacks have been arrested in the last 70 years for violations. ■

MARCH 2, 1986

Swedish Premier Assassinated on Stockholm Street

James F. Clarity, Milt Freudenhelm and Richard Levine

Olof Palme, the Prime Minister of Sweden and an internationally prominent left-wing activist, was shot and killed by a gunman Friday night on a brightly lit street corner in downtown Stockholm. He had dismissed his security guards and was walking with his wife after attending a movie premiere.

The assailant escaped, apparently in a car driven by an accomplice; the police said they had no evidence of a motive. In a call to a news agency in London, however, a terrorist group called the Holger Meins Commando claimed responsibility.

It was the first assassination of a Swedish head of government or state in more than 200 years. The last European leader killed while holding office was the Prime Minister of Spain, Luis Carrero Blanco, in 1973, who died in a car-bombing attributed to Basque separatists.

Mr. Palme, who was 59 years old, led his Socialist Party for 17 years, serving as Prime Minister from 1969 to 1976, when he lost an election, and regaining the office in 1982. Educated at Kenyon College in Ohio, he was a frequent and sharp critic of United States policies. In 1968 he marched alongside a North Vietnamese diplomat in a demonstration against the American war in Vietnam, and he campaigned vigorously against deployment of American nuclear weapons in Europe.

He was faulted for muting criticism of the Soviet Union, even when Soviet submarines were repeatedly sighted in Swedish waters. But Sweden, which proclaims itself a neutral nation, remained Western-oriented in trade, culture and democratic institutions.

President Reagan sent condolences, denouncing the murder as "a senseless act of violence." He praised Mr. Palme for "his devotion to democratic values and his untiring efforts to promote peace." ■

APRIL 29, 1986

SOVIET ANNOUNCES NUCLEAR ACCIDENT AT ELECTRIC PLANT

Serge Schmemann

MOSCOW, April 28—The Soviet Union announced today that there had been an accident at a nuclear power plant in the Ukraine and that "aid is being given to those affected."

The severity of the accident, which spread discernable radioactive material over Scandinavia, was not immediately clear. But the terse statement, distributed by the Tass press agency and read on the evening television news, suggested a major accident.

The phrasing also suggested that the problem had not been brought under full control at the nuclear plant, which the Soviet announcement identified as the Chernobyl station. It is situated at the new town of Pripyat, near Chernobyl and 60 miles north of Kiev.

The announcement, the first official disclosure of a nuclear accident ever by the Soviet Union, came hours after Sweden, Finland and Denmark reported abnormally high radioactivity levels in their skies. The readings initially led those countries to think radioactive material had been leaking from one of their own reactors.

The Soviet announcement, made on behalf of the Council of Ministers, after Sweden had demanded information, said in its entirety:

"An accident has occurred at the Chernobyl nuclear power plant as one of the reactors was damaged. Measures are being taken to eliminate the consequences of the accident. Aid is being given to those affected. A Government commission has been set up."

The Chernobyl plant, with four 1,000-megawatt reactors in operation, is one of the largest and oldest of the 15 or so Soviet civilian nuclear stations. Nuclear power has been a matter of high priority in the Soviet Union, and capacity has been going into service as fast as reactors can be built. Pripyat, where the Chernobyl plant is situated, is a settlement of 25,000 to 30,000 people that was built in the 1970's along with the station. It is home to construction workers, service personnel and their families.

A British reporter returning from Kiev reported seeing no activity in the Ukrainian capital that would suggest any alarm. No other information was immediately available from the area.

But reports from across Scandinavia, areas more than 800 miles to the north, spoke of increases in radioactivity over the last 24 hours.

The first alarm was raised in Sweden when workers arriving at the Forsmark nuclear power station, 60 miles north of Stockholm, set off warnings during a routine radioactivity check. The plant was evacuated, Swedish officials said. When other nuclear power plants reported similar happenings, the authorities turned their attention to the Soviet Union, from which the winds were coming.

A Swedish diplomat here said he had telephoned three Soviet Government agencies—the State Committee for Utilization of Atomic Energy, the Ministry of Electric Power and the three-year-old State Committee for Safety in the Atomic Power Industry—asking them to explain the high readings over Scandinavia. All said they had no explanation, the diplomat said. ■

Repairs being carried out on the Chernobyl nuclear plant in the Ukraine, following a major explosion in April of 1986 which, according to official statistics, affected 3,235,984 Ukrainians and sent radioactive clouds all over Europe.

Muammar el-Qaddafi in 1985.

JANUARY 9, 1986

PRESIDENT FREEZES ALL LIBYAN ASSETS HELD IN THE U.S.

Gerald Boyd

WASHINGTON, Jan. 8—President Reagan today ordered Libyan assets in the United States frozen, and the State Department issued a report giving details of its charges that Col. Muammar el-Qaddafi's Government supported terrorism around the world.

The action came a day after the President announced measures virtually severing all economic ties with Libya and ordered Americans living there to depart.

The report charging Libyan complicity in terrorism included some new allegations about assistance given to terrorist groups by Colonel Qaddafi. It was issued in an effort to bolster the Government's case for a worldwide boycott of Libya.

But the American appeal for cooperation received a tepid response from European governments and Japan, all of which expressed doubts about the merits of economic sanctions. At the same time, the Federal Bureau of Investigation said it had prevented six potential terrorist attacks last year within the United States that were to be carried out by terrorists from abroad. Three of the incidents involved a Libyan diplomat who the F.B.I. said had entered this country to coordinate violence against Libyan dissidents.

In Libya, the state radio described the new United States moves as proof that President Reagan "and his intelligence services are involved in lowly conspiracies" to overthrow the Qaddafi Government.

The State Department report issued today accused Colonel Qaddafi of using terrorism as "one of the primary instruments of his foreign policy."

Included in the "white paper" report, prepared by the Central Intelligence Agency,

OBITUARY

MAY 10, 1986

TENZING NORKAY, 72, IS DEAD: CLIMBED EVEREST WITH HILLARY

DARJEELING, India, May 9—Tenzing Norkay, the Sherpa who stood atop the world on Mount Everest with Sir Edmund Hillary in 1953, died here today of a lung infection. He was 72 years old.

He and Sir Edmund, the New Zealander who was knighted for his feat, became the first to climb the world's highest mountain when they reached the summit of Everest on May 29, 1953. The Sherpa who began as a climber's porter became an inspiration to a generation of mountaineers.

Tenzing Norkay died at dawn today at his home at this picturesque resort about 310 miles north of Calcutta. He had been ill for two years and served as an adviser to the Himalayan Mountaineering Institute.

Sir Edmund, now New Zealand's Ambassador to India, said the death of his partner in the successful assault on the 29,028-foot-high crest was "an unexpected shock."

Prime Minister Rajiv Gandhi called the Sherpa a "simple man of indomitable spirit who inspired the Indian youth to take to mountaineering."

"The entire country will mourn the passing away of the legendary figure," Mr. Gandhi said.

The mountaineer lived in a three-story villa with his wife, several of their 6 children and 25 dogs. He once complained that, even many years after the expedition, so many people sought him out that he had to post a mastiff on his door to keep them away.

The one question he consistently refused to answer was probably the one he was asked most often: Who stepped on the summit first, Tenzing or Sir Edmund?

"This is teamwork; actually, we climbed together," he said. "Whatever Hillary say, I don't care, but I say, teamwork. There shouldn't be controversy there."

Tenzing Norkay was born in 1914 in the Sherpa village of Solo Khumbu in Nepal, one of 13 children. He was unsure of his birthdate and there were no records, but he reckoned it to be in May.

His name at birth was Namgyal Wangdi, but he said a Buddhist holy man insisted he was the reincarnation of a rich man who had recently died. The holy man suggested he be renamed Tenzing Norkay, which means "wealthy-fortunate follower of religion."

It was while herding his family's yaks, he said, that his dream of climbing Everest took shape.

Members of the small Sherpa tribe, which has no written language and a forgotten history, generally work as attendants and porters for mountaineers. Tenzing was one of the few to become a full-fledged climber.

George Michael Westmacott, a British member of the history-making climb, said today that others in the party were "disappointed, but not resentful" that Lord Hunt, the leader, chose Tenzing to make the final drive to the summit.

"He was different from most Sherpas because he wanted to get to the top of the mountain," Mr. Westmacott said. "The others were quite happy to carry the loads." ■

were several charges of Libyan support for guerrilla groups throughout the world and other terrorist actions. For example, it said that Libya had sent planeloads of gunmen to Saudi Arabia in 1984 and 1985 to try and disrupt the annual Moslem pilgrimage to Mecca.

The paper confirmed for the first time that Egypt had thwarted a plot of Libyan-backed Palestinians to blow up the American Embassy in Cairo with a truck bomb in May. In addition, it said that several known Libyan terrorists have been assigned to the Libyan Embassy in the Sudan and that Libya had provided arms to Sudanese revolutionary committees dedicated to overthrowing the Sudanese Government. The White House spokesman, Larry Speakes, said there had been 695 terrorist incidents last year, with about 200 directed at Americans. In addition, he said, there were 126 aborted terrorism incidents last year, including 23 in the United States. ■

OCTOBER 13, 1986

REAGAN-GORBACHEV TALKS END IN STALEMATE AS U.S. REJECTS DEMAND TO CURB 'STAR WARS'

Bernard Gwertzman

REYKJAVIK, Iceland, Oct. 12—President Reagan and Mikhail S. Gorbachev ended two days of talks here today with no agreement on arms control and no date for a full-fledged summit meeting in the United States.

While officials said that the two leaders had succeeded in developing tentative understandings on most arms control issues, a possible accord foundered over Soviet insistence that the United States scrap its space-based missile-defense plans.

Mr. Reagan, speaking to American forces at the Keflavik Air Base near here, before returning home, said, "We came to Iceland to advance the cause of peace and, though we put on the table the most far-reaching arms control proposal in history, the General Secretary rejected it."

Mr. Gorbachev, at a news conference, attributed the failure to American intransigence on the plan for a space-based missile defense, known officially as the Strategic Defense Initiative, and popularly as "Star Wars." The Soviet leader said he had told the President at the end of their meeting: "We missed a historic chance. Never have our positions been so close."

When the Iceland meeting was first arranged, it was expected to set a date for a regular summit meeting in the United States in the coming months, as called for by the two leaders at their first meeting in Geneva last year.

MAY 31, 1987

Teenager's Flight to Kremlin Wall Jolts Politburo

James F. Clarity and Milt Freudenheim

To the amazement of all and the consternation of Soviet authorities, a 19-year-old amateur pilot from West Germany flew a tiny single-engine plane across more than 400 miles of heavily guarded Soviet territory last week and landed next to the Kremlin wall at the foot of Red Square.

Matthias Rust, a vacationing computer operator, took off in a rented Cessna 172 from Helsinki, Finland, ostensibly bound for Stockholm. Then he made an abrupt U-turn toward Moscow, where he reportedly circled the main Government palaces before landing on a cobblestone square amid startled strollers Thursday evening. Passers-by got the pilot's autograph, and an artist painted the blue-and-white plane parked near the famous onion domes of St. Basil's Cathedral. The police took Mr. Rust into custody.

Soviet authorities were not amused. The ruling Poliburo called a special meeting yesterday and removed the 76-year-old Defense Minister, Marshal Sergei L. Sokolov, and Aleksandr Koldunov, an aide who headed Soviet air defense forces.

Moscow television said air defense radar had spotted the Cessna as it approached the border. "Soviet fighters twice flew around it," the broadcast said. "The Politburo noted that the commanders of the air defense forces manifested an unpermissible carelessness and indecisiveness," it added, and they criticized the "absence of proper alertness and discipline and major failures in management of troops from the Ministry of Defense."

A Western attache was gentler. "We can't paint them as dumb," he said. "Is the profile of a sporting aircraft at low altitude the same as the profile of a cruise missile?"

Flipping the dials of their short-wave radios last week, Soviet listeners encountered a surprising absence of the customary Kremlin-sponsored drone overpowering the Voice of America's programs in Russian, Ukrainian, Uzbek and six other languages. Officials in Washington said Moscow had stopped jamming the Voice's Soviet-language programs for the first time since 1980. ■

Mathias Rust arrives in a Moscow court on September 4, 1987. He was sentenced to four years in a labour camp for violating Soviet airspace.

Prime Minister of Great Britain, Margaret Thatcher, waves to supporters during her victory on election night June 11, 1987, in London.

JUNE 12, 1987

THATCHER CLAIMS HER THIRD VICTORY, BUT MARGIN DROPS

Howell Raines

After a bruising campaign, Margaret Thatcher claimed victory this morning in the British general election and a place in history as the first Prime Minister in this century to win three consecutive terms.

At dawn, the count stood at Conservatives 345, Labor 225, and the Alliance parties 13.

In the popular vote, Mrs. Thatcher had 42.9 percent, up half a point from 1983. Labor got 32.3, up more than four points. The Alliance got 22.7 percent, a slippage of almost three points.

In claiming victory, Mrs. Thatcher declared it a "day of history."

"It is wonderful to be entrusted with the Government of this great country once again," Mrs. Thatcher told a cheering crowd at Conservative Central Office at 3:15 this morning. She reminded them that her platform called for extending her free-market principles to Labor's strongholds in the decaying "inner cities."

Throughout the campaign, the Labor leader, Neil Kinnock, had hammered at Mrs. Thatcher as an advocate of a country "divided by privilege." In the election, the Conservatives scored heavily in London, prosperous southern England and across the Midlands, while Labor was strong in areas of economic decline in Wales, Scotland and the north.

"I think what we're witnessing is an a even greater abyss of division than that which we've witnessed previously," Mr. Kinnock said in a grudging acknowledgement of Mrs. Thatcher's victory. Referring to his own victory in his home constituency, Mr. Kinnock said, "We shall work for the day when not just we shall win, but England shall win."

After a campaign in which Mr. Kinnock's stinging oratory and polished use of television had clearly rattled Mrs. Thatcher, Labor was disappointed by the modesty of its gains over the 206 seats it had held. ■

JUNE 13, 1987

RAZE BERLIN WALL, REAGAN URGES SOVIET

Gerald M. Boyd

WEST BERLIN, June 12—President Reagan sought today to undercut Europe's perception of Mikhail S. Gorbachev as a leader of peace, bluntly challenging the Soviet leader to tear down the Berlin wall.

Speaking 100 yards from the wall that was thrown up in 1961 to thwart an exodus to the West, Mr. Reagan made the wall a metaphor for ideological and economic differences separating East and West.

"There is one sign the Soviets can make that would be unmistakable, that would advance dramatically the cause of freedom and peace," the President said.

"Secretary General Gorbachev, if you seek peace—if you seek prosperity for the Soviet Union and Eastern Europe—if you seek liberalization: come here, to this gate. Mr. Gorbachev, open this gate. Mr. Gorbachev, tear down this wall."

Mr. Reagan made the remarks with the Brandenburg Gate in East Berlin in the background. An East Berlin security post was in view.

The Berlin police estimated that 20,000 people had turned out to hear the President, but some observers thought the crowd was smaller than that. ■

JULY 4, 1987

French Court Finds Barbie Guilty and Orders Him To Prison For Life

Richard Bernstein

Klaus Barbie, the wartime Gestapo chief of Lyons, was convicted early today of crimes against humanity and was sentenced to life imprisonment.

Mr. Barbie, who walked out of the trial on its third day, nearly two months ago, and had returned only twice since then, was brought into the courtroom just after midnight for the reading of the verdict.

He stood motionless and without expression, his head bowed slightly toward his court interpreter, as the presiding judge, Andre Cerdini, pronounced him guilty on all 341 separate items of the indictment, involving the deportation, unlawful imprisonment and torture of Jews and members of the French Resistance during the German occupation of Lyons between 1942 and 1944.

The life sentence means that Mr. Barbie, 73 years old, will be eligible for parole in 15 years, when he will be 88.

France abolished the death penalty in 1981. French courts had convicted Mr. Barbie of war crimes twice in absentia and sentenced him to death, but the statute of limitations in those cases expired before he could be returned to France. Trial Riveted the Country

The verdict, after six hours of deliberation by the panel of three judges and nine jurors, ended an eight-week trial, the first in a French court on a charge of crimes against humanity. The proceedings had commanded the attention of this country, first by several weeks of often gripping and dramatic testimony and then by a bitter, often angry contest between prosecution and defense lawyers.

"This shows that the French people have not forgotten," Serge Klarsfeld, a lawyer and Nazi crimes researcher, said after the verdict.

Mr. Klarsfeld, who led a 10-year campaign to have Mr. Barbie brought to France from a 32-year refuge in South America, said: "There was an exceptional crime, and this was an exceptional trial. And because memory is related to justice, it means that the children of Izieu will not die away in memory. They will not be forgotten."

Mr. Klarsfeld was referring to 44 Jewish children who were taken by the Gestapo from a rural hiding place just east of here and sent to their deaths in the Nazi concentration camps.

Mr. Barbie, who came to be known as the Butcher of Lyons, was the chief of the Gestapo here from late 1942 until the Germans were driven from this part of France in August 1944. He was brought to France four years ago from Bolivia, where he had lived under the assumed name Klaus Altmann since escaping from Europe in 1951.

His trial, more than 40 years after the German defeat, had been heralded by many here as a historic event and one whose purpose was not only to bring a presumed Nazi criminal to justice, but also to enrich the memory of the wartime persecution of Jews—more than 60,000 of whom died in deportation—and members of the Resistance. ■

OBITUARY

AUGUST 18, 1987

Rudolf Hess Is Dead; Last of the Hitler Inner Circle

Rudolf Hess, the onetime deputy to Hitler who early in World War II parachuted into a Scottish meadow in what he called an attempt to make peace between Nazi Germany and Britain, died yesterday in West Berlin. He was 93 years old.

Hess, once one of Hitler's designated successors, was the last survivor of the 19 German officials convicted by the International Military Tribunal at Nuremberg in 1946. Given a life sentence, he had been an inmate of Spandau Prison in West Berlin since 1947; for the last two decades, Hess had been Spandau's only occupant.

Hess's son, Wolf-Rudiger, was informed by British authorities yesterday afternoon that his father died at the British Military Hospital in West Berlin. Allied officials said he was taken there earlier in the day from Spandau.

There was no immediate report on the cause of death. Hess had been treated at the British hospital last spring for a heart condition.

With Hess's death, Allied officials said Spandau Prison would be torn down.

"The purpose of Spandau Allied War-Crimes Prison has ceased with the death of Rudolf Hess," the Allied Prison Administration said in a statement. "In accordance with the decision of representatives of Great Britain, France, the U.S.A. and the U.S.S.R., the Allied Prison Administration will be terminated and the prison will be demolished."

Allied sources have said in the past that the prison would be demolished promptly to prevent its becoming a focus of neo-Nazi sentiments.

A disgruntled World War I veteran, Hess became an early member of the Nazi Party and, in the 1920's, Hitler's secretary and bodyguard. He rose to be head of the party's Political Central Commission in 1932. When Hitler gained power in Germany in 1933, he made Hess his deputy as chief of the Nazi Party—formally, the National Socialist German Workers' Party—and brought him into his Cabinet as a Minister Without Portfolio. He also, in 1939, declared Hess second in the line of succession, after Hermann Goring.

Hess has been called shy, bland and unintelligent by historians. He also had a reputation for dogged loyalty to Hitler, and he recalled his Nazi career proudly in a statement he made before being sentenced at Nuremberg:

"I am happy to know that I have done my duty to my people, my duty as a German, as a National Socialist, as a loyal follower of my Fuhrer. I do not regret anything."

In the last decades of his life, Hess was one of the world's best-known and most controversial inmates, particularly as the number of surviving Nazi leaders dwindled.

Details of Hess's prison life were occasionally reported: how he suffered from pneumonia and pleurisy and, in 1977, apparently tried to kill himself; how he was sometimes sent to a British military hospital in West Berlin; and how his son visited him once a month and campaigned in vain to have him set free.

Over the years, the United States, Britain, France and West Germany made appeals to have Hess freed on humanitarian grounds.

The requests generated some controversy. Noting that Hess signed the infamous Nuremberg laws that stripped German Jews of their civil rights, a key event in the Holocaust, Rabbis Marvin Hier and Abraham Cooper of the Simon Wiesenthal Center in Los Angeles, a center for the study of the Holocaust, wrote some years ago:

"A life sentence for this unrepentent Nazi is an act of compassion in comparison with the fate suffered by the millions who were redefined as subhuman by a stroke of Hess's pen."

The Germans insisted that Hess was "the victim of hallucinations." Several British and American psychiatrists contended that Hess was insane, noting his dealings with astrologers, his paranoia and his lapses of memory.

Hess did not testify at Nuremberg, and did not seem to have interest in the trial. Sometimes he read a book in court, sometimes he appeared to follow the testimony; mostly he sat, apparently lost in meditation.

In later years, historians tended to doubt that Hess was crazy. "He just had a bee in his bonnet," said A. J. P. Taylor, the British historian, "a strong conviction that war between England and Germany was a mistake and that if he came over himself he could influence the British to make peace." ■

Rudolph Hess, Joachim Von Ribbentrop and Hermann Goring sitting in the defendents box at the Nuremberg Trials in 1946.

DECEMBER 17, 1987

338 GUILTY IN SICILY IN A MAFIA TRIAL; 19 GET LIFE TERMS

Roberto Suro

The largest Mafia trial in history ended today with guilty verdicts against 338 of 452 defendants accused of running a vast criminal empire financed largely with heroin trafficking to the United States.

The jury ordered life sentences, the maximum penalty, for 19 men, including the foremost leaders of the Sicilian Cosa Nostra and professional killers who did their bidding.

Among them was Michele Greco, nicknamed the Pope because of his place atop the Mafia hierarchy. Mr. Greco was found guilty of ordering 78 homicides, including the assassinations of several important government officials.

The most important evidence came from two informers, Tommaso Buscetta and Salvatore Contorno, who have also testified at New York Mafia trials. The prosecutor, Giuseppe Ayala, told reporters tonight, "Their testimony was accepted when other facts confirmed it."

On the basis of that testimony, for the first time in Sicily the Mafia was prosecuted as a single, unified orgnanization with its own leadership.

Most of the specific crimes cited in the trial occurred in the early 1980's, when the Sicilian Mafia provided 50 percent of the heroin reaching the American East coast, the United States Justice Department estimated.

The "maxi-trial," as it became known, was viewed throughout Italy as a demonstration of the state's willingness to strike back at a criminal organization that grew steadily more powerful and murderous as it expanded its lucrative drug trade.

Much of the reaction to the verdict by public authorities was subdued in recognition of the fact that the Mafia is still very much alive in Sicily. Proof of that arrived less than four hours after the sentencing when one of the defendants declared innocent, Antonino Ciulla, was murdered immediately after he was released from custody.

About a thousand lawyers, defendants and spectators had been waiting for three hours when Presiding Judge Alfonso Giordano entered the amphitheater-shaped courtroom and began, "In the name of the Italian people . . ."

The short, plump judge, who grew a beard during the 35 days he guided jury deliberations, read as fast as he could. A nearly indecipherable stream of names and legal citations poured forth. Gradually it became apparent that men once considered untouchable were being sent to jail. ■

DECEMBER 9, 1987

THE SUMMIT; REAGAN AND GORBACHEV SIGN MISSILE TREATY AND VOW TO WORK FOR GREATER REDUCTIONS

David K. Shipler

U.S. President Ronald Reagan with Soviet leader Mikhail Gorbachev during welcoming ceremonies at the White House on the first day of their summit in 1987.

With fervent calls for a new era of peaceful understanding, President Reagan and Mikhail S. Gorbachev today signed the first treaty reducing the size of their nations' nuclear arsenals.

The President and the Soviet leader, beginning three days of talks aimed at even broader reductions, pledged to build on the accord by striving toward what Mr. Gorbachev called "the more important goal," reducing long-range nuclear weapons.

In their White House conversations, the leaders were said to have reviewed their previous proposals aimed at furthering those negotiations, and they established an arms-control working group of ranking officials to hold parallel sessions.

An immediate mood of warmth was established as the two leaders agreed this morning to call each other by their first names, a White House official said. He quoted the President as telling Mr. Gorbachev, "My first name is Ron."

Mr. Gorbachev answered, "Mine is Mikhail."

"When we're working in private session," Mr. Reagan reportedly said, "we can call each other that."

The new treaty, which provides for the dismantling of all Soviet and American medium- and shorter-range missiles, establishes the most extensive system of weapons inspection ever negotiated by the two countries, including placing technicians at sensitive sites on each other's territory.

The visit to Washington by Mr. Gorbachev was the first by a Soviet leader since Leonid I. Brezhnev was here 14 years ago, and it took on immediate drama as Mr. Reagan, who entered office with deep suspicions of the Soviet Union, welcomed Mr. Gorbachev on the South Lawn of the White House.

"IIf approved by the Senate, the accord would require the dismantling within three years of all 1,752 Soviet and 859 American missiles with ranges of 300 to 3,400 miles and their nuclear warheads. It also provides for stationing inspection teams at sensitive sites on each other's soil, with the right to make a certain number of short-notice inspections elsewhere each year for 13 years. ■

DECEMBER 20, 1987

IN CHINA, THE BUCK STARTS HERE

Nicholas D. Kristof

Her life has changed in many ways since she became a tycoon. There is the stereo to play Chinese opera, and a refrigerator to keep drinks cold.

But Yip Hongcheung, a 36-year-old capitalistic Communist, slyly points to her greatest triumph: an indoor bathroom with running water. "It's a big improvement," she explains cheerfully. "Before, I could only dream of such a thing."

Mrs. Yip and her husband are Chinese "Rockefellers": sunburned, mud-between-the-toes landlords with 40 acres and 60 laborers under them; they pay their workers about $50 a month, and earn more than $100,000 a year by raising chickens; rabbits; fish, in ponds; fruit, and young fruit trees destined to be planted in orchards elsewhere.

Forty years ago, the local Communist Party might have shot them; now it gives them a 30-year lease on the land. It is no wonder that Mrs. Yip is so enthusiastic: "Everyone's becoming richer in Guangdong. Everybody's living a better life."

It is propaganda, but it is true. Guangdong Province, a region almost the size of the British Isles and a bit more populous, is China's vanguard, awakening from a few hundred years' economic slumber to set a frenetic pace as one of the fastest-growing economies in the world. Step into a New York shop and a product with a "Made in China" label—a purse, a sweater, a pair of shoes—probably comes from Guangdong. The province's agricultural bounty does not get as far as New York, but most of the fish, crabs, bananas and lychee fruit overflowing in Hong Kong's markets are harvested by Guangdong's peasants.

A crowded patchwork of rice paddies, banana plantations and brick villages, Guangdong surrounds Hong Kong and, perhaps as a result, is the most open, most capitalistic and most prosperous part of China. Guangdong has nearly tripled its economic output in eight years, and more and more Asia experts think that if China continues on its present course of economic liberalization, Guangdong could become the "next Taiwan" or the "next Korea."

Last month, China announced that the Communist Party had designated Guangdong Province an "experimental region" for political and economic reform. The announcement appeared to confirm the province's role as a trailblazer, but it also suggested that Guangdong is different from the rest of the country, that it has been given more rope—to prove itself or hang itself. Even if the province continues to flourish, the regulators in Beijing may decide that the methods are ill-suited for the rest of the nation, or that, though promising, they are too risky to be generally prescribed.

Meanwhile, Guangdong these days is an exhilarating tapestry of progress, where families that have toiled for hundreds of generations only to get nowhere suddenly are bounding toward what is, to them, unimaginable prosperity. A largely flat, fertile agricultural land, the province brims with sugar cane, bananas, peanuts and pigs. The province is home to 63 million people, roughly three-quarters of whom are peasants, the elderly ones gnarled like driftwood.

A bustling street in the city of Canton, China, which is in the Guangdong province.

AUGUST 21, 1988

Cease-Fire Takes Effect in 8-Year Iran-Iraq War

Alan Cowell

After almost eight years of a war that has claimed an estimated one million lives, a cease-fire between Iran and Iraq was reported holding tonight.

The truce, arranged by the United Nations, went into effect today at 7 A.M. local time. By nightfall, there were no reports of violations.

"I really think both countries are serious," the United Nations Secretary General, Javier Perez de Cuellar, told reporters in London, where he was on his way to formal peace talks between the two nations in Geneva starting Thursday. "They are committed to the cease-fire."

A team of 350 United Nations observers spread out along the 740-mile border between the combatants.

"They are on the ground in large numbers from north to south, and the cease-fire is holding," Col. William Phillips, the Irish operations chief of the 24-nation Iran-Iraq Military Observer Group said.

The war—fought on land and in the air, in the oil lanes of the Persian Gulf and with missile and chemical weapons attacks—produced no major territorial gains for either side.

Yet Iraq, which invaded Iran on Sept. 22, 1980, has proclaimed victory. Motorists and demonstrators poured onto the streets of Baghdad overnight, blowing horns, beating tambourines and spraying water.

The response in Teheran, the capital of Iran—which accepted United Nations peace terms last month after delaying for a year—was more cautious. It reflected the uncertainties provoked by an Iranian about-face described by Ayatollah Ruhollah Khomeini, the Iranian leader, as deadlier than poison.

"We will abide by the cease-fire completely, and there will be no shooting," the Iranian President, Hojatolislam Ali Khamenei, reportedly told Iranian soldiers.

Hojatolislam Hashemi Rafsanjani, Speaker of the Iranian Parliament, said on the Teheran radio, "There should be no violations on the front, and God forbid not one unauthorized bullet should be fired."

But he cautioned: "We have not yet arrived at peace. God willing, if we reach that day, we will declare it ourselves."

The sudden string of Iraqi victories, war weariness in Iran, depleted military supplies and Teheran's increasing isolation in the face of Arab, United States and other Western backing for Iraq are widely thought to have spurred Iran to seek peace. ■

SEPTEMBER 9, 1988

U.S. ASSERTS IRAQ USED POISON GAS AGAINST THE KURDS

Julie Johnson

The United States said today that it was convinced Iraq had used poison gas against Kurdish guerrillas and condemned the action as "abhorrent and unjustifiable."

American officials had maintained until today that the Government had no conclusive proof that Iraq had renewed its use of chemical weapons.

An Iraqi Foreign Ministry official, leaving a meeting at the State Department, characterized the charge as "absolutely baseless."

Since 1984 in its war against Iran, Iraq has been accused of using mustard gas, which burns, blisters and blackens the skin and can be lethal if inhaled. Iraq also has used, to a lesser extent, a lethal nerve gas called Tabun, which prompts convulsions and foaming and bleeding at the mouth before death. Cyanide gas also has been used by both sides in the war.

The State Department spokesman, Charles E. Redman, said the United States was certain of Iraq's use of such weapons within its own borders.

"As a result of our evaluation of the situation, the United States Government is convinced that Iraq has used chemical weapons in its military campaign against Kurdish guerrillas," Mr. Redman said. "Any use in this context is abhorrent and unjustifiable."

Officials at the White House and State Department did not specify the extent, frequency or type of gas that Iraq had used against the Kurds. Citing the need to protect intelligence sources, they declined to describe in any detail the evidence on which the American accusation and condemnation were based.

A State Department spokesman said today that a United States Embassy official from Ankara had spent two days assessing the situation in eastern Turkey. Thousands of Kurdish refugees have crossed the Iraqi border into Turkey, fleeing a new offensive against Kurds started by the Iraqi Government of President Saddam Hussein after the Aug. 20 cease-fire in the Iran-Iraq war.

Iraq issued a denial last weekend, through Foreign Minister Tariq Aziz, that it had used chemical weapons against the Kurds. ■

DECEMBER 20, 1988

JETLINER CARRYING 258 TO U.S. CRASHES IN SCOTTISH TOWN; ALL BELIEVED DEAD

Craig R. Whitney

LONDON, Dec. 21—A Pan Am Boeing 747 on a flight from London to New York with 258 people aboard crashed tonight in a southern Scottish village, British military authorities reported. The airline said it knew of no survivors.

The plane was flying at 31,000 feet when it suddenly disappeared from radar and crashed into two rows of houses, setting them on fire. There was no immediate indication of the cause of the crash. British officials would not respond to speculation by some about a structural failure or an onboard explosion in the jumbo jet.

Pat Coffey, a spokesman for the British Royal Air Force, said the plane, Pan American World Airways Flight 103, left Heathrow Airport outside London after originating at Frankfurt, West Germany, and was bound for Kennedy International Airport.

Among those on board was the chief administrative officer of the United Nations' Council for Namibia, Bernt Carlsson of Sweden, who was flying to New York for the signing of an accord on Namibian independence, aides to Mr. Carlsson said. Others included executives of Volksagen and The Associated Press. There were also unconfirmed reports that six members of the State Department's Diplomatic Security Service were aboard.

Pan Am officials in New York said it was the worst single-plane disaster in the airline's history.

The plane left Heathrow about 25 minutes behind schedule at 6:25 P.M. (1:25 P.M., New York time). It disappeared from air controllers' radar scopes 52 minutes later, shortly before a series of explosions and fires were reported on the ground in the Scottish village of Lockerbie, according to witnesses and official accounts.

"The aircraft is reported to have hit two rows of houses, which have been demolished by the impact, and also to have hit vehicles on the highway," said a spokesman for the Royal Air Force's rescue and coordination center near Edinburgh. Houses and cars along the highway to Glasgow were still blazing fiercely several hours after the crash, he said. There were no survivors in these houses, about 40 in all, The Associated Press reported.

The airplane had a capacity of 412 passengers. There were 243 passengers on board, and 15 crew members, Pan Am said. Jeff Kreindler, a Pan Am spokesman in New York, said there was "no sign at all" of adverse weather that might have been a factor.

Mr. Kreindler, the Pan Am spokesman, said, "There was no indication of any problems on board that aircraft or with the machine itself," Asked whether the plane's crew had received any bomb threats, he said, "There were no threats." ■

A policeman walks near the cockpit of the 747 Pan Am Boeing that exploded in December, 1988.

JANUARY 7, 1989

HIROHITO, 124TH EMPEROR OF JAPAN, IS DEAD AT 87

Susan Chira

Emperor Hirohito, the last of the World War II leaders and Japan's longest-reigning monarch, died today at the Imperial Palace. He was 87 years old.

In his 62-year reign, the Emperor presided over the most tumultuous era in Japan's modern history, although like most of the 123 emperors before him, he watched more than he acted. During his reign, his nation embraced militarism, conquered much of Asia, waged war on the Allied Powers, suffered the world's first atomic bombing, and painfully rebuilt, rising in just four decades to become the world's most vibrant economic power.

Hirohito's death came after more than a year of declining health. He had been confined to his bed for more than three months.

Because Japanese tradition decrees that the Chrysanthemum Throne may not be empty, Crown Prince Akihito, Hirohito's 55-year-old son, became Japan's 125th Emperor. In a ceremony as ancient as his title, Akihito received two of the Imperial treasures—a sword and a jewel—and received the Imperial seal and the seal of state.

Shoichi Fujimori, the grand steward of the Imperial Household Agency, announced the Emperor's death at 7:55 A.M. and revealed for the first time that Hirohito had been suffering from cancer of the duodenum, a section of the small intestine.

"The whole nation is deeply saddened by his death," the steward said, using a special honorific verb reserved for the death of an emperor. "Despite the concerted efforts of medical treatment, finally today His Majesty passed away from a tumor in the duodenum."

As news of Hirohito's death spread, many Japanese throughout Tokyo put flags outside their homes and businesses. An elderly woman hoisted a flag to half-staff outside a sushi shop, radio stations played classical music and a crowd gathered near the Imperial Palace. A large contingent of riot police officers were deployed to guard against anti-imperial demonstrations or the possibility that avid followers might commit suicide.

When Hirohito ascended the throne, his subjects revered him as a descendant of Amaterasu, the sun goddess who, according to Japanese mythology, created the Japanese archipelago from the drops of water that fell from her spear. Fueled by militarist propaganda that drew on these myths, more than two million soldiers died in his name. But on Aug. 15, 1945, that myth was shattered as his subjects heard Hirohito's voice for the first time. He announced Japan's surrender on the radio and called on the Japanese to "endure the unendurable." Now, he told his countrymen in a second precedent-shattering announcement five months later, the people were sovereign and the Emperor was not divine.

Emperor Hirohito in his kimono coronation robe in 1926.

Thus Akihito becomes the first Emperor to be installed since Japan was transformed into a constitutional democracy under the American Occupation at the end of World War II.

The whole nation is deeply saddened

Eleven years old at the end of the war, the young Crown Prince diligently prepared himself to become Emperor in the new democratic era, studying English with an American tutor and becoming the first heir to the throne to marry a commoner.

The new Emperor is only the fourth in 120 years since Japan opened itself to the world, abandoned feudalism and began its industrial drive under his great-grandfather, the Emperor Meiji.

This morning, Prime Minister Noboru Takeshita said: "Our country has since pursued the realization of peace and democracy under the new constitution. It has achieved remarkable progress by virtue of the untiring efforts of our people and has now become an important member of the international community. I feel most keenly that these achievements have been made possible by the presence of His Late Majesty as the symbol of the state and of the unity of the people." ■

FEBRUARY 16, 1989

Last Soviet Soldiers Leave Afghanistan

Bill Keller

MOSCOW—The last Soviet soldier came home from Afghanistan this morning, the Soviet Union announced, leaving behind a war that had become a domestic burden and an international embarrassment for Moscow.

The final Soviet departure came on the day set as a deadline by the Geneva accords last April. It left two heavily armed adversaries, the Kremlin-backed Government of President Najibullah and a fractious but powerful array of Muslim insurgents, backed by the United States and Pakistan, to conclude their civil war on their own.

Lieut. Gen. Boris V. Gromov, the commander of the Soviet forces in Afghanistan, walked across the steel Friendship Bridge to the border city of Termez, in Uzbekistan, at 11:55 A.M. local time (1:55 A.M., Eastern time), 9 years and 50 days after Soviet troops intervened to support a coup by a Marxist ally.

"There is not a single Soviet soldier or officer left behind me," General Gromov told a Soviet television reporter waiting on the bridge. "Our nine-year stay ends with this."

Today's final departure is the end of a steady process of withdrawal since last spring, when Moscow says there were 100,300 Soviet troops in Afghanistan. At the height of the Soviet commitment, according to Western intelligence estimates, there were 115,000 troops deployed.

The weekly Literaturnaya Gazeta described the killing of a carload of Afghan civilians, including women and children, and the order by a commander to cover it up.

The article was a foretaste of recriminations expected in the months ahead.

The war cost the Soviet Union roughly 15,000 lives and undisclosed billions of rubles. It scarred a generation of young people and undermined the cherished image of an invincible Soviet Army. Moscow's involvement in Afghanistan was often compared to the American experience in the Vietnam War, in which more than 58,000 Americans died.

"The day that millions of Soviet people have waited for has come," General Gromov said to an army rally in Termez, Reuters reported. "In spite of our sacrifices and losses, we have totally fulfilled our internationalist duty." ■

MAY 3, 1989

Hungary Dismantling Its Barbed-Wire Curtain

Two soldiers help dismantle the iron curtain in Hungary on May 1, 1989.

APRIL 6, 1989

VIETNAM PROMISES TROOPS WILL LEAVE CAMBODIA BY FALL

Steven Erlanger

Ten years and three months after its soldiers invaded Cambodia and installed a new Government in Phnom Penh, Vietnam announced today that it would unconditionally withdraw the rest of its troops by the end of September.

Vietnam had previously insisted that a troop withdrawal by that time would have to be linked to a cutoff of all foreign military aid to the three factions that oppose Hanoi's ally in Phnom Penh, Prime Minister Hun Sen.

Otherwise, Vietnam had said, it would not withdraw its troops until the end of 1990. Hanoi says those troops number 50,000 and American officials estimate them to be 60,000 to 70,000.

Vietnam's occupation of Cambodia has been, along with the Soviet presence in Afghanistan, one of the major East-West issues. China had vowed not to improve relations with Moscow until the Vietnamese left Cambodia. And Vietnam's own efforts to obtain aid and recognition from the United States in the aftermath of the Vietnam war were frustrated by Washington's insistence that Hanoi withdraw its troops from Cambodia first.

Today, instead of waiting for aid to the opposition guerrillas to cease, Vietnam urged the supporters of the opposition guerrillas, most notably China, to honor promises to stop all military aid when Vietnam withdraws.

In a joint declaration, Vietnam, Cambodia and Laos reserved the right of Phnom Penh to request further "assistance" if military aid to the opposition did not stop. The declaration also said the nations of the world should take responsibility for insuring that the Cambodian civil war ends and that the "genocidal Pol Pot regime" not be allowed to take power again in Cambodia.

According to Vietnamese officials, five to seven Vietnamese soldiers are wounded or killed every day in Cambodia. Since 1978, there have been about 55,000 Vietnamese casualties, a third of whom were killed. ■

Cambodians bid farewell to Vietnamese troops leaving Cambodia in the city of Battambang in September 1989.

JUNE 4, 1989

CRACKDOWN IN BEIJING; TROOPS ATTACK AND CRUSH BEIJING PROTEST; SCORES ARE KILLED

Nicholas D. Kristof

Tens of thousands of Chinese troops retook the center of the capital early this morning from pro-democracy protesters, killing scores of students and workers and wounding hundreds more as they fired submachine guns at crowds of people who tried to resist.

Troops marched along the main roads surrounding central Tiananmen Square, sometimes firing in the air and sometimes firing directly at crowds of men and women who refused to move out of the way.

Early this morning, the troops finally cleared the square after first sweeping the area around it. Several thousand students who had remained on the square throughout the shooting left peacefully, still waving the banners of their universities. Several armed personnel carriers ran over their tents and destroyed the encampment.

Most of the dead had been shot, but some had been run over by armored personnel carriers that forced their way through barricades erected by local residents.

The official news programs this morning reported that the People's Liberation Army had crushed a "counter-revolutionary rebellion" in the capital. They said that more than 1,000 police and troops had been injured and some killed, and that civilians had been killed, but did not give details.

Changan Avenue, or the Avenue of Eternal Peace, Beijing's main east-west thoroughfare, echoed with screams this morning as young people carried the bodies of their friends away from the front lines. The dead or seriously wounded were heaped on the backs of bicycles or tricycle rickshaws and supported by friends who rushed through the crowds, sometimes sobbing as they ran.

The avenue was lit by the glow of several trucks and two armed personnel carriers that students and workers set afire, and bullets swooshed overhead or glanced off buildings. The air crackled almost constantly with gunfire and tear gas grenades.

"General strike!" people roared, in bitterness and outrage, as they ran from Tiananmen Square, which pro-democracy demonstrators had occupied for three weeks.

While hundreds of thousands of people had turned out to the streets Saturday and early today to show support for the democracy movement, it was not clear if the call for a general strike would be successful. The Government had been fearful that a crackdown on the movement would lead to strikes, but its willingness to shoot students suggested that it was also capable of putting considerable pressure on workers to stay on the job.

Many of those killed were throwing bricks at the soldiers, but others were simply watching passively or standing at barricades when soldiers fired directly at them.

It was also impossible to determine how many civilians had been killed or injured. Beijing Fuxing Hospital, 3.3 miles to the west of Tiananmen Square, reported more than 38 deaths and more than 100 wounded, and said that many more bodies had yet to be taken to its morgue. A doctor at the Beijing Union Medical College Hospital, two miles northeast of the square, reported 17 deaths. Beijing Tongren Hospital, one mile southeast of the square, reported 13 deaths and more than 100 critically wounded.

"As doctors, we often see deaths," said a doctor at the Tongren Hospital. "But we've never seen such a tragedy like this. Every room in the hospital is covered with blood. We are terribly short of blood, but citizens are lining up outside to give blood."

Most Chinese seemed convinced that the tanks and troops had been ordered into the city to crush the pro-democracy demonstrations once and for all. The immediate result of the first clashes was to revitalize the pro-democracy movement, which had been losing momentum over the last 10 days, and to erase the sense that life in the capital was returning to normal. But the use of tanks and guns came later, and it was not clear if they would succeed in ending the movement or would lead to such measures as a general strike.

The tension was exacerbated by an extraordinary announcement on television Saturday night, ordering citizens to "stay at home to protect your lives." In particular, the announcement ordered people to stay off the streets and away from Tiananmen Square. ■

A lone demonstrator stands down a column of tanks June 5, 1989, at the entrance to Tiananmen Square in Beijing.

OBITUARY

JUNE 4, 1989

Ayatollah Ruhollah Khomeini, 89, Unwavering Iranian Spiritual Leader

Raymond H. Anderson

The life of Ayatollah Ruhollah Khomeini was so shadowy, so overlain with myth and rumor, that there was lingering disagreement or uncertainty about his ancestry, his true name and his date of birth.

But when he returned in triumph to Teheran on Feb. 1, 1979—after almost 15 years in exile—the imposing man in a black robe with a white beard and intense dark eyes left little doubt about who he was, or what he wanted for his ancient land.

Ayatollah Khomeini felt a holy mission to rid Iran of what he saw as Western corruption and degeneracy and to return the country, under an Islamic theocracy, to religious purity.

The Islamic Shiite leader's fervor helped drive Shah Mohammed Riza Pahlevi from the Peacock Throne on Jan. 15, 1979, and into foreign exile. The Shah's eventual arrival in the United States for cancer treatment was the spark that set off the American hostage crisis.

Under the Ayatollah, Iran was wrenched backward from widespread economic development and social change and onto a path that was broadly hostile to the Western world.

The Ayatollah's path also led to eight years of bloody, costly, inconclusive war between Iran and its Arab neighbor Iraq. He demanded that his country fight unrelentingly after Iraq invaded Iran in September 1980, but he eventually accepted a truce in 1988.

Many longtime Iranian opponents of the Shah hoped that the Ayatollah would turn over power and allow a democratic society to emerge. But he held to his dream of an Islamic republic and retained his Islamic fervor—scuttling a tentative economic and political opening to the West with his call for the killing of a British author, Salman Rushdie, whose novel "The Satanic Verses" was deemed to have blasphemed the faith.

A month later, he dismissed Ayatollah Hussein Ali Montazeri, a relative moderate who had been designated as his political heir. There has been speculation that Ayatollah Khomeini's son, Hojatolislam Ahmad Khomeini, is emerging from a power struggle as a prime contender to inherit his authority.

There was no one in Iran with sufficient authority to challenge the Ayatollah successfully. In the aftermath of the revolution, he moved relentlessly toward his theocratic goal, consolidating power and silencing the opposition.

In a frenzy of political retribution and Islamic purification, thousands of people were executed in public, including the Shah's officials, torturers, criminals, homosexuals and prostitutes.

A 1987 report of the United Nations Commission on Human Rights estimated that as many as 7,000 people were shot, hanged, stoned or burned to death after the 1979 revolution. ■

The Islamic Revolution's founder Ayatollah Ruhollah Khomeini in 1979 in Tehran by his supporters.

SEPTEMBER 11, 1989

HUNGARY ALLOWS 7,000 EAST GERMANS TO EMIGRATE WEST

Serge Schmemann

Hungary announced today that it is allowing thousands of East Germans who have refused to return home to leave for West Germany. It was another chapter, and a dramatic one, in a summerlong exodus through the new Hungarian gap in the Communist frontier.

The announcement cleared the way for more than 7,000 East Germans, who have said they wanted to go west, to do so beginning at midnight. But it was possible that this number might substantially increase as other East Germans, now in Hungary as tourists, take advantage of the new opportunity. Hungary's Foreign Minister said there are 60,000 people in this category.

A declaration by the Hungarian Government said that because of the "unbearable situation" created by the tide of East Germans trying to leave their country, Hungary has decided to temporarily suspend a 20-year-old agreement with East Germany and to allow the refugees free passage "to a country of their choice."

"It's like Christmas," said a young worker as he hugged his teary-eyed girlfriend in a flood of television lights. Next to them, a mother stood in silent embrace with three daughters. And all around, scores of children continued to romp among the tents, trailers and piles of knapsacks.

Late last night, the first of the departing East Germans, honking their car horns and cheering wildly, began pouring across the Hungarian border. For virtually all those who are refusing to return to East Germany, the destination is West Germany, where they are eligible for automatic and instant citizenship.

The agreement marked the first break by a Warsaw Pact country in the customary cooperation in blocking citizens from going to the West. In so doing, it dramatized the gap that has developed in the Eastern bloc between countries eager to embrace Western ways and those clinging to the old orthodoxy. ■

SEPTEMBER 28, 1989

Johannesburg Acts to Ease Segregation

Christopher S. Wren

The city of Johannesburg opened swimming pools and recreational centers to all races today and proceeded with plans to desegregate buses.

The city's action came after the Johannesburg City Council decided Tuesday night to eliminate the final remnants of what is called "petty apartheid" here. The council voted after a survey conducted among the city's 271,000 white voters showed general approval for such a move.

At a news conference today, Jan Burger, the leader of the National Party councillors who control the council, said President F. W. de Klerk had been informed of the decision and had raised no objections. Mr. Burger said the repeal of the segregation laws was consistent with Mr. de Klerk's promises of evolutionary change.

Restaurants, hotels and sports stadiums in Johannesburg and other major cities have opened to all races in recent years, but most public accommodations had remained technically closed to nonwhites.

Johannesburg is not the first city in South Africa to desegregate its public accommodations. Cape Town did so through the 1980's and petitioned the Government last March for exemption from the Group Areas Act, which mandates residential segregation throughout South Africa, so it could admit nonwhite residents. The Government has withheld such permission.

Johannesburg and other cities are still bound by the Group Areas Act, though some downtown neighborhoods like Hillbrow and Berea have had an influx of blacks from the overcrowded townships. The Government has agreed in principle to designate such integrated areas "free settlement areas" open to all races.

The Separate Amenities Act, another basic law of apartheid that allows segregation of publicly owned accommodations, has fallen into increasing disuse, though it is still enforced in Pretoria and other more conservative cities. Mr. Burger said the act gave municipalities, including Johannesburg, the option to enforce or ignore it. ■

OCTOBER 2, 1989

Rights for Gay Couples in Denmark

Sheila Rule

In what gay rights advocates hailed as the first unions of their kind in the world, six homosexual couples were legally joined today in "registered partnerships" that gave them most rights of married heterosexuals, but not the right to adopt or obtain joint custody of a child.

Each of the couples entered a small room in the ornate City Hall, and in civil rites that differed from those of heterosexuals only in the description of the union were asked by Mayor Tom Ahlberg if they wanted to be "in partnership" with each other. After saying "I do," the couples, all of them male, were given certificates of their partnership.

The ceremonies, followed by the traditional throwing of rice and confetti, were held on the day a new national law went into effect making Denmark the first country to legalize homosexual unions.

Members of Parliament passed the measure in May by a vote of 71 to 47, after a 40-year campaign by gay rights advocates. In this country where Government has traditionally been sympathetic toward minorities, opposition has come mainly from the small Christian People's Party, which called the legislation unnatural, unethical and dramatically at odds with the laws of other countries.

Although the law stops short of calling the unions marriages, it gives homosexual couples most of the advantages and disadvantages of marriage. Partners—at least one must be a resident Danish citizen—are liable for each other's maintenance. They also have the automatic right to inherit the other's property, and must undertake legal divorce proceedings to dissolve the partnership. They can also be forced to pay alimony, and in some circumstances, a partner can be held responsible for the other's tax liabilities.

Advocates said that Sweden last year became the first country to provide some minimum rights to homosexual couples, including rights involving inheritance, but that the Swedish law equates homosexual couples with unmarried heterosexual couples.

NOVEMBER 10, 1989

EAST GERMANY OPENS FRONTIER TO THE WEST FOR MIGRATION OR TRAVEL; THOUSANDS CROSS

Serge Schmemann

East Germany on Thursday lifted restrictions on emigration or travel to the West, and within hours tens of thousands of East and West Berliners swarmed across the infamous Berlin Wall for a boisterous celebration.

Border guards at Bornholmer Strasse crossing, Checkpoint Charlie and several other crossings abandoned all efforts to check credentials, even though the new regulations said East Germans would still need passports and permission to get across. Some guards smiled and took snapshots, assuring passers-by that they were just recording a historic event.

The mass crossing began about two hours after Gunter Schabowski, a member of the Politburo, had announced at a press conference that permission to travel or emigrate would be granted quickly and without preconditions, and that East Germans would be allowed to cross at any crossing into West Germany or West Berlin.

Once Mr. Schabowski's announcement was read on radio and television, a tentative trickle of East Germans testing the

Berlin Wall opening in Germany on November 10, 1989.

new regulations quickly turned into an jubilant horde, which joined at the border crossings with crowds of flag-waving, cheering West Germans. Thousands of Berliners clambered across the wall at the Brandenburg Gate, passing through the historic arch that for so long had been inaccessible to Berliners of either side.

Similar scenes were reported in Lubeck, the only other East German city touching the border, and at other border crossings along the inter-German frontier.

All through the night and into the early morning, celebrating East Berliners filled the Kurfurstendamm, West Berlin's "great white way," blowing trumpets, dancing, laughing and absorbing a glittering scene that until now they could glimpse only on television.

Many East Germans said they planned to return home the same night. The Mayor of West Berlin, Walter Momper, toured border crossings in a police radio truck and urged East Berliners to return.

The extraordinary breach of what had been the most infamous stretch of the Iron Curtain marked the culmination of an extraordinary month that has seen the virtual transformation of East Germany under the dual pressures of unceasing flight and continuing demonstrations. It also marked a breach of a wall that had become the premier symbol of Stalinist oppression and of the divisions of Europe and Germany into hostile camps after World War II.

The Berlin wall—first raised on Aug. 13, 1961, to halt a vast hemorrhage of East Germans to the West—evolved into a double row of eight-foot-high concrete walls with watchtowers, electronic sensors and a no man's land in between. Frequent attempts to breach the barrier often ended in death, and the very sophistication of the wall became a standing indictment of the system that could hold its people only with such extraordinary means.

In West Berlin, Eberhard Diepgen, the former mayor, said: "This is a day I have been awaiting since Aug. 13, 1961. With this the wall has lost its function. It can and must be torn down." ■

Some guards smiled and took snapshots

THE BORDER IS OPEN; JOYOUS EAST GERMANS POUR THROUGH WALL; PARTY PLEDGES FREEDOMS, AND CITY EXULTS

Serge Schmemann

The Berlin Wall opening in Berlin, Germany, in November 1989.

As hundreds of thousands of East Berliners romped through the newly porous wall in an unending celebration, West German leaders today proclaimed this the moment Germans had yearned for through 40 years of division.

At the same time, change continued unabated in East Berlin, where the Communist Party's Central Committee concluded a three-day session with the announcement of a program of radical changes. They included "free, democratic and secret elections," a "socialist planned economy oriented to market conditions," separation of party and state, parliamentary supervision of state security, freedom of assembly and a new law on the press and broadcasting.

"The German Democratic Republic is in the midst of an awakening," the Central Committee declared in the prologue to the newly adopted program. "A revolutionary people's movement has brought into motion a process of great change."

Though the West Berlin police could give no estimate of the numbers of East Berliners who crossed over in the last 24 hours, the authorities said that only 1,500 so far had announced their intention to stay.

Beyond Berlin, only one of many points along the border between the two Germanys where people could cross, 55,500 East Germans crossed over the border between the two Germanys since the wall was opened on Thursday, and 3,250 remained in West Germany, the West German Interior Ministry said.

Chancellor Helmut Kohl, who interrupted a state visit to Poland to come to West Berlin, told an emotional crowd of East and West Berliners gathered outside the West Berlin city hall: "I want to call out to all in the German Democratic Republic: We're on your side, we are and remain one nation. We belong together."

Speaking on the steps of the city hall, from which President John F. Kennedy had made his "Ich bin ein Berliner" speech shortly after the wall was raised, Mr. Kohl declared: "Long live a free German fatherland! Long live a united Europe!"

In a development that gave further evidence of the figurative crumbling of the wall, East Germany announced the opening of five new crossings. One was at the Glienicke Bridge, famed as the site of past exchanges of captured spies between East and West, and another was at Potsdammer Platz, once the heart of Berlin.

The arrival of an army bulldozer at Eberswalder Strasse to drill another new opening quickly attracted a crowd on both sides and sent rumors through the city that the East German Army was breaking down the wall. When the machine finally broke through, West Berliners handed flowers to the driver and rushed to pick up pieces of the wall for souvenirs.

At the Potsdammer Platz crossing site, West Berliners mounted the wall to chip away pieces while East German workers laid paving stones in the no-man's land, watched by about 50 soldiers.

In the giddiness of the grand reunion, German reunification was in the air. "We've done it! The wall is open!" proclaimed the popular tabloid Bild in a giant headline. ■

DECEMBER 23, 1989

Upheaval in the East: Cheers as Brandenburg Gate Reopens

Serge Schmemann

Leaders of the two Germanys reopened the Brandenburg Gate today, breaching a barrier that more than any other had come to symbolize the division of the nation.

Tens of thousands of Germans, oblivious to a steady drizzle, packed both sides of Berlin's most famous gate to celebrate the formal inauguration of two new pedestrian crossings by West Germany's Chancellor, Helmut Kohl, and East Germany's new Prime Minister, Hans Modrow.

Although it has been six weeks since the Berlin wall fell open and at least half the East Germans have visited the West, the reopening of the two-century-old landmark offered symbolic confirmation that the German nation was again seeking to become whole.

come together

Almost immediately, great numbers of East Germans began flowing through the new opening and across the previously sealed square on which the gate stands. They overwhelmed security barriers, happily mobbing the dignitaries and clambering on top of the wall. The new crossings were opened to the left and right of the gate, leaving a broad, flat arc of wall directly in front intact for now.

A similar mass of West Germans on the other side joined in the cheers and celebrations, though for two more days only East Germans will be able to pass through freely.

Hundreds of Berliners on both sides carried banners or West German flags. "Berlin is one city. Germany is one nation," one placard read. Another said in English, "Come Together." ■

DECEMBER 23, 1989

CEAUSESCU FLEES A REVOLT IN RUMANIA, DIVIDED SECURITY FORCES FIGHT ON

David Binder

Rumanian civilians jubilate during a rally in Bucharest, holding newspapers announcing the arrest of Nicolae Ceaucescu on December 24, 1989. The communist dictator Nicolae Ceausescu and his wife, Elena, were deposed and executed by a firing squad the next day.

After ruling Rumania as a dictator for a quarter of a century, President Nicolae Ceausescu was forced to flee Bucharest Friday when angry crowds of anti-Government demonstrators, backed by army units, took over large sections of the capital.

Reports spoke of fierce fighting in the capital between the army and the pro-Ceausescu security police, but by early today the army appeared to be gaining the upper hand.

Bucharest radio said the head of the security police changed sides and ordered his forces to support the army and the Rumanian people, Reuters reported Friday evening. The broadcast also said the Interior Minister and a Deputy Prime Minister had been arrested by anti-Ceausescu forces.

"The forces of democracy are in the ascendant," a State Department official who is following the situation said Friday evening.

Loyalist forces also were reported Friday evening to be attacking Timisoara, the western city where the uprising began last Saturday. But the army said that it had repulsed that attack.

Early today, Maj. Gen. Stefan Gusa, the Army Chief of Staff, said regular army units opposing Mr. Ceausescu had taken control of almost the entire country from security police forces, Reuters reported.

Open graves were discovered in Timisoara Friday with what were believed to be as many as 4,500 bodies, many of them women and children, who were believed killed by security forces over the weekend.

Once Mr. Ceausescu and his wife, Elena, fled, the changes that took place in Rumania were more sudden and dramatic than any in Eastern Europe.

Early today, the Bucharest Radio reported that all Rumanian political prisoners had been freed.

The television and press, which yesterday had been the most rigidly controlled in

(cont'd. next page)

(continued from previous page)
Eastern Europe, declared their freedom. Viewers around the world saw live images of demonstrations and heard calls for freedom and change that had been inconceivable before. But shortly after midnight in Bucharest, the television station went off the air while heavy fighting was going on in the vicinity.

Asked to explain the forces that came together to bring about his downfall, one of the United States Government's leading analysts of Rumanian affairs said today:

"I think it was a people in despair of their physical survival under Ceausescu, facing at last the choice to die fast or die slowly."

The analyst, who asked not to be identified, said a combination of desires for "religious rights and wanting to live like human beings finally reached a stage where helplessness was replaced by rage." ■

DECEMBER 23, 1989

'The Year of Democracy' Still Leaves Unanswered Questions

R. W. Apple Jr.

The armed rebellion against Nicolae Ceausescu in Rumania demonstrates that no hard-line Communist regime in Eastern Europe can evade the popular wrath sweeping the region.

Already gone are the hard-line regimes in Poland, Hungary, Czechoslovakia, East Germany and Bulgaria, and now Rumania appears to be in the throes of revolution. These regimes jailed dissidents, disdained truth and scorned justice. Through long, dark decades, they seemed immutable, but they all began to founder in a matter of months.

The bloody and still-incomplete revolution in Rumania, the opening of the Berlin Wall at the Brandenburg Gate and the invasion of Panama, all within the final 10 days of 1989, provided a fitting denouement to a turbulent, dramatic, fascinating year in international affairs. Many called it "the year of democracy"—the most important 12 months, perhaps, since 1968, with all its rebellions, and worthy of comparison even with the annus mirabilis of 1848.

But like 1848, it leaves behind many problems, many questions and many signs of instability, especially in the main cockpit of change, the area between the Elbe and the Urals.

The tides of change are lapping dangerouThe swiftness of events in Rumania—even faster than in Czechslovakia -was what was so stunning. One day the regime looked resolute, impregnable. Then suddenly, "the coming unrest spread its thunderclouds under the eyes of the government." as Victor Hugo wrote of the French revolution in "Les Miserables."

But it is far easier to topple tired and rotten political and economic structures, as revolutionaries have discovered time and again over the centruies, than it is to build shiny, efficient, lasting new ones.

And building new ones will cause distress to the millions in Eastern Europe who want democracy but also want to keep at least part of their socialist safety net intact. Inevitably, as they lose their guaranteed employment when obsolete factories are closed, as they lose food and rent subsidies, severe tensions will develop. People may become disillusioned with the new way.

But even in economic disarray, East Germany, Czechosolovakia and Hungary together have a gross national product larger than China's. The potential is there. Help from the West is assured, coordinated by the European Community with the full approval of the United States in what Europeans are only now beginning to see as an historic decision reached at Paris this summer.

Political questions may be almost as difficult as the economic problems. Which German unification—or consolidation or amalgamation—seems inevitable to many scholars and diplomats, either in fact or in law. But what will the terms be? Which way will the new Germany look and think and feel? Can it find ways to avoid frightening, elephant-like, the smaller animals in its forest?

Such questions and their qualified, partial, contradictory answers, so slow to emerge, are less stirring than revolutions, and hence less likely to command the world's continuing interest and help. Washington and other world capitals, which have a tendency to let their attention wander after a while, will find their patience and commitment sorely tested in the months ahead. ■

A couple knocking stones out of the Berlin wall in 1989.

Business

It was a spectacle for the ages. The normally buttoned-down business world, propelled by the galloping pace of globalization and deregulation, delivered enough drama to light up every theater on Broadway.

Even with Howard J. Ruff's doomsaying book, "How to Prosper During the Coming Bad Years," still on the best-seller lists, the Dow Jones reached dizzying heights, breaking records every week, or so it seemed, and radiating the excitement of a casino. It was the decade of the hostile takeover. Wall Street buccaneers, audacious and swaggering, engineered a stunning series of acquisitions that rocked the financial world. It was high-stakes drama as mammoth corporations swallowed each other one by one, making media stars not only of the dealmakers but also of the journalists who covered them.

Risk arbitrager Ivan Boesky in his office in the early 1980s.

A trader on the New York Stock Exchange watches as the Dow Jones Industrial Average plunges in October of 1987.

Michael Douglas posing as Gordon Gekko from the movie "Wall Street."

It was a gambler's dream come true until, in 1987, the market plunged earthward at a terrifying speed.

The decade cried out for a Balzac to capture the drama, and it found one in Tom Wolfe. His satirical novel "The Bonfire of the Vanities" captured the ethos of the decade, the vaunting ambition and unbridled acquisitiveness epitomized by the Wall Street traders he called "masters of the universe." On film, the director Oliver Stone dramatized the financial free-for-all through the character of Gordon Gekko, a ruthless arbitrageur whose motto, "greed is good," became one of the catchphrases of the decade.

The once-staid world of the Fortune 500 reached a frenzied boil. A Supreme Court decision forced AT&T to break up the Bell System, a telephone monopoly that Americans had thought of as immutable. Deregulation opened the way for new airlines like People Express and crippled venerable carriers like Eastern, TWA and Pan Am, which were in their death throes by the end of the decade.

It was the heyday of the corporate raider. Risk-takers like Carl Icahn, T. Boone Pickens and Saul Steinberg made an art of the hostile takeover, using debt as a tool to acquire big companies for relatively little upfront cash in a maneuver that soon became known to one and all: the leveraged buyout. At the investment banking firm of Drexel Burnham Lambert, whiz kid Michael Milken made his name by financing takeovers with the speculative, high-yield instruments known by the undignified name of junk bonds.

As the federal government relaxed its antitrust regulations, merger and acquisition mania took hold. Capital Cities Communications bought ABC, General Electric bought RCA and Philip Morris bought Kraft Foods. Time Inc. merged with Warner Communications, Bristol-Myers with Squibb, Bridgestone with Firestone. And in the largest leveraged buyout ever seen, the private equity firm Kohlberg Kravis Roberts paid $25 billion for RJR Nabisco, itself a product of the 1985 merger of R.J. Reynolds Tobacco and Nabisco Brands.

The whole world seemed intoxicated by financial wheeling and dealing. In a newly deregulated Britain, London emerged as a linchpin for global finance. Even China, awakening from the spell of Mao and the Communist Revolution, put a modest chip on the table, establishing its own stock exchange.

London's Stock Exchange in the 1980s.

U.S. Attorney Rudolph Giuliani (right) and SEC Sleuth Gary Lynch, special investigator, announcing one of the many insider trading indictments in the late 1980s.

It all seemed too good to be true, and it was. The stock market boomed. Real estate prices shot sky-high in New York, Paris and London. Art fetched record prices at the auction houses. Great fortunes were made. It all seemed too good to be true, and it was. The government prosecutors began looking at insider trading, unscrupulous deals and fraud.

In a foreshadowing of things to come, the arbitrageur Ivan Boesky, who had amassed a huge fortune by betting on corporate takeover, was convicted of insider trading and sentenced to prison in 1986.

As the decade wound to a close, Michael Milken faced the music too. The junk-bond king, widely assumed to be the model for Gordon Gekko, was indicted on 98 counts of racketeering and securities fraud in 1989. After pleading guilty to lesser charges, he was sentenced to 10 years in prison and barred for life from working in the securities industry.

It was a symbolic moment, and seen as such. The masters of the universe, at decade's end, were in retreat. It seemed only fitting that a best-seller by James R. Stewart describing their exploits should be titled "Den of Thieves."

DECEMBER 24, 1980

Japan Tops U.S. in 1980 Car Output

Mike Tharp

TOKYO, Dec. 23—Japan has become the world's largest vehicle producer, the Japan Automobile Manufacturers Association said today.

Through the first 11 months of the year, Japanese vehicle production, including cars, trucks and buses, reached a record 10.1 million units, association officials said. The figure represents a 15.1 percent increase over 1979.

During the same period, the association said, United States production fell to about 7.4 million units, down from 10.9 million in 1979.

From January to November 1980, Japanese auto makers produced 6.4 million cars, up 14.4 percent over a year earlier; 3.6 million trucks, up 15.9 percent, and 82,620 buses, up 46.5 percent. ■

A view of Japanese Honda cars being offloaded from a freighter.

APRIL 26, 1981

HOW TO START AN AIRLINE: People Express Poised to Fly

Daniel F. Cuff

Customers boarding People Express plane for their first $69 flight from Newark to Dallas/Ft. Worth.

"There it goes now," said Gerald L. Gitner. The Boeing 737 roared on takeoff past the second-floor corner office window at Newark Airport's North Terminal. Mr. Gitner and Donald C. Burr watched like proud fathers. The gleaming jet, the first in their proposed fleet, was undergoing tests last week by a team from the Federal Aviation Agency. Mr. Burr, 39, and Mr. Gitner, 36, plan to give birth to an airline this Thursday.

Its name is People Express Airlines, and its goal is to make money by flying people cheaply from Newark to such places as Buffalo, Norfolk and Columbus and back. Mr. Burr, who is chairman and chief executive, and Mr. Gitner, president and chief operating officer, say they can fly people for less than the price of driving or taking the bus. They will charge $23 to Buffalo and Norfolk and $35 to Columbus on weekends and evenings.

That is a lot less than the current fares charged by other airlines of $99 to Buffalo, $82 to Norfolk and $146 to Columbus. But the airlines that fly these routes are slashing ticket prices to meet the People Express competition. On the Buffalo route, for example, US Air will meet the People Express

(cont'd. next page)

(continued from previous page)
fare and Piedmont will do the same on the Norfolk run.

Thus it appears that People Express is in for a ferocious fight as it tries to get a toe-hold in the busy Northeast market. Parts of the airline business these days are beginning to resemble the pioneering era when barnstormers-turned-businessmen scrambled to found the mail lines that became the nation's major air carriers. Today, airlines like People Express are springing up as a result of the Government's 1978 deregulation of fares and route structures, and the competition is fierce. They are trying to copy the earlier fare-cutting successes of PSA in California and Southwest Airlines in Texas in the days when those airlines operated within state lines to stay out of Washington's regulatory clutches.

"The Deregulation Act looked like a whole new thing," Mr. Burr said. "Now, even more, it's clear that we're only on the leading edges of a new era not dissimilar in a sense from the old days when airlines got under way."

Some of these aggressive new airlines are Midway in Chicago and Air Florida. In this region, Eastern Airlines is already locked in combat for its shuttle business with New York Air, a subsidiary of the Texas Air Corporation, which also operates Texas International Airlines. New York Air has plans to expand cut-rate service to other Northeast cities. ■

JANUARY 9, 1982

U.S. SETTLES PHONE SUIT, A.T.& T. TO SPLIT UP, TRANSFORMING INDUSTRY

Ernest Holsendolph

WASHINGTON, Jan. 8—The American Telephone and Telegraph Company settled the Justice Department's antitrust lawsuit today by agreeing to give up the 22 Bell System companies that provide most of the nation's local telephone service.

On a landmark antitrust day, the Justice Department also dropped its marathon case against the International Business Machines Corporation that had sought to break up the company that has dominated the computer industry. The Justice Department said the suit was "without merit and should be dismissed."

The A.T.& T. agreement, if finally approved by a federal court, would be the largest and most significant antitrust settlement in decades. It is likely to be compared with the 1911 settlement that divided the Rockefeller family's Standard Oil Company into 33 subsidiaries, some of them huge oil companies in their own right.

The heart of the agreement requires A.T.& T. to give up all its wholly owned local telephone subsidiaries, which are worth $80 billion, or two-thirds of the company's total assets. That would radically alter a company that has accounted for more than 80 percent of the nation's telephone service, changing the course of the industry.

But A.T.& T. would be free to enter such previously prohibited fields as data processing, communications between computers and the sale of telephone and computer terminal equipment, all rapidly growing and a profitable aspect of the telecommunications industry. And it would retain its long-distance service.

A critical aspect of the proposed settlement is that it would sever a key source of the giant company's economic and political power, namely the phone companies that blanket nearly every major metropolitan area of the nation and provide a protected market for the parent company's equipment production and facilitated the long distance service. A number of analysts speculated that A.T.& T. agreed to the huge divestiture because the company feared that Judge Greene, who was expected to rule on the case early this summer, would find the phone company guilty of antitrust law violations and perhaps force it to give up other subsidiaries as well.

The phone companies that would be spun off include the following: Bell Telephone of Nevada, Illinois Bell Telephone, Indiana Bell Telephone, Michigan Bell Telephone, New England Bell Telephone and Telegraph, New Jersey Bell Telephone and New York Telephone.

Many of the actual and potential competitors of A.T.& T. are expected to have much to say. For instance, Thomas E. Wheeler, president of the National Cable Television Association, which has always dreaded A.T.&T.'s possible entry into that business, criticized the "closed-door agreement" and said that only Congress should be allowed to restructure the industry. ■

OCTOBER 8, 1982

EUPHORIC DAY FOR WALL STREET

Robert J. Cole

From the president of the New York Stock Exchange to a trainee on the floor of the American Exchange, Wall Street workers concluded yesterday that, despite record-breaking volume, the industry breezed through what might soon become just another day at the corner of Broad and Wall.

"We can handle 250 million to 300 million shares a day," asserted John J. Phelan Jr., president of the New York exchange, "whether it's all big financial institutions or all individual retail orders or any mix of both."

Asked how he could be so confident—particularly in view of yesterday's 147-million-share volume—Mr. Phelan replied: "Because we've built models and tested them up to about 300 million shares and 250,000 transactions. That's twice the volume today and five times the number of transactions."

On the Big Board trading floor, where the sound level intensified dramatically in the final hour of activity, traders waved at photographers, reporters and others present to record the historic event. Some blew police whistles. Others tossed sheets of paper into the air. At the 4 P.M. close of trading, the traditional shout normally associated with such big events rang out across the huge arena, partly to please the news media, and the exchange's fire bell brought the day to a dramatic close.

Ronald Pompei, a 23-year-old Amex floor trainee from Elmsford, N.Y., described the heavy trading there as "like being in the middle of a subway in rush hour."

On the Big Board trading floor, Robert Guarino, a floor member of Wedbush, Noble, Cooke, said: "I'm so busy I can't even take phone calls. This morning we had a lot of buying. This afternoon we had a lot of selling because of profit taking."

The public also seemed to be caught up in the general euphoria, characterized by Michael Sylvester, a phone clerk for Boettcher & Company, as "the electricity and excitement in the air." At Grand Central Station, the lines in front of Merrill Lynch's stock price video screens were longer than those in front of the commuter information boards.

But yesterday, the "regulars" were joined by executives in pin stripes—often with briefcase in one hand, ice cream cone in the other.

Those at the Merrill Lynch bubble gave President Reagan and his economic program little credit for the market's rally. Many attributed it to the approaching November elections, and there was a widespread feeling that the rally would be short-lived.

"To me as a layman, there is no sound underlying economic reason for this volume and rise in good issue stocks," said John L. Tabakman, 70, a retired train dispatcher. "It's the politicians, the elections," he continued. The rally would not help the Republicans in November, he said in response to a question, because "too many people are out of work."

Overview of the New York Stock Exchange in the early 1980's.

OBITUARY

JANUARY 15, 1984

RAY A. KROC DIES AT 81; BUILT MCDONALD'S CHAIN

Eric Pace

Ray A. Kroc, the builder of the McDonald's hamburger empire, who helped change American business and eating habits by deftly orchestrating the purveying of billions of small beef patties, died yesterday in San Diego. He was 81 years old and lived in La Jolla, Calif.

Mr. Kroc, who also owned the San Diego Padres baseball team, died of a heart ailment at Scripps Memorial Hopsital in San Diego, a McDonald's spokesman said. At his death he was senior chairman of McDonald's.

Mr. Kroc, a former piano player and salesman of paper cups and milkshake machines, built up a family fortune worth $500 million or more through his tireless, inspired tinkering with the management of the McDonald's drive-ins and restaurants, which specialize in hamburgers and other fast-food items.

He was a pioneer in automating and standardizing operations in the fiercely competitive, multibillion-dollar fast-food industry. He concentrated on swiftly growing suburban areas, where family visits to the local McDonald's became something like tribal rituals.

He started his first McDonald's in Chicago in 1955 and the chain now has 7,500 outlets in the United States and 31 other countries and territories. The total systemwide sales of its restaurants were more than $8 billion in 1983. Three-quarters of its outlets are run by franchise-holders.

What made Mr. Kroc so successful was the variety of virtuoso refinements he brought to fast-food retailing. He carefully chose the recipients of his McDonald's franchises, seeking managers who were skilled at personal relations; he relentlessly stressed quality, banning from his hamburgers such filler materials as soybeans.

Mr. Kroc also made extensive, innovative use of part-time teenage help; he struggled to keep operating costs down to make McDonald's perennially low prices possible, and he applied complex team techniques to food preparation that were reminiscent of professional football.

Ray Albert Kroc went to public schools in Oak Park, but did not graduate from high school. In World War I, like his fellow Oak Parker, Ernest Hemingway, he served as an amublance driver. Then, after holding various jobs, he spent 17 years with the Lily Tulip Cup Company, becoming sales manager for the Middle West.

By 1941 he became the exclusive sales agent for a machine that could prepare five milkshakes at a time.

Then, in 1954, Mr. Kroc heard about Richard and Maurice McDonald, the owners of a fast-food emporium in San Bernadino, Calif., that was using several of his mixers. As a milkshake specialist, Mr. Kroc later explained, "I had to see what kind of an operation was making 40 at one time."

Mr. Kroc talked to the McDonald brothers about opening franchise outlets patterned on their restaurant, which sold hamburgers for 15 cents, french fries for 10 cents and milkshakes for 20 cents.

Eventually, the McDonalds and Mr. Kroc worked out a deal whereby he was to give them a small percentage of the gross of his operation. In due course the first of Mr. Kroc's restaurants was opened in Des Plaines, another Chicago suburb, long famous as the site of an annual Methodist encampment.

Business proved excellent, and Mr. Kroc soon set about opening other restaurants. The second and third, both in California, opened later in 1955; in five years there were 228, and in 1961 he bought out the McDonald brothers.

Under Mr. Kroc's persistent goading, McDonald's insisted that franchise owners run their own outlets. It also poured hundreds of millions of dollars into advertising—to the point where the head of another fast-food company said in 1978 that consumers were "so preconditioned by McDonald's advertising blanket that the hamburger would taste good even if they left the meat out."

Mr. Kroc suffered a stroke in December 1979 and soon afterward entered an alcoholism treatment center in Orange, Calif., because, he said at the time, "I am required to take medication which is incompatible with the use of alcohol."

HELPED CHANGE AMERICAN EATING HABITS

JANUARY 27, 1985

On Language; Beware the Junk-Bond Bust-Up Takeover

William Safire

"The combination of bust-up takeover threats with greenmail has become a national scandal," writes Martin Lipton, a lawyer, in The New York Law Journal. He adds, ominously, "The junk-bond bust-up takeover is replacing the two-tier bootstrap bust-up takeover."

"National scandal" is the only phrase I recognize in that burst of tycoonspeak. "The new vocabulary of our business," the investment banker Felix G. Rohatyn has written, reflects a go-go atmosphere in which "two-tier tender offers, Pac-Man and poison-pill defenses, crown-jewel options, greenmail, golden parachutes, self-tenders all have become part of our everyday business."

Let us master that lexicon by considering the individual words and phrases. (This will be a lexical bust-up takeover.) When Brian Fernandez of Normura Securities is quoted in Newsweek as saying, "I'm sure I.T.T. has a mine field of poison pills and shark repellent to keep people away," what does he mean?

Shark repellent is the action taken by a company's board of directors to shoo away raiders—the "sharks" circling the company and hoping to chew it up. (The much-derogated sharks can be investors wanting virtuously to throw out inefficient management that has been living off the stockholders' backs, but let's look at takeovers from the point of view of the fearful company.)

"One way to repel sharks is to stagger the board of directors," reports Fred R. Bleakley of The New York Times. "Instead of having the terms expire for all the board members at the same time, making a takeover easier, the staggering might mean that only one member's term expires at any given time," which might try a shark's patience. Another repellent is a fair-price amendment to the company's bylaws, preventing the shark from offering different prices on bids to different stockholders for their shares. Yet another is the crown-jewel option, selling off the most profitable segment of the company; this comes from the figurative use of "the jewel in the crown," now the title of a television series having nothing to do with the world of big business.

My favorite repellent is the poison pill, taken from the world of espionage, in which the agent is supposed to bite a pellet of cyanide rather than permit torture after capture (the Central Intelligence Agency finds it hard to get agents to do that anymore). To make a stock less attractive to sharks, a new class of stock may be issued: this is "a preferred stock or warrant," Arthur Liman, a lawyer, informs me, "that becomes valuable only if another company acquires control. Because it becomes valuable to the target, it becomes costly to the buyer: when the buyer takes the bite, to follow the metaphor, he has to swallow the poison pill."

A junk bond is a high-yield, high-risk security specially designed to finance a takeover; this is supposed to enable the issuer of the bond to get enough bank financing to offer stockholders cash for all the stock in the company. "Following the takeover," writes Mr. Lipton, "the target is busted up to retire part of the takeover financing. Plants are closed, assets are sold, employees are thrown out of work and pension plans are terminated." That's what comes of a junk-bond bust-up takeover.

In extremis, a corporate survivor can try greenmail. First the shark swims around the company, showing its wicked fin and making menacing splashes; the shark keeps buying stock, but not enough to take over. Then the shark offers the frightened directors on the life raft a deal: use company assets to buy in the shark-held stock at a premium, higher than the market price. Big profit for shark, safe jobs for management, and only the other company stockholders get hurt. This is the sort of thing the labor racketeer Louis (Lepke) Buchalter did for garment-center operators in the good old days: the shark sells protection from shark bites. The essence of greenmail is the bonus paid over the market price: "We certainly don't identify it as greenmail," said T. Boone Pickens Jr. of his withdrawn bid to take over Phillips Petroleum, "because we negotiated substantially the same deal for the stockholders as we got for ourselves."

"Greenmail is patterned on blackmail, with the green representing greenbacks," reports Sol Steinmetz, a lexicographer, of Barnhart Books. "It may have been inspired by the earlier graymail." That is a threat by a defense attorney to force the government to drop an espionage case by demanding the exposure of secrets.

I am not going into two-tier tender offers or Pac-Man defenses because it is not my intent to steal students from the Harvard Graduate School of Business, but the golden parachute deserves etymological examination. This agreement to pay an executive his salary and benefits, even if the company is taken over by somebody who wants to heave him into shark-infested waters, is based on golden handcuffs, coined in 1976 to mean "incentives offered executives to keep them from moving to other jobs." In turn, this was based on the British golden handshake, a 1960 term for a whopping sum given as severance pay.

You are now prepared for a raid on a medium-size lemonade stand. If in trouble, get yourself a White Knight, which is either a friendly bidder or a washday miracle. ■

MARCH 19, 1985

ABC IS BEING SOLD FOR $3.5 BILLION

N. R. Kleinfield

The American Broadcasting Companies agreed yesterday to be sold to Capital Cities Communications Inc. for more than $3.5 billion.

The surprise deal represents the first time that ownership of any of the nation's three major networks has changed hands. It also represents the biggest acquisition outside the oil industry in corporate history.

ABC, with 214 affiliated stations, has been a major cultural force in the nation, broadcasting such popular programs as "Dynasty" and "Hotel" and capturing a wide audience with its Olympics programming last summer. Capital Cities, a little-known but ambitious stalker of broadcast and publishing properties, owns television and cable TV systems, the Fairchild Publications business newspaper group and several daily newspapers.

(cont'd. next page)

(continued from previous page)

Thomas S. Murphy, the 59-year-old cost-conscious chairman and chief executive of Capital Cities, and Leonard Goldenson, the strong-willed 79-year-old chairman and chief executive of ABC, said they had been talking on and off since early December, though the deal was essentially patched together over the last two weekends.

"We just thought it was a natural fit between the two companies," Mr. Murphy said in an interview yesterday, "and we thought we'd have an opportunity to handle the new possibilities coming up in the electronics fields better together."

But the agreement, approved by both companies' boards of directors, means the twilight of the long reign of Mr. Goldenson, the chief builder who put ABC together. Once the merger is completed, he will be reduced to chairman of the consolidated company's executive committee.

"That is my wish," Mr. Goldenson said. "I feel that the company I built from scratch is in good hands and that it will be carried on, and that's important to me."

To get ABC, a company four times its size, Capital Cities is offering to pay ABC's stockholders a hefty $118 a share in cash plus warrants to buy Capital Cities stock at a set price. ABC's stock rose $31.375 yesterday, closing at $105.375. As a result of this sizable outlay, however, Capital Cities will gain entry to the glamorous and powerful world of network broadcasting.

"There are certainly cross-ownership questions," said James McKinney, chief of the F.C.C.'s mass media bureau, the division with responsibility for broadcasting oversight. "I would guess they will come in with a plan fairly shortly."

Elsewhere, Ted Turner, the owner of Turner Broadcasting System Inc., is reported to be considering a bid for the CBS network. Meanwhile, a conservative group, with the backing of Senator Jesse Helms, Republican of North Carolina, was put together to raise cash to buy CBS stock as a way of challenging what the group calls the liberal bias of CBS News.

CBS said it had no comment on the ABC-Capital Cities agreement. NBC said only that it wished both companies well. ■

Clockwise from the top left: Frederick S. Pierce, President ABC, Inc.; Daniel B. Burke, President of Capital Cities/ABC, Inc; Leonard H. Goldenson, Chairman, ABC, Inc.; and Thomas S. Murphy, Chief Executive Officer, Capital Cities/ABC, Inc.

Microsoft owner and founder Bill Gates poses in front of hundreds of boxed Microsoft products in 1986.

AUGUST 22, 1985

MICROSOFT AND I.B.M. JOIN FORCES

Andrew Pollack

SAN FRANCISCO, Aug. 21—The International Business Machines Corporation has agreed with the Microsoft Corporation, a key software supplier, to develop fundamental software for personal computers, the companies said today.

But Microsoft will be able to sell the jointly developed operating systems to other computer manufacturers, which should allay industry fears that I.B.M. would one day migrate to its own, proprietary operating system. That could have locked others in the industry out of the market and made it impossible for existing software to run on future I.B.M. computers.

The agreement states that I.B.M. and Microsoft will work together on personal computer operating systems, the software that directs the computer in performance of basic operations such as retrieving information from data storage disks. Microsoft already supplies the MS-DOS operating system used in I.B.M. computers and other computers compatible with the I.B.M. machines.

As to the industry fears that I.B.M. will lock out its competitors, "If anything will eliminate it, this will eliminate it," said William H. Gates, the chairman and chief executive of Microsoft. "It's very clear that this is a reaffirmation of the importance of DOS."

"I think it's good for us from an outside perception viewpoint," said Ben Rosen, the chairman of the Compaq Computer Corporation, the leading supplier of I.B.M.-compatible personal computers. He said the agreement would help assure customers of what Compaq has always believed—that I.B.M. will not desert the open MS-DOS operating system.

The agreement calls for the two companies to cooperate on the development of operating systems and other systems software products. While future versions of MS-DOS are included, the companies did not specify what else might be included. But it is likely the agreement calls for them to work on computer programming language, networks for connecting computers together and "windowing environments" that allow several tasks to appear on the screen at the same time, each in its own little "window." Microsoft is already working on future versions of its operating systems, known as versions 4.0 and 5.0, that will take advantage of more powerful computers now being built.

The new versions are expected to allow several tasks to be performed at once on the computer, whereas the existing MS-DOS can only handle one application at a time. The new versions will also be able to handle more computer memory. The current versions can only handle up to 640,000 characters of memory, whereas it is not uncommon now for computers to have one million characters of storage or more.

Microsoft, based in Bellevue, Wash., was catapulted to the lead in the software business when I.B.M. chose its operating system five years ago. Since then it has grown to $140 million in revenues and diversified. MS-DOS sales now represent about 20 percent of its revenues. Its sales to I.B.M. account for less than 10 percent, Mr. Gates said. ■

SEPTEMBER 19, 1985

APPLE COMPUTER ENTREPRENEUR'S RISE AND FALL

Andrew Pollack

Steve Jobs with the Lisa computer in 1983.

SAN FRANCISCO, Sept. 18—In his years of guiding Apple Computer Inc., Steven P. Jobs had become the epitome of the American entrepreneur, a symbol of the wealth and power that can arise almost overnight in California's Silicon Valley.

Even President Reagan, in a recent address, urged the nation's youth to "follow in the footsteps of those two college students who launched one of America's great computer firms from the garage behind their house."

The tale of Mr. Jobs's visionary leadership at Apple came to a bitter end on Tuesday when he resigned as the company's chairman after disclosure of his plans to start a new company.

Mr. Jobs would not comment in detail today on the developments that led to his fall from grace at Apple.

But according to associates, the same vision, drive and ego that helped Mr. Jobs make Apple into a leading personal computer company also prevented him from heeding the advice of others to the point that Apple, which at one time seemed unstoppable, is in worse financial shape than it has ever been.

"He only trusted himself to be the high leader," said Stephen Wozniak, who founded Apple with Mr. Jobs in 1976 and has since seen his relations sour with his former partner.

Mr. Jobs, at 30 years old a millionaire many times over, lost operating authority of the company in the spring, but remained its largest shareholder and chairman of the board. His impatience with this reduced role led him, in the best Silicon Valley spirit, to do what entrepreneurs do best: start a new company. It was this that caused the final rift with Apple's current management.

Apple is not considered to be in danger of failing, although some computer analysts say the company, in a weakened condition, may be a takeover target. But the job of guiding Apple now belongs more

(cont'd. next page)

than ever to John Sculley, the president and chief executive officer recruited from Pepsico two years ago by Mr. Jobs personally.

Mr. Jobs's resignation culminates a tumultuous power struggle with Mr. Sculley that began earlier this year as Apple's fortunes started to decline, a power struggle that Mr. Sculley has compared to a real-life version of "Dynasty," the television program.

Mr. Jobs's resignation from that position was precipitated by a dispute over plans to start his own company to make unspecified computer products for the higher education market. Apple officials say they feel betrayed that Mr. Jobs might compete with Apple, since the higher education market is one of Apple's strongholds. In addition, Mr. Jobs plans to hire five Apple employees.

Like many legends, the story of Apple is somewhat exaggerated, even by President Reagan. Mr. Jobs and Mr. Wozniak were not college students, but were college dropouts who hung around together in the garage at the home of Mr. Jobs's parents, tinkering with electronics. Some of their first devices were boxes that allowed them to make long-distance calls without paying.

It was Mr. Wozniak who actually did the engineering work to design the Apple II computer, which became a best-seller. But Mr. Jobs was the one who wanted to start a company and blustered his way into getting Apple a supply of parts and a top-notch public relations firm before the company was hardly out of the garage.

He became the company's visionary, conceptualizing products like the Macintosh. "He seemed to be able to see slightly beyond the horizon when other people couldn't see beyond the end of their nose," said Michael Moritz, senior editor of the Technologic Computer Letter, an industry newsletter, and author of "The Little Kingdom," a history of Apple.

Mr. Jobs could inspire and charm, getting people to follow him down any path. "He was always so persuasive the way he would say things," said Mr. Wozniak, who, despite his falling out with Mr. Jobs, called him "the finest technical leader Apple has ever had."

But Mr. Jobs could also be arrogant and alienate people who worked with him and take revenge on people who crossed him. Former Apple employees say they were afraid to disagree with Mr. Jobs.

Apple, while having a solid management, still might miss Mr. Jobs. The company is weak in top engineering talent to guide product development. Moreover, more traditional managers like Mr. Sculley have often proved no more adept at running technology companies than the original entrepreneurs. Some analysts and former employees are worried that Apple is losing its spark and becoming stodgy, a process some refer to as "Scullification."

"The great sadness and the great tragedy" of the departure of Mr. Jobs from Apple, Mr. Moritz said, "is that both the company and he personally would be better off if they were still together." ■

DECEMBER 12, 1985

G.E. WILL PURCHASE RCA IN A CASH DEAL WORTH $6.3 BILLION

John Crudele

The General Electric (GE) building, formally known as the RCA building, in Rockefeller Center, New York City.

The General Electric Company agreed yesterday to acquire the RCA Corporation, owner of the NBC television network and a leading defense and consumer electronics company, in a cash deal worth nearly $6.3 billion.

The announcement was the second this year of a network takeover. The acquisition of the American Broadcasting Companies for $3.5 billion by Capital Cities Communications was announced in March.

Word of the merger agreement between G.E., a broadly based electronics firm founded by Thomas Alva Edison, and RCA, which G.E. helped found in 1919, was apparently less of a surprise to the financial community. Before the news yesterday, the price of RCA's stock jumped nearly 20 percent on extraordinarily heavy volume of 5.1 million shares.

The agreement reunites two companies that helped each other grow from the end of World War I, but became fierce competitors in pursuit of communications technology. Their combined revenues would make them together the nation's seventh-largest industrial corporation, sandwiched between the International Business Machines Corporation and the du Pont Company.

While details of the merger were sketchy, G.E. said it would pay $66.50 a share in cash for RCA's 94.4 million shares. The total price of $6.28 billion matches the transaction for the largest non-oil company acquisition. Earlier this year, Kohlberg, Kravis, Roberts & Company agreed to buy the Beatrice Companies, a Chicago-based consumer products company, for $6.2 billion.

an excellent strategic opportunity

In a statement last night, the companies said the merger is "an excellent strategic opportunity for both companies that will help America's competitiveness in world markets."

The transaction may have been helped along by the fact that executives from both companies know each other well.

G.E. chairman chairman, John F. Welch Jr, who is 50 years old and took over as head of the company in 1981, is expected to remain in charge of the combined company. Also likely to stay on is Robert R. Frederick, president and chief executive of RCA, who was formerly a G.E. executive. ■

MAY 16, 1986

SALE OF BINGHAM PAPERS NEARS

Alex S. Jones

LOUISVILLE, Ky., May 15—In a rare break with tradition, the elegant breakfast usually given by the Bingham family on the morning of the Kentucky Derby did not take place this year.

At The Courier-Journal and The Louisville Times, the newspapers that are the heart of the Bingham family's communications empire, mordant staff members have set up betting pools on who will acquire the newspapers, and at what price.

In this atmosphere of anxiety, sadness and circus, on Friday the warring members of the Bingham clan will gather to try to select a new owner for The Courier-Journal and The Louisville Times, thus ending the nearly 70-year reign of the Binghams, whose Kentucky communications empire made them one of the state's most powerful families. The deliberations could go into next week.

While those submitting bids for the newspapers have not been identified, they are thought to include the Gannett Company, the Washington Post Company and the Tribune Company of Chicago.

"It's the passing of an era that we'll never see again," said Harvey I. Sloane, county judge executive of Jefferson County, which includes Louisville.

The decision to sell all the family holdings was announced on Jan. 9 by Barry Bingham Sr., the 80-year-old patriarch and chairman of the family companies. That decision, which came after years of bitter feuding over the family business by his three children, was immediately denounced as a "betrayal" by Barry Bingham Jr., his only surviving son and the operational head of the family enterprises.

While the Louisville newspapers are considered editorial plums, analysts say they come encumbered with economic drawbacks such as a flat Louisville economy and expensive statewide circulation that has been maintained more for prestige and tradition than for profit. A new printing plant that some analysts say is needed could cost $75 million, and the new owner will likely merge the newspapers into one, which could mean the elimination of a hundred editorial jobs or more. ■

NOVEMBER 15, 1986

BIG TRADER TO PAY U.S. $100 MILLION FOR INSIDER ABUSES

Peter T. Kilborn

WASHINGTON, Nov. 14—Ivan F. Boesky, one of the biggest and best-known speculators on Wall Street, has agreed to pay a $100 million penalty for illegal insider trading, the Government announced today.

The sum was by far the largest ever assessed against someone who has reaped "ill-gotten gains," said John S. R. Shad, the chairman of the Securities and Exchange Commission, which announced the penalty. Half of the sum represents illegal profits, the other half a civil penalty.

In addition to the financial penalty, Mr. Boesky, chief executive of Ivan F. Boesky & Company, an investment firm, after an 18-month phase-out period, will be barred for life from the American securities industry.

The investigation arose out of a case against Dennis B. Levine, the merger specialist at the center of a trading scandal, who has cooperated with the Government, as Mr. Boesky is doing now. According to the S.E.C., Mr. Boesky had agreed to pay Mr. Levine 5 percent of the profits made on some of his biggest transactions.

The Government said Mr. Levine, a former managing director of the Wall Street firm of Drexel Burnham Lambert Inc., gave Mr. Boesky inside information concerning takeover and other activity surrounding Nabisco Brands, American Natural Resources, Union Carbide, General Foods and other big companies. Insider trading takes place when securities are bought or sold on the basis of information that is not yet available to the public.

Mr. Boesky is a specialist in the high-tension, high-stakes world of risk arbitrage, where stocks are bought in anticipation of a takeover, a merger or change in corporate ownership. The son of a Russian immigrant delicatessen owner in Detroit, Ivan Boesky was known as a loner among other risk arbitragers, a man called "Ivan the Terrible" for his apparent success in trading stocks.

Newspaper reports put his personal wealth in excess of $250 million. He was said to have a 300-button telephone console in his office, and three phones in his chauffeur-driven car. As a trader, he realized profits of legendary proportions in such takeovers as Chevron's purchase of Gulf Oil and Texaco's purchase of Getty Oil. Those were two of the biggest such transactions ever, and both predated the period covered by the S.E.C. complaint.

"Risk arbitrage is not illegal," Mr. Shad, the S.E.C. chairman, told a news conference. "But it is illegal to trade on material, nonpublic information."

Mr. Shad added: "This will have a significant impact on many of the people engaged in risk arbitrage, in making sure they don't step over the line." ■

Ivan Boesky leaves the New York District U.S. Courthouse after pleading guilty on April 23, 1987.

DECEMBER 19, 1987

BOESKY SENTENCED TO 3 YEARS IN JAIL IN INSIDER SCANDAL

James Sterngold

Ivan F. Boesky, once among the financial world's most powerful speculators and now a symbol of Wall Street's excesses, was sentenced yesterday to three years in prison for conspiring to file false stock trading records.

According to records kept by the United States Attorney's office in Manhattan, the three-year term is the third longest to have been imposed in a case related to insider trading. Mr. Boesky had faced a maximum penalty of five years in jail and a $250,000 fine.

Comments by the judge, the United States Attorney and Mr. Boesky's lawyer underscored both the enormity of Mr. Boesky's crimes, the unimagined scope of the corruption on Wall Street that he exposed to the Government and the extent to which his cooperation led to a broadening of the insider trading scandal.

Judge Lasker said he believed that Mr. Boesky had reformed, but emphasized that a prison term was necessary to try and stanch what he characterized as widespread disregard for the law in business and government.

"Ivan Boesky's offense cannot go unpunished," Judge Lasker said. "Its scope was too great, its influence too profound, its seriousness too substantial merely to forgive and forget."

"Recent history has shown that the kind of erosion of morals and standards and obedience to the law involved in a case such as this is unhappily widespread in both business and government," he added. "The time has come when it is totally unacceptable for courts to act as if prison is unthinkable for white-collar defendants but a matter of routine in other cases. Breaking the law is breaking the law."

During the hearing Mr. Boesky spoke in an almost inaudible whisper, telling the judge that he had expressed his remorse at a pre-sentencing hearing on Dec. 3. "I felt it deeply then and I feel it even more deeply now," he told the court yesterday.

U.S. Attorney Rudolph Giuliani announces Ivan Boesky's jail sentence for inside trading at Federal Courthouse in New York City.

APRIL 27, 1987

A Debate in China Over Stock Trading

Nicholas D. Kristof

Before the Communist victory in 1949 exorcised almost all traces of capitalism from China, this city boasted of having the biggest stock market in Asia. Now, as the nation tentatively rediscovers the need for capital markets, Shanghai has a new stock exchange—one that lists four stocks and two bonds.

When one of the bond issues went on sale in late January, more than 3,000 would-be customers, some of whom had lined up the day before, nearly broke down the iron gate in front of the bank.

But whether the public will be allowed to satisfy its craving to invest in bonds and stocks—which in China sometimes look more like debt instruments—is still open to question. A debate continues in the highest levels of the Communist Party over the suitability of trading securities in a socialist economy.

Shenyang became the first city in China to reopen a stock exchange

Just a few months ago the trend seemed to favor shareholding. Last August the northeastern city of Shenyang became the first city in China to reopen a stock exchange, and since then exchanges have opened in Shanghai, Beijing, Wuhan and Tianjin. When the chairman of the New York Stock Exchange, John J. Phelan Jr., visited China last fall, he was granted a long audience with the country's supreme leader, Deng Xiaoping.

In an article in the official Beijing Review in December, a Beijing University economist predicted a vast expansion of shareholding. The economist, Li Yining, proposed what amounted to the privatization of China: turning state-owned companies into stock-issuing concerns owned by their shareholders.

Foreigners so far are not permitted to participate in the securities market—although prominent visitors are allowed to buy a single share as a souvenir. For that reason, and because any securities profits would be in local currency and could not be converted, international securities firms have not paid much attention to the stock markets in China.

For companies, the great advantage of issuing stocks or bonds is being able to grow without the uncertainties of arranging bank loans. According to official figures, more than 6,000 companies throughout China have issued shares worth $1.6 billion, but that equals only 1 percent of the loans last year in the banking system. ■

Shares of stock traded on the Shanghai stock exchange.

DECEMBER 13, 1985

G.E.'S DEMANDING CHAIRMAN

Thomas J. Lueck

STAMFORD, Conn., Dec. 12—In four years as the chairman of the General Electric Company, John F. Welch Jr. has become known simultaneously as one of the nation's toughest executives, as an intellectually astute manager and as a man more inclined to demand action immediately than wait for a second opinion.

Mr. Welch has made his mark on G.E., where sharp cost cutting, plant modernization and a host of management changes have made him something of a guru in business circles.

Still, one of the questions that loomed large in the wake of Wednesday's merger announcement by G.E. and the RCA Corporation was whether he has the diplomatic skills to mesh the assets and personalities of two major companies.

"Diplomacy?" remarked the 50-year-old Mr. Welch today. "I don't think anybody could recall a more diplomatic merger." He added: "This was not a takeover. This is a merger that makes great strategic sense to both sides."

Indeed, in telephone interviews late today, Mr. Welch and other senior G.E. officers said that they would not have agreed to merge with RCA unless they were convinced that the two companies could be combined without a major change in RCA's business or management style.

"This is a merger of two similar cultures; I don't see any major conflict," said Michael Carpenter, G.E.'s director of planning, who in the past has been an outspoken critic of the wave of mergers and acquisitions on Wall Street.

"My job is to give them the resources they need to win," said Mr. Welch, who has

John F. (Jack) Welch Jr.

pruned layers of middle-level management at G.E., closed down dozens of its plants and reduced overall employment by about 20 percent. At the same time, he has funneled more than $8 billion in capital spending into the automation, reorganization and growth of the company's remaining businesses.

Even beyond the General Electric headquarters near here in Fairfield, Conn., Mr. Welch's demanding style has become well known. A chemical engineer by training, Mr. Welch normally works 12-to-14-hour days in shirt-sleeves. He insists on fresh, entrepreneurial insight from his executives, often in spontaneous meetings.

Mr. Welch quickly changed things. The company's planning department, under Mr. Carpenter, has shrunk to eight employees. And those who have left are among more than 100 employees at the Fairfield headquarters who have resigned, or been discharged, under Mr. Welch. About 600 remain. ■

Traffic and pedestrians in front of the New York Stock Exchange in 1987.

APRIL 24, 1987

EXCHANGE SEAT SELLS FOR $1 MILLION

Phillip H. Wiggins

A seat on the New York Stock Exchange was sold yesterday for $1 million, the highest price ever paid for what has become one of the hottest properties on Wall Street.

The record price eclipses the $850,000 paid for a seat only last Monday. Analysts said the sale showed confidence in the market's strength in the face of the dollar's weakness and interest-rate uncertainty.

The New York Stock Exchange does not disclose the participants in the sale of a seat. But the buyer was identified on Wall Street as Stern Brothers, a small brokerage and specialist firm based in New York, and the seller was said to be Irwin Herling, a New Jersey resident.

Mr. Herling could not be reached for comment. In June 1964, when he was admitted to the exchange, four seats were sold, one for $205,000, one for $210,000, and two for $207,000. Officials at Stern Brothers declined to comment on the sale.

"The price of the seat reflects supply and demand," said Richard Torrenzano, chief spokesman for the Big Board, as the New York Stock Exchange is known. "There is a great deal of demand right now, which seems to imply that we have reached the strongest level of optimism in our history about the strength and future of the New York Stock Exchange."

There are 1,366 seats on the New York Stock Exchange, a number that has been fixed for decades, and 611 member organizations hold seats. Since seats are held in individual's names, some firms hold several seats. Some seats may be leased, and some are held as investments. ■

AUGUST 4, 1987

SENATE, BY 91 TO 2, BACKS GREENSPAN AS FED CHIEF

Nathaniel C. Nash

The Senate today approved the nomination of Alan Greenspan to be the chairman of the Federal Reserve Board.

Mr. Greenspan, who until recently ran his own economic consulting firm in New York, Townsend-Greenspan & Company, was approved by a 91-to-2 vote.

He will replace the current chairman, Paul A. Volcker, whose term expires on Thursday.

Voting against the nomination were Senator Bill Bradley, Democrat of New Jersey, and Senator Kent Conrad, Democrat of North Dakota.

Mr. Greenspan's approval by the Senate was never seriously in doubt since President Reagan announced early in June that he would appoint the economist to succeed Mr. Volcker. But Mr. Greenspan's views on deregulation caused some concern among senators, as did his close political ties with the Republican Party, and his lack of international exposure.

Senator William Proxmire, Democrat of Wisconsin and chairman of the Senate Banking Committee, on several occasions expressed his disagreement with Mr. Greenspan's views that the banking industry should undergo considerably more deregulation. But Mr. Proxmire supported the nomination, noting that he expected Mr. Greenspan to be as vigorous an inflation-fighter as was Mr. Volcker.

President Ronald Reagan announcing Alan Greenspan (left) as Federal Reserve Board Chairman replacement for Paul Volcker (right).

OCTOBER 20, 1987

STOCKS PLUNGE 508 POINTS, A DROP OF 22.6%; 604 MILLION VOLUME NEARLY DOUBLES RECORD

Lawrence J. De Maria

Stock market prices plunged in a tumultuous wave of selling yesterday, giving Wall Street its worst day in history and raising fears of a recession.

The Dow Jones industrial average, considered a benchmark of the market's health, plummeted a record 508 points, to 1,738.74, based on preliminary calculations. That 22.6 percent decline was the worst since World War I and far greater than the 12.82 percent drop on Oct. 28, 1929, that along with the next day's 11.7 percent decline preceded the Great Depression.

Since hitting a record 2,722.42 on Aug. 25, the Dow has fallen almost 1,000 points, or 36 percent, putting the blue-chip indicator 157.5 points below the level at which it started the year. With Friday's plunge of 108.35 points, the Dow has fallen more than 26 percent in the last two sessions.

Yesterday's frenzied trading on the nation's stock exchanges lifted volume to unheard of levels. On the New York Stock Exchange, an estimated 604.3 million shares changed hands, almost double the previous record of 338.5 million shares set just last Friday.

Yesterday's big losers included International Business Machines, the bluest of the blue chips, which dropped $31, to $104. In August the stock was at $176. The other big losers among the blue chips were General Motors, which lost $13.875, to $52.125, and Exxon, which dropped $10.25, to $33.50.

According to Wilshire Associates, which tracks more than 5,000 stocks, the rout obliterated more than $500 billion in equity value from the nation's stock portfolios. That equity value now stands at $2.311 trillion. Since late summer, more than $1 trillion in stock values has been lost.

The losses were so great they sent shock waves to markets around the world, and many foreign exchanges posted record losses. In a sign of the continuing effect, the Tokyo Stock Exchange fell sharply today. The Nikkei Dow Jones average plummeted a record 3,395.95 yen, to 22,350.61, a drop of 13.2 percent, by late afternoon. Also, the Hong Kong exchange decided to close for the week.

Stock market analysts scrambled for explanations, which ranged from rising interest rates to the falling dollar to the possibility of war between the United States and Iran.

But many experts seemed to think that a major catalyst was fears of a breakdown in accords to maintain trading and currency stability between the United States and its major trading partners.

Stock prices around the world plummeted, taking their cue from Wall Street. Panic selling swamped stock exchanges in Tokyo, Hong Kong, London, Frankfurt, Amsterdam, Mexico City and other centers.

The stock market's incredible decline, analysts said, might have repercussions far beyond the immediate ones. The stock market has often portended economic declines. What a decline such as has occurred may mean is hard to imagine.

Tens of millions of Americans are tied to the stock market, either directly, or through mutual funds, or through pension funds that invest in equities.

In addition, rumors began to spread yesterday that some financial institutions might have lost heavily in the frantic trading, and might be in trouble. Small firms may have liquidity problems, and be forced to close. Individual traders and investors have undoubtedly been wiped out. Large firms may have to cut back, and it is not inconceivable that the ripples may spread to the banking community, which has been edging into the securities business.

That could lead to layoffs, and further economic dislocations.

"One word is operative out there now," said one very shaken trader. "Fright."

A trader on the New York Stock Exchange bows his head during Black Monday.

OCTOBER 20, 1987

THE MARKET PLUNGE

DAY TO REMEMBER IN FINANCIAL DISTRICT

Alison Leigh Cowan

Wall Street workers heading home after the stock market crash.

From the trading floors of the big brokerage firms to the stock exchanges to the shoeshine stands in the heart of the financial district, it was clear that yesterday would be a day etched in people's memories for years to come.

The genuine fear and panic rippling through the markets was reflected in the agitation of strangers stopping each other in the street to inquire about the market, in the stony-faced traders whose sense of humor had abandoned them and in the exhaustion of stock exchange employees struggling to maintain orderly trading.

Joel L. Lovett, a trader for Jacee Securities, stepped outside of the American Stock Exchange yesterday at the end of a session that eclipsed the 1929 crash and mopped the sweat from his forehead.

"I've been down here for 30 years," he said. "I thought pandemonium set in when John F. Kennedy was assassinated. But I've never seen anything like this. I thought there would be a correction in the market. But this is shocking. There's hysteria and fear. It's absolute fear."

It's absolute fear.

Normally calm offices needed lessons in crowd control. Investors lined up outside the Fidelity Investments office in Boston to redeem their shares, and passers-by stood in front of Fidelity Investments' Park Avenue investors center in midtown Manhattan with their faces pressed against the glass even though there was nothing to see. The branch's ticker tape had been broken for several days and the electronic bulletin board that had been flashing market quotes jammed at 1:56 P.M.

At midday, Craig Curtiss, an employee of Adler Coleman & Company who works on the New York Stock Exchange floor, observed: "Everything is out of control. Clerks and teletypists might be here till 7 o'clock."

His firm trades 150,000 shares on a normal day. By noontime, it had already done half a million shares. "It's crazy," he said. He ordered a shish kebab from the hot-dog cart outside the exchange and asked for hot sauce just to "get a little more fire in the belly" before going back inside.

Wall Street traders are usually quick with the wisecracks following everyone else's disasters, but the market's unprecedented plunge yesterday left many of them with an unprecedented loss for words.

When somebody on Drexel Burnham Lambert's trading desk asked if anyone had a joke to lighten things up, a bewildered pall fell over the usually glib crowd as the equities traders stared at each other blankly.

"This was not a laughing matter," said Mark Mehl, head of Drexel's equities desk. On second thought, he said, "I'd like to hear some jokes if you've got some."

"Jokes?" said Jack Conlon, head trader at Nikko Securities. "Not a one. There's nothing funny about what's going on."

Many traders and investment bankers expressed mock relief that most firms' windows were sealed. Some Shearson Lehman Brothers traders posted a sign over their desk saying, "To the lifeboats." ■

DECEMBER 10, 1987

Wall Street Reviews 'Wall Street'

Geraldine Fabrikant

For many investment banking luminaries at a private screening of "Wall Street" on Monday night, watching the new film was like watching home movies.

There were familiar deals and familiar faces, with cameo roles by pals and colleagues, in the movie about wheeling, dealing and crime on Wall Street. People in the audience at the uptown Manhattan theater nudged one another when Kenneth Lipper, the investment banker and former Deputy Mayor of New York, appeared on screen. They nudged each other again when Jeff Beck of Drexel Burnham Lambert came on.

There was an undercurrent of excitement in the audience, which included Bruce Wasserstein and Joseph R. Perella, co-heads of investment banking at the First Boston Corporation; Donald G. Drapkin, a lieutenant of Ronald O. Perelman, the chairman of Revlon Inc. and multimillionaire investor; Laurence A. Tisch, chief executive of CBS Inc.; and Paul E. Tierney Jr., the financier of Coniston Partners.

Long the grist for newspaper and society columns, Wall Street's leaders had finally made it in Hollywood—even if it was as larger-than-life villains.

After the lights came up, many in the audience said they had found the movie, which opens tomorrow, dramatic and entertaining. And Stephen A. Schwarzman, a partner at the Blackstone Group, an investment banking firm, added: "The film captured the mood of the trading rooms. They tried to capture something about the deal-oriented side of Wall Street and they succeeded."

Certainly the film is timely, coming in the wake of the insider trading scandals and the Oct. 19 collapse of the stock market. "Wall Street" is the story of a relentlessly evil Wall Street mogul named Gordon Gekko, played by Michael Douglas, who ensnares Bud Fox, an ambitious, and weak, young stockbroker, played by Charlie Sheen.

Mr. Fox courts Mr. Gekko's business. Then Mr. Gekko easily seduces him into illegally gathering inside information for him. Mr. Fox, whose nose is pressed against the glass of the good life, is desperate to build his own fortune.

Ultimately, Mr. Gekko betrays him. Mr. Fox then comes to his senses and tries to rectify what he has done. In doing so, he incriminates Mr. Gekko.

Despite the audience's enthusiasm, few were convinced that "Wall Street" would be a blockbuster, in part because its subject matter was too alien for many moviegoers.

As William E. Mayer, a managing director of First Boston, put it: "It's too foreign to be a hit elsewhere in the U.S. You have people on farms in Iowa going to movies. How can they relate to this?"

The 130 people who attended the dinner at the Regency Hotel following the screening may have debated the merits of the film, which was directed by Oliver Stone. But most did not quibble with its technical accuracy.

"The screaming is typical," Mr. Schwarzman said, referring to scenes in which deals started to go bad. "When deals go wrong, you have no one else to blame so you yell at yourself and you yell at others."

At least one arbitrager, however, said the film captured the prevailing mood on Wall Street. "It laid bare the real motivations," said this viewer, who requested anonymity. "People pretend that they are doing something noble, raising capital to support America's businesses, but Wall Street is just about making money."

Praise for the film was not universal. Mr. Drapkin, Revlon's vice chairman, found the plot difficult to follow and said the story was not gripping. And he said the lack of a sympathetic character was a weakness.

"It is upsetting because it makes the excesses of Wall Street look like an everyday occurrence," said Leonard N. Stern, chairman of Hartz, the pet food and real estate concern.

But given the damage already done by the insider trading scandal and the stock market crash, Mr. Schwarzman asked, "How can the image of Wall Street be hurt any more?"

Director Oliver Stone (right) sitting with actor Charlie Sheen on set of movie "Wall Street."

MURDOCH'S GLOBAL POWER PLAY

William H. Meyers

Media baron Rupert Murdoch in his office in 1985.

A fiery-red lotus roars out of the driveway of the Bel-Air Hotel in Los Angeles. Knees tucked under the dashboard, Rupert Murdoch guns the low-slung two-seater through the twisting turns on Stone Canyon Road—simultaneously shifting, steering and tracking down his subordinates on the car telephone. At precisely 8 o'clock on this balmy January morning, the Lotus rolls through the gates of 20th Century-Fox, Murdoch's television and motion picture studio.

Murdoch storms into his office, his double-breasted blazer flapping, and confronts the stacks of letters and faxes on his mahogany desk. They are the outpourings of the News Corporation Ltd., a $4.2 billion global empire that encompasses 150 newspapers and magazines, a satellite cable channel, book publishers, an airline, television stations, a hotel reservation service, even a sheep farm in the Australian outback. Normally, Murdoch would devour these documents, but he impatiently shoves them aside. He wants to concentrate all his considerable energies and anger on the target of the day: Senator Edward M. Kennedy, Democrat of Massachusetts.

At Kennedy's urging, a special measure had quietly been attached to a catchall spending bill and signed into law. It closed the door on any chance Murdoch might have of escaping a Federal ban against cross-ownership of newspapers and television stations in the same city—in his case, The Boston Herald and WFXT-TV, in Boston, and The New York Post and WNYW-TV, in New York. "The process was an outrage," says Murdoch, his hard-edged Australian vowels asserting themselves. He calls it an exercise in "liberal totalitarianism," an attack against papers that have frequently criticized the Senator.

Over the next days, Murdoch will mount the kind of brass-knuckle attack that has made the Melbourne-born publisher the most intimidating media mogul since William Randolph Hearst. "People are afraid of him," says Sir William Rees-Mogg, former editor of The Times of London.

In an era when giant corporate and financial institutions increasingly compete on a worldwide basis, Keith Rupert Murdoch stands poised to create the first global communications network. The pieces are already in place on four continents.

His newspapers control 60 percent of the market in Australia, more than a third of the market in Britain. The South China Morning Post, his toehold in Asia, commands the lion's share of Hong Kong's English-language newspaper circulation. He owns television or cable operations in the United States and Europe, upscale magazines such as New York and Epicurean in Melbourne and major interests in book publishing houses such as William Collins Sons & Co. in London and Harper & Row in New York. He has a significant financial stake in Reuters, the international news service, and in Pearson P.L.C. of London, whose holdings include The Financial Times and the Penguin Publishing Company.

The News Corporation's revenues have grown at a startling pace, driven by a 10-year string of acquisitions. But its debt has mounted even faster; it has reached $5.6 billion—$4.3 billion in direct borrowings, plus an additional $1.3 billion in convertible debt. The company's huge cash flow easily services that debt and enables News Corp. to take on more.

Deft exploitation of the differences in Australian, British and American tax and accounting rules permit the company to borrow far more than its competitors while avoiding dilution of Rupert Murdoch's holdings. Through such borrowings, Murdoch has extended his realm, one giant step at a time:

A. In March 1977, after snapping up The New York Post for $30 million, he purchased the New York Magazine Company for $17 million.

B. In Feb. 1981, he gained control of the venerable Times of London and The Sunday Times for $28 million.

C. In April 1985, he purchased 50 percent of 20th Century-Fox from Marvin Davis, the Denver oilman, for $250 million and soon after secured seven television stations from Metromedia for $2 billion. In December, Murdoch bought Davis's remaining share of Fox for $350 million.

D. In March 1987, he took over Australia's Herald and Weekly Times group for $1.6 billion, and then Harper & Row, the publisher, with a $300 million offer.

E. In Jan. 1988, he revealed a $600 million, 20.4 percent, holding in Pearson P.L.C., owner of The Financial Times, making the News Corporation the largest shareholder. ■

OCTOBER 21, 1988

Bid for RJR Nabisco Jolts Bonds

Kenneth N. Gilpin

The corporate bond market was jolted yesterday by the $17 billion leveraged buyout offer for RJR Nabisco.

The movement in RJR bonds was merely the latest takeover-related drop that has occurred this week. Earlier, prices of outstanding Philip Morris securities fell sharply after the company made an unsolicited offer for the Kraft Company.

"Over the last 30 days or so it has become increasingly obvious that there is an increasing level of event risk in the bond market because stock market prices are so low," said James Ednie, corporate vice president and senior industrial corporate bond trader at Drexel Burnham Lambert. "Bondholders suffer from those sorts of transactions, because securities become increasingly attractive to raiders and management. It is clear that the industrial bond market cannot benefit from this deal."

Underscoring Mr. Ednie's point were the actions taken by the two major ratings services, Moody's and Standard & Poor's, in the wake of the RJR announcement. Yesterday afternoon both agencies said they were monitoring the company and suggested that ratings might be downgraded on RJR's $5 billion in outstanding debt. The company currently is rated A by both services.

The ripples that spread from the RJR announcement were big enough to overcome a rise in the secondary Treasury bond market and caused prices of many other industrial bond issues to ease by about one-quarter of a point, traders said. ■

SEPTEMBER 8, 1988

DREXEL BURNHAM CHARGED BY S.E.C. WITH STOCK FRAUD

Stephen Labaton

The Securities and Exchange Commission charged yesterday that Drexel Burnham Lambert Inc. had engaged in a secret agreement with Ivan F. Boesky to defraud Drexel clients, trade illegally on insider information, manipulate the prices of stocks and violate a host of other securities regulations.

Although some of the charges against Drexel, one of Wall Street's most powerful firms, had been anticipated for some time, the nature of other allegations were more serious than had been generally expected.

The 184-page civil complaint, filed in Federal District Court in Manhattan after the stock markets closed, named Drexel and four of its employees, including Michael Milken, the head of the firm's high-yield "junk bond" department. The complaint recounts Drexel's role in a litany of high-powered corporate mergers and restructurings involving such names as MGM/UA Entertainment, MCA Inc., Diamond Shamrock, the Wickes Companies and the Stone Container Corporation.

In its filing, the agency accused the Miami industrialist Victor Posner and his son Steven N. Posner of violating Federal securities laws by scheming with Drexel to conceal the ownership of securities, an illegal practice known as stock parking.

While the complaint does not spell out precise fines, S.E.C. lawyers said yesterday that if they were successful Drexel could be penalized hundreds of millions of dollars.

In addition, all the defendants could be forced out of the securities business after an administrative proceeding, which typically follows cases brought by the S.E.C.

Mr. Boesky has been a crucial element of the Government's investigation of Drexel, and he is expected to be the star witness for the S.E.C. and Federal prosecutors if their cases make it to trial.

OCTOBER 31, 1988

KRAFT BEING SOLD TO PHILIP MORRIS FOR $13.1 BILLION

Robert J. Cole

In one of the biggest takeovers to date, two of the nation's best-known makers of consumer goods, Philip Morris Companies and Kraft Inc., yesterday agreed to merge in a deal valued at $13.1 billion in cash.

Kraft's stockholders will get $106 a share, $9.50 higher than the shares closed on Friday and $40.875 higher than they were trading for before the offer was made on Oct. 17.

The combined company would knock Unilever, the British-Dutch company, out of first place as the world's largest producer of consumer goods.

In making the announcement late yesterday with Kraft, Hamish Maxwell, chairman and chief executive of Philip Morris, said: "As we have stated from the outset, we

(cont'd. next page)

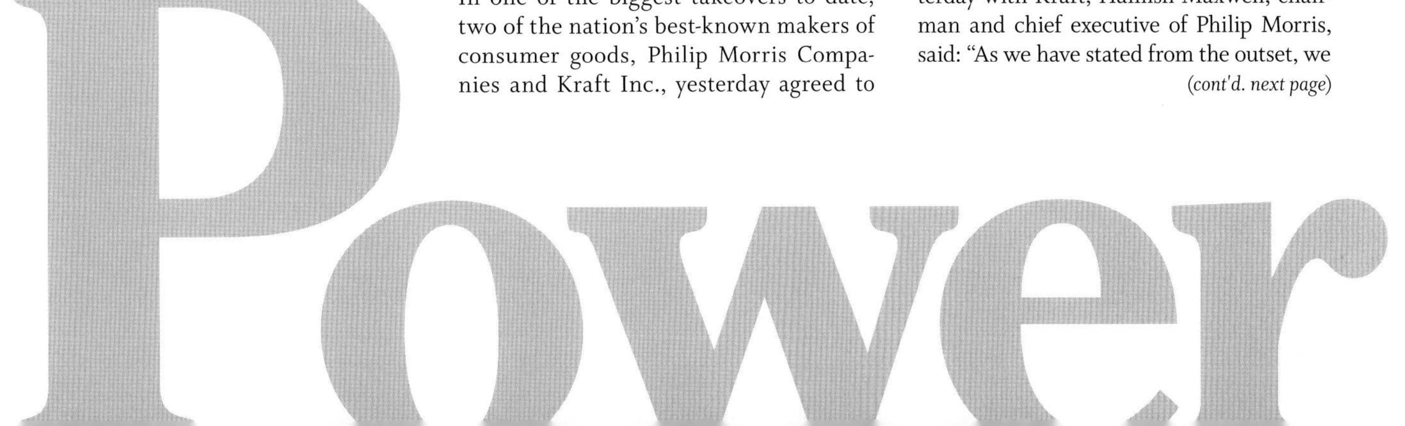

(continued from previous page)
believe the combination of Philip Morris and Kraft will create a U.S.-based food company that will compete more effectively in world food markets. Kraft's products provide an excellent complement to our existing product lines and position us to capitalize on marketing opportunities worldwide."

Philip Morris is the maker of Marlboro cigarettes, Miller beer, Maxwell House coffee and Ronzoni spaghetti, among other products. In addition to Kraft cheeses, including Philadelphia and Velveeta, Philip Morris will now add such other well-known Kraft brand names as Sealtest ice cream, Parkay margarine, Light n' Lively yogurt and Miracle Whip salad dressing.

Kraft executives and employees may not see much change in the combined company, except for the new ownership. Mr. Richman will remain Kraft's chairman and also become a Philip Morris vice chairman. Michael A. Miles, Kraft's president and chief operating officer, will remain president of Kraft but take on the additional title of chief executive officer, continuing to report to Mr. Richman. Philip Morris and Kraft have also agreed that Kraft's headquarters will remain in Glenview, Ill., for at least two years.

Kraft's enormously valuable name will survive as a subsidiary of Philip Morris while the Philip Morris parent company will continue to operate as it did before.

Asked in an interview if he had any more takeover deals in mind, Mr. Maxwell said with a chuckle, "No, this is enough for this year." ■

MARCH 5, 1989

TIME INC. AND WARNER TO MERGE, CREATING LARGEST MEDIA COMPANY

Floyd Norris

Time Inc. and Warner Communications Inc. announced yesterday that they plan to merge, creating the largest media and entertainment conglomerate in the world.

Time's chairman, J. Richard Munro, said the new company would seek to grow even larger by acquiring other businesses.

Time is a leading book and magazine publisher with extensive cable television holdings, and Warner is a major producer of movies and records and has a large cable-television operation. The merger would create a new company, Time Warner Inc., with a stock market value of $15.2 billion and revenue of $10 billion a year.

The merger would insure Time Warner a place in the 1990's as one of a handful of global media giants able to produce and distribute information in virtually any medium. The companies said the deal would help the United States compete against major European and Asian companies.

"Only strong American companies will survive after the formation of a unified European market in 1992," said Steven J. Ross, chairman of Warner.

Time Warner would replace Bertelsmann A. G., a privately held German publisher known primarily for its book division, as the world's largest communications company in terms of revenue. Bertelsmann's 1987 revenue was more than $6 billion.

The merger would unify two huge media companies that have felt the pressure of demands for performance and have long been the subjects of takeover rumors on Wall Street. The much larger merged company would be a more difficult takeover target.

An analyst for Drexel Burnham Lambert Inc., John Reidy, called the deal "mind-boggling."

"What you've got is a company that will be the largest magazine publisher in the country, the world's most profitable record company, a cable television entity with more than 5.5 million cable subscribers, one of the world's largest book-publishing operations and the country's largest supplier of pay-cable programming," he said.

Time's properties include Time, People, Money and Sports Illustrated, as well as Home Box Office, the pay-television operator; Time-Life Books, and Book-of-the-Month Club.

Warner owns Warner Bros., a major film producer, and a large record company, a major paperback book publisher and cable-television systems.

One person who attended the Time board meeting said that after a day of reviewing financial data, board members applauded when shown a video of Warner programming, including excerpts from its new "Batman" movie. ■

DECEMBER 22, 1988

Michael Milken: Legendary Wall Street Outsider at Center of U.S. Inquiry

James Sterngold

One of the few things the highly competitive and often contentious executives in the financial world can agree on is that the 1980's would have been a different era were it not for the energy and obsession for control of one person: Michael R. Milken.

Certainly Drexel Burnham Lambert would not have been in the position of forfeiting $650 million to settle securities law charges were it not for its involvement in activities overseen by Mr. Milken's area of operations.

By extolling the rewards of high-yield "junk bonds" over their risks, Mr. Milken promoted a market that now amounts to $175 billion. In the process, his firm raised billions of dollars in capital for young companies and helped fuel the takeover boom with deals financed by junk bonds. At the same time, though, Mr. Milken's unorthodox sales practices and network of investors raised serious questions about the propriety of his techniques.

One would never guess at Mr. Milken's almost legendary image by looking at him.

Mr. Milken is self-effacing and modest in appearance. He favors sport coats over suits and wears a less than subtle toupee, providing a thatch of dark hair over his boyish face and deep-set, dark eyes.

He has also cultivated an image as an outsider. Mr. Milken once labored in something close to obscurity out of an office in Beverly Hills, Calif., near where he grew up but about as far from Wall Street as one could get.

That was the facade. Behind it was a man whose intense, slightly high-pitched voice over a telephone could cause some of the flashiest, wealthiest and most powerful financiers to snap into action and do precisely as he directed, whether it was buying tens of millions of dollars of junk bonds issued by one of his clients or helping finance a takeover. That, in fact, was Mr. Milken's real genius and possibly the cause of his downfall. It was not what he did with his own money, or even the way he singlehandedly created the junk bond market, but the network of wealth he could marshal to consummate the deals he dreamed up.

Michael Milken being questioned by reporters in 1998.

It was an awesome financial force that he orchestrated with the deftness of a philharmonic conductor. It was also a network that no other Wall Street firm could match, or crack, and that Government investigators spent two years trying to unravel.

Mr. Milken worked not with the Fortune 500 companies that make up the

(cont'd. next page)

(continued from previous page)
corporate establishment, but with entrepreneurs like Nelson Peltz, Ronald Perelman, Ivan F. Boesky and T. Boone Pickens, who were little known before Mr. Milken's junk bond revolution was unleashed in the early 1980's.

Mr. Milken was able to turn his clients into multimillionaires. He also made certain that they understood just who was responsible for producing that bounty, creating powerful allegiances that he could call upon when needed.

And Mr. Milken was more than just a financier, say those who worked closely with him. He was, they say, a salesman with an unequaled ability to make those in his financial orbit feel they were part of a mission, with his inspired sermons on the power of junk bonds.

At the heart of the legend was what many called "the Milken experience."

In his heyday, this is the way it typically worked. The chief executives of three to seven companies would be sent to different conference rooms in Mr. Milken's Beverly Hills office.

Surrounded by a phalanx of aides, Mr. Milken would march from one room to the next, delivering in each an inspired discussion of the chief executive's company, its prospects, its needs and what Drexel would do for it.

The session would last just a few minutes, and would include a few words from Mr. Milken on his views of the general business climate or the global financial situation. Mr. Milken would then shake the hand of the awed executive, leave a few aides with him to tie up the details of a deal, and then move on to the next meeting.

"The focus and intensity are amazing," said a senior figure at a major buyout firm. "It's like a beam is focused on you and the rest of the room is dark."

Mr. Milken is now active in anti-drug campaigns and other charities focusing on young people, said Harry Horowitz, who has been one of Mr. Milken's closest friends since the two were in fifth grade.

He added that Mr. Milken is something of a health nut who has never drunk coffee, alcohol or even soda, and has never smoked.

"He's a boring guy on New Year's," Mr. Horowitz said.. ■

MARCH 30, 1989

'JUNK BOND' LEADER INDICTED BY U.S. IN CRIMINAL ACTION

Stephen Labaton

In the largest criminal action against a Wall Street figure, a Federal grand jury today indicted Michael R. Milken, the Drexel Burnham Lambert Inc. executive who transformed corporate takeovers through the pioneering use of high-yield "junk bonds."

Prosecutors said they would seek an unprecedented financial penalty against individuals, totaling $1.8 billion in forfeitures from Mr. Milken and two other defendants for violations of the Federal racketeering law.

Mr. Milken said through a spokesman that he believed he would be vindicated. And lawyers for Mr. Milken and his two co-defendants said they would plead not guilty. The other defendants are Michael Milken's brother, Lowell, a senior Drexel executive, and Bruce L. Newberg, a former Drexel trader in the high-yield, high-risk bonds.

The Milkens will take a leave of absence from the firm.

Part of the most extensive criminal securities fraud inquiry ever undertaken by the Federal Government, the long-expected indictment is based in large part on information supplied by Ivan F. Boesky, the arbitrager who settled insider-trading charges and is now serving a prison term.

A conviction on even a single count could end Michael Milken's career.

Mr. Milken, 42 years old, built a junk-bond empire that brought him more than $1 billion from 1983 to 1987 and provided financing for hundreds of corporations and takeovers.

Along the way, prosecutors said, Mr. Milken cheated clients and stockholders, manipulated the marketplace and tricked a corporation into being taken over.

"The three-year investigation has uncovered substantial fraud in a very significant segment of the American financial community," said Benito Romano, Acting United States Attorney in Manhattan. "A serious criminal problem has infected Wall Street."

Listing 98 felony counts, today's indictment said that from 1984 to 1986 Mr. Milken violated laws on securities and mail fraud, insider trading, making false statements to the Government and racketeering. The criminal racketeering charges represent the broadest use yet of that statute on Wall Street.

If the defendants are convicted on the racketeering charges alone, the Government can theoretically seek more than $11 billion in forfeitures and fines. In addition, Mr. Milken faces a maximum prison sentence of 520 years. ■

New York

Ed Koch, New York's ebullient mayor for most of the 1980's, saw himself as a cheerleader-in-chief. His style was encapsulated in a famously self-congratulatory catchphrase: "How am I doin'?"

Ed Koch in 1982.

It was the wrong question to ask in 1980, when the city was hit with a crippling transit strike. Bicyclists squeezed their way between angry motorists. Workers streamed like refugees across the East River bridges. This was the moment when working women put their high heels in a purse or tote bag and tied up the laces on a pair of running shoes. The style continued after the strike ended.

Better news was just around the corner. New York, still reeling from near-bankruptcy in the mid-1970's, was struggling to regain its economic footing and recover the brash self-confidence that had long made it the most hated city in the United States, a status that residents prized.

It managed to do both. After weathering a severe recession, Wall Street came roaring back after 1982, embarking on a bull run of historic magnitude. The shower of gold in the financial markets worked wonders. Suddenly, the city was awash in money, and it showed. Not since the Gilded Age had New York seen such unbridled displays of wealth, as a wave of freshly minted billionaires preened and strutted, fighting their way into the upper reaches of society by funneling their wealth into charity balls and clamoring to join the boards of august institutions like the Metropolitan Museum of Art and the New York Public Library.

Socialite Nan Kempner attends Tiffany's 150th Anniversary Gala at the Metropolitan Museum of Art in New York City in 1987.

Commuters walking across the Brooklyn Bridge on the first day of 1980 transit strike.

They liked to collect art. Their money helped float the Whitney Museum of American Art and Museum of Modern Art. It kept the hammers pounding relentlessly at Christie's and Sotheby's. It touched off a boom in high-end galleries of contemporary art and made instant millionaires of artists like the Neo-Expressionists Eric Fischl, David Salle and Julian Schnabel. All of them showed at Mary Boone, the gallery of the decade.

The city's sports franchises did their bit to keep spirits high. The once omnipotent Yankees sank into the doldrums, but the lowly Mets, who had not won a World Series since 1969, staged a comeback and won the big prize in 1986. That same year, the New York Giants finished at the top of the NFC and went on to defeat the Denver Broncos in Super Bowl XXI. Meanwhile, the New York Islanders emerged as a powerhouse in the National Hockey League, winning the Stanley Cup every year from 1980 through 1983. Yes, the Islanders played in Nassau County. The Giants played in New Jersey, but New York took credit anyway.

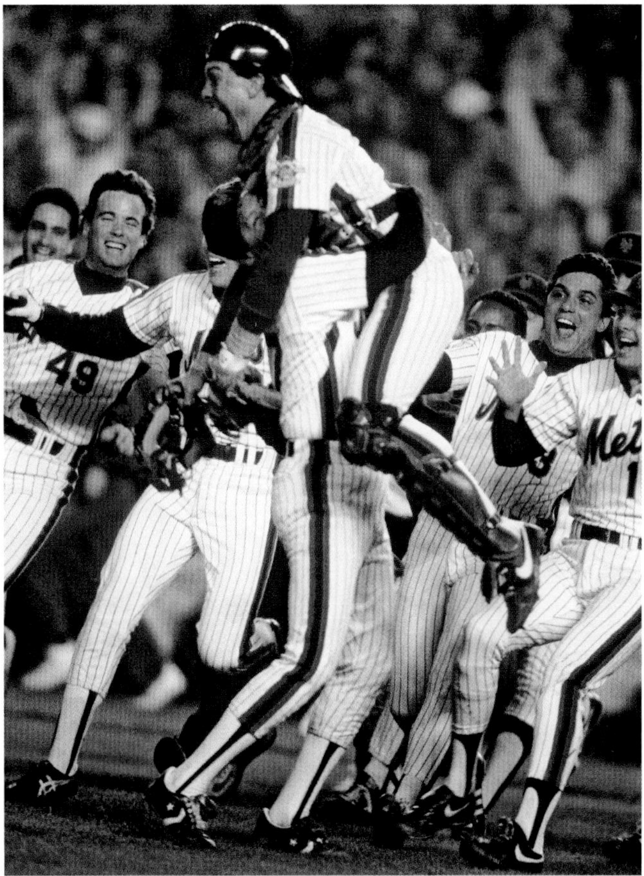

The New York Mets celebrate their 1986 World Series victory.

It was a heady time. The Brooklyn Bridge celebrated its hundredth anniversary. The Statue of Liberty got a makeover. New York was back, or so it seemed.

But two specters darkened the city's streets. Rising real estate prices and the continued erosion of the city's manufacturing base led to an epidemic of homelessness and the widespread use of a new drug, crack cocaine. In the gay community, a mysterious pneumonia-like disease took hold. Once identified, AIDS became the modern-day equivalent of the Black Death, attacking an entire generation of gay men.

Police patrol walking past a homeless man in Tompkins Square Park.

Mayor David Dinkins with wife, Joyce, giving acceptance speech after winning the mayoral election in 1989.

In addition, racial divisions remained an ugly scar. On three occasions, young black men who had strayed into the wrong Brooklyn neighborhoods were set upon and beaten to death by local thugs. Bernhard Goetz, a thin, bespectacled white man dubbed the Subway Vigilante, pulled out a handgun and shot four black teenagers who mugged him on the No. 2 train. In 1989, however, the city elected its first black mayor, David Dinkins.

New York has always been a city of extremes. In the 1980's the extremes widened. After its near-death experience in the 1970's, when it fell into receivership, the city came back to life. But now it was both richer and poorer, safer and more desperate, more exciting and more hopeless. It was New York, only more so.

DECEMBER 9, 1980

CROWDS OF LENNON FANS GATHER QUICKLY AT THE DAKOTA AND HOSPITAL

A crowd began to gather at West 72nd Street and Central Park West immediately after John Lennon, the former Beatles star, was shot and killed last night. Some of the first people to gather were eyewitnesses to the murder. Others had been only a block away.

By midnight, the crowd of mostly young people at that corner outside the Dakota, where Mr. Lennon lived with his family, had grown to several hundred, and by 1 A.M. it grew to nearly 1,000.

Many were crying and they were all asking questions about the shooting. Some said that they had come to the scene from other boroughs and others said that they had come from surrounding communities.

The scene resembled a pilgrimage, with cars double-parked as young men, some of them on roller skates, and women, some in slippers and housecoats, stood on the street.

Some of the people were singing and humming the lyrics of "All My Loving" in soft voices. "Tomorrow I'll miss you / remember I'll always be true / and while I'm away / I'll write home ever day ... ." Then people in the crowd joined in and sang out, "And I'll send all my loving to you."

Yoko Ono is helped by David Geffen as she leaves Roosevelt Hospital after learning her husband, John Lennon, had died after being shot by Mark Chapman.

DECEMBER 10, 1980

POLICE TRACE TANGLED PATH LEADING TO LENNON'S SLAYING AT THE DAKOTA

Paul L. Montgomery

While John Lennon was mourned yesterday by millions around the world, the New York City police were trying to understand the erratic behavior of the 25-year-old former mental patient who is accused of fatally shooting the musician Monday night at the entrance to the Dakota apartments on Central Park West at 72nd Street.

The accused assailant, Mark David Chapman of Honolulu, was arraigned yesterday afternoon in Manhattan Criminal Court on charges of second-degree murder and criminal possession of a revolver he bought for $169 in Hawaii six weeks ago.

The police said Mr. Chapman had been seen loitering around the arched 72d Street entrance to the Dakota on both Saturday and Sunday.

About 5 P.M. on Monday, the police said, Mr. Lennon and Miss Ono left the Dakota for a recording studio. Mr. Chapman approached Mr. Lennon for an autograph, the police said, and he scribbled one on the cover of his new album, "Double Fantasy," recorded with Miss Ono and released two weeks ago.

The Lennons returned to the Dakota at about 10:50 P.M., alighting from their limousine on the 72d Street curb although the car could have driven through the entrance and into the courtyard.

As the couple walked by, Chief Sullivan said, Mr. Chapman called, "Mr. Lennon." Then, he said, the assailant dropped into "a combat stance" and emptied his pistol at the singer. According to the autopsy, four shots struck Mr. Lennon, two in the left side of his back and two in his left shoulder. All four caused internal damage and bleeding.

According to the police, Mr. Lennon staggered up six steps to the room at the end of the entrance used by the concierge, said, "I'm shot," then fell face down.

The first policemen at the scene were Officers Steve Spiro and Peter Cullen, who were in their patrol car at 72d Street and Broadway when they heard a report of shots fired at the Dakota. According to Chief Sullivan, the officers found Mr. Chapman standing "very calmly" where he had been.

The police said he had dropped the revolver after firing it; the elevator operator took it for safekeeping. The police said Mr. Chapman had a paperback book, J.D. Salinger's 1950's novel "Catcher in the Rye," and a cassette recorder with 14 hours of Beatles tapes.

The musician's last interview was with RKO Radio, recorded a few hours before his murder. He talked of his love for his wife, his new music and the peace he was trying to find.

"I'm really talking to the people who grew up with me," he said. "I'm saying, 'Here I am now, how are you? How's your relationship going? Did you get through it all? Wasn't the 70's a drag? Here we are, let's try to make it through the 80's, you know?' " ■

SEPTEMBER 20, 1981

SIMON-GARFUNKEL REUNION JAMS CENTRAL PARK

Paul L. Montgomery

Paul Simon and Art Garfunkel performing in Central Park.

In weather carrying more than a hint of autumn, several hundred thousand people seeking remembrance of the 1960's carpeted the Great Lawn of Central Park yesterday evening for the free reunion concert of Paul Simon and Art Garfunkel.

As the singers, who had parted company 11 years ago, joined their voices once again in "Mrs. Robinson," "Homeward Bound," "Bridge Over Troubled Water" and other wistful anthems of a rebellious decade, cheers of recognition rolled in from the vast gathering, put at 400,000 by the police.

There were couples who had fallen in love to Simon and Garfunkel and who sat on blankets holding hands, and there were younger people whose only perspective of the 60's had been from the seat of a stroller.

For as far as one could see on the level ground, there were people sprawled, surrounded by beach chairs, ice chests and other paraphernalia of a long wait. Midway through the concert, Mr. Garfunkel shaded his eyes and looked out at the multitudes. "I thought it might be somewhat crowded," the singer said, "but we seem to have filled the place."

The crowd, called by officials the largest in the history of free concerts in the park, had begun gathering in the morning for the reunion, which began at dusk. A number of people in the front, pressed against the barricades in front of the stage, had to be helped out to get some air.

Mr. Simon said he had originally intended to give a solo concert, then asked Mr. Garfunkel to join him in a few numbers—something the singers have done a few times since they decided to pursue separate careers in 1970. By the time negotiations were completed, it was to be Simon and Garfunkel together for half the program.

"Then I realized I would be the opening act for that show and I didn't want to be the opening act," Mr. Simon recalled. "People are always talking about reunions. Now we'll find out if it's really satisfying."

Mr. Garfunkel said he was excited about rejoining Mr. Simon, with whom he first began harmonizing when they were in junior high school in Forest Hills, Queens. "It feels like the biggest show I ever did in my life," Mr. Garfunkel said. "I'm dying to hit the stage. I feel like a swimmer who's been on the edge of the pool for weeks. I love the event. Everything about it seems to have a positive energy." ■

NOVEMBER 4, 1981

MAYOR TAKES 75%

FRANK LYNN

Mayor Koch, carrying Democratic and Republican endorsements, won a second term in a landslide yesterday as Democrats swept citywide and boroughwide offices.

The 56-year-old Mayor and his two Democratic running mates, City Council President Carol Bellamy and Comptroller Harrison J. Goldin, overwhelmed their opponents with at least 75 percent of the vote.

The Mayor won every Assembly District in the city, including black and Hispanic districts. During the campaign, minority politicians and some of Mr. Koch's opponents had charged that he was insensitive to the city's minorities. Eighty percent of his vote was on the Democratic line and the remainder on the Republican line.

The Mayor's experience in the 1977 and 1981 election campaigns was a case study in the shifting fortunes of a politician. Four years ago, he started out his mayoral campaign as a decided underdog with no discernible major power base. He was known as a liberal from Manhattan, but that was already being questioned by the so-called reform Democrats with whom he had started his political career.

AUGUST 8, 1982

A DISEASE'S SPREAD PROVOKES ANXIETY

Robin Herman

The persistence of a serious disease whose victims are primarily homosexual men has touched off anxiety among homosexuals in New York City, where nearly half of the nation's cases have been reported.

Doctors treating homosexuals say they are being flooded with telephone calls from old and new patients with minor complaints. Clinics offering testing for the disease are oversubscribed. And homosexual men speak of great confusion over how to adjust their health habits to avoid the disease, which remains largely mysterious in its symptoms and causes.

The disease—called acquired immune deficiency syndrome, or A.I.D.S.—produces a suppression of the body's natural defenses and sets the stage for the intrusion of several deadly afflictions, including a rare form of cancer called Kaposi's sarcoma and a rare pneumonia.

The Centers for Disease Control in Atlanta have recorded 505 cases of the syndrome coupled with the cancer, pneumonia or other opportunistic infections since the national facility began gathering data on cases in June of last year. Of those people, 202 have died, or 40 percent. The cases include 243 residents of New York City.

Reports of the disease have not abated. About two new cases a day are recorded at the disease control center. Officials there attribute the increase both to improved reporting and to a real rise in cases. The disease has already killed more people than reported cases of toxic shock syndrome and the original outbreak of Legionnaire's disease, and it has engendered as much fear.

Dr. David J. Sencer, New York City's Health Commissioner, has termed the immune deficiency syndrome "a major health problem." He emphasized that groups other than homosexual men were involved. Groups afflicted with the syndrome include more than 60 heterosexual men and women who were drug abusers and used intravenous needles; 30 male and female immigrants from Haiti, all heterosexual, and some hemophiliacs who use blood products to combat their illness.

The National Gay Task Force is coordinating a conference on the disease, and publications for homosexuals, including The Advocate, Christopher Street and New York Native, have been printing extensive articles about it.

"It's basically frightening because no one knows what's causing it," said John Kolman, a 28-year-old law student who went to the St. Mark's Clinic in Greenwich Village last week complaining of persistent swollen glands, thought to be one early symptom of the disease. "Every week a new theory comes out about how you're going to spread it."

Physicians say they are seeing panic-stricken patients who display skin lesions that turn out to be bug bites, poison ivy, black and blue marks or freckles of no medical consequence.

"There's tremendous anxiety and it translates into panic behavior," said Dr. Roger W. Enlow, a clinical researcher at the Hospital for Joint Diseases, Beth Israel Medical Center, who helps run the all-volunteer St. Mark's Clinic.

Dr. Sencer, the Health Commissioner, said: "It's unfortunate we don't have anything positive to recommend to people at the present time. We just don't know." ■

JULY 2, 1982

4,000 FOLLOWERS OF MOON WED AT THE GARDEN

Paul L. Montgomery

Four thousand followers of the Rev. Sun Myung Moon, most of them selected for each other by him, were married amid flags and balloons yesterday in a mass ceremony at Madison Square Garden.

The floor of the arena, carpeted in white for the occasion, was a sea of bridegrooms dressed identically in blue suits and brides in identical lace and satin gowns made by the church. Mr. Moon and his wife, Hak Ja Han, called the "true parents" of mankind by his Unification Church, aspersed the couples with water as they passed in rows to the strains of Mendelssohn's Wedding March.

Some of the couples had met only a few weeks ago at mass ceremonies the church calls "matchings." A number of couples—particularly those in which Koreans or Japanese were matched with Americans—had no common language and had spoken to each other only through an interpreter.

In the church's teaching, people matched by the leader must have been members for at least three years and must have practiced chastity. After the marriage, called a "blessing," there is a 40-day period of "purification" and separation before the union can be consummated. In the Garden seats were 6,000 parents, friends and invited guests who had passed through metal detectors before entering. Some parents waved and smiled at the couples as they marched in.

Unification Church leader Sun Myung Moon presiding over the mass wedding ceremony at Madison Square Garden.

My mother can't even talk about it without crying.

Others seemed bewildered as they searched for their children in the rows of faces. A number were crying. and some conceded that it was not with joy.

One of those married yesterday was Bruce Burris, 24 years old, of Nebraska. His bride, Sanae Tsuchida, 25, of Japan, was selected for him by Mr. Moon on June 24. The bride had arrived in the United States that day. Mr. Burris said he had talked with her for "a few hours" through an interpreter and both had decided to take the step.

"It was wonderful," said the bridegroom of the mass ceremony. "The marriage vows were very impressive." Mr. Burris was asked whether he would live with Mrs. Burris after the 40-day waiting period. "I think so," he replied. "Yeah. I'm pretty sure."

The mass wedding was the first of a series Mr. Moon says he will conduct around the world. Mr. Moon, who was convicted in Federal District Court here last May 18 of conspiracy to defraud the Government and filing false tax returns, faces sentencing in two weeks. He could get five years in prison on the conspiracy charge and three years on each of three tax charges.

The Unification Church has 10,000 "core missionaries," or full-time workers, and 30,000 "home members."

Critics of the church say that normal family and sexual relationships are disrupted by fiat of the leader as part of the church's efforts to control the minds of its members. Several dozen former members and parents demonstrated outside the arena, carrying signs like "Let Our Children Go!" and "Hitler, Jim Jones, Moon."

"My sister's been a member nine years and she's down there somewhere," said Maryanne Wagner of Memphis, one of the relatives at yesterday's ceremony.

She pointed at Mr. Moon, robed in white on a crimson dais and said: "That man has caused more heartache in my family and everybody else's than anybody I can think of. My mother can't even talk about it without crying." ■

MAY 24, 1983

BROOKLYN BRIDGE, 'THE ONLY BRIDGE OF POWER, LIFE AND JOY,' TURNS 100 TODAY

Deirdre Carmody

Tens of thousands of New York City residents and out-of-town New York City buffs will flock into lower Manhattan and Brooklyn this morning and onto the banks of the East River tonight to pay joyful homage to the Brooklyn Bridge, which is 100 years old today.

Tributes and visitors poured in all day yesterday in preparation for the ceremonies.

A 60- by 90-foot American flag was being prepared to be hung today from the George Washington Bridge, the Hudson River arriviste that is a mere half-century old.

"What bridge?" wrote Thomas Wolfe. "Great God, the only bridge of power, life and joy, the bridge that was a span, a cry, an ecstasy—that was America."

In the evening there will be street fairs and formal ceremonies; a harbor craft parade on the East River; a Sound and Light Spectacle on the bridge's south face, and a half-hour of fireworks billed as one of the biggest pyrotechnic displays in American history.

New Yorkers have a reputation for being cynical about many aspects of the daily life of their city. But when it comes to the celebration of their history and of their monuments, they are as softhearted and as corny as any small-town resident in the rest of the country.

New Yorkers stunned out-of-towners with their old-fashioned good humor and outpourings of enthusiasm on the day of the Bicentennial, and all indications yesterday were that they were eager to do the same again for their beloved Brooklyn Bridge.

Ferry service is being suspended because many boats are expected to mass in the river to toot their horns and set off jets of spray. That, too, will be reminiscent of opening day 100 years ago, when at least 50,000 people came into the city by train and probably an additional 50,000 arrived by boat to see the world's longest suspension bridge.

"Our most durable monument," wrote Montgomery Schuyler in the Harper's Weekly dated May 24, 1883. It is that very durability that is being celebrated today.

Fireworks filling the sky over Brooklyn Bridge during Centennial celebration festivities.

AUGUST 7, 1983

The Empire and Ego of Donald Trump

Marylin Bender

Donald Trump shown here in the mid-1980s.

He made his presence known on the island of Manhattan in the mid-70's, a brash Adonis from the outer boroughs bent on placing his imprint on the golden rock. Donald John Trump exhibited a flair for self-promotion, grandiose schemes—and, perhaps not surprisingly, for provoking fury along the way.

Senior realty titans scoffed, believing that braggadocio was the sum and substance of the blond, blue-eyed, six-footer who wore maroon suits and matching loafers, frequented Elaine's and Regine's in the company of fashion models, and was not abashed to take his armed bodyguard-chauffeur into a meeting with an investment banker.

The essence of entrepreneurial capitalism, real estate is a business with a tradition of high-rolling megalomania, of master builders striving to erect monuments to their visions. It is also typically dynastic, with businesses being transmitted from fathers to sons and grandsons, and carried on by siblings. In New York, the names of Tishman, Lefrak, Rudin, Fisher, Zeckendorf come to mind.

And now there is Trump, a name that has in the last few years become an internationally recognized symbol of New York City as mecca for the world's super rich.

"Not many sons have been able to escape their fathers," said Donald Trump, the president of the Trump Organization, by way of interpreting his accomplishments. Three of them, built since 1976, stand out amidst the crowded midtown landscape: the 68-story Trump Tower, with its six-story Atrium housing some of the world's most elegant stores; the 1,400-room Grand Hyatt Hotel, and Trump Plaza, a $125 million cooperative apartment. And more is on the way.

"At 37, no one has done more than I in the last seven years," Mr. Trump asserted.

Fifteen years ago, he joined his father's business, an empire of middle-class apartment houses in Brooklyn, Queens and Staten Island then worth roughly $40 million. Today, the Trump Organization controls assets worth about $1 billion.

Mr. Trump assiduously cultivates a more conservative public image now, a gentleman of taste in a navy-blue suit with discreetly striped shirts and blue ties, who weekends with his family in Greenwich, Conn. Last spring he forsook the Hamptons, his former habitat, to buy an estate in the conservative community.

I don't like to lose

But Mr. Trump prides himself on being street smart and boasted that Brooklyn and Queens, where he was raised, are among "the toughest, smartest places in the world." Mr. Trump prefers the vocabulary of war and sports to document his exploits, acknowledging "I don't like to lose."

His alternating skills of charming some individuals and riding roughshod over others has earned Donald Trump a reputation in some quarters as someone not to be trusted. He reneged, for example, on a promise to donate to a museum the Art Deco bas-reliefs on the facade of Bonwit Teller's—bulldozed to make way for Trump Tower. It was a sin deemed unforgivable by landmark preservationists. But the only negative comments about Donald Trump these days are given off the record.

Backed initially by his father, Mr. Trump has operated as a lone wolf in Manhattan for nearly the last decade. He acquires properties through Trump Enterprises or Wembly Realty Inc. and has them transferred to Donald J. Trump so that he can personally take the huge tax write-offs from real estate projects rather than having them "wasted," as he called it, on a corporation. He also said he saves corporate and franchise taxes.

For major deals, he forges a partnership with a single gilt-edged financial institution or hotel chain. Holiday Inns, for example, is his co-venturer in the $200 million Harrah's hotel casino scheduled to open in Atlantic City next May, the largest gaming palace in the New Jersey resort.

The most striking evidence of Mr. Trump's entrepreneurship, however, is in New York.

There is the Grand Hyatt Hotel, reconstituted with a facade of mirrored glass on the skeleton of the Commodore Hotel adjoining Grand Central Terminal. Since it opened in 1980, it has been credited with reversing the deterioration of East 42nd Street.

Then, of course, Trump Tower, a skinny bronze and glass skyscraper at 725 Fifth Avenue, atop the former site of Bonwit Teller at the corner of 56th Street. Its Atrium, a vertical shopping mall rendered in peach marble and bronze with an 80-foot cascade, is a showcase for 40 purveyors of super luxury wares such as Loewe of Madrid, Asprey's of London and the jewelers, Cartier, Harry Winston and Buccellati. Purchasers of condominium apartments—91 are priced above $1 million—will start moving in later this month. ■

TIMES SQ. ALSO BECKONS WITH LESS SINISTER JOYS

Times Square in the mid-1980's.

Martin Gottlieb

One of the less-publicized al fresco facts of life in Manhattan is that on a sunny spring weekend, the block of 42nd Street between Seventh and Eighth Avenues is likely to attract larger crowds than the most popular pasture in Central Park. And even more surprising is that many of the strollers are ordinary people out for a good time, in search of a cheap double bill, a fast-food dinner and a glimpse of glitter and excitement.

Last Sunday, for example, with the temperature hovering in the 60's and the sun throwing deep shadows off the block's 15 hulking movie and peep-show marquees, streams of people eight deep strolled past sex shops, drug dealers and loud and sometimes raunchy displays for movies featuring ax murderers and women touted as "the roughest, toughest, dirtiest babes around."

For many New Yorkers—particularly those with fond recollections of the Times Square of the 1940's and 50's—this block may well be the most foreboding in the city.

"On no other block in the city is crime as prevalent," says the 880-page draft environmental impact statement for the proposed $1.6 billion plan to rebuild Times Square. "On no other block is there the collection of drug dealers and users, alcoholics and derelicts, prostitutes and other hustlers drawn there by the overall street environment."

Yet for tens of thousands of others, the block has become what the impact statement defines as the only "regional, low-income entertainment center" in the area. They are drawn by what is probably the densest collection of movie theaters in the world—14 across two 800-foot-long blockfronts—some of the cheapest ticket prices in the city—$2 to $4 for double and triple features with as many as eight consecutive previews thrown in—and the closing of scores of theaters in the last decade in poorer neighborhoods.

If the Times Square plan, sponsored by the city and the state's Urban Development Corporation, is approved, the theaters, which date to the early years of the century and are of some architectural and historical note, would be restored for use as legitimate and first-run movie theaters. This, proponents of the plan believe, would attract a much different, more middle-class crowd to Times Square and go a long way toward making over the block.

But the owners of the largest theater chain on the block disagree. Terming the project "ill-conceived and not calculated to remedy the problems that the U.D.C. and the city claim to exist," Robert Brandt, a spokesman for the Brandt Organization, which operates seven of the theaters, said this week that his company "will vigorously oppose the project at every level of proceeding on up through the courts."

"People go there for the same reasons they did when we were kids," said William Kornblum, professor of sociology at the City University of New York, who headed a study team that analyzed street life on 42nd Street for the U.D.C. "You come in from another borough or from uptown looking for some fun. You grab a burger and you go to a movie."

Hope Proctor, 22, a student at Westchester Community College, and her friend

THE CITY SEES NO SOLUTIONS FOR HOMELESS

Deirdre Carmody

A record $100 million will be spent this year to provide food and shelter for the growing numbers of single homeless people in New York, but city officials say they still have no solution for those who live in the street and refuse assistance.

These people, the hard-core homeless, have become one of the city's most visible social problems.

Once mainly found sleeping in parks and in abandoned buildings, thousands of these destitute men and women now live in doorways or on sidewalks throughout the city, including such affluent areas as Madison Avenue and Park Avenue.

The street people, many of whom are chronically mentally ill, make up only a small percentage of the city's homeless population. But because they have become an inescapable presence in the lives of most New Yorkers, they are a major concern as city officials prepare to house and feed record numbers of homeless people this winter.

If projections prove correct, there will be nights when nearly 10,000 homeless men and women will be housed in the city's public shelters and in the 90 churches and synagogues that provide beds and services for the homeless.

"We are in a situation that totally overwhelms us," said City Council President Carol Bellamy, who refers to the city's homeless as "this tidal wave of human beings."

No one knows the total number of homeless people in New York, but officials and advocates agree that the number continues to increase dramatically. In 1978 the city had three shelters that housed 2,000 people. Last year, on peak nights, the city housed 6,500 people in 18 shelters while 1,000 more homeless men and women were given beds in churches and synagogues.

"We see over 30,000 individuals in our shelters in the course of a year," said Robert Trobe, who heads the Family and Adult Services office of the welfare agency.

These numbers do not include the members of 3,000 homeless families who have been evicted or burned out of their homes and are housed by the city in about 50 hotels.

Of all the homeless, the street people are the most difficult to count. Often they are known to social workers only as "Chanter," "Poor Hearing" or "Painted Jeans." Project HELP, a crisis intervention group set up by the city to reach these people, has made a list of 1,200 individuals in Manhattan south of 96th Street, with 30 to 40 people being added every month. *(cont'd. next page)*

Charles Plummer completed a sightseeing tour with a debate over which of three first-run movies to see. Somehow, they wound up at the Selwyn Theater, where "10 Violent Women" was sharing the bill with "Chesty Anderson, U.S.N." Mr. Plummer's opinion of the former: "Cheap, sloppily put together, no stars, and there were only three or four violent women." Of the latter, he observed, "Her chest wasn't that big."

Herbert J. Gans, a Columbia University sociology professor who has been retained by the Brandt Organization, has charged that the environmental statement is "full of biases" designed to justify a plan "to move out lower-income citizens and taxpayers and to replace them with more affluent ones."

Out on 42nd Street, Mr. Plummer weighed the possibilities.

"It could be a plus in that they would attract higher-income people with more money to spend," he said, "but it could also be a loss, in that if they try to totally clean up this block, they could have a riot on their hands." ■

Blind beggar on Fifth Avenue in New York in Christmas 1982.

(continued from previous page)

Many of them are chronically mentally ill. Some are severely psychotic. Their behavior is often bizarre, and even menacing, as they stumble about addressing strangers on the street or unseen deities in the sky, sometimes shouting obscenities or urinating against buildings in view of passers-by.

A woman known as Judy sits under an awning at 63rd Street and Second Avenue, surrounded by her possessions. She sits, docile, all day. At about 11 P.M. she usually starts to scream. Sometimes she continues for hours, screaming obscenities and intimate details about her life.

"At first I felt compassion," said Jane Kosarin, who lives nearby. "After all, she's in the street and she needs help. But you can hear her with your windows closed and I haven't slept for nights because of her. It's affected my life and I'm on medication as a result."

The crux of the problem is that little can be done to help someone who needs psychiatric help but refuses assistance. Under New York State's Mental Hygiene Law, no one can be involuntarily admitted to a psychiatric facility unless he or she has "a mental illness for which immediate inpatient care and treatment in a hospital is appropriate and which is likely to result in serious harm to himself or to others."

Under the law, "serious harm" means, in effect, that the person is either homicidal or suicidal.

Officials say that this is a difficult standard to meet and that most street people, mentally disturbed or psychotic as they may be, do not meet it.

Mental health experts say that even if standards for admission were changed, hospitalization would be too extreme a treatment for most mentally-ill street people. They add that mental hospitals remain so overcrowded that beds would not be available.

"We need housing," Governor Cuomo said in an interview. "We need capital sources. Can we find a way to generate the capital strength we need to build housing for the homeless? President Reagan is saying that the national government does not deal with the homeless problem and he is getting away with it."

Mayor Koch, describing the dimensions of the problem, said, "You have to understand that there is a limit to what we can do when the Federal Government moves out of low-income housing." ■

DECEMBER 23, 1984

A GUNMAN WOUNDS 4 ON IRT TRAIN, THEN ESCAPES

Robert D. McFadden

A middle-aged man with a silver-colored pistol strode into a subway car rolling through lower Manhattan yesterday and shot four young men he had apparently singled out from among the passengers, the Transit Authority police reported.

As the victims collapsed, all bleeding profusely from wounds of the upper body, a dozen other passengers, screaming and sobbing, fell on the floor or herded into the next car. The train, a No. 2 Seventh Avenue IRT express, halted just north of the Chambers Street station at about 1:45 P.M.

Then, in a bizarre twist to what transit authorities called one of the worst crimes of the year in the subways, the gunman discussed the shootings briefly with a conductor, according to investigators, one of whom described a colloquy.

"Are you a cop?" the conductor was said to have asked as he approached the man, who had shoved the gun into his waistband and was bending over and saying something to a victim.

"No," the gunman replied. "They tried to rip me off."

The gunman, who was described as "calm, cool and collected," then noticed two trembling women lying on the floor and, along with the conductor, helped them up.

As the women fled into the next car, the conductor, whose name was not released, turned again to the assailant.

"Give me the gun," he urged.

But the gunman turned without responding and stepped through the door at the end of the car. The conductor tried to grab him, the police said, but he leaped to the tracks from between cars and vanished in the dark tunnel.

"He picked out these four guys and shot every one of them," said Capt. John Kelly of the Transit Authority police. "He knew what he was doing. He was not just shooting indiscriminately. He was either harassed or robbed by these guys earlier on the train."

The police said two of the wounded young men, interviewed later in the hospitals, denied robbing or harassing the man who shot them. ■

JANUARY 6, 1985

GOETZ: A PRIVATE MAN IN A PUBLIC DEBATE

Robert D. McFadden

Subway vigilante Bernard Goetz leaves the Manhattan District Attorney's office March 26, 1985.

Mafia Chief, Paul Castellano (Big Paul) is escorted by FBI Agents after he surrendered himself at his attorneys office in March of 1985.

FEBRUARY 27, 1985

U.S. INDICTMENT SAYS 9 GOVERNED NEW YORK MAFIA

Arnold H. Lubasch

A Federal racketeering indictment charged nine men yesterday with participating in a "commission" that governs the five organized-crime "families" in New York City.

Five of the defendants were identified in the indictment as the bosses or acting bosses of "the five La Cosa Nostra families."

The 15-count indictment said the commission regulated a wide range of illegal activities that included narcotics trafficking, loansharking, gambling, labor racketeering and extortion against construction companies.

According to the indictment, which was filed in Manhattan, the commission resolved a 1979 dispute in the Bonanno crime group by "authorizing the murder" of the group's boss, Carmine Galante, and four associates. *(cont'd. next page)* ■

To his admirers, Bernhard Hugo Goetz is a personable, scholarly, self-reliant man who cares about his neighbors and his community, despises hoodlums and has long been frustrated by what he sees as a drift toward criminal anarchy.

To his detractors, he is a captive of naive idealism, a profoundly introverted and secretive man whose friendliness falls short of real friendships and whose outspoken views on crime mask a darker personality obsessed by irrational fears.

The emerging picture of Mr. Goetz is a kaleidoscope of clashing opinions reflecting the harshness, if not the scope, of the debate over vigilantism and public safety that has arisen since he shot four youths who harassed him on a Manhattan subway train Dec. 22.

Interviews with relatives, acquaintances, former teachers and others in recent days have drawn the portrait of an inward-looking, socially awkward man who was raised in small-town comfort and educated in private schools, who divorced once, succeeded in his own electronics business, but was frustrated in his efforts to fight drugs, crime and filth in the city.

It is also a picture of a lonely 37-year-old man who has sustained two major traumas in his life—criminal charges against his father, and a 1981 mugging that shattered his faith in the administration of justice.

It happened about 2:30 P.M. on Jan. 26, 1981, in a subway station on Canal Street. Mr. Goetz had just bought equipment valued at $800 to $1,000 at a nearby store and he was taking it home, he recalled at the hearing in 1982 on his application for a pistol permit.

"Three fellows jumped me," he said, "and I ran. They took—they took the items I was carrying. I ran out of the subway station up the steps. They came after me. Fortunately for myself, a police officer was on the street. He apprehended one of the perpetrators. The other two took the things I was carrying, put them down and ran away. They were very clever."

Later, he amplified his remarks: "The arresting officer saw him strike me, knock me down, and he ran into me, knocking me into a plate-glass window, which fortunately didn't break. But the door handle hit me in the chest and it tore cartilage and connecting tissue in my chest."

Painful as the injury was, it was the aftermath of the mugging that appeared to bother Mr. Goetz most.

The apprehended suspect, 16-year- old Fred Clarke of Brooklyn, was taken to Criminal Court. "He was kept for 2 hours and 35 minutes," Mr. Goetz recalled. "Now, I was there in the Criminal Court Building for 6 hours and 5 minutes, along with the police officer who made the arrest.

Citing the mugging and his frequent need to carry large sums of cash, Mr. Goetz applied for a pistol permit later in 1981, but was turned down on the ground that he had failed to show sufficient need. His appeal of that decision to Sergeant Charleman also was rejected.

"He was physically hurt," his neighbor, Mr. Horwitz, recalled. "He was beaten to a certain extent. Then he was hurt a second time when the police did nothing about it."

The police believe that Mr. Goetz, blocked from owning a legal weapon, went to Florida, where it was not difficult to buy the chrome-plated, .38-caliber revolver used in the subway shootings. ■

(continued from previous page)

The indictment, containing the first Federal charges to focus on the commission, was announced at an elaborate news conference attended by 17 law-enforcement officials, including William H. Webster, the director of the Federal Bureau of Investigation.

Mr. Webster said the indictment focused on "the symbol of power" in organized crime, striking a significant blow at some notorious figures who were under intensive investigation for a long time.

Rudolph W. Giuliani, the United States Attorney in Manhattan, conducted the news conference in the Federal office building, at 26 Federal Plaza, across the street from the United States Court House at Foley Square.

"This case charges more Mafia bosses in one indictment than ever before," Mr. Giuliani said. He described the commission as "the Mafia's ruling council here in New York City and other cities." Following are the nine defendants, identified with the positions that the indictment attributed to them in the five traditional crime families called Gambino, Genovese, Colombo, Lucchese and Bonanno: GAMBINO: Paul Castellano (known to his associates as Big Paul), 69 years old, the boss, and Aniello Dellacroce (Neil), 70, the underboss, both of Staten Island.

GENOVESE: Anthony Salerno (Fat Tony), 73, of Rhinebeck, N.Y., the boss.

COLOMBO: Gennaro Langella (Gerry Lang), 46, of Brooklyn, the acting boss. Also Ralph Scopo, 56, of Queens, a Colombo member and president of the District Council of Cement and Concrete Workers.

LUCCHESE: Anthony Corallo (Tony Ducks), 72, of South Oyster Bay Cove, L.I., the boss; Salvatore Santoro (Tom Mix), 69, of the Bronx, underboss; Christopher Furnari (Christie Tick), 60, of Staten Island, consigliere, or counselor.

BONANNO: Philip Rastelli (Rusty), 67, of Brooklyn, the boss.

There was no mention of Carmine Persico (The Snake), who was in jail during most of the activities described in the indictment and who has been named as the Colombo boss in another indictment. Several of the other defendants were also named in recent indictments.

Recounting a history of organized crime, the indictment said a criminal society called "La Cosa Nostra or the Mafia" operated through groups known as families. It said each family was headed by a boss, an underboss and a consigliere, with capos, or captains, in charge of "soldiers" and associates.

In 1931, the indictment said, the commission was formed as "the council for La Cosa Nostra families." At times, it added, the commission also included bosses from families in Chicago, Detroit, Philadelphia and New Jersey.

If convicted, they could face up to 20 years in prison on each charge. ■

NOVEMBER 6, 1985

KOCH WINS A THIRD TERM, 3 TO 1; VOWS TO COMBAT 'INEQUITIES'

Frank Lynn

Mayor Koch easily won a third term at City Hall yesterday, leading a Democratic sweep of virtually every city office at stake in the election.

Although he faced two major-party opponents—City Council President Carol Bellamy and Diane McGrath—and six lesser-known rivals, the 60-year-old Mr. Koch was winning by more than three to one and capturing every Assembly District in the city.

With 99 percent of 5,129 districts reporting, the vote was:

Koch 854,048 Bellamy 161,113 McGrath 108,529

Mr. Koch won with 75 percent of the vote, the same vote percentage as his landslide victory in 1981, when he ran on both the Republican and Democratic lines. But he fell short of his 753,000-vote plurality in 1981, largely because of low turnout yesterday.

Mayor Koch told several hundred cheering supporters at the Sheraton Centre hotel that in his next term he would address "the superpriorities of education, housing, transportation and to reduce the inequities caused by poverty."

"I am committed over the next four years to do what I can, to come as close as I can in that four-year term, to achieve those aspirations for all the people in this town without regard to race, religion, national origin or sexual orientation," he said.

New York City Mayor Ed Koch during his run for third term.

NOVEMBER 29, 1985

A NEW, PURIFIED FORM OF COCAINE CAUSES ALARM AS ABUSE INCREASES

Jane Gross

A new form of cocaine is for sale on the streets of New York, alarming law-enforcement officials and rehabilitation experts because of its tendency to accelerate abuse of the drug, particularly among adolescents.

The substance, known as crack, is already processed into the purified form that enables cocaine users to smoke, or free-base, the powerful stimulant of the central nervous system.

Previously, free-basers had to reduce cocaine powder themselves to its unadulterated form by combining it with baking soda or ether and evaporating the resulting paste over a flame.

Since crack appeared on the streets of the Bronx last year, spreading throughout the city and its suburbs, new cocaine users have graduated more quickly from inhaling to free-basing, the most addictive form of cocaine abuse.

In addition, dealers in crack have found a ready market in people reluctant to intensify their intake by intravenous injection of cocaine because of the fear of AIDS, or acquired immune deficiency syndrome, a fatal affliction that is spread by contaminated needles.

As the use of crack has increased, Federal drug officials have begun raiding "factories" where the cocaine powder is processed into pure beige crystals known as "rocks" and then packed into transparent vials resembling large vitamin capsules.

Meanwhile, narcotics officers of the New York City Police Department have shut down a few of the so-called crack houses, the rough equivalent of heroin-shooting galleries, where sales are made and users gather for smoking binges that can last for several days.

Two of the crack houses, also known as base houses, were raided recently in the Tremont section of the Bronx, according to Lieut. John Creegan, one of them in an apartment and the other in a rooming house.

"I talked to one of the women there," Lieutenant Creegan said, "and it was almost like her mind was burned out. She told me all she does is do crack all day."

"Unlike normal cocaine, people who free-base can't stop," said Mr. Hopkins. "They free-base until all their money is used up. The way crack is spreading is almost verification of that. It pays as a distributor to free-base it, because it makes you sell your brand quicker than somebody else."

"It's a new, improved product," said Dr. Arnold M. Washton, the director of addiction research and treatment at Regent Hospital on East 61st Street in Manhattan and Stony Lodge Hospital in Ossining, N.Y. "No mess, no bother, no delay—and addicts have never been any good at delayed gratification."

Buying crack is safer than making it and often cheaper. A kit of free-base equipment—beaker, bunsen burner and pipe—costs about $14 and the chemicals are volatile, sometimes causing explosions like the one that injured the comedian Richard Pryor in 1980.

The crack sold on the street in New York ranges in cost from $2 to $50 depending on the number of rocks in the vial and, paradoxically, is sometimes less expensive than the amount of powder, currently retailing at $75 to $100 a gram, necessary to produce the equivalent free-base. ■

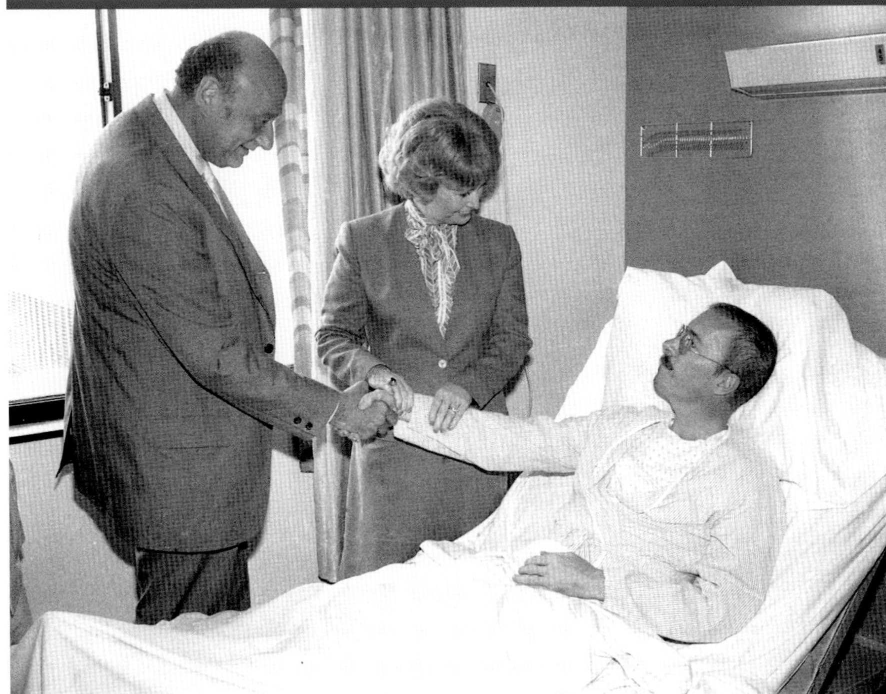

Secretary of Health and Human Services Margaret Heckler joins Mayor Koch at bedside of AIDS victim Peter Justice.

DECEMBER 23, 1985

Aids: Bellevue Tries to Cope with Disease it Cannot Cure

Ronald Sullivan

The AIDS epidemic has transformed Bellevue Hospital Center to such an extent that the fatal disorder of the immune system is now the municipal hospital's single most common medical diagnosis.

Although the fear of contagion that initially gripped the hospital has abated in recent months, Bellevue still faces the grim reality of treating a disorder it cannot cure and accommodating itself to large numbers of deaths it cannot prevent.

(cont'd. next page)

(continued from previous page)

While soaring costs are a major concern, the numbing realization that nothing can be done to prevent the fatal course of AIDS is inflicting mounting emotional casualties on Bellevue's medical and nursing staff.

The hospital's elevators, emergency rooms and clinics are as busy and as crowded as usual, and the quiet bustle on the medical and surgical floors seems the same as ever.

But Bellevue's appearance is misleading, said Dorothy Shayan, the director of nursing.

"We are losing large numbers of young men and children to this disease, and the psychological and emotional stress on everyone is devastating," she said. "Patients die in hospitals; we know that. But never before like this."

As a result, AIDS, acquired immune deficiency syndrome, is redefining the way Bellevue doctors and nurses confront death and a ravaging terminal illness.

Bellevue, the country's oldest public hospital and world famous for its 250 years of medical and surgical achievements, is where young doctors are trained to do everything they can to keep life going. Now, however, there is a growing emphasis on allowing AIDS patients to forgo heroic measures and die with as much dignity as possible.

The greatest changes at Bellevue have occurred in the 200-bed department of medicine, where every fourth patient is an AIDS victim. The department accounts for about a fourth of the hospital's 850 patients, including those in the surgical, obstetric, pediatric and psychiatric departments.

Although there has been no reported case thus far of a nurse, doctor or hospital worker contracting AIDS on the job, there are still certain risks.

For example, 20 staff members at Bellevue have thus far suffered accidental needle punctures from syringes used on AIDS patients. They are being closely monitored to see if any of them contracts the disorder.

Dr. Robert Holzman, a Bellevue specialist in infectious disease and an expert on AIDS, said the chances of contracting AIDS from a needle puncture "are extremely small; the odds are more than a 100 to 1."

Camille Caracappa, a 23-year-old nurse, knows the odds. But when she stuck her finger accidentally on Dec. 3 with a syringe she had just used on an AIDS patient, she said she quickly forgot the odds favored her.

"In an instant, all I could feel was a wave of fear," she said in an interview on Bellevue's 16th floor, where many of the hospital's AIDS patients are treated.

Health officials estimate that about 300 AIDS patients are hospitalized in New York City—half of them in municipal hospitals and half in the city's private hospitals.

Before AIDS became epidemic, the most common diagnoses among Bellevue's 850 patients were psychiatric disorders, asthma and traumatic injuries. All told, Bellevue has treated more than 400 AIDS patients this year, many of whom died either in the hospital or soon after being discharged.

Thus far, 15,403 cases of AIDS have been reported nationally since the disorder was first identified in 1981, almost a third of them here.

Federal health officials say they expect 6,000 new AIDS cases in this country to be reported by the end of this year and twice as many next year.

Thus far, more than half of AIDS patients have died from the diseases and infections that overwhelm the body as a result of a complete breakdown of the immune system. AIDS, a viral disorder, is regarded as ultimately fatal in virtually every case, usually within a year after the first hospitalization. ■

AUGUST 27, 1986

SLAIN WOMAN FOUND IN PARK; SUSPECT SEIZED

Crystal Nix

An 18-year-old woman who graduated last spring from the Baldwin School was found slain yesterday morning in Central Park. The police said she had apparently been sexually abused and strangled.

The police said early today that they had arrested a suspect, Robert Chambers, 19, of 11 East 90th Street. They said the suspect, who knew the woman, was charged with second-degree murder.

The body of the victim, Jennifer Dawn Levin of 84 Mercer Street in SoHo, was found by a bicyclist at about 6:15 A.M. off Park Drive East near 81st Street, just behind the Metropolitan Museum of Art, according to Capt. Harold J. Wischerth of the Manhattan North Zone No. 4 detective unit.

"She was bubbly and very social—she was just a kid," said her uncle, Dan Levin, as he stood outside the Mercer Street building where she had lived with her father, Steven Levin, and stepmother, Arlene. "She loved life."

Detectives on the case said they thought Miss Levin was probably killed elsewhere and dumped in the park. A car was seen on Park Drive East, speeding south on a northbound street. There were tire tracks in the grass by the body, the police said.

The suspect lives in a luxury four-story brick building just off Fifth Avenue and next to the Cooper-Hewitt Museum—less than a half mile from where the body was found. ■

epidemic

AUGUST 28, 1986

DARKNESS BENEATH THE GLITTER: LIFE OF SUSPECT IN PARK SLAYING

Samuel G. Freedman

Both the victim and the suspect in the strangling death Tuesday of an 18-year-old woman moved in the same Manhattan circle of privileged young people, a circle centered on the Upper East Side singles bar where the two spent the hours before the murder, the police and others close to the case say.

For Jennifer Dawn Levin and Robert E. Chambers Jr., life was private schools, fancy apartments, foreign vacations and underage drinking at a preppy hangout called Dorrian's Red Hand. But for Mr. Chambers, it was also unemployment, academic futility and signs of cocaine abuse.

The two had known each other for about two months and dated several times, the police said, before they met early Tuesday morning at Dorrian's Red Hand, at 300 East 84th Street. The owner, Jack Dorrian, said he knew both as regulars.

Mr. Chambers and Miss Levin each had arrived with a separate group of friends, but they left together at 4:30 A.M., exchanging "boy-girl talk" as they walked toward Central Park, the police said. It was there, the police believe, that she was killed.

Less than two hours later, a passer-by found Miss Levin's body—strangled with her bra and apparently sexually abused, according to the authorities—in the park, just behind the Metropolitan Museum of Art. An autopsy yesterday confirmed that she was strangled, and further tests were to be conducted today.

Early this morning, Mr. Chambers was arraigned on a charge of second-degree murder.

The details of both Mr. Chambers's life and Miss Levin's began to emerge yesterday—details that contradicted Mr. Chambers's golden-boy image and revealed a naivete beneath Miss Levin's worldly exterior.

Mr. Chambers, in the recollection of friends, possessed charisma and mature good looks rare for a 19-year-old. He stood 6 feet 4 inches tall, weighed 220 pounds and was a gifted athlete, who had played for three years on the soccer team at York Preparatory School, 116 East 85th Street.

"Nothing less than total success," said the caption beneath Mr. Chambers's photograph in his yearbook.

But self-discipline, it appears, was something Mr. Chambers lacked. If anything, he seemed to try to coast on his good looks and charm—and, in academic settings, not always with success.

"He was bright, charming and not a particularly good student," recalled Ronald P. Stewart, the York headmaster, in an interview yesterday.

The bar owner described Mr. Chambers as "the nicest kid you'd want to meet," someone who would help calm rowdy customers and pick up litter or broken glass from the floor. But he added that Mr. Chambers had "a drug problem" and had gone to treatment program in Michigan about three months ago.

Miss Levin, meanwhile, was a young woman who "was always happy," said Eric Barger, the manager of Flutie's Pier 17, the restaurant in the South Street Seaport where she worked as a hostess this summer.

Robert Chambers, accused killer of Jennifer Levin, in court in 1986.

"Never once, from the time I hired her, did I ever see her come to work with anything but a smile," he said.

This fall Miss Levin was going to enter Chamberlayne Junior College in Boston—an expensive, two-year school that does not require Scholastic Aptitude Tests for admission. Miss Levin's father, Steven, said yesterday that his daughter was "always the straight kid of her crowd" and that "maybe she was too trusting."

Still, Mr. Levin acknowledged that his daughter "liked to go out at night." Mr. Dorrian said she came into his bar two or three times a week. And amid Miss Levin's belongings at the murder scene, the police found a learner's driving permit giving her age as 22.

It had been her passport into Dorrian's Red Hand.

MARCH 14, 1986

MANES IS A SUICIDE, STABBING HIMSELF AT HOME IN QUEENS

Robert D. Mcfadden

Donald R. Manes, who resigned as Queens Borough President last month after an apparent suicide attempt and widening allegations of corruption against him, died last night of a self-inflicted knife wound of the heart, the police said.

Mr. Manes, who sought the Democratic nomination for Governor in 1974 and until this year was one of the city's most powerful politicians, was pronounced dead at Booth Memorial Medical Center in Flushing, Queens, at 11 P.M., after an hour of frantic medical efforts to save him.

Despondent for months, facing almost certain indictment in the city's worst corruption scandals in decades, the 52-year-old former official stabbed himself once in the chest with a 12-inch knife in the kitchen of his home at 80-65 Chevy Chase Street in Jamaica Estates, Queens, the authorities said.

Alice T. McGillion, the Deputy Police Commissioner in charge of public information, said Mr. Manes was found lying face up on the kitchen floor by his wife, Marlene, at 9:52 P.M., after their daughter, Lauren, 25, saw him talking on a telephone and fumbling erratically in a kitchen drawer.

"This is an enormous tragedy," Mayor Koch said in a statement. "And under these circumstances, and after death, we should also remember the good things Donald Manes did."

In the early morning hours of Jan. 10, seven hours after he left a function at Queens Borough Hall, Mr. Manes was found dazed and bleeding from slashes of the wrist and ankle and wildly weaving in his car on the Grand Central Parkway in Queens.

Rushed by the police to Booth Memorial Medical Center, he also suffered a heart attack that night.

Shortly after Mr. Manes's first suicide attempt, a longtime friend of Mr. Manes, Geoffrey G. Lindenauer, the deputy director of the city's Parking Violations Bureau, was arrested and charged with taking a $5,000 bribe from the president of a company hired by the bureau to collect overdue parking fines.

Within a week, an executive of another collection company, Michael G. Dowd, a Queens lawyer, told authorities that he paid bribes to Mr. Lindenauer on instructions from Mr. Manes.

Mr. Manes, under increasing pressure as the scandal spread, took a leave of absence on Jan. 28. Claire Shulman, who was Mr. Manes's deputy, served as acting borough president for six weeks.

This week, she was selected unanimously in a special vote by the borough's nine City Council members, to serve as borough president for the remainder of this year. ■

JULY 4, 1986

NATION REKINDLES STATUE OF LIBERTY AS BEACON OF HOPE; ACROSS U.S., A CEREMONY FOR HISTORY

Sara Rimer

The Statue of Liberty wreathed in light during fireworks display for Liberty Weekend, to celebrate the statue's restoration and centenary.

OCTOBER 28, 1986

METS GET THE MAGIC BACK, TAKE 7TH GAME IN THE WORLD SERIES

Joseph Durso

The Mets brought their season of splendor to a stunning finish last night when they rallied twice to defeat the Boston Red Sox, 8-5, and win their first World Series in 17 years.

They did it with all the magic that carried them to 116 victories during the season and beyond, and that revived their fortunes after they had lost the first two games of the Series. And they shook Shea Stadium with roaring cheers, but with no postgame disorder, from the 55,032 people who watched the Mets bring down the curtain on one of the most successful seasons in baseball history.

They won their championship in the seventh game of the 83rd Series and the 175th game of their baseball year, and they won it by sweeping the final two games with rousing rallies in late innings. They were two runs down in the 10th inning Saturday night, and scored three and won. They were three runs down to Bruce Hurst, the Red Sox's starting pitcher, last night, but stormed back with three runs in the sixth and three more in the seventh, and won it all.

"We were destined to win," said Ron Darling, the Mets' pitcher who threw two home-run pitches to the Red Sox in the second inning. "We were destined to win after finishing second the last two years. Somehow, some way, we got it done."

"We had to win four out of five going to Boston one week ago," said Keith Hernandez, who ignited the Mets' comeback with a two-run single in the sixth inning. "But the ability to bounce back from adversity marks this club. It's the very symbol of this club."

"It is unbelievable," said Roger McDowell, who became the winning pitcher even though he endured one damaging inning. "I have no idea how we kept rallying in the playoff and in the last two games here." ■

Bill Buckner's (of the Boston Red Sox) famous error at the bottom of the 10 inning, in Game 6 of the 1986 World Series. The New York Mets went on to win that game and Game 7.

NOVEMBER 26, 1986

FRIEDMAN IS GUILTY WITH 3 IN SCANDAL

Richard J. Meislin

NEW HAVEN, Nov. 25—A jury today returned guilty verdicts against Stanley M. Friedman, the Bronx Democratic leader and long one of New York City's most powerful political figures, on all charges against him in the first Federal trial stemming from New York City's corruption scandal.

Three other defendants were also found guilty of charges including racketeering, conspiracy and mail fraud for their participation in a "racketeering enterprise" that transformed the city's Parking Violations Bureau into a tool for their corrupt personal profit.

The 12 jurors, their expressions grim, delivered the verdict at 11:11 A.M. after deliberating for three days on the eight weeks of testimony and argument in the case. The jury found Mr. Friedman and each of his co-defendants guilty of racketeering, conspiracy and mail fraud charges carrying lengthy prison sentences and heavy financial penalties.

In addition to Mr. Friedman, those found guilty were Lester N. Shafran, the former director of the Parking Violations Bureau; Michael J. Lazar, a real-estate developer and former city transportation administrator; and Marvin B. Kaplan, the chairman of Citisource Inc., a company chosen to manufacture hand-held computers to issue summonses for the parking bureau. Mr. Kaplan was also found guilty of having perjured himself while testifying before the Securities and Exchange Commission last February.

Mr. Friedman, surrounded by his wife and children and looking drained, said that "to say we were shocked would be an understatement," and vowed to seek vindication in a higher court. "As far as I'm concerned, the fight is out of you when they close the box," Mr. Friedman said, "and I have no intention of quitting. I never quit a fight in my life, and this fight is far from over."

As a convicted felon, Mr. Friedman, a lawyer, faces possible disbarment.

On the counts on which they were found guilty, Mr. Friedman, Mr. Lazar and Mr. Shafran each face a maximum prison sentence of 50 years; Mr. Kaplan faces 52 years. ■

DECEMBER 21, 1986

BLACK MAN DIES AFTER BEATING BY WHITES IN QUEENS

Robert D. McFadden

A 23-year-old black man was struck and killed by a car on a Queens highway early yesterday after being severely beaten twice by 9 to 12 white men who chased him and two other black men through the streets of Howard Beach in what the police called a racial attack.

The dead man, Michael Griffith, of 1650 Pacific Street in the Bedford-Stuyvesant section of Brooklyn, was found shortly after 1 A.M. lying on the Shore Parkway at Cross Bay Boulevard. He had been struck by a car whose driver, the son of a New York City police officer whose name was not released, apparently had no connection to the assailants, the police said.

When he was struck, Mr. Griffith was fleeing from the beatings—one outside a pizza parlor on Cross Bay Boulevard at 157th Avenue and another at 158th Avenue and 84th Street—by a gang who accosted the black men after their car had broken down.

"Niggers, you don't belong here!" the white men shouted as they set on the black men with fists and bats outside the pizzeria, according to Cedric Sandiford, a companion of the dead man.

The pizza shop is in the predominately white, middle-class Howard Beach neighborhood, just west of Kennedy International Airport and north of the marshes and waterfowl refuges of Jamaica Bay.

"All crimes are terrible, but crimes involving racial bigotry are the absolute worst," Mayor Koch said at an afternoon news conference at the 106th Precinct station house. "The survivors were chased like animals through the streets, with one of them being killed on the highway."

Noting that a $10,000 reward had been posted for the capture of the assailants, the Mayor added, "This incident can only be talked about as rivaling the kind of lynching party that took place in the Deep South—this is the No. 1 case in the city."

Police Commissioner Benjamin Ward, who assigned 50 investigators to hunt for the attackers, said the beatings had been carried out by "locals" in Howard Beach, a community of 18,000 people where civic pride mingles with an insular spirit and concern over crime has led to the creation of private street patrols that stop and question strangers.

Mr. Ward said the whites responsible for the beatings "lived in the area and frequented the pizza parlor" where the first attack occurred. He called for residents of the area to "come forward and identify" those responsible for the incident. ■

JANUARY 26, 1987

SUPER BOWL XXI; GIANTS ROUT BRONCOS IN THE SUPER BOWL

Frank Litsky

Head coach Bill Parcells of the New York Giants raises his fist in victory as he is carried off the field after winning Super Bowl XXI.

The garbage barge floats by Coney Island in 1987.

APRIL 18, 1987

Unwanted, 3,100 Tons of L.I. Garbage Sail into Gulf of Mexico in Search of a Dump

Philip S. Gutis

As yet, no one has compared the almost monthlong journey of a barge full of Long Island garbage to the decade-long wanderings of Odysseus so carefully detailed by Homer.

But the similarities are clear. Odysseus's expedition was marked by unusual changes of fortune. And the barge—laden with 3,100 tons of industrial waste from Islip, Long Island—is meeting a similiar fate in her nearly 1,400-mile search for a dump to call home.

The barge, which has quickly become a symbol of the region's growing problems with trash, was barred by court order from docking in Morehead City, N.C. She has made front-page headlines in New Orleans, as government officials gathered to insure that the fly-covered craft stayed far from the Louisiana shore.

The barge began her journey March 22 from Long Island City, Queens. She was waiting today in about 18 feet of water in Grand Path, a portion of the Mississippi Delta about two miles south of Venice, La.

Official attention to the barge did not wane today, even though all government offices were closed for Good Friday. A representative of the Plaquemines Parish Port Authority, Ernie Dobson, stood guard over the barge. "If it takes off and leaves, we want to know where it is going," he said.

On Thursday, Gov. Edwin W. Edwards of Louisiana told reporters in New Orleans, "We certainly have notified the company we do not feel it is the proper use of our facilities, and we suggest it go back from whence they came.

"If we don't have the legal authority, then we can't line the National Guard on the banks of the river and shoot at them. That would be an improper and illegal act."

The trail of trash essentially began last November, when the Islip Town Board voted to bar all industrial waste from its 75-acre landfill in Hauppauge. The dump is almost full. At that point, a company, Waste Alternatives, was formed to remove trash generated by businesses here.

Waste Alternatives, according to the chief engineer of the Islip Resource Recovery Agency, Charles H. Weidner, had been shipping the trash to a large landfill in Dunmore, Pa. But when the dump recently stopped accepting trash from all out-of-state haulers, companies and municipalities across the region were left with no place to put their garbage.

That is when, according to Islip officials, Lowell Harrelson took control of the trash, pledging to ship it by barge to North Carolina. There, he hoped to bury the garbage in a landfill, where it would be used to produce methane.

Officials in North Carolina, however, obtained a court order banning the barge, which then set off for Louisiana in hopes of dumping the waste in a private landfill there.

Back on Long Island, the new Islip Supervisor, Frank Jones, is removed enough from the barge to see the problem as a "godsend." Islip has been involved for years in a battle with the State Department of Environmental Conservation over the 20-year-old landfill in Hauppauge. Although Islip is building an incinerator, the state has refused to allow the town to expand the landfill until the new plant opens.

"They have told us to take our trash out of town," Mr. Jones said. "Now that idea might just mean that we have to send it to the moon. In my judgment, within a month there will not be a state in the country that will take anybody's else's garbage." ■

MAY 31, 1987

NEW YORK WILL START GIVING OUT CONDOMS IN BARS AND MOVIES

Ronald Sullivan

Beginning this summer, a team from the New York City Department of Health will give out free condoms at singles bars, pornographic-movie theaters, massage parlors and sex clubs throughout the city to warn of the dangers of casual sex.

The move is a further attempt to fight the spread of AIDS, which the City Health Commissioner, Dr. Stephen C. Joseph, has said has infected as many as 500,000 people in the city.

Dr. Joseph said the team's efforts will represent a new approach in the department's educational efforts to stem the spread of the AIDS epidemic. "We want to reach out to heterosexual people before they engage in unsafe sexual practices," he said.

The department's initial educational efforts were aimed at sexually active homosexuals and it led to the closing of several homosexual bath houses and nightclubs that the department said permitted unsafe sex.

Other efforts were aimed at intravenous drug users who, with homosexuals, constitute the two major risk groups for the fatal illness. An educational program was also presented in local high schools.

The most recent effort is an advertising campaign aimed at heterosexuals warning that casual sex placed them at risk. The television and newspaper advertisements emphasize the use of condoms to prevent infection by the HIV virus, which causes acquired immune deficiency syndrome.

The city's assistant health commissioner for AIDS program services, Peggy Clarke, said the team will seek permission from the owners of the singles bars and other places they visit before they distribute AIDS prevention literature and free condoms.

She said she anticipated a positive response.

Ms. Clarke said the department would also try to persuade the managers of escort services and houses of prostitution to distribute free condoms. ■

AIDS demonstrators stage a protest at St. Patrick's Cathedral in 1989.

AUGUST 25, 1987

Garbage Barge's 155-Day Odyssey Comes to an End

The barge Mobro was docked yesterday near the Southwest Brooklyn Incinerator in Bensonhurst, ending an epic quest for a place to deposit its contents. The trip began March 22 in Long Island City and included rejections in North Carolina, Alabama, Mississippi, Louisiana, Texas, Florida, Mexico, Belize and the Bahamas. The barge is to be unloaded later this week and the trash inspected for infectious waste. It will then be recycled or incinerated and the ash taken to a landfill in Islip, L.I. ■

OCTOBER 9, 1987

RESTAURANTS: Le Cirque

Bryan Miller

After 13 years and 50,000 chivalrous hand pecks to the ladies, Sirio Maccioni is still wowing them. A consummate impresario and choreographer, he is forever refining his international act known as Le Cirque. Like any showman riding a long-run hit, the Italian-born owner brings changes to his production ever so carefully. Those he has added in the past year, including an astonishingly versatile young chef, have boosted the restaurant's performance to four-star heights—joining the exalted galaxy that includes Le Bernardin, Chanterelle, Lutece and the Quilted Giraffe.

That Le Cirque is the most glamorous and electrifying setting in New York goes without saying. Not the room particularly, a brightly lighted, tightly cramped rococo den with its zany monkey murals and peculiar bouquet sconces that could have come from a suburban lawn-and-garden center. Le Cirque's unparalleled spirit springs from the staff and customers who fill it. On any evening the celebrity scorecard overflows. There may be Lee Iacocca holding court over a veal chop, Paul Bocuse and Roger Verge sampling everything on the menu, the King of Spain and his retinue marveling at the wine list,

Mick Jagger trying to look comfortable—and all, amazingly, appearing inconspicuous amid the glittering colony of habitues.

Late last year, Alain Sailhac, Le Cirque's chef for eight years, passed the baton to the 32-year-old Lyons native Daniel Boulud, who trained at some of the greatest kitchens in France before doing stints here at Le Regence in the Hotel Plaza-Athenee and at the Polo in the Hotel Westbury. If a generalization can be made about changes on this awesomely varied menu, it is that, on the whole, the approach is lighter, more rustic Provencal than polished Parisian.

One unforgettable dish is called sea scallops fantasy in black tie, an individual silver casserole dish of exquisite sliced sea scallops layered with black truffles, moistened with buttery vermouth and truffle juice. Next to that you can find something as unabashedly earthy as a cold terrine of beef shanks with leeks in a faintly piquant raifort sauce speckled with diced vegetables, or tissue-thin carpaccio of red snapper glossed with truffle oil and under a cover of arugula and fresh chervil. Foie gras comes in no fewer than two dozen costumes, depending on Mr. Boulud's whim (sauteed with Concord grapes and cranberries was inspired).

Trying to describe Mr. Boulud's vast lunch and dinner entree repertory in this space would be like itemizing the fall exhibitions at the Metropolitan Museum of Art on a postcard.

Le Cirque's three-ring performance, like a family trapeze act, has become even more dazzling and sure-handed over time. And Mr. Maccioni seems to do it with the greatest of ease.

Le Cirque: **** 58 East 65th Street.

Atmosphere: Plush, densely packed room done in a rococo style. Good acoustics despite large crowds.

Service: Unflappably seasoned European staff, highly professional and cordial.

Recommended dishes: Sea scallops and truffles, terrine of beef shanks and leeks, carpaccio of snapper, foie gras, escargot in white wine and herbs, roasted sea bass in potato crust, grilled salmon with walnuts, navarin of lamb, magret of duck with plum, venison with three purees, raspberry napoleon, sugar basket with fresh figs, mango curls with mango ice cream, creme brulee.

Price range: Lunch: prix fixe $29.75, a la carte appetizers $8.75 to $27, main courses $17 to $26.50; dinner: appetizers $9.75 to $26.50, main courses $21 to $29. ■

John Gotti arrives for the funeral of bodyguard Anthony J. (Shorty) Mascuzzlo. On the right is Salvatore (Sammy the Bull) Gravano.

APRIL 2, 1989

JOHN GOTTI RUNNING THE MOB

Selwyn Raab

Every workday about noon, with ritual pomp, a gleaming limousine glides into the driveway of a modest, split-level house in the Howard Beach section of Queens. Emerging from the house is John Joseph Gotti, a spring to his step, his shoulders squared like a West Point plebe. He is dressed impeccably: muted solid-colored double-breasted suit, creamy white shirt and silk tie with matching breast-pocket handkerchief. Behind the wheel of the waiting Mercedes-Benz or Lincoln is one of three driver-bodyguards who rotate in chauffeuring Gotti around New York.

The 48-year-old Gotti lists his occupation as a roving salesman for a plumbing contracting company. In court records, however, prosecutors brand him as the reigning head of the Gambino family, the largest Mafia or Cosa Nostra group in the country. Since 1984, convictions obtained under the Racketeering Influenced and Corrupt Organizations—or RICO—Act have dismantled most of the nation's 24 organized crime families. Now, for law-enforcement officials, Gotti represents the most formidable roadblock left in a campaign to dislodge the Mafia from its remaining stronghold—the New York region.

F.B.I. and local investigators believe Gotti seized control of the Gambino family after he arranged for the previous boss, Paul Castellano, to be gunned down on a Manhattan street in December 1985. At that time, Gotti was an obscure, middle-level capo regime, or captain, in the crime family.

Since taking over an empire that experts estimate grosses at least $500 million yearly from illegal enterprises, Gotti has become organized crime's most significant symbol of resistance to law-enforcement since Al Capone cavorted in Chicago 60 years ago. As he makes his predictable daily round of meetings from dingy storefront hangouts to elegant restaurants, he boldly displays his contempt of investigators who have been thus far unable to convince a jury that he is engaged in criminal

(cont'd. next page)

(continued from previous page)

activities. Upon spotting detectives on stakeouts, he has been known to rub one index finger against another at them, mouthing the words: "Naughty, naughty."

Gotti's notoriety generates intense and, at times, divisive competition among prosecutors over who will get a crack at convicting him. The next legal battle will be handled jointly by the Manhattan District Attorney's office and the New York State Organized Crime Task Force, which obtained an indictment accusing Gotti of ordering the shooting and wounding of a carpenter's union official in 1986. Arrested for the shooting in January, Gotti reiterated his disdain. "Three to one I beat this charge," he joked to the arresting officers. The next day he was freed on $100,000 bail.

Despite his bravado, Federal and local investigators view Gotti's ascension as a sign of decay within the Mafia. Before he vaulted to the top, his criminal profile, sketched in Federal Bureau of Investigation and New York Police Department records, was that of a thug with a bulky arrest record who had served two prison sentences for bungled crimes. And investigators evaluate him as less capable of running a criminal conglomerate than the cadre of high-ranking mobsters who have been eliminated, in recent years, by prosecution and by death.

Appraising Gotti's three years at the summit, investigators say he still lacks the skills to resuscitate or expand the mob's more sophisticated enterprises, such as extorting kickbacks for rigging contracts in the construction and garment industries. Payoffs to Gotti are said to be dwindling. Investigators believe he relies increasingly on what he knows best: strong-armed profits from loan sharking, gambling and narcotics deals.

Jules J. Bonavolonta, the F.B.I. special agent in charge of the organized-crime branch in New York, contends that a vivid clue to Gotti's character can be gleaned from confidential reports in which Gotti reportedly disclosed that his childhood idol was Albert Anastasia, a founder of Murder Inc. According to Bonavolonta, Gotti is "a former two-bit hijacker and a degenerate gambler who rules right now because he is ruthless and vicious." ■

APRIL 21, 1989

Youths Rape and Beat Central Park Jogger

Craig Wolff

A young woman, jogging on her usual nighttime path in Central Park, was raped, severely beaten and left unconscious in an attack by as many as 12 youths, who roamed the park in a vicious rampage Wednesday night, the police said.

The woman, a 30-year-old investment banker, was found in the early morning wearing only a bra, her hands bound with her sweatshirt and her mouth gagged. Her body temperature, the police said, dropped to 80 degrees while she lay bleeding in a puddle for nearly four hours about 200 yards from where she had been set upon.

The woman, who was found by two passers-by at 1:30 yesterday morning, was listed in critical condition yesterday at Metropolitan Hospital with two skull fractures.

The attack was apparently the last of a burst of random assaults by the youths in the northern reaches of the 840-acre park. That area has not yet seen the vast rehabilitation that has touched many other sections of the park in recent years.

Five youths were arrested in connection with another attack Wednesday evening, and the police said that they were considered suspects in the assault on the jogger.

The teenagers began marauding shortly after 9 P.M., with the robbery of a 52-year-old man at 102d Street on the East Drive. The youths got away with just a sandwich, and the police were unsure how the man, who was walking and carrying a shopping bag, was able to fend them off.

In the next hour, they threw rocks at a taxicab, chased a man and woman riding a tandem bicycle at 100th Street on the East Drive and attacked a 40-year-old jogger, hitting him on the head with a lead pipe, the police said. The jogger told the police that the group turned on him after he came upon them as they attacked a woman on the bridle path about 96th Street, just east of the jogging track around the Reservoir. The man was not seriously injured.

At 10 o'clock, the police said, the group came upon the female jogger as she was running on a desolate transverse, closed to cars, at 102d Street, adjacent to North Meadow softball fields, The police said that the youths numbered as many as 20 when the attacks began and that as many as 12 assaulted the jogger.

Central Park has been the site of other attacks by groups of youths.

Many of the recent renovations of neglected areas of the park—including the rebuilding of Bethesda Terrace, the reopening of the Wollman Memorial Ice Skaing Rink and the rebuilt Central Park Zoo—have been intended to make the park less forbidding.

But the northern part, has not had as many improvements. ■

A bouquet of flowers marks the spot in Central Park where a jogger was attacked in 1989.

AUGUST 27, 1989

A New Generation of Racism Is Seen

Kirk Johnson

The killing of a black teenager Wednesday night in the Bensonhurst section of Brooklyn is but the most searing example of what sociologists and civil rights groups say is a renewed and rising tide of racial intolerance among teen-agers and young adults across the country.

Why that spirit of prejudice crossed the line from slurs and stereotyping to violence in Bensonhurst remains speculative. But those who have studied race relations and teen-age violence say there are common threads.

The group of 10 to 30 bat-wielding whites who the police said killed Yusef Hawkins in the mistaken belief that he had shown up to date a white girl all apparently came from a white working-class enclave; in this case, Bensonhurst.

Although renewed prejudice has been reported across all income levels and classes in recent years, experts said racism has particularly taken root in white working-class areas wrenched by the economic dislocations of the 1980's, and among young people with no memory of the civil rights struggles of the 60's and 70's.

In addition, most of the Brooklyn attackers were under 20 years of age, reflecting a pattern in New York City in which 70 percent of all bias incidents are committed by people under 19, according to the Police Department.

Growing racial intolerance among the young "is one of the most significant trends of the last few years," said Janet Caldwell, a program associate at the Center for Democratic Renewal, an Atlanta-based research group that monitors the Ku Klux Klan and other hate groups.

Justice Department figures show that the number of cases it investigated as "racial incidents" fell slightly between 1986 and 1987, but that racial incidents classified as "school related" rose by almost 50 percent.

Janet Caldwell, at the Center for Democratic Renewal, said she believes the change in attitudes among many young people is rooted in both reality and myth.

The reality, she said, is that young people with no memory of the struggle that led to racial quotas in colleges and in the work place are coming of age in a world where job competition is increasing, where "it is very easy to fall through the cracks if you can't climb into the technocracy."

The myth is that those changes have resulted in "a loss of white-skin privilege," she said.

"Young whites are facing things they never had to face before," she said. "The high-paying post-industrial jobs are not there for them."

Another important element, she believes, are the efforts by groups like the neo-Nazis, the Klan and the Skinheads to influence the young through white-power rock and roll, cartoons and other methods. In addition, she said, most schools are not teaching about the evils of racism to counter those efforts.

The question that many say hangs over the Bensonhurst incident is why race relations appear to be worsening in New York City. From 1984, when Bernhard H. Goetz shot four black teenagers on a subway car, through the 1986 death of a black man in Howard Beach, Queens, after he was chased onto a highway by a group of whites, to the Bensonhurst case, tension between the races has risen by almost any measure.

Yet community leaders in Bensonhurst and police investigators also say that cooperation among residents has been better than in some past bias investigations, including that of the Howard Beach attack.

A large crowd attends the funeral of Yusuf Hawkins, the victim of a racially motivated killing.

SEPTEMBER 13, 1989

Dinkins and Friends Exult in Victory

Celestine Bohlen

Mayor-elect David Dinkins gives his victory speech on November 7, 1989 in New York City.

Not long after the image of Mayor Edward I. Koch faded from a giant television screen above the Hotel Penta Grand Ballroom just after midnight, David N. Dinkins mounted the stage to the cheers of several thousand supporters to claim victory in the Democratic mayoral primary.

"You voted your hopes and not your fears, and in so doing you said something profound today about the soul and character of this town," Mr. Dinkins, the first black mayoral nominee of the Democratic Party in New York City, said early today. "You, the people of New York, made history today."

Mr. Dinkins quickly set about fashioning his approach to running against Rudolph W. Giuliani, the Republican nominee. A former Federal prosecutor, Mr. Giuliani is expected to emphasize his ability to deal with the city's drug and crime problems. "With your help," Mr. Dinkins said, "I intend to restore the rule of law in our streets, in our schools and in our subways.

"There is no excuse for stealing, for violence, for urban terrorism. I intend to be the toughest mayor on crime this city has ever seen." Before Mr. Dinkins took the stage, the loudest cheers were for the Rev. Jesse Jackson, who described Mr. Dinkins's nomination as squarely in the tradition of the civil rights movement.

"David Dinkins's victory sends a good message to all of America," said Mr. Jackson, who noted that Democratic leaders had recently gathered to search for the party's message for the 1990's. "The message is in New York," he said.

Mr. Jackson linked the Dinkins victory to the reaction to the killing last month of a black teenager who was confronted by a gang of young white men in the Bensonhurst neighborhood of Brooklyn.

Mr. Jackson said voters had chosen "to turn pain into power." He likened Mr. Dinkins's victory to a resurrection after the trauma of the racial killing.

By the time the polls closed three hours earlier, the crowd was already elated, convinced that their candidate had won.

"It's the biggest thing since Joe Louis beat Max Schmeling," said Clementine Pugh, a Dinkins supporter from Harlem, as she rushed to kiss Jim Bell, a Dinkins volunteer from the United Auto Workers Union. "You could feel it—you could feel it all day. The people could smell their own power."

"I'm rejoicing," said Ekua Wilson Sampson, a math teacher at Junior High School 145 in the Bronx. "Koch has been in too long."

Several speakers began laying the groundwork for a polite reception of Mayor Koch—all in the name of party unity in the face of Mr. Giuliani's campaign for the Nov. 7 election. ■

The Channel Gardens in Rockefeller Center during the 1989 holiday season.

OCTOBER 31, 1989

Japanese Buy New York Cachet with Deal for Rockefeller Center

Robert J. Cole

The Rockefeller Group, the owner of Rockefeller Center, Radio City Music Hall and other mid-Manhattan office buildings, said yesterday that it had sold control of the company to the Mitsubishi Estate Company of Tokyo, one of the world's biggest real estate developers.

Richard A. Voell, Rockefeller's president and chief executive, said Mitsubishi would pay $846 million in cash for a 51 percent interest. The proceeds will go into the family trusts established by John D. Rockefeller Jr. in 1934 and be used to diversify the family's holdings.

The deal, which comes almost exactly 50 years after Rockefeller Center opened on Nov. 1, 1939, is only the latest instance of the Japanese buying a vital piece of the American landscape, from Hollywood to Wall Street. In September, the Sony Corporation bought Columbia Pictures for $3.4 billion.

David Rockefeller, the company's chairman, said in a statement that the agreement "preserves the abiding commitment to Rockefeller Center and New York City which my father made more than 50 years ago, and which present generations of the family continue to feel." There has been talk that the 88 Rockefeller descendants, all beneficiaries of the 1934 trusts, had wanted to take advantage of high Manhattan property values and turn their stakes into cash.

Jotaro Takagi, president of Mitsubishi Estate, said: "There is no business address in the world that has the same cachet as Rockefeller Center. It is synonymous with excellence. We are making this investment with the objective of continuing this tradition into the 21st century, sharing with the Rockefeller family the vision of the center as a very special place in New York City, and of the city itself as a world capital of business and culture."

Since the 1930's, Columbia University had owned the land under the original

Rockefeller Center running down the east side of the Avenue of Americas to Fifth Avenue and from 48th Street to 51st Street. But the Rockefeller Group bought it in 1985 for $400 million.

Mr. Rockefeller, who is 74 years old, is one of two surviving children of John D. Rockefeller Jr., who had five sons and one daughter. The other is Laurance S. Rockefeller, 79, owner of the Woodstock Inn in Woodstock, Vt., and former chairman of Rock Resorts.

In Rockefeller Center, Mitsubishi will become the landlord of some of the biggest names in the country: General Electric, NBC, Time Warner, Price Waterhouse and Morgan Stanley. ■

HELMSLEY GETS 4-YEAR TERM FOR TAX FRAUD

William Glaberson

Leona Helmsley leaving the New York Federal Court House in 1989.

Saying that Leona Helmsley had been motivated by "naked greed," a Federal judge in Manhattan sentenced her yesterday to a four-year prison term and fined her $7.1 million for tax fraud. Mrs. Helmsley, who described herself in advertisements as the queen of the Helmsley hotel chain, would be eligible for parole after 16 months in prison.

In imposing what many lawyers viewed as stern sentences on Mrs. Helmsley and two former employees, whose conspiracy trial became national theater last summer, Judge John M. Walker Jr. said, "I trust that the sentences today will make it very clear that no person, no matter how wealthy or prominent, stands above the law."

Judge Walker pronounced the sentence in a courtroom packed with more than 300 spectators after an emotional plea by the 69-year-old Mrs. Helmsley. It was the first time the woman who was portrayed as a "tough bitch" by her own lawyer during the trial had spoken publicly about the charges of falsifying documents and illicit billing practices.

Her face drawn, Mrs. Helmsley stood at a lectern in Federal District Court in Manhattan and sobbed uncontrollably as she addressed the judge, begging not to be separated from her husband, Harry B. Helmsley, the billionaire real-estate entrepreneur who sat impassively in the third row.

But Mrs. Helmsley did not acknowledge that she had done anything wrong. "I am more humiliated and ashamed than anybody could ever imagine that I have been found guilty of a serious crime," Mrs. Helmsley said, her voice breaking. "I feel as though I'm in the middle of a nightmare."

When he spoke later, Judge Walker looked directly at Mrs. Helmsley and said she was fully responsible for the scheme that included billing Helmsley businesses for more than $3 million in furnishings for Dunnellen Hall, the couple's 26-acre estate in Greenwich, Conn.

In addition to the fine, Judge Walker said Mrs. Helmsley would have to perform 750 hours of community service during her probation. The judge also said she would have to pay $1.2 million in federal taxes and $469,300 in state taxes. He also said she would have to pay the costs of prosecution. Federal prosecutors said that amount had not yet been determined.

Lawyers said the jail term was on the high end of the range of possible sentences, especially considering Mrs. Helmsley's age and the poor health of Mr. Helmsley, 80 years old, who was also charged in the case but was excused from the case when Judge Walker found that he was mentally incompetent to stand trial.

There was little doubt yesterday in Federal District Court that the sentencing, like the trial in July and August, was being watched carefully all over the country. More than an hour before the scheduled 2 P.M. court session, more than 100 members of the public lined up quietly outside the fifth-floor courtroom with reporters to watch the sentencing of the woman whose faults and foibles were daily headlines in the heat of the summer.

The crowd was made up of people who talked to each other about such details as the $29 Itty-Bitty Book Light that Mrs. Helmsley billed to one of her businesses and the $45,681 clock in the shape of the Helmsley Building that she had made for her husband.

The single bit of testimony that many people have said crystallized the message of the trial came from Elizabeth Baum, a former housekeeper who joined a long line of former employees who testified. Her boss, Mrs. Baum testified, told her: "We don't pay taxes. Only the little people pay taxes."

When the proceeding was over yesterday, Mrs. Helmsley and her husband descended the 17 front steps of the Foley Square courthouse in lower Manhattan. People in a crowd on the sidewalk taunted them with shouts about jail time. Then the couple's bodyguards shoved them into a waiting Lincoln and they rode off into a light snow. ■

A DECADE ENDS, AND THE NOUVELLES OF NEW YORK ARE NOT INVITED

Georgia Dullea

There was a moment in December 1980, when then President-elect Ronald Reagan was kneeling on the floor of Brooke Astor's Park Avenue apartment after one of her important black-tie dinners. He was looking for a diamond earring she had dropped and together they were laughing. It was an oddly glamorous moment, the philanthropist, the President and the lost diamond.

Soon after that there appeared on the New York social scene the first glints of the gilded era of the 80's. This was a lavish spectacle of wealth and the props of wealth fueled by the sort of fast money from Wall Street that made the word millionaire obsolete. Parties were the thing in this era, million-dollar birthday parties for the middle-aged.

"In my day, a million was a lot," said Mrs. Astor, who put the rich-rich on the charity circuit. "Today, a billion is more like it."

The pace setters of the decade were a handful of financial wizards and their younger second or third wives. Suddenly they were everywhere—in the flesh and in print. One could turn to the business section and read about the deals they did and the money they made and then, flipping to the gossip columns, read about the showy ways in which they spent the money.

Glossy magazines devoted articles and even cover stories to their enchanted life styles. One could be at home—a Rubens in the drawing room, a Renoir in the bath—with Gayfryd and Saul Steinberg. Or John and Susan Gutfreund, who entertain with four kinds of caviar. Or Henry Kravis and Carolyne Roehm, who eats Oreos for breakfast.

In their conspicuous consumption, the Nouvelles were consumed by the public and served up by a press for whom the point of the story increasingly became not how lovely, but how much. The cake for the wedding of Laura Steinberg and Jonathan Tisch reportedly cost $17,000. Ummm, delicious. Taste that money.

Signs that the social spectacle might be souring came in 1986, when Felix and Elizabeth Rohatyn, a couple with social clout, questioned the opulence of charity balls. The biggest balls were run not by the Nouvelles, but by Old Guard figures like Mrs. Astor, Pat Buckley and Annette Reed.

Yet the Nouvelles, with their big-money connections, were selling $100,000 worth of tables and their friends wouldn't come to dowdy parties. The Rohatyns were squelched.

Then came Oct. 13, 1987, the stock market plunge and Wall Street jitters. Never mind. A week later Nouvelle socialites stepped out in $25,000 poufs to welcome Christian Lacroix, with his couture collection, Luxe, to New York.

In other ways, the Nouvelles seemed the purest expression of the Reagan economic philosophy, which celebrated personal wealth. If this philosophy blurred class distinctions, press agentry buried them.

After all those stories about all those parties, the public could hardly be expected to discern any difference between Pat Buckley of the Old Guard and Ivana Trump of the Nouvelles—not with Mrs. Buckley and friends posing for the paparazzi on the Trump yacht.

Nor did the public really care. But the Old Guard did, and by the summer of 1988 its members were being stung by the Nouvelle excesses.

Everybody agreed it was time to tone down, at least in public.

The Reagans left the White House. Jerry Zipkin, Nancy Reagan's confidant and permanent representative to New York, though, was still squiring women whose husbands were too busy or too bored to take them to parties. The spring social season was somewhat muted. The Nouvelles had gone underground.

Suddenly last summer, back-to-back fantasy parties broke out. The revels were miles from New York, but news of Nouvelles travels. First was the $1 million party Gayfryd Steinberg gave for her husband in Quogue, N.Y. The next week brought reports of the $2 million-plus party Malcolm Forbes gave for himself in Tangier, Morocco.

That did it. More criticism. More satire. In November 1989, Mrs. Astor, again in diamonds, presided at another important black-tie dinner. As the cameras clicked, she covered her necklace with a chiffon scarf. Her photo appeared in Women's Wear Daily, with those of other women wearing the discreet jewelry of the new Soft Society.

"Forget the hard flash of the Nouvelle Society Eighties," said an article accompanying the photographs. "People are fed up with opulent excess and social showoffs." ■

Donald Trump, shown here with his wife Ivana, purchased the Sultan of Brunei Adnan Khashoggi's yacht, "Nabila," for 30 million dollars and renamed it 'The Princess Trump" in 1988.

Science, Technology and Health

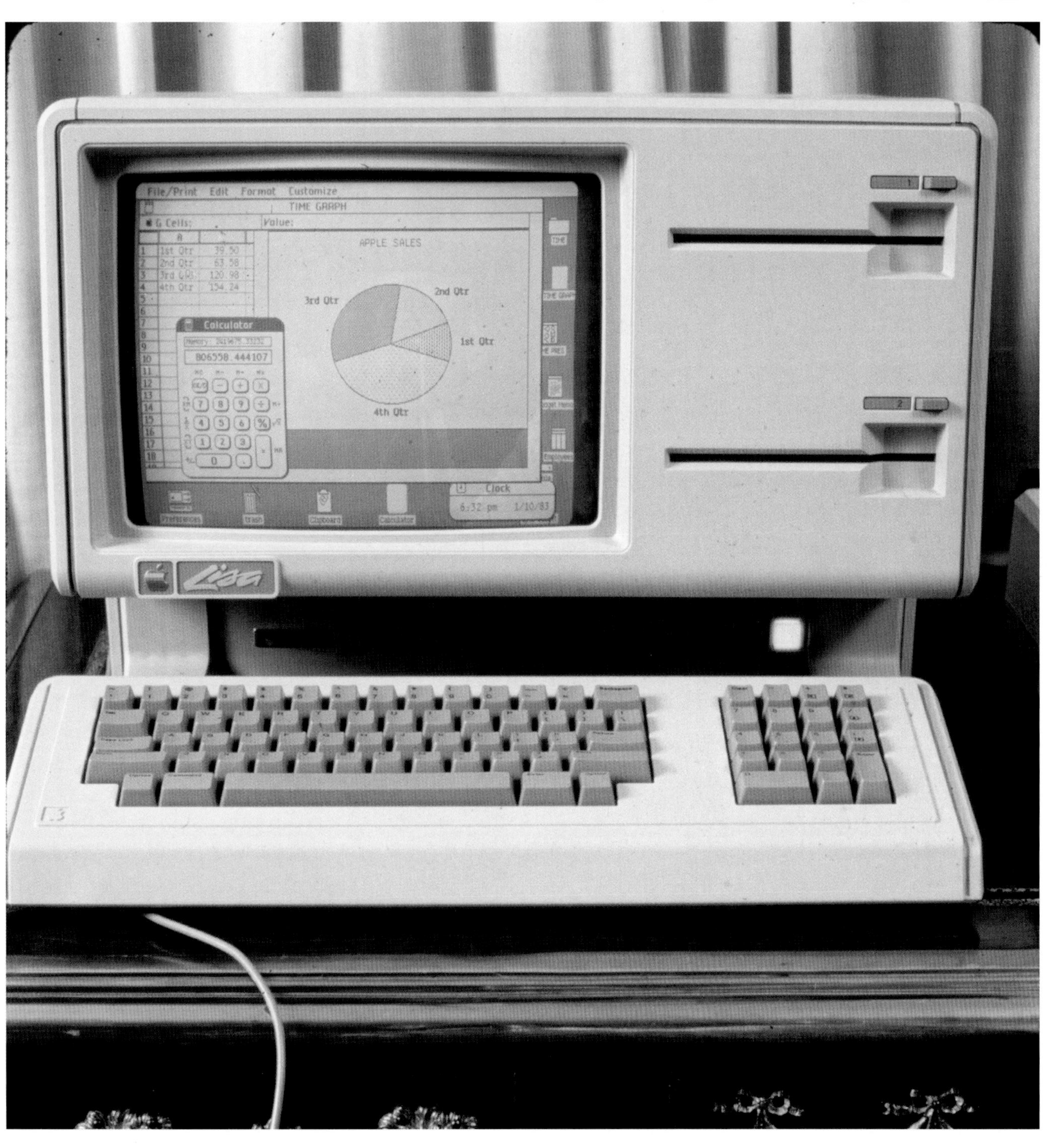

No one alive can recall the wrenching transformations of the Industrial Revolution. But nearly everyone on earth has witnessed the dawn of the Internet age, its modern-day equivalent. The globe-shrinking, empowering series of innovations that has transformed lives throughout the world and continues to shape communications, entertainment, leisure time and the workplace first took hold in the 1980's.

Technicians inspect a new military remote-controlled plane at the Edwards Air Force Base, California, in 1981.

There was no Wright Brothers moment. The Internet advanced stealthily, the province of academic researchers and specialists at vast government-funded computer projects like the Defense Advanced Research Projects Agency in the United States and the European Center for Nuclear Research, known by its French acronym, CERN, in Switzerland.

The world little noted but has long remembered, for example, the moment in 1980 when Tim Berners-Lee, an independent contractor with CERN, wrote the hypertext software code he named Enquire. It corralled the disparate provinces of the documentation systems then in existence and united them in a single entity he called the World Wide Web.

British physicist-turned-programmer Tim Berners-Lee.

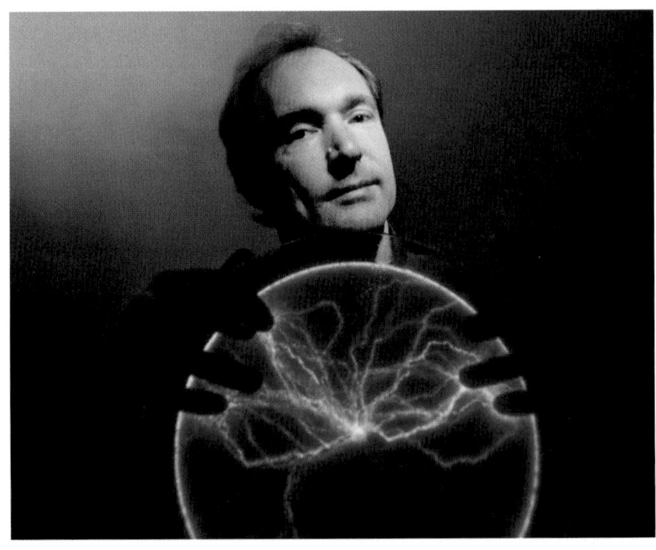

The launch of space shuttle Columbia in 1981.

The personal computer advanced by leaps and bounds. The do-it-yourself kits of the 1970's evolved into preassembled computers with processing power that expanded exponentially. Entrepreneurs like Bill Gates of Microsoft and Steve Jobs of Apple developed new programs and hardware that made the personal computer as familiar as a television set by the end of the decade.

Users learned to operate a funny little gadget called a mouse, mastered the art of sending electronic mail — or e-mail, for short — and took part in chat lines in the cyberspace gathering places known as virtual communities. They learned to fear a mysterious enemy called a virus. They looked forward to the day, apparently not far off, when everyone could work at home and telecommute.

The space program still sent astronauts aloft, but the focus shifted to the orbital craft known as space shuttles, like the Columbia, the Discovery and the Challenger, to transport satellites and spare parts for space stations.

The shuttles ascended to an altitude between 200 and 400 miles, a short hike compared with the moon missions of yesteryear but with dangers just as threatening. Less than two minutes after take-off on Jan. 28, 1986, the Challenger disintegrated over the Atlantic Ocean, killing all seven crew members.

The unmanned Voyager 1 spacecraft reached the far ends of the solar system, sending back stunning photographs of the moons and rings of Saturn before traveling onward to Uranus and reaching Neptune by the end of the decade.

Dione, one of the moons of Saturn, photographed by Voyager 1, 1980.

Medical research advanced on several fronts, most notably in cancer research, but the frantic search for a cause and a cure for AIDS dominated the headlines. The disease, first noted in the early 1980's, remained a mystery until Robert Gallo in the United States and Luc Montagnier in France simultaneously identified the retrovirus, HIV, that causes the deadly immune deficiency. By the end of the decade, AZT, the first drug to treat the disease, had been developed and approved for adult use by the FDA.

Luc Montagnier, Jean-Claude Chermann and Françoise Barre-Sinoussi, the three Franch scientists who helped to discover the causes of AIDS, in 1984.

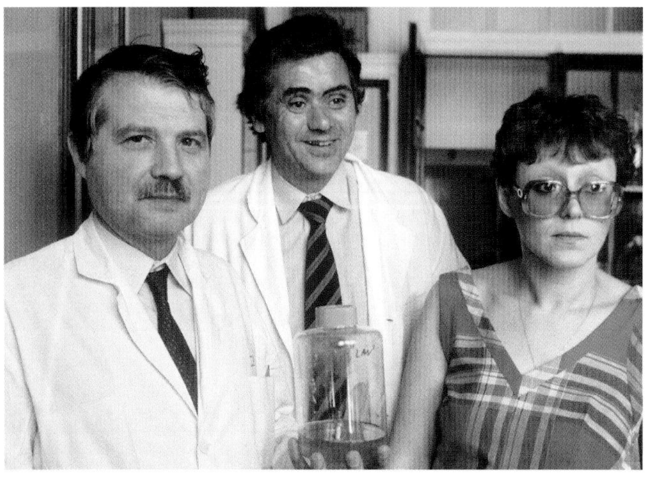

It was a decade of startling breakthroughs and exciting new research projects. Surgeons began opening up clogged arteries with a minimally invasive procedure called a balloon angioplasty. In Salt Lake City, Dr. Robert K. Jarvik successfully implanted an artificial heart of his own design in the chest of a retired dentist named Barney Clark.

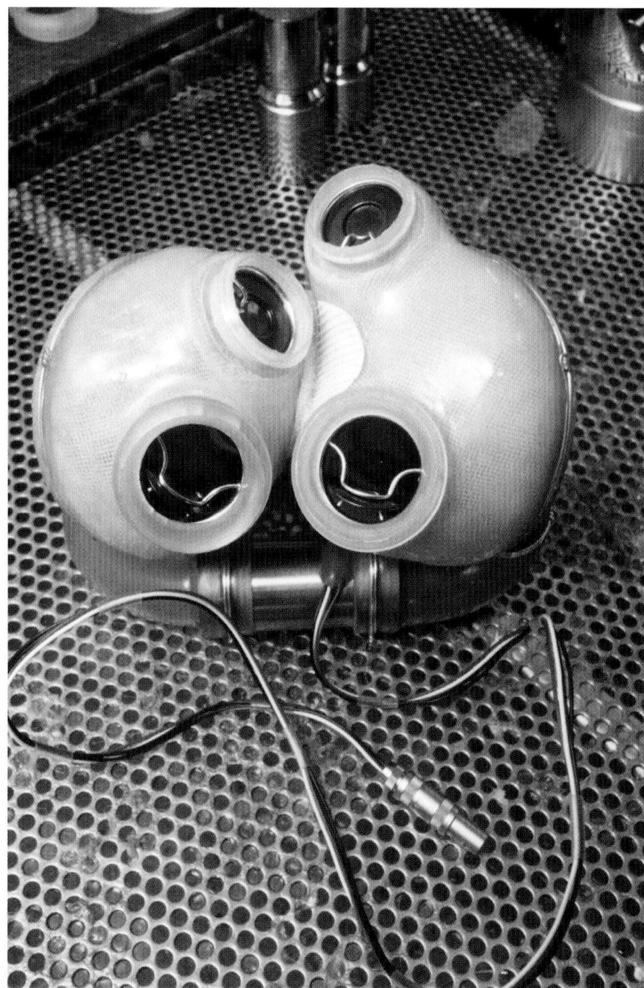

The artificial heart in 1981.

In 1980, the World Health Organization announced that smallpox had been eradicated, pronouncing the final word on a disease that had afflicted mankind for more than 10,000 years. It was an unforgettable moment that lit a spark of hope. If smallpox could be vanquished, surely AIDS could not be far behind.

DECEMBER 22, 1980

The E.P.A. Gets Tough on Waste

Barnaby J. Feder

Chemical industry executives were calling 1980 "the year of Hazardous waste" even before President Carter signed legislation this month that will create a $1.6 billion "superfund" to clean up dangerous toxic waste dumps and chemical spills.

The reason is that the Environmental Protection Agency last month imposed long-delayed regulations governing the handling of hazardous wastes from the moment of their creation to their final disposal. While the "superfund" is aimed at cleaning up such hazardous waste disasters as Love Canal, the agency regulations have the broader goal of preventing them.

"This is the most comprehensive set of environmental regulations ever developed," declared Ben Woodhouse, manager of regulatory affairs for the United States marketing division of the Dow Chemical Company.

The scope of the regulations is indicated by the 13 pages the E.P.A. needed in the Federal Register simply to outline the criteria for determining whether a waste is hazardous. The regulations extend beyond toxic wastes to include substances that are considered dangerous because they are corrosive, easily ignitable or highly reactive.

The clean-up bill requires industry to pay excise taxes on basic chemicals and crude oil that will raise $1.38 billion of the total over five years. The new regulations, which became effective Nov. 19, will probably cost as least that much annually, according to the agency's analysis. In combination with existing air and water pollution control laws, they are intended to close the circle on industrial pollution problems that have caused increasing public concern in the last decade. ■

NOVEMBER 10, 1980

MORE COLORFUL VIEW OF SATURN EMERGING

John Noble Wilford

Pasadena, Calif., Nov 9—Voyager 1, now 2.5 million miles from Saturn speed, has returned new photographs showing contrasting bands of pale yellow, golden brown and reddish brown running parallel to the planet's equator, as well as high-speed jet streams coursing through the hydrogen-helium atmosphere.

The multi-hued world of Saturn emerging in the Voyager photography is in striking contrast to its pale yellow image seen in the best Earth-based telescopes.

Saturn's rings continued to surprise and puzzle scientists as new Voyager photographs, processed to show how the right particles reflect ultraviolet light, highlighted what appeared to be some fundamental difference between the innermost ring and the other two major rings. In ultraviolet light, the inner or C ring has a bluish tint, as against the whiter A and B rings.

The 10,000-mile wide C ring is the least visible from Earth of the three major rings. Between the C ring and the cloud tops of Saturn, a distance of about 8,000 miles, lies a region apparently free of orbiting debris. ■

Image of Saturn taken by Voyager 2 spacecraft.

SHUTTLE ROCKETS INTO ORBIT ON FIRST FLIGHT

John Noble Wilford

CAPE CANAVERAL, Fla., April 12—The space shuttle Columbia, its rockets spewing orange fire and a long trail of white vapor, blasted its way into earth orbit today, carrying two American astronauts on a daring journey to test the world's first re-usable spaceship.

Soon after they settled into orbit, John W. Young, a civilian, and Capt. Robert L. Crippen of the Navy focused a television camera on the Columbia's tail section and discovered that more than a dozen heat-shielding tiles had ripped off, possibly because of the stresses of launching.

Project officials said that the tile loss should not shorten the flight or endanger the lives of the astronauts when the Columbia plunges back into the atmosphere, glowing red-hot from frictional heat, to attempt a runway landing Tuesday. The projected 36-orbit, 54 1/2-hour flight is scheduled to end at Edwards Air Force Base in California.

"I'm just not concerned about it," Neil B. Hutchinson, a flight director at Mission Control in Houston, said in discussing the tile problem at a news conference this afternoon. "We've got a super vehicle up there."

The mission is the first of four planned orbital tests of the space shuttle, a revolutionary complex of machinery designed to take off like a rocket, cruise in orbit like a spacecraft and return to earth like a giant glider. No other space vehicle has been reflown.

If the shuttle lives up to expectations, the Columbia and three sister ships now under construction should each be capable of making as many as 100 round trips into space, deploying and servicing satellites and also carrying scientific laboratories and planetary probes.

It was the first launching of American astronauts in nearly six years, and officials at the Kennedy Space Center were elated and visibly relieved. Controllers in the firing room waved small American flags as soon as they received assurances that Mr. Young and Captain Crippen were safely in orbit.

George F. Page, the director of shuttle operations, arrived at a post-liftoff news conference, smiling and waving his flag. "I've been on a lot of first launches," he said. "I've been in the business 20 years, and I never felt anything like today." Neither did Captain Crippen, the 43-year-old astronaut who made his first trip into space after waiting 15 years. His heart rate jumped to 130 beats a minute, from a normal 60, in the 12-minute ascent. The increased heart rate was not unusual for astronauts in a critical phase of a mission.

"That was one fantastic ride!" he exclaimed. "I highly recommend it." Though busy checking out the shuttle systems, Captain Crippen stole a few glances out the cockpit window at the earth and the airless space all around, remarking: "Oh, man, that is so pretty!"

Starting as a 4.5-million-pound, 184-foot-high complex of machinery, consisting of the orbiter Columbia attached to a huge external fuel tank and two solid-fuel rockets, the space shuttle struggled upward to achieve orbit. ■

The age of the Space Shuttle begins with the launch of Columbia on the STS-1 mission. Commander John Young and Pilot Robert Crippen were at the controls.

JUNE 19, 1983

COOL, VERSATILE ASTRONAUT: SALLY KRISTEN RIDE

William J. Broad

The celebration over sending the first American woman into orbit has tended to overshadow the fact that Dr. Sally K. Ride is to be the first person to perform one of the most significant tasks of the space age. Reaching into the void with a 50-foot robotic arm, she plans to capture a satellite as it hurtles about the earth and, using mechanical might conferred by gears and motors, bring it safely to rest in the cargo bay of the space shuttle.

Her aerial exercise points to the not-so-distant future when it could be routine to grasp satellites, mine asteroids, build space stations—in short, to clutch and shape instead of just to pass through space as an awestruck visitor. It marks a new stage in the taming of the high frontier.

Even before liftoff, Dr. Ride had achieved world renown as the woman designated to break the all-male barrier in the American space program. There are now seven women in the astronaut corps.

Dr. Ride will also play an important role in preparation for future missions. She will act as a liaison agent between the Government and private companies when clients from aerospace and military industries contract for space aboard the shuttle.

On the second shuttle flight Dr. Ride had the highly visible job of capsule communicator, the person on the ground who relays messages to the astronauts. Soon after that she was named mission specialist for the seventh flight of the shuttle.

In her pioneering role, Dr. Ride has been subjected to a host of personal questions, such as whether she would wear a brassiere in orbit and whether she feared the flight would adversely affect her reproductive organs. Through it all she has remained unrattled, direct and concise.

"It's too bad this is such a big deal," she remarked at a NASA news conference. "It's too bad our society isn't further along." ■

Astronaut Sally Kristen Ride inspects the array of tools at her disposal during her earth orbit in the Challenger shuttle STS-7.

AUGUST 31, 1983

First U.S. Black in Space

William J. Broad

The first black American to soar into space, Lieut. Col. Guion S. Bluford Jr., has in his career followed a trajectory as sure and graceful as that of the Challenger. Fascinated as a child with things that fly, he pursued his interest to the point of taking a doctorate in aerospace engineering. A reluctant hero on the issue of racial barriers, the 40-year-old Air Force officer acknowledged his pioneering role at a recent news conference, but he stressed that he was more excited about being able to fly on the Challenger.

He has nonetheless gone out of his way to share with black students his devotion to the art of aerospace engineering.

This year he visited a predominantly black high school in Camden, N.J., which built an experiment to be carried aboard the Challenger. "The students went wild when Colonel Bluford came," said one teen-ager who worked on the experiment. "He said: 'I'm an engineer, and I'm black and I'm lonely out there.' "

With almost no hope of success, Colonel Bluford in 1978 applied to the astronaut program, along with 8,078 others. He said he was puzzled when an official of the National Aeronautics and Space Administration called to chat about the Texas sunshine, until he was asked if he would like to be an astronaut.

The next year he became eligible for a mission. "It really proved to be better than I expected," he said after entering the program. "It gives me a chance to use all my skills and do something that is pretty exciting. The job is so fantastic, you don't need a hobby. The hobby is going to work."

Colonel Bluford, who prefers to be called Guy, is a mission specialist, one of the new breed of scientific pioneers who are taking an increasing share of the limelight from the pilot astronauts.

Aboard the Challenger, he will perform experiments with electrophoresis, a way to separate biological materials according to their surface electrical charge by passing them through an electric field. The technique may yield new drugs. He will also help launch a communications and weather satellite for India and put the shuttle's mechanical arm through tests with an 8,000-pound weight

Though he is the first American black in space, he is not the first black; the Soviet Union placed Arnaldo Tamayo Mendez, who is Cuban, into orbit in 1980 aboard Soyuz 38. Waiting to follow Colonel Bluford into space are three other black American astronauts.

The comedian Bill Cosby said the historic flight was a breakthrough for the Federal Government. "This is someone who had earned the mission," he said. "Our race is one which has been quite qualified for a long time. The people who have allowed him to make this mission are the ones that have passed the test."

Colonel Bluford lives in Houston with his wife, an accountant with an oil concern. Both his sons are science students in college. "I try to keep them from feeling pressured that they have to accomplish more than I have," he said. "I want them to be happy. That's what is most important." ■

AUGUST 31, 1984

NEWEST SHUTTLE FIRED INTO ORBIT AFTER 3 DELAYS

John Noble Wilford

CAPE CANAVERAL, Fla., Aug. 30—After three postponements over two months, the space shuttle Discovery rocketed into orbit today on its maiden flight and successfully deployed the first of three communication satellites in its cargo.

The launching, which came just seconds before 8:42 A.M., was delayed almost seven minutes by the intrusion of a small private aircraft in the restricted airspace surrounding the Kennedy Space Center. The countdown was halted while an Air Force plane intercepted the intruder that was holding up the $1.2-billion spaceship and escorted it out of harm's way.

On the ground the reaction to the successful launching was more exuberant. The nation's 12th shuttle mission, and the Discovery's first, was postponed twice in June, once because of a computer malfunction and then because a fuel valve failed to open in the final seconds before liftoff. One of the engines that had already ignited had to shut down.

Then, with these problems behind them, launching crews uncovered a potential problem in transmitting critical ascent commands through the spaceship's master events controller. This forced a one-day postponement in the launching, which had been scheduled for Wednesday.

At a post-launching news conference, Robert B. Sieck, the launching director, said: "We're happy the orbiter and its crew finally left town. The launch team is ecstatic. The only way to get over an abort and two postponements is to have a successful launch."

Astronaut Dale Gardner approaches the Westar 6 satellite, using the Manned Manoeuvring Unit (MMU), prior to capturing it and bringing it back to Discovery's cargo bay.

MARCH 5, 1985

E.P.A. ORDERS 90 PERCENT CUT IN LEAD CONTENT OF GASOLINE BY 1986

Philip Shabecoff

WASHINGTON, March 4—The Environmental Protection Agency said today that it was considering a total ban on leaded gasoline by 1988. It issued final rules for removing 90 percent of the lead currently in automobile fuel by the end of this year.

The agency said last year that it was contemplating a flat prohibition on lead in gasoline by 1992.

Lee M. Thomas, Administrator of the environmental agency, said that an accelerated schedule for barring all lead in gasoline was being considered in large part because of new information about the adverse effects on human health of lead in the air. In particular, he noted that new studies suggest that lead from gasoline is a significant cause of high blood pressure among adults.

"There is no doubt in my mind that lead in the environment is still a national health problem and that gasoline is a major contributor to lead exposure," Mr. Thomas said at a news conference at his headquarters this morning. "These standards," he said, "will significantly reduce the adverse health effects that result from using lead in gasoline and will reduce the misuse of leaded gasoline in vehicles designed for unleaded fuel."

Agency data show that the use of leaded gas is 67 percent higher than was forecast in 1982 when the current standard of 1.1 grams per gallon was adopted. Much of that increase, according to the agency, is because some motorists are using the cheaper leaded gasoline in vehicles with engines designed to use only lead-free gasoline.

Mr. Thomas said that it was estimated the new rules put in place today would add about 2 cents a gallon to the cost of producing gasoline. He said he did not know how that increase would translate at the pump. ■

APRIL 28, 1985

This Journey Comes Once in 76.3 Years

Robert Merkin

Travelers dream of spectacular destinations throughout the world, but the next major trek for as many as 10,000 North American adventurers may be to gaze at something entirely beyond this world—the return of Halley's comet next April.

The best seats on the planet will be in the Southern Hemisphere. But no one will be forced to travel below the Equator for a good show, according to the astronomer Stephen J. Edberg, coordinator for amateur observations at the Jet Propulsion Laboratory in Pasadena, Calif., and unofficial high lama for every amateur Halley hunter on the continent.

"For those willing to make some effort," he says, "there'll be a very satisfactory view in the Northern Hemisphere." The effort will require an exodus from urban areas to the nearest desert or clear rural or wilderness skies, but once there, Halley's comet, nucleus and tail, should be visible to the naked eye and clear and detailed through ordinary binoculars.

But stay-at-home or globetrotter, you might as well kiss the comet goodbye if you don't catch it in 1986; it returns to this neighborhood roughly once each 76.3 years. If a 10-year-old child is old enough to understand what he or she is viewing and remember it, that child will be 86 years old when the next opportunity knocks, around 2062. (It could be worse. The Great Comet of 1864 won't be back for about 3 million years.) The British Astronomer Royal, Edmund Halley, calculated his comet's average period, or circuit time around the sun, during its 1682 visit, but this period can be as short as 74 or as long as 79 years.

As soon as California's Mount Palomar telescope confirmed, in October 1982, that Halley's comet was back in the neighborhood, knowledgeable comet watchers were able to calculate its closest approach to earth and make their reservations accordingly. The full moon interferes with good viewing, so its dark phases will leave a best-observation window from April 4 or 5 through April 20. (The comet will be visible to a greater or lesser extent from January through April. March and April will be the best months. February will be the poorest because the comet will be too close to the sun.)

Before Dr. Halley, comets appeared without warning or prediction, and the most common explanation was that they were omens of nasty historic events on the horizon. ■

Halley's Comet in 1986.

Mother ship Atlantis II of Woods Hole Oceanographic Institution returning home after expedition to site of wreckage of luxury liner Titanic.

SEPTEMBER 3, 1985

WRECKAGE OF TITANIC REPORTED DISCOVERED 12,000 FEET DOWN

William J. Broad

A team of American and French researchers was reported yesterday to have found the hulk of the luxury liner Titanic south of Newfoundland.

After combing the site with new undersea robots, the team was able to verify the ship's identity with cameras and sonar early Sunday morning, according to American and French officials. A French

(cont'd. next page)

(continued from previous page)

announcement said the wreck was found at a depth of more than 12,000 feet.

The discovery came more than 73 years after the luxury liner, said to be unsinkable, struck an iceberg on her maiden voyage and went down, resulting in the loss of more than 1,500 lives. The ship was the biggest and most luxurious liner of her day.

Dr. Robert D. Ballard of the Woods Hole Oceanographic Institution in Massachusetts, the leader of the joint expedition, said in a ship-to-shore interview that pieces of the ship were found early Sunday.

She took more than 1,500 to their death

The Titanic's wreckage had eluded at least three teams who set out to find it. Researchers have come back with only dim, tantalizing hints.

The Titanic sank on her way from Southampton, England, to New York after striking an iceberg April 14, 1912. She took more than 1,500 of her approximately 2,200 passengers and crew to their death.

The Titanic was carrying some of the richest of the world's rich, including John Jacob Astor and his wife, who bore his child after Astor went down with the ship. They were aboard in a suite that cost $4,000 for the one-way voyage.

Isidor Straus of Macy's was lost, as was Mrs. Straus, who refused to leave her husband of many years to enter a lifeboat.

The researchers worked at finding the wreck with advanced robots that use remote-controlled television, photography and sonar-mapping systems that can survive crushing pressure and pierce the darkness miles under the ocean surface. ■

FEBRUARY 4, 1986

NEW DNA TEST OFFERS BIOLOGICAL 'FINGERPRINTS' FOR CRIME FIGHT

Lawrence K. Altman

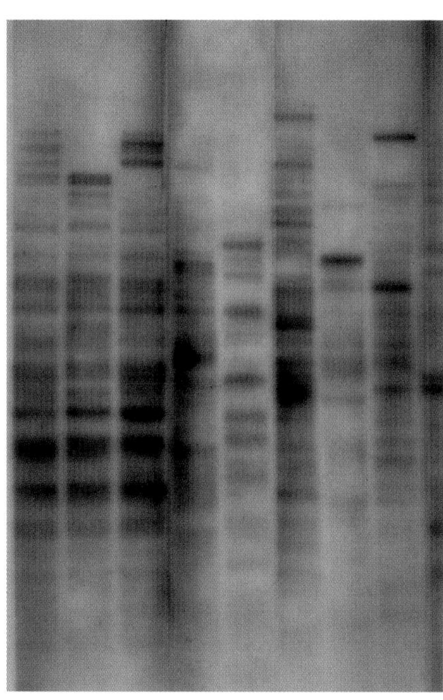

An autoradiograph of the first genetic fingerprint.

A new biological test promises to change radically the way criminologists track down murderers, rapists and muggers.

Virtually foolproof identification of any person is now believed possible through the powerful new laboratory test that detects genetic "fingerprints" in tiny samples of blood, semen and hair roots.

The test can help solve mix-ups of newborn babies in hospitals, aid in identifying lost people, help determine parentage and alter immigration procedures. The test may also provide scientists with new methods to detect hereditary disorders and to determine the functions of large portions of the genetic material DNA in the body.

The test is called DNA fingerprinting. DNA, or deoxyribonucleic acid, is contained in every cell and is different in each person.

The British scientists who developed it calculate that the chances of two people having the same test results are measured in the billions. The only known exceptions are identical twins. Experts say that DNA fingerprinting might someday have greater application than conventional fingerprints and be done routinely at birth.

DNA fingerprints for blood and sperm appear to be the same. Because there are severe limitations on identifying the origin of sperm through existing techniques and because spermatozoa are largely composed of DNA, criminology experts said they suspect that the main use of the new test will be in rape cases. According to the developers of the test, it should be possible to match a DNA fingerprint of sperm from a victim or clothing with that of blood or sperm from a suspected rapist.

The test was developed at the University of Leicester by Dr. Alec J. Jeffreys and reported in a recent issue of the British journal Nature. It was adapted for criminology use by Dr. Peter Gill and Dr. Werrett of the British Home Office's Forensic Science Service in Aldermaston, working in collaboration with Dr. Jeffreys.

Other forensic scientists, such as Dr. Gilbert E. Corrigan of the Veterans Administration Hospital in St. Louis, called the test "phenomenal."

So far the test is apparently being done only in England. Some experts said they believed a few laboratories in the United States would begin experimenting with it in about a year.

James Kearney, a forensic science specialist at the Federal Bureau of Investigation in Washington, said his agency was taking the development seriously, had assigned a researcher to study its potential and has been collaborating with scientists at the National Institutes of Health to develop a similar test.

Mr. Kearney said it would take "from two to five years" to overcome the hurdles and to adapt the test for routine testing, according to estimates made by F.B.I. specialists. ■

MARCH 14, 1986

2 SOVIET ASTRONAUTS LOFTED TOWARD NEW SPACE STATION

Serge Schmemann

MOSCOW, March 13—The Soviet Union launched two astronauts today toward a rendezvous with the new space station Mir, and in a rare move the takeoff was shown live on national television.

At exactly 3:33 P.M. (7:33 A.M., New York time), flames belched from the huge boosters and the rocket lifted smoothly over the snow-dappled Central Asian steppes at the Baikonur launching site.

Fifty seconds later, as the voice of the controller reported that "the flight is normal," the television shifted to cameras inside the Soyuz T-15 craft and showed Col. Leonid D. Kizim, the commander, and Vladimir Solovyov, the flight engineer, cradled in their space suits and apparently at ease.

At 120 seconds, as the controller announced the separation of the first stage, the astronauts were visibly jolted. The transmission continued until the 270th second, when the crew was reported safely in orbit.

The launching was only the fourth that the Russians have shown live on television. The three previous televised shots involved foreigners, directly or indirectly: the Soyuz crew that linked up with an American Apollo spacecraft in 1975, and Soviet-French and Soviet-Indian crews in 1982 and 1984.

Some Western diplomats surmised that the launching was broadcast to demonstrate the reliability of Soviet equipment after the catastrophic explosion of the American space shuttle Challenger Jan. 28, with the loss of seven lives. The Soviet press has commented at length on the Challenger disaster and the subsequent investigation, sometimes arguing that it demonstrates the dangers of President Reagan's proposed reliance on a space-based defense against nuclear missiles.

The publicized launching of the two astronauts followed hard on the successful rendezvous of two unmanned Soviet space probes, Vega 1 and 2, with Halley's comet. First Vega 1 on Thursday, then Vega 2 on Sunday flew by the comet to record and measure its nucleus and its coma of dust.

The Vega missions involved participation by experts from a dozen countries and were given extensive publicity in an apparent effort to demonstrate Soviet dedication to peaceful and cooperative exploration of outer space. ■

Russian Mir Space Station.

MARCH 25, 1986

GLOBAL EFFORT URGED FOR OZONE

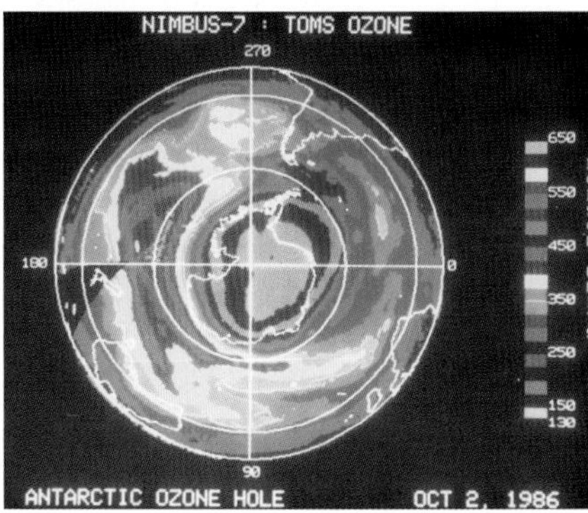

Total Ozone Mapping Spectrometer (TOMS) false color image showing ozone depletion over Antarctic taken from NASA's NIMBUS-7 SATELLITE in 1986.

MEDFORD, Mass., March 24—International laws banning the use of products containing chlorofluorocarbons has been urged at a conference on the global environment.

Senator John H. Chafee, a Rhode Island Republican who was one of 10 speakers at the New England Environmental Conference at Tufts University, said the laws were needed to protect the ozone layer in the upper atmosphere.

Chlorofluorocarbons are believed to damage the ozone layer's shielding effect, allowing the sun's harmful ultraviolet rays to penetrate the atmosphere Mr. Chafee told the 1,200 participants at the conference, which was sponsored by more than 180 organizations, that without international laws preventing the use of products containing these chemicals, there could be increased incidences of skin cancer and other diseases along with the extinction of certain plants and animals.

"Many people assume that we solved the problem when in 1978 the United States prohibited the use of CFC's in spray cans," Mr. Chafee said Sunday. "Unfortunately, many nations in the world have not enacted such prohibitions."

He also warned of "extraordinary changes in climate" from the "greenhouse effect," the warming of the planet caused by burning fuels and dangerously high levels of carbon dioxide.

"Shifts in rainfall, growing season and temperature in our Midwest could dramatically alter our ability to continue as a world leader in food production," he said, adding that the melting of the polar ice cap would raise the sea level to dangerous heights. "Coastal New England would be particularly hard hit," he said.

Mr. Chafee drew mixed reaction from the audience when he suggested that "the need to find nonfossil fuels may even make us swallow hard and move toward nuclear energy." ■

DECEMBER 13, 1987

THE GENOME PROJECT

Robert Kanigel

It would be the biggest, costliest, most provocative biomedical research project in history, and the United States must embark on it immediately. That was how Walter Gilbert, Nobel Prize-winning biology professor at Harvard University, heard the genome project described at scientific meetings all through 1985 and 1986. The undertaking—which would reveal the precise biochemical makeup of the entire genetic material, or genome, of a human being—would, he heard, revolutionize medicine. It would answer the Japanese challenge in biotechnology. It would grant insight into human biology previously held only by God.

At meetings in California and New Mexico, in New York and Washington, Gilbert watched the billion-dollar national project seize the imagination of scientists—yet threaten to stall over the form it should take and the speed at which it should proceed. So one day, as he sat through yet another meeting, it struck him that since the genome project had to be done, and it was going to be years, if ever, before the Government marshaled the resources and the will to undertake it, he, Walter Gilbert, would have to do it.

Early this year, Gilbert announced he would launch a new biotech venture, the Genome Corporation, whose sole purpose would be to "read" the human genome and sell the information that is deciphered. Gilbert's plans stirred immediate controversy. How, it was asked, could someone "own" the human genome? By what moral yardstick could it be exploited for private gain?

A robustly built, 55-year-old man with a gap-toothed Cheshire cat grin, Gilbert brims over with the intellectual mischievousness that has always steered him toward the hottest game in town. In the 1960's, he gave up a promising career in physics and charged into the emerging field of molecular biology. Later, without a lick of business experience, he helped start one of the first big biotech companies, Biogen, and made millions for himself and others—before being unceremoniously dismissed.

Is he now, as some suspect, trying to recreate in the Genome Corporation the heady excitement of the early Biogen days and to overturn his reputation as a brilliant scientist but failed businessman?

Gilbert has yet to line up financial backing and many are skeptical about his plans. But whether or not his company becomes a reality, most observers agree that the genome project, in one form or another, will happen anyway—and that when it does, it will change the face of biomedicine. It will set off, predicts Jack B. McConnell, director of advanced technology at Johnson & Johnson, a "third revolution in biotechnology." The first, McConnell says, brought vaccines, antibiotics, new drugs; the second, artificial hips, pacemakers and other such devices; the third could help speed the development of new treatments or possible cures for Down's syndrome, cystic fibrosis and the host of other genetic diseases (about 4,000), and could spark high-tech spinoffs on a scale not seen since the moon program.

In the new understanding it promises to give humans about themselves, the genome project also raises philosophical questions going back to Eden and the Tree of Knowledge: Can we know too much? For it would place in human hands the actual blueprints—in unremitting, look-it-up-in-the-dictionary detail—for how human beings are made, how they grow, how they differ among themselves and from other animals.

The elephants, polar bears and other animals chiseled into the brick walls surrounding the large central court of Harvard's Biological Laboratories once gave fair notice of the building's function. But in this building, where Walter Gilbert has made most of his discoveries and where his lab remains, researchers today explore not just living animals but the molecules that give them life. Foremost among them is the molecule that makes elephants elephants and humans human—the master molecule, DNA.

In the mid-1970's, Walter Gilbert developed with Allan Maxam (then a lab technician) a technique that, by chemically cutting DNA into segments of varying lengths, vastly simplified the reading of DNA messages. This rapid-sequencing method, together with a similar one developed by the British scientist Frederick Sanger, increased by a thousandfold the rate at which DNA information could be read, accelerating the pace of genetics research—and also earning both Gilbert and Sanger the Nobel Prize in Chemistry in 1980.

Yet today, only about 500 human genes (less than 1 percent of the total) have been decoded. Scientists are slogging through the human genome like a third-grader reading Kierkegaard. Even a steady rise in the rate of sequencing would leave the job unfinished until the 22nd century. The genome project would transform the whole scale of that effort. Making use of new sequencing machines and relying on large computers to store and manipulate the information, it would complete all three billion DNA bases by the year 2000 or soon after. ■

A cancer researchers uses ultraviolet light to study DNA in 1987.

APRIL 13, 1988

Harvard Gets Mouse Patent, a World First

Keith Schneider

Calling it a "singularly historic event," the United States today issued to Harvard University the world's first patent for a higher form of life, a mouse specially developed by researchers at the Harvard Medical School through techniques of genetic manipulation.

The United States Patent and Trademark Office issued patent No. 4,736,866 for "transgenic nonhuman mammals" developed by Dr. Philip Leder, a 53-year-old geneticist at Harvard Medical School, and Dr. Timothy A. Stewart, 35, a former Harvard researcher who is a senior scientist at Genentech Inc., a leading biotechnology company in South San Francisco.

The two scientists isolated a gene that causes cancer in many mammals, including humans, injected it into fertilized mouse eggs and developed a new breed of genetically altered mice.

Because half the females develop cancer, the altered breed serves as a more effective model for studying how genes contribute to cancer, particularly breast cancer, Dr. Leder said.

Other experts said the invention presented scientists with a more efficient biological system for testing new drugs and therapies to treat cancer, and for determining whether chemicals and other toxic substances found in food or the environment are harmful.

The announcement elated researchers and biotechnology industry executives who said it would attract more investments for research and lead to safer and more effective biological inventions in medicine, agriculture, forestry and other industries.

But critics, including several powerful members of Congress, protested the decision, arguing that a handful of officials appointed by the Reagan Administration had in a single act determined a new and important public policy without a public debate and in defiance of a request from Congress to delay the action.

The Patent Office decision recognizes the quickening pace of developments in biotechnology, particularly in creating and duplicating new forms of animals. Along with genetically engineered pigs, cattle and sheep that have been produced in laboratories across the country, scientists are also beginning to transform aquatic species.

A transgenic mouse, who has had alien genes introduced into its DNA for research purposes, on palm of Dr. Philip Leder, a Harvard Medical School Molecular geneticist.

JANUARY 3, 1989

Scientists Link '88 Drought to Natural Cycle in Tropical Pacific

William K. Stevens

Last year's killing drought in the United States was caused by massive, naturally occurring climatic forces in the tropical Pacific Ocean and had little to do with global warming caused by the greenhouse effect, according to new evidence.

The same complex forces, involving large-scale shifts in ocean temperatures and winds in the equatorial Pacific, affected not only North America. They also made themselves felt on the other side of the world, scientists say, causing the unusually heavy monsoon rains that in 1988 brought record floods, death and misery to Bangladesh.

These broad, intricately interconnected relationships between the ocean and the atmosphere have been only dimly understood in the past. But now climatologists are making major strides in understanding the ways in which such relationships in one part of the world drastically affect weather conditions, lives and fortunes in another.

While most climate experts believe that the greenhouse effect, a global warming caused by pollutants in the atmosphere, will have a major impact in the decades ahead, even those who argue most strongly for that point of view agree that last year's drought was overwhelmingly a product of natural forces. Even if a warming trend is already under way, as some experts believe, on a year-to-year basis events such as last year's changes in the Pacific exert a far stronger influence on the weather, scientists say.

The tropical Pacific is emerging in some scientists' minds as perhaps the planet's most important source of short-term climatic changes.

This is the territory of El Nino, the massive strip of abnormally warm water that from time to time stretches westward along the Equator from South America and that sometimes plays havoc with the weather in various parts of the world. But El Nino is only part of the story.

(cont'd. next page)

(continued from previous page)

Climatologists now recognize that it is not just a random phenomenon. It appears periodically, alternating with what has only recently been identified as its opposite twin: an abnormally cold stretch of equatorial water.

Scientists disagree on what to call the cold cycle. It was first dubbed La Nina, Spanish for "the girl," to distinguish it from El Nino, which means "the boy," or Christ Child, so named because the warm cycle appears near Christmas. Some scientists objected to La Nina as sexist, however, and substituted El Viejo, "the old man," as in Old Man Winter. Still others prefer to avoid all this by simply calling the cycles warm events and cold events.

It was this cold cycle in the eastern Pacific, some scientists now say, that played a major role in creating the great North American drought of 1988 and the devastating floods that inundated Bangladesh.

Precisely what triggers a warm or cold phase is not yet perfectly understood, but scientists believe they know much about the general processes at work. A cold phase, such as now exists, develops when strong trade winds, blowing from the east, drive warm surface water to the western Pacific. At the same time, there is an increased upwelling of cold water from the ocean depths off South America. ■

Climatologists now recognize that it is not just a random phenomenon

MARCH 25, 1989

LARGEST U.S. TANKER SPILL SPEWS 270,000 BARRELS OF OIL OFF ALASKA

Philip Shabecoff

Tugboats tow the oil tanker Exxon Valdez off Bligh Reef in Prince William Sound.

A tanker filled to capacity with crude oil ran aground and ruptured yesterday 25 miles from the southern end of the Trans Alaska Pipeline, spewing her cargo into water rich in marine life.

By evening the ship, the Exxon Valdez, had sent more than 270,000 barrels, or about 38,500 tons, of oil into Prince William Sound, making this the largest tanker spill in United States history.

Opponents of further development of Arctic oilfields quickly seized on the spill as evidence of what they perceive as the environmental risks involved.

By early evening the spill was about 5 miles long and 500 feet wide, said Petty Officer John Gonzales, a spokesman for the Coast Guard station at the port of Valdez, from which the Exxon Valdez departed late Thursday, bound for Long Beach, Calif., with her load of 1,260,000 barrels.

Petty Officer Gonzales said no one had died or been injured in the accident. He said the Exxon Valdez had been maneuvering around icebergs when she ran aground on Bligh Reef, 25 miles south of the port, about 10:30 A.M. yesterday, Eastern standard time. Whether the maneuvering was the cause of the accident is under investigation, he said.

David Parish, a spokesman for Exxon, said the company did not expect major environmental damage as a result of the spill.

But environmentalists and marine biologists expressed fear that the spill would cause drastic damage to the abundant marine life in Prince William Sound, including otters, whales, porpoises, sea birds and fish. They said the spill could mean severe losses to Alaska's fishermen, because in this season pink salmon are migrating from the coast to the ocean and herring are moving in toward the shore.

Several environmentalists said the spill raised anew questions about the wisdom of continuing to develop oil on Alaska's North Slope, sending it south across the state through the pipeline and loading it onto tankers. They insisted that this kind of accident provided another argument against the Government's plans to open up the Arctic National Wildlife Refuge on the North Slope to oil development.

The spokesman said bird experts from the Fish and Wildlife Service had been sent to Alaska to try to save an undetermined number of sea birds already fouled by the oil.

The oil industry has contended that its safety and environmental record in Alaska is excellent and that the fears of opponents of North Slope oil development have failed to materialize in the 12 years since the Trans Alaska Pipeline was opened. ■

AUGUST 20, 1989

VOYAGER CAMERAS DISCOVER A TURBULENT BLUE NEPTUNE

John Noble Wilford

As Voyager 2 closes in for the first fly-by of Neptune on Thursday night, its cameras are already giving scientists a clear view of the planet, a beautiful blue orb in dark space, and discovering it to be a surprisingly dynamic world of thick gases roiled by 400-mile-an-hour winds and a storm system the size of Mars.

The spacecraft has also just detected intense natural radio emissions from Neptune, indicating that it has a magnetic field generated by fluid motions in a planet's core. The emissions are produced around planets by high-velocity charged particles as they spiral along magnetic field lines into the planet's atmosphere.

Photographs transmitted by Voyager in the last few days have especially surprised and confounded scientists. Because heat drives planetary weather, the scientists found it astonishing that a planet out where the sunlight is dim could muster the energy to generate such violent winds and storms.

"It's just amazing," said Dr. Andrew Ingersoll, a planetary meteorologist at the California Institute of Technology. "The energy for winds is weaker at Neptune than at Jupiter, and yet the turbulent atmosphere there is similar to Jupiter's."

The scientists have no theories yet on why the atmosphere is so turbulent. The most recent pictures, made public today, showed in the greatest detail yet the huge storm system, known as the Great Dark Spot, in Neptune's southern hemisphere. Discovered in early pictures three months ago, the storm can now be tracked in time-lapse sequences as it pulsates and twists with cyclonic force.

At Neptune, its last planetary target, Voyager will be almost 2.8 billion miles from Earth, a distance so great that it takes 4 hours and 6 minutes for the radio signals bearing its pictures and data to arrive at tracking stations. Neptune is currently the farthest planet from the Sun. Pluto, with its elongated orbit, moved closer to the Sun than Neptune in 1979 and will again move farther away in 1999. ■

A view of Neptune taken from Voyager 2 spacecraft.

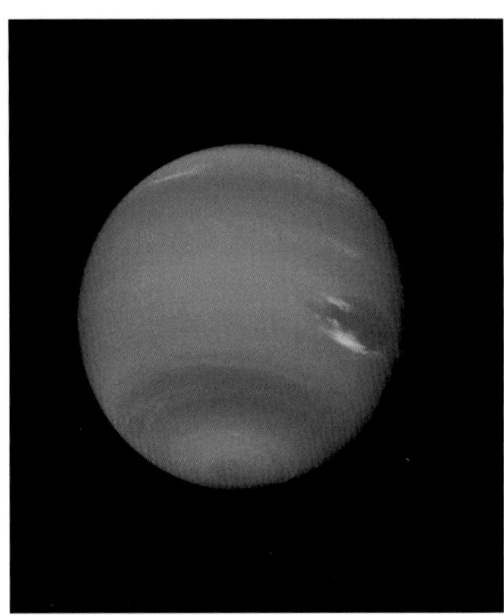

Rival Scientists Decide Universe Is Composed of 3 Types of Matter

By Malcolm W. Browne

Using two giant particle accelerators, one in Europe and the other in California, rival teams of scientists have established beyond reasonable doubt that the universe contains no more than three fundamental types of matter.

The discovery, reported yesterday by the Stanford Linear Accelerator Center in California and by the European Laboratory for Particle Physics in Geneva, is a scientific landmark with far-reaching implications for physics, astronomy and cosmology.

Settling the question of how many types of matter the universe might embody has long been a major quest of physicists. But the equipment needed to perform the necessary experiments was beyond the reach of technology until recently. The completion of new, powerful particle accelerators finally achieved the goal.

There had been evidence over the last few months that the number of types of matter was three, but with yesterday's announcement this assumption became a virtual certainty.

The nearly simultaneous disclosures by the two laboratories reflect the intensity of the competition between them, in which Nobel prizes and other rewards might be at stake. Scientists at Stanford held a news conference yesterday to report their achievement, and scientists in Europe promptly accused the Stanford group of trying to upstage their own results, which were scheduled to be made public today.

The new accelerator results strongly reinforce theories about how the universe developed after its violent birth.

It has long been known that matter consists of more than 100 different kinds of particles, but in the last two decades, physicists realized that this bewildering array is made up of combinations of a handful of "fundamental" particles. Physicists have been able to group these particles in three distinct "families."

The first family, from which all familiar matter is made, consists of "up" and "down" quarks, the constituents of the protons and neutrons in atomic nuclei; the electron, and a particle called the electron neutrino. Neutrinos have no electric charge and no measured mass as yet, and as such are very difficult to study. They nevertheless play crucial roles in the structure of matter and the entire universe.

Two other families of fundamental particles have been discovered in special kinds of matter, those created by high-energy particle accelerators or carried by cosmic rays. The second family includes "charmed" and "strange" quarks, the muon, and the muon neutrino. The third family consists of "top" and "bottom" quarks, the first of which has yet to be detected; the tau particle, and the tau neutrino. ■

OCTOBER 19, 1989

Shuttle Launched After Delay and Galileo Is Sent to Jupiter

John Noble Wilford

The space shuttle Atlantis rocketed into orbit today to send the Galileo spacecraft on its planned six-year, 2.5-billion-mile journey to Jupiter.

On the fifth orbit, the crew of Atlantis released the 2.5-ton Galileo from the cargo bay at 7:15 P.M. The astronauts maneuvered the shuttle out of the way, and an hour later, the rocket attached to Galileo fired to boost the spacecraft out of Earth orbit.

Minutes later, the second stage of the solid-fuel rocket was fired, sending the spacecraft on its interplanetary trajectory.

Operations of the Galileo rocket were controlled by an Air Force center in Sunnyvale, Calif., 37 miles south of San Francisco. The center suffered some minor damage in the earthquake but was restored to normal service early today.

Jubilant scientists hailed the launching of the long-delayed Galileo mission to orbit Jupiter, the largest planet. During the mission, an instrumented probe will be fired into the Jovian atmosphere.

Lennard A. Fisk, the space agency's associate administrator for science, called this the beginning of "the second golden age in the exploration of the solar system."

Scientists believe that Galileo's 745-pound probe, which is to penetrate deep into the dense hydrogen atmosphere, could give them important clues about primordial conditions in the solar system and perhaps insights into the validity of the "big bang" theories of the creation of the universe. ■

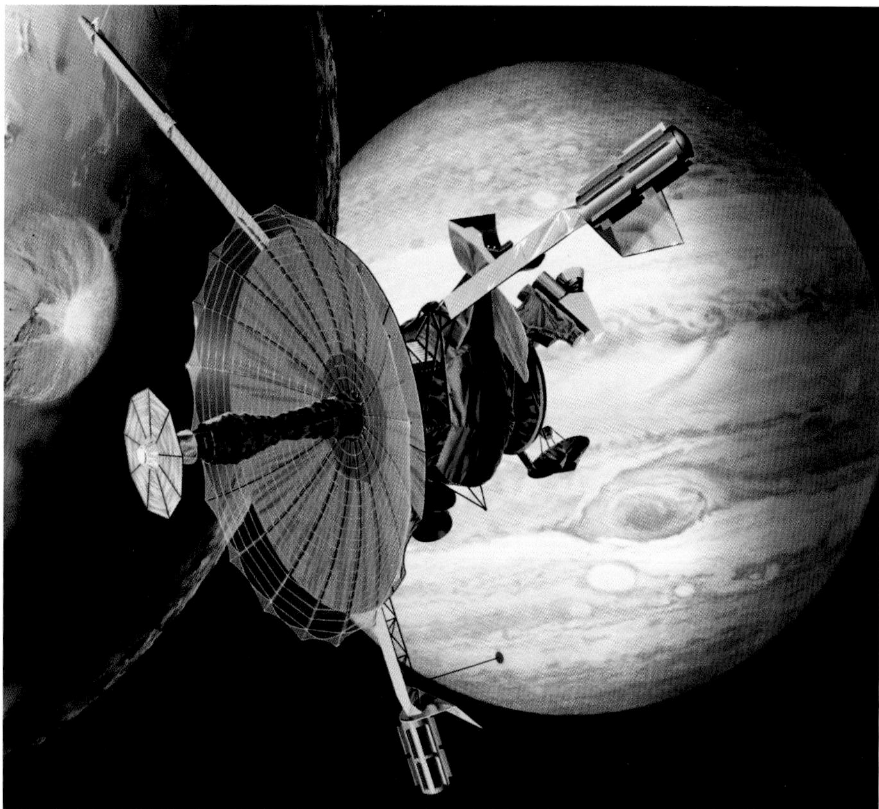

NASA's Galileo probe passing over one of Jupiter's 16 moons.

DECEMBER 12, 1989

South Pole Emerging as Center of Astronomy

Malcolm W. Browne

Fighting chronic fatigue caused by thin air and deadly cold, scientists here are assembling a new type of telescope that may reveal the mysterious origin of cosmic rays.

The new instrument is the first large telescope ever brought to the South Pole. It is part of a concerted campaign begun recently to exploit Antarctica's unique physical qualities for astronomical research.

Among the other new Antarctic projects expected to shed light on cosmic rays will be the launching from Ross Island later this month of a gigantic balloon.

The balloon, flown by the National Aeronautics and Space Administration, will carry four astronomical experiments, including two cosmic-ray analyzers built at the University of California at Berkeley. Scientists expect the winds at altitudes more than 100,000 feet to carry the balloon westward along the 78th parallel completely around the world in about 15 days, perhaps returning to within a few hundred miles of its launching site.

The South Pole is now basking in 24-hour-a-day summer sun at the relatively mild temperature of about minus-10 degrees Fahrenheit, and many scientists shed their red National Science Foundation parkas while working outdoors. But the touch of an unprotected fingertip to cold metal can produce pain and frostbite.

Another problem is the altitude. The South Pole is 9,300 feet high, and because the air is very cold, it is as thin as the air on top of an 11,000-foot-high elevation in a temperate zone. People living at the Pole grow accustomed to having a difficult time sleeping, tiring quickly and becoming absent-minded. A lack of oxygen makes a few of them sick.

But despite the discomforts and the monotonous view of the featureless polar plateau, astronomers are delighted with the scientific advantages of the site.

"The time has finally come when Antarctica is coming into its own as a major center for important astronomical research," said Dr. Robert M. Morse of the University of Wisconsin. ■

FEBRUARY 28, 1980

Small Computer Software Gains

Peter J. Schuyten

There is something new and novel in publishing these days, and the name is computer software. Although in its infancy, this is a business, according to some observers, that in time could produce the next Doubleday or Harper & Row. But these are not conventional publishing houses like a Doubleday. Rather, they are small independent companies whose sole or main business is the production of computer software for those smallest of data procession machines—the "personal" computer.

The companies, there are only a handful of them, produce five-inch record-like computer disks, known as "floppies" containing the software instructions that govern the operations of these machines. They are sold at retail, typically in a computer store.

Despite early and overly optimistic notices, the market for these computers has not exploded. Rather, these machines have remained pretty much the province of the hobbyist or technically inclined layman whose primary motivation in owning a computer is to learn about data processing. And to hear some in the industry tell it, the market is near saturation point. The problem is that even people who perceive the need for a small computer don't want to learn the programming.

"There is no such thing as a real personal computer yet," said Daniel H. Fylstra, a founder and president of Personal Software, based in Sunnydale, Calif. "We won't see the emergence of a mass market until there are computer programs that are easy to use and intuitive from a user's point of view." ■

SEPTEMBER 23, 1980

CHESS COMPUTERS MOVE TOWARD MASTERY OVER HUMANS

Joseph Williams

Down a bishop and two pawns, peering at the board from behind a pair of spectacles, the chess player had a carefully hidden plan. Patiently, he waited for the computer to act. Then, when he was handed a printout of the computer's next move, his face crinkled with a smirk of delight. Quickly he took the rook pawn with his queen, checkmating his mechanical opponent. Man had won. Computer had lost. Again.

The lesson was an old one: Chess mastery does not come easily, even for computers. Man—at least, the most skilled of his kind—is still better than the very best computer. But the world computer chess championships starting Thursday in Linz, Austria, will provide a significant indication of how far computers have come and how intense the race is to improve their playing ability.

The four-day tournament will put forward an international field of 16 computer programs. Some programs will be run on portable computers at the tournament site; others will be at fixed locations in their home countries, with moves transmitted by telephone.

On another front, programmers are undoubtedly working more intensely these days because of a recently announced $100,000 prize for the first computer program to beat humans in the traditional world championship. That prize will be provided by the Fredkin Foundation of Cambridge Mass., and administered by Carnegie-Mellon University in Pittsburgh.

Ken Thompson of Bell Laboratories in Murray Hill, N.J., has opted for this intense searching technique, and he has achieved notable success in a program named Belle. The program will compete in the Linz tournament.

The heart of the Belle program is its hardware. Mr. Thompson has 10 hard-wired modules connected to his computer which he said enables the computer to analyze "about 100,000 positions per second" to a depth of seven or eight piles, or about 18 million positions in three minutes.

Experts are optimistic about the future of chess-playing computers. Many of the portable microcomputer chess games available in stores can beat the average player, but tackling grandmasters will be more difficult.

Hans Berliner (right front) with his Hitech computer and Robert Hyatt (left front) with Cray XMP 48 computer using his "Blitz" program during a computer chess tournament in which Hitech won in 1986.

OCTOBER 23, 1980

Manufacturers Using Robots

Agis Salpukas

At most of the nation's plants that turn out planes, tractors, trucks, machine tools or motors in quantities that do not lend themselves to large assembly-line production, the methods of manufacturing have changed little since World War II.

Most of the great variety of parts needed for such products are cast, machined and assembled by hand in batches, usually about 10 batches a day of about 20 parts per batch. It is this type of manufacturing that has been difficult and expensive to automate and thus has remained largely in the hands of blue-collar workers whose productivity has shown little grown. But, increasingly, companies have been turning to the use of automated robots to perform such tasks.

Dennis E. Wisnosky, manager of the Manufacturing Organization and Automation Technology Center at the International Harvester Corporation, told a symposium on Industrial Automation and Robotics last week that his company was planning to spend about $2 billion in the next five years in an attempt to bring major improvements in many of its plants.

Mr. Wisnosky said that American manufacturers had little choice but to update the manufacturing process, since Japan, its major competitor, was already ahead of the rest of the world in applying robots. In terms of the number of advanced robots already on the plant floor, Japan has about 7,500, the United States 5,000 and Western Europe 4,000.

Up to now, most of the industrial robots put into use have been what Phillippe Villers, president of Automatix Inc., called "dumb" robots—those that can do a series of programmed tasks but cannot adapt to changes in their environment. But the greatest growth in robot manufacturing, he said, will come in robots that are "smart." Such robots could have some ability of sight or touch, such as being able to pick the right parts off a conveyor belt and put them into a computer-controlled machine tool.

Sparks flying as robots weld raw metal car frames on an assembly line at a Honda plant in the early 1980s.

Texas Instruments Inc., he noted, has already set up a system of robots to test small calculators. A nimble robot picks up the calculators from test machines while another presses keys in a predetermined way. A third robot "reads" to see if the calculator has come up with the right answers. ■

AUGUST 27, 1980

DISCLOSURE ON RADAR-EVADING PLANE ASSAILED AT HOUSE PANEL'S HEARING

Richard Burt

Washington, Aug. 27—Members of a House subcommittee charged today that secret information on an experimental aircraft able to evade Soviet radar detection was leaked to a journalist so that the Defense Department could justify announcing the existence of the plane.

The charge was made after the journalist, Benjamin F. Schemmer, told members of the House Armed Services subcommittee on research and development that senior Pentagon aide disclosed details of the Air Force's "stealth" aircraft program and encouraged him to write an article about it last week. Mr. Schemmer, editor of the Armed Forces Journal, said he was given details about the aircraft four days before Secretary of Defense Harold R. Brown held a news conference on the subject.

Mr. Schemmer said in sworn testimony that in a Pentagon briefing he was told that Mr. Brown would not announce the project until his article appeared. The disclosure that Mr. Schemmer apparently received an officially sanctioned leak is almost certain to fuel the growing debate over whether the Carter Administration is misusing sensitive national security information for political purposes.

In today's hearing, several members of Congress made similar charges, suggesting that Mr. Schemmer had been given information on the "stealth" program so that the Pentagon would have some justification for announcing that it was working on a new generation of aircraft. The chairman of the subcommittee, Representative Samuel S. Stratton, Democrat of New York, said that "it is clear from information that has been given us that the Department of Defense is more interested in convincing the public that it is doing a great job than in keeping our secrets from the Soviet Union." ■

AUGUST 23, 1981

NEXT, A COMPUTER ON EVERY DESK

IBM PC Model 5150 with printer, 1981.

Andrew Pollack

It used to be that a little money and a little inventiveness would go a long way in the personal computer business. Apple Computer, it is now legend, was started by two college dropouts working in a garage. The Tandy Corporation, now one of the industry's leaders, invested just $150,000 to develop its first computer.

Now the ante is rising dramatically. The race is intensifying, and the personal computer industry is seeing an influx of participants. In June, the Xerox Corporation became the first major office equipment company to enter the market. Then, 11 days ago, the biggest of them all, the International Business Machines Corporation, jumped in. Other large computer and office equipment companies will likely enter the fray, and many Japanese companies are waiting in the wings.

In particular, I.B.M.'s entry erased any lingering doubts that personal computers are serious business and no place for the puny or the mere tinkerer, except around the edges of the market.

Worldwide, some 500,000 computers costing less than $5,000 were sold last year at a total value of $730 million, according to Dataquest Inc., a Cupertino, Calif., market research firm. That total will grow at least 40 percent annually, to 3.7 million units, valued at $3.9 billion, in 1985, the firm estimates.

And with computer power becoming available to the masses, entire new businesses are opening up around it. Such services as electronic information retrieval and the writing of programs, or software, allow businessmen, engineers, schoolchildren and housewives to make greater use of the machines.

The entry of many big companies like I.B.M. will change the market, but it also reflects changes already occurring. The industry is moving to a second generation of machines, which will use microprocessors capable of handling 16 "bits," or units of information, at the same time, twice the processing power of existing 8-bit machines.

I.B.M.'s machine was one of the first by a major manufacturer to use the 16-bit microprocessor, but most others in the industry are expected to match that eventually. The new generation will thus be faster and capable of handling more complex tasks and larger memories.

(cont'd. next page)

(continued from previous page)

Alternatively—and much more important, according to some experts—the new generation of machines could be used to perform the same tasks computers now do but be much easier to use. In effect, the machine would do more of the work and the user less. Instead of having to type detailed instructions on a keyboard, using a special language, in a few years users will be able to communicate with computers more like they do with fellow human beings. Computers might develop the ability to understand the particular nuances and style of their owners.

"They will have as much stored knowledge of what you know, what you've said, what you've done than any friend would have the patience to learn," predicts William H. Gates, president of Microsoft, a Bellevue, Wash., company that has designed software for many personal computer manufacturers, including I.B.M.

The market for personal computers is also changing and is segmenting. While personal computers are often thought of as home computers, the industry definition is of any machine inexpensive enough for one person to own and use, whether at home or at work. And while the personal computer started as a device for the computer hobbyist, its major market by far has turned out to be the small business user and professionals, such as doctors, writers and farmers who use the computer for their accounting, inventory, mailing lists and word processing, either at home or in the office. According to Future Computing, a Dallas consulting firm, small business use accounts for nearly half the sales of under-$10,000 units.

Personal computers are also finding a place in large corporations. A large company might give all its analysts or engineers personal computers to replace or supplement a larger computer they all had to share. Computers can be linked together in networks so that workers can send memos to one another electronically.

A separate market seems to be emerging, directed at the home market. Whereas computers used for business sell for at least $2,000 and have one or more disk storage devices to hold programs and files, the computers aimed at the home market are clustered at $300 to $600. Such machines, offered now by Tandy, Commodore, Atari and Texas Instruments, are merely electronic keyboards that attach to one's television set and emphasize games and education.

Experts generally do not expect the home market really to start growing until 1985 because there is not much that can be done with them yet.

The presence of hundreds of programs and numerous peripherals for the Apple, as well as the fact that Apple is carried by 1,000 of the 1,500 computer retail stores, give Apple great momentum.

Apple, however, has recently run into several problems as a result of its rapid growth. The Apple III, which was designed to be a larger version of the Apple II, was introduced in May 1980, but ran into manufacturing problems and was plagued by technical flaws. Apple finally got the product to market last March but there is still not much software available. The system is selling at a rate of 1,000 a month, compared to more than 15,000 a month for the Apple II. Because it is not firmly established, and because of its higher price, the Apple III is considered much more vulnerable to attack by I.B.M. than the Apple II. If Apple introduces a 16-bit machine within a year, it will further undermine its sales of the Apple III.

OCTOBER 11, 1981

Word Processors Spell Out a New Role for Clerical Staff

Sharon Johnson

The growing business reliance on word processors, those small computers with typewriter-like keyboards designed to complete routine reports and other rote clerical chores, has barely begun, but it already is having a profound effect on the office of the present as well as the future.

Where there was one word processor for every 10 clerical workers last year, by mid-decade the figure will be one for every three.

Experts predict a radical restructuring of work, including a devaluation of current work skills and the creation of new ones.

"The emphasis on typing speed also will decline because these machines make it possible for secretaries to handle more work in less time," said John J. Connell, executive director of the Office Technology Research Group, a Pasadena, Calif., organization of managers from 44 foreign and domestic companies concerned with managing change in the office. "Instead of spending 20 percent of her day typing, the typical secretary will spend only 10 percent in the years ahead. Secretaries will have more time to devote to intellectual tasks that are now done by their bosses and other managers."

One of the biggest problems to be overcome is worker resistance. "The use of word processors has meant a slight improvement in the working lives of some clerical workers because it has removed the drudgery of repetitive typing," said Karen Nussbaum, director of Working Women, a group representing female office workers. "But for millions of others, it has meant that they are assigned to centers where they do nothing but baby-sit machines for eight hours." ■

compute

NOVEMBER 15, 1981

VIDEO GAMES: A GLUTTON FOR GLOBS...AND QUARTERS

Katya Goncharoff

There are no fire buttons, warp buttons or hyperspace buttons. Bombers, fighter planes, mutants, asteroids and space invaders are nowhere to be seen.

For a year now, the best seller in the $5-billion-a-year video-game market has been Pac-man, a hide-and-seek game that has to do with eating fruit, gobbling energy dots, and eluding amorphous monster globs. It is made by the Midway division of the Bally Corporation.

"At first blush, Pac-man seems like a kid's game, but anyone can be entranced by it," says Ray E. Tilley, managing editor of Playmeter, a trade magazine that reports on coin-operated amusements.

Since Pac-man was introduced in October 1980, the video game playing public has been entranced in excess of $1 billion, according to industry analysts. That adds up to more than four billion quarters consumed by Pac-man alone. The price of a Pac-man ranges from $2,500 to $3,000, depending on the model.

"Pac-man is the most popular video game ever," says Harold Vogel, games analyst at Merrill Lynch. "It's had an unusual life span already. With 100,000 units out there, that's an all-time record."

On some college campuses and at resorts, games like Pac-man can earn up to $500 a week. For that reason, pinball and video-game arcades usually have five or six or more Pac-mans, and video games can now be found at suburban family entertainment centers, in college dormitories, in movie theater lobbies, at supermarkets and airports—even at a taco stand on 72nd Street on the West Side of Manhattan.

Wherever a Pac-man game appears, it is often a standout not only because it makes money but because, unlike most successful video games, it has nothing to do with war, space or shooting. According to a Paine Webber report entitled "Video Games: A New Growth Industry," these are three activities that appeal especially to men. The report points out that the Pac-man game appeals to nearly as many women as men and thus has a broader player base.

The game itself is difficult to describe. As one player, a snack bar manager who averages seven to eight hours of video game play a week, explains it, "It is so simple, but it has no relation to reality. It's different from space games, tank games and war games. The motivation is eating. This creature moves and eats dots."

Pac Man video game screen.

129

FEBRUARY 15, 1982

Big Plans for Little Computer

HAYWARD, Calif.— In an industry in which egos frequently are as large as the products are small, Adam Osborne may take the prize for each.

Mr. Osborne is the founder and president of the Osborne Computer Corporation, which makes a portable, mass-marketed personal computer that is quickly gaining popularity.

Mr. Osborne, at 42 years of age one of the "old-timers" in the personal computer industry, obviously perceives a hole in the market. He founded the privately held company with $250,000 of his own money in 1980 and rapidly produced a microcomputer that folds up to the size of a suitcase, fits under an airplane seat and weighs just 24 pounds.

Shipments began last summer, and between June and November, Osborne recorded $1 million in sales and quickly became profitable. With a 25-month backlog of orders, Mr. Osborne is boldly predicting now that he will sell $200 million worth of computers by the end of 1982, a total that would be more than half the revenues posted by Apple Computer Inc. in 1981, its fifth year.

Mr. Osborne said he was currently shipping more than 120 machines a day, but expected to be at a 1,000-a-day rate by the end of the year. That would put his company at the same shipping rate as the industry's largest manufacturers.

Osborne, which employs 150 persons, "may have the steepest sales slope of any company," said Ben Rosen, a New York electronics industry analyst whose venture capital fund has invested a small amount of money in Osborne Computer.

The Osborne 1 sells for $1,795. Packaged all in one case, the microcomputer, built around an eight-bit microprocessor, includes a five-inch display screen and two floppy-disk drives for storing data. By comparison, most other computers with similar equipment, but perhaps with potential for more data storage, sell for about $2,500.

Besides portability and low price, Mr. Osborne brought a third new feature to the personal computer marketplace: Included in the price are two applications software packages, one for word processing and one for financial analysis.

Mr. Osborne said his next step would be to introduce more computer products at the low end of the price range. He would not give details of his plans, but said he would drop "a cherry bomb" when competition moved into his territory. ■

Osborne 01 microcomputer system, 1982.

NOVEMBER 2, 1983

THE DEBUT OF I.B.M.'S JUNIOR

Andrew Pollack

The International Business Machines Corporation yesterday introduced its first computer designed specifically for use in the home, but said the $700 machine would not be available for the upcoming holiday buying season.

Consumers will not be able to buy the long anticipated computer, called the PCjr (pronounced PC Junior), until early next year and it will be in limited supply even then, the company said.

The home computer industry has been characterized by severe price cutting, which helped lead to last week's announcement by the Texas Instruments Corporation that it was quitting the business. There is also a growing disenchantment among consumers who are finding that the machines, many of which carry base prices of $200 and less, can do little more than play games.

The PCjr, long known in the industry as the "Peanut," will come in two versions. The basic machine will have 64K bytes, or 64,000 characters, of internal memory and will sell for $700. It will have two slots for cartridges, similar to video game cartridges, that contain programs for the computer. A television or a special video monitor, not included in the price, could be used as a screen.

The enhanced version, which will sell for $1,300, will have 128K bytes, or 128,000 characters, of memory and a disk drive capable of storing an additional 360,000 characters. It will also include the cartridge slots.

The basic Apple IIe, with 64,000 characters of memory, has a list price of $1,400, without the disk drive needed to run programs. That compares with the basic $700 PCjr. Apple, which has already lost market share to the I.B.M. PC in the office market, is expected to have to cut the price of the IIe to remain competitive in the home and education market. ■

DECEMBER 6, 1983

'WINDOWS' AND 'GATEWAYS' LOOM IN NEAR FUTURE

Erik Sandberg-Diment

The Computer Dealers Exposition, or Comdex, was held in Las Vegas this year.

Comdex, if not guaranteed to provide ultimate answers, at least lays out all the potential new candidates in one huge exhibition, flowing out of the Las Vegas Convention Center and onto the floors and ballrooms of nearby hotels.

Gateways were to this year's show what mice were to last year's. Then everyone was unofficially demonstrating his own version of the mouse, the cigarette-pack-sized pointer that, attached by its tail of cable to the computer, allows the cursor on the screen to be moved without using the keyboard.

Me-too competition was keenly evident in the software world of windows. "Windows" is the current (or soon to be so) buzzword in user-friendliness. They allow your personal computer to become the ultimate messy desk, at least metaphorically. You can pile all the paperwork in your drawers, files and shoeboxes into layers and layers of electronic papers on your screen.

For you to get at this material, the display is split into numerous smaller screens, or windows, each providing a glimpse of enough to let you determine more or less what's hidden and whether you want to deal with it at the moment.

Windows will be available sometime in 1984. At the moment three major software houses—Visicorp, Microsoft and Quarterdeck—are attempting to convince buyers that their particular windows, once they manage to get them open, are the only ones through which to view the world.

My own feeling is that windows are as likely to lead some computer owners to defenestration as to success in dealing with data. Still, windows may find a niche in business computing. Technology always seems to find a place for itself somewhere—well, perhaps not always. ■

JANUARY 16, 1984

APPLE EXPANDS PRODUCT LINE

Andrew Pollack

The Apple III computer.

LOS ANGELES, Jan. 15—One year ago Apple Computer Inc. hoped to dazzle the computer world with a revolutionary new machine called Lisa that was said to be the key to the company's future. But Lisa turned out to be a poor seller, and Apple's earnings and its leadership in the personal computer market crumpled under an attack from the International Business Machines Corporation.

Now Apple is preparing to try again with another new machine called Macintosh, which will be introduced at the company's annual meeting on Jan. 24. The stakes for Apple are even higher now, especially if it wants to remain a force in the computer business. It is Apple's third and probably last chance to reduce its dependence on its Apple II line, which is nearly seven years old.

Macintosh, which is expected to sell for $2,500, is only part of Apple's strategy. The company is also announcing newer, faster versions of its Lisa with an entry price as low as $3,500. And later in the year the company is expected to announce two new versions of its Apple IIe and to push that product more strongly into the home market.

Apple had a number of setbacks in 1983 after several years of breakneck growth. I.B.M., which entered the personal computer business in 1981, quickly surged to the lead in terms of revenues and significance. Apple actually sold more computers than I.B.M. did last year—but at a lower price as I.B.M. forced Apple out of the profitable office market and into the home and educational markets. Apple had no mainstream office computer with which to respond, since its Apple III had never caught on, and the Lisa, priced initially at $10,000, was too expensive.

Meanwhile, Apple's earnings plunged. The company earned only $5.1 million in the quarter ended last Sept. 30. That was 73 percent below the level of a year earlier. John Sculley, Apple's president and chief executive officer, who was hired from Pepsico Inc. last spring, has said low earnings would continue for two more quarters.

Apple declines to comment on forthcoming announcements, but industry sources indicate that the basic Macintosh will sell for $2,500. It will include 128,000 characters of memory, a high-resolution black-and-white nine-inch screen and one disk drive storing about 400,000 characters of information. The disks will be 3 1/2 inches in diameter, compared with the traditional 5 1/4 inches.

The development of Macintosh was headed by Steven P. Jobs, Apple's chairman. Macintosh will use the same technology as Lisa. Thus users will be able to accomplish various tasks by pointing to symbols on the screen with a palm-sized device called a "mouse."

However, Macintosh's relatively small memory is expected to limit its capacity, especially compared with Lisa, to simultaneously display different programs in different "windows" on the screen and to move information from one program to another. Such transfer between programs is useful, for instance, if someone wants to take budget projections calculated with a program called a spreadsheet and insert them into a letter being written using a word-processing program.

Sources say the computer at first will come with two programs: MacWrite, a word-processing program, and MacPaint, which allows users to draw images on the screen by moving the mouse. A dot matrix printer capable of printing the images drawn on the screen as well as text will be included for an extra $500 in the introductory offer.

Macintosh is expected to weigh slightly less than 20 pounds and to come with an optional cloth carrying case. ■

MARCH 28, 1984

ELECTRONIC OFFICE CONJURING WONDERS, LONELINESS AND TEDIUM

William Serrin

Rebecca Alford arrives each weekday at 7 A.M. for her job processing health claims at a life insurance company in Syracuse. For the next nine hours, except for breaks and lunch, her day is dominated by a computer.

Mrs. Alford says her job at the Equitable Life Assurance Company is monotonous and is paced by strict output standards, and that workers are intensely scrutinized by superiors. "If you stop working, they ask you what you are stopping for," she says. "Pinning you to a computer, I don't like that at all."

She works at a video display terminal alongside some 55 workers in the department, processing 70 claims a day. She gets a 15-minute break in the morning and a hour off for lunch.

Mrs. Alford, who is 30 years old, earns $217 to $400 a week, depending on production. She says the pay standards, a form of piece work, are so complicated that workers do not know how much they will earn each week.

Her work environment is a manifestation of the electronic office, in which many tasks are performed with the help of computers and other new technologies.

As typewriters and other office equipment are replaced by video display terminals all over the country, clerical workers and, to an increasing extent, professional and management workers are feeling the effects. Many, like Mrs. Alford, find the work monotonous and boring. But many others are pleased and say the new technologies make the work less time-consuming by removing tedious tasks of the past.

The technologies, which many experts say constitute one of the more important developments in the workplace in the 1980's, are bringing fundamental changes in the way office work is organized and performed in general business offices, insurance companies, brokerage houses, banks and the like.

In recent years, the number of electronic work stations in use has risen markedly, and it is expected to increase substantially, authorities say. Today some 12.7 million video display terminals, personal computers, word processors and the like are in use in the United States, with the number expected to rise to 41 million by 1987, according to International Data Corporation, a market research company in Framingham, Mass.

The computerization, some experts say, means a continuing decline in what has been called the social office. Doris McLaughlin, a technology specialist at the University of Michigan, says the technologies "are making work a lot more lonely."

"It's tedious, it's boring," Gladys Hunter, 45 years old, says of her clerical job at a Cleveland bank. "Some girls are bringing in radios, with headphones, to get them through the night," she says.

"We're not talking about eliminating the human factor," says Randy J. Goldfield, a computer consultant with Omni Group. "All we can do is have the machines do the grunt work a lot faster. We're talking about removing a lot of the low-level work from the desks of secretaries and even professionals and having it automated, and presumably providing a bonus factor of available time in which people can be more creative and productive."

Five office workers at Harvard University said they enjoyed a number of aspects of the new technologies. "It's a joy not to have to retype," said Christina Knapp, a Harvard secretary.

Anne Miller, a worker at the Widener Library, said the machines offered explosive gains in the collection of information and making information available to scholars and the general public.

Barbara Lewis, a secretary at Harvard, said, "I feel I'm doing six days' work in five."

The women contended that many university workers feared job loss because of the technologies.

Miss Knapp said, "If you're not quick, you're shunted to other work." She says the issue is participation. "We would welcome the technologies if we felt we could feel some control over what happens to us," she said.

APRIL 9, 1984

APPLE PLANS PORTABLE COMPUTER

David E. Sanger

In two weeks Apple Computer Inc. plans to introduce a briefcase-size, battery-operated version of its popular Apple IIe that analysts say could pose a significant challenge to the International Business Machine Corporation's PCjr home computer.

The new Apple IIc, the company's first portable computer, will be shown to the public on April 24 in San Francisco. Its introduction, at a base price of $1,295, marks the second major product announcement by Apple in three months aimed directly at I.B.M.'s growing share of the personal computer market; the Macintosh, Apple's powerful and so far highly successful entry against the I.B.M. Personal Computer, was brought out in late January.

Apple officials decline to discuss the new IIc publicly, but they have already allowed some industry analysts brief glimpses of the machine. By all accounts, it weighs about 7 1/2 pounds, excluding a 5-pound battery pack, and includes 128,000 characters of internal memory. It also feature a full- sized keyboard, and an optional "mouse," a handheld pointer device similar to the one used on Apple's Lisa and Macintosh machines to control the movement of a cursor on the computer's screen.

The computer also comes with a single floppy disk drive, for permanent data storage, tucked into the side of the machine. A $300 printer, capable of reproducing seven colors, is also expected. ■

Apple Macintosh portable computer, 1989.

MAY 31, 1987

KEEP THE PICTURE, BUT TOSS THE CAMERA

"In the past the camera was one of our most important icons, as significant as the picture itself. Now it's convenience and the picture that counts."

The words are those of Ray Brown, professor of popular culture at Bowling Green State University. But they could just as easily have come from executives at the Eastman Kodak Company and Fuji Photo Film U.S.A. Both companies are touting disposable cameras that do the picture-taking job effectively, if not artistically.

Kodak's Fling and Fuji's Quick Snap are clearly aimed at the same buyers. Each weighs just a few ounces, comes with a fixed focus, a miniature lens and viewfinder, and a manual advance system. Both are constructed of plastic, are intended for use outdoors, and are to be discarded when the roll of film is taken out to be developed.

Fuji U.S.A. already has experience with throwaway cameras. Last year its parent company, the Fuji Photo Film Company, Tokyo, introduced the throwaway camera in Japan and sold 1.5 million cameras in six months.

Neither Fuji nor Kodak is pushing disposables as an alternative to expensive cameras. "The value is there for an enjoyable picture but certainly not a professional frame," said Jack Powers, general manager of Kodak's consumer products division.

Similarly, Paul Hudak, director of marketing for Fuji Photo Film, U.S.A., said disposables were "aimed at people who might otherwise miss out on a photographic opportunity because they were reluctant to bring their camera's along."

He added that amateur photographers already snap about four billion outdoor photographs a year. He estimated that by 1990 disposable cameras will raise that figure by 15 percent.

But much will depend on many stores carry disposable camera. "If they're selling the convenience of a disposable product, then the challenge is to have broad distribution," said Richard Winger, manager of The Boston Consulting Group. ■

AUGUST 20, 1988

NEXT OFFICE REVOLUTION: 'VOICE MAIL'

Andrew Pollack

At many companies, the interoffice memo has learned to talk. A new generation of telephone answering machines is replacing the memo and the message slip, uprooting office folkways in the process.

These computer-based systems, dubbed "voice mail," can answer a company's phones, route callers, and dispense information. They allow senders to shower the same oral messages on dozens or even hundreds of recipients at once, to be heard at their convenience.

Some people find such systems impersonal, intimidating, even infuriating. Callers can find themselves bounced from one recorded response to another, unable to break through to a human being, a situation that has been dubbed "voice mail jail." Even regular users can become befuddled. One man in Los Angeles pressed the wrong buttons on his phone and transmitted a private love message to his entire department.

Others find the systems intriguing, invaluable, even indispensable. They eliminate the frustrations of busy signals and "telephone tag"—a situation in which callers keep missing each other. "It's the most important technology since photocopying," said Gus Bender, a telecommunications specialist at the Travelers Companies, the Hartford insurance concern, where 10,000 employees use voice mail.

Almost everyone seems to agree that they are becoming inescapable. Even the Vatican is installing one, to allow callers to hear messages from the Pope.

The result is that, far more than with mere answering machines, people no longer have to talk to each other directly to communicate by phone. Indeed, voice mail users now talk about two kinds of telephone communications -voice mail, which is communicating by message, and "real-time" communications, once known as conversation, in which both parties are on the line at the same time.

"I may talk to a salesman for as long as a week only through the message box," said Bill Caparelli, vice president of sales and marketing at VLSI.

Voice mail supporters say it offers great savings in costs and time. Secretaries and receptionists can be eliminated or diverted to other tasks, and the phones are always answered. "We have entire departments without secretaries," said Paula Jones, a spokeswoman for VLSI. Telephone tag and ubiquitous message slips can be reduced. People can retrieve and send messages 24 hours a day from any place, a great help for people who must communicate across time zones.

Voice mail systems are specialized computers that convert speech into digital bits. The digital speech can be stored on magnetic disks, copied and manipulated just like other computer data.

As answering machines, they are more versatile than tape recorders. They can take a message even when the phone is in use. Moreover, a person hearing a message from another voice mail user can immediately dictate a reply into the phone, which will automatically send it to the caller's phone mailbox.

Messages can also be transferred from one person to another, or circulated like in-house memos, with each listener appending oral comments.

Perhaps the feature that is most obvious to outsiders, however, is the "automated attendant," in which the computer answers the phone and routes the call to a particular individual or to pre-recorded information. Voice mail systems are now used to dispense information ranging from airline flight schedules to the menu at Harvard dining halls to 976 services like dial-a-porn ("Press 1 for hot raw ecstasy," etc.). At the Republican National Convention this week, a voice mail system dispensed convention news and local traffic and weather reports.

Voice mail systems have been in use since 1980, but met with a mixed reception. Some early users abandoned their systems out of frustration or because they offended customers. But the systems have become popular more recently as prices have dropped and the technology has improved.

Prices for voice mail systems range from $3,000 to $500,000, depending on capacity, or about $50 to $200 per phone mailbox. Some companies sell circuit boards for $300 that turn personal computers into voice mail systems. ■

SEPTEMBER 18, 1980

TAMPON BRAND TIED TO SHOCK SYNDROME

Karen DeWitt

Use of the Rely brand tampons may increase the risk of a serious, sometimes fatal disorder in women called toxic shock syndrome, the Government's Center for Disease Control in Atlanta said today.

The center said a review of women who contracted the disorder last July and August found that about 70 percent of them used Rely tampons. The study also affirmed earlier findings that indicated a link between toxic shock syndrome and the use of tampons generally.

Toxic shock syndrome is a recently recognized illness that occurs primarily in women under 30, particularly during or just after their menstrual periods. The illness is characterized by sudden onset of high fever, vomiting, diarrhea, a rapid drop in blood pressure, sometimes leading to shock, and a sunburnlike rash followed by peeling skin, especially on fingers and toes.

The risk of contracting the disorder, apparently an infection from the bacteria known as staphylococcus aureus, is low, however. Only about three out of 100,000 women of menstruating age are affected annually. Since last January, the Center for Disease Control has received reports of 299 cases, 285 of them in women. Ninety-five percent of the cases in women occurred during their menstrual cycle. Since 1975, 25 deaths, all women, have been attributed to toxic shock syndrome.

Last June, the Center for Disease Control reported that use of tampons seemed to be a contributing factor to the disorder. The new center study, however, indicated that the syndrome was associated with Rely tampons more frequently than with other brands.

Infectious Disease Specialist Dr. Edward H. Kass holding a beaker with Tampon fibers which he believes causes Toxic Shock Syndrome.

JULY 3, 1981

RARE CANCER SEEN IN 41 HOMOSEXUALS

Lawrence K. Altman

Doctors in New York and California have diagnosed among homosexual men 41 cases of a rare and often rapidly fatal form of cancer. Eight of the victims died less than 24 months after the diagnosis was made.

The cause of the outbreak is unknown, and there is as yet no evidence of contagion. But the doctors who have made the diagnoses, mostly in New York City and the San Francisco Bay area, are alerting other physicians who treat large numbers of homosexual men to the problem in an effort to help identify more cases and to reduce the delay in offering chemotherapy treatment.

The sudden appearance of the cancer, called Kaposi's Sarcoma, has prompted a medical investigation that experts say could have as much scientific as public health importance because of what it may teach about determining the causes of more common types of cancer.

Doctors have been taught in the past that the cancer usually appeared first in spots on the legs and that the disease took a slow course of up to 10 years. But these recent cases have shown that it appears in one or more violet-colored spots anywhere on the body. The spots generally do not itch or cause other symptoms, often can be mistaken for bruises, sometimes appear as lumps and can turn brown after a period of time.

Doctors investigating the outbreak believe that many cases have gone undetected because of the rarity of the condition and the difficulty even dermatologists may have in diagnosing it.

Dr. Alvin E. Friedman-Kien of New York University Medical Center, said he had tested nine of the victims and found severe defects in their immunological systems. The patients had serious malfunctions of two types of cells called T and B cell lymphocytes, which have important roles in fighting infections and cancer. ■

DECEMBER 1, 1981

A BALLOON DEVICE AVERTS SURGERY FOR CORONARY DISORDERS

Lawrence K. Altman

To spare many patients painful and costly surgery, doctors are turning to a technique that involves inflating a balloon in arteries clogged by fatty deposits from arteriosclerosis.

The balloon, inflated after being introduced into the damaged area of a blood vessel, compresses obstructions and allows more oxygen-rich blood to flow to an organ. In some instances, the technique is relieving cramps and saving legs by removing obstructions to the blood supply to the lower limbs. In others, it relieves the obstructions that produce the chest discomfort called angina and might also lead to heart attacks.

In addition, this method (known technically as percutaneous transluminal angioplasty) is treating, and even curing, some cases of a type of high blood pressure that results from blockage of an artery feeding the kidneys. Although such blockages cause only a small percentage of all cases of high blood pressure, the therapy can be dramatically successful, freeing the patient entirely from drug therapy.

Until four years ago, radiologists who were experienced in using angioplasty for several ailments were unable to flatten obstructions in the coronary arteries, which are the ones that nourish the heart. Heart attacks can result when coronary arteries are blocked by fatty substances.

Now this technique, in addition to all its other applications, is becoming more commonly used to compress obstructions in coronary arteries. Although coronary angioplasty generally is still considered experimental, it is becoming a standard practice at a few hospitals.

Three doctors who have compressed obstructions in the coronary arteries of more than 1,100 patients have the longest experience with the technique. They are Dr. Andreas Gruntzig, who devised the technique at the University of Zurich and now works at Emory University in Atlanta; Dr. Simon H. Stertzer at Lenox Hill Hospital in New York; and Dr. Richard K. Myler at St. Mary's Hospital in San Francisco.

Angioplasty removes the blockage caused by atherosclerotic plaques, or the accumulation of fatty substances on the inside wall of an artery.

In about four of five patients, the balloon technique removes the obstruction and immediately relieves the symptoms. And about 84 percent of such patients will maintain their success after three years, according to data collected in a registry at the National Institutes of Health and reported at a meeting of the American Heart Association in Dallas two weeks ago. ■

Heart specialist Dr. Andreas Gruntzig holding a balloon catheter.

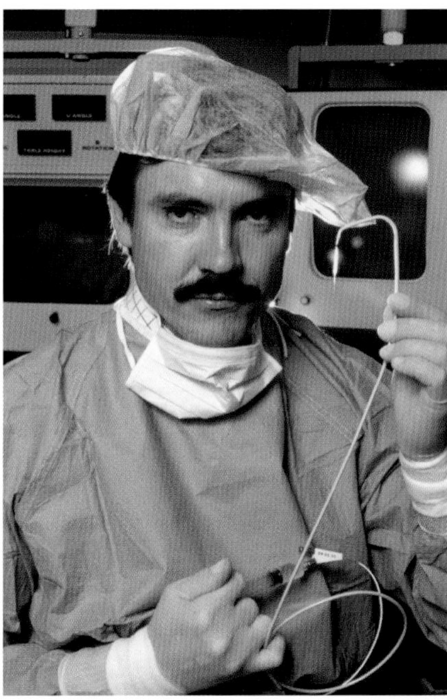

Dr. Robert Jarvik, the inventor of the artificial heart.

DECEMBER 2, 1982

Artificial Heart Implant Is Begun in Salt Lake

George Raine

SALT LAKE CITY, Dec. 1—A retired Seattle dentist suffering from inoperable heart disease underwent surgery late tonight for what was to be the first transplant of a permanent artificial heart.

Barney Clark, 61 years old, had been scheduled to receive the fistsized polyurethane device Thursday morning at the Utah Medical Center, but his rapidly deteriorating condition led doctors to begin an emergency operation at 10:30 P.M. The operation by a team of University of Utah doctors was expected to last three to four hours.

Dr. Clark suffered from cardiomyopathy, a degenerate disease of the heart muscle. He was among 10 prospective recipients of the revolutionary device, called the Jarvik-7, for Dr. Robert Jarvik of the university's Artificial Organs Division, who developed the device.

Because Dr. Clark's condition satisfied the rule established by the University of Utah and the Federal Food and Drug Administration, he was selected as the first recipient of a permanent artificial heart.

Hundreds of animals have survived for up to nine months with the Jarvik-7 heart, but Dr. Clark is the first human recipient. The surgical team was headed by Dr. William C. DeVries, chief of cardiothoracic surgery at the University of Utah Medical Center, who is the only surgeon authorized by the Government to implant the Jarvik-7 heart. Recipients of the heart, which is driven by an external air com-

FEBRUARY 6, 1983

AIDS: A NEW DISEASE'S DEADLY ODYSSEY

Robin Marantz Henig

Cards representing AIDS victims held aloft during interdenominational service in Central Park last night in 1983.

pressor, will have to spend the rest of their lives tethered to the compressor by two six-foot hoses, doctors say.

In recent months, while he was in better health, Dr. Clark visited the medical center to observe parts of artificial hearts in place in calves and sheep. He returned here Monday, in serious condition, and immediately signed a letter of authorization for doctors to implant the device. He signed a second authorization a day later.

Since Tuesday, Dr. Clark's heart rate has deteriorated and the decision to proceed with the operation at an earlier time was made by Dr. DeVries and other attending physicians at about 8 o'clock this evening.

"His attitude prior to surgery was marvelous," said Dr. Chase N. Peterson, the vice president for health sciences at the University of Utah. "He turned to his wife, Unaloy, and said, 'I'm a little nervous'." ■

Medical detectives are calling it the century's most virulent epidemic. It is as relentless as leukemia, as contagious as hepatitis, and its cause has eluded researchers for more than two years. Acquired immune deficiency syndrome, or AIDS, was first seen in homosexual men—particularly those who were promiscuous—but it has now struck so many different groups that its course cannot be predicted.

And despite a massive nationwide microbe hunt involving hundreds of investigators and millions of dollars, scientists simply cannot catch up with it. "We're always a few steps behind," says Dr. William W. Darrow, a research sociologist with the Centers for Disease Control (C.D.C.) in Atlanta, "and that makes us very, very concerned. The disease could be anywhere now."

While AIDS has continued to rage in big-city homosexual communities with terrifying and deadly results, it has also struck Haitian men and women, intravenous-drug users, female partners of drug users, and infants and children. AIDS has become the second leading cause of death—after uncontrollable bleeding—in hemophiliacs, and, most recently, a number of surgical patients who have received blood transfusions have contracted AIDS, raising fears among some observers about the nation's blood supply.

The mysterious AIDS organism is generally thought to be a virus or other infectious agent (as opposed to a bacterium) and to be spread in bodily secretions, especially blood and semen. It is responsible for the near-total collapse of the body's immune system, leaving the victim prey to cancers and opportunistic infections that the body is unable to defend against. And, while some of the diseases associated with AIDS can be successfully treated, the underlying immune problem is, apparently, irreversible. The AIDS patient may survive his first bizarre infection, or his second, but

(cont'd. next page)

(continued from previous page)

he remains vulnerable to successive infections, one of which is likely to kill him.

AIDS is deadly. According to the C.D.C.'s figures for late January, it has struck 958 individuals since it was first seen in 1979, and it has killed 365, a mortality rate of 38 percent; of the cases reported before June 1981, 75 percent are dead. Although these earlier cases probably received less experienced treatment than AIDS patients get today, some fear that the five-year death rate will be higher than 65 percent. Smallpox, by comparison, killed 25 percent of its victims.

In the fall of 1981, the C.D.C. studied the sexual habits of 50 homosexual victims of AIDS. The investigators did not ask for the names of their partners.

Epidemiologists developed many theories about why homosexual men were at risk for these rare infections and cancers. Sexually active homosexuals are prone to a host of diseases: syphilis, gonorrhea, genital herpes, hepatitis, amebiasis (one of the most common diseases in what doctors call the "gay bowel syndrome") and infections caused by fungi and protozoa usually seen only in the tropics.

As the syndrome spread to other groups, however, early theories that attempted to explain the outbreak among homosexuals were discarded. Within months, intravenous-drug users—both men and women—who were not homosexuals were showing the same signs of immune suppression and developing the same unusual opportunistic infections. Then came Haitians, in both the United States and Haiti, who said they were neither homosexuals nor drug users but who developed what appeared to be an identical syndrome of acquired immune deficiency.

In the spring of 1982, the C.D.C. received its first reports of AIDS in hemophiliacs. Some of these patients were probably exposed to the AIDS agent in a blood-clotting medication called factor VIII concentrate that is made from the blood of thousands of donors. Anywhere from 2,500 to 22,000 blood donors are used to make just one lot of this widely used product; one lot treats about 100 patients. To date, the C.D.C. has received a total of eight confirmed reports of hemophiliacs with AIDS, six of whom have died. All used factor VIII concentrate rather than an older, less convenient blood product called cryoprecipitate, which is made from the blood of a handful of donors. In view of the AIDS threat, some hemophilia experts are urging a return to cryoprecipitate, especially in mild or newly diagnosed cases.

In the summer of 1982, the C.D.C. received reports of three patients who contracted AIDS after receiving blood transfusions. Two of those patients were adults from the Northeast and the third was an infant in San Francisco who needed a transfusion to correct an Rhfactor incompatibility. Four more cases of possible transmission of AIDS through blood transfusions are now being investigated.

By mid-January, the C.D.C. had received five reports of AIDS that had spread to female sexual partners of drug abusers. In four of those cases, the male partners had not even been sick. Thus, AIDS qualified as a sexually transmitted disease among heterosexuals. It also began to be clear that individuals could be identified who might be carriers of the AIDS agent, able to infect other people without themselves developing symptoms.

Dr. James Oleske, a pediatric immunologist and associate professor at the University of Medicine and Dentistry of New Jersey, has treated eight young patients since 1979, four of whom have died. He believes the disease is passed on either in the womb or through normal contact between mother and child after birth. "It's a tragedy," he says of the cases he has seen. "The only thing to be said for it is that eventually AIDS will help us understand more about the immune system." Homosexual men still represent 75 percent of the disease's victims, and the specter of AIDS haunts every member of the homosexual community, especially in the cities where it is most prevalent (they are, in descending order, New York, San Francisco, Los Angeles, Miami, Newark, Houston, Chicago, Boston, Washington and Philadelphia).

"You don't know what it's like to be gay and living in New York," says Larry Kramer, 47, a novelist and screen writer and the cofounder of Gay Men's Health Crisis, an educational and fund-raising group for AIDS victims. "It's like being in wartime. We don't know when the bomb is going to fall. I've had 18 friends die in the last year and a half from AIDS," Mr. Kramer says. "Another 12 are now seriously ill, and six of them are in the hospital. Doctors and psychiatrists are pleading with the community to learn a new way of socializing. They're begging us, in the name of all who died, to learn how to date."

And, in fact, behavioral changes are currently the only prudent advice physicians can offer. Some doctors hesitate to urge celibacy or monogamy on patients for whom casual sex is a way of life, but most seem to think the evidence is compelling enough to advocate just that. "I strongly recommend that my patients be very circumspect and cautious in their future sexual contacts," says Dr. Dan William, a Manhattan internist who treats primarily homosexual men. In his practice of some 2,000 patients, he has seen 24 cases of AIDS.

"I tell my patients what the epidemiologists know—which isn't much," says Dr. William. "We are more or less convinced that we are dealing with a sexually transmissible agent. Large numbers of contacts—or a small number of indiscriminate contacts—increase the probability of exposure. In addition, a patient's susceptibility to any infectious disease is much greater." Dr. William counsels monogamy, and, he adds, "It's important for a patient to emphasize to his sex contact that he must not bring any new diseases home with him."

The incubation period for AIDS is thought to be at least six to eight months and could be as long as two years. This means that people who have already been infected might not know it until sometime between mid-1983 and the end of 1984. By then, each carrier might have unknowingly infected hundreds more individuals—through sexual contact, through blood donations, or through some yet unimagined route.

"Most epidemics behave better than this," says the C.D.C.'s Dr. Curran. "Like detective stories, they come eventually to a merciful end—even if they remain unsolved." But with acquired immune deficiency, more than two years after the first case was reported, there is still no end in sight. ■

NOVEMBER 29, 1983

AIDS NOW SEEN AS A WORLDWIDE HEALTH PROBLEM

Lawrence K. Altman

Geneva acquired immune deficiency syndrome (AIDS) has become a worldwide problem with cases now being reported in 33 countries and all inhabited continents.

Of particular concern is a spurt in cases diagnosed in Europe, where the number has doubled in the last year, as it did soon after the disease became known in the United States in 1981.

And there are indications that in Africa the disease may be striking heterosexual men and women in equal numbers, unlike the situation in the industrialized countries, where AIDS predominantly strikes homosexual men and intravenous drug users. The disease is occurring in several countries in central and western Africa to a much greater extent than was previously recognized.

Although AIDS has been diagnosed worldwide, the reports have been somewhat spotty, according to Dr. Walter Dowdle of the national Centers for Disease Control in Atlanta, who was chairman of an international gathering of scientists here last weekend, the first meeting to discuss the global impact of AIDS.

Dr. Dowdle emphasized that the new findings that emerged from that meeting should not be greeted with undue alarm. "AIDS is not a mysterious disease that is going to sweep the whole world," he said. "It is increasing, but not at a rate alarming for the general public."

The 38 scientists who met at the World Health Organization's headquarters represented all the specialties involved in AIDS research.

The 15 European countries reporting to the World Health Organization now account for about 10 percent of all AIDS cases. Of the 267 AIDS cases that have been reported in Europe, 164—or about 60 percent—were diagnosed from January to October of this year.

Preliminary results of a new study in central Africa have led some AIDS experts to suspect that the disease may generally be transmitted heterosexually in some of the less developed areas of the world. The study also suggests, however, that this may be because of inadequately sterilized needles and syringes used in everyday medical practice.

In some countries, only a few AIDS cases have been diagnosed. Australia has reported four cases and Japan, the only Asian country to report the disease, two.

Despite the small number of cases reported in some countries, many participants said they suspected the true incidence of AIDS was more widespread than believed. They said the incidence of AIDS might be many times greater than the official worldwide total of about 3,000 cases.

The 2,753 AIDS cases reported from the United States make it the country with by far the largest reported incidence of the disease. However, recent health statistics from New York have hinted that the so-called "doubling phenomenon," in which the number of new cases doubles about every six months, may be easing off. "What this means, we're really not sure," Dr. Dowdle said. "But we certainly hope it means something."

Meanwhile, however, the doubling phenomenon has appeared in Canada as well as Europe.

Of the 50 AIDS cases reported so far in Canada, 15 were reported in 1982, 15 in the first six months of 1983 and 20 from July to October, Dr. Alastair J. Clayton, an official of the Laboratory for Disease Control in Ottawa, said.

The doubling phenomenon is evident from the European statistics in which the number of diagnosed cases rose from 2 in 1979 to 10 in 1980, 17 in 1981, 67 in 1982 and 164 so far this year.

One bright note in an otherwise bleak situation was a report about hepatitis B, a health problem that threatens many of the same people who are at high risk of contracting AIDS.

Researchers reported that, despite earlier fears, there was no evidence that AIDS or any other infection could be spread by hepatitis B vaccine. Those fears had arisen because the licensed hepatitis B vaccine is derived from the blood of chronic hepatitis B carriers, many of whom are homosexual men.

Nevertheless, the potential spread of AIDS through other blood products, as well as whole-blood transfusions, still concerns many doctors. ■

APRIL 22, 1984

FEDERAL OFFICIAL SAYS HE BELIEVES CAUSE OF AIDS HAS BEEN FOUND

Lawrence K. Altman

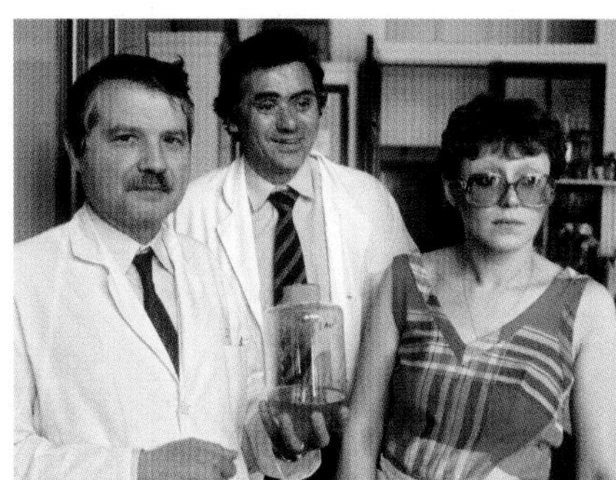

Luc Montagnier, Jean-Claude Chermann and Françoise Barre-Sinoussi, the three Franch scientists who helped to discover the causes of AIDS in Pasteur Institute of Paris.

ATLANTA, April 21—Dr. James O. Mason, head of the Federal Centers for Disease Control, said today that he believed a virus discovered in France was the cause of acquired immune deficiency syndrome, or AIDS.

The French virus is called LAV, for lymphadenopathy-associated virus. It is a member of the retrovirus family, which over the past year has been the leading candidate as the cause of AIDS.

"We cannot know for sure now that the LAV virus is the agent that causes AIDS, but the pattern it follows in the human body makes us believe it is," Dr. Mason said.

According to the Centers for Disease Control, 4,087 cases were reported in the United States as of Monday, and 1,758 patients have died.

Dr. Mason predicted that in time the new findings would lead to development of a diagnostic test for AIDS as well as a test to help in prevention. For one thing, he said a test might be developed to screen out AIDS-contaminated blood before it was transfused to patients.

One reason for believing that the virus is the cause of AIDS, Dr. Mason said, is that tests first done in France have shown that the LAV attacks the same white blood cells, called OKT4, or helper T-cells, that are destroyed by the disease.

SEPTEMBER 13, 1983

ON TRAIL OF CANCER: DISCOVERIES REACH A CRESCENDO

Harold M. Schmeck Jr.

Scientists who study biology at its most basic level are in the midst of a crescendo of new discoveries that seem to be unraveling of the mystery of the cancer process.

In the last few months, they have added to the list of known human cancer genes, identified new significance in the breakage and rearrangement of chromosomes, begun to see the function of cancer genes' counterparts in the normal body, and identified a two-stage sequence in which two cancer genes of different classes act in step to produce a malignancy.

So fast and furious is the pace of discovery that some experts say informally that more has probably been learned in the past few years than in the previous quarter century.

"With the new molecular tools, so many things are just coming together," said Dr. George F, Vande Woude of the National Cancer Institute, one of the experts in the field.

Most of this increasing wealth of knowledge has to do with the genes, the basic hereditary messages carried in the form of DNA (deoxyribonucleic acid) in all living cells, and with the chromosomes, the tiny threadlike structures that carry those genes somewhat like beads on a string.

Some of the newest and most provocative findings link certain genes, called oncogenes, or cancer genes, with changes in chromosomes in a fashion that suggests plausible hypotheses to link the changes to the beginnings of cancer.

In recent months scientists have also, for the first time, linked a cancer gene to a known product in the body, a growth factor that helps the body make platelets, blood substances that are called into action to heal wounds. The apparent link between such a growth factor and the normal counterpart of an oncogene seems significant to many research workers because cancer has long been defined as a state in which cell growth often accelerates wildly having somehow lost its normal controls. ■

JUNE 1, 1984

Hepatitis Vaccine Produced by Gene-Splicing

Harold M. Schmeck Jr.

The first experimental vaccine for humans produced through gene-splicing methods has given healthy adults immunity to hepatitis B virus, a major cause of liver disease throughout the world, scientists reported yesterday in The Journal of the American Medical Association.

The importance of such a vaccine, made artificially in the laboratory, is that it could be produced in virtually limitless quantity, probably at relatively low cost, and would be free from the risk of contamination by substances from human blood.

Furthermore the promise shown by the experimental vaccine against hepatitis B virus also suggests that other vaccines against important human diseases may be made by gene-splicing technology in the future.

The need for such a vaccine is great. Today there are estimated to be more than 200 million cases of liver disease worldwide that are caused by the virus. At least that many people are carriers of the virus and are capable of passing it on to others.

In regions of Asia and Africa where hepatitis B virus is most common as a cause of liver infection, liver cancer is the leading cause of cancer death among males. Experts believe infection with the virus is a factor in the cause of most of those cancers. ■

Scientist Michael Houghton wearing latex gloves holding up a series of vials in a laboratory where he performs hepatitis non-A, non-B test procedures involving isolation and cloning of proteins.

DECEMBER 12, 1984

MOVEMENT SEEKS TO ADVANCE RIGHTS OF DYING

Andrew H. Malcolm

Every day several sacks of mail arrive at the front door of a small rented house in suburban Los Angeles and in two crowded offices on West 57th Street in Manhattan. From the quarters of these three little-known organizations a continent apart comes much of the current impetus for a better-known movement advocating the "right to die."

A good deal of attention has been captured by those who call themselves the "right to life" movement: activists who seek to protect the unborn by opposing abortion. But at the other end of life, where machines and drugs can prolong life often beyond the will of patients to live it, hundreds of thousands of people are organizing to secure the rights of patients who want "death with dignity."

On the surface, there is little controversy over granting dignity to a dying person. Without issuing broad policy statements, medical groups generally agree that in some terminal cases, technology merely prolongs the dying process, and such groups leave individual decisions to the physicians involved. The painful and increasingly complex conflicts come when the desire for a natural death by an individual or his family clashes with a whole host of legal, moral and ethical concerns of hospitals afraid of lawsuits, of doctors who control life-support machines and regard a patient's death as a professional failure and of emotional relatives under stress.

There are also some who fear that making it easy for patients or relatives to have

Larry Kramer at the Village Voice AIDS conference on June 6, 1987 in New York City.

life-sustaining machinery turned off could lead to abuses under the name of euthanasia, or mercy killing.

Although their precise goals and strategies differ, the Society for the Right to Die and other such groups are striving, with some apparent success, to change the way American society looks at death. In their view, death is no longer a simple inevitability. With machines that can pump and clean blood, fill and empty lungs with air and restart hearts, man can often control the time of death, although not always the quality of prolonged life.

For a hopelessly ill person to choose a natural death instead of lingering on a machine, the groups maintain, is as much a moral and legal right as the right, long established in law, to consent to initial medical treatment.

The three large organizations working to design and rewrite state laws, to alter public perceptions and to assist individuals and families in the emotional and legal confrontations that frequently erupt are the Society for the Right to Die, Concern for Dying and the Hemlock Society.

The Hemlock Society appears to be the most radical group. Its 10,000 members believe that individuals who want to commit suicide, which the society calls "self-deliverance," ought to be able to receive active assistance as well as to have medical treatment stopped on demand.

Both Concern for Dying and the Society for the Right to Die shun advocating active euthanasia and instead emphasize education of doctors, legislators, patients and their families to the rights of patients.

"The patient's wishes should be paramount," said Alice Mehling, executive director of the Society for the Right to Die. ■

JULY 22, 1985

IMPACT OF AIDS: PATTERNS OF HOMOSEXUAL LIFE CHANGING

Glenn Collins

Four years since the public first became aware of AIDS, the lethal viral disease has brought profound changes to the lives of homosexual men in New York.

It has had a pervasive effect on homosexual life styles, relationships, sexual patterns and self-images. Many believe the changes to be permanent, and some feel that the disease has led to a redefinition of contemporary homosexual life.

Successive stages of panic and apathy about AIDS have seized homosexuals since 1981. The years have taken their toll. "I think the gay community is still reeling from the devastation of this disease," said Dr. Stuart E. Nichols Jr., a psychiatrist at Beth Israel Medical Center who has treated and studied AIDS patients since 1981. "It's a personal disease for any gay man, and the ability to deny is not there anymore for the majority of gays."

For many, it has entailed the emotional cost of repeatedly coming to terms with death at an early age. "A man I know said to me today, 'I know 150 people who've died of AIDS'—150 people!" said Larry Kramer, author of "The Normal Heart," an Off Broadway play about AIDS.

Currently AIDS, acquired immune deficiency syndrome, is the leading cause of death among men aged 25 to 44 in New York City, supplanting the usual causes in this age group such as suicide, accident and homicide. According to the City Health Department, 3,926 cases of AIDS have been reported in the city, 59 percent of them among homosexual or bisexual men; most of the rest come from a variety of risk groups, including intravenous drug users and the sex partners or children of those who have AIDS. Since 1978, 2,033 of the AIDS victims in the city have died—52 percent of the reported cases.

Many of those interviewed agreed that AIDS has led to change in several areas,

(cont'd. next page)

(continued from previous page)
including modifications in sexual activity, a trend toward long-term relationships and a realignment in relation to the nonhomosexual part of the community. However, such changes have been complex, said Dr. Emery S. Hetrick, an assistant professor of clinical psychiatry at New York University Medical Center. He is a member of the State Task Force on Gay and Lesbian Issues appointed by Governor Cuomo.

It is hard to generalize about "extremely diverse" people, he said, noting that the impact of AIDS is only one aspect of life among homosexuals of different ages, social class and ethnicity.

"Many people have limited having sex to one's life partner, or are practicing 'safe sex,'" said Dr. Hetrick. He was referring to techniques such as limiting the number of sexual partners; using prophylactics and avoiding exchanges of body fluids that have been linked with transmission of the virus that is believed to cause AIDS; getting regular physicians' checkups, and avoiding drugs that suppress the body's immune system or reduce inhibitions about high-risk sexual behavior.

Dr. Hetrick emphasized, though, that sexual patterns were varied before the advent of AIDS. "A number of men were extremely sexually promiscuous, and a proportion engaged in acts that could be dangerous," he said. "But a sizable number had been in stable relationships, and were not at risk at all. Some others were in primarily stable relationships, with perhaps an occasional trip to the baths."

All those interviewed said that the widely reported panic that crested in 1983 has abated, and that it is no longer common for nonhomosexuals to express fear that hairdressers or waiters will give them AIDS.

Opinions differ about the lessons that can be drawn from the response to AIDS and about whether the struggle has transcended traditional divisions among homosexuals. "It's a big dark cloud, but there's a real silver lining to it," said Judge Failla. "The community has matured and taken responsibility for itself."

But Mr. Kramer, a founder of the Gay Men's Health Crisis, said, "AIDS hasn't coalesced the gay community one single bit—anyone who claims that is deaf, dumb and blind."

He added: "The gay community is totally and utterly unorganized. We have no political power in this society, and no lobbying power in Washington. That's obvious from the response to this horrible disease."

Mr. Dunne said he found Mr. Kramer's play "profoundly moving" but it made him "profoundly angry."

"He says there are no heroes," Mr. Dunne said. "But I see them and work with them all the time—the physicians and nurses and volunteers bearing terrible burdens, and the people who are dying from AIDS and have been so heroic in the way they struggle with it." ■

MARCH 11, 1986

FETAL TESTS CAN NOW FIND MANY MORE GENETIC FLAWS

Harold M. Schmeck Jr.

The couple already had two children afflicted with the grim reality of cystic fibrosis. They could not face having another. The disease causes digestive problems, breathing problems, lung infections, with an almost continual threat of death from early childhood onward. The woman ended her next pregnancy by abortion.

But now she is pregnant again and plans to have this baby. Genetic testing that has become available only within the last several months has given her solid assurance that the child will be free of the disease.

This is the human side of a revolution in diagnosis of genetic diseases that is unfolding today because of scientists' growing ability to find and interpret the messages of the human genes. Today such diagnoses are becoming available for an ever increasing roster of disorders caused by a fault in one or another single gene among the 50,000 to 100,000 that humans possess. Individually, most of these diseases are quite rare, although cystic fibrosis afflicts an estimated 30,000 Americans and Duchenne's muscular dystrophy appears about once in every 5,000 males born alive.

Prenatal detection of the classic form of hemophilia has become possible within the last year, as has been the case with cystilemma fibrosis. What one expert called "reasonably good" detection of muscular dystrophy has been possible since last fall. Phenylketonuria, an important cause of mental retardation usually known as PKU, has been detectable in the fetus for about two years; the blood diseases sickle cell anemia and thalassemia, also known as Cooley's anemia, have been detectable longer.

Earlier methods have allowed detection of at least 50 other genetic diseases, including Down's syndrome and Tay-Sachs disease. But the new DNA studies are safer for the fetus than some of the earlier techniques and have added important diseases never before detectable in the womb.

With the new predictive abilities come some sobering ethical and social problems of which specialists are very much aware. Only a handful of laboratories today are capable of doing the new tests, and they are expensive, yet many thousands of people might benefit. Furthermore, the ever-increasing ability to detect genetic disease early in fetal life is likely to sharpen the debate over abortion and generally exacerbate the dilemma of parents and doctors when diseases that used to be unforeseeable "acts of God" can now be predicted in advance. ■

AUGUST 9, 1986

U.S. FILES FIRST AIDS DISCRIMINATION CHARGE

Robert Pear

WASHINGTON, Aug. 8—The Federal Government has for the first time accused an employer of illegally discriminating against a person with AIDS, Federal officials said today.

The charge was made by the Department of Health and Human Services, which said that a North Carolina hospital had violated a man's civil rights by dismissing him from his job as a registered nurse and then refusing to consider him for any other job.

The Government said the Charlotte Memorial Hospital and Medical Center had violated the law "by discriminatorily denying the complainant individualized consideration for possible re-employment."

The Government's action is significant because it sets a precedent demonstrating that people with acquired immune deficiency syndrome may be able to protect their rights despite a restrictive interpretation of the relevant law by the Justice Department. In addition, lawyers said, the ruling underscores the need for employers to be cautious in taking action against workers with AIDS.

The law in question, Section 504 of the Rehabilitation Act of 1973, prohibits discrimination on the basis of handicap in any program or activity that receives Federal financial assistance.

Charlotte Memorial Hospital, a 777-bed nonprofit facility, receives Federal funds through Medicare and Medicaid, the programs for the elderly and poor. ■

NOVEMBER 3, 1987

Last Samples of Smallpox Pose a Quandary

Harold M. Schmeck

Ten years after smallpox ceased to exist as a human disease, virus experts and public health officials are in a strange and unprecedented quandary: what to do with the last surviving smallpox viruses.

These viruses, the most fearsome endangered species on earth, exist today in only two places, high security laboratories in Moscow and at the Centers for Disease Control in Atlanta.

Now, on the 10th anniversary of the eradication of smallpox, the experts are questioning whether or not those last stocks of variola virus—the cause of smallpox—should finally be destroyed.

"No scientist is working with viable variola virus or is likely to be allowed to do so," said Dr. Keith Dumbell, of University of Cape Town, in South Africa, writing in The Lancet, a medical journal. "To the best of our knowledge," he added, "destruction of all remaining laboratory stocks of variola virus would set the final seal on the attempt to rid the world of this infectious scourge."

But some specialists have argued that the virus should not be erased altogether from the world, partly because unforeseen research uses might arise in the future and partly simply because once it was destroyed, it could never be raised from extinction. Philosophically, the deliberate extinction of a species would be an unprecedented step.

But this is a species that, over thousands of years, has killed many millions of people and has spread panic and destruction in its wake, often killing one in five of those infected in any outbreak and disfiguring many of the survivors.

Now the only surviving representatives of the virus are stored in little vials kept in freezer lockers at minus 94 degrees Fahrenheit, waiting only for some hypothetical future use.

The last naturally transmitted case of smallpox occurred in Merka, Somalia, in late October 1977. It is from this case that the 10-year anniversary is dated. The next year, two cases occurred in England because the virus accidentally escaped from a research laboratory. There have been many rumors but no actual cases of smallpox anywhere since then.

Dr. Dumbell questioned his fellow virologists throughout the world about the desirability of destroying the virus. Of the 61 scientists in 22 countries who responded, only five thought the virus stocks should be preserved indefinitely.

Those five offered two fundamental reasons: first, that the virus could be kept in storage with minimal risk and that this should be continued to preserve specimens of the species; and second, that the preservation of openly retained stocks was preferable to destroying them and leaving the possibility that some country was keeping secret stocks for possible use in biological warfare.

Such rumors of clandestine virus supplies are fueled by the fact that some countries, notably the United States and the Soviet Union, continue to vaccinate military personnel even though there is no present risk of the disease smallpox anywhere.

Dr. Donald A. Henderson, who was head of the World Health Organization's global smallpox eradication program from 1966 until its successful conclusion, said yesterday he could see both sides of the quandary. He does not consider the safety of maintaining stocks a major issue.

"As a scientist I would say let's keep it," he said, "but looking at the reality of concerns, I think we would be politically well advised to destroy it." ■

MARCH 21, 1987

U.S. APPROVES DRUG TO PROLONG LIVES OF AIDS PATIENTS

Irvin Molotsky

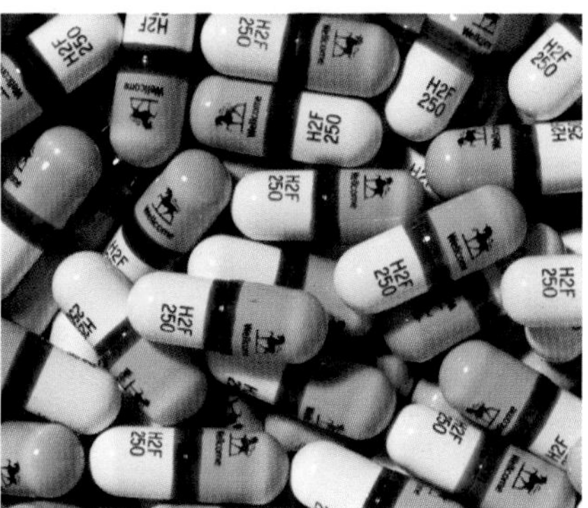

3'-azido-3'-deoxythymidine (AZT), the drug used to treat HIV.

The first drug proved to prolong the lives of AIDS patients was given Federal approval today. Both Government and drug company officials emphasized, however, that the drug was not a cure for the fatal disorder of the immune system, which has struck 33,000 Americans.

The drug is azidothymidine, or AZT, an antiviral drug made by the Burroughs Wellcome Company under the brand name Retrovir. Its approval, which means it can be prescribed by doctors, had been expected since January, when the company made its presentation before the Food and Drug Administration.

Even before today's approval, the drug had been made available to more than 5,000 patients in clinical tests and in a special program to many of the most severely ill patients with acquired immune deficiency syndrome.

Because of concern over the drug's potentially severe side effects and limitations in supply, Burroughs Wellcome said it would limit distribution in the coming months to selected categories of patients. These will include, in addition to thousands of AIDS

(cont'd. next page)

(continued from previous page)

patients who have suffered a particular form of pneumonia, many thousands more with a severe form of AIDS-related complex, or ARC, a subgroup whose white blood cells have been severely depleted.

The drug works by inhibiting the ability of the AIDS virus to duplicate inside body cells. It apparently is not completely successful at this, however, because for unknown reasons, the condition of some patients on the drug continues to deteriorate. The drug does not rid the body of the virus.

Physicians and AIDS patients said they were pleased by today's announcement but concerned by the high price of the drug, estimated at $8,000 to $10,000 a year for a patient. They say this will force many people to exhaust their savings and go on the welfare rolls, relying on programs such as Medicaid to pay for the drug.

The Gay Men's Health Crisis, a voluntary organization in New York that assists AIDS victims, said it was pleased by the licensing of AZT but concerned about the price.

"This licensing represents another step forward in the research on AIDS," the group said. "We are, however, outraged at the extreme high cost of the drug and the fact that a person with AIDS may be forced to spend down all their assets in order to afford this excellent drug."

Archie Harrison, a New York AIDS patient who has been taking AZT for 17 weeks, said that he felt the drug had helped him, and that he personally had not suffered the bad side effects some patients had. But he, too, expressed concern about the cost.

"I think it's outrageous, in a life-threatening situation," said Mr. Harrison, a 32-year-old man who was diagnosed with AIDS in February 1986. He noted that many patients on AZT were living on fixed incomes, such as Social Security disability, and would be unable to pay for AZT by themselves.

The New York State Department of Health said the drug would be covered under Medicaid, which pays for the health care of poor people. As with other drugs, the program will pay pharmacists the wholesale cost plus a nominal dispensing fee.

The state's view is that "if the treatment is effective then it should be available to all residents of the state," said Frances Tarleton, a spokeswoman for the department.

Medicaid is a joint Federal-state program administered by the states. Each state will decide its policy on payment for AZT. ■

JULY 28, 1987

Fatigue 'Virus' Has Experts More Baffled and Skeptical than Ever

Philip M. Boffey

Medical experts are struggling, with only limited success, to understand a mysterious illness that leaves its victims exhausted for months or years at a time.

The ailment, known as chronic Epstein-Barr virus infection, chronic mononucleosis or chronic fatigue syndrome, has stirred rising concern in public and medical circles over the last two years.

The illness has already caused one highly publicized but sharply disputed "epidemic" at a resort community at Lake Tahoe, Nev., from 1984 to 1986. It may have caused an outbreak of 100 cases in the small Nevada town of Yerington from late 1985 to early 1986, according to Dr. Anthony L. Komaroff, director of general medicine at the Brigham and Women's Hospital in Boston.

"Whatever it is, it seems to be growing in frequency," said Dr. Komaroff, whose group has studied more than 500 patients suffering from the syndrome. "Literally every time I say to a friend that I'm studying this illness, and then describe it, they say 'Oh, my God. My niece has it, or my next-door neighbor, or my boss.'"

Although the syndrome has apparently never been fatal, it can unquestionably be devastating to many of those affected. Virtually all suffer persistent fatigue, in some cases so overwhelming that it curtails work, restricts social life or even becomes totally disabling. Most victims also experience low-grade fever, muscle pains, depression, headaches, recurrent sore throats, swollen lymph glands and allergies. And many victims are unable to think clearly or to concentrate. Some have likened their condition to feeling like a Raggedy Ann doll with the stuffing knocked out or to an endless bout of flu with the added mental confusion of Alzheimer's disease.

Some experts suspect that "chronic Epstein-Barr virus syndrome" has become the latest fad diagnosis, replacing iron-poor blood, low blood sugar and thyroid problems as a catch-all explanation for symptoms that cannot otherwise be explained.

"I don't think it's clear that there's an epidemic of this," said Dr. George Miller, a professor of pediatric infectious diseases, epidemiology and molecular biochemistry at the Yale University medical school. "I would say there might be an epidemic of diagnosis."

Dr. Gary Holmes, an epidemiologist at the Federal Centers for Disease Control who studied the Lake Tahoe outbreak, said, "A lot more is being made of this by the lay press than it probably deserves," adding, "The problem is that almost every person in the United States has symptoms that are compatible with symptoms of the syndrome."

The ailment strikes women twice as often as men, for reasons that are not understood. It also disproportionately afflicts nurses, doctors and other health personnel. The most visible victims are often professionals in fast-paced jobs, leading quipsters to dub it "the Yuppie plague" or "Yuppie flu." ■

FEBRUARY 16, 1988

Drug Combination Gains Support as Alternative to Surgical Abortion

Gina Kolata

Drugs that induce miscarriages may eventually replace traditional surgical abortions in the first three months of pregnancy, according to a World Health Organization official. In particular, a panel that recently evaluated international drug tests determined that a specific two-drug combination was safe and effective when used early in pregnancy.

The combination included a relatively new compound, called RU 486, that induces abortions and has been tested in Europe as a "morning after" pill. The other drug, prostaglandin, is older and already on the market.

The combination is about 95 percent effective in causing abortions in the first three months of pregnancy, according to the panel, which was convened by the W.H.O. and which will be publish its report in two months.

The drug combination is "a major advance," said Dr. Irving Spitz, director of clinical research at the Population Council in New York City. The drugs "certainly will have a very major impact, absolutely," he added.

At the same time, Dr. Spitz and others noted that drug companies might not choose to market the drugs in this country out of fear of opposition from those who object to abortions.

A woman is given an RU 486 pill and two days later gets an injection of prostaglandin or a prostaglandin suppository. The woman then has a miscarriage; her uterus contracts and expels the fetus. The experience is like a heavy menstrual period, often accompanied by some cramps.

The drugs produce "very, very minimal side effects," Dr. Barzelatto said. "There is not an significant increase in nausea over the amount pregnant women feel anyway, the women don't have diarrhea, and the abdominal pain is not severe."

Dr. Spitz said Ru 486 induces abortions in 80 to 85 percent of women who take it in the first six weeks of pregnancy, but its effectiveness falls substantially after that. By the 9 or 10th week of pregnancy, "only one-third respond," Dr. Spitz said. ■

Dr. Etienne-Emile Baulieu holds RU-486 pills he developed.

Supporters and opponents of the drug RU 486 demonstrate outside the French Embassy.

FEBRUARY 22, 1988

BOYCOTT THREAT BLOCKING SALE OF ABORTION-INDUCING DRUG

Gina Kolata

While a new abortion-inducing drug is expected to be sold in France, China, England and other countries, opponents of abortion are blocking sale of the drug in this country.

The fate of the drug, RU 486, which has a potential for other medical conditions, mostly affecting women, is focusing new attention on the influence of the anti-abortion movement on medical decisions.

National Right to Life and other groups opposed to abortion have served notice to drug companies that if any company sold an abortion-inducing drug the millions of Americans who oppose abortion will boycott all the company's products. This happened to the Upjohn Company of Kalamazoo, Mich., when it tried to develop abortion-inducing drugs several years ago.

Pharmaceutical companies say they have no plans to seek the Food and Drug Administration approval that is necessary to sell abortion-inducing drugs in the United States. They say publicly that they are not cowed by the anti-abortion movement and that they had other reasons for not selling such drugs. Privately, however, drug makers speak differently.

"The reasons are obvious," said one company executive who asked not to be named. He said his company feared that if it sold such a drug, it would suffer greatly from a boycott by the millions of members of National Right to Life and by "all the physicians, pharmacists and lay people who don't believe in abortions."

The power of anti-abortion groups "is very upsetting," said Dr. Irving Spitz, director of clinical research at the Population Council in New York City. Dr. Daniel Mishell, professor and chairman of obstetrics and gynecology at the University

(cont'd. next page)

(continued from previous page)
of Southern California School of Medicine, said he thought it was "medically wrong" that RU 486 would not be available to women in this country.

Dr. Mishell said abortions would be safer with RU 486. Surgical abortions, performed by suction and by dilation and curettage, carry risks of blood loss, perforation of the uterus, complications from anesthesia and perforation of the bowel or other organs. Although these things rarely occur, they would be avoided altogether in a drug-induced abortion.

RU 486 causes abortions by blocking progesterone, a hormone needed to maintain a pregnancy. By itself, the drug induces abortions in 80 to 85 percent of women who take it very early in pregnancy, within the first six weeks after their last menstrual period. But its effectiveness then starts to drop sharply so that by nine weeks after a woman's last period, there is only one chance in three that abortion will occur.

Researchers in Europe and China foIn 1985, Upjohn stopped all research on drugs to induce abortions or prevent pregnancy, after two years of a boycott of all Upjohn products by National Right to Life. An Upjohn spokesman said the company decided to stop its fertility research program because of "the adverse regulatory climate in the United States" and because of the "litigious climate" here.

Dr. C. Wayne Bardin, who is vice president and director of biomedical research at the Population Council, and others also say the boycott was a principal reason that Upjohn stopped its fertility program.

Dr. Hodgen is concerned that the abortion issue will preclude marketing RU 486, even for the uses that have nothing to do with stopping or preventing pregnancy. "Groups that oppose abortions will oppose the marketing of this drug, even if the drug cured the common cold," he said. "Let's be real about that."

Dr. Hodgen added that the emergence of RU 486 poses a new issue for American society. If a drug can provide so many benefits, should it be kept off the market because it also can induce abortions? "We have to weigh risks and benefits of a social nature," he said. ■

FEBRUARY 28, 1988

THE HIGH COST OF THINNESS

Robin Marantz Henig

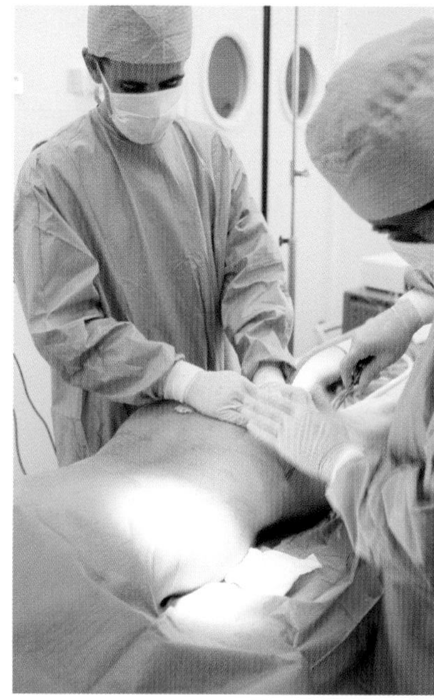

Suctioning fat from the thighs, rump, knees and face may seem an extreme way to pursue good looks. But the American Society of Plastic and Reconstructive Surgery announced recently that this technique, called liposuction, is "safe and effective."

Liposuction has become the most common form of cosmetic surgery done in the United States: more common than face lifts, nose jobs, skin buffs, wrinkle fills or eyebag removals. In 1986 alone, nearly 100,000 liposuctions were performed, most of them on people who weren't, in any medical sense of the word, obese. They were people who generally run none of the ordinary health risks of being fat, such as high blood pressure, heart disease or diabetes. Their only problem was that, in their opinions, they were not slim enough.

So here we have a potentially deadly, expensive antifat operation that is, according to advocates like Dr. Robert Bernard of the New York Regional Society of Plastic and Reconstructive Surgery, "very definitely not for the overweight." Here is an operation that works best on the people who need it least (the more fat removed, the higher the risk); that, among other things, can lead to disability from fat clots, blood clots or severe depletion of bodily fluids; that doesn't always even improve the patient's looks.

Yet this is the operation that has become the most popular cosmetic surgery of our time, because so many people seem to want an easy way to look thinner. But beyond the cute names and euphemisms, which make the procedure sound as simple as vacuuming a closet, is the truth about liposuction. It is major surgery. The patient faces a one- to two-hour operation, most often under general anesthesia and most often requiring an overnight hospital stay, followed by six weeks or more of limited activity—including wearing a tight girdle so the skin won't sag later. Pain, numbness, bruising, discoloration, depigmentation and other transient complications can linger for as long as six months.

As for the severest risk, death, it is true that 11 deaths is a low mortality rate, on the order of .01 percent. (Eleven is the number of deaths brought to the attention of the surgery society's ad hoc committee on new procedures; the actual total may be higher.) But low mortality rate or not, 11 deaths is 11 deaths too many. Should anyone die in the name of vanity? These 11 patients—not to mention the thousands incapacitated or inconvenienced—were healthy when they went in for their operations.

"These are usually young people," says Dr. Kenneth Christman, an Ohio plastic surgeon whose first—and last—liposuction resulted in his patient's death. "The patients getting liposuction are 20, 30, 40 years old; these are people who have no business dying."

SEPTEMBER 6, 1988

Gene Studies Emerging as Key Engine of Science

Harold M. Schmeck, Jr

The science of genetics is fast becoming what geneticists always knew it was: the central and most provocative science of life.

How far and fast the field has come was abundantly apparent at a recent major international meeting in Toronto. Many, perhaps most, of the scientific reports given there would have been incomprehensible to geneticists as recently as a decade ago. Some would have been derided as fantasy.

But today the revolution of modern genetics that began 35 years ago when the structure of the genetic material DNA was discovered has entered a new time of acceleration.

"Genetics is a great engine driving the advancement of knowledge in a whole host of fields in biology," said Dr. Philip Leder of Harvard Medical School, a major figure in modern research on gene functions.

In an interview last week he cited many such fields in human genetics alone. He noted that there has been improved diagnosis of a wide range of diseases and treatment of some; better understanding of the biology of the brain and central nervous system, and discovery and production on a large scale of many rare human substances that are coming into use to treat a wide range of ills, including such major killers as cancer and heart disease.

At the Toronto meeting, the 16th International Congress of Genetics, one of the most heavily attended scientific workshops was on transgenic mice—animals with foreign genes, sometimes human, sometimes of other species, that were transplanted into them as embryos. The animals are proving valuable to science in many ways; for example, they provide fresh understanding of how genes called oncogenes contribute to the cancer process.

The first human oncogene was isolated and reproduced in the laboratory in 1982 and the first success in transplanting genes into embryos of mammals occurred two years earlier. Not many years before that first successful transplantation, eminent scientists had scorned the idea that it might be achieved before the 21st century.

The numbers are evidence of how vigorous and expanding the science of genetics has become, Dr. Haynes said. "Today genes can be identified, weighed, measured, counted, manipulated, replicated and mutated in test tubes, and shuttled from cell to cell, even across species barriers," Dr. Haynes said in his opening address.

The processes of splicing, analyzing and rebuilding genes are today so routine and so largely automated that a major topic of the Toronto meeting was how to carry out a huge project to translate the chemical messages of all the three billion subunits of the human DNA. That project is controversial today, but not because anyone doubts that it can be done.

Some geneticists believe the project would become an immense source of valuable new insights to be mined for decades by scientists exploring the biology of human health and disease. Others believe there are better ways of using their efforts to push back the frontiers of knowledge.

Both camps are convinced that their branch of science is only just beginning to exert its full potential impact for the better understanding of life and for improving the human condition. ■

DNA molecular model kit from 1986.

OCTOBER 17, 1989

CRITICS CHALLENGE RELIANCE ON DRUGS IN PSYCHIATRY

Daniel Goleman

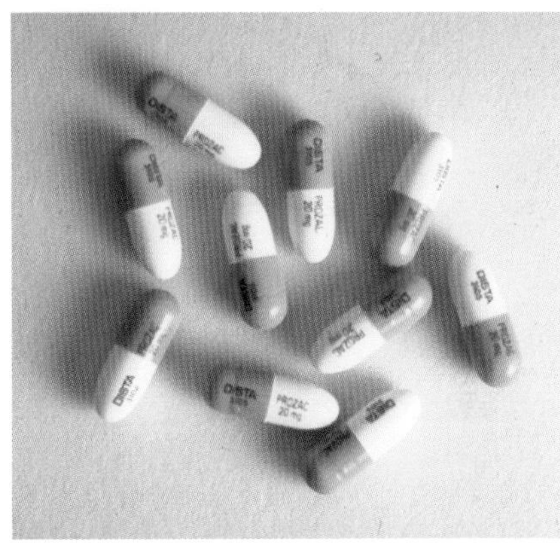

The United States Food and Drug Association approved the prescription anti-depressant medication Prozac in 1987.

The movement among psychiatrists to rely more and more on using drugs to treat mental disorders is coming under strong attack. Critics contend that scientific studies evaluating the effectiveness of psychiatric drugs have been systematically biased, exaggerating the medications' potency.

The drugs under challenge include many of the main medicines used to treat anxiety, depression and schizophrenia. Critics say close scrutiny of the scientific literature suggests that many studies of such medications are flawed and that their results should be regarded with skepticism. Further, they say, the scientific debates and professional doubts on the question have been isolated in the professional community, and patients have been left in the dark.

The challenge is disputed by advocates of biological psychiatry, who see mental disorders as diseases of the brain that can best be treated with medication rather than psychotherapy. They say the critiques make too much out of minor technical

(cont'd. next page)

(continued from previous page)
matters and ignore an overwhelming body of data supporting the effectiveness of medication.

The debate is, in part, another skirmish in the battle for patients between psychiatrists, who can prescribe medications, and psychologists, clinical social workers and other psychotherapists, who cannot.

In the last decade or so, many psychiatrists have shifted toward more treatment by drugs. But a spate of new studies raise questions about that trend. The most recent, published in the October issue of The American Journal of Psychiatry, showed that 45 severely depressed patients who received cognitive-behavioral therapy in addition to drug treatment fared better a year later than those who received drugs alone.

"The answer to all psychiatric problems does not lie in drugs; the magnitude of their effect is far less than the public has been led to believe," said Roger P. Greenberg, a psychologist in the department of psychiatry at the State University of New York Health Center in Syracuse. "We're not arguing that medications do nothing; there's a place for drugs for some people, but they are overrated and overprescribed. In comparisons of psychotherapy and drugs, by and large drugs do not appear to be the superior treatment."

While some psychiatrists worry that a public debate over the efficacy of psychiatric drugs may lead some patients to stop taking drugs they need, others see the debate as useful.

"There are some abuses of drugs, just as there are some careless charges," said E. Fuller Torry, a psychiatrist in Washington. "But it's a healthy dialogue that needs to go on. You shouldn't leave all the decisions to the psychiatrists." ■

NOVEMBER 28, 1989

SURGEONS COMPLETE HISTORIC TRANSPLANT

Gina Kolata

CHICAGO, Nov. 27—The nation's first liver transplant using a living donor had an unexpected complication today as surgeons removing one-third of the donor's liver accidentally nicked her spleen, making it necessary for them to remove it.

Nevertheless, surgeons said tonight that the complicated procedure was generally going well. After seven tense hours of surgery, they had removed the donated tissue from Teresa A. Smith, 29 years old, of Shertz, Tex., and had begun transplanting it into her 21-month-old daughter, Alyssa.

As it began to appear that the operation would be a success, the atmosphere noticeably lightened. In contrast to the first part of the procedure, carried out virtually in silence in the blue-tiled operating room as rock music played.

"This is really the fun part," said Dr. Christopher E. Broelsch, the leader of the surgical team at the University of Chicago Medical Center, as he prepared to implant the donated liver.

The operation was completed at 8:30 P.M., more than 12 hours after it began. "It went extremely well," Dr. Broelsch said. "I am quite excited about it."

Although four similar transplant operations involving live donors have been performed in other countries, until now, all liver transplants in this country have involved livers from cadavers.

Liver transplant surgeons elsewhere in the country said that they were eager to try living donor transplants themselves but that they wanted to see how the procedure fared at Chicago. In such cases, surgeons prefer that the donor be a close relative so there will be less of a chance that the recipient's body will reject the new organ.

Dr. Broelsch said that he would know within 24 to 48 hours after the completion of the transplant whether the liver was functioning normally. He said he would know within one week whether there would be a severe rejection of the new organ by Alyssa's body.

But he added: "This liver is going to function right away. I can tell."

Fashion, Life & Style

In the little-seen film "Rude Awakening," released in 1989, two former hippies return to the New York of the 1980's and discover a new America in which idealism has given way to materialism and political protest has vanished. In one telling scene, three icons of the era—Jerry Rubin, Bobby Seale and Timothy Leary—argue over a business deal. The revolution was truly over.

The voyages of self-discovery and personal fulfillment that typified the 1970's, dubbed the Me Decade, reached their final stops by the beginning of Ronald Reagan's first term. As baby boomers reached their thirties and forties, the itch to acquire took hold. The years of recession and inflation receded, giving way to an economic boom that encouraged wealth accumulation and conspicuous consumption.

The style setters of the Reagan era provided a marked contrast to the muted tones of the Carter administration. Nancy Reagan, surrounded by an entourage of California tycoons and their wives, cultivated a court style that favored designers like Adolfo, James Galanos and Bill Blass.

Glitter and display ruled the upper reaches of Manhattan's social world as well. Wall Street wealth translated into a non-stop pageant of charity balls, A-list receptions at the Temple of Dendur in the Metropolitan Museum of Art, and a fevered competition to serve on the boards of the best museums. The new money launched the careers of society decorators like Mark Hampton and Mario Buatta, known as the Prince of Chintz for his lavish use of floral patterns.

Ronald Reagan And Nancy Reagan

Fashion was on the move, speaking in unfamiliar accents and drawing inspiration from unexpected sources. A new generation of Japanese couturiers emerged, led by Rei Kawakubo and Yohji Yamamoto, captivating fashion critics with designs that recalled abstract geometric paintings.

At the same time, street fashion influenced style every bit as much as the runway shows in Paris and Milan did. Stars like Madonna picked up on the clothing trends in Manhattan nightclubs, then displayed them to an audience of millions through the new medium of music videos. Suddenly, teenagers wanted to wear fingerless lace gloves, crucifix jewelry and underwear as outerwear. California mall rats invented the Valley Girl look. Later in the decade, rap music and hip-hop brought the street styles of Harlem and L.A.'s South Central neighborhood to eager fans.

The fitness boom, reflected in the popularity of Jane Fonda's phenomenally successful "Workout Book," had a profound influence on fashion, forcing designers to rethink the female body and the changing social role of women. Azzedine Alaïa made his name with body-hugging dresses that earned him the nickname King of Cling, while Claude Montana came up with one of the decade's signature looks: big shoulders and tight waists that endowed the female form with a linebacker's power.

Fashion designer Isaac Mizrahi, fashion designer Oscar de la Renta, actress/singer Liza Minnelli and actress Audrey Hepburn ay a reception at the Metropolitan Museum of Art in 1989.

The women from the cast of "Dynasty" show off their shoulder pads.

Most women did not buy Alaïa or Montana. Their designers were Calvin Klein and Donna Karan. They learned to love the big-shoulder look by watching the hit television series "Dynasty," where Hollywood designer Nolan Miller outfitted Linda Evans and Joan Collins with shoulder pads that seemed to take up the entire screen. Films like "Flashdance" popularized fitness fashion—dance-rehearsal clothes like leg warmers and sweatshirts, or tracksuits.

Commercial fashion relied on advertising and marketing, not couture shows. Calvin Klein became a household name thanks to a series of brilliant advertising campaigns for his jeans, featuring models like Brooke Shields and Andie MacDowell and directed by fashion photographers like Bruce Weber and Richard Avedon.

Men got their taste of casual glamour from shows like "Miami Vice," where Don Johnson wore T-shirts under unconstructed jackets, voluminous pleated linen trousers, loafers without socks, Ray-Ban Wayfarers and lots of pastel.

More conservative buyers opted for the preppy look, a reinterpretation of old-guard establishment style championed by Ralph Lauren, a former Brooks Brothers salesman. The impulse was international. In Britain, it was favored by the tribe known as the Sloane Rangers, epitomized by Diana Spencer, a Sloane icon before her marriage to the Prince of Wales. In France, the look was known as "bon chic, bon genre"—or BCBG, for short.

Americans wanted to live well, and Martha Stewart sympathized. Her first book, "Entertaining," published in 1982, catered to the same fantasies of the good life as did Ralph Lauren's clothing designs. Every generation requires an official guide to good taste and gracious living. Stewart stepped into the role in the 1980's, addressing a surprisingly broad audience. Kmart, sensing Stewart's mass appeal, signed her up to produce a signature line for its bargain-priced stores.

Food and fine dining, once the preoccupation of a small eccentric subculture, began to attract large numbers of the affluent, pleasure-seeking tribe known as yuppies, who haunted the latest restaurants and swore allegiance to fine wine. The food revolution that began in California at Chez Panisse gathered steam, and a new American cooking style emerged. Chefs like Paul Prudhomme and Larry Forgione showed the potential of traditional American ingredients and regional styles. France no longer dominated the culinary conversation.

A sample meal at Chez Panisse.

The appetite for good food coexisted, sometimes uneasily, with a strict mandate handed down by fashion magazines and advertisers: be thin. A rash of diet books and workout manuals showed how to stay svelte and toned all the way to old age. The federal government came to the rescue when the FDA approved a new artificial sweetener, aspartame. Lean Cuisine, introduced in 1981, tapped into a growing market when it offered low-calorie frozen meals. The American waistline continued to expand regardless.

Nintendo's Game Boy was introduced in 1989.

Video games did not help. Children who, in days of yore, would have played sports instead spent their time with arcade and computer games like Pac-Man, Donkey Kong and Super Mario Brothers. Rubik's Cube, a puzzle with moveable parts, required a certain amount of manual labor, but its heyday was brief. The expansion of cable television made it even more difficult to move from the couch.

What you saw depended on where you stood. The same America that witnessed an alarming dramatic rise in cocaine use among the middle classes also experienced a revival of evangelical Christianity, a conservative shift that would dramatically reshape national politics for years to come. In the end, there was only one thing that Americans could agree on in the 1980's: when the Coca-Cola Company, with great fanfare and a marketing blitz, introduced New Coke in 1985, the public rejected it unanimously

NOVEMBER 5, 1980

THOSE PRECOCIOUS ADS

Sandra Salmans

Fifteen-year-old Calvin Klein model Brooke Shields in 1980.

He has winsome brown eyes, she has tumbling blond curls, and neither of them is a day over 11 years old. "You've got the look I want to know better," he sings to her. Leaning toward him intently, she sings back, "You've got the look that's all together."

The "look" is Jordache jeans for children, and the 30-second television commercial is an example of a new—and highly controversia—generation of advertising. While advertisers have long exploited sex and youth to sell their products, recently they have begun to pitch that appeal to ever-younger markets. In the last few months, it is widely believed, there has been an explosion in sexually suggestive commercials using child models and aiming at the prepuberty set.

One of the most controversial series of commercials, for Calvin Klein jeans, is actually aimed at adults but features a 15-year-old film star, Brooke Shields, who made her debut a few years ago as the nymphet of "Pretty Baby." In the seven commercials, the teen-ager is given such double-entendre lines as "What comes between me and my Calvins? Nothing!" and "If my Calvins could talk, I'd be ruined."

Such commercials have offended a number of adult viewers. "We've been getting an awful lot of letters from all over the country," said Evelyn Dee, a staff member of Morality in Media, an antipornography group. "A lot of people think Brooke Shields is being exploited."

Manufacturers acknowledge that they also have received protests, but they note that it is hard to quarrel with the commercials' apparent success. "We got a negative reaction," said Warren Hirsh, former president of Puritan Fashions, which manufactures Calvin Klein jeans. "But I'll be frank: Our business was quite good." ■

Nancy Reagan chose a single-shoulder James Galanos gown for the 1981 inaugural ball.

JANUARY 21, 1981

WITH A NEW FIRST LADY, A NEW STYLE

Leslie Bennetts

When her husband was inaugurated as the 39th President, Rosalynn Carter decided not to buy a new gown for the ball; she wore an old blue chiffon she had purchased six years earlier and worn for Mr. Carter's inauguration as Governor of Georgia.

After Ronald Reagan became the nation's 40th President yesterday, Mrs. Reagan prepared to appear at the inaugural balls in a handbeaded gown designed by James Galanos. Its cost is estimated by industry experts to approach five figures and the overall price of Mrs. Reagan's inaugural wardrobe is said to be around $25,000.

Such differences bring into sharp focus the contrast between Mrs. Carter's style and that of Nancy Reagan, who is already being hailed by some as a glamorous paragon of chic and criticized by others for exercising her opulent tastes in an economy that is inflicting hardship on so many.

Fashion designers are ecstatic about Mrs. Reagan's emphasis on clothes and effusive in their descriptions of her personal style. "She represents what I would call a thoroughbred American look: elegant, affluent, a well-bred, chic American look," said Adolfo, one of Mrs. Reagan's favorite designers. "She has very feminine taste, but not cute, not frumpy. If she has a blouse with a little ruffle, it's elegant, it's not overbearing. She herself is more important than what she has on. She has expensive taste, but it's an image of good taste. I think there are many women who would like to look like her."

Many fashion figures expect the impeccably groomed Mrs. Reagan to stimulate their industry. "She's going to have a great influence on fashion," said Mollie Parnis, who has designed clothes for every First Lady in the past thirty years, although she has not yet designed anything for Mrs. Reagan. "She likes clothes, she entertains beautifully, she will be wearing the right thing at the right time, and it has to filter down." ■

JULY 6, 1981

An Abundance of Hair on City's Streets

Angela Taylor

Hair—the real thing, not the musical—is having a big revival this summer. What seems to be tons of hair can be seen bouncing around the city, more of it than has been fashionable for decades.

Hair was long in the 1940's when Rosie the Riveter was required to wrap it up in a scarf so she wouldn't get tangled in the production line machinery. It was long again in the hippy 60's, but then it was either ironed straight or frizzed into Afros. This year, it is long and wildly curly and the woman with a wealth of tresses is stopping traffic on the city streets.

The naturally curly-haired woman is, of course, especially blessed. But for her straight-haired sisters, there is always the beauty salon. Hairdressers are dusting off techniques they haven't used in years: setting hair on rollers, or rag curlers, or contraptions that look like twisted macaroni.

Teasing—it's called back combing these days—is back. And hair stylists sometimes cheat for photography by using 1960's fake "falls" or propping hair up with horsehair "rats." Salons are reporting a brisk business in permanent waves to give hair the body required for the current effects.

What women say they like best about longer hair, in addition to the fact that it goes with this year's luxurious, sexy fashions, is the possibility of variations. Madeline Stone, a songwriter, explained that she was born with curly hair. "I don't do a thing to it after I wash it," she said. "I'm so glad to be in fashion again." ■

JULY 30, 1981

THE DRESS: Silk Taffeta with Sequins and Pearls

Susan Heller Anderson

LONDON, July 29—For her long walk up the aisle that transformed her into a princess, Lady Diana Spencer, in the most romantic storybook tradition, wore a sequin-and-pearl-incrusted dress with a 25-foot train.

Made of ivory silk taffeta produced by Britain's only silk farm, the dress was hand-embroidered with old lace panels on the front and back of the tightly fitting boned bodice. A wide frill edged the scooped neckline, and the loose, full sleeves were caught at the elbow with taffeta bows. A multilayered tulle crinoline propped up the diaphanous skirt.

A diamond tiara belonging to Earl Spencer, Lady Diana's father, anchored her ivory tulle veil, aglitter with thousands of hand-sewn sequins. Also borrowed was a pair of diamond drop earrings from Lady Diana's mother, Frances Shand-Kydd.

For the final tradition-bound item -something blue—a blue bow was sewn into the waistband of the dress. A fiercely and successfully kept secret, the dress had been guarded day and night by a security organization at the workrooms of the designers, David and Elizabeth Emanuel. A final fitting, necessitated by Lady Diana's loss of 15 pounds in the last four weeks, was held last week at Buckingham Palace. Emmanuel-designed wedding dresses sell for about $3,700 at Harrods, the London department store. But a dress manufacturer in Cardiff, Wales, had already produced two copies of the gown by 4:30 P.M. today. In three days, the company said, it will make 90 more copies selling for $500.

Queen Elizabeth's dress, coat and hat, by Ian Thomas, were bright acquamarine crepe de chine, worn with a double strand of bird's-eggsized pearls and a large diamond brooch. Festooned with a fluffy hat of osprey feathers, Queen Elizabeth the Queen Mother chose vivid sea green silk georgette with floaty panels by her favorite designer, Hartnell. Princess Anne and Princess Margaret were both colorful, the former in a white dress with buttercup yellow flowers, the latter in deep peach georgette.

A popular choice was cornflower blue, now being called "Lady Diana blue" after the suit she wore in her widely published engagement photograph. Mrs. Shand-Kydd, Princess Alexandra and the Princess of Wales's former roommates chose similar shades of blue, as did the Countess Spencer, stepmother of the Princess, and Prime Minister Margaret Thatcher. ■

FEBRUARY 17, 1982

NANCY REAGAN GIVES UP DRESS DESIGNER LOANS

Hedrick Smith

WASHINGTON, Feb. 16—Do clothes make the woman? Not necessarily. Not when they are expensive designer gowns on loan to the White House. Not when they stir a public controversy. Not when the First Lady is involved.

Hurt by public criticism of her practice of accepting expensive dresses and later giving them to museums, Nancy Reagan has found a graceful way out. She is phoning her designers and is also informing the general public that she will no longer accept loans of clothes from fashion designers.

In the last few days, the White House has sent out nearly 40 letters to people who have written to comment, both positively and negatively, about Mrs. Reagan's acceptance of dresses from designers such as Galanos, Adolfo, Bill Blass and David Hayes and then donating 13 of their dresses to museums.

she felt she was helping the American clothing industry

"She really just got tired of it all, of people misinterpreting what she was doing," said one close personal aide who requested anonymity. "She felt she was helping the American design industry and the American clothing industry by publicizing American fashions. But it was beginning to take a bad slant, as if she didn't have any wardrobe of her own, which is ridiculous. It got to her."

The letter, signed by the First Lady's special assistant, Elaine D. Crispen, explains that for many years in California as well as in the White House, Mrs. Reagan has given her clothing to museums "because she believes that the clothing of any particular era is a visual story of the people of that period."

And, in response to some public suspicions, the letter emphasizes that in the past, "neither she nor the designers have taken a tax deduction" for the donated dresses. ■

JULY 31, 1983

MUCH ADO ABOUT THE JAPANESE

Carrie Donovan

The commotion is widespread, though the clothes are just beginning to be. They come from Japan and involve, in particular, the work of three designers born, bred and trained there: Issey Miyake (say me-yak-ee), Rei Kawakubo (ray cow-wa-coo-bo) and Yojhi Yamamoto (Yo-ge ya-ma-mo-toe). Though there are several other talents whose designs are spreading commercially—among them Matsuda and Kansai—it is this trio that is spearheading a startlingly original fashion movement.

THE COMMOTION IS WIDESPREAD

It is a movement that has an established foundation: Miyake has, since 1972, been presenting collections in Paris or New York and selling to a few avant-garde boutiques, among them Charivari in New York. But it is only in the last year or so that the Japanese movement has gained momentum, as Miyake has been joined by fellow countrymen in introducing their collections at the widely attended and reported pret-a-porter showings in Paris.

Last March, at the presentations for fall 1983, the Japanese look suddenly was very apparent, almost overshadowing the rather mild French offerings. As a result, it made headlines, conversations and controversy. The Japanese had "arrived" and fashion-conscious customers everywhere were extremely curious to know and see all about the movement.

But fashion followers, critics and store buyers seem to be split in their opinions. Either the Japanese movement is the most exciting thing to happen to fashion in years, or it's an outrage, a travesty of what clothes are supposed to be about. The believers of the latter are dismayed at such things as sweaters sprouting holes, albeit carefully calculated ones; at coats and dresses cut with slits here and there and hemlines that dip down and up in a seemingly haphazard way; at sleeves that slip well down over the hands and sometimes come four to one garment. They cannot conceive of women wanting to engulf themselves—most of these clothes are cut on the voluminous side—in something so strange, so never before seen.

Understandably, the big American department and specialty stores have moved very cautiously in investing money and space in something so violently at odds with the rest of today's fashion picture that is safe and predictable. It is still not easy for the curious customer to locate the new Japanese clothes in these big stores, even in one as forward-thinking as Bloomingdale's.

Yet these qualities of newness, strangeness, inventiveness, of surprisingly fresh thinking are drawing an ever-increasing number of admirers to the Japanese designs. This Japanese infusion—or intrusion, depending on the viewer's interpretation—is serious and far-reaching. It questions what is balance and symmetry and what is drama and sophistication. What these clothes—particularly those of Miyake and Kawakubo—possess above all else is strength and elegance. They are never unsure, or, for that matter, flamboyant. And while they certainly do not satisfy accepted Western standards of coquetry and allure, they establish their own vocabulary for initiating the same emotions.

The young, with their sense of adventure, are also drawn to these Japanese designs, often despite their high price. Karl Lagerfeld, Paris's premier avant-garde creative talent, has commented that the new fashion for the 1980's "will come from the Japanese. . . . They are so much better educated for the future. They can be happy in a changing world. They don't compare clothes to the past as we do. They want the future." ■

MARCH 25, 1984

ON THE TRAIL OF LONDON'S SLOANE RANGERS

Caroline is squeaky clean, freshfaced and easy to identify by the string of (real) pearls, which she wears at all times. Henry is cleancut and pink-cheeked, and can be spotted from a distance by his too-large coat (handed down from his father). Closer inspection will reveal either a red- or blue-and-white boldly-striped shirt (during business hours) or a good, plain, but frayed, one (in off-duty hours). Both are Sloane Rangers.

Sloane Rangers have been a distinct species for years, but it took two journalists, Anne Barr and Peter York, to come up with the collective noun—and Caroline and Henry as the archetypal names—a few years ago. Official recognition came with the publication of their "Sloane Ranger Handbook" just over a year ago and, more recently, the "Sloane Ranger Diary."

Visitors to London wishing to study the breed should simply take a walk through Sloane Ranger land—known to the Post Office as the SW 3,5,7 and 10 districts, and to the general public as Knightsbridge, South Kensington and Chelsea—where they will find them thick on the ground: at work, rest and play in their natural habitat.

Sloane Rangers congregate there because they feel safest among their own kind. Named for Sloane Street and Sloane Square, the hub of their universe, Rangers are upper-class men and women who come "up from the country" to live in London after finishing school or university. Their object is marriage. By definition, they are young for, once married, they may stay in town until the first little Sloane arrives, but then it's back to the country, Land Rover and Labrador.

In the meantime, most work (although the women will stop as soon as possible after the wedding) and most share flats, as the Princess of Wales did. "POW," as the Princess is known among those who used to be her peers, is Super Sloane and the fashions she set during her engagement were simply the standard Sloane Ranger uniform. She has progressed, but they have stayed the same. Sloane Rangers are conservative, conventional and insular.

To see them in their greatest concentration, if time is limited, walk down Beauchamp (pronounced Beecham) Place past one bijou boutique after another. Caroline will have a mane of thick (but manageable) hair, held back perhaps by a 1960's velvet-covered hairband. There will be a Hermes scarf somewhere in evidence (perhaps tied around the strap of her shoulder bag). In winter, she will be wearing a Loden coat; in summer a dress (probably Liberty print). The sportif Caroline will wear a lambswool crewneck sweater in a clear color with the lace collar of a blouse turned over it. She may wear jeans or a skirt in navy, burgundy or olive with colored pantyhose and low-heeled Gucci shoes.

Henry will be wearing a bespoke suit, dotted tie and silk handkerchief (probably also spotted). Or, perhaps, he will sport his casual garb: jeans, decent tweed jacket and either a navy Guernsey or olive army sweater; sometimes he will brighten the outfit with a yellow pullover.

Princess Diana, Sloane Ranger, in 1982.

Madoona at the 12th Annual American Music Awards in 1985.

JUNE 7, 1985

Madonna and Her Clones

She uses only one name, but no matter. Only those who have been residing on the planet Jupiter for the last several years need to ask Madonna who? Rock's hottest female star, whose hits include "Borderline," "Material Girl" and "Like a Virgin," is in New York for performances at Radio City Music Hall and Madison Square Garden.

She is leaving her mark not only on popular music but on popular style as well. Madonna's style of dress might best be characterized as part Jayne Mansfield, part street urchin. It emphasizes a low neckline and, often, a bare midriff, lace tights, anklets, thrift-shop jewelry, fingerless lace gloves and more.

How much more? Well, flower-print tight pants, a gold crucifix, Merry Widow black lace bras, chiffon strips as hair bows and jeweled belts. A tumble of disheveled curls tops it all off.

For those who want a little historical perspective, the popularity of this mode has been traced all the way back to 1983, when Cyndi Lauper, a rock star with a sense of humor, first put all the pieces together. But while Miss Lauper carved out a niche for the look, Madonna has turned it into a bona fide fad, taken up by legions of adolescents and post-teenagers such as those below.

This week, Madonna, left, was window-shopping on Madison Avenue, ice cream in hand, a camera-shy bodyguard at her side, and typically decked out. Her ensemble included tight flower-print black pants, Merry Widow top, bare shoulders, assorted rosaries and sunglasses. The girl had all her material. ■

NOVEMBER 13, 1985

Fashion Experts Rate Princess's Style

Michael Gross

From the moment Princess Diana landed on American soil, the big names of America's fashion world were watching. As usual, they found little to agree on but this: "She is," said Lynn Manulis, president of Martha, "the most charismatic fashion figure that's come down the pike since Jackie O."

Diana's clothing choices are, of course, limited by royal protocol. But Evangeline Bruce, who sat next to Prince Charles at the National Gallery dinner in Washington Monday night, said, "I have the feeling the title bit doesn't come into her dressing." Mrs. Bruce is the widow of David K. E. Bruce, who was Ambassador to Britain.

Diana's style gave some fashion arbiters pause, though their criticism was often couched in awe. "She is just an overwhelming personality," said Geoffrey Beene. "It doesn't matter what she wears. I don't think the clothes are that good, some of the design is not on target to me as a professional, but who cares? Her presence overcomes any banalities of dress."

Like the winds that kept Diana clutching at them, some blew cold over the Princess's hats. "I just think they're terrible," said Eileen Ford, co-founder of Ford Models.

The designer Mary McFadden disagreed. "I love her flying saucer hats," she said.

Michael Katz, another designer, joined in Miss McFadden's approval. "I don't like all of them," he said, "but it's good and it's new."

While no observer was willing to call Diana a pacesetter, some thought there were lessons to be learned from her wardrobe. "The essence of being well dressed is to be appropriate for every occasion," said Amy Levin, editor of Mademoiselle. "She does that. Maybe her things could be a little bit racier or more modern, but I think she's great."

"I don't know what appropriate means," said Grace Mirabella, the editor of Vogue. "You've got a 23-year-old who is in a special place, so appropriate becomes rather different." She found the Princess "marvelous" in gowns, but thought her days clothes seemed "a little less than glamorous."

"There's nothing dowdy about her," Diana Vreeland said. "She's got radiance. What she wears is incidental but she has wonderful taste. Aura is everything. It's the essence of the woman. You can buy the town out and not get off the ground, but if you've got the personal aura, you just shine, you give pleasure."

Indeed, Diana gives pleasure, but the key may not be her clothes. "It's difficult for her not to look well," said Bill Blass. "Her youth counteracts her clothes. You don't notice her clothes as much as her. There's a lot to be said for youth, kid." ■

Diana, Princess of Wales, wearing a red silk taffeta evening dress designed by fashion designer Jan Van Velden.

MARCH 18, 1986

THE MAKING OF A DESIGNER

Lisa Belkin

Tommy Hilfiger is headed for the top—just ask him.

"I think I am the next great American designer," he said. "The next Ralph Lauren or Calvin Klein."

The 34-year-old Mr. Hilfiger is not shy about sharing his vision of his future. For three months a Times Square billboard compared him to those designers, with Perry Ellis thrown in for good measure. Now a 10-second television commercial and a six-page magazine ad announce: "First there was Geoffrey Beene, Bill Blass and Stanley Blacker. Then Calvin Klein, Perry Ellis and Ralph Lauren. Today, it's Tommy."

In an industry where reputations usually take root slowly, Mr. Hilfiger's is being created from scratch in less than two years. Eighteen months ago he was a freelance designer with no formal training and a handful of clients. Today he is a project of Murjani International Ltd., a leading apparel manufacturer, which has spent up to $20 million, and plans to spend millions more, to make his name a household word.

The strategy is raising eyebrows—and a few voices—in the fashion industry.

"I give it a year," said Jack Hyde, consulting head of the Menswear and Marketing Division at the Fashion Institute of Technology. "He's not a designer, he's a creation."

But Mr. Hilfiger and his backers express confidence in their plan.

"I think they felt I was the natural all-American-looking, promotable type of person with the right charisma," said Mr. Hilfiger, who bounces when he talks. "I'm that person. I'm a marketing vehicle."

The company calls the look "The New American Classics"—oversized oxford shirts with large pockets, khaki pants with a signature button over the zipper, bright red blazers with contrasting lining. Shirts sell for $40 to $50, slacks from $45 to $55, jackets for $90 to $160. The first shipments, made largely in the Far East, arrived in the stores last spring.

Reaction to the collection has been mixed. "Calvin Klein did that four years ago, Polo did that last year, that was big in Europe four years ago, that's long gone," Mr. Hyde said as a model paraded before the Fashion Institute audience in a series of Tommy Hilfiger outfits.

Right now, it seems, Mr. Hilfiger's advertisements are better known than Mr. Hilfiger's clothes. The campaign was developed by George Lois, of the advertising firm of Lois, Pitts & Gershon, who arrived at a planning meeting carrying samples of ads for such designers as Calvin Klein, Ralph Lauren, Perry Ellis, Alexander Julian, Robert Stock and Giorgio Armani.

"We bought every telephone booth in New York," said Matthew Rubel, vice president of Tommy Hilfiger. "We bought the billboard in Times Square."

The company expects sales of $16 million this year, about as much as it has spent to promote the line in the last 18 months. "It's in its infancy," Mr. Hilfiger said. Soon, Mr. Horowitz said, the Tommy Hilfiger name will be licensed on such items as dress shirts and accessories. In June, Mr. Hilfiger will introduce his women's apparel line.

"We think we've found the formula," Mr. Hilfiger said. "We found the way to tell the public we're here without being too arrogant. We created a whole fame."

DESIGNER DONNA KARAN: HOW A FASHION STAR IS BORN

Carrie Donovan

Donna Karan at an event at the Metropolitan Museum of Art in 1986.

For a designer of clothes on New York's Seventh Avenue, the capital of this country's women's fashion industry and the center of a $20 billion business, a car and driver is a sure sign of success. Each weekday evening near 39th Street, in the vicinity of 550 Seventh Avenue, the most elite building in the garment district, the chauffeurs and limousines can be seen arriving in clusters.

A few months ago, the industry noted that someone new had joined this group. A driver named Marvin Morris began showing up in a beige Lincoln Town Car, waiting patiently each evening near 550 for his boss, Donna Karan, who is generally considered by the fashion press and retailers to be the newest industry star.

In just 12 months, Donna Karan, New York, has become the designer label that sells out in the stores faster than any other. The Karan clothes are a prime resource in 120 of the most prestigious stores in America, among them Saks Fifth Avenue, Bloomingdale's, I. Magnin and Bergdorf Goodman. According to Bergdorf's chairman, Ira Neimark, the Donna Karan boutique—the area of the sales floor in which her designs are sold—produces "the highest sales per square foot of any American designer space in the store." Saks Fifth Avenue concurs—a particularly significant declaration because Saks has devoted more square feet to the Karan clothes that any other store and has the boutiques in 11 of its 41 branches. Marvin Traub, chairman of Bloomingdale's, says, "Our first-year Karan sales figures are close to $2 million, and they would be even better if we had them in all our stores."

Miss Karan takes on her own label at a time when the risks are high. A young designer named Stephen Sprouse, for example, was discovered in 1983, was hailed as the latest fashion superstar in 1984 and disappeared in mid-1985. His fall collection for that year, dubbed a success by the fashion press, was never manufactured, because his company owed at least $600,000 to creditors. "Fashion," says Jay Meltzer, an apparel analyst for Goldman, Sachs & Company, "is a high-risk investment. If it works, it's wonderful." The fact that most women now work in offices has had an enormous effect on clothes and the money made from them, as anyone familiar with the histories of Calvin Klein, Anne Klein & Company and Liz Claiborne knows well. But Donna Karan's clothes push the working woman idea further. They are made, the designer says, for the needs of top professional women—women in charge, women so sure of themselves and their careers that, even at work, they can enjoy clothes that are sophisticatedly curvy and, as opposed to those of, say, Anne Klein, a bit sexy. Not all the women who buy the clothes hold down an executive job, of course, or a job of any kind. But the interesting fact is that they seem to want to look as if they do.

Women first encountered the clothes that Donna Karan designed for her own label at a showing at the Bergdorf Goodman store in New York on June 18, 1985. Because fashion is a business in which a tiny change, a nuance of design, can have important consequences, Miss Karan's designs were hailed as a totally new concept of dressing. Although that was an overstatement, the idea behind these clothes obviously filled a void. The outfits begin with a pair of semi-opaque, dark, waist-length tights. Next comes a garment called a bodysuit, a slip-on of Italian-made jersey or knit. It has long sleeves, pulls on over the head, fits snugly and fastens with snaps at the crotch. This serves to replace a conventional sweater or blouse. Donna Karan has designed more than a dozen versions, most with pads to shape the shoulders. Over all this the designer wraps, or ties, skirts, shawls, jackets and coats, most made of fabric from the superb mills of northern Italy and all draped and shaped with luxurious folds.

These clothes retail from $180 for some of the bodysuits to as high as $2,200 for one of this fall's new baby llama coats. Most of the outfits can be assembled for about $1,000, and another $1,000 or so is needed to accessorize them the way Miss Karan intends.

The fashion press was impressed by the clothes last year. The designs were featured many times in Women's Wear Daily and shown twice on the covers of Vogue and the Fairchild Publications' fashion newspaper, W. There has been extensive coverage in Harper's Bazaar, The New York Times Magazine, Elle and in leading British and French fashion magazines.

The clothes she creates, Donna Karan says, are made to enhance her own figure. She is constantly concerned about her trim, but not rail-thin, body. Every day she spends 12 minutes on an exercise bike, and three mornings a week she works out for an hour under the eye of a personal trainer. "I must, I must, I must improve my bust," she chants at one point. Reflecting this concern, her designs have a way of emphasizing the curve of the waist and the hips without stringently outlining them. The shawls and jackets are camouflage for bumps or protrusions. ■

JUNE 13, 1986

BRACES: HIDDEN ASSETS GO PUBLIC

Michael Gross

It's hot and muggy, and all around town a sartorial secret of some of New York's most conservative men is being revealed as they doff their jackets on steamy streets.

Suspenders—or braces—in wild stripes, polka dots and plaids are emerging from beneath conservative business suits. Nude women and acrobats and devils and dollar signs stream down starched shirts. Why? Well, basically to hold up their trousers. But that is far from their only appeal.

Many men say they wear flashy braces as a counterpoint to their serious business lives.

Call them braces or suspenders—the words are used interchangeably, though with a strong preference for the former among the affluent and assured. Either way, they are now big business, high style and an easy last-minute gift for Father's Day.

Nowadays, suspender stocks go far beyond the traditional solids, jacquards, brocades, foulards, florals and paisleys, stripes, spots and plaids. While some snappy dressers such as Philip B. Miller, chairman of Marshall Field's in Chicago, still favor simple solid colors, today's best-selling brace styles are motifs: roosters, parrots, devils, owls, Confederate flags, playing cards, bulls and bears dripping ticker tape, cupids and acrobats.

America's most conservative men are the leaders of this resurgence. "Your more affluent people wear braces," said Elliott Rabin, co-owner of Peter Elliott (1383 Third Avenue at 79th Street), a speciality shop.

"I wear naked ladies," said Sewantana Kironde, a director of the Chase Investment Bank. He calls his collection of 20 braces "a sartorial pretension."

That pretension is often passed down through generations. Jack Heller, the Foreston Development's president, whose grandfather always wore braces, said: "They put humor into an otherwise serious life." ■

OCTOBER 1, 1986

LIFE IN THE 30'S

An 80's fashion staple: leggings and high-top sneakers.

Anna Quindlen

Who are these people who can take a pair of black pants and a black sweater and an important jewel and turn it into a fashion statement anyway? I want to meet one. I don't know these people. I know people like me who buy outfits—the kind of people who have a party to go to and panic, and in that panic run out and make a kamikaze attack on a dressing room and buy themselves an outfit. Three months later, they run into that outfit in the closet and say, like the caterpillar in Wonderland, "Whoooo are Yooooou?"

This is why I need a fashion arbiter. You've read about fashion arbiters in the newspapers, people in black pants and important jewels who come out twice a year and say something like "bolero jackets." And there you are. Six months later you're squeezing into a bolero jacket and wondering where all that thigh came from.

Luckily my fashion arbiter is not exactly like that. My fashion arbiter is my sister. She is young, hip and on a budget, so she always knows which young, hip and cheap things are coming along. She knows my strengths and weaknesses.

My strength is that I have credit cards and will do what she says. My weakness is that I am old. She can't come in and say, "Things with big holes in them and a rosary around the neck," because I just won't listen. My other weakness is that I can easily get bogged down in fashion trends and embarrass her by slogging around in big shirts a full year after big shirts have become passe. (Of course, there was a time when I never did anything but slog around in big shirts or their dress equivalent. But my sister does not handle maternity trends.) Twice a year, my sister comes into my kitchen and says something like this:

"Reeboks. With heavy crew socks scrunched down."

That was last year. Imagine my surprise to find out that the trend of the season was an antelope. How would I wear it? What would I wear with it? Where would I keep it? Would the dogs like it? And what about the crew socks? Were they for me, or the antelope?

(cont'd. next page)

(continued from previous page)

"They're sneakers," my sister said. "Leather. White. Black. Pink. Preferably high tops with a velcro close." "What do I wear them with?" I said. "Stirrup pants." "Stirrup pants? What are stirrup pants?" "They're like made of stretch fabric and they have stirrups that go under your foot and you wear them with scrunched down crew socks and the Reeboks."

"Wait a minute," I said. "These sound like stretch pants. I know what stretch pants are. People wore them in the 1960's and everyone looked terrible in them except for Marilyn Monroe."

"They are just like stretch pants except they look good," my sister patiently explained. "Get a big sweater. Get Reeboks. Get scrunched down crew socks."

So I have to stick with my sister no matter what. Not long ago she came into my kitchen and said, "Shells."

I said nothing. My immediate impulse had been to ask about sand and mollusks and whether lobsters were included, but I was still stinging from the antelopes. "And hoop earrings," she added. "You don't mean shells as in blouses, do you?" I said. "No sleeves? Round neck? Ban lon?" "What is Ban lon?" my sister asked. "Never mind. Those shells?"

"Yes, those shells," my sister said. "With a short straight skirt. Big hoop earrings. And flats."

My whole life began to pass before my eyes. For a moment I thought longingly of taffeta and bustles as I realized that if I took this advice I was going to be wearing approximately the same outfit I had worn to a particularly dreadful junior high school sock hop when I was 13 years old.

"I did this 20 years ago," I said. "But 20 years ago I had no thighs. Now I have children. I already did shells and short skirts and big hoop earrings."

"Well," said my fashion arbiter, "I think you're going to do it again." ■

AUGUST 2, 1987

On Campus, the Look Is, Well, Studied

Lisa W. Foderaro

The collegians of the 1980's have in fact become cleaner cut and more clothes-conscious than those of the 70's. Even those completing their schooling on campuses with a Bohemian flair say the number of students wearing baggy, earth-colored clothes has dwindled in the last few years and that more students are adopting a sportier, more conservative appearance.

"In the 1970's, the idea of caring about your college wardrobe was outmoded," observed Sandy Horvitz, fashion director at Mademoiselle magazine. "But this is the 80's, and people seem more into clothing and being a little chic."

Fashion experts have already forecast a number of campus-bound fads for fall—from kilt pins skewered through Oxford shoes instead of laces for an offbeat preppy look for women to oversize button-downs in prewrinkled cotton for a more-rumpled-than-thou look for men.

Students in or near an urban area seem more willing to experiment with styles and accessories. "Most people dress for effect—political, social or otherwise," said Morris Panner, now a third-year student at Harvard Law School. "You see a lot of classic L.L. Bean dressing, as well as the latest styles out of New York."

On the West Coast, trendiness reigns. In southern California, especially in the Los Angeles vicinity, dressing draws its inspiration from the surfer culture as well as from national currents. For the moment, several styles rage: oversized, wildly patterned and brightly hued shorts; huge T-shirts and sweaters; stone-washed denim jackets; pastel sweatpants and sweatshirts and "micro" mini-skirts in denim, suede and leather. In northern California, however, where the weather is more variable, campus clothes largely resemble those of the Northeast.

There is one kind of student that seems rather hardened to the vicissitudes of style—the graduate student. The lack of interest usually reflects these students' concerns with more weighty matters, namely gearing up for the career track. Yet a certain self-assurance appears to take hold at that stage as well.

"You already have your own identity, and you know that image is not going to make or ruin your graduate-school career," said Chris Reid, a first-year student at Georgetown Law School.

SEPTEMBER 6, 1987

THE SWAGGER OF CHRISTIAN LACROIX

Carrie Donovan

It is a hot August afternoon in the south of France. A gypsy woman stands in a shady doorway off the sunlit village street. She beckons to the woman, who approaches and gives her some coins. She reads his palm. Then Lacroix turns and, with a big smile, reports to his friends:

"She says I'll be famous in six months."

Everyone has a good laugh. Six months! What an out-of-date gypsy! The French news magazine Paris Match is on the stands this very August day with a big spread about Lacroix's spectacular rise to the top of the fashion world. Newspaper stories, some with front-page headlines, have just appeared in France, Britain, Italy and the United States. Radio broadcasts and television spots from all over have been pouring out ardent enthusiasm for Lacroix's first couture collection.

People who follow fashion are saying that no reputation has ever been made as quickly as Lacroix's, no new direction set so suddenly. True, they say, Lacroix has come out of the Paris couture, that rarified old world of made-to-order clothes for superrich women, but they are certain his ideas will be copied everywhere. They contend his influence will be evident soon in the stores, no later than this winter, when millions of women will begin to dress his way: in clothes that are unabashedly glamorous and theatrical.

Last January, he left his job at the Paris couture house of Jean Patou, where for the past few years he had been designing dramatic couture clothes that created a stir. In 1986, in particular, he introduced bouffant (or "pouf," or "bubble") cocktail dresses that were so widely copied that they quickly changed—from slinky to effervescent—the way many fashionable women looked in the evening.

On July 26, Lacroix showed 60 luxurious outfits to the world's fashion press and to key figures in the fashion industry. They were mostly dresses he had designed for women to wear to the fanciest social occasions—in his words, "a dress for one woman for one occasion." All were made of sumptuous materials—satins, velvets, laces, embroidery and furs—and with shapes and details inspired by the traditional flouncy costumes of southwest France. He employed unusual geometric patterns and mixed such colors as orange, scarlet, fuchsia and purple. He decorated the clothes with thick embroidery, and with braid, beads and jewel-like trimmings. Necklines plunged in shawl-like vees, and the silhouettes were bouncy and curvy. The clothes matched in theatrical thrust the music Lacroix's models strutted to—Andalusian themes full of trumpet calls and assertive flair. Nothing was sedate or retiring. Lacroix's performance made the critics gasp.

Designer Christian Lacroix showing his Haute-Couture, Fall-Winter collection in Paris, France, on July 26, 1987.

American stores went to battle to be the first to offer a garment bearing the Lacroix label. Bloomingdale's won. On Wednesday, Sept. 16, as guests arrive at sunset for a party in the New York store, a single outfit from the Lacroix couture collection—No. 27, a brown, chartreuse and pink satin cocktail dress in size 6—will be unveiled in a Bloomingdale's Lexington Avenue window. The dress will go on sale after 10 the next morning—for $15,000.

Asked where he wants to be in five years, Lacroix says, "I want to deserve all the success of this couture, to prove that Agache did not make a mistake. I think I have to be careful with success, to remain young. Perhaps the secret is enthusiasm. We have to stay passionate, to have joy and happiness with our work. We hope not to take ourselves too seriously. Well," he makes a quick gesture with his hand and smiles, "perhaps just a little serious in business." ■

OCTOBER 21, 1987

Acid Wash Gives a Lift to 7th Avenue

Isadore Barmash

The surprisingly simple technology of washing jeans in chlorine to reduce the stiffness and abrasiveness of the cotton denim has been a boon to the often-depressed garment industry. The chlorine removes dyes, giving the garments a lighter, worn appearance while softening them.

First used two years ago by the Italian company of Rifle Jeans, the process was dubbed acid wash, reflecting the streaked appearance of the finished product, as a sales tool. In fact, no acid is involved. "The term acid wash is a complete misnomer," said Joyce Bustindy, a spokeswoman for Levi Strauss & Company. "We call our process white wash."

The process was quickly picked up in the United States, according to New York garment makers, and has figured in the sale of millions of jeans, jackets and skirts.

"Acid-washed clothing is the most important thing that has come along in the men's and women's garment industry in years," said Jack Taylor, divisional merchandise manager of Gottschalk's Inc., a retail chain in Fresno, Calif. "We're selling thousands of them a week in our 11 stores, in all price brackets. They're extremely popular for the 14- to 26-year-old market."

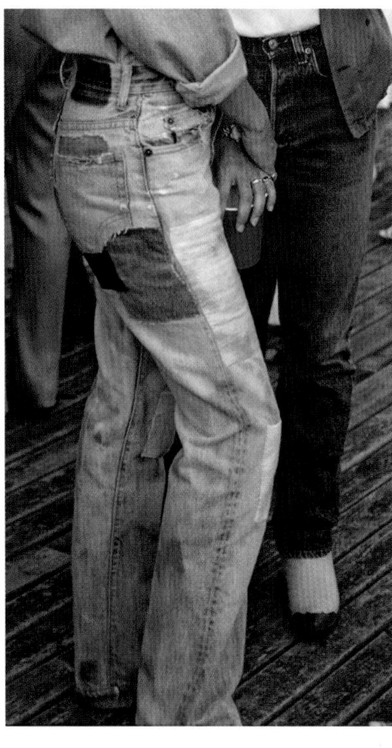

MAY 8, 1988

MEN'S STYLE; BULLS AND BEARS

Ruth La Ferla

Jay Spieler says he's still partial to the vivid shirts, paisley ties and plaid suits he wore in the giddy days before Black Monday. Spieler, a broker with Drexel Burnham Lambert, insists last October's market collapse hasn't caused him to change his image by a thread. But others, still feeling last October's aftershocks, are trading in their showy plumage for something more subdued.

Wall Street, to be sure, has traditionally been viewed as a bulwark of sartorial conservatism. And though its somber image has grown livelier in recent years, that trend has, to some extent, reversed itself. Does this mean the era of "imperious excess" described by Tom Wolfe in "The Bonfire of the Vanities" is on its way out?

Some people think so. "Seasoned and sophisticated men are dressing less ostentatiously," says Robert Minicucci, a young investment banker at Shearson Lehman Hutton. "Corporate America is looking more for good ideas than for gladhanders who have their suits made in Savile Row."

Similarly lofty sentiments echo along corporate corridors and issue from the

JANUARY 24, 1988

THE SHOULDER PAD: LIKE IT OR LUMP IT

Stephanie Sakson-Ford

This will be remembered as the year of the shoulder pads. As fast as I could take them out, designers and manufacturers were putting them in.

Wearing what is in effect prosthetic devices says a lot about our society. Contact lenses are in, glasses are out. Our bodies have to appear perfect, slim, muscular. Shoulder pads must be surrogate muscles. On those of us foolish enough to leave them in, it can backfire. A bag slung over one's shoulder can cause the pad to migrate onto the edge of the shoulder, giving away the fashion secret. Worse yet, washed ones can lump up and create an unusual silhouette.

But the thing that annoys me most is what they attempt to transform women into: men.

A stylish suit with straight, quarterback shoulders and a slim, tubular skirt is entirely antithetical to the shape of a woman's body.

I'd like to ban on shoulder pads for environmental reasons as well. Foam does not deteriorate as fast as fabric, leather or even vinyl, as anyone who has ever sat in a 10-year-old car seat knows. Years from now, archeologists will unearth hundreds of foam triangles attached to tattered shreds of linen and ask, "Why ruin this nice piece of fabric with a hunk of foam? ■

Joan collins wearing her iconic large shoulder pads!

lips of merchants who cater to a downtown trade. Some believe Wall Street's renewed tendency to dress down predates Black Monday, and owes its revival to a mix of factors, not the least of which are last year's insider trading scandals. "After the Boesky thing," says Jay J. Cohen, an executive vice president of Taylor & Ives, a corporate design and financial advertising firm, "everyone wanted to keep a low profile." To that end, he believes, some men have adopted a calculatedly nondescript style, donning muted sack suits and immaculate white shirts as a form of sartorial camouflage. The object, says Cohen, is to create a persona that "blends in with the crowd."

More telling, perhaps, is Ralph Lauren's decision to issue the sack suit. For fall, he is showing a natty, squarish model complete with soft shoulders, three buttons, a back vent and flat-front trousers.

But there are limits to all this sobriety. Heavy-soled brogues, plain shirts and muted patterns may, ironically, be riding the crest of fashion's new wave. Yet spending hasn't suffered visibly.

A seasoned Wall Street banker with sensitive fashion antennae interprets this news in more human terms. His friends, he says, are swapping their gold-banded watches for leather-strapped vintage models, exchanging their suspenders for crocodile belts and other old-money artifacts. "The look," he notes, "is understated, but it still costs." ■

JUNE 12, 1988

TO START WITH...; AN ARTFUL PLOY

Hermes ties.

Hermes silk neckties have survived the market crash as Wall Street status symbols, firmly knotted around the necks of investment bankers, bond traders and other highfliers.

Recently, a group of investment bankers was observed in the firm's executive dining room, pondering the subject of the Hermes tie over broiled swordfish steaks and Diet Cokes.

The conversation suggested arbitrage as the bankers compared the prices they pay for the only item of sartorial splendor Tom Wolfe ignored in "The Bonfire of the Vanities." The duty-free shop at the Tokyo airport used to have the best price and selection, one man said, but the strong Japanese yen has made shopping there all but prohibitive. The duty-free shop in the Paris airport is good in a pinch, volunteered another, but it doesn't have the best patterns. A third banker spoke up: The Hermes boutique on 57th Street in Manhattan offers 50 patterns in a range of 12 colors. (There aren't any regimental stripes, though. The French go to England for those.) Fifty-seventh is fine, commented still another banker, if you are inclined to pay $75 for a tie.

John Giroux, a senior partner in the law firm of Dumler & Giroux and a man who often wears Hermes ties, counsels, "Anyone you could conceivably want to impress would already know it's Hermes." ■

JANUARY 15, 1989

IT'S A SMALL WORLD

Ruth La Ferla

Angel Antonio Sanchez-Cabanas turns away from the glare of Madrid's midday sun and leans his frame against a wall, the better to show off his garb. He wears a snug-fitting toreador-style jacket, a black ribbon tie—the sort of thing that Zorro might have fancied—and a Mexican belt with a hand-tooled silver buckle. He mates this all-Latin composite with American khaki trousers and a pair of fancy snakeskin cowboy boots, a present from a friend in Oklahoma.

At the Burghy, a popular fast-food restaurant in Milan's Piazza San Babila, schoolgirls sip Cokes, preen and display their own variation of Euro-American chic. Here the requisite uniform is usually an oversized tweed sport coat pinched from papa, a demure white blouse with a Peter Pan collar and slim jeans that are faded to robin's-egg blue. High-High-top sneakers, clunky Doc Martens shoes or slightly beat-up Top-Siders complete the look.

Prague has its own answer to the Burghy: the Moskva Arbat, a neon-lit, Eastern-bloc-style McDonald's. Jan Zvonechek sits on a bench visitor, "America is very far away." You wouldn't know it from his outfit: he wears a black leather motorcyclist's jacket, a pocket-size denim pouch hanging around his neck and a pair of loose, battered-looking jeans.

In metropolitan centers as far-flung and diverse as Shanghai, Bonn and Buenos Aires, there appears to be a consensus among the style-conscious young about what's hip, hot or current on the street. These days it's hard at a glance to distinguish a schoolgirl in Hong Kong from her leather or denim-clad counterpart in another part of the world.

It isn't precisely that these kids look alike. But young iconclasts—who tend to spearhead trends—have forged a common fashion language whose vocabulary might include such oddly assorted elements as a fringed American cowboy jacket, German track shoes, a Soviet Army trench coat, a kilim-patterned vest, or dainty Edwardian knickers picked up at a London flea market.

The style derived from combining such items might best be described as a global melange. It is both the byproduct and the

(cont'd. next page)

(continued from previous page)
most visible expression of an international cultural synthesis trend watchers say has been long in the making. In the early 1970's, Herman Kahn, the writer and futurologist, argued that with the spread of the Beatles' influence, "pop" culture, which had previously been a strictly American phenomenon, became internationalized. "This sort of thing is going to continue," Kahn predicted. "Perhaps in 1985, an Italian, Tanzanian, Bolivian or Turk will listen to an Icelandic pop singer on a Thai-made transistor radio, wearing clothes first designed in a boutique in Seoul."

Kahn's forecast for the 80's wasn't far off the mark. These days information travels with a speed even he might not have imagined. At a time when vanguard American rock groups play and record in the Soviet Union; when an architect working in Tokyo can instantaneously "fax" a series of drawings to his office in London, and when designs by fashion innovators like France's Jean-Paul Gaultier or England's Vivienne Westwood are splashed across the pages of magazines from Athens to Atlanta, it's clear that young people draw their ideas from a common image bank.

"We find that young women everywhere have similar interests and preoccupations," says Robert A. Gutwillig of Hachette, the publisher of Elle magazine.

For New Yorkers at fashion's cutting edge, making fun of the norm is one way to stand out from the herd. At Patricia Field's East Eighth Street boutique, which serves as an afternoon meeting house for many of the same young people who haunt Manhattan's clubs late at night, a young woman with a starlet pout seems to consciously send up her own Long Island upbringing when she sweeps through the shop in a much-too-large mink coat. Field says a lot of her customers meld influences from sources as diverse as Harlem and St. Moritz for a similarly satiric effect. A typical look might consist of black stovepipe jeans, an acid green ski jacket and festoons of gold rope chains.

It may differ in its details, but what passes as street style varies little from place to place around the world, Field contends. She recalls a recent visit from a Soviet fashion editor, who, much to Field's surprise, had never been to New York, but seemed to grasp intuitively what was hip by downtown standards. "The world," Field says, "is a very small place." ■

A young couple wearing leather jackets and 80's clothing in London, 1980.

JULY 9, 1989

GUYS AND DOLLS AT THE MALLS

Ruth La Ferla

The prevailing wisdom has it that the mall is the great societal leveler of our time, where fashion is reduced to formula. Indeed, a casual observer of the youth scene in any one of the nation's 32,000-plus shopping centers is tempted to agree with Joan Didion, who has called malls "toy garden cities . . . profound equalizers, the perfect fusion of the profit motive and the egalitarian ideal." At Smith Haven Mall, a middle-income shopping center in Lake Grove, L.I., a group of 14-year-old girls, all coifed to resemble some hybrid of Rod Stewart and Farrah Fawcett, line up at the ladies' room mirror and, with synchronized movements, mist their hair with fixative.

Mall kids tend to take their style cues from city kids. Indeed, at no time in memory have progressive—and often provocative—urban fashions been so speedily absorbed into the mainstream. These days, an onlooker might be hard pressed to tell a stylishly funky Manhattan East Villager from her equally stylish counterpart in Short Hills, N.J., or Plano, Tex.

One reason is that stores like the Limited, Benetton, Aeropostale, Units and Banana Republic—most of which once were exclusively urban, offering such style staples as pre-aged denims, canvas knapsacks, bandanna-print shorts, pocket T-shirts, tube skirts and leggings—now have outposts in malls across the country.

Mall girls, as a rule, cultivate a look of innocence, a buttoned-up but lightly teasing alternative to Madonna's aggressively sexual lingerie chic. The newer style is espoused by pop performers like Debbie Gibson, who arrays herself in floral vests and flounced skirts over leggings, when she isn't wearing tomboyish jeans cut off at the knees. Boys lean toward denim and leather, worn over T-shirts with loud skateboard-style graphics. The truly hip, though, pay homage to Rick Astley. The British rock star likes to wear double-breasted retro suits, patterned 1940's ties and a modified pompadour reminiscent of the 1950's.

Still, it wouldn't be fair to accuse these kids of mechanically aping their idols. To use a word they tend to overwork, most aim for a look that has "quirk." A trait that's hard to isolate, quirk is expressed in the cartoonishly overscaled, but nonetheless elegant, tan linen suit worn by Shahal Khan of Bridgewater, N.J. Or in Amanda Gingery's purple hose and close-clipped platinum hair, both of which contrast smartly with her thigh-high black knit dress. "I wear black a lot," says the worldly 14-year-old from New Jersey. "It brings more attention to my face." Who does she strive to look like? "Oh, nobody special," she replies, a little vaguely. Gingery, too, likes to "make up" her look as she goes. ■

APRIL 16, 1989

If Fashion Is Changing, it Must Be Almost 1990

Bernadine Morris

Working on the collections introduced in Europe last month and in New York last week, fashion designers had more to think about than just making pretty clothes that sell. For those who see themselves as pacesetters and who try to anticipate how women would like to look before women think of it themselves, there was another consideration: These were the first collections that would be sold and worn in the 1990's.

The 1980's were a fairly nondescript period, which helps explain why Christian Lacroix's poufs and bubble skirts, brilliant colors and inventive designs captured the attention of the fashion world two years ago. His wildly exuberant designs and costume party look loosened the shackles of restraint from other designers, and fashion was off on a binge. The bubble burst, but the Lacroix legacy remains: he has made the world safe for short skirts.

Most designers in this country and abroad have stopped their skirt hems just above the knees.

But hemlines alone do not make lasting fashion news. The next major change will come out of the test tube, says Geoffrey Beene, one of this country's most innovative designers.

He foresees new fabrics that bond together, are warm without weight or are cooler for summer.

He has been focusing on short skirts for the last five years on purely logical grounds. Short skirts are easier to get around in and weigh less than long ones, he points out. He has sought out the lightest fabrics available.

It is a look already adopted by fashionable young women in the streets of Milan and Paris, and it has been featured by other designers, including Jean-Paul Gaultier in Paris and Donna Karan and Carolyne Roehm in this country.

The disappearance of the skirt and the unencumbered design of clothes in general will influence the look of the early 1990's, at least. They may pave the way for truly modern clothes that reflect the new roles of modern women. ■

NOVEMBER 12, 1989

THE MODELS AND THE GLAMOUR TRADE

Woody Hochswender

The search for "the look," the magic that will make lipsticks jump into pocketbooks and magazines walk off newsstands, is endless and truly global. Start with the lips. Lips are big right now. Today's hot models—Cordulla, Christy, Michaela, Naomi—all have full, seductive lips. It used to be the eyes that did the selling, but now the fashion magazines send out big wet kisses to the unsuspecting passerby.

Then there is height: 5 feet 9 inches is the minimum at most agencies, and several leading models are 6 feet or more.

Finally, the hair: it's got to be a bob. Ever since Linda Evangelista, a gamine figure on countless catwalks and magazine pages, cut her hair this year and her career zoomed, the cool have got cropped.

It could be just that fluky. For all the money involved, the modeling industry is remarkably fortuitous and chaotic. When you call a modeling agency in New York, you immediately sense the frenetic pace of the enterprise. The receptionists and bookers answer breathlessly. Nervous energy buzzes through the line.

For a recent photo session, Naomi Campbell, a lithe 19-year-old model, was running four hours late. While the photographer, editor, stylist, and makeup artist pondered an empty set in a rented studio, her booker at Elite kept insisting Ms. Campbell had been delayed at the hairdresser. When she finally showed up, her hair didn't look done.

The British-born Ms. Campbell looks deceptively ordinary off camera but comes alive when the flash begins to pop, conveying a manic Josephine Baker-style energy. She has recently hit the big time—covers for Vogue, fashion shows for all the top designers and much-publicized nights on the town with Iron Mike. That kind of success is extremely rare and far from the workaday reality of the modeling business.

There are around 3,000 working models in New York—from cover girls to showroom and runway mannequins to production fit girls—toting portfolios, heading for go-sees, dashing from fashion show to fashion show. There are perhaps another million wanna-bes.

For several seasons, the designer shows have been dominated by an elite group of models, an A-team of tall, stately walkers, among them Iman, Dalma, Ilonka (many models are known professionally by first names, perhaps to enhance their mystique but also to protect their privacy), Anna Bayle, Ally Dunne, Magaret Donahoe, Naomi Campbell, Linda Evangelista, Melanie Landestoy, Maureen Gallagher, Vanessa Duve, Louise Vyent and Veronica Webb.

This group, and a few others, are booked way in advance by the leading designers, and they appear in show after show, like some barnstorming basketball team. Samples are cut to fit their bodies. Cars are provided to shuttle them between assignments. Designers want to be certain their collections are shown in the best possible light—store buyers, being human, are not immune to glamour—even if it means paying $2,000 a day, including time for fittings, hair and makeup, for each model. ■

Model Naomi Campbell

NOVEMBER 9, 1980

A NEW WHITE HOUSE STYLE IS ON THE WAY

Enid Nemy

American President Ronald Reagan (1911–2004) and First Lady Nancy Reagan relax in the sitting area of their White House bedroom, Washington, DC, November 1981.

Whether they're in or out, intimates or sideliners, thrilled or able to contain their joy, the men and women around First Lady-elect Nancy Reagan agree on one thing: The White House is in for a change of style.

There will be, they say, considerably more social activity encompassing more people of diverse interests and occupations, imaginative and elegant parties, small dinners, and what several described as "a return of dignity."

"Nancy has her own imprint," said Harriet Deutsch, a friend who lives in Beverly Hills, echoing numerous others. "She has flair and style, and she won't be like any other First Lady," said Bonita Wrather, wife of Jack Wrather, a Los Angeles entertainment executive who is on the Reagan transition team.

There was, too, a general belief that Mrs. Reagan would not be as active politically as her predecessor, and that although she would be likely to influence fashion, it would not be through any conscious attempt.

"Her dinner parties are lovely, formal but casual with great warmth," said Jerome Zipkin of New York, the social moth who flutters between coasts and continents and was with the Reagans the night of the election. "And Ronnie always makes an amusing toast that is pertinent."

The White House menus would be neither faddish nor hokey, Mr. Fine predicted. "She doesn't like to cook, but she likes to eat, and she knows food," said Monsieur Marc, the hairdresser Mrs. Reagan visits in New York. "This will not be a Coca-Cola and ketchup White House."

Another friend, describing the Reagan "warmth and style," used the President-elect as an illustration. She was one of the guests at the election night dinner party given for the Reagans and their intimate friends by Mr and Mrs. Jorgensen.

"When the results were obvious," she said, "Ronnie turned to all of us and said, 'You were all so good to me when I was unemployed, and I'm not going to change a bit now that I've got a job.'"

Four UCLA students model the latest in college "preppie" fashion in 1981.

JANUARY 4, 1981

BEHIND THE BEST SELLERS; 'PREPPY HANDBOOK'

Dudley Clendinen

Last spring, Jonathan Roberts was 25 years old, a graduate of the Cambridge School in Boston and Brown, a funny young man who wanted to write. "Usually, people tell you to write what you know," he says. "For years, I thought—'What do I know? I'm just a Preppy.'"

Then he thought again and confided his idea for a book to three Preppy friends, all single, clever, mid-twentyish and residents of Manhattan: Lisa Birnbach of the Riverdale School and Brown, Carol McD. Wallace of Country Day and Princeton and Mason Wiley of The Episcopal School and Columbia University. They agreed

JULY 14, 1981

Big Hopes for Pudding Pops

Sandra Salmans

WHITE PLAINS, July 9—First, there was Jell-O, a gelatin dessert, and its sales were good. Then General Foods created Jell-O pudding. Now, if the giant food company has its way, there will be Jell-O Pudding Pops, frozen pudding on a stick.

Conceived four years ago, test-marketed since 1978, Pudding Pops promises to be one of the most successful products to emerge in recent years from the General Foods kitchens. The company refuses to say when it will be introduced nationwide. But General Foods, which has already sunk millions of dollars into the new product, clearly has great hopes for Pudding Pops.

"It's potentially a very large business," said Peter Rosow, general manager of the company's desserts division, who predicts that it will make major inroads on the lucrative ice cream market.

Pudding Pops is only one new product at General Foods, which introduces several each year. Currently, it is also testing Jell-O Slice Creme, a freezer cake mix, and Jell-O Gelatin Pops, whipped gelatin on a stick.

While mothers still wanted its "wholesome goodness" for their children, Mr. Rosow said, afternoon snacks such as ice cream and packaged cakes were usurping the place of conventional desserts that were not readily portable and required preparation time. "The question was, 'How can we put pudding in the path of the afternoon snack opportunity'?" said Mr. Rosow. "What we did was to freeze it and put it on a stick."

Even its flavors were borrowed from traditional Jell-O pudding: chocolate, vanilla, banana and butterscotch. The reason, Mr. Rosow said, is that "its credentials are pudding credentials."

General Foods scientists say that the development of Pudding Pops was not quite that simple, but the technology involved was certainly less sophisticated than that of other new General Foods products such as Lean Strips, a textured protein substitute for bacon, or frozen Crispy Cookin' french fries. The dessert division does have some higher-technology products under development, but with Pudding Pops, Mr. Rosow conceded, "it is hardly the Manhattan Project." ■

it's hardly the Manhatten Project

to collaborate. Miss Birnbach took on the chores of editor, writer and manager of the budget. She paid everyone else out of a checkbook imprinted with her nickname, "Bunny," and a stemmed martini glass.

What emerged in September from the Workman Publishing house was "The Official Preppy Handbook," by its own definition, the "In book of the season." It is about Mummy and Daddy, whose lives and family rooms are imprinted decorously with the repeated images of ducks, whose Saturdays in the fall are given to tailgate picnics before the old school game, whose children are nicknamed Muffy or Missy or Buffy, Skip or Chip or Kip.

By the time Muffy and Skip become Mummy and Daddy, they will have mastered these and the million other details involved in living the elite and proper life of Prep. Or they can buy this book. Anyone can. "You don't have to be a registered Republican," the preface says invitingly. "In a true democracy, everyone can be upper class and live in Connecticut. It's only fair."

That may or may not be true, but it is funny. On the other hand, its authors say the book itself, 224 pages of wry detail, is a true account of being Preppy. "Our feeling was that it is such an inherently amusing subject that we don't have to make jokes about it," says Mr. Roberts. "All we have to do is tell the truth." Who cares? Anyone to whom it matters, or who wants a laugh. ■

JANUARY 27, 1982

HOW THE 'LIGHT' FOODS ARE CONQUERING AMERICA

Bryan Miller

So many new "light" products have appeared on the market in recent months that light foods and beverages represent the major growth field in the American food industry. Such items as light canned fruit, light pancake mix, light spaghetti sauce, light salad dressing, light ketchup, light frozen dinners, light wine and light cocoa mix can be found on supermarket shelves. Other light fare that is to appear soon includes potato chips, snack foods, fruit drinks and cookies.

Industry executives and market analysts predict that the upsurge of light foods, which has been under way for two years, will continue and they venture that when the scramble to offer new products is over, low-calorie foods could constitute up to 10 percent of the $300 billion American food market.

"Light" (or the more trim spelling "lite") is a loosely defined term to describe food and drink that contain less than the normal amount of something—sugar, starch, salt, alcohol—and, hence, fewer calories.

The Quaker Oats Company, which introduced its Aunt Jemima Lite Syrup in the summer of 1980, says it has increased syrup sales by 50 percent.

Del Monte reports sales of its light canned fruits—50 calories a half-cup serving against 85 for its regular products—"right on target." Fernando R. Gumucio, head of the company's grocery products division, said he believed that the fruits, which have less sugar in their packing syrup, would soon make up 15 to 20 percent of Del Monte's sales of canned fruit.

Three nutrition and diet specialists who were interviewed said that light products might provide some help to people trying to reduce sugar or other elements in their diet but that the products were without much merit as weight-reduction aids.

"I don't think all these products have really made a dent in the obesity problem in this country," said Dr. Myron Winick, director of the Institute of Human Nutrition at the Columbia University College of Physicians and Surgeons. ■

JULY 21, 1981

A CUBE POPULAR IN ALL CIRCLES

Ron Alexander

The summer's most popular cubes are not the colorless frozen water kind that do nothing but melt lazily in chilled glasses filled with tea, Perrier or Kir. No: This summer's big cube is a maddening Mondrian-colored plastic puzzle, composed of 27 subcubes that rotate on horizontal and vertical axes. It's called Rubik's Cube, after Erno Rubik, a teacher of architecture and design at the School for Commercial Artists in Budapest.

The object of his addictive invention is to scramble the solid-color sides by twisting and turning the rows of cubes on their inner axes and eventually return them to their original places. New Yorkers are currently twisting and turning Rubik's creation on streets, stoops, subways, buses, benches and beaches—and in bars, beds and, no doubt, hot tubs.

And the first regional competition for the title of United States Rubik's Cube champion will be held Saturday in Burlington, Mass., near Boston.

According to Ideal, more than 10 million cubes have been sold worldwide since May 1980. Not all purchasers become as violent as the man who flung his cube from the window of a Fifth Avenue bus one scorching day last week, shouting "The hell with it. It's impossible." Actually, it's not.

Benji Fisher, 18, a student at the Bronx High School of Science, says he can solve the puzzle in two and a half minutes. Mr. Fisher, one of eight United States representatives in the recent International Mathematical Olympiad, does not recommend haphazard twisting and turning. "If you make one move every second, you'll probably get the cube back to the way it was in a few billion years," he explains. Mr. Fisher, who says he did not use formal mathematics in reaching his solution, offers this advice: "Don't be afraid to mess up something that looks good; find simple maneuvers that leave most of it unchanged; remember precisely what those moves do."

B. Dalton Fifth Avenue began stocking the cube and gets $6.95, but prices vary all over town. It's $9.95 at F.A.O. Schwarz, $10 at Macy's and Bloomingdale's, $4.94 at the Toys "R" Us stores and $13 at the Museum of Modern Art, which recently accepted the cube for its Design Collection.

Children, according to the observations of Hilda Griesfeller of F.A.O. Schwarz, are the ideal "cubies." "They have infinitely more patience," she says.

Well, not all of them. When Dayvonne Anderson, 11, of Riverdale, found Ideal's solution pamphlet to be as infuriating for her as the puzzle itself, she promptly tossed the cube in warm water, removed all 54 of the colored plastic coverings and rearranged them so that all six sides of the cube were once again a solid color. Then, with a sigh of satisfaction, she proudly announced, "I won!"

MARCH 14, 1982

Mainstream U.S. Evangelicals Surge In Protestant Influence

Kenneth A. Briggs

Often overshadowed by fundamentalism and shunned by church liberals, the mainstream of evangelical Christians has emerged as the most powerful new force in American Protestantism.

These evangelicals, mostly moderate in theology and politics, have been growing in numbers for years. But now they are

Rev. Jerry Falwell with then-Vice President George H.W. Bush.

strengthening their own institutions and making deep inroads in the 50-year-old liberal leadership of the major Protestant denominations.

The signs of evangelical vitality are seen in the robustness of student movements, in the enthusiasm of lay people and in the clergy, which is well-equipped by education and outlook to bring the historic tenets of the Protestant faith to bear on 20th-century problems.

In essence, evangelicals stand between liberals and fundamentalists. They stress a personal commitment to Jesus, confidence in the Bible and enthusiasm for spreading the word and seeking converts. Evangelicals tend to hold in high importance the Second Coming of Christ, the saving act of Christ's death, the Virgin Birth and the physical Resurrection.

In comparison, liberals do not hold so uniformly to this set of beliefs and are less absolutist and literal-minded on questions of doctrine. While evangelicals share many beliefs with fundamentalists, and the lines sometimes blur, the fundamentalists tend to be more absolutist in their approach to Christian theology.

Evangelicalism was the hallmark of 19th-century Protestantism. It was a blend of Reformation doctrine, exuberance for the democratic ethos and hope that people and societies could change for the better under God's will. Evangelicals today maintain they are on this historical trunk line.

Since the 1980 elections, when fundamentalists such as the Rev. Jerry Falwell put effort and money into a campaign to influence voters, the moderates have felt an increased need to press their own cause. Many evangelicals and fundamentalists have made vigorous efforts to define themselves as separate from each other. Relations have become strained.

Dr. Timothy Smith, a church historian at Johns Hopkins University, believes there are 12 streams of evangelicals. Among them are Pentecostals, members of transplanted European ethnic churches, and Baptists, in addition to the millions of conservatives in the liberal denominations. "Fundamentalism," Dr. Smith noted in an article written in conjunction with Cullen Murphy in a recent issue of the Woodrow Wilson Quarterly, "is merely a subculture within 'mainstream' evangelicalism, a relatively young and extreme movement within an older moderate one." ■

MARCH 24, 1982

COOKING IS BECOMING A CHOICE AMERICAN CAREER

Marian Burros

The French-born chef-owner of La Cote Basque in Manhattan, Jean-Jacques Rachou, has 21 chefs in his restaurant kitchen and 16 of them are American. "I know this will get me in trouble," he said recently, "but American chefs are better than French. They have a good education. They're smart. They learn fast. They respect you. They really want to learn."

The Americans at La Cote Basque are part of a burgeoning phenomenon, a new breed of young men and women who have chosen careers in cooking. In recent years their impact has been widely felt: Professional cooking schools, which once went looking for students, have long waiting lists even though the number of schools has increased dramatically in the last five years. Americans are taking over the kitchens of some of the finest restaurants, once the domain of Europeans, most of them French. In 1973 Johnson & Wales College in Providence, R.I., had 141 students in its new culinary-arts program; this year there are 1,600. According to the United States Labor Department, there will be 86,000 cook's and chef's jobs in the next decade, almost double the openings in the last 10 years.

There are a number of reasons for the boom in the cooking profession. A decade ago French chefs imported Frenchmen to cook in American kitchens. Then in 1969 the Federal Government severely restricted the admission of foreign chefs, so restaurants were forced to hire Americans. At the same time more and more Americans were traveling, eating out, buying cookbooks, taking lessons and cooking seriously. Cooking became an increasingly chic hobby for men; choosing a chef's toque over a doctor's stethescope or lawyer's briefcase became respectable.

Today the chef is seen as a romantic figure. Jonathan Waxman, chef at Michael's Restaurant in Santa Monica, Calif., credits three-star chefs like Paul Bocuse, Michel Guerard and the Troisgros brothers for the new image.

Most chefs and student chefs say they have chosen the field because it offers an outlet for creativity. Mr. Knerr said that cooking for a dining room full of customers was like being in the theater. "There is a feeling of excitement," he said. "I guess it's the same thing an actor or a dancer feels when there's a full house. You are performing. Only, the people smell it, they taste it and they feel it." ■

An executive chef instructs a student in the kitchen at the New England Culinary Institute, Vermont, in the 1980s.

MAY 2, 1982

TAPPING THE HOMOSEXUAL MARKET

Karen Stabiner

Major film studios made a hedged bet this season that the healthy, wealthy and-or wise homosexual was a marketable commodity. Paramount Pictures's "Partners," which opened this weekend, is a comedy about two New York cops (one's straight, the other isn't) who pretend to be lovers to solve a murder. It follows: 20th-Century Fox's "Making Love" (a doctor leaves his wife for another man); Warner Bros.'s "Personal Best" (two female Olympic teammates fall in love), and M-G-M/U.A.'s "Victor, Victoria," in which Julie Andrews finishes off her nun and governess image by playing a woman pretending to be a man who is a female impersonator.

Today, the studios advertise alongside Heublein, Seagram, Perrier, Harper & Row and others, primarily wooing an economically attractive segment of the consumer population—the white, single, well educated, well-paid man who happens to be homosexual.

In tight-money 1982, men with high earning power and low financial obligations are making purveyors of luxury items and leisure services take a second look. While these men are a small percentage of the national homosexual population—one market researcher refers to them as "the upscale tip of the iceberg"—they are, according to The Advocate's publisher, Peter Frisch, a "recession-proof market."

Retailers felt they could no longer ignore the fact that the mainstream population was adopting styles, in dress, decorating and even drinks, from affluent homosexuals. The male homosexual with money was doubly attractive: He spent, and his selections seemed to influence others who spent.

"It was true in the 1930's, the 40's, the 50's and the 60's that we had more discretionary income than other men," says Michael Denneny, an editor at St. Martin's Press and an associate editor of Christopher Street. "But it wasn't until the 1970's that style began being heavily exported from the gay world to the rest of the culture."

One observer, surveying the Los Angeles bar scene, predicts that the sweet drinks currently in favor at bars frequented by homosexuals will be next year's major trend. In fashion, Frisch lists cotton housepainters' pants and aspects of "the western look" as crossovers.

"They're the first to do things," says Barry Lorie, Fox senior vice president, publicity and promotion, who worked on the "Making Love" campaign. "That's a given."

Joe Di Sabato, in addition to serving as an advertising representative, calls himself a "gay-marketing consultant," and is president of Rivendell Marketing. He devotes his professional life to the perpetuation of a particular, if narrow, group image.

"The old image of the gay," he says, "was gay radicals and transvestites. Now it's someone who drives a Maserati and has an Advent TV screen."

What advertisers have yet to do is construct a homosexual prototype to take his or her place in the family of national-advertising characters. McDonald's does television commercials with all-black casts. Stouffer's frozen foods have a long-running series that features a harried career woman. On television and in print, ethnic characters sell everything from Italian food products to Pentax cameras.

But a television commercial has yet to portray two childless, attractive men as they turn off their dual alarm, or brush their teeth side by side at double sinks, or discuss the aroma of the morning's coffee or the crunch of their breakfast cereal and imitation low cholesterol bacon. One man does not kiss another man goodbye as he gets behind the wheel of his low-mileage car.

Will they ever—or is this to continue as a secret courtship? Roger Stone of the Marshalk Agency takes the good-business approach to the issue of two men and toothpaste in television's future. "Of course, you'll have gay men," he says. "In terms of dollars, it's a bigger market than the black market."

Jerry Della Femina pronounces judgment without hesitation. "Not in our lifetime," he says. He is likely right. There is an analogy to be made, however uncomfortable the business community might be about the connection, between the homosexual population and business's attitude toward it. The highly visible, ghettoized male homosexual lives apart from other homosexuals in this country; he is a distinct minority, as are the advertisers who go after him. Like the still-closeted homosexual population—fearful of the ramifications of a public declaration, and unconvinced of the benefits—most providers of goods and services choose either to deny their interest or evade the issue altogether. ■

Actors Robert Preston and Julie Andrews in "Victor/Victoria."

JUNE 10, 1982

CHINTZ FLOWERS IN GRAND REVIVAL

Suzanne Slesin

A bedroom decorated with a Chintz flowered pattern.

Chintz. Just the word conjures up a number of decorating worlds: gracious rooms by such legendary designers as Elsie de Wolfe and Sybil Colefax, cozy morning rooms in English country houses and the currently popular amalgam of these two styles, as evidenced in the work of several prominent New York designers, including Mario Buatta, Thomas Fleming and his partner, Keith Irvine, and Mark Hampton. In these modern adaptations, as well as their predecessors, the overall image is fresh and flowery—rooms festooned with flounced draperies, skirted tables, pillow-laden canopied beds and flounced slipper chairs.

According to Tom Parr, a senior partner of Colefax & Fowler Designs Ltd., the prestigious London-based decorating and fabrics firm, which is known for its high-glaze chintz, the word "chintz" is based on the Hindu word "chint," which became "chintes" and "chintz" in English. The patterned Indian cotton fabric—originally a dressmaking cloth—was first used in Europe in the beginning of the 17th century and had its greatest flowering at the end of the 18th and beginning of the 19th centuries.

In the past, the patterns were hand-blocked, a process that has virtually disappeared today. There are few craftsmen left to do this costly and time-consuming printing process, and the printing of the patterns is now done either by hand silk-screening or by machine.

"Not only does chintz come in patterns of every scale but the colors are always a little off, never primaries, which allows one to use different chintzes together," said Mr. Fleming.

"Nowadays, we refer to chintz as plain or printed cotton," said Christopher Adlington, styling director of Lee/Jofa, a to-the-trade fabric house that recently introduced a range of more abstract, pastel-hued and glazed designs. "They're still chintzes," asserted Mr. Adlington. ■

JULY 2, 1983

SEARLE SWEETENER WINS APPROVAL FOR SOFT DRINKS

Pamela G. Hollie

In the early 1980s, Equal and its European counterpart, Canderel, were the first aspartame-based sweeteners to be sold to the public.

The Food and Drug Administration said yesterday that it had approved the use of aspartame, the low-calorie sweetener of G.D. Searle & Company, for use in soft drinks in the United States. Aspartame, the first sweetener to be approved in 25 years, now becomes the only rival to saccharin in the $4 billion diet soft-drink market.

Until now, saccharin has had a monopoly in the soft-drink market, which accounts for 70 percent of its sales, or about $115 million a year.

"We are working with major soft-drink companies to help them bring their products to market as quickly as possible," said Robert Shapiro, president of the Searle Nutrasweet group. Nutrasweet is the trade name for aspartame. The sweetener is already being used in soft drinks in Canada, Denmark, Sweden and Ireland.

A spokesman for Coca-Cola USA said yesterday that the company had not made a decision on using aspartame in its diet products, but he noted that the company puts the sweetener in its low-calorie drinks in Canada, where saccharin is not approved for such use.

(cont'd. next page)

(continued from previous page)

First approved by the F.D.A. in 1974, aspartame ran afoul of the agency when reports that it might cause brain damage resulted in a stay of approval. No evidence that aspartame caused brain damage was found.

Although aspartame is 300 times sweeter than saccharin and, unlike saccharin, has not been linked with cancer, its high cost may be an obstacle to a large-scale move to aspartame in the soft-drink industry. It costs about $85 a pound compared with about $4 a pound for saccharin. ■

NOVEMBER 29, 1983

'ADOPTABLE' DOLLS AREN'T HAVING ANY TROUBLE FINDING HOMES

David Bird

After two months of searching and getting up early and standing in lines with others on the same mission, Michaline Perez of Passaic Park, N.J., was in luck yesterday. She was able to buy a Cabbage Patch Kids doll.

"I can hardly believe it," Mrs. Perez said as she handed over $50, more than twice the regular price, for the doll. "I finally won."

Mrs. Perez was luckier than thousands of other prospective buyers across the country who have endured shoving, trampling, mauling and long waits in the cold for a chance to buy a doll that everyone seems to want this season.

In Charleston, W. Va., 5,000 shoppers bent on getting one of the 120 dolls available at Hills Department Store started a near-riot, said Scott Belcher, the store's manager.

"They knocked over tables, fighting with each other—there were people in midair," he said. "It got ugly."

In Wilkes-Barre, Pa., a woman suffered a broken leg and four others were injured when 1,000 people, some of whom had been waiting for eight hours, rushed into the Zayre department store to snatch up the few Cabbage Patch Kids available.

The store manager, William Shigo, armed himself with a baseball bat. "This is my life that's in danger," he said from behind a protective counter.

The doll is basically an 18-inch plastic body that comes in male and female models and a variety of clothing, hair styles and features. It has a face of soft plastic that at least one woman described as "homely, beautiful homely, something only a mother could love."

Mrs. Perez finally got her doll at a store in Clifton, N.J., called the Rowe-Manse Emporium. It had run newspaper advertisements saying it would buy the dolls for $40 and sell them for $50.

"The response has been incredible," Olga Vapner, a vice president of the store, said yesterday. "We've been jammed. The phone hasn't stopped ringing. They were lined up in the rain this morning waiting for us to open."

Parents say part of the attraction of the dolls is that each comes with "adoption papers" that the child fills out as well as a name, like Mike Jacie, Berton Pat, Nigel Maynard and Luna Trudy. But the child can put any name desired on the papers.

Asked why she liked the doll, Eileen said, "She has a real bellybutton." ■

FEBRUARY 10, 1984

Tv Dinners Seek Gourmet Market

The continuing success of low-calorie and so-called gourmet frozen foods has revived a market whose palate was dulled by traditional TV dinners. And this year promises an even broader range of entries as the nation's leading frozen food marketers fight for a bigger chunk of what is now the industry's fastest-growing and most profitable sector.

The industry calls them "premium frozen meals." And so far, analysts say, the three leaders are the Stouffer Corporation's Lean Cuisine, Swanson Foods' Le Menu and Armour Food's Dinner Classics. Weight Watchers' entrees and the Banquet Foods Corporation's Light and Elegant are a somewhat distant fourth and fifth.

Indeed, sales of these premium frozen meals—a category that includes both dinners and entrees—have exploded in the last year, spurring sizable jumps in the sale of traditional frozen meals as well.

Frozen Food Age, a trade publication, called 1983 the frozen food industry's best year in the last six. After relatively flat results in that period, retail frozen food sales climbed above $13 billion last year, up from $12.3 billion in 1982.

And the main reason, the publication and industry analysts say, is this relatively new generation of premium frozen meals designed to appeal to the younger, more affluent, more health conscious and sophisticated shopper, a target much sought after these days.

That target includes the nation's growing population of working women and consumers in general who have less time to cook but are looking for and can afford more imaginative meals.

"As more women join the work force and there's more emphasis on convenience and quality in food, our user base has broadened dramatically," said Marguerite Dannemiller, a spokesman for Stouffer's. "Lean Cuisine was a significant reason for this." Campbell now forecasts that sales of Le Menu will approach $200 million in this fiscal year, about double its original estimate. ■

MAY 23, 1984

PROLIFERATION OF THE SALAD BAR

Florence Fabricant

It happens mostly around midday and late in the afternoon.

Shoppers in food markets scoop slices of raw carrot and cucumber, shredded cabbage, canned baby corn and bamboo shoots, spinach leaves, bean sprouts, cauliflower, raisins and croutons into oblong plastic or foil containers. They are preparing lunch or dinner.

Serve-yourself salad bars, featured in restaurant chains since the 1960's, have now been added to supermarkets and, more recently, to many of the small produce shops owned by Koreans. "We have a lot of young professional people in the neighborhood and they don't like to cook after work," said John Lee, who installed an elaborate salad bar about five weeks ago in his store, Han's Oriental Market, 2150 Broadway, at 76th Street.

The salad bar at Han's, advertised on a sign suspended from the store's canopy, offers more than 60 items, from lettuce, tomatoes, watercress, celery and radishes to pickled ginger root, cubes of tofu, tuna salad, sunflower seeds and canned peas.

Six or seven kinds of dressings are also available at the free-standing refrigerated counter that fills the center of the store. The price for any assortment is $2.79 a pound.

"I suppose it's a little overpriced but it's convenient," said Tracey Snyder, who was serving herself from the salad bar at Broadway Gardens, 2343 Broadway, at 86th Street, where salad is $2.39 a pound.

The salad-bar experiment was first tried in restaurants about 20 years ago and proved to be extremely successful, according to Charles Bernstein, editor of the trade publication Nations Restaurant News. "It hit really big in the 1970's," Mr. Bernstein said, "but many people in the industry thought it was a fad that would run its course. It looks like it may be bigger still in the 1980's." ■

SEPTEMBER 26, 1984

WHAT ALICE TAUGHT THEM: DISCIPLES OF CHEZ PANISSE

Marian Burros

Alice Waters

More than any other single figure, Miss Waters has been instrumental in developing the exciting and imaginative style that has been labeled New American Cuisine. Its trademarks—apparent in a wide range of dishes that include such marvelous inventions as whole baked garlic with white cheese and peasant bread, smoked trout and chervil butter, and ragout of wild mushrooms with veal stock and red wine—are an adventurous, often improvisational use of the finest American ingredients and an exquisitely simple and straightforward approach to their preparation.

In the last five years Chez Panisse has spread its influence by way of a family tree whose branches reach a number of the country's most exciting new restaurants. Jonathan Waxman at Jams in New York; Mark Peel at Spago in Los Angeles; and Charlene Rollins at the New Boonville Hotel in Boonville, Calif., all worked in the Chez Panisse kitchens. So did Mark Miller of the Fourth Street Grill in Berkeley; Steven Sullivan of the Acme Bread Company in Berkeley; Judy Rogers, who until earlier

(cont'd. next page)

foodie

(continued from previous page)

this year was the chef at the Union Hotel in Benicia, Calif.; and a half-dozen others who have settled from the West Coast to Rome.

Miss Waters quickly acknowledges her own debt to the French: Chez Panisse began in 1971 as a French restaurant, emphasizing the earthy cooking of Provence. But in time she began to experiment. Soon the traditional dishes were lightened, and ingredients indigenous to California were used. She insisted that those ingredients be impeccably fresh and prepared to highlight, rather than mask, their flavor.

From the beginning, this philosophy has attracted talented, creative, young people—most in their late 20's and 30's—who loved good food and appreciated Miss Waters's intellectual approach to it. Few had any formal culinary training. Her one-time partner and first chef, Mr. Tower, had studied design at Harvard as an undergraduate and graduate student. Others studied English literature, philosophy and Chinese art history and anthropology.

The atmosphere in the kitchen was hectic and frequently chaotic, but those who came to work at Chez Panisse soon discovered that Miss Waters was an exceptional teacher. Mr. Waxman, whose restaurant on East 79th Street in Manhattan is noted for its grilled foods and fresh vegetables, says: "She teaches by example, not by lecture. She is not classically trained, but she is an intellectual chef. She understands food and presents it in an alive and healthy manner."

"Every night at Chez Panisse the menu changed, and every night I was scared," Mr. Waxman recalled. "There is an air of excellence, and everyone is entitled to criticize. I learned that you don't serve a dish unless it's perfect. If you have to go through 16 cases of red leaf lettuce to find the finest, you do it." He discovered that he had to "taste things and taste things—you don't just look at them."

Miss Rogers, now a caterer in the Bay area, worked at Chez Panisse for two years. She describes Miss Waters as "the kind of cook who is visceral instead of one who quantifies."

"It means," she said, "that I never learned to keep my knives sharp or how to convert grams to ounces. I never learned how to fillet a fish."

"Some technical stuff has been undervalued," she said.

"We've always been a little loose around the edges," Miss Waters acknowledges.

Then why her fantastic success and continuing influence?

"Alice can harness people's creative outlet," Mr. Sullivan said.

Mr. Miller credits Miss Waters with teaching him "to understand a lot about my own abilities."

"She always pushes you to the edge," he said, "to be really adventurous." ■

JUNE 12, 1985

FANS OF OLD COKE SAY THE NEW IS NOT IT

James Barron

Seven weeks after the Coca-Cola Company changed its longtime recipe, many frustrated Coke drinkers are complaining that the new taste is just not the real thing.

"It's a taste tragedy," said Robert Hester, a writer in Jacksonville, Fla.

"It's flat and too sweet," said Kathy Kapture, a Detroit waitress. "It doesn't have the same fizz, it doesn't quench your thirst and I'm not buying it."

"Completely devoid of any character at all," declared the humorist Jean Shephard, who has been lacing his one-man shows with Coca-Cola jokes.

All this may sound like a tempest in a cola can, but from Montreal to Monterey, Calif., diehard fans of old Coke are angrily denouncing the idea of tampering with their favorite, hoarding whole cases and paying up to $1.25 for a 6 1/2-ounce bottle.

And the company that makes Coke says it has been getting 1,500 phone calls a day, mostly from people who dislike the new taste.

"Obviously, it is an area of concern," said Brian Dyson, the president of Coca-Cola USA. "We want everybody to be absolutely pleased."

Some old Coke devotees have been stockpiling it. Melanie Smeade of Seattle bought 10 cases of 12-ounce cans, while Dan Lauck, a reporter with KMOL-TV in San Antonio, spent $972 for 110 cases of 6 1/2 ounce bottles. He has yet to try the new version.

In Beverly Hills, Calif., a wine shop began selling old Coke by the case for $30, triple the usual price.

SEPTEMBER 14, 1986

WHERE, OH, WHERE TO EMPTY THE TRASH?

A pile of newspapers waiting for recycling at the Santa Monica Community Center, CA.

Scott Bronstein

The outskirts of Boulder, Colo., are usually quiet this time of year. But on one small, industrial lot, the silence of the Rocky Mountain morning is sporadically shattered by a loud, crunching noise. Eco-Cycle's shredding machine, familiarly called the "bone crusher" by staff workers, is warming up.

Piles of used newspapers, collected from hundreds of Boulder homes, climb up a long conveyer belt, disappearing into the building containing the shredder. There, they are beaten, pummeled, pushed, and finally baled into cubes. Before the day is out, more than 45,000 pounds of those cubes will be en route by truck to a paper mill in Oregon, where they will be recycled into new paper products.

The Adolph Coors Company, meanwhile, has promised to buy Eco-Cycle's crushed glass, while Reynolds Aluminum will take the baled aluminum.

The prices these companies pay cover only about 80 percent of the cost of collecting and recycling the materials. In fact, Eco-Cycle, a non-profit community organization, has been losing some $15,000 a month.

Nonetheless, Boulder, like thousands of other communities across the country, is stepping up its trash recycling efforts. The reason: too much garbage and too little landfill space to put it in.

"What we have come up against is a solid-waste crisis, and it's the responsibility of government to address this problem," said Mary T. Sheil, director of the New Jersey Office of Recycling, which is pushing for state-wide mandatory recycling.

A number of states, including Rhode Island, Michigan, Illinois and Massachusetts, have enacted or are considering legislation mandating the recycling of trash. In Oregon, recycling is mandatory for communities of more than 4,000 people.

Recycling of glass and aluminum has climbed more dramatically. A decade ago, some 137,000 tons of aluminum were recovered, making 27 percent of the total. Today, some 650,000 tons are recycled, or 53 percent of the used cans around.

Ten years ago, 368,000 tons of glass were recycled annually, barely 3 percent of the total glass containers. Today, that figure is nearly 1.25 million tons, or just under 10 percent of the total.

SEPTEMBER 7, 1986

THE EVER-FATTER BUSINESS OF THINNESS

N. R. Kleinfield

"Thousands of Women Get Back Girlish Figures on Incredible Super Diet." . . . "New Medical Breakthrough! Lose Up to 50 Pounds Without Dieting." . . . "All the Figure Toning of 3,000 Sit-Ups Without Moving an Inch."

On and on go the advertising siren calls, sounding the wonders of a mammoth and bewildering industry that thrives on the American obsession with trim waistlines. The chance to make dollars off diets has attracted a remarkable assortment of businesses, from solid corporations such as Ciba-Geigy and Carnation to fly-by-night enterprises with box-number addresses. Some of the products are preposterous, like the pajamas that purportedly melt off pounds as you sleep. Some are dangerous, like the notorious tapeworm pills of years ago.

But neither scandals nor deaths nor fears of being duped seem to dampen the consumer mania for thinness without pain. And, ironically, the very fact that so many weight-control products ultimately leave people as tubby as ever guarantees the vitality of the diet industry.

"Everything is go," remarks the ever-upbeat Charles Berger, the president of Weight Watchers International, one of the most successful weight-reducing companies. "Our research shows that over 60 percent of American women are dieting at some point in a year and that number seems to keep edging upward."

Various market researchers estimate that Americans spend more than $10 billion a year on diet drugs, exercise tapes, diet books, diet meals, weight-loss classes, fat farms and devices like body wraps.

For many large Americans, the road to slenderness is paved with diet pills.

Can the Amazing Japanese Super Pill help you lose without dieting? Well, maybe if you don't eat. Rivers of diet aids flow on and off the market, advertising in the backs of women's magazines, with copy that promises weight removal in poundage just short of miraculous. Their manufacturers are often fly-by-night companies no one has ever heard of, usually reachable only through post office boxes.

Both the F.D.A. and the Council of Better Business Bureaus have begun attacking through brochures and outright prohibitions fraudulent weight-reducing aids. The F.D.A. has tested hundreds of diet pills and found strange ingredients in a lot of them, including things like freeze-dried cow brains. It has looked at grapefruit diet pills and at pills that produce bulk in the body, such as Glucomannan, the key ingredient in the Amazing Japanese Super Pill, and said that there isn't any valid evidence that they work.

Still, the tiny companies selling these shadowy products go on bragging about their wonders. A spokesman for Amitol Industries, distributor of the Japanese Super Pill, says that the company has "400,000 satisfied customers. I've seen lots and lots of glowing testimony on it. One person claimed she lost 90 pounds."

The F.D.A. has also assailed devices that purport to melt off pounds. There are body wraps, bands of rubber or plastic material worn around the hips, waist and thighs, as well as "sauna suits" or "reducing pajamas" that enclose the entire body. One product that the F.D.A. examined was a plastic band that was inflated with air from an electric hair dryer and that, when wrapped around a fat person's waist, supposedly melts pounds off. The F.D.A. says that these enclosures will temporarily produce weight loss from the heavy perspiration they cause; the catch is that the weight is quickly packed back on by drinking or eating. It also warns that they can cause severe dehydration or circulatory constriction. "You could wake up slimmer," notes an F.D.A. spokesman, "but you might also wake up dead." ■

A client walks towards an entrance to a Weight Watchers meeting location in Arlington Heights, Illinois.

AUGUST 23, 1987

K MART HIRES A CELEBRITY HOSTESS

Linnea Lannon

Martha Stewart stands behind a table full of her creations, surrounded by students at one of her seminars on entertaining in 1988.

Many strange combinations have come out of American kitchens in the 80's, but K Mart may have served up the piece de resistance with its recent announcement that entertainment guru Martha Stewart has signed a five-year contract to be its national spokeswoman and a consultant for home fashions.

For many who are familiar with Mrs. Stewart's brand of stylish partygiving, conveyed in five lavishly illustrated books, the link with the nation's largest discount retailer might have seemed an odd combination—but then, people once laughed at goat cheese pizza, too.

As trend-conscious hostesses know, Mrs. Stewart, 44, is an energetic former stockbroker who turned to catering in 1976—and deftly began the process of turning her life style into a cottage industry. Since 1982, when "Entertaining" hit the beautiful cookbook market, Mrs. Stewart has become something of a phenomenon in the food industry. All of her five offerings—the latest being "Weddings," priced at a steep $50—consistently appear in the top 100 current titles list of Crown Publishers, whose Clarkson Potter division prints her books.

In conversation, Mrs. Stewart is quick and direct, almost brusque. But it soon becomes clear that being Martha Stewart occasionally requires brusqueness and almost always demands stamina and organization. She says that some of her assistants consider her a slave driver. And a recent day in the kitchen proved that a slave driver is required, on occasion.

Mrs. Stewart is not worried about what K Mart will do to her high-toned, if occasionally precious, image. "I'm not changing the quality of the books, of what I do," she said.

She is approaching the next five years with gusto. And realism.

"I'm not going to tell K Mart customers to go to Wolfgang Puck's for dinner," she said, referring to one of her favorite chefs and the owner of Los Angeles' chic Spago restaurant. "But I might give them a recipe for one of his pizzas." ■

APRIL 13, 1988

Classroom Focus Shifting to the Art of Thinking

Joseph Berger

Children in kindergarten here are learning how to think. Not just to read and write and spell, but to think.

"What's inside the box?" asks the teacher, Robin Mosley Keffer, holding up a foot-long blue box sealed with tape. The 5-year-olds make some wild guesses: an egg, a fake animal, a big book, a balloon, high-heeled shoes, a cookie, spaghetti.

Ms. Keffer passes the box around and lets the children shake it, listen to it, smell it. She prods them to use their "powers of analysis" to eliminate some possibilities. The children decide the object is not a cookie because they could have smelled it. It is not an egg because an egg would have broken. A furry toy animal would not have made the rustling noise heard when the box was shaken.

The children never do guess that the box contains snapshots of them. But the wave of giggles when they peek inside suggests they have savored the thrill of deduction with the zest of Sherlock Holmes. They have practiced making inferences and learned how to support their hunches with a well-reasoned argument.

An increasing number of teachers, from kindergarten through college, have altered lesson plans to include the art of thinking. Many others are being trained so they can shift the classroom emphasis away from just giving pupils information and more toward making them think about the issues raised by that information.

These educators say that American students have become obsessed with getting the right answers on tests and are weak at analyzing what they are learning and at grasping implications. These weaknesses, the educators say, will affect the students' ability to make future decisions about career and marriage, what candidates to vote for and what products to buy.

While schools have always assumed that thinking was part of their mission, educators are making the teaching of thinking skills a more formal part of their programs.

(cont'd. next page)

(continued from previous page)

Articles on teaching the concept of "critical thinking" have flourished since the late 1970's, and there has been a dramatic push in the last few years by at least 28 states and hundreds of school districts to re-train teachers and revise curriculums.

Advocates say their movement has gained new strength as a response to an exaggerated stress on memorized information created by the pressure to raise student performance on standardized tests. That stress, they say, is one of the unseen and harmful consequences of the "back to basics" calls of the 1970's.

"It's not just the ability to remember things and feed them back on tests that determines how well you're going to do in life," said Dr. Heidi Jacobs, a professor at Teachers College at Columbia University. "It's the ability to solve problems and reflect and to, in fact, think critically." ■

A first grade class in 1988.

JULY 2, 1988

Rough-Edged Ads Sell 'Reality'

Randall Rothenberg

With its out-of-focus close-ups, drifting camera and grainy shots of teenagers spraying one another with soda and sashaying between cans, the current television commercial for Sprite looks like a home movie—which is no accident.

The promotion for the Coca-Cola Company soft drink is one of at least four national ad campaigns employing the home-movie approach and is one way advertisers are trying to contend with what many sociologists and market researchers say is a consumer backlash against glitziness and authority figures in advertising.

Dismissed as a fad when it was introduced two years ago, "reality" advertising—which features ordinary people in natural settings or circumstances—has become a dominant thrust in American marketing.

Among the forms of this reality advertising are these:

- Grim and gritty "slice of death" commercials like those about small companies losing business because managers did not choose systems from the American Telephone and Telegraph Company.
- Improvisational ads like the new promotions for Surf laundry detergent that were filmed without scripts or story boards and feature actual families camping, gardening or playing sports.
- Homemade commercials like the exuberant Sprite spot, which was "produced by students, directed by students, featuring students," as its opening shot proclaims.
- Slice-of-life "docudramas" like the ad featuring a young father cuddling his newborn daughter and projecting her future in one of the "Real Life, Real Answers" ads for the John Hancock Mutual Life Insurance Company, the pioneer in the genre.

Sociologists and market researchers say the ads depicting real people and real situations may appeal to consumers because their faith in institutions and authority has diminished.

Disaffection has become pronounced in the last two years because of events like the space shuttle disaster, the Iran-contra affair and the spread of acquired immune deficiency syndrome, said Charles J. Hess, president of Inferential Focus, a research organization that analyzes cultural and political trends for politicians and business.

Even as the consumer revolt against authority was building, a parallel rebellion was gaining momentum among the creative people in advertising. It developed in response to the glossy commercials of the early to mid-1980's—called "Pepsi-style" ads by some in the profession, after the song-and-dance spots starring Michael Jackson, the pop star. ■

"reality" advertising has become a dominant thrust in American Marketing

FEBRUARY 10, 1988

'FRUGAL GOURMET': A Minister Makes Food His Mission

Glenn Collins

On a misty morning, just up the steep hill from Puget Sound, Jeff Smith was charging through the bustle of the Pike Place Market here, working his way from steelhead to salmon to squid. He was brought to a halt in front of Jack's Fish Spot and Crab Pot by a stranger who stuck out his hand and introduced himself as Chris Peters of Seattle. "You're Jeff Smith, the Frugal Gourmet," Mr. Peters said. "I watch you religiously."

"That's just the word," said Mr. Smith.

The 6-foot-3 Mr. Smith, all wire-rims, white goatee and idiosyncratic enthusiasm, is a United Methodist minister who has become the nation's first food evangelist.

Later in his office, half a block from the market, Mr. Smith, who grew up in Seattle, said: "The cooking is just a front. I really run a storefront church on TV."

Some storefront: his half-hour television show is the Public Broadcasting Service's most popular cooking show, viewed by an average of 4.4 million people a week, according to the Nielsen Television Index. His three cookbooks are a publishing phenomenon, having sold 3 million copies since 1984, nearly 2.3 million in hard cover. All three books have reached the top of The New York Times's best-seller list for advice, how-to and miscellaneous hard-cover books, including Mr. Smith's latest title, "The Frugal Gourmet Cooks American," which has sold 500,000 copies since November.

The remarkable popularity of the 49-year-old Mr. Smith has been greeted with puzzlement by those in the food industry who cannot understand his appeal. His megastar status has also provoked criticism from some in the cooking establishment who find his recipes simplistic and who tend to dismiss him as a television huckster. "The food people are jealous," said Maria Guarnaschelli, Mr. Smith's editor at William Morrow & Company. "It's a small world, and they all know each other and snipe at each other, and Jeff suddenly appears and transcends all that." ■

MARCH 9, 1988

A Revival for Makers of Classic Toys

Stung by its failure to continue churning out blockbuster hits like the Cabbage Patch kids and the Teddy Ruxpin talking bear, the toy industry is shifting back to basics. Classics like building blocks, trains and cars are regaining popularity and some middle-tier companies best known for their old favorites are enjoying a renaissance.

The "megahit" toy, perhaps best exemplified by Coleco's Cabbage Patch dolls, rocked the industry in the mid-1980's, earning enormous profits for the company that could catch the fancy of millions of American children. But as the best sellers lost their commercial appeal, manufacturers scrambled to find new hits and failed, generating enormous losses and even some bankruptcies.

"Manufacturers and retailers have rediscovered board games, die-cast figures and model toys," said Tom Kully, an analyst with William Blair & Company. "If it's basic, then the odds are that it's doing rather well."

Blockbuster toys that failed have also taught the industry some bitter lessons about growing too fast, analysts and manufacturers said.

Worlds of Wonder Inc., which enjoyed overnight success with the Teddy Ruxpin bear in 1985, suffered just the sort of fate that Mr. Killgallon fears. After spending much of its Teddy Ruxpin profits on research and development, the company failed to produce another big hit and filed for bankruptcy last year.

As it shifts its focus, the toy industry also must contend with the growing popularity of video games. Although not considered toys by many in the industry, the games have made a comeback over the last year. Nintendo, the Japanese company that has a 70 percent share of the market, sold more than $500 million in hardware and software in 1987, and sales continue to rise.

"Video product sales could be in excess of $1 billion next year, and with total toy industry sales figures estimated at $8 billion or $9 billion, video games are something the toy companies will have to reckon with," said Barry Rothberg, an analyst with Mabon, Nugent & Company.

Not that companies have given up looking for blockbusters. "The expectations for the blockbuster have decreased," Sean McGowan, a toy analyst with Balis, Zorn, Gerard Inc said, "but if one happens to come along, it will be the gravy now, and not the roast." ■

In the late 1980's toy fads like Teddy Ruxpin, My Buddy and Pound Puppies began to lose popularity.

FEBRUARY 15, 1989

The Happy Face Has a Nice New Day

James Hirsch

When the "smile" face became a fad in 1970, it was like a lighthearted punctuation mark at the end of a tumultuous decade. Now, after nearly 20 years in eclipse, the happy face is back, its 100-watt smile lighting up T-shirts, canvas tote bags, spandex cycling shorts and other merchandise in newly opened shops at Macy's and Bloomingdale's stores in New York and Chicago. Happy-face goods have also surfaced in kiosks and specialty stores in New York and other cities.

The embrace of the merchandisers reflects the shortage of trends, even as it provides a glimpse into how fashion movements travel from the cultural fringes into the mainstream.

As is often the case in retro fashion, historical accuracy is somewhat beside the point. An icon of the 70's, the yellow disk with the line-drawn face is being sold as hippie fashion, stamped on peace-sign necklaces that say "Feelin' Groovy." In Macy's happy-face shop, six television screens show the movie "Woodstock."

"No self-respecting hippie would wear a smiley face," said Charlie Alzamora, program director for WMCA, a New York radio station that used a version of the logo in the early 1960's years before it went national. The hippie-inspired remake of the happy face, he said, "is the confusion of two cultures by marketing experts."

In London last year, the smiling logo was the most visible sign of a resurgence of 1960's-style music, colorful clothes and youthful restlessness. This movement emerged from the underground "acid house" music phenomenon that began in the late 70's, evolved in clubs in New York, Chicago and London, and later merged with retro-hippie fashions in the balmy Balearic Islands off Spain.

The trajectory is familiar. In the last 15 years disco music, punk fashion, break dancing and rap music started outside the mainstream and were integrated into popular culture.

"Subculture is the eternal source of ideas," said Rudolph, who has learned a few things about subculture as the director of Manhattan nightclubs like Danceteria, the Tunnel and now Mars. "It's much easier for Bloomie's to capitalize on something after everyone has read about it," said Rudolph, who uses only his first name. Once a trend reaches the public, he asserted, it has lost its cachet among "the cool." ■

MAY 3, 1989

IN SEATTLE, ESPRESSO IS RAISED TO AN ART

Marian Burros

In ordinary American cities the aroma of espresso does not emanate from local department stores. Nor can it be purchased on street corners and in libraries. But Seattle is no ordinary American city.

Those who know it well find nothing unusual in the fact that you can smell the espresso from Nordstrom's, its best-known and most prestigious department store, a block before you see the building. That's at the downtown store. Should you look through the windows of Nordstrom's branch in the University District you will see people sitting at little tables, right next to the shoe department, drinking espresso, cappuccino and more than a dozen other variations on the espresso theme.

One block from Nordstrom's, there are five places to buy a cup of espresso, including Bulldog News and Fast Espresso, which specializes in newspapers and magazines, and the Haagen-Dazs ice-cream store. No trip to the local supermarket is complete without a stop at the espresso stand outside the door. Espresso is sold in movie theaters, alongside videotapes and with slices of pizza.

No need to labor the point. The picture is clear. The residents of Seattle are nuts about their espresso. From the man in the hard hat on his way to his construction job at 7 A.M. to the society matron on an afternoon shopping trip, espresso is to Seattle what bagels are to New York. One couple, who spend their winters in Hawaii, take their espresso maker with them on the plane, carefully cradled in the wife's lap.

No one knows how Seattle got this way. Theories abound: the damp weather; the large Scandinavian population known for its love of good coffee; the particular quality-consciousness of the city; or the presence of two coffee roasters in the city for the last 18 years.

Kent Bakke, owner of Visions Espresso, an importer and distributor of coffee and espresso equipment, said the quality of the coffee was a key. "In the late 60's and early 70's we were developing our palates in Seattle," he said. "All things related to food and wine—and coffee is part of it."

Debra Hackett, who is a sales manager for S.B.C., one of the city's large roasters, says her company and the other big roaster, Starbucks Coffee Company, "have been responsible for educating the public about quality coffee, to appreciate that it is better to have one good cup than five or six poor ones."

Other cities have pubs; Seattle has coffeehouses, not unlike those of 18th-century European cities or America in the 1950's. The first, Cafe Allegro, built in 1975, is still the best known. On weekend mornings, it's standing room only on the cement floor or leaning against the brick walls. People are reading newspapers, books or magazines, doing homework or crossword puzzles or talking in small groups.

"You can read here; you can talk here," said one Saturday morning regular, Bruce Weaver, an artist. "You can order a triple

Elizabeth Taylor and Malcolm Forbes celebrating his 70th birthday.

macchiato and you don't have to explain what it is."

While espresso carts are a novelty to the rest of the country, a second generation of espresso bars has already made an appearance in Seattle. Instead of selling sweets, they offer panini, the traditional Italian sandwich served in Italy at espresso bars. The most mouthwatering of these sandwiches, made with focaccia, is found at the Botticelli Cafe, where Torrefazione coffee is also served. The classic version of panini contains prosciutto, fontina cheese and parsley sauce.

The Pacific Northwest reportedly has the highest number of coffee drinkers. And Seattle certainly has more espresso drinkers than anywhere else in the United States. It's no wonder that a truck bearing an advertisement for house calls on ailing espresso machines has been spotted around the city recently. ■

AUGUST 21, 1989

As in Old Days, the Jet Set Comes in for a Landing

Alan Riding

As police sirens led air-conditioned buses and dark-windowed limousines through the streets of Tangier on Saturday night, few people here seemed to care whether the big bash at the palace on the hill was a real birthday party or simply a huge marketing extravaganza.

It also mattered little that, among the 600 or so rich or famous invited over by Malcolm S. Forbes, the millionaire owner of the magazine that carries his name, probably only Morocco's Crown Prince Mohammed, Elizabeth Taylor and Henry A. Kissinger were household names to most locals.

Rather, for many who remembered the good old days before, during and after World War II when Tangier prospered as a center of glamour and intrigue, it was simply an occasion for nostalgia. And for those younger, it stirred hopes that Mr. Forbes had put the town back on the jet set's party circuit.

Morocco's delight at the publicity surrounding the party helped Mr. Forbes justify the expenditure of an estimated $2 million on celebrating his 70th birthday. "It's an opportunity for so many of our friends to get to know a country that has long been a friend of the United States," he told the gathering.

"I'm here because so many of my friends are here," former Secretary of State Kissinger said as he left a yacht chartered by the press and television lord Rupert Murdoch, and walked over to a yacht owned by Giovanni Agnelli, the chairman of Fiat. "Of course, there are some people here who want to make sure everyone knows they're invited."

The guests seemed to fall naturally into categories. Some clearly added to the publicity generated by the party, such as Elizabeth Taylor, Walter Cronkite, Barbara Walters, Betsy Bloomingdale, Oscar de la Renta, Calvin Klein, Dr. Kissinger and the Governors of California, New Jersey, Rhode Island and Puerto Rico.

There were also powerful figures from the world of publishing: not only Mr. Murdoch, but also the British newspaper titan Robert Maxwell, who dressed like a sultan; Katharine Graham, chairman of The Washington Post Company; Mortimer Zuckerman, chairman of U.S. News & World Report; Jann Wenner, publisher of Rolling Stone; and senior editors from several other publications.

A good number of the Fortune 500 corporations were represented by their C.E.O.'s, ranging from Lee Iacocca, chairman of the Chrysler Corporation, and Roger Smith, chairman of General Motors, to Henry Kravis of Kohlberg Kravis Roberts and John Kluge, chairman of Metromedia.

The party itself resembled an Arabian feast on a Hollywood set, with hundreds of dancers, drummers and horsemen and three photogenic camels receiving guests as they lined up to enter the palace. Inside, Mr. Forbes's five children acted as hosts in different tents decorated with chandeliers. Then, after an Arab dinner and toasts, Beverly Sills led the singing of "Happy Birthday" that preceded a fireworks display.

Odder, though, was the fact that Elizabeth Taylor played the role of hostess even though no one here seemed to be

(cont'd. next page)

(continued from previous page)

lieve occasional reports that Mr. Forbes was her latest escort. In a night that buzzed with gossip for all tastes, there were those who suggested that they were joined mainly by a desire for publicity.

Was a surprise wedding in the cards, reporters shouted out. "No," he replied. "You don't have to marry everyone you have fun with." What did Miss Taylor give him as a present, he was asked. "I'm not saying," he answered, then added a bit of promotion for his friend's perfumes: "Actually, she gave me Elizabeth Taylor's Passion for Men." ■

NOVEMBER 29, 1989

THE PAST IS NOW THE LATEST CRAZE

Randall Rothenberg

A booming market in nostalgia is turning yesterday—when all our troubles seemed so far away—into the latest craze in the communications and consumer products industries.

In their latest attempt to cater to the postwar baby boom, the largest generation of consumers the world has ever known, numerous publishers and packaged-goods manufacturers now believe that the way it was is the way it is.

"Nostalgia waxes and wanes, and it's certainly waxing now, as the baby-boom generation passes into phases of life that create conditions that can elicit nostalgic responses," said Fred Davis, a professor at the University of California at San Diego.

Those hoping to capitalize on nostalgic appeals have generally reached back to the baby-boom generation's adolescent years, a period of life Professor Davis calls "the chief reservoir of nostalgia." Indeed, the Nickelodeon cable television network programs its daily "Nick at Nite" segment, which features reruns of such old television staples as Rowan and Martin's "Laugh-In" and "My Three Sons," by picking the top-rated shows of 15 to 20 years ago, when its core audience was 12 years old.

Advertising agencies began testing nostalgic appeals to young professionals in the mid-1980's. In 1985, for example, Young & Rubicam secured rights to the 1965 Beatles' song "Help" for an advertising campaign for the Ford Motor Company's Lincoln-Mercury division. These tentative pokes at the past have lately become a flood.

"I thought nostalgia was a fad at first, but I'm convinced it's a phenomenon," said Michael D. Drexler, an executive vice president at the Bozell advertising agency. "The size of the market is big enough now to capitalize on it as a business."

Sociologists and marketing experts who have studied the current passion for the past generally agree that peoples' desire to relive earlier times, even times before they were born, is in large measure a response to the rapid pace of social and technological change.

Robert Goldman, an associate professor of sociology at Lewis and Clark College in Portland, Ore., who studies advertising themes, said he had noticed two predominant motifs in contemporary advertising: love of the past, and images of fear and death. Both, he said, attract "a population that is unsure how to deal with the present."

Professor Davis of the University of California said nostalgic feelings were a result of "identity discontinuity," the sense that the experiences that anchor peoples' lives are in constant flux. "We turn to the past," he said, "for psychological security and comfort, which present times deny us." ■

nostalgia

Arts & Entertainment

When record numbers of Americans tuned into watch the final episode of "MASH" in 1983, the cozy, communal ritual of family viewing was already in the throes of a revolution. The old world of three major networks and high-minded scripted dramas was in its final days, as the spread of cable television fractured the viewing audience into thousands of constituencies, each with its own set of preferences and, thanks to the remote control, the power to dictate terms.

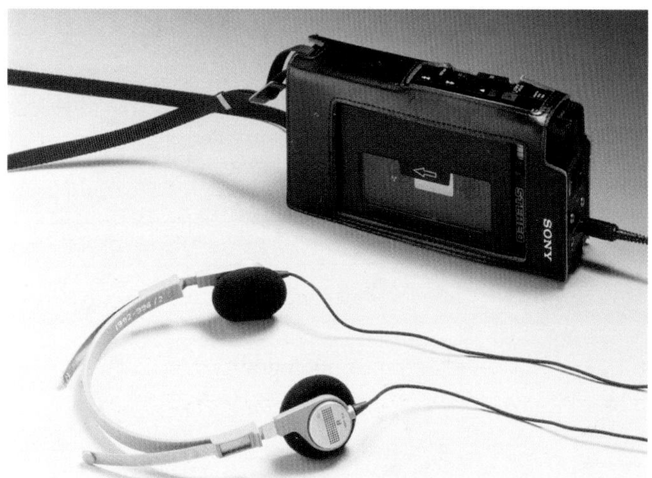

The original 'Walkman,' model TCS 300, made by Sony of Japan in 1980.

In all the arts, choice proliferated and habits of consumption changed. Sometimes new technology altered the landscape. The Sony Walkman allowed music fans to listen on the move. The compact disc, which instantly made the vinyl LP obsolete, improved sound quality and made storage easier. With the camcorder, introduced by Sony in 1982, anyone could make a video.

Television viewers faced a new world of seemingly infinite variety. The same small screen accommodated "Masterpiece Theater" and programs like "Married . . . With Children," a raunchy new comedy on the fledgling Fox Network that pushed the boundaries of good taste.

MTV, a startup channel that broadcast music videos round the clock, turned out to be something more than a modern version of "American Bandstand." It was a showcase for the latest street fashions, a training ground for aspiring directors, and a cinematographic innovator. Its hectic visual style, with constant quick cuts, had an immediate impact on longer-form television shows and film.

MTV VJ Downtown Julie Brown on the set in MTV's New York Studio in 1988.

Projection of a Robert Mapplethorpe self-portrait during a protest at the Corcoran Gallery of Art in 1989.

Culture became a battleground, reflecting the same divisions that would split the country evenly between red and blue states. Rock music loomed a moral threat in a way it had not since the days of Elvis Presley. Alarmed at the salaciousness and profanity she heard in rock songs, Tipper Gore joined forces with several other prominent political wives to form the Parents Music Resource Center. The organization lobbied the music industry to attach warning labels to records with sexually explicit or profane lyrics. The issue became more heated with the growing popularity of rap music, especially gangsta rap and groups like Public Enemy.

The motion picture industry faced similar concerns. In 1984 it introduced a new rating, PG, to alert parents that a film contained language or images that might not be suitable for younger viewers.

The visual arts, not normally a hotbed of social controversy, inflamed passions, especially on Capitol Hill, when a new breed of political artists began showing at publicly supported museums. Robert Mapplethorpe's elegant, shockingly sexual photographs of gay men caused a furor when they were included in an exhibition at the Corcoran Gallery of Art in Washington that was funded, in part, by the National Endowment for the Arts. Andres Serrano's photograph "Piss Christ," which shows a crucifix immersed in a glass vessel filled with urine, set off a storm of controversy and set the stage for the "culture war" between the art world, the endowment, and conservative lawmakers in Washington.

Strife and contention, although fierce, was intermittent. For most audiences the arts delivered pleasure, pure and simple. Hollywood film in particular fell into an easy rhythm of action movies, horror films and many, many sequels.

The 70's had been a golden age of sorts, with challenging films both domestic and foreign. Martin Scorsese continued to flourish in the 1980's, making what many critics called his finest film, "Raging Bull," but the big box-office hits tended to be franchise films like "Beverly Hills Cop," "Lethal Weapon," "Airplane" and "Halloween," which generated sequel after sequel. The "Star Wars" juggernaut continued to roll in "The Empire

Strikes Back" and "Return of the Jedi," both phenomenally successful, but still not as big as Steven Spielberg's "E.T. the Extra-Terrestrial."

The target audience was, increasingly, young. John Hughes's gentle comedies about teen life, like "The Breakfast Club" and "Pretty in Pink," made instant stars out of Molly Ringwald and the young actors dubbed the "Brat Pack." The growing sophistication of computer-generated special effects narrowed the differences between film and video games. "Tron," a 1982 science-fiction film inspired by video games, marked a cinematic turning point. Actors faced a new dawn in which they ran a distant second to digitally produced images and explosions.

Actresses, Debra Burrell, Sheryl Lee Ralph & Loretta Devine from the cast of Dreamgirls.

The big-budget blockbusters still left room for quirky independent films, which gained box-office credibility after the low-budget "Sex, Lies, and Videotape" took in millions at the box office. Directors like Jonathan Demme, in films like "Melvin and Howard" and "Something Wild," and David Lynch, in "Blue Velvet," showed that the renegade spirit of the previous decade had not died.

In pop music, Michael Jackson emerged as a megastar. "Thriller," released in 1982, became the best-selling album of all time. Madonna began her climb to international celebrity. In a memorable demonstration of celebrity power, the biggest names in rock 'n' roll staged an epic benefit concert, Live Aid, to raise money to alleviate the famine in Ethiopia.

Jazz showed surprising resiliency. Miles Davis staged a comeback early in the decade, and a group of young traditionalists, led by a trumpet player from New Orleans, Wynton Marsalis, revived interest in the traditional jazz music of the 1930's. Lincoln Center staged a series of concerts that led to the creation of a permanent jazz program.

A British invasion swept over Broadway. One after another, lavish musicals like "Cats," "Les Miserables" and "Phantom of the Opera" opened to rapturous applause and never left, running year after year. The homegrown Broadway musical, one of America's great gifts to the world, seemed exhausted, although national honor was saved with the triumphant opening of "Dreamgirls." The show, loosely based on the story of the Supremes, proved that Andrew Lloyd Webber did not have an absolute monopoly on the genre.

The Thatcher era, with its new mercantile spirit, provoked a response in politically minded playwrights like David Hare and Caryl Churchill, whose piercing looks at contemporary Britain impressed critics on both sides of the Atlantic. In the United States, Larry Kramer put the tragedy of AIDS on the stage with his groundbreaking play "The Normal Heart."

The dance world lost two giant figures, George Balanchine and Alvin Ailey. Suzanne Farrell, one of the century's greatest dancers, retired. But there was also an influx of fresh talent. Mark Morris assembled a company of dancers that brought a new sense of wit and invention to the stage, and Twyla Tharp entered into a brilliant creative partnership with Mikhail Baryshnikov, who took over as artistic director of the American Ballet Theatre at the beginning of the decade. Darci Kistler, a protégé of Balanchine, became a principal dancer at the New York City Ballet, the youngest in its history at only 17.

Cable television diminished the power of the networks, and the advent of CNN, not to mention the retirement of Walter Cronkite as anchor of "The CBS Evening News," foretold the end of network dominance in the news. But the networks could still produce enormously popular comedies and dramas. Prime-time soaps like "Dallas" and "Dynasty" kept Americans glued to the set, and innovative series like "Cheers" and "Hill Street Blues" stretched the boundaries of their genres. "The Cosby Show" in particular was a landmark, a comedy series that presented black Americans in the round, endowed with the full range of human complexities, problems and emotions.

The visual arts took center stage, and not just because of the culture wars. A brash new style of painting, Neo-Expressionism, brought a new generation of artists to public attention. A flood of Wall Street money fueled sky-high prices for all forms of art, but artists like Julian Schnabel and Jeff Koons showed a distinct flair for marketing and media manipulation, proof that the lesson of Andy Warhol had been

The 1981 cast of "Hill Street Blues."

closely studied. Artists and their dealers no longer labored quietly; artists wanted to be famous, and their handlers took pains to make that happen. Never had the machinery of art, fashion, money and celebrity meshed so tightly.

The Nobel Prize in Literature, often awarded to esoteric writers in past decades, redeemed itself in the 1980's, honoring the likes of Joseph Brodsky, Czeslaw Milosz, Gabriel Garcia Marquez and Wole Soyinka. At the same time, younger writers staked their claim. In the United States, a literary brat pack—Jay McInerney, Tama Janowitz and Bret Easton Ellis—looked like the 1980's answer to the Beats of the 1950's.

Commentators worried about declining literacy and the degeneration of the English language. The spread of Valley Girl dialect did not help. Allan Bloom, a classics professor at the University of Chicago, made the best-seller list with "The Closing of the American Mind," a prolonged lament about the failure of higher education and the sorry state of American culture. E.D. Hirsch, another academic, put the case starkly in his best-selling "Cultural Literacy," arguing that Americans simply did not know the facts that an educated person should know.

Both books set off a fierce debate. Were Americans under-educated, ill-informed, uncouth? If so, why did the 1980's offer such rich pickings in art, music, theater, literature and dance? The decade was turbulent and confusing. The cultural friction was undeniable, so were the achievements.

Tama Janowitz at her book party for "A Cannibal In Manhattan" in 1987.

MAY 18, 1980

A Show That Might Even Have Dazzled Picasso; Picasso at the Modern

Grace Glueck

MOMA painting and sculpture director William S. Rubin in front of Pablo Picasso's "Les Demoiselles d'Avignon" in 1984.

"I want people to go out of here reeling, to have a sense of 'How could he do it?'" says William Rubin, who assembled the cornucopian Picasso show—one of the largest and most important art displays of our time that will cram the Museum of Modern Art's entire building from May 22 through Sept. 16.

The exhibition, a near-$2-million extravaganza formally entitled "Picasso: A Retrospective" presenting almost 1,000 works in every medium by the protean Spanish artist, who is generally acknowledged as the dominant figure of 20th century art, will undoubtedly be Mr. Rubin's curatorial *chef d'oeuvre.* About 300 of the works have never been seen before in this country, and 30 works have never been seen anywhere, including a 1956 wood version of a sculpture group called "The Bathers," lent by one of Picasso's heirs.

On the eve of the 100th anniversary of his birth in 1881, Picasso is seen, in the main body of critical opinion, as the towering progenitor of the art of our time, a position achieved not only by the immense fertility of his invention that led to the revolutionary style of Cubism, but also the sheer prodigality of his output. In the artist's estate at his death, for example, were 1,855 paintings, 1,228 sculptures, 7,089 drawings, 3,222 ceramic works, 17,411 prints, and 11 tapestries. "No artist invented so much in one lifetime," says Mr. Rubin. "There's enough material in the MOMA show to make 50 other careers."

The show was proposed by Mr. Rubin on a visit to Picasso shortly before the artist's death in 1973. Picasso was "amused" by the notion of a museum-wide show, according to Mr. Rubin, and agreed to collaborate. But the artist's death a few months later brought preparations to a halt. Only after the recent resolution of his tangled estate could the project again be seen as a possibility.

The show is certainly the most comprehensive Picasso exhibition ever mounted. "But the unbelievable thing is that you could fill the museum again with terrific Picassos that are not in the show," notes Mr. Rubin. ■

SEPTEMBER 28, 1980

BUILDING ON EMOTIONS

Paul Goldberger

There are many terms for it—romanticism, neo-eclecticism, a return to ornament, postmodernism. They do not mean the same thing, but they are all attempts to explain, in one way or another, a certain feeling that has been in the air for some time now. Architects and decorators talk willingly today of pleasure, of delight, of prettiness even. They seem to talk less of rules and more of whims, less of order and more of randomness, less of physical structure and more of spirit and mood. Even the most rigorous modernist seems compelled to say a word or two about emotional content when defending his or her work, and he or she who speaks only in terms of purity of space and structure, the words of modernism's gospel, is likely to sound rather old-fashioned.

It is tempting, when one ponders the situation, to say that the world of architecture and design has been turned upside down. After all, two years ago Philip Johnson, once modernism's leader, and John Burgee designed a limestone-fronted structure, complete with classical moldings, for the apartment house at 1001 Fifth Avenue in New York City. When one looks at this curious building and then looks back at, say, Ludwig Mies van der Rohe's great 860-880 Lake Shore Drive apartments in Chicago of 1950, it is a startling comparison: The new building is what looks old-fashioned, while the "modern" building, the box of steel and glass, turns out to be 30 years old.

No more. Now, not only is Philip Johnson going about creating classical ornament, but we also have architects like Allan Greenberg, who is designing a "real" Georgian manse; Charles Moore, who has been mixing elements from various cultures and periods for some time and now does so with more exuberance than ever; Robert Stern, whose mix of classical allusions and

(cont'd. next page)

(continued from previous page)
elements from the Shingle Style is increasingly articulate; Michael Graves, whose rich colors and subtle forms, derived from classicism but highly personal, are nothing if not romantic. There are many other, younger architects working in similar directions.

This sort of romanticism is what we might call the romanticism of aspiration—it uses historical details and historical style in the hope of conveying certain qualities of a past period. It is a kind of design with a social goal as much as a purely visual one, and it often has a pleasing kind of innocence to it.

All of this is, at bottom, a reaction against modernism. Its austerity, we have finally realized, served too narrow a range of the human psyche; without a certain kind of attention to the broader range of human emotions, service to the eye has insufficient meaning.

This does not mean that modern design is finished, that we will see no more of it—far from it. But what we will see are more and more variations on modernist themes, such as a designer like Saladino offers or, as, say, Kevin Roche created in his sparkling, decorative, yet utterly modernist United Nations Plaza Hotel, an attempt to bring a level of emotional content to the modern design vocabulary. ■

JULY 12, 1981

EXPRESSIONISM RETURNS TO PAINTING

Hilton Kramer

In art, every authentic style comprehends a distinctive point of view. It exalts certain emotions, and upholds certain attitudes. It makes a judgment about the medium, and a judgment about life. Upon its emergence it proffers a revision of existing ideas about art, and thus—either by implication or by direct assault—represents a challenge to the prevailing orthodoxies. Every genuine change of style may therefore be seen as a barometer of changes greater than itself. It signals a shift in the life of the culture—in the whole complex of ideas, emotions and dispositions that at any given moment governs our outlook on art and experience.

In the visual arts, a change of this sort is now apparently upon us in the form of an energetic wave of Neo-Expressionist painting. This burgeoning movement has swiftly achieved a remarkable success on both sides of the Atlantic—for it is as much a European as it is an American movement—and it is now the focus of a good deal of critical discussion and acclaim.

In this country, for example, the outstanding figures at the moment are Julian Schnabel, Susan Rothenberg and the British-born painter Malcolm Morley—three very individual artists whose work does not seem to have much in common until placed in the perspective of the conventions they have vigorously repudiated.

In Italy, where the movement has erupted with particular force, its leaders appear to be Francesco Clemente, Sandro Chia and Enzo Cucchi—though they are themselves part of a larger group whose work has already been shown at museums in Basel, Essen and Amsterdam. In Germany, not surprisingly, the Neo-Expressionists have won a great deal of attention, for it was in Germany that the Expressionist movement originated some 75 years ago, and its revival is therefore seen as, among other things, a vindication of a national artistic tradition.

But what, as they say, is it all about?

One thing it is about, surely, is the legitimization of a mode of painting that exults in the physical properties of the medium, and in its capacity to generate images and stir the emotions. This is painting that makes a very frank appeal to the senses at the same time that it addresses itself without embarrassment to our appetite for poetry, fantasy and mystery. It swamps the eye with surfaces that are shameless in their exploitation of tactile effects, and with vivid images that are not always susceptible to easy explanation or understanding. It is painting that relies more on instinct and imagination than on careful design and the powers of ratiocination. It shuns the immaculate and the austere in favor of energy, physicality and surfeit.

Against the "closed" styles so long in fashion, the Neo-Expressionists offer us painting that is nothing if not "open"—painting that releases the medium from the restraints of high-minded theory in order to allow fantasy and emotion to play a more forthright role in determining the boundaries of pictorial discourse. ■

MAY 15, 1983

ARTISTS GRAPPLE WITH NEW REALITIES

Michael Brenson

Cindy Sherman with Andy Warhol in 1982.

There is no question in most artists' minds that the art world has changed dramatically in the last few years. It is bigger, faster and more conspicuous than before. There are more artists, dealers, collectors, agents, promoters and people writing about art. There is more to be won and lost now, at an earlier age.

In short, the art world has become big-time. With the emergence of a $2 billion a year art market in New York alone and the institutionalization of the avant-garde, not only by museums, where work is often on the walls while the radical edge is still hot, but also by universities, where more and more avant-garde artists have been hired to teach more and more studio art programs, art has entered the mainstream of American life.

What these changes mean for art, however, how they affect the making of art and the artists, is a matter of ongoing discussion and sometimes urgent concern. As art has entered the mainstream of American life, the mainstream of American life, with its turbulent as well as its bracing currents, has edged deeper and deeper into the world of art. On the one hand, the art world has probably never generated so much excitement and interest and touched off so many dreams. The audience for art continues to increase. With the success of such artists as David Salle, Julian Schnabel, Robert Longo and Cindy Sherman, all around 30 years old, and Keith Haring and Jean Michel Basquiat, still in their early twenties, artists now begin their careers knowing they have a chance for fame and fortune at an age that was almost unthinkable even ten years ago.

On the other hand, there is a widespread belief that worldliness, big money, instant stardom and art are incompatible—and that if they do co-exist, the integrity and scope of the art must suffer. There is no doubt that as the stakes increase, the pressures, distractions and temptations with which artists in New York now live have become more and more intimidating. Furthermore, as the media wait impatiently for the next "hot" artist and more and more collectors' limousines roll into SoHo to line up for work that has not yet been created, there is also an increasing danger of artists becoming themselves commodities. "There's this using up," said the 31-year old sculptor Timothy Woodman. "You're discovered, you're used up, you're out."

The questions being raised about the art world now could not be more consequential. Is it still possible, given the conditions which have generated so much interest and made so much possible, to create work with the integrity and purpose that have always given art its necessity? With the pressure to "make it," the possibility of something like immediate gratification, and the distorting amount of attention successful artists may receive, can artists continue to reach for something beyond vanity and the moment?

For some artists, whatever the situation, the issue has been and always will be the strength and will of the individual. "I really believe the pressure comes from me and not the art world," Mr. Salle said. "I don't think anything today has changed the difficulty of making significant art and the steep odds against it." ■

JANUARY 8, 1984

PHILIP JOHNSON DESIGNS FOR A PLURALISTIC AGE

Joseph Giovannini

Several years ago, as it started to rain at an architects' picnic in Princeton, one of those present suggested that the group call Philip Johnson and "ask him to have it stop raining."

No one made the call, but the anecdote is telling. "He is the most powerful architect since Bernini," says the New York architect Peter Eisenman. To many observers, Mr. Johnson is a figure of enormous power—an architect whose reputation is an issue almost independent of his buildings, and possibly one of his most impressive constructions.

But the appreciation is not entirely unmixed. The outspoken James Marston Fitch, professor emeritus at the Columbia University School of Architecture, says "he is impregnable," even though "fundamentally frivolous."

Mr. Johnson is perhaps now somewhere between being more controversial than ever and beyond controversy: the architect is attracting the most substantial commissions of his career—such as the proposal for four new towers he recently presented for the revitalization of Times Square. He is responding with designs, pleasing for some people, merely glib to others, but that are certainly expanding the traditionally conservative corporate palette.

One of the few elements that ties Mr. Johnson's widely divergent buildings together is, in fact, their pinstriped urbanity—their elegant finish helps mask the architectural shock that few other architects would be able to get away with. Besides the Chippendale top of the A. T.& T. Building, he has designed a Gothic skyscraper for Pittsburg Plate Glass, a Dutch-gabled high-rise in Texas, and is now working on a high-rise Welsh castle apartment building with a crenellated top for Donald Trump. Other than their sophisticated level of finish and detailing, a certain light Cole Porter wit, and their efficient interior planning, there are remarkably few characteristics common to these buildings—and none that might add up to a consistent system of belief.

As an architect who "cannot not know history," Mr. Johnson has thoughts about his place in it, and as usual he is of several minds. On the one hand, he says, "we think we're creating architectural history." But on the other hand, "I don't see myself as important, but I might eventually be considered important. With these startling commissions in different cities—like the Pennzoil—I'm getting a different level of acceptance than I used to."

The A. T. & T. Building in New York City, designed by Philip Johnson and John Burgee.

OBITUARY

MARCH 7, 1986

GEORGIA O' KEEFFE DEAD AT 98;

SHAPER OF MODERN ART IN U.S.

Edith Evans Asbury

Georgia O'Keeffe adjusting a canvas from her "Pelvis Series- Red With Yellow," in Albuquerque, New Mexico, 1960.

Georgia O'Keeffe, the undisputed doyenne of American painting and a leader, with her husband, Alfred Stieglitz, of a crucial phase in the development and dissemination of American modernism, died yesterday at St. Vincent Hospital in Santa Fe, N.M. She was 98 years old, and had lived in Santa Fe since 1984, when she moved from her longtime home and studio in Abiquiu, N.M.

As an artist, as a reclusive but overwhelming personality and as a woman in what was for a long time a man's world, Georgia O'Keeffe was a key figure in the American 20th century. As much as anyone since Mary Cassatt, she raised the awareness of the American public to the fact that a woman could be the equal of any man in her chosen field.

Miss O'Keeffe burst upon the art world in 1916, under auspices most likely to attract attention at the time: in a one-woman show of her paintings at the famous "291" gallery of Alfred Stieglitz, the world-renowned pioneer in photography and sponsor of newly emerging modern art.

From then on, Miss O'Keeffe was in the spotlight, shifting from one audacious way of presenting a subject to another, and usually succeeding with each new experiment. Her colors dazzled, her erotic implications provoked and stimulated, her subjects astonished and amused.

The artist painted as she pleased, and sold virtually as often as she liked, for very good prices. She joined the elite, avant-garde, inner circle of modern American artists around Stieglitz, whom she married in 1924.

Long after Stieglitz had died, in 1946, after Miss O'Keeffe forsook New York for the mountains and deserts of New Mexico, she was discovered all over again and proclaimed a pioneering artist of great individuality, power and historic significance.

Miss O'Keeffe had never stopped painting, never stopped winning critical acclaim, never stopped being written about as an interesting "character." But her paintings were so diverse, so uniquely her own and so unrelated to trends or schools that they had not attracted much close attention from New York critics.

Then, in 1970, when she was 83 years old, a retrospective exhibition of her work was held at the Whitney Museum of American Art. The New York critics and collectors and a new generation of students, artists and aficionados made an astonishing discovery. The artist who had been joyously painting as she pleased had been a step ahead of everyone, all the time. ■

JUNE 3, 1986

THE LOWER EAST SIDE'S NEW ARTISTS

Douglas C. McGill

In the early 1980's, Meyer Vaisman and Peter Nagy were young artists in Manhattan, both in their early 20's and both recently graduated from art school. And both, when unable to find an existing commercial gallery in New York to show their work, took an increasingly common step for young artists in Manhattan: they started their own galleries.

Today, Mr. Vaisman's gallery, International With Monument, and Mr. Nagy's, Nature Morte, are two of the most successful on the Lower East Side, a thriving new commercial art district in New York. And the two young men have become quite successful as artists, as well.

Their story typifies a change that has taken place in New York's contemporary art scene, which in recent years has been transformed from a relatively small and cloistered world to a thriving industry that makes stars of unknowns and has spawned growing numbers of galleries, trade publications and entrepreneurs.

There were around 200 art galleries in the New York metropolitan area in 1976, mostly in the traditional art districts of 57th Street and SoHo, according to the Gallery Guide, which lists New York art galleries. Today, the guide lists 560 galleries in the New York area, including such Manhattan neighborhoods as the Upper East Side, NoHo, Tribeca and the Lower East Side. The Art Dealers Association of America estimates that there are $1 billion a year in fine-art transactions in New York City.

The breeding ground for many of the new artists has been the Lower East Side, which, in the last five years, has been the fastest growing of all the art districts of New York. Although there were virtually no art galleries there in 1980, there are nearly 100 there today. In tiny storefronts previously occupied by Ukrainian- and Polish-American shops, dozens of new art galleries have been started each year by young entrepreneurs, many of them young artists.

Some days, the Lower East Side, which is called the East Village by many, looks like a cultural version of the garment district, with artists and art handlers carrying canvases still wet with paint from their apartment studios to nearby galleries to display. The local cafes, which have proliferated along with the galleries, are filled with artists and dealers, and gallery owners frequently take groups of collectors to artists' studios to try to interest them in works that are still in progress.

It is in this environment that many young artists have recently made their start in the art world—and done so with a splash. ■

FEBRUARY 10, 1985

NEW ART, NEW MONEY

Cathleen McGuigan

When Jean Michel Basquiat walks into Mr. Chow's on East 57th Street in Manhattan, the waiters all greet him as a favorite regular. Before he became a big success, the owners, Michael and Tina Chow, bought his artwork and later commissioned him to paint their portraits. He goes to the restaurant a lot. One night, for example, he was having a quiet dinner near the bar with a small group of people. While Andy Warhol chatted with Nick Rhodes, the British rock star from Duran Duran, on one side of the table, Basquiat sat across from them, talking to the artist Keith Haring. Haring's images of a crawling baby or a barking dog have become ubiquitous icons of graffiti art, a style that first grew out of the scribblings (most citizens call them defacement) on New York's subway cars and walls. Over Mr. Chow's plates of steaming black mushrooms and abalone, Basquiat drank a kir royale and swapped stories with Haring about their early days on the New York art scene. For both artists, the early days were a scant half dozen years ago.

Visitors stand among paintings by artist Jean Michel Basquiat which are part of an exhibition of 150 works of art by Basquiat, at Musee d'Art Moderne on October 15, 2010 in Paris, France.

That was when the contemporary art world began to heat up after a lull of nearly a decade, when a new market for painting began to make itself felt, when dealers refined their marketing strategies to take advantage of the audience's interest and when much of the art itself began to reveal a

(cont'd. next page)

(continued from previous page)

change from the cool and cerebral to the volatile and passionate.

But today, contemporary art is evolving under the avid scrutiny of the public and an ever-increasing pool of collectors in the United States, Europe and Japan; and it is heavily publicized in the mass media. Barely disturbed by occasional dips in the economy, the art market has been booming steadily.

Take Basquiat. Five years ago, he didn't have a place to live. He slept on the couch of one friend after another. He lacked money to buy art supplies. Now, at 24, he is making paintings that sell for $10,000 to $25,000. They are reproduced in art magazines and also as part of fashion layouts, or in photographs of chic private homes in House & Garden. They are in the collections of the publisher S. I. Newhouse, Richard Gere, Paul Simon and the Whitney Museum of American Art.

His color-drenched canvases are peopled with primitive figures wearing menacing masklike faces, painted against fields jammed with arrows, grids, crowns, skyscrapers, rockets and words. "There are about 30 words around you all the time, like 'thread' or 'exit,'" he explains. He uses words "like brushstrokes," he says. The pictures have earned him serious critical affirmation. In reviewing a group show of drawings last year, John Russell, chief art critic of The New York Times, noted that "Basquiat proceeds by disjunction—that is, by making marks that seem quite unrelated, but that turn out to get on very well together." His drawings and paintings are edgy and raw, yet they resonate with the knowledge of such modern masters as Dubuffet, Cy Twombly or even Jasper Johns. What is "remarkable," wrote Vivien Raynor in The Times, "is the educated quality of Basquiat's line and the stateliness of his compositions, both of which bespeak a formal training that, in fact, he never had."

In the last year or so, Basquiat has established a friendship with an artist who probably understands the power of celebrity better than anyone else in the culture. Once when he was trying to sell his photocopied postcards on a SoHo streetcorner, he followed Andy Warhol and Henry Geldzahler into a restaurant. Warhol bought one of the cards for $1. Later, when Basquiat had graduated to painting sweatshirts, he went to Warhol's Factory one day. "I just wanted to meet him, he was an art hero of mine," he recalls. Warhol looked at his sweatshirts and gave him some money to buy more.

Their friendship seems symbiotic. As the elder statesman of the avant-garde, Warhol stamps the newcomer Basquiat with approval and has probably been able to give him excellent business advice. In social circles and through his magazine, Interview, he has given Basquiat a good deal of exposure. Though Warhol teases Basquiat about his girlfriends, Basquiat finds the time to go with Warhol to parties and openings. In return, Basquiat is Warhol's link to the current scene in contemporary art, and he finds Basquiat's youth invigorating. "Jean Michel has so much energy," he says. One acquaintance suggests that the paternal concern Warhol shows for Basquiat—for example, he urges the younger artist to pursue healthful habits and exercise—is a way for Warhol to redeem something in himself. When asked how Warhol has influenced him, Basquiat says, "I wear clean pants all the time now." ■

FEBRUARY 10, 1985

IN LONDON, A FINE HOME FOR A MAJOR COLLECTION

John Russell

One of the more unpredictable places in which recent art of high quality can henceforth be seen in ideal conditions is on Boundary Road in Northwest London. As its name suggests, Boundary Road is somewhat on the edge of things. Lightly trafficked, it has a metropolitan bit, a suburban bit and a villagey bit. The villagey bit includes a betting shop, a take-out Tandoori shop, and in fact a whole clutch of the diminutive, highly characterized one-family stores that George Orwell described so well in the 1930's. It also has, or had, a little factory tucked away at the back not far from the junction of Boundary Road and Abbey Road.

That factory was a rundown sort of place when it was bought a year or two ago by Charles Saatchi, who is best known as the cofounder in first youth of Saatchi & Saatchi, an advertising agency that does a multimillion-dollar business in many parts of the world. Charles Saatchi is also well known—some would say notorious—in the international contemporary art establishment for the collection of recent art that he and his wife have been forming since the late 1960's.

The private collector of new art, as he existed in pre-revolutionary Moscow, in Switzerland in the first half of this century and in the United States today, has had few parallels in England. It was, therefore, thought in London to be in rather bad form—pushy, if not actually disreputable—when the Saatchis not only bought the paintings and sculptures that they most liked, but bought them in large numbers. No one knew exactly what they had, but in major international loan exhibitions they made their mark as lenders over and over again.

It did not endear them to English artists, who have a hard time scratching a living from local collectors, that they spent a lot of time in the United States and bought heavily in the domain of American art. Nor did it endear them to American artists that more recently they have bought heavily in the domain of German and Italian art.

This situation was further complicated by the fact that although in his professional activity Charles Saatchi is a laconic lord of language who can make one word do the work of 50, he has never in his life given an interview, whether about the collection or about anything else. Nor is he going to start doing so now. It is also pertinent that the four-volume catalogue is entitled "Art of Our Time" in very large letters, and subtitled "The Saatchi Collection" in very small ones. It includes appreciations of the artists by many good writers—among them Hilton Kramer, Peter Schjeldahl, Robert Rosenblum, Rudi Fuchs and Jean-Christophe Ammann—but the Saatchis themselves are never mentioned.

Given that the collection as catalogued includes nearly 500 works by 45 artists—of which perhaps one-tenth at most can be shown at any one time—the inaugural show could have been a promiscuous catchall. But the Saatchis have opted for plain grand statement, and for the presentation in depth of four artists—Donald Judd, Andy Warhol, Cy Twombly and Brice Marden. The result suggests that a golden age in art can take many forms, and that one of them can be found in the achievement of the 1960's and 70's.

Doubtless these matters will be debated as long as the Saatchis are an active force in the art market. Meanwhile, two things need to be said. One is that Max Gordon has contrived for them one of the most blissful spaces of its kind that this visitor has ever trodden. The other is that on the evidence of the catalogue there is material in the collection for a series of densely thought-through and sometimes definitive exhibitions that could continue for five or six years at least.

The unnamed gallery at 98a Boundary Road, London N.W.8. is at present open by appointment only. Anyone who is interested to go can telephone London O1-624-8299 as of now. ■

NOVEMBER 17, 1985

YOUTH—ART—HYPE:

A DIFFERENT BOHEMIA

Maureen Dowd

Ann Magnuson sits on a worn couch in her East Village apartment, rummaging in the junkyard of American culture. She talks, with affectionate mockery, about icons and totems and slogans, past and present. Her allusions spill out like the contents of some crazed time capsule—Steve and Eydie, "The Beverly Hillbillies," Patty Hearst, Gidget, Wonder bread, Amway, TV evangelists, Lawrence Welk, Jim Morrison and the Doors, Chicken McNuggets, high-fiber diets, midstate pork princesses, Mantovani, Mr. Spock and "Beyond the Valley of the Dolls."

Recently christened "the Funny Girl of the avant-garde" by People magazine, the 28-year-old conjures up these spirits in her satirical skits for downtown clubs such as Area, Danceteria and the Pyramid. Her characters include Mrs. Rambo, who shoots her way through Bloomingdale's to save Nancy Reagan from getting a New Wave makeup job at the Yves St. Laurent counter, and Fallopia, Prince's new protégé, who is really Delores Jean Humpshnoodleburger, a graduate of the Rose-Marie School of Baton and Tap in Duluth.

She is a performance artist with a cult following and the area where she lives and works is simply called downtown.

She is at the center of the vivid New York arts community that has captured international attention spinning what has come to be known as "the downtown style." The artists cannibalize high art and the mass culture of the last three decades—television, suburbia, pornography, Saturday morning cartoons, comic books, Hollywood gossip magazines, spirituality, science fiction, horror movies, grocery lists and top-40 lists.

"It's everything turned inside of itself, it's sensory overload," Ann Magnuson says. "It's a postmodern conglomeration of all styles. You steal everything."

Although there are one or two outposts above 14th Street, the community begins there and moves fitfully down Manhattan, through the East Village, the Lower East Side and, on the West Side, down through TriBeCa to the Battery. It tends to hug the edges of the island and carefully avoids that older artists' haunt, Greenwich Village.

Just as irony is the hallmark of the downtown style, the word bohemia takes on an ironic twist when used to describe this arts community. For this is a bohemia, to use Ann Magnuson's phrase, that is turned inside of itself, different from any that have preceded it. While past bohemians were rebels with contempt for the middle class and the mercantile culture, many of the current breed share the same values as the yuppies uptown.

This is a blue-chip bohemia where artists talk tax shelters more than politics, and where American Express Gold Cards are more emblematic than garrets. In this Day-Glo Disneyland, the esthetic embrace of poverty has given way to a bourgeois longing for fame and money. It is a world where nightclubs have art curators and public-relations directors are considered artists.

"Bohemia used to be a place to hide," says John Russell, the chief art critic of The New York Times. "Now it's a place to hustle."

"It's not chic to be a starving artist any more," agreed Joe Dolce, a writer and publicist for the downtown nightclub Area. "It's more chic to be making millions. Bohemia meets David Stockman."

American actress, performance artist and nightclub performer Ann Magnuson.

NOVEMBER 24, 1986

NEW BREED OF HIGH-STAKES BUYER PUSHES ART-AUCTION PRICES TO LIMIT

Douglas C. McGill

A new species of auction goer—people of recently acquired wealth who have become high-stakes collectors of art—are responsible in large part for the series of record-shattering art auctions at Sotheby's and Christie's that took in more than $155 million in the last two weeks.

The influence of these new collectors, who work in such fields as finance and real estate, has become one of the most controversial subjects in the art world—a debate fueled by the prices of this month's auctions. At the top of the record-setting sales for a two-week period were a Leonardo sketch for $3.6 million, a Mondrian painting for $5 million and a work by the contemporary artist Jasper Johns for $3.6 million.

Art has been collected as investment for at least the last three decades, and experts agree that several other factors besides the new collectors played a role in creating an environment ripe for sales of such proportions. Prime among them were changing tax laws that take effect Jan. 1, after which capital gains will be taxed at a higher level.

In addition, a weakness of the dollar against several foreign currencies, especially the yen, has increased the number of foreign buyers at the auctions. One of the highest prices in the recent sales, for instance, the $5 million for the Mondrian, was offered by a New York dealer bidding for a group of private Japanese collectors. ■

OBITUARY

FEBRUARY 23, 1987

ANDY WARHOL, POP ARTIST, DIES

Douglas C. McGill

Andy Warhol, a founder of Pop Art whose paintings and prints of Presidents, movie stars, soup cans and other icons of America made him one of the most famous artists in the world, died yesterday. He was believed to be 58 years old.

The artist died at the New York Hospital-Cornell Medical Center in Manhattan, where he underwent gall bladder surgery Saturday. His condition was stable after the operation, according to a hospital spokeswoman, Ricki Glantz, but he had a heart attack in his sleep around 5:30 A.M.

Though best known for his earliest works—including his silk-screen image of a Campbell's soup can and a wood sculpture painted like a box of Brillo pads—Mr. Warhol's career included successful forays into photography, movie making, writing and magazine publishing.

He founded Interview magazine in 1969, and in recent years both he and his work were increasingly in the public eye—on national magazine covers, in society columns and in television advertisements for computers, cars, cameras and liquors.

In all these endeavors, Mr. Warhol's keenest talents were for attracting publicity, for uttering the unforgettable quote and for finding the single visual image that would most shock and endure. That his art could attract and maintain the public interest made him among the most influential and widely emulated artists of his time.

Although himself shy and quiet, Mr. Warhol attracted dozens of followers who were anything but quiet, and the combination of his genius and their energy produced dozens of notorious events throughout his career. In the mid-1960's, he sometimes sent a Warhol look alike to speak for him at lecture engagements, and his Manhattan studio, "the Factory," was a legendary hangout for other artists and hangers-on.

In the 1980's, after a relatively quiet period in his career, Mr. Warhol burst back onto the contemporary art scene as a mentor and friend to young artists, including Keith Haring, Kenny Scharf and Jean Michel Basquiat.

"He had this wry, sardonic knack for dismissing history and putting his finger on public taste, which to me was evidence of living in the present," said the sculptor George Segal. "Every generation of artists has the huge problem of finding their own language and talking about their own experience. He was out front with several others of his generation in pinning down how it was to live in the 60's, 70's and 80's."

In his book, "The Philosophy of Andy Warhol," the artist wrote a short chapter entitled "Death" that consisted almost entirely of these words: "I'm so sorry to hear about it. I just thought that things were magic and that it would never happen." ■

MAY 24, 1987

PROTECTING 'NEW' SISTINE CEILING: A DEBATE FLARES

Roberto Suro

More than midway through their 12-year project, the restorers of the Sistine Chapel frescoes seem to have dampened a debate over the use of solvents to strip away old varnish and five centuries' accumulation of soot.

But the controversy seems to have entered a new phase, this time over how best to protect what now is being revealed. Some critics contend that as the Michelangelo masterpiece is exposed again to the light, it also faces greater exposure to humidity and airborne pollutants that could damage the frescoes.

The Vatican's restoration project, begun in 1980, was sure to generate debates if only because it is altering the appearance of one of the world's best-known masterpieces, Michelangelo's epic depiction of history from the world's creation to its end.

The restoration is being done one section at a time. This summer the workers will reach the "Creation of Adam," which, with its outstretched hands, is perhaps the most famous pictorial image produced by Western culture.

Disagreements began over the removal of the 16th-century animal glue varnish that had combined with candle soot and dust to form a dark patina over the plaster. Critics protested that the workers' solvents were wiping away some of Michelangelo's original work and that, since no new protective coating is being applied in place of the old varnish, the frescoes could be damaged by exposure to the air.

The Vatican commissioned a study of the Sistine Chapel in 1982 and 1983 by Dario Camuffo, a physicist at Italy's National Research Council. Mr. Camuffo measured the variations in temperature and humidity caused when tourists crowd into the chapel for a few hours a day.

With an average of about 6,000, and a maximum of up to 18,000, visitors a day crowding through the chapel, Mr. Camuffo said the frescoes were constantly being weakened and that tiny cracks were spreading across the plaster. He said a major cause of these cracks was the changes in temperature and humidity caused by the crowds.

So far, the Vatican has put into effect some, but not all, of Mr. Camuffo's recommendations. Low-heat lighting has been installed, and so has an electrostatic carpet that collects dust from tourists' shoes. He also recommended that tourists be prohibited from carrying wet umbrellas and raincoats into the chapel, but this point was rejected.

According to Walter Persegati, secretary-treasurer of the Vatican Museums, the system will control temperature and humidity and thoroughly filter the air going into the chapel.

Those who share this view say they believe the Vatican will eventually have to limit the influx of warm, humid human bodies that perhaps pose the greatest danger to the frescoes.

Restricting public access to the chapel is something that the Vatican has been unwilling to consider so far, and if other alternatives, like the climate control system, do not succeed, the guardians of Michelangelo's frescoes may have to face an extremely difficult decision. ■

NOVEMBER 12, 1987

Van Gogh's 'Irises' Sells for $53.9 Million

Rita Reif

Van Gogh's glowing "Irises"—painted in 1889 during the artist's first week at the asylum at St.-Remy—was sold at Sotheby's in New York last night for $53.9 million, the highest price ever paid for an artwork at auction.

The fierce bidding for the Van Gogh masterpiece was witnessed by an international gathering of about 2,200 collectors, dealers, museum curators and officials, a standing-room-only crowd that watched the proceedings in person and over closed-circuit television. Taking bids by telephone at the front of the room were two Sotheby's employees, David Nash, head of fine-art sales, and Geraldine Nager, who is in the bids department.

There was a gasp throughout the room as John L. Marion, chairman of Sotheby's North America and the auctioneer, began the bidding at $15 million. Bidding progressed in $1-million increments between the two telephones and was sold to Mr. Nash, who was bidding for a European agent of an unidentified collector.

These are the 10 most expensive works of art sold at auction. Dollar figures are as of the date of the sale.

1. "Irises" by Van Gogh. Sotheby's New York. 1987. $53.9 million.
2. "Sunflowers" by Van Gogh. Christie's London. 1987. $39.9 million.
3. "The Bridge of Trinquetaille" by Van Gogh. Christie's London. 1987. $20.2 million.
4. The Gospels of Henry the Lion, a 12th-century illuminated manuscript. Sotheby's London. 1983. $11.9 million.
5. "Adoration of the Magi" by Mantegna. Christie's London. 1985. $8.1 million, or $10.4 million.
6. "Rue Mosnier With Street Pavers" by Manet. Christie's London. 1966. $7.7 million, or $11 million.
7. "Portrait of a Young Girl Wearing a Gold-Trimmed Cloak" by Rembrandt. Sotheby's London. 1986. $10.3 million.
8. "Seascape: Folkestone" by Turner. Sotheby's London. 1984. $10 million.
9. "Landscape With Rising Sun," by Van Gogh. Sotheby's New York. 1985. $9.9 million.
10. "Woman Reading" by Braque. Sotheby's London. 1986. $9.5 million. ■

Buyers bid for Vincent Van Gogh's "Irises" at an auction at Sotheby's in New York on November 11, 1987.

OBITUARY

AUGUST 15, 1988

Jean Michel Basquiat, 27, An Artist of Words And Angular Images

Constance L. Hays

Jean Michel Basquiat, a Brooklyn-born artist whose brief career leaped from graffiti scrawled on SoHo foundations to one-man shows in galleries around the world, died Friday at his home in the East Village. He was 27 years old.

A woman looks at Jean Michel Basquiat's "Portrait of the Artist as a Young Derelict" at the Modern Arts museum in Paris.

NOVEMBER 13, 1988

80'S DESIGN: WALLOWING IN OPULENCE AND LUXURY

Paul Goldberger

The architecture of the last decade has been marked by a consistently high level of concern for appearances; it has been lavish in its use of materials, active in its use of ornament, and highly dependent on the forms of history, particularly those of classicism.

This has been a decade—and here we come back, inevitably, to the fact of these having been the Reagan years—in which architecture has been luxurious, even sumptuous, but in which it has also been not a little self-indulgent. These have been great years for the marble shippers of Italy and the granite quarries of New England; the office buildings of the 1980's have been celebrations of luxury such as we have not seen for half a century. Opulence has been the order of the day—from the A.T.& T. Building by Philip Johnson and John Burgee in New York; to the same architects' towers in Boston, Chicago, Houston and Dallas; to buildings such as Kohn Pedersen Fox's Procter & Gamble headquarters in Cincinnati, Edward Larrabee Barnes's Equitable Tower in New York, and Skidmore, Owings & Merrill's modestly named One Magnificent Mile in Chicago.

Some of these buildings have been good and some of them have been terrible, but taken as a group, the good and the bad present a remarkable sense of a time concerned primarily with recapturing a sense of lavishness from the past.

Post-modernism began, after all, a decade or more before the Reagan era, with the work of such theorists as Robert Venturi, who one presumes would be appalled to think of any connection between his ideas and the conservative tastes of the Reagan years. He was arguing against the utopianism of modernism, and against its austerity and indifference to popular taste; his alternative, of course, was a highly studied architecture that comments ironically on the architecture of the past and, in its irony, asserts itself firmly as work of our time.

Post-modern architects began by looking at the past to seek to express connections to a broader culture that modern architecture had denied them; by the mid-1980's, many of them were looking back just for the ease and comfort of it. The career of Robert A. M. Stern stands as a perfect example of this: a student of Robert Venturi, Mr. Stern in the 1970's sprinkled his work with Venturiesque irony. But in the 1980's he became more and more a designer of lavish, highly traditional houses for the well-to-do; he moved from commenting on the Shingle Style to attempting to echo its forms literally. In the last couple of years, Mr. Stern has designed sumptuous Georgian and Shingle Style mansions that could almost pass for leftovers from the 1920's.

OPPULENCE HAS BEEN THE ORDER OF THE DAY

Perhaps the real design symbol of these years has not been Philip Johnson or Robert Stern but Ralph Lauren, who produces impeccable stage sets of traditional design; they exude luxury and ease. Ralph Lauren has become a kind of one-man Bauhaus, a producer of everything from fabrics to furniture to buildings, all of which, taken together, form a composite, a fully designed life. But where the Bauhaus sought to challenge established standards, to break out of the bourgeois symbols of the age, Ralph Lauren celebrates them. Design is not a matter of challenge but of comfort.

The challenge of the next decade will not be to supplant post-modernism but to bring it back to its beginnings—to try to re-establish the connection between post-modernism and seriousness of intent that Robert Venturi gave it in its beginnings, while not losing sight of the social goals that have become more important in the last couple of years. It is not an easy agenda—but there never was anything easy about making architecture in the real world, in this time or any other. ■

MARCH 29, 1989

Pei Pyramid and New Louvre Open Today

Paul Goldberger

PARIS, March 25—Not since Gustave Eiffel made the first climb to the top of his tower 100 years ago has the inauguration of a structure in Paris been as eagerly awaited as the opening of I. M. Pei's glass pyramid in the middle of the courtyard of the Louvre.

And Wednesday afternoon, more than five years after the unveiling of its design provoked international controversy and accusations that an American architect was destroying the very heart of Paris, President Francois Mitterrand is to quietly snip a ribbon, officially opening the pyramid.

The news from Paris is that the Louvre is still there, although it is now a dramatically different museum. The pyramid does not so much alter the Louvre as hover gently beside it, coexisting as if it came from another dimension.

The pyramid itself is a technological tour de force: it is exquisitely detailed, light and nearly transparent. Yet it is also a monument intended to take its place in the city's grandly scaled urban fabric, a structure that, for all its overt modernism, has a strictly geometric formal quality that ties it to the Parisian cityscape.

The story of this 71-foot-high structure of glass and metal, which now serves as the main public entrance to a significantly remodeled Louvre, bears other resemblances to that of the Eiffel Tower. Like the tower, the pyramid was at first bitterly denounced by many prominent people in the arts, who viewed it as an unwelcome intrusion of harsh modernism into the sacred precincts of Paris. But also as with the tower, the Parisian mood mellowed as construction proceeded. Now that the pyramid is finished, its sharpest critics seem to have retreated, and it has become fashionable in this city not only to accept the building but even to express genuine enthusiasm for it.

The vast new underground Louvre contains a 29-foot-high main hall beneath the glass pyramid, shops, cafeterias, an auditorium and education and information facilities for visitors, and storage and work areas for the staff.

Beginning Thursday, the first day the public will be admitted to the renovated Louvre, visitors will enter the museum through the pyramid, stopping first on a triangular ground-level entry platform, then descending via an escalator, a spiral staircase or a round open platform elevator to the new main vestibule, called the Hall Napoleon. ■

JUNE 14, 1989

CORCORAN, TO FOIL DISPUTE, DROPS MAPPLETHORPE SHOW

Barbara Gamarekian

The Corcoran Gallery of Art has canceled a planned retrospective of the work of the photographer Robert Mapplethorpe, anticipating that its content would trigger a political storm on Capitol Hill.

"Robert Mapplethorpe: The Perfect Moment," an exhibition of more than 150 works, many of them explicit homoerotic and violent images, was partly financed with a grant of $30,000 from the National Endowment for the Arts, an agency already under fire from Congress for its grant policies. The exhibition was to have opened on July 1.

"Citizen and Congressional concerns—on both sides of the issue of public funds supporting controversial art—are now pulling the Corcoran into the political domain," said the director of the Corcoran, Dr. Christina Orr-Cahall.

Organized by the Institute of Contemporary Art at the University of Pennsylvania, the show has appeared in Philadelphia and Chicago, and is to travel to Hartford; Berkeley, Calif.; and Boston. Another extensive exhibition of Mapplethorpe's work was on view last year at the Whitney Museum of American Art in Manhattan. The photographer died of AIDS in March at the age of 42.

Dr. Orr-Cahall said that the gallery had not yet received Congressional pressure, but that gallery officials had been "monitoring" the situation and felt that a major Congressional dispute was shaping up over the National Endowment's support of the exhibition. The Corcoran received $292,000 in Federal funds in 1988 and the gallery is involved in a campaign to increase its endowment from $2 million to $12.5 million.

The controversy comes at a time when the arts endowment's budget is up for review and it faces reauthorization legislation. The endowment has been severely criticized in recent months by members of Congress regarding a grant made to an artist through the Southeastern Center for Contemporary Art. The work under fire, by Andres Serrano, is a photograph of Christ on a crucifix submerged in the artist's urine.

Senator Alfonse M. D'Amato, Republican of New York, took to the floor of the Senate on May 18 to express outrage. Twenty-five members of the Senate, across the political spectrum, co-signed a letter written by Senator D'Amato to Hugh Southern, the acting chairman of the arts endowment, asking that the endowment change its procedures.

Senator Jesse Helms, a Republican of North Carolina, joined with Mr. D'Amato on the Senate floor in expressing his outrage over the Serrano photograph and "the blasphemy of the so-called artwork."

"I'm appalled by the decision," said the director of the Washington Project, Jock Reynolds. "It is an outright cave-in to conservative political forces who are once again trying to muzzle freedom of expression in the arts. The Corcoran should look to the inscription that is carved over its entrance: 'Dedicated to Art.' They should stand by their motto and let Mapplethorpe's work speak for itself."

MARCH 2, 1980

THE PACKAGING OF JUDITH KRANTZ

Natalie Gittelson

In a publishing world worried about huge sums paid to popular writers, the author of "Scruples" has sold the reprint rights to her novel, "Princess Daisy," for a record $3.2 million.

APRIL 5, 1981

London Literary Life; Let Me In, Let Me In!

Martin Amis

Martin Amis poses at home on September 25, 1987, in London, England.

Not long ago, I traveled to Cambridge to give a reading from a novel I had just published. In the pub afterward, surrounded by pleasantly deferential students, I was asked about the London literary world. The students' preconceptions about London were, of course, as naive and fantastic as were mine about Cambridge: "Is Clive James really a millionaire? Do you know Angus Wilson? Is Ian McEwan really having an affair with Princess Margaret?" I exaggerate, but the questions all presupposed a febrile metropolis of vast monetary gain, blazing celebrity and keen socio-sexual selfbetterment.

The London literary world does not exist. The London literary world is chimerical. "I am a chimera," I always think, when people assume I belong to it. The London literary world is a collective fantasy of eager literary aspirants, and the fantasy contains strong elements of paranoia.

Years ago I made the mistake of writing the "One Man's Week" guest column in the London Sunday Times. In this article I described a regular London lunch which is informally attended by myself, one or two novelists, a cartoonist, the odd poet and assorted literary layabouts. The piece was written in terms of comic hyperbole'a London literary lunch as it might be imagined by, say, an embittered provincial schoolmaster with a crate of unpublished novels in his garden shed. Under the restaurant's sparkling chandeliers, the assembled tricksters and careerists gorged themselves on expensive food and drink, offering bribes to venal literary editors, crafting ecstatic reviews of each other's books, condemning rivals to obscurity, hollering at the waiters, staggering out drunk at 5 o'clock, and so on.

Practically everyone took the piece seriously as a confession or a boast. At last, people thought, they're coming out into the open.

"I was only kidding," I pleaded but to no avail. In a sense, the lesson of this literary sketch, and its attendant hate mail, is an old one: Never overestimate the obviousness of your own irony. But perhaps the response also reflects a general hunger to believe in an elite that coldly excludes oneself. Would-be writers may actually prefer to think of the London literary world as a hive of toadyism and malpractice. Such an impression adds considerable poignancy to the presupposition of neglect.

In the British view of the trans-Atlantic literary world, the beleaguered poets and novelists of America live in turreted fortresses or are reduced to spectral, subterranean existences. This version exaggerates reality, but suggests real differences too. When Norman Mailer published "The Naked and the Dead," he instantly saw himself as "a node in a new electronic landscape of celebrity, personality and status."

But there is no such landscape in England. There can be no more than half-a-dozen serious British writers who could live by their books alone. We are always forced out into the world mainly because we are looking for extra work. Here we tangle with the odd overzealous fan, and with each other; but there is no feeling of intellectual community or consensus. We are just a lot of people writing in rooms and meeting occasionally for lunch. ■

APRIL 15, 1981

PULITZER NOVEL'S PUBLICATION IS TALE IN ITSELF

Reginald Stuart

NEW ORLEANS, April 14—"I don't like fame," 79-year-old Thelma Toole said. "But I'm happy for my son." Her unrelenting belief in the writing of John Kennedy Toole, her late son, led to the publication last year of a manuscript over which he had toiled for years and, yesterday, to the crowning of his work with a Pulitzer Prize for fiction.

"I was in a transcendental mood because I had tried for so many years," Mrs. Toole, a retired teacher of the dramatic arts, said in summing up nearly 15 years of struggle that resulted in the publication of the book, a comic novel about life in New Orleans entitled "A Confederacy of Dunces."

The book was praised in The New York Times Book Review as "a masterwork of comedy" and it was selected by The Los Angeles Times as one of the five best novels of the year. The Chicago Sun-Times called it "a foot-stomping wonder."

The story behind this book is perhaps a familiar one, up to a point. It is of an unknown young writer convinced that he can be an author and of his romance with a New York publishing company. His inability to win publication is believed by his mother to have contributed to his suicide in March 1969 at the age of 32.

"It's beautiful and it's full of pain and anxiety," Mrs. Toole said of the entire experience, ranging from the time her son presented her with a manuscript he wrote while in the Army through the very moments that she recalled the ordeal here today for a reporter, occasionally interrupting her account to answer the phone.

The time was in the mid-1960's, when prospects were perhaps not the greatest for a manuscript focusing on the life of poor whites and their encounters with the rest of New Orleans society. But John Toole set out to have his manuscript published with one house only—Simon & Schuster.

The manuscript came to Robert A. Gottlieb, at the time an editor at Simon & Schuster. Mr. Gottlieb, now president and editor in chief of Albert A. Knopf, contacted this afternoon by telephone, said that he did not remember the man, the manuscript or the book.

As Mrs. Toole explains it, the writer-editor relationship kept her son John "on tenterhooks" for some months before he accepted repeated suggestions for manuscript changes by Mr. Gottlieb.

"Gottlieb would write and say the manuscript needed work but it still would not sell," said Mrs. Toole.

After nearly two years, her son asked for the manuscript back. It sat dormant for nearly three years and in 1969, while in Biloxi, Miss., John Kennedy Toole died in his car of carbon monoxide poisoning. The death was ruled a suicide.

"After my son died, I took the manuscript and said to myself 'something has to be done,'" said Mrs. Toole. She tried several other publishers but had no luck.

She then turned to the novelist Walker Percy, who was teaching a creative writing course at Loyola University in New Orleans. "I suppose I put forth such a fervent plea, I suppose he might have been touched," said Mrs. Toole. A week later Mr. Percy sent a postcard praising the book. Eventually, he helped secure its publication by the Louisiana State University Press in Baton Rouge, the state capital, about 75 miles from here.

"When I got the book in my hand, I called Walker and said it's so much richer," said Mrs. Toole. "He said that was because it was in print."

Mr. Percy said in a brief telephone interview today that the manuscript looked "physically shabby" when he received it and he at first felt he could get rid of Mrs. Toole in relatively quick order. But, he recalled, after he started reading the manuscript he could not put it down. "It didn't take long to recognize that there was something of quality here although I admit I felt it was a book that would only have regional appeal," said Mr. Percy. "Frankly I was astonished at the national response."

Mr. Percy also said that, except for editing, few changes were made in the manuscript. The book is in its sixth printing, according to officials at L.S.U. Press, with sales exceeding 45,000 copies in hardback and paperback. The movie rights have been sold. ■

OBITUARY

JUNE 19, 1982

JOHN CHEEVER IS DEAD AT 70; NOVELIST WON PULITZER PRIZE

Michiko Kakutani

John Cheever at his home in Ossining, New York, October 1979.

John Cheever, whose poised, elegant prose established him as one of America's finest storytellers, died yesterday at his home in Ossining, N.Y. He was 70 years old and had been afflicted with cancer for several months.

Long regarded by critics as a kind of American Chekhov, Mr. Cheever possessed the ability to find spiritual resonance in the seemingly inconsequential events of daily life.

In four novels, "The Wapshot Chronicle," "The Wapshot Scandal," "Bullet Park" and "Falconer," and more than 100 short stories, he chronicled both the delights and dissonances of contemporary life with beauty and compassion.

It was an achievement recognized by a Pulitzer Prize, a National Book Award, a

(cont'd. next page)

National Book Critics Circle Award and the Edward MacDowell Medal. Last April he also received the National Medal for Literature, in recognition of his "distinguished and continuing contribution to American letters."

One of the few collections of short fiction ever to make The New York Times best-seller list, his collected stories published in 1978 established him as a writer with a popular audience as well. A new novella, "Oh What a Paradise It Seems," was published by Alfred A. Knopf last March.

His voice was the voice of a New England gentleman—generous, graceful, at times amused, and always preoccupied with the fundamental decencies of life.

"The constants that I look for," Mr. Cheever once wrote, "are a love of light and a determination to trace some moral chain of being."

Flooded in light—river light, morning light and late autumn light—his stories were also illuminated with a spiritual radiance. Indeed, for all his meditations on the sad, sometimes humorous inadequacies of modern America, Mr. Cheever was, at heart, a moralist, concerned with what he called "the enduring past" and the nostalgia created by memory and desire. ■

OCTOBER 10, 1982

A TALK WITH DON DELILLO

Robert R. Harris

During the last 11 years Don DeLillo has published seven novels of wit and intelligence. He has examined advertising ("Americana," 1971), football ("End Zone," 1972), the rock music scene ("Great Jones Street," 1973), science and mathematics ("Ratner's Star," 1976), terrorism ("Players," 1977), the conventional espionage thriller ("Running Dog," 1978) and, in his new novel, "The Names," Americans living abroad.

Yet despite his unusual versatility and inventiveness, it seems that relatively few readers other than the critics clamor for Mr. DeLillo's work. He is able to earn a living from his writing, but he has not had a large commercial success.

"I don't know what happens out there," he says. "I don't know how the machinery works or what curious chemical change has to take place before that sort of thing happens. I wouldn't speculate. I've always tried to maintain a certain detachment. I put everything into the book and very little into what happens after I've finished it."

Mr. DeLillo's new novel explores how Americans work and live abroad. The protagonist, James Axton, a "risk analyst" for a company with C.I.A. ties, becomes obsessed with a bizarre murderous cult whose members select their victims by their initials.

Like "Ratner's Star," a book in which Mr. DeLillo says he tried to "produce a piece of mathematics," "The Names" is complexly structured and layered. It concludes with an excerpt from a novel in progress by Axton's 9-year-old son, Tap. Inspiration for the ending came from Atticus Lish, the young son of Mr. DeLillo's friend Gordon Lish, an editor.

Critic Diane Johnson has written that Mr. DeLillo's books have gone unread because "they deal with deeply shocking things about America that people would rather not face."

"I do try to confront realities," Mr. DeLillo responds. "But people would rather read about their own marriages and separations and trips to Tanglewood. There's an entire school of American fiction which might be called around-the-house-and-in-the-yard. And I think people like to read this kind of work because it adds a certain luster, a certain significance to their own lives."

The best reader, is one who is most open to human possibility

Mr. DeLillo believes that it is vital that readers make the effort. "The best reader," he says, "is one who is most open to human possibility, to understanding the great range of plausibility in human actions. It's not true that modern life is too fantastic to be written about successfully. It's that the most successful work is so demanding." It is, he adds, as though our better writers "feel that the novel's vitality requires risks not only by them but by readers as well. Maybe it's not writers alone who keep the novel alive but a more serious kind of reader." ■

MARCH 20, 1983

Directors Join the S.E. Hinton Fan Club

Stephen Farber

Matt Dillon with S.E. Hinton in the movie "Tex," September 1982.

The novelist S.E. (Susan Eloise) Hinton has lived in Tulsa, Okla., for most of her 34 years. But these days she cannot help seeing her hometown as a giant movie sound stage. Three of her four books have been filmed in Tulsa in the last year and a half.

"Tex," the first to be released, attracted good reviews last fall. "The Outsiders," directed by Francis Coppola, opens in 800 theaters across the country on Friday.

Miss Hinton writes books for what is called the Young Adult market; her books have sold seven million copies to teenagers, and teenagers happen to be the core audience for movies these days. She is in demand because Hollywood believes that her stories can entice the kids who determine today's blockbusters.

Both "Tex" and "The Outsiders" were turned into films because of pressure from

Miss Hinton's adolescent readers. A group of students in a California high school sent a petition to Francis Coppola stating that "The Outsiders" was their favorite book and nominating him to direct the movie version. Intrigued, Mr. Coppola asked his producer, Fred Roos, to read the novel, and Mr. Roos recommended it highly as a project for Mr. Coppola's Zoetrope Studios.

Miss Hinton's novelistic universe is a distinctive one. All four of her books are set in and around Tulsa, and they are unusual among teenage novels because of their sensitivity to class conflicts between rich kids and poor kids. In her stories the parents are largely absent; intense teenage friendships and sibling rivalries provide much of the dramatic material. Perhaps most surprisingly, all four books center on boys and are told from a male narrator's point of view.

"That's the point of view I'm most comfortable with," Miss Hinton asserts. "When I was growing up, most of my close friends were boys. In those days, girls were mainly concerned about getting their hair done and lining their eyes. It was such a passive society. Girls got their status from their boyfriends. They weren't interested in doing anything on their own. I didn't understand what they were talking about."

The reason that Miss Hinton originally used her initials rather than her full name was that she didn't want her readers to question the authenticity of her books by knowing the author was a woman. When Matt Dillon first met her, he paid her what he thought was the ultimate compliment: "From reading your books, Susie, I thought you were a man." ■

APRIL 24, 1983

SOUTHERN ACCENT GARNISHES THE PULITZER PRIZES

Wayne Biddle and Margot Slade

Pulitzer prize winning author Alice Walker, at her home in San Francisco, 1989.

Speaking with the same brutal honesty through characters seeking to control their own lives, two women of the South received Pulitzer Prizes last week—Alice Walker cited for a novel "at once political and spiritual," and Marsha Norman for a "deeply moving" drama.

"I suppose what I was saying is this: Although we don't get each other's messages, we can still have faith in each other," Miss Walker once said of her book, "The Color Purple." The story concerns two black women: Celie, a child-wife living in the South, and her younger sister Netti, a missionary in Africa. Between world wars, they sustain themselves and each other by writing letters they never actually receive. The story focuses on Celie, at first a poor girl enslaved and abused by black men, in the end freed and endowed with a sense of self-worth by two rebellious black women. Miss Walker is the first black woman to win the fiction award.

Jessie Cates understands herself too well at the start of Miss Norman's play, "'Night, Mother." That is why she is intent on suicide. But not before she makes her mother, Thelma, face the emptiness of their home and daily rituals. Self-revelation, here, is a double-edged sword infinitely reflected. Jessie discovers that her interior life is "lost" but still hers to "stop, shut down, turn off," while Thelma's awakening to her daughter's condition acknowledges the inexorable logic of the suicide.

JUNE 8, 1985

THE YOUNG AND UGLY

Michiko Kakutani

Bret Easton Ellis

LESS THAN ZERO. By Bret Easton Ellis. 208 pages.

This is one of the most disturbing novels I've read in a long time. It's disturbing because the 20-year-old author draws a knowing portrait of adolescence that is almost entirely defined by hard drugs, kinky sex and expensive clothes. And it's disturbing because these kids—who are as young as 13 and 14—are not only living a life out of a Harold Robbins novel, but have also acquired, at their brief age, a cynicism that makes, say, James Dean in "Rebel Without a Cause" seem like a Pollyanna.

According to the book jacket, Bret Easton Ellis is a student at Bennington College who grew up in Los Angeles, and his slick, first-person narrative encourages one to read the novel as a largely autobiographical account of what it's like to grow up, rich and jaded, in Beverly Hills today. If Mr. Ellis's story seems grossly sensationalistic at times—among the events described are a gang-rape of a 12-year-old girl—it also possesses an unnerving air of documentary reality, underlined by the author's cool, deadpan prose.

The narrator, Clay, and his friends—who have names like Rip, Blair, Kim, Cliff, Trent and Alana—all drive BMW's and Porsches, hang out at the Polo Lounge and Spago, and spend their trust funds on designer clothing, porno films and, of course, liquor and drugs. None of them, so far as the reader can tell, has any ambitions, aspirations, or interest in the world at large. And their philosophy, if they have any at all, represents a particularly nasty combination of EST and Machiavelli: "If you want something, you have the right to take it. If you want to do something, you have the right to do it."

Mr. Ellis has a good ear for the sort of dumb exchange of non sequiturs, bad jokes and half-hearted shrugs that pass for conversation between Clay and his friends; and while his descriptions of Los Angeles carry a few too many echoes of Raymond Chandler, Joan Didion and Nathanael West—his novel contains all the requisite references to driving the highways, listening to the desert wind and watching beach houses slide into the sea—they nonetheless demonstrate a keen eye for grim details (the dead fish in the Jacuzzi, the cigarette butt stubbed out on the kitchen floor, and so on) and a sure sense of the absurd.

Still, "Less Than Zero" ends up feeling more like a "60 Minutes" documentary on desperate youth than a full-fledged novel. Its narrative, told in fast-paced, video-like clips, devolves into a litany of predictable scenes involving sex, drugs and rock-and-roll. And the characters remain so alike in their aimlessness and disaffection that the reader has a pretty hard time of it telling them apart.

Mr. Ellis clearly possesses talent—and the drive to do something with his gifts. Perhaps in his next novel, he will bring them to real fruition—and write a story that doesn't merely depress us with sociological reports, but also moves us with the force of its imaginative transactions. ■

OCTOBER 13, 1986

IN PUBLISHING, THE NAME IS THE GAME

Michiko Kakutani

A glace at yesterday's New York Times best-seller list shows that 7 of the top 15 nonfiction books were written by people best known for something other than writing. There are five autobiographies: "Mayflower Madam," by Sydney Biddle Barrows, with William Novak; "Snake" by Ken Stabler, the retired Oakland Raiders quarterback, and Berry Stainback; "I, Tina," by the singer Tina Turner, with Kurt Loder; "McMahon!," by Jim McMahon, the quarterback for the Chicago Bears, with Bob Verdi; and "And So It Goes," by Linda Ellerbee, the television commentator. The other two books are less memoirs than meditations: Bill Cosby on being a parent ("Fatherhood") and the former Oakland Raiders coach John Madden (with Dave Anderson) on—what else?—football ("One Knee Equals Two Feet").

Also recently published or forthcoming are autobiographies by Gelsey Kirkland, Jose Napoleon Duarte, Hugh Downs, Joan Baez, Alicia Markova, Jill Ireland Bronson, Phil Niekro, Liberace, Carol Burnett, Eugene McCarthy, Joan Sutherland, Franco Zeffirelli, Margaret Whiting, Mary Wilson and Joe Montana.

Certainly this People magazine approach to publishing isn't an entirely new phenomenon, and in cases where the individual possesses a substantial story or literary gifts (or, most happily, both), the result can be a compelling book. Many of these new autobiographies by public figures, however, are little but slapped-together narratives, designed to be sold—like sportswear or cosmetics—on the basis of their author's fame.

Because such books are frequently written with a ghostwriter or collaborator, the bylines that appear on a given title page can take oddly convoluted forms: "Football for Young Players and Parents" was written "by Joe Namath," "created and produced with Bob Oates Jr.," with "illustrations by Todd Treadway," and "special photography by Rob Brown." And the mystery-thriller "Murder at the Super Bowl" was written by Fran Tarkenton with Herb Resnicow, from a "concept by Bill Adler." Such a litany sounds more like the roll of credits on a movie than the byline of a novel—a form once regarded as the supreme province of the individual writer's voice. But given publishers' new emphasis on packaging—and the apparent belief that anyone can write a book—it probably won't be long before we see novels crediting assistants for such matters as stunts, special effects and maybe even additional dialogue. ■

NEW YORK'S SPINNING LITERARY CIRCLES

Caryn James

American novelist, Jay McInerney (center) having afternoon tea with reporters from "Private Eye" and publicist Caroline Michel (right) in 1988.

A writer's life may be one of dreary solitude, but the Literary Life—ah, the Literary Life promises glamour, fame, a seat next to Hemingway as he scribbles immortal prose in a Paris cafe. The myth is so alluring it can survive even the most scaled-down atmosphere. On a typical New York night, for instance, David Leavitt, Meg Wolitzer and Gary Glickman—all novelists in their 20's and the best of friends—are likely to be having dinner at their favorite restaurant, a dingy, hole in the wall in the West Village. "Even as we sit there," Glickman says, "I sometimes wonder, 'Is this it? Is it the Cafe de Flore?'" As Hemingway might have said, isn't it pretty to think so?

A different twist on the literary life in 1980's New York clubs replacing cafes, and roaming bands of authors stalking the night streets from Area to Palladium to Nell's. Jay McInerney's best-selling 1984 novel, "Bright Lights, Big City," with its aspiring-writer hero, created a hip New York where late-night clubs and cocaine blurs collide with literary ambition. Tama Janowitz's "Slaves of New York," published last year, carries on the image, in stories full of struggling artists, devious gallery owners, desperate hangers-on, all willfully imprisoned by their need to be trendy in the city. But these muddled, hard-partying characters—when would they ever find the time, or the clearheadedness, to write?—are fictional exaggerations.

In reality, for many young writers today, New York is a base where they can strive and grow until they become successful enough, or frustrated enough, to leave for a while—to spend the summer at a tranquil writers' colony or to make money teaching for a year—always returning to replenish themselves in the literary waters, and hit some gossip-filled book parties to make contacts with editors, agents and publishers.

There is a dense network of overlapping circles, formed from tiny cells: Jay McInerney and his friends, the flashy, successful editors Gary Fisketjon, and Morgan Entrekin; the trio of precocious whiz kids, Leavitt, Wolitzer and Glickman—whose first novel, "Years From Now," will be published this summer—and a larger clan of authors in their late 20's and 30's who have passed through Columbia University's writing courses.

The glitzy image of New York as a club-filled amusement park is not pure hype, though, any more than it is the simple truth. Look at the video Tama Janowitz made. Billed as "the first literary video," it was a brief commercial for "Slaves of New York" that appeared on cable television last fall. Tama, with her antique-shop, disheveled, early-Madonna look, is seen strutting down the street, dining with Andy Warhol and the rock star Debbie Harry, sitting in a pink crinoline skirt at a desk in the tiny Horatio Street studio apartment where she then lived. A voice-over that brings to mind "Life Styles of the Rich and Famous" entices viewers to read about: "New York's art scene! The color! The characters! The relationships!" Is this Tama Janowitz's life?

"Put it this way, I don't wake up in the morning and put on a tutu and have makeup artists come over while I'm sitting there typing. Real life might be one day of me sitting there typing and just making some horrible dinner and then watching TV, and the next night might be the night I go to dinner with Andy," she said a few months before the pop artist's death. ■

JANUARY 3, 1988

CHICAGO'S GRUMPY GURU

James Atlas

Until a few months ago, Allan Bloom was an obscure academic. Students of Plato knew him as the author of a highly idiosyncratic translation of "The Republic"; students of Rousseau may have used his translation of "Emile" in a college course. In 1983, Simon & Schuster had signed him up to write a book on the crisis in higher education, offering a $10,000 advance; if the book did well, they calculated, it might sell a few thousand copies. Four years later, "The Closing of the American Mind" made its way to the top of The New York Times best-seller list and stayed there for 10 weeks. By the time I arrived in Chicago, it had been on the list 31 weeks and sold close to half a million copies.

"The Closing of the American Mind" has provoked a fantastic amount of debate. Even now, 10 months after its publication, large-scale attacks continue unabated.

Bad reviews are one thing; the responses to Bloom's book have been charged with a hostility that transcends the usual mean-spiritedness of reviewers. "How good a philosopher, then, is Allan Bloom?" demanded Martha Nussbaum, a classics professor at Brown.

"The answer is, we cannot say, and we are given no reason to think him one at all." This was mild compared to the objurgations of David Rieff, a senior editor at Farrar, Straus & Giroux. Bloom, he charged, was an academic version of Lieut. Col. Oliver L. North: vengeful, reactionary, antidemocratic. "The Closing of the American Mind," he concluded, was a book "decent people would be ashamed of having written."

What is it about this book that kindles such fury? For one thing, Bloom isn't so mild-mannered himself. In his survey of the American scene, he finds much that is contemptible. Contemporary students are ignorant; they don't read books; they're corrupted in adolescence by primitive rock music. One of Bloom's most notorious images is of a hypothetical 13-year-old boy doing his math homework while listening to the "orgasmic rhythms" of a "drag-queen" (Mick Jagger) on his Walkman. "In short," declares Bloom, "life is made into a nonstop, commercially prepackaged masturbational fantasy." But it isn't just "the young" who besmirch America; the culture as a whole is mediocre, "a Disneyland version of the Weimar Republic for the whole family."

How does the university figure in Bloom's scheme of things? His book is subtitled, "How Higher Education Has Failed Democracy and Impoverished the Souls of Today's Students." Like E. D. Hirsch Jr., whose "Cultural Literacy" was another unlikely book high on the best-seller lists for months, Bloom deplores the low standards that prevail on American campuses. Who's to blame? College administrators, who've abdicated their civilizing role by acquiescing to the demand for "relevance." Black studies, Deconstructionism, the popularization of German philosophy in the works of Herbert Marcuse and others: it's all a plot to discredit what are called around Chicago the Great Books.

This fierce polemic is hedged about with a lot of very heavy philosophizing. For Bloom, the corruption of the modern world can be variously traced to Locke, whose theory of rights prepared the way for liberalism; to Nietzsche, whose critique of bourgeois culture was appropriated by the American left; to Heidegger, who gave philosophical credence to Nazism; and to many other intellectual villains, both witting and unwitting.

My theory is that Bloom appeals to the perennial student in so many of us'that yearning, after years out in the busy world, to restore for a brief moment the innocence of our undergraduate days, the long nights in the library spent struggling through "The Social Contract." His book is about the joys of education: how to live in the world without losing one's soul. Bloom is a Socrates figure; he wants to go among his pupils debating the great ideas. And Chicago is his Athens.

NOVEMBER 9, 1988

LESSONS

Edward B. Fiske

This is the year the term "cultural literacy" became part of cultural literacy.

First came E. D. Hirsch Jr.'s "Cultural Literacy: What Every American Needs to Know." The book became a surprise best seller by arguing that American schoolchildren lack the basic information that is part of being an educated person. Too many of them, he said, think that the Alamo was a play by Homer or that the Great Gatsby was a magician.

Now Mr. Hirsch, a professor of English at the University of Virginia, has published "The Dictionary of Cultural Literacy," a list of 7,500 cultural tidbits, from a cappella to zygote, that "form the common heritage of all literate Americans." Still to come is a children's dictionary and tests of cultural literacy for sixth and twelfth graders.

His first battle is with those who argue that the main purpose of education is to teach certain skills like reading, calculating and thinking, and that these skills can be taught in isolation from any particular content. That philosophy underlies both the "cafeteria" curriculums of the 1970's and today's movement toward "critical thinking."

Mr. Hirsch's second battle is with the cultural left, which has accused him of promoting prevailing American cultural values at the expense of information about non-Western cultures and the experience of women, ethnic minorities and other groups.

But Mr. Hirsch says that his critics confuse culture and politics. "I consider myself a political liberal because I want to give disadvantaged children the same opportunities that others have," he said. "I'm all for evolution in the content of what educated people know." ■

APRIL 1, 1988

For Morrison, Prize Silences Gossip

Herbert Mitgang

Toni Morrison in her office at Princeton University.

Responding to the first call yesterday afternoon informing her that she had won the Pulitzer Prize for fiction, Toni Morrison caught her breath, asked for a few minutes to form her thoughts, then said:

"I think I know what I feel. It's true that I had no doubt about the value of the book and that it was really worth serious recognition. But I had some dark thoughts about whether the book's merits would be allowed to be the only consideration of the Pulitzer committee. The book had begun to take on a responsibility, an extra-literary responsibility that it was never designed for."

By "extra-literary responsibility," Ms. Morrison was referring to the controversy surrounding a statement on her behalf, signed by 48 black writers and published in The New York Times Book Review last January. The statement, prompted by Ms. Morrison's having not won the 1987 National Book Award, for which she had been a finalist, decried the fact that she had never won the Book Award or the Pulitzer Prize.

Literary figures agreed yesterday that "Beloved" had won the Pulitzer Prize on its own much-deserved merits as a novel. Ms. Morrison herself said she believed that the award was made despite "gossip and speculation."

"In the end I feel as though I have served the characters in the book well, and I have served the readers well, and I hope the Pulitzer people are as proud of me as I am of them," Ms. Morrison said. ■

FEBRUARY 16, 1989

IRANIANS PROTEST OVER BANNED BOOK

Sheila Rule

Demonstration against Salman Rushdie for his book "The Satanic Verses" in Paris, France, in November 1989.

Thousands of people reportedly threw stones and waved pictures of Ayatollah Ruhollah Khomeini outside the British Embassy in Teheran today in protest against a book that has been deemed offensive to Islam.

The demonstration came as an aide to Ayatollah Khomeini, the Iranian revolutionary leader, was quoted as offering a $1 million reward to anyone who killed the book's author, Salman Rushdie. The reward was to be tripled if the killer was Iranian.

Mr. Rushdie's novel, "The Satanic Verses," has prompted violent protests this week by Muslims in India and Pakistan.

The police today were guarding Mr. Rushdie's house in north London, as well as the offices of the book's publisher, Viking Penguin. Telephone calls to Mr. Rushdie's residence went unanswered, and the Press Association, Britain's domestic news agency, said the author was believed to be in hiding with 24-hour armed police guards.

The official Iranian press agency quoted Fakhreddin Hejazi, a member of the Iranian Parliament, as telling demonstrators in Teheran that Britain was "the enemy of the Koran and Islam and the manifestation of all things evil."

A spokesman in the British Foreign Office said the police in Teheran were out in force and kept the crowd across the road from the embassy.

Mr. Rushdie, a British subject, was born into a Kashmiri Muslim family in Bombay. Today was declared a day of mourning in Iran in protest against "The Satanic Verses," which many Muslims contend is blasphemous.

Hojatolislam Hashemi Rafsanjani, the Speaker of the Iranian Parliament, was quoted by Iran's press agency as saying that what had angered Ayatollah Khomeini was not "merely the publication of a book or novel against Islam."

A Reuters report from Nicosia, Cyprus, said the Iranian state television had broken into a news broadcast to report that Hassan Sanei, an aide to Ayatollah Khomeini, had offered a reward to "anyone who would punish this mercenary of colonialism for his shameful act."

APRIL 16, 1989

ODE ON AN OED

Hugh Kenner

THE OXFORD ENGLISH DICTIONARY Second Edition. Prepared by J. A. Simpson and E. S. C. Weiner. 20 volumes. 21,728 pp. New York: Clarendon Press/Oxford University Press. $2,500.

So here it is at last, the distinguished thing, and at 11.5 cents a page not really overpriced. For these pages average 2,300 words. Thus Stephen King's hard-cover publisher charges more per word for phrasing far less meticulously thought out. "Meticulously"? That contains the Latin "metus," fear, and it used to connote timid fussing such as you'd smirk at. But the Oxford English Dictionary's dated citations permit you to watch as in the 20th-century meticulousness slides toward the admirable: "careful, punctilious, scrupulous, precise."

All four of those words apply to any OED entry. Take "adamant," which my favorite one-volume dictionary, Webster's Ninth New Collegiate, disposes of in six lines. In the Oxford they accord it half a page, from which we learn that its Greek root means "untamable"; that Greeks and then Romans applied it to the hardest substances they knew of (ultimately the diamond); then that "early med.L. writers" got hung up on "adamare," Latin for "to love deeply," and took to using "Lapidem Adamantem," the Attracting Stone, for the new-fangled magnet.

In the first edition, the citations for "adamant" stop at 1878, well before anyone was stating adamantly. That was because Oxford published the first part of "A" as long ago as 1884, and kept it locked in type. From then clear to 1928 the work emerged piecemeal, in units of (normally) 64 pages, collected by thrifty folk for future binding. By the time the whole dictionary was available in a 12-volume set (1933), so much new material had flooded in that the earlier portions were already obsolete. So the same year saw a supplementary volume; and when a second (four-volume) Supplement got added (1972-86), meticulous users found themselves consulting three alphabets. It was time, they decided at Oxford, to consolidate.

Briefly: with generous help from I.B.M.-United Kingdom Ltd., the whole huge bank of knowledge got computerized, the supplementary entries now made integral with what they'd once supplemented. Henceforward, no more of tacking new stuff on at the end. A novelty inserted in its proper place now nudges everything to its right further rightward. In the process some 5,000 new words (and new uses of old words) got added: "acid rain," "daisy-wheel," "Amex," "Visa," "CAT," "brain-dead," "dingbat"; the computerist's sense of "Pascal," the mathematician's of "set." I've made that all sound easier than it was. The keyboarding, subcontracted to a firm outside Philadelphia in Fort Washington, Pa., took 180 people 18 months. Custom software nicknamed Oedipus Lex (OED Integration, Proofing and Updating System) got written in England, while at the University of Waterloo, in Ontario, people devised the data base code to keep track of structural "tags," more or less the elements typography sorts out on the page: pronunciations, etymologies, subdivisions of senses, instances ordered by date. At one stage the eyeglasses of fully five dozen proofreaders were being wiped with unreckonable Kleenexes. The result is so up-to-now it's even captured "fax."

Don't think of it as a dictionary; think of it as five cartons, each about 10 by 16 by 12 inches and weighing 30 pounds, piled up on your doorstep by United Parcel Service, all the way from a warehouse in Fairlawn, N.J., four to six weeks after you order the Second Edition of the Oxford English Dictionary. All you have to do to cause this to happen is dial (800) 451-7556 and give Oxford University Press a credit card number that's good for $2,500—the price of the 20 volumes—plus $75 for shipping charges. As of early this month, Oxford had sold 841 sets in the United States, out of the total print run of 10,000 sets.

The original 12 volumes of the First Edition, issued from 1884 to 1928, were sold by subscription in paperbound segments as they became available, and you can still have the First Edition in computer-readable form (on CD-ROM, I.B.M. compatible) from Oxford for $995. The First Edition is also still available photographically reduced into two large volumes of tiny type, magnifying glass included, for $27.95 through the Book-of-the-Month Club as a premium for joining, or from Oxford for $195.

There are no other ways of purchasing the new Second Edition—for the time being at least, it's all or nothing at all.

But it may be possible to find discounts at local booksellers. One neighborhood store in Brooklyn, for instance, Bookcourt at 163 Court Street, will order it for you at 15 percent off—$2,125. ■

MAY 11, 1989

'Lonesome Dove' Dispute Highlights Growth in Books on Tape

Aljean Harmetz

Aactors Danny Glover (left), Rick Schroder (center), and Robert Duvall in the television mini-series "Lonesome Dove."

Larry McMurtry's Pulitzer Prize-winning novel "Lonesome Dove" provided CBS with a mini-series that attracted large audiences earlier this year. Now a legal battle has erupted over rights to an audio version of the novel.

Simon & Schuster, which will publish the authorized audio version this year, has sued Dove Books-on-Tape, which has already shipped an abridged version of the soundtrack of the mini-series. Last week, Simon & Schuster, a division of Gulf and Western Inc., won a temporary restraining order prohibiting Dove from shipping its remaining 2,000 tapes.

The lawsuit, on the ground of copyright

JULY 4, 1989

How Stories Written for Mother Became Amy Tan's Best Seller

Julie Lew

Amy Tan

Finding one's voice in writing fiction is crucial for a beginning writer, but for Amy Tan, it seemed as if the voice found her first.

From the start, when she wrote the stories that eventually became her first novel, the best-selling "Joy Luck Club," Ms. Tan said she felt as if she were merely taking dictation from an invisible storyteller.

"The Joy Luck Club" is a collage of interwoven stories told from the viewpoints of four Chinese mothers, members of the Joy Luck Club, a mah-jongg club, and their Chinese-American daughters. Unlike the eccentric characters in "Tripmaster Monkey," Maxine Hong Kingston's new novel about the Chinese-American experience, the women in "The Joy Luck Club" could belong to any immigrant group.

"The Joy Luck Club" has won glowing reviews, and paperback rights were sold to Vintage Books for $1.2 million.

Ms. Tan said she set out to write the stories for her mother to explain all the disagreements and turbulent moments of their lives together.

"When I was writing, it was so much for my mother and myself," she said. "I wanted her to know what I thought about China and what I thought about growing up in this country. And I wanted those words to almost fall off the page so that she could just see the story, that the language would be simple enough, almost like a little curtain that would fall away."

Ms. Tan's relationship with her mother had deteriorated after the deaths of her father, an electrical engineer and Baptist minister, and her brother, both of whom died of brain tumors when she was 15. Her mother took her and a younger brother away from the "diseased" house to Europe and eventually settled in Montreux, Switzerland.

Ms. Tan crammed as many courses as she could into a year and graduated early from high school there. When they returned to the United States, settling in the Bay Area, Ms. Tan enrolled in Linfield College, a Baptist school in Oregon, one of two her mother had picked out for her. But Ms. Tan left the school to follow her boyfriend to San Jose State University and changed her major from pre-med to English.

Mother and daughter stopped speaking to each other for six months.

I had always wanted to be a writer

"My mother was convinced she had lost me," she said. "I was so determined not to have anything to do with her." Ms. Tan eventually married the boyfriend, Lou De Mattei, who became a tax lawyer. She received a master's in linguistics.

"I had always wanted to be a writer," she said. "I used to write little fantasy stories to myself. Sometimes I wrote these stories to friends in the guise of a letter. But I also had the practical sense that a person doesn't make a lot of money being a writer, and I couldn't do that except as an indulgence, as a hobby."

Some of the details of her life have been woven into her book, like the discovery that her mother had left behind two other daughters, Ms. Tan's half-sisters, when she came to the United States from Shanghai in 1949.

"It includes details of stories I've heard," Ms. Tan said. She recalled one anecdote her mother told her about a friend who was fleeing from the Japanese in the war. "She had all these bags in her hands and she started dropping these bags along the road, one by one."

That image later surfaced in the book in a story about a woman who, after dropping the bags of necessities and food, was finally forced, out of sheer fatigue, to leave her two babies along the road.

The author and her mother are closer, but Ms. Tan's generational and cultural conflicts are a constant discovery process, she said.

"I think that if everything were neatly resolved," she said, "I would have no more stories to write." ■

---

infringement, illustrates the growing importance of a publishing field that barely existed five years ago. The defendant, Michael Viner, co-owner of Dove Books-on-Tape, said he believed the suit was the first of its type in the fledgling industry.

Speaking of the industry's annual revenues, Jim Milliot, executive editor for Knowledge Industry Publications, a research concern, said: "There are no hard numbers, no industry data, just seat-of-the-pants guesstimates. The ball park figure is $250 million in sales divided equally between retail and mail order."

John Zinsser, who is in charge of audio book reviews for Publishers Weekly, estimates the size of the market for audio books—also known as spoken-word publishing—at $100 million in 1988, with fiction providing about 40 percent of the sales.

Mr. Viner, who started Dove Books-on-Tape in his garage six years ago with his wife, Deborah Raffin, an actress, said he expects $6 million in sales this year. Among Dove's coming releases are the best-selling novels "The Joy Luck Club" by Amy Tan and "The Long Dark Tea-Time of the Soul" by Douglas Adams, read by the authors, and novelizations of the new movies "Batman," read by the actor Roddy McDowell, and "Indiana Jones and the Last Crusade," read by William Conrad. ■

OBITUARY

DECEMBER 27, 1989

SAMUEL BECKETT IS DEAD AT 83;
His 'Godot' Changed Theater

Mel Gussow

Samuel Beckett, a towering figure in drama and fiction who altered the course of contemporary theater, died in Paris on Friday at the age of 83. He died of respiratory problems in a Paris hospital, where he had been moved from a nursing home. He was buried yesterday at the Montparnasse cemetery after a private funeral.

Explaining the secrecy surrounding his illness, hospitalization and death, Irene Lindon, representing the author's Paris publisher, Editions de Minuit, said it was "what he would have wanted."

Beckett's plays became the cornerstone of 20th-century theater beginning with "Waiting for Godot," which was first produced in 1953. As the play's two tramps wait for a salvation that never comes, they exchange vaudeville routines and metaphysical musings'and comedy rises to tragedy.

Before Beckett there was a naturalistic tradition. After him, scores of playwrights were encouraged to experiment with the underlying meaning of their work as well as with an absurdist style. As the Beckett scholar Ruby Cohn wrote: "After 'Godot,' plots could be minimal; exposition, expendable; characters, contradictory; settings, unlocalized, and dialogue, unpredictable. Blatant farce could jostle tragedy."

At the same time, his novels, in particular his trilogy, "Molloy," "Malone Dies" and "The Unnamable," inspired by James Joyce, move subliminally into the minds of the characters. The novels are among the most experimental and most profound in Western literature.

For his accomplishments in both drama and fiction, the Irish author, who wrote first in English and later in French, received the Nobel Prize in Literature in 1969.

At the root of his art was a philosophy of the deepest yet most courageous pessimism, exploring man's relationship with his God. With Beckett, one searched for hope amid despair and continued living with a kind of stoicism, as illustrated by the final words of his novel, "The Unnamable": "You must go on, I can't go on, I'll go on." Or as he wrote in "Worstward Ho," one of his later works of fiction: "Try again. Fail again. Fail better."

Though his name in the adjectival form, Beckettian, entered the English language as a synonym for bleakness, he was a man of great humor and compassion, in his life as in his work. He was a tragicomic playwright whose art was consistently instilled with mordant wit. As scholars and critics scrutinized his writing for metaphor and ulterior meaning, he refrained from all analysis or even explanation. As he wrote to his favorite director, Alan Schneider: "If people want to have headaches among the overtones, let them. And provide their own aspirin." When Mr. Schneider rashly asked Beckett who Godot was, the playwright answered, "If I knew, I would have said so in the play." ■

NOVEMBER 18, 1980

DARCI KISTLER BALLET DEBUT

Anna Kisselgoff

Every so often—it happens about once a decade—George Balanchine singles out a very young dancer for special attention in his New York City Ballet. In the present instance it is the 16-year-old Darci Kistler, who joined the corps de ballet only last spring, but who was, most unusually, seen in a series of major debuts last weekend in Balanchine ballets at the New York State Theater.

The most prominent role was that of the ballerina in the second movement of "Symphony in C" on Sunday night. In the afternoon, she also danced for the first time as the supporting soloist in "Walpurgi snacht Ballet."

This kind of exposure within the first year in a company is unorthodox for any dancer, not to speak of an inexperienced 16-year-old barely out of ballet school. Yet, as the past has shown, Mr. Balanchine does not take such chances lightly. The truth is that he is taking no chance at all—his own experience functions as a preselection process that zeroes in on foolproof potential. The very attention he pays to such a very promising few enables them to develop beyond their present capabilities.

Miss Kistler is a "natural" dancer. When she walks about the stage, she does so with a little lope, knees bent and on half toe. This coltish quality separates her from others in the Balanchine mold—and she is instantly recognizable as a Balanchine dancer. In other companies, her elongated line, fabulous leg extension and lunges into arabesque might be considered extreme departures from the norm.

Yet this kind of dancing serves the creative needs of a Balanchine ballet, and it was seen to best effect in "Walpurgisnacht Ballet." Her harp solo looked newly lyrical, infused with a beautiful effortlessness, clearly shaped in every movement and firm in the jumps on toe. ■

OCTOBER 25, 1981

PHILIP GLASS BREAKS THROUGH

Robert Coe

Five years ago, when it received its American premiere at the Metropolitan Opera, "Einstein On the Beach," a controversial collaboration between the composer Philip Glass and the playwright-director Robert Wilson, exploded operatic conventions with amplified instruments played at rock-and-roll volume and a bizarre libretto of solfege syllables, counted numbers and stream-of-consciousness monologues. Hundreds in attendance at the two sold-out performances stalked out of the Met, handing their ticket stubs to hundreds of people waiting just as eagerly to get in.

Glass's new opera, "Satyagraha," which arrives at the Brooklyn Academy of Music on Nov. 6 for five performances with the Brooklyn Philharmonia, departs as radically as "Einstein" from much of the familiar ground of contemporary Western opera. The libretto, adapted from the Bhagavad-Gita—the inspiration for the political theory of "satya" (truth) and "agraha" (firmness)—is sung by six principals and a chorus of 40 in the original, vowel-rich Sanskrit.

Glass's score—three hours of perpetual motion for voices, strings, woodwinds and electric organ—sustains the dreamlike serenity of the staging and language, with shimmering harmonies and super-Romantic melodic lines surfacing and submerging in cyclic variation. One long scene is based on 143 repeats of a simple fourchord progression, and, at another point, Gandhi wanders among his sleeping comrades, singing a scale from E to E, 30 times over.

But while Glass's needle-in-the-groove compositions remain for some critics simply boring—or, worse, a form of sonic torture—serious musical appreciation of his work is growing, and so is popular acceptance. Several months ago, Glass signed the first exclusive composer's contract with CBS Masterworks since Aaron Copland—and before Copland, Igor Stravinsky. Glass's ability to bring together unexpectedly diverse audiences has resulted in one of the widest followings—and certainly the most eclectic—of any serious composer writing today.

Philip Glass

OCTOBER 11, 1981

THE DEARTH OF GREAT OPERA SINGERS

Donal Henahan

Many years ago, in the dawn of the Stereo Age, some farsighted impresario in the record business put out a series called "Opera Without Words." An orchestra and a conductor whose names escape me at the moment performed voiceless versions of "La Traviata," "La Boheme" and other popular favorites, presumably for the audience that liked operatic music but could not bear to hear it sung. At the time, some of us were already so sophisticated that we could not only listen to whole operas, voices and all, but detect the difference between Hans Hotter and Russell Oberlin. We whooped in derision at the oafs who bought and presumably played these wordless operas, which stood in connoisseur esteem just one level below records bearing such titles as "The Heart of the Concerto."

Now, however, I wonder if opera without words may not have been an idea ahead of its time and one now worth reviving. That melancholy thought occurs in the wake of a couple of weeks of listening at the Metropolitan Opera, during which we had a "Norma" without a vocally plausible Norma, a "Siegfried" without a vocally plausible Siegfried and a "Butterfly" without a vocally plausible Butterfly.

Before the season is over, of course, we are bound to hear some voices that at least remind us of the real article. That might even happen tomorrow night when Birgit Nilsson visits the Met all too fleetingly in "Die Frauohne Schatten."

The return of Miss Nilsson comes just in time to remind us that opera with words has not always been a hopeless notion. However, her presence also is a sobering reminder of how few genuine Wagnerians there have been during her generation and how dismal is the outlook right now for the immediate future.

Every voice enthusiast has reasons to offer for this famine, and they have been discussed often in these pages. Actually, the voice crisis is not confined to Wagner but extends to an older, grander style of operatic singing in general. Worth an especially respectful hearing is the opinion of J.B. Steane, whose "The Grand Tradition" is an astute account of the ups and downs of singing as reflected on recordings between 1900 and 1970. Mr. Steane thinks that the grandopera vocal style may not be dead and could even be starting to revive somewhat. But he contends that it is doomed unless composers go back to writing for the tradition and a new generation of young listeners finds something to value in the idea of vocal grandeur.

Tenor Jose Carreras as Rodolfo and soprano Teresa Stratas as Mimi in Puccini's La Boheme on stage at the Metropolitan Opera.

"Perhaps consignment to the museum is the inevitable fate both of grand opera and the tradition of singing associated with it," Mr. Steane says. Modern pop culture has given an entirely new meaning to singing, so that "to the average youngster the sound of the operatic soprano voice on records or television is now quite actively unpleasant: it sounds unnatural, being so high above the speaking voice, it sounds assertive, unfriendly and uncomfortably loud in its power, and its quality carries a mental image that is somewhat comical." ■

SEPTEMBER 28, 1983

JESSYE NORMAN IN WAKE OF A TRIUMPH

Bernard Holland

Jessye Norman

Jessye Norman celebrated her great success at the Metropolitan Opera's opening night Monday with Chinese food and an hour and a half of sleep.

Her debut at the Met as Cassandra in Berlioz's "Troyens" won over Monday night's audience and Tuesday morning's critics.

Berlioz kills off his Cassandra at the end of Act I, but the opera is so massive—five hours plus—that Miss Norman had plenty of room to make a grand impression during her time on stage. It is a vocally demanding role, but afterwards Miss Norman felt vocally healthy, "a little exhausted but very elated." "I felt like I ought to go right out and sing it again," she said.

For the current run of "Les Troyens" Miss Norman and Tatiana Troyanos will alternate in the roles of Dido and Cassandra. They will also cover for each other—that is, in case one is ill, the other will sing both roles. "At some point, I would really like to sing the two parts, and you do have a good half hour between the first- and second-act appearances," said Miss Norman. "You're so wound up after singing Cassandra, you feel like keeping on. And Dido is a very different kind of role; it's much more lyrical and makes for a wonderful change."

"I was finished by 9 o'clock, and my family and friends went across the street from Lincoln Center and had some lovely Chinese food," Miss Norman said. "When we got back, the Met was still at it, and though they didn't finish until well after midnight, it was lovely that so many people waited to the end to come back and see me." ■

MAY 1, 1983

BARYSHNIKOV PUTS HIS STAMP ON BALLET THEATER

Anna Kisselgoff

When American Ballet Theater opens an unusually long season—11 weeks—tomorrow night at the Metropolitan Opera House, it will be the third year the company will be seen in New York with Mikhail Baryshnikov at the helm. As Ballet Theater's artistic director since Sept. 1, 1980, Mr. Baryshnikov—to keep the nautical image—is still adamantly steering the course he first predicted. And yet he is, perhaps surprisingly, also willing to trim his sails.

He is, for instance, ready to accept that some criticisms of his controversial revisions of the 19th-century classics were well taken. In contrast to his statements in 1981, he is also less apt to mention Leningrad's Kirov Ballet, his former company before he became a superstar in the West, as a reference point for his own stagings and concepts.

Asked to appraise his own first two and a half years as artistic director, Mr. Baryshnikov offered the following reflection: "The company is at the end of its first cycle of transition and it points to how I would like to see the company in the future. Stylistically, there have been some painful moments. When you work on style and you're correcting all the time, it's a pretty boring process. It's like raising a child and you will see the result in five, six years."

To those who expected a clean sweep—a total break with the policies of Lucia Chase, the company's previous director—the Baryshnikov line of advance might look like two steps forward, one step back. Nonetheless there are significant differences—a shift away from a looser artistic profile toward a stronger consistency regarding both repertory and style.

Mikhail Baryshnikov in 1981.

The cornerstone of Mr. Baryshnikov's policy, as demonstrated in his first two seasons, is to turn Ballet Theater into an ensemble oriented troupe in which the ballet on view, rather than any individual dancer, is the chief attraction. This is clearly the most significant change in policy, although it has never been formally enunciated as such. In practice, it has meant a dilution in star impact among the principal dancers when younger dancers share their roles, and it has meant an increase in works that stress group choreography. Understandably this evolution, still in progress, has been a shock to a public that has its favorites (among whom Mr. Baryshnikov, willingly or not, is a top draw). ■

there have been some painful moments

OBITUARY

MAY 1, 1983

GEORGE BALANCHINE, 79, DIES IN NEW YORK

Anna Kisselgoff

George Balanchine, one of the greatest choreographers in the history of ballet and the co-founder and artistic director of the New York City Ballet, died yesterday.

Mr. Balanchine, who was 79 years old, died at Roosevelt Hospital of pneumonia, a complication that arose from a progressive neurological disorder.

In guiding the New York City Ballet to international pre-eminence, Mr. Balanchine established one of the foremost artistic enterprises the United States has called its own. As a 20th-century master, his personal contribution loomed even larger.

More than anyone else, he elevated choreography in ballet to an independent art. The plotless ballet became a synonym for Balanchine ballet. In an age when ballet had been dependent on a synthesis of spectacle, storytelling, decor, mime, acting and music, and only partly on dancing, George Balanchine insisted that the dance element come first.

In his dictum that the material of dance is dance itself, he taught dancers and the public to look at ballet in a new way. In his attraction to the very essence of dance—movement, steps and combinations of steps—he enlarged the ballet vocabulary as had no other 20th-century choreographer.

And because his choreography was so closely related to the music, a Balanchine work, in his words, became an invitation to "see the music and hear the dancing."

Like Stravinsky and Picasso, the 20th-century modern artists with whom he has been ranked, Mr. Balanchine was an innovator who came out of a classical tradition.

The hallmark of the Balanchine style was, indeed, its conscious use of tradition as a base. The idiom in which Mr. Balanchine chose to work was the 400-year-old academic movement vocabulary he had learned as a child in his native Russia at the Maryinsky Theater.

It was at this imperial theater in St. Petersburg that the 19th-century French-Russian choreographer Marius Petipa created his greatest works, including "The Sleeping Beauty."

Tradition was the base for renewal, and radical innovation could come only from those steeped in tradition. This belief was central to Mr. Balanchine's work, and it was reiterated in print by Lincoln Kirstein, the distinguished dance scholar who became Mr. Balanchine's patron and co-founder of the City Ballet and its precursor companies.

Together they established the School of American Ballet in 1934 and embarked on a venture that helped raise ballet to the highest status it has ever enjoyed in the performing arts.

The result was a creative output that raised the total of major Balanchine ballets to more than 200, only a few of them dating from the choreographer's years in Russia or in Serge Diaghilev's Ballets Russes and other European companies.

Throughout his career in the United States, the clarity of Mr. Balanchine's artistic vision remained remarkably consistent. The goal was a school and an American Classical company with its own new works rather than 19th-century classics and revivals. The museum concept was ruled out. Spectacle would be subordinate to dancing.

It was a commonplace to say that Mr. Balanchine choreographed better for women than men. There was no doubt that he believed his own often-repeated remark that "ballet is woman." Whether they were trained by him or not, a galaxy of ballerinas would always be identified with his works or the City Ballet. Among them were Miss Tallchief, Marie Jeanne, Miss LeClercq, Melissa Hayden, Patricia Wilde, Diana Adams, Allegra Kent, Violette Verdy, Patricia McBride, Kay Mazzo and Suzanne Farrell.

In a remarkable summation of his beliefs in this matter and in his attitude toward life, Mr. Balanchine gave the following interpretation of his "Don Quixote," in which he had once cast himself as the Don and Miss Farrell as Dulcinea:

"My interest in 'Don Quixote' has always been the hero's finding something to live for and sacrifice and serve. Every man wants an inspiration. For the Don, it was Dulcinea. I myself think that the same is true in life, that everything a man does he does for his ideal woman. You live only one life and you believe in something, and I believe in that." ■

George Balanchine dancing in 1983.

OBITUARY

AUGUST 18, 1983

IRA GERSHWIN, LYRICIST, DIES; SONGS EMBODIED BROADWAY

John S. Wilson

Ira Gershwin, the lyricist who collaborated with his brother, George, on the scores for Broadway musicals that included "Porgy and Bess" and "Of Thee I Sing," died yesterday at his home in Beverly Hills, Calif. He was 86 years old.

Mr. Gershwin, who wrote the lyrics of such Gershwin brothers songs as "Embraceable You," "Strike Up the Band," "The Man I Love," " 'S Wonderful," "Somebody Loves Me" and "I Got Rhythm," had a heart disease and had been in frail health for several years. He died in his sleep.

His biographer, Robert Kimball, said yesterday that Mr. Gershwin had been unable to attend the Broadway opening last spring of the hit musical "My One and Only," whose score relies entirely on George and Ira Gershwin songs from other shows.

Although he was best known for his collaboration with his brother, Mr. Gershwin also furnished lyrics for Kurt Weill's songs for "Lady in the Dark," Harold Arlen's compositions for the musical remake of the movie "A Star Is Born," and Jerome Kern's songs for the movie "Cover Girl."

The Gershwin brothers' "Of Thee I Sing," in 1932, was the first musical, and Mr. Gershwin the first lyricist, to win a Pulitzer Prize for drama. The show's memorable score included the songs "Who Cares?" and "Love Is Sweeping the Country." Mr. Gershwin was also a member of the Songwriters Hall of Fame.

The words written by Mr. Gershwin to accompany the music of some of the leading song composers of the time had a wit, polish, freshness and depth of feeling that set them far above the ordinary run of popular lyrics.

Collaborating with his brother, Mr. Gershwin wrote the words for such songs as "Our Love Is Here to Stay," "Oh, Lady Be Good," "They Can't Take That Away From Me" and "Funny Face."

With Kurt Weill, in addition to "Lady in the Dark," he wrote the musical show "The Firebrand of Florence," and with Arthur Schwartz he wrote "Park Avenue." In Hollywood, he worked with Jerome Kern on the outstanding score for "Cover Girl."

For many years, Mr. Gershwin lived in the shadow of his younger brother, whose music had captured the imagination of America. Ira used the name "Arthur Francis" to avoid confusing matters.

For five years, beginning in 1920, whenever anyone wanted to meet the nebulous "Arthur Francis" who wrote such wonderful lyrics, George Gershwin would reply, "Mr. Francis is too busy working to be disturbed," and let it go at that.

Finally, in 1924, George Gershwin admitted that he had a brother who worked with him, and for the first time the billboards on Broadway proclaimed a show by the team of George and Ira Gershwin. It was the smash hit "Lady Be Good."

There followed in rapid succession "Tip Toes," "Oh Kay," "Funny Face," "Rosalie," "Treasure Girl," "Show Girl" and "Girl Crazy." The titles conformed to a George Gershwin superstition: They should have not more than two words and should, if possible, have something to do with a girl. ■

JUNE 13, 1984

BAUSCH TROUPE MAKES NEW YORK DEBUT

Anna Kisselgoff

The word was out, the place was mobbed. Pina Bausch, from West Germany, is the most talked-about choreographer in Europe and it was obvious that her reputation had preceded her at the Brooklyn Academy of Music last night, where the Pina Bausch Wuppertaler Tanztheater made its New York debut.

(cont'd. next page)

Pina Bausch

(continued from previous page)

When the last blackout eclipsed the final moment in her version of "The Rite of Spring," the mostly young audience rose to give the 43-year-old Miss Bausch and her company a cheering ovation. This first program, which opened with Miss Bausch's theater piece, "Cafe Müller," is one of three that will be on view during the company's two-week run at the academy.

Miss Bausch is a major talent and an exciting one. This is clear even from a program that was designed by the academy to ease us gently into Miss Bausch's more extreme experiments. Anyone who has followed her career through the European press can expect talk of real police dogs ringing a stage, stuntmen dropping four stories to the ground, dancers performing in tanks of water and stages filled with women in lingerie.

Her view of Stravinsky's "Rite of Spring," although performed on a dirt-covered floor, turns out, however, to be a recension rooted in a conventional idea, the battle of the sexes. And "Cafe Müller," with its imagery of emotional pain, most of it self-inflicted, would not be startling to anyone familiar with Expressionist forms, Italian films about couples unable to communicate or both.

The performers are exceptional. Their hallmark is to avoid recognition of each other on stage and as Dominique Mercy and Beatrice Libonati hurl each other against a wall or repeatedly fall out of an embrace, they do so nearly as strangers. Their lips meet but whether they kiss is another matter.

When Jean Sasportes crashes through the furniture, he seemingly goes unacknowledged, and his destination is always undefined. When Meryl Tankard's fearful scurries dot the action, she too becomes an unimportant bystander. In Jan Minarik, Miss Bausch—whose background solos serve as an abstraction of the drama—has a powerful perfomer who needs only to stand still to hold the stage. ■

NOVEMBER 30, 1984

MARK MORRIS,
A New Force in Dance World, Hurtles on Stage

Jennifer Dunning

"Mark Morris: The Next of the Major Moderns?" a dance magazine trumpeted recently on its cover. Mr. Morris, a 28-year-old choreographer now based in his hometown of Seattle, first engaged New York audiences in 1980, when he showed his dances in one of the city's downtown studio spaces. This weekend, he and his dancers are performing in the Brooklyn Academy's prestigious Next Wave Festival—recognition of the fact that Mr. Morris is now considered one of the most gifted choreographers of his era.

His dances are musical, intelligent, lushly physical and informed by an endearing mixture of flamboyance and humanity. They also tend to defy categorization. This weekend, for example, audiences will see his "Gloria," a richly textured pure-dance piece; "O Rangasayee," a 20-minute workout of a new solo for himself set to music by Sri Tyagaraja; and his new "Championship Wrestling After Roland Barthes," a group work set to synthesizer music composed by Herschel Garfein.

The first two dances were inspired, typically, by music. Mr. Morris had been carrying the Vivaldi score around in his head since his high school days, when he sang in a choir, studied ballet and flamenco and immersed himself in Balkan folk dancing, which he performed from the age of 14. At 20, he left Seattle for New York, where he found work with the companies of such choreographers as Eliot Feld, Twyla Tharp, Lar Lubovitch and Hannah Kahn.

Mr. Morris returned to Seattle last year so that he could work more spontaneously and informally. How does he feel about being the possible crown prince of modern dance? "I need a manager in a raccoon coat," he says ruefully.

Mark Morris & Teri Weksler in scene from Mark Morris Dance Group performance of "One Charming Night" in 1985.

dance

SEPTEMBER 24, 1985

PAVAROTTI REFLECTS UPON THE CELEBRATED VOICE

Will Crutchfield

Opera has known careers as remarkable as Luciano Pavarotti's, but not many, and rarely more than one in any generation. The beloved Italian singer approached last night's Metropolitan Opera opening as a star not only at the top of his profession, but one who has reached beyond it to a public not normally concerned with opera. He has taken his knocks, as well as garnering his laurels, along the way.

On a recent morning before the rehearsals for last night's "Tosca" at the Met, Mr. Pavarotti sat in the bare studio of his large Central Park South apartment and talked about age, the future, the lonely profession of opera—and, naturally, "the voice."

Mr. Pavarotti is approaching his 50th birthday (Oct. 12) and his 25th anniversary in opera, and "the voice" that represents opera to the world at large is still basically fresh and lyrical.

In a generation when too many singers reach their half-century in the grip of wobble, souring of tone and general distress, the only really significant change in the Pavarotti sound has been a certain erosion of the high notes. For some years now, he has avoided the high C that he used to deliver nine times in a single aria in "Daughter of the Regiment."

A bout of vocal trouble did shadow the Pavarotti career a few years back—not the crisis that some singers undergo, but enough to cause concern. The singer was quite frank about its cause: "I took too many sleepy pill. It should make you sleep and recuperate, but when you take them every day as I did, there comes una sonnolenza nelle corde vocale—the vocal cords were sleepy. One day the sound was not so good, the next day worse. But it is now three years that I don't take any. I don't sleep as good, but I feel very healthy."

Luciano Pavarotti before a performance.

However healthy, though, Mr. Pavarotti is at the stage where any singer must begin to reflect on the fact that voices do not last forever. Some tenors have gone on singing well through their 50's and beyond, but more have not. The battered little notebook he carries with him reads "Luciano 1984-89," and actually holds engagements up to 1990 ("too far"). And beyond that? "I am cautious," he said, "but I think I may have good endurance. When I began to study, I made lists of all the roles I wanted to sing, and the age at which I planned to sing them. At the top I put 'Rodolfo—22.' I did it at 26. Everything has come later than I planned, and I am not sorry. I thought to retire myself at 55, but for now the voice feels . . . ." His words trail off and he knocks wood, but a grin on the famous face lets you know exactly how the voice feels. ■

OCTOBER 13, 1985

There's New Passion in Music-Making

John Rockwell

Sometimes conventional wisdom turns out not to be so wise, after all. Cliches codify what everyone knows, to the point of banality, but sometimes cliched assumptions become outmoded; they aren't even trivially true any more. Take the widespread notion that young instrumental virtuosos these days, while technically proficient, are bland, conservative and utterly lacking in individuality, "soul" or "heart."

But what if this widely held thesis isn't valid? Or, more likely, that while it accurately described much of the previous generation, it is losing its aptness for the best young performers in their 20's and 30's who are now gaining favor with the musical public?

There is no point in worrying overmuch about just who belongs within the magic circle of those dubbed "soulful" and those (young or old) who should still be branded as mechanistic. Here, just for argument's sake, is a short list, all familiar to New York concertgoers. They range, among the pianists, from the Romantically communicative Radu Lupu to the willfully flamboyant Ivo Pogorelich to the introvertedly intense Youri Egorov to the coolly mystical, experimentally offbeat Peter Serkin to the manneristicaly swooning Keith Jarrett, who made his fame in jazz and is now carving out a Romantic niche for himself as a Classical pianist.

Among the young violinists there are Gidon Kremer, restlessly curious and imposingly musical; the wonderfully poetic Elmar Oliveira; the big-toned and exciting Kyung-Wha Chung; the still evolving, eagerly commanding Nadia Salerno-Sonnenberg. There is the preeminent young cellist, Yo-Yo Ma, masterly in standard repertory and willing to branch out into the jazz-flavored compositions of Claude Bolling. There is the clarinetist Richard Stoltzman, who offends some purist technicians but who takes all sorts of invigorating risks with his art.

There is no need here to engage again in that age-old argument about whether the younger players stack up adequately next to the masters. Maybe Hofmann or Lhevinne or Rubinstein or Cortot were "better." Or maybe the differences of Zeitgeist make such comparisons suspect in the first place. The point is that as a group, we have better, more personable, more engaging instrumentalists today than we had in the generations that came to the fore in the 1950's, 60's and 70's.

The issue, it should be stressed, is distinctive personality, not style. The best young soloists today hardly all sound alike—in fact, their very differentness reinforces the thesis. That said, however, a prevailing shift can be detected away from a faceless modernist reductionism, a too-sober concern for getting the notes "right" and eschewing expressivity as willful indulgence, and toward a greater flamboyance, color and poetic intensity. In short, a shift from Classicism to a contemporary kind of Romanticism. ■

DECEMBER 21, 1986

THE DEATH AND LIFE OF MINIMALISM

John Rockwell

Love it or loathe it, Minimalist music, with its patterned repetition, seemingly endless length and stubborn refusal to come to conventional climaxes, is everywhere these days. Right now, the fifth act of Robert Wilson's controversial "CIVIL warS," a full-blown opera with music by Philip Glass, is in the midst of a run at the Brooklyn Academy of Music. But no matter where one turns, Minimalism is being enjoyed by eager young devotees and denounced by rival composers and unsympathetic critics.

For critical observers, the current ubiquity of Minimalism offers certain ironies. The best-known Minimalist composers, Mr. Glass and Steve Reich, now reject the term as irrelevant to the music they have composed since the late 1960's. Whether one accepts that rejection—composers are notoriously nervous about labels—it still seems accurate to place Minimalist music's creative peak at least 15 years ago.

But a true exploration of Minimalism must transcend their music, which hardly encompasses all or even the purest forms of the Minimalist esthetic. The exploration must even transcend music itself. Minimalism as a movement—never formally organized but still a tangible linking of like-minded artists—embraced all the arts, starting with painting and sculpture and quickly spreading to dance and music and beyond.

More generally still, Minimalism can be seen as a tendency that inflected (or infected) much of our cultural life in the 60's and 70's, including popular music and jazz, films, plays, poetry and novels, often by artists who never even conceived of the term, at least as applied to themselves. Beyond that, a case can be made for a Minimalist politics, a Minimalist cuisine, Minimalist fashions and even Minimalist lifestyles.

The fact that Minimalist music is so pervasive today can be explained in part by the fact that music lags behind the other arts; painting and dance are now in the full throes of a post-Modernist reaction that makes Minimalist art of this sort seem old hat, indeed. But the success of Mr. Reich and Mr. Glass has more to do with the inevitable momentum of careers: Mr. Reich is 50 years old and Mr. Glass turns 50 next month, and their artistry and influence took time to make their full impact. Now that it's finally done so, and lesser youngsters are dutifully aping their styles, others in the younger generation may well be provoked into a reaction against them.

The irony of Minimalism's popularity today is that by the terms of any true Mimimalist, a gigantic spectacle like Mr. Wilson's "CIVIL warS," with its plethora of events and its operatic score by Mr. Glass, would hardly qualify as Minimalist at all. Mr. Reich is composing symphonic and choral works. So as audiences are puzzled and pleased, you can be sure that lurking in the theater are younger artists who angrily resent what they perceive as its post-Modernist inflation of rhetoric and lavishness of imagery. Even now, they dream of some new form of spare, serious, mystically involving art. "Post-Minimalism," anyone? ■

JUNE 23, 1987

FRED ASTAIRE, THE ULTIMATE DANCER, DIES

Richard F. Shepard

Fred Astaire, whose flashing feet and limber legs not only made him America's most popular dancer but also set standards for motion picture musical comedies that have rarely been met and never exceeded, died of pneumonia yesterday at Century City Hospital in Los Angeles. He was 88 years old.

Mr. Astaire blithely danced his way into the heart of an America tormented by the Depression and edging toward World War II. His deceptively easy-looking light-footedness, warm smile, top hat, cane, charm and talent helped people to forget the real world that nagged at them outside the movie house.

The Astaire legend, which spanned more than six performing decades on stage, screen and television, began before he was 10 years old when his mother paired him as a dancer with his sister, Adele, the partner with whom he first found success.

Mr. Astaire starred in more than 30 film musicals between 1933 and 1968. Eleven of these co-starred Ginger Rogers, his most durable dancing partner. The music they danced to was written by the cream of the popular-music world, including Cole Porter, Irving Berlin, Jerome Kern and George and Ira Gershwin.

His dance numbers fit neatly within the bounds of a movie screen, but they gave the illusion of being boundless, without regard for the laws of gravity or the limitations of a set.

He was also a paragon among his professional peers. George Balanchine, the artistic director of the New York City Ballet and a man whose supreme standards rarely allowed for superlatives, called him, simply, "the greatest dancer in the world."

Anna Kisselgoff, dance critic of The New York Times, gave this description of the Astaire genius: "At its most basic, Mr. Astaire's technique has three elements—tap, ballet and ballroom dancing. The ballet training, by his account, was brief but came at a crucial, early age. He has sometimes been classed as a tap dancer, but he was never the hoofer he has jokingly called himself. Much of the choreographic outline of his dancing with his ladies—be it Miss Rogers or Rita Hayworth—is ballroom. But of course, no ballroom dancer could dance like this." ■

OBITUARY

SEPTEMBER 24, 1987

BOB FOSSE, DIRECTOR AND CHOREOGRAPHER, DIES

John T. McQuiston

Robert Louis Fosse was born in Chicago on June 23, 1927, the son of a vaudeville entertainer. He began performing on the vaudeville circuit as a child, and by the age of 13 he was a seasoned veteran of many burlesque shows.

After World War II, he formed a dance team with his first wife, Mary-Ann Niles, appearing in nightclubs and stage musicals. In the early 1950's, he was a dancer and actor in several films, including "Kiss Me Kate" and "My Sister Eileen." During that period he married his second wife, Joan McCracken.

In 1954, he began a successful run as a Broadway choreographer, winning a Tony Award for his first venture, "The Pajama Game." He also choreographed the film version of the hit musical. He had a similar success with the Broadway stage and film productions of the musical "Damn Yankees."

In 1959 he directed his first Broadway musical, "Redhead," which starred his third wife, dancer Gwen Verdon. He went on to direct such hits as "How to Succeed in Business Without Really Trying," "Sweet Charity," "Pippin" and "Chicago," all of which he choreographed in his characteristically jazzy style.

In his 1978 Tony Award-winning production of "Dancin'," Mr. Fosse presented a celebration of dance in all its varied forms. Among the performers was Jill Cook, who recalled that she decided to be a dancer after seeing "Sweet Charity."

After the death in 1980 of the choreographer Gower Champion, Frank Rich of The New York Times wrote that Mr. Fosse "may now be the last active theater choreographer who knows how to assemble an old-fashioned, roof-raising showstopper in which every step bears the unmistakable signature of its creator."

Joseph Papp, producer of the New York Shakespeare Festival, recalled last night that Mr. Fosse, as a young sailor in the Pacific during World War II, performed in variety shows put together by Mr. Papp.

"I saw at once that he was footjoy, carefree, jaunty," Mr. Papp said. "He loved to dance. On some islands he would perform in the hot sun for five or six hours. He'd go on until he nearly collapsed from the heat."

"With the death of Michael Bennett in July, and now Bob Fosse, the musical theater has lost two giants, two great choreographers," Mr. Papp said. ■

Dancers perform during the rehearsal of Fred Ebb and Bob Fosse's musical "Chicago."

NOVEMBER 2, 1987

New and Mighty Piano Makes Carnegie Debut

Harold C. Schonberg

Yesterday's Carnegie Hall concert of the Leningrad Philharmonic, conducted by Aleksandr Dmitriev, was completely traditional. But not so the instrument upon which Lazar Berman played the Liszt Piano Concerto in A. It was a Fazioli F 308 concert grand, a 10-foot-2-inch monster with four pedals, a tripartite lid propped by three sticks and a fighting weight of 1,518 pounds. If nothing else this weight makes it the heavyweight champion of contemporary grand pianos. In recent weeks there has been much word of mouth about this new entry, and even something of a media blitz. In the audience were representatives of major piano companies.

There are only three F 308's in the world, though a fourth is under construction. The Fazioli is something new in the pianoforte world. The company was formed in Sacile, a city near Venice, in 1981 by Paolo Fazioli, a concert pianist who went into engineering and started researching piano manufacture in the 1970's.

The F 308 is not cheap. At $77,000 or so it tops the 1,058-pound Bosendorfer Imperial, which sells for around $75,000. The two major American concert grand pianos, Steinway and Baldwin, are priced close to $50,000.

The F 308 sounded impressive in its American debut. It had a clear, singing treble and plenty of power. Its bass may take some getting used to; it is not as firm as the Steinway bass, and it had pronounced overtones. None of this was annoying, and there could be no denying the impact of the instrument. Of course, it will have to be put through the usual tests before any kind of judgment can be made.

After the performance Mr. Berman described it as "a bel canto piano," as befits the Italian tradition of song. He said that the instrument was still in an experimental stage and that he had not stopped loving his Steinway. Nor will he ever. But he was happy to try out the Fazioli in New York. He said he liked its sonority and power. But he is not happy with the three-part lid. And, as for the four pedals, Mr. Berman was a bit dubious.

"It will take a lot of practicing," he said. ■

NOVEMBER 29, 1987

Unlikely Team Behind an Unlikely Opera

Diane Solway

It is a steamy day in Houston, where in a warehouse across the street from the Southern Noodle Company, the director Peter Sellars is running through a scene from "Nixon in China," John Adam's opera about Richard Nixon's 1972 landmark visit to the People's Republic of China. The scene is Pat Nixon's tour of a Peking glass factory, and the cast includes the soprano Carolyann Page as Pat Nixon and three contraltos known as the "Maoettes," a Motown-style back up group comprised of Mao Zedong's private secretaries, who echo his pronouncements like a Greek chorus.

One of the most trumpeted avant-garde events of the season, "Nixon in China" comes to the Brooklyn Academy of Music's Next Wave Festival for a two-week run beginning Friday, following it's inaugural performances last month at the Houston Grand Opera's new Wortham Center, where it drew sharply divided critical response. Some critics took issues with Mr. Adam's music, calling it tedious and superficial. Others, however, have called the opera heroic. ■

NOVEMBER 20, 1988

CITY BALLET AT 40: Balanchine's Legacy Lives

Anna Kisselgoff

George Balanchine is dead. Any appraisal of the New York City Ballet on its 40th anniversary must begin with this fact and its finality. As the City Ballet prepares to celebrate its first four decades, the question of its future direction becomes as important as its contribution to the past.

The truth—for many, so hard to face—is that five years after Balanchine's death the City Ballet is no longer Balanchine's company: Young dancers who never knew the troupe's founding choreographer have begun to fill the ranks and, although thoroughly schooled in the style of his ballets, they are also affected by the new choreography they dance. While maintaining his repertory and paying allegiance to his moral and stylistic inspiration, Balanchine's successors are justifiably determined not to look only to the past. The troupe they direct remains the world's preeminent model of contemporary classicism.

On Tuesday night, the company established by Balanchine and Lincoln Kirstein opens a new season at the New York State Theater by "re-creating" the first program that marked its official beginning. On Oct. 11, 1948, at the City Center of Music and Drama, the young creative troupe presented three Balanchine ballets that will now be seen in the same order: "Concerto Barocco," "Orpheus" and "Symphony in C."

No straight line has charted the course of the company's history. Obviously, the City Ballet of today—Mr. Kirstein is general director, Peter Martins and Jerome Robbins jointly are artistic directors—is not the same troupe that existed 40 years ago or even at Balanchine's death on April 30, 1983. For the first time, the City Ballet seems finally to be emerging from a state of transition, albeit one masked by an esthetic continuity stemming from Balanchine's especially strong legacy. As the Danish-born Mr. Martins (clearly no New York native) puts it, "It's as if you're in the Holland Tunnel with the windows closed and all you

(cont'd. next page)

(continued from previous page)

want to see is New Jersey. All of a sudden, it's there. We have gone through what seemed an endless tunnel."

Certainly, the company has been affected by the fact that one of the greatest choreographers of all time is no longer pouring new ballets into its repertory. At the same time, the Balanchine ballets that still make up City Ballet's profile continue to define the high standards that ennoble the company. Somewhat unfairly, these same standards imply that Balanchine's successors will always be compared to him. The company still boasts one of the 20th century's major choreographers in Mr. Robbins. And while Mr. Martins—the best of the neo-Balanchine choreographers—will probably rank higher in reputation than is now apparent, his contribution lies also in his superior knowledge of classical technique. ■

JANUARY 1, 1989

Twyla Tharp: Turning Sharp Corners

Diane Solway

"This year is an extraordinary set of circumstances. It's what I think of as a shakedown," says the choreographer Twyla Tharp who, for the first time in 23 years, is without a dance company that bears her name or her singular stamp. This past July, Ms. Tharp announced that she was disbanding the modern-dance troupe she began in 1965 and accepting the invitation of American Ballet Theater's artistic director Mikhail Baryshnikov to join A.B.T.

Ms. Tharp's arrangement with Ballet Theater—which has taken on 7 of the 15 members of Twyla Tharp Dance—has led many to wonder how the choreographer will maintain her creative identity and make her mark within a large established ballet company, and whether Ms. Tharp and Mr. Baryshnikov—forceful personalities in their own right—will develop an environment in which both can thrive.

Mr. Baryshnikov believes the presence of Ms. Tharp and her dancers at Ballet Theater will stimulate its classically rooted dancers and extend their stylistic range. He also suspects that the choreographer's close association with a major classical ballet company will "stretch Twyla's horizons" and bring both the company and Ms. Tharp new audiences. Several of the choreographer's earlier works are to be added to the Ballet Theater repertory. ■

Twyla Tharp rehearses a move, back-to-back with dancer Kevin O'Day.

FEBRUARY 3, 1980

London to Broadway: How a Culture Shapes a Show

Mel Gussow

At present, four recent London successes are in New York—Harold Pinter's "Betrayal," Martin Sherman's "Bent" (an American play that received its first production in London), Tom Stoppard's "Night and Day" and the Andrew Lloyd Webber-Tim Rice musical, "Evita."

In varying degrees, each has suffered—and survived—a sea change. It was enlightening to have seen the plays in both cities. The contrasting productions say something about the incompatibility of British and American attitudes not only toward theater but also toward society and personal relationships.

"Betrayal" is the most recent transfer. Despite Pinter's position in the top rank of contemporary British playwrights, he has not, until now, had great commercial success of the American stage.

The excellent British actors who originated their roles at the National Theater—Daniel Massey and Penelope Wilton as the married couple, Michael Gambon as the husband's best friend who is also the wife's lover—may not have been considered stars of international magnitude. In the United States, the roles are played by Roy Schneider, Blythe Banner and Raul Julia. The director, Peter Hall, and the designer John Bury, and the play are the same. ■

JULY 6, 1980

AN 'EPIC' DRAMATIZATION OF A DICKENS NOVEL

Mel Gussow

The Royal Shakespeare Company's production of Charles Dickens's "Nicholas Nickleby" is a monumental theatrical experience. Performed in two parts in alternating repertory over a period of eight and one half hours, the play, as adapted by David Edgar, synthesizes the book's 65 chapters into five densely textured, incident-filled acts. Every major character in the novel is represented on stage—some 150 played by 45 quick-changing actors.

This is as close to a complete "Nicholas Nickleby" as one could imagine within the boundaries of theatrical artifice. A collaborative venture among the actors, the adaptor and the co-directors, Trevor Nunn and John Caird, it is a kind of live "Masterpiece Theater" mini-series—and something more.

Most of the dialogue is direct from Dickens; it is ornate without being fustian. Wisely, Mr. Edgar has also retained a taste of the original descriptive text. In an exemplary use of the Story Theater method, actors issue occasional commentary on their actions and those of others, underscore attitudes and stitch transitions. As chorus, singly and in unison, the company characterizes "this wilderness of London," where wealth and poverty stand side by side. The play does not shortchange Dickens's pronounced social conscience, showing, among other things, how the burden of money affects those who need it as well as those have it.

The production is a paradigm of the art of transformation—from actors into a diversity of characters, from theater today into England of the 1830's, from narrative into drama. The work has an authenticity that surpasses that in any other stage adaptation of Dickens that I have seen. The wretchedness of actual conditions is juxtaposed next to the remembered bliss of "bygone days and childhood times." Dastardly evil is vanquished by selfless heroism. The latter is, of course, incarnated by the title character.

The production is a paradigm of the art of transformation

Each half of the play is self-sustaining and can be seen separately. The second half begins with a speedy recapitulation of the preceding events. However, for maximum enjoyment the work should be seen in sequence in its entirety. I saw it all in one day, at a matinee and an evening performance, beginning at 2 P.M. and ending at 11:30 P.M., with one hour for dinner. My feeling at the end of the doubleheader was one of satisfaction, not satiety.

As the actors took the last of many curtain calls, it appeared as if they were as reluctant to leave our company as we were to leave theirs. Even though all wrongs were righted and all plot strands were knitted neatly together, one still hoped that there could be more to the story, which is, of course, the reaction we have when we read the book. The R.S.C.'s "Nicholas Nickleby" is a great novel turned into grand theater. ■

SEPTEMBER 7, 1980

'42ND STREET' LOG-THE MAKING OF A HIT

CLIFF JAHR

It was one of the most stunning moments in the history of Broadway theater. Stunning in the literal sense. The opening night audience at the Winter Garden on Aug. 25 had just given 10 rousing curtain calls to the cast of "42nd Street," the new David Merrick-Gower Champion musical hit, when Mr. Merrick himself entered the stage from the wings. The audience was already on its feet, and Mr. Merrick, who had made a point of keeping out of the public eye during rehearsals and tryouts, received an ovation. "I'm sorry to have to report. . ." he said, but was cut off by a roar of applause. "No, no, it's very tragic," he continued, this time being interrupted by laughter and applause. "You don't understand," he continued almost angrily, "Gower Champion died this morning."

It was an astounding finale. But even had Mr. Champion not died the very day of his opening, the story behind "42nd Street"—from its conception four years ago to its Broadway opening—was destined to become a theater classic.

The idea for the new Broadway musical came to librettist Michael Stewart ("Hello, Dolly!") some four years ago while he was watching the old movie one night at a West Side revival house. "I was gripped," he remembers, "by this grandaddy of the backstage stories and how valid it still is." Mark Bramble, however, with whom he was then developing "Barnum," felt "reluctant" about the idea until he became enchanted by the Harry Warren-Al Dubin oeuvre (22 movies) filled with sunny tunes like "We're in the Money" and "Lullaby of Broadway." Any of these songs, he realized, could be drawn upon to comprise a new musical based on "42nd Street."

One bright August afternoon in 1978, over lunch at the Plaza, Mr. Stewart and Mr. Bramble showed what they had to David Merrick, whose office boy Mr. Bramble had once been. Mr. Merrick first offered "42nd Street" in the spring of last year to director-choreographer Gower Champion, with whom he had collaborated on seven musicals including one called "Hello, Dolly!," which ran seven years.

On the last night in Washington, Mr. Champion told Mr. Merrick about his illness. "It was a difficult speech," recalls the producer, who was willing to discuss this meeting but declined to comment on other aspects of the production. "Gower had no notion he had a short time to live. Nor did his doctor. He just described some blood ailment he had."

At his apartment one afternoon with Wanda Richert, an actress in the show, Mr. Champion admitted off-handedly: "You know, this disease could kill me. But if I go, I'm going out in style, I hope."

The following day, Miss Richert found Mr. Champion at home in a dazed condition and rushed him to the hospital. He died at 1 p.m. on Aug. 25, the day the show was to open. Mr. Merrick was one of the first to be given the news, and he took it upon himself to direct everyone, including hospital authorities, to withhold the announcement until after the opening.

The next morning, all seven of the major New York critics gave the show high praise, especially its musical production numbers. Frank Rich of The Times, who found fault with the book, saluted "Gower Champion's final display of blazing theatrical fireworks."

As for Mr. Merrick, his bold gamble created a profit gusher. Since he owns the entire show, his personal income as long as "42nd Street" plays to sold-out houses will exceed $50,000 a week. Subsidiary rights and road companies will generate enormous additional income, but just the Broadway production alone, after a five-year capacity run, would net Mr. Merrick more than $11 million. ■

Jerry (right) and the cast of the Broadway musical "42nd Street" looking on as the show's producer David Merrick (center), at the curtain call, announces that the show's director, Gower Champion, had died of a rare blood disease some hours earlier.

DECEMBER 21. 1981

'DREAMGIRLS,' Michael Bennet's New Musical, Opens

Frank Rich

When Broadway history is being made, you can feel it. What you feel is a seismic emotional jolt that sends the audience, as one, right out of its wits. While such moments are uncommonly rare these days, I'm here to report that one popped up at the Imperial last night. Broadway history was made at the end of the first act of Michael Bennett's beautiful and heartbreaking new musical, "Dreamgirls."

"Dreamgirls" is the story of a black singing group that rises from the ghetto to national fame and fortune during the 1960's. Like the Supremes, to which they bear more than a passing resemblance, the Dreams have their share of obstacles to overcome on the way up. At the end of Act I, the heroines are beginning to make it in Las Vegas, but there's some nasty business to be dealt with backstage. The act's hard-driving manager, Curtis (Ben Harney), has come into the Dreams' dressing room to inform Effie, who is both his lover and the group's best singer, that she is through.

It's at this point that Jennifer Holliday, the actress who plays Effie, begs Curtis to let her stay, in a song titled "And I Am Telling You I'm Not Going." Miss Holliday is a young woman with a broad face and an ample body. Somewhere in that body—or everywhere—is a voice that, like Effie herself, won't take no for an answer. As Miss Holliday physically tries to restrain her lover from leaving, her heart pours out in a dark and gutsy blues; then, without pause, her voice rises into a strangled cry.

"Dreamgirls" is a musical with almost 40 numbers, and virtually everything, from record-contract negotiations to lovers' quarrels, is sung.

Perhaps inevitably the cast's two standouts are those who play characters who do not sell out and who suffer a more redemptive form of anguish: Miss Holliday's Effie and Cleavant Derricks, as a James Brown-like star whose career collapses as new musical fashions pass him by. Like Miss Holliday, Mr. Derricks is a charismatic singer, who conveys wounding, heartfelt innocence.

Is "Dreamgirls" a great musical? Well, one could quarrel with a few lapses of clarity, some minor sags, the overpat and frantic plot resolutions of Act II. But Mr. Bennett and Miss Holliday have staked their claim to greatness. ■

JUNE 22, 1982

LONDON'S 'CATS,' A NEW WEBBER MUSICAL

Frank Rich

Ensemble scene from the musical "Cats" at the Winter Garden Theatre in New York.

Over the last decade, the young composer Andrew Lloyd Webber conducted a tireless campaign to prove that, yes, the British can create contemporary musicals as sleek and snazzy as Broadway's. Certainly it can be argued that he has made his case. With two successful shows in New York right now, "Evita" and "Joseph and the Amazing Technicolor Dreamcoat," and a third, "Cats," arriving at the Winter Garden next October, Mr. Webber is almost as dominant a force in the American musical theater as he is in England's.

In "Cats," Mr. Webber has his best lyricist ever—by the name of T.S. Eliot. The show is a nearly complete musicalization of the whimsical "Old Possum's Book of Practical Cats," with an inspirational climax thrown in for last-minute plot's sake. "Cats" is a true phenomenon here. Even a year into the run, tickets are sold out six weeks in advance, and there are so many "Cats" souvenir hawkers in the lobby of the New London Theater that the whole enterprise resembles a gold rush.

This commercial success could be repeated in New York. The set is a cat's eye, junk-heap vision of London that, with its three-sided arena configuration, recreates the intimate feel of Mr. Prince's "Candide" even as it looks like an Anglicized "Hair." As in those musicals—and "Nickleby"—cast members circulate among the audience, prodding it to purr. Presumably architects will dismantle the cavernous Winter Garden to recreate this crucial ambience for Broadway.

But "Cats" is, at heart, simply a series of feline song-and dance variety turns, and Mr. Webber and Mr. Nunn need a third collaborator, a choreographer, to keep the fur flying as entertainingly as their formula will allow. The British musical theater hasn't produced any showbiz choreographers at the top American level, and the one who did "Cats," Gillian Lynne, hasn't made her dances as distinctive and varied as Eliot's verses and a full-length dancing show demand.

In New York, Miss Lynne will have some valuable allies: a chorus of Broadway dancers rather than their less proficient and stylish West End counterparts. Her ability to join with them to raise the pizazz quotient of "Cats" may determine whether Andrew Lloyd Webber captures New York's fancy once more. ■

JULY 14, 1982

FIERSTEIN AND 'TORCH SONG': A DARING CLIMB FROM OBSCURITY

Michiko Kakutani

Certainly it is one of the most daring and anomalous plays to ever move to Broadway. A four-hour drama in three parts, Harvey Fierstein's "Torch Song Trilogy" recounts the story of Arnold Beckoff, a nice Jewish boy of "great wit and want," who also happens to be an avowed homosexual and a transvestite who makes his living by appearing on stage.

In addition to garnering critical acclaim, the play—which recently moved from an Off Broadway house to the Little Theater—has also brought its author and star sudden recognition. After years of working in obscurity Off Off Broadway, Mr. Fierstein, at the age of 28, finds himself giving interviews at Sardi's, posing for Richard Avedon and sorting through offers from Hollywood directors. He feels, he says, "like Cinderella."

"When I started in drag, there were other people doing it," he explains in a husky whisper, "but only for each other, and I knew I had to make my own place. I knew I had to keep doing it, keep hitting the doors myself and not let them slam in my face. This time, they didn't slam the door, and it was a shock."

Only a short time ago, of course, "Torch Song Trilogy" itself would have been cause for shock on the part of some Broadway theatergoers. Although Mr. Fierstein says that he modulates his performance in response to audience reaction—he can let the seduction scene run anywhere from 4 to 10 minutes—the text of the play possesses a willful candor that makes such older plays as "Tea and Sympathy" and "The Boys in the Band" seem cautious and condescending.

Indeed, it is only in recent years that playwrights and authors have been able to deal openly with homosexual themes; in the past, such subjects were couched in metaphors and allusions, and characters who deviated from accepted norms of sexual propriety usually underwent conversion, died or were condemned to lasting unhappiness.

Matthew Broderick (left) starred in Harry Fierstein's "Torch Song Trilogy" in 1982.

Mr. Fierstein began performing as a transvestite at a Lower East Side club while he was still a teenager. He weighed 270 pounds at the time and specialized in impersonating Ethel Merman.

The drag-club appearances led to a theatrical debut in Andy Warhol's "Pork" at La Mama in 1971, and by 1973 Mr. Fierstein had turned from acting to playwriting. His first two plays, like "Torch Song," drew on the homosexual milieu—one of them served as a comment on the Continental Baths, and "Flatbush Tosca" turned the famous diva into a transvestite—but the playwright's next project, "Spookhouse," is less parochial in theme.

For the time being, though, Mr. Fierstein is appearing every night on stage as Arnold—an exhausting role that keeps him on stage almost continually during the play's four hours. "I'm tired, very tired," he says, "but I wouldn't trade it for anything. If 'Torch Song' were done in the 50's, it would have played in a little cafe, and that would have been it—an artist can create his own world, but he can't remake the world. So it's very gratifying in that a breakthrough has at last been made; there's at last a real live, out-of-the-closet queer on Broadway. But for me, it doesn't really matter where I work—as long as I work somewhere." ■

OCTOBER 18, 1982

Shepard's 'West' Revived and Restored

Mel Gussow

The production of Sam Shepard's "True West" that opened last night at the Cherry Lane Theater is an act of theatrical restitution and restoration. Two seasons ago, the Public Theater presented the New York premiere of this comedy—a production that was disclaimed in absentia by the playwright—and the work seemed, for the freewheeling Mr. Shepard, uncharacteristically heavy-handed.

Seeing the play in revival, one realizes that it was the production not the play that was originally at fault. The new version—using the same script—is an exhilarating confluence of writing, acting and staging. As performed by John Malkovich and Gary Sinese, two members of Chicago's Steppenwolf Theater Company making their New York debuts, and as directed by Mr. Sinise, this is the true "True West." The compass needle is unwavering.

One sees now that the play is a rambunctious and spontaneous tale about sibling rivalry and the cronyism of popular culture. It shares with an earlier Shepard, "Angel City," a sardonic concern with the seductiveness of Hollywood and with the battle between art and business. The play's principal characters, Lee and Austin, are fraternal opposites. Lee is a scurvy desert rat, Austin a hot shot intellectual screenwriter. They are country and city mouse, or the old and the new West.

No one forgets that the playwright means to be playful, and the stage business—including the transformation of a spotless kitchen into a trash bin of beer cans and plastic crockery—is made to seem organic (though not biodegradable). Credit should be given to the modular authenticity of the set design by Kevin Rigdon and Deb Gohr, resident designers with the Steppenwolf Theater, and to the nimbleness of the unseen stagehands.

"True West," revivified, should now take its rightful place in the company of the best of Shepard—along with "The Tooth of Crime," "The Curse of the Starving Class" and "Buried Child." ■

AUGUST 7, 1983

HAS THE REGIONAL THEATER FULFILLED ITS PROMISE?

Don Shewey

Theater in America used to mean Broadway. The great playwrights wrote for Broadway and Broadway was their showcase, the place where things began. All that has changed. Partly, economics have made it practically unthinkable for a straight play to originate on Broadway. But if Broadway is no longer synonymous with the theater in America, that is largely because of the regional theater movement that took root in this country over the last 25 years. That movement has created opportunities for theater artists to live and work in such cities as Atlanta, San Francisco, Chicago, Louisville and Seattle, instead of having to migrate to New York to be where the action is. It has nurtured writers as diverse as Sam Shepard and Beth Henley, David Mamet and Lanford Wilson, Marsha Norman and Charles Fuller. Many of the plays that go to Broadway have originated in one of these regional theaters, and an entire repertory of American drama of merit has sprung up from all over the country, which has made it possible for a play to have a life without ever treading the Great White Way.

But despite its undoubted influence, the regional theater movement a quarter of a century after it has begun, is in a state of flux. Many of its founders have died, and a number of their successors feel a need to take time off to renew themselves. Meanwhile, a new generation of artistic directors is questioning whether the regional theater has fulfilled or subverted its original intentions—namely, to establish an alternative to the commercial theater, to nurture companies of resident artists, and to bring quality theater to cities across the United States.

For many of the regional theaters, the problem is in balancing artistic and institutional concerns. The 18-year old American Conservatory Theater in San Francisco is the only combined conservatory and classical repertory company in America. But the very size and structure of such an organization causes problems, and A. C. T. suffered a severe financial crisis two years ago. "We had to hire fewer actors, do smaller plays, and rearrange our program," says founder and general director William Ball.

"There is a danger of allowing artistic product to take second place to an institution," says Liviu Ciulei, artistic director of the Guthrie Theater in Minneapolis. The Guthrie doesn't do new plays, and Mr. Ciulei feels that is a lack. "We don't dare to present many new American plays on this huge stage. We're trying to find a temporary solution and possibly build a second stage," he says. "That takes money."

"Regional theater is in a state of flux now," says Gordon Davidson, who has just completed a year-long sabbatical from his post as artisitic director of the Mark Taper Forum in Los Angeles. "There's a lot of concern that the quality of the work is adequate but not good enough. Theater isn't dealing with the life of the society. I'm concerned about a number of social and political questions that are not being written about. How do I help stimulate the quality of subject matter?"

"I'm one of the people who thinks there will never be a single national theater," Arvin Brown, artistic director of the Long Wharf Theater in New Haven, says. "We are the American theater, and like everything else in America, it's a polyglot." ■

APRIL 21, 1985

THE GRITTY ELOQUENCE OF DAVID MAMET

Samuel G. Freedman

David Mamet

Over the last decade, Mamet has proved as prolific and as successful as any American playwright. After bursting onto the scene as a wunderkind with "American Buffalo"—written and produced in 1975, when he was 27—he has demonstrated a staying power rare in a field of fickle acclaim. Mamet endured some critical doubts in mid-career over plays like "The Woods," "Lone Canoe" and "Edmond," but he continued to write every day in his

(cont'd. next page)

(continued from previous page)
workmanlike way—if not a play, then an essay; if not an essay, then a magazine article; if not an article, then a letter to his sister. "The idea that one can become a better writer, a more famous writer, a richer writer, has been the ruination of many many writers," Mamet says, "and I do not plan to be one. It's like a guy who makes chairs. It's something I can do and I can do well. And obviously if I keep at it, within the limits of the form, I should get better at it in small increments. But the important thing is not my becoming a better chair maker, but the chair. You don't become better in general, the chairs become better." In the last three years, Mamet's regimen has yielded the highly regarded screenplay for "The Verdict" and the caustic comedy "Glengarry Glen Ross," for which he won both the Pulitzer Prize and the New York Drama Critics Circle Award as the best American play of 1984. He won Tony nominations last year for both "Glengarry" as the best drama and "American Buffalo" as the best revival, a rare achievement. This year, Mamet has renewed his traditional ties to the Goodman Theater in Chicago. The theater staged his adaptation of Chekhov's "The Cherry Orchard" in March. Mamet's latest plays, the one-act dramas "The Shawl" and "The Spanish Prisoner," began performances two days ago at the Goodman's New Theater Company—an offshoot devoted to new American plays—and a revival of "The Water Engine" is to begin Friday on the Goodman's main stage. It amounts to a Chicago Mamet festival. That is appropriate, for there is no better place to begin to talk about Mamet than Chicago. He grew up there, and references to the city pervade his plays. In the Goodman Theater and in its artistic director, Gregory Mosher—who has directed all but one of Mamet's 12 plays at the Goodman—Mamet has found a security few playwrights enjoy. Although Mamet now divides his time between a Chelsea town house and a Vermont farm, he still belongs to the lineage of Chicago writers. He echoes their direct style and their loathing of pretense. His street denizens recall Saul Bellow's Augie March and James T. Farrell's Studs Lonigan. Whenever Mamet eats at the Berghoff Restaurant, near the Goodman, he wonders if it was the restaurant that Hurstwood managed in Theodore Dreiser's "Sister Carrie."

Now he faces the different difficulty—in others' minds, if not his own—of following up on "Glengarry," his most accomplished and most rewarded work. "The Shawl" and "The Spanish Prisoner" are thematically similar to Mamet's earlier plays, but they represent a stylistic departure. They trade more on words than on action; they are cryptic and brooding; plays like "Glengarry" were volatile and literal. Mamet has kiddingly called "The Shawl" "my 'Twilight Zone' episode." The actor Mike Nussbaum said that he read "The Spanish Prisoner" and told Mamet he did not understand it. The playwright shrugged: "Yeah, my writing's been pretty weird lately." ■

FEBRUARY 6, 1983

BROADWAY VS. WEST END

Frank Rich

I don't know a single American who saw Michael Frayn's "Benefactors" in London, myself included, who imagined that the play would last a month in New York. Even those who liked "Benefactors" couldn't picture a large Broadway audience for a muted Chekhovian piece in which the metaphorical cherry orchard is a slum London neighborhood to be cleared for mass housing. The play was too parochially English—possibly "too intellectual" and, worse, "too brittle." Yet "Benefactors" has proved the most highly attended play of the Broadway season.

This surprise success is a sign that there may actually still be a hungry Broadway audience for serious theater, ready to support those productions courageous enough to provide it. The positive response to "Benefactors" may also say something about the often discussed differences between American and English acting. Unlike "The Real Thing"—which was restaged, redesigned and partly rewritten in its improved New York edition—"Benefactors" arrived on Broadway with no visible alterations. The set, the text and the staging (by Michael Blakemore) are as they were in London's West End. But "Benefactors" seems less muted, intellectual, brittle on Broadway—less English, if national stereotypes are to be believed.

Lest anyone conclude that the American actor's supposed propensity for heart over mind serves all material, however, one need look only to "The Caretaker," where Chicago's Steppenwolf troupe has injected so much sentimentality that Harold Pinter's jagged, ash-colored comedy disintegrates almost as soon as it begins. The same phenomenon was visible in the misbegotten film version of David Hare's "Plenty," in which Meryl Streep, by pumping up the weepy neuroticism of the heroine, softened an alienated, antagonizing representative of England's postwar decline into a sensitive, depoliticized martyr—an incongruous Sylvia Plath of Suez.

The English, meanwhile, have their own cultural blind spots to bear. These people just don't quite understand musicals. The only excitingly staged English musical I've ever seen—"Evita"—was directed by an American, Harold Prince. The imaginative spectacle of "Cats," which sometimes seemed inanimate in London, benefited enormously from the injection of American performing expertise in New York. When the English try to perform Broadway material—well, forget it. The unintentional comic highpoint of the season may have occurred in the London revue, "Jerome Kern Goes to Hollywood," where "Ol' Man River" was delivered as if it had been written for Mayfair swells rather than a black Southern laborer.

MARCH 29, 1987

THE EMPIRE STRIKES BACK

Frank Rich

A New York theatergoer stricken by an inferiority complex in London could perennially take solace in the one American beachhead along the West End—the musical. For all its classical glories, London has long been dependent on New York for that levitating synthesis of song, dance, drama and performance that is Broadway's one undisputed contribution to world theater.

Now, however, the world seems to be turning upside down. New York has not produced a single hit musical of its own this season, and no further American musicals are even contemplated for production by summer. The trans-Atlantic jet stream of talent has dramatically reversed direction. Instead of creating musicals that might be exported to the West End, Broadway is frantically mounting duplicates of London hits—some of which star dancing or singing English actors, such as Robert Lindsay and Colm Wilkinson, of the highest caliber. "Les Miserables," an English adaptation of a French spectacle, and "Me and My Girl," a retooled revival of a 1937 London favorite previously unknown to New York, are among the season's most popular productions with both the critics and the public.

According to the trade paper Variety, one of every three Broadway ticket-buyers in mid-March was attending one of those two shows or two other London musical imports, Andrew Lloyd Webber's "Cats" and "Starlight Express." Of 22 attractions on Broadway, these four musicals were the only productions not reduced to dumping unsold tickets at the half-price booth.

The Broadway scene, however depleted, still boasts many active composers—Stephen Sondheim, Cy Coleman, Jerry Herman, Charles Strouse, John Kander and Marvin Hamlisch, among others—while the London roster ends with only a couple of fairly obscure names following that of the ubiquitous Mr. Lloyd Webber. Successful as Mr. Lloyd Webber is, his work can't yet be compared seriously with Broadway's best of any period. He's primarily a canny, melodic pastiche artist, and his music has declined sharply since he lost the lyrics of his original collaborator Tim Rice (who parted ways after "Evita") and T. S. Eliot (the unwitting lyricist of "Cats").

Along with Mr. Lloyd Webber's ability to connect with mass taste, the other key to the English musical's new success is its shift in emphasis in musical staging. Unable to compete with Broadway's high-powered choreography, the English musical had to turn elsewhere for kinetic energy. The option chosen was spectacle: If the performers can't dance, why not let the scenery do so instead?

There are 14 musicals running in London right now: half are British, half are American. Given America's postwar domination of the form, this parity is remarkable. Of the seven American musicals, three are small-scale Off Broadway imports while the other four (including "42nd Street" and "Cabaret") contain no music written later than 1966. Broadway's current dearth of native hits is directly reflected in the West End product. ■

APRIL 19, 1987

'LES MISERABLES': The Distinctive and Stirring Version Is Still Victor Hugo's

John Gross

"Les Miserables" on Broadway in New York City.

There were people who told me "Les Miserables" was going to be wonderful and people who told me it was going to be terrible. The truth—or my reactions, at least—turned out to lie somewhere in the middle. If the lyrics were often little more than doggerel, and if the score often seemed the musical equivalent of doggerel, there were compensations in Colm Wilkinson's rightly acclaimed Jean Valjean, in a few of the supporting performances, in the scenery and lighting, and, every now and then, in a genuinely striking dramatic effect. But none of it added up to Victor Hugo.

How could it have done? The novel is vast and sprawling and dense with detail; any dramatization, however skillful, is bound to sacrifice an enormous amount, and there are important episodes—the Waterloo chapters in particular, which the musical understandably skips—that it is very hard to imagine being successfully transferred to the stage.

It would be asking too much for any dramatization to match either the prodigious flow of comment that Hugo keeps up or his range of historical reference. What might reasonably be hoped for, on the other hand, is a counterpart to the poetic force of his narrative. This certainly won't

(cont'd. next page)

(continued from previous page)
seem an impossibility to anyone who has seen the 1935 movie version with Fredric March and Charles Laughton.

The most obvious resource that a musical version has for rivaling the impact of the original ought to be music. Unfortunately the Royal Shakespeare adaptation lets us down; and though a few strong images linger on (the stage barricades are all that barricades should be, the scene in the sewers is surprisingly effective), the production as a whole seems to me to convey little of the novel's power.

For in spite of everything that has been said about Hugo's sense of history, "Les Miserables"—the novel—is as much an immense psychodrama as a historical epic, one in which Hugo acts out his private feelings and frustrations. And some of the deepest of those feelings, as a number of commentators have pointed out, express themselves as a form of incest, in Valjean's more-than-fatherly love for Cosette and (until his change of heart) in his hatred of Marius. None of which is very apparent in the musical. ■

MARCH 21, 1988

'M. Butterfly,' a Story of a Strange Love, Conflict and Betrayal

Frank Rich

It didn't require genius for David Henry Hwang to see that there were the makings of a compelling play in the 1986 newspaper story that prompted him to write "M. Butterfly." Here was the incredible true-life tale of a career French foreign service officer brought to ruin—conviction for espionage—by a bizarre 20-year affair with a Beijing Opera diva. Not only had the French diplomat failed to recognize that his lover was a spy; he'd also failed to figure out that "she" was a he in drag. "It was dark, and she was very modest," says Gallimard (John Lithgow), Mr. Hwang's fictionalized protagonist, by half-joking way of explanation. When we meet him in the prison cell where he reviews his life, Gallimard has become, according to own understatement, "the patron saint of the socially inept."

But if this story is a corker, what is it about, exactly? That's where Mr. Hwang's imagination, one of the most striking to emerge in the American theater in this decade, comes in, and his answer has nothing to do with journalism. This playwright, the author of "The Dance and the Railroad" and "Family Devotions," does not tease us with obvious questions such as is she or isn't she?, or does he know or doesn't he? Mr. Hwang isn't overly concerned with how the opera singer, named Song Liling (B. D. Wong), pulled his hocus-pocus in the boudoir, and he refuses to explain away Gallimard by making him a closeted, self-denying homosexual. An inversion of Puccini's "Madama Butterfly," "M. Butterfly" is also the inverse of most American plays. Instead of reducing the world to an easily digested cluster of sexual or familial relationships, Mr. Hwang cracks open a liaison to reveal a sweeping, universal meditation on two of the most heated conflicts—men versus women, East versus West—of this or any other time. ■

Larry Kramer posing in front of a bookshelf in his home.

OCTOBER 9, 1988

Larry Kramer's Update on the War at Home

Stephen Holden

"I don't consider myself a playwright or a novelist but a writer who tries to find the best form to get the message out," declared Larry Kramer, who brought the boiling-hot politics of the AIDS crisis to the theatrical mainstream with his 1985 play "The Normal Heart." "I write out of anger, and of course for anyone who's gay now there's a lot to be angry about."

His newest play, "Just Say No," now in previews and opening next Sunday at the WPA Theater, is billed as a farce. But beneath the brittle, pun-filled dialogue his rage against people in high places still simmers.

Since 1981, even before AIDS had a name, Mr. Kramer has been sounding the alarm about a disease that had begun taking the lives of his friends. His cries escalated to an accusatory howl in his drama, "The Normal Heart." First produced at the Public Theater, the drama accused government and the media of recalcitrance in dealing with an epidemic that Mr. Kramer still believes could have been contained had the warnings been sounded earlier. Initially viewed by many, including some in the gay community, as a hysterical prophet of doom, Mr. Kramer is now widely respected as a prescient artist/activist whose rhetoric may have been inflammatory but whose grim message was tragically accurate.

Sitting in the living room of his cluttered Manhattan apartment, the trim, bearded 53-year-old author was surrounded by books that he characterized as "research" for his new play. Among the volumes stacked on sofas were "Reagan's America" by Garry Wills, "Dark Victory: Ronald Reagan, MCA and the Mob" by Dan E. Moldea, Laurence Leamer's "Make Believe, The Story of Nancy and Ronald Reagan" and "Vicki," Joyce Milton and Ann L. Bardach's biography of Vicki Morgan, the murdered mistress of the late Alfred Bloomingdale.

Troupe members from the Steppenwolf Theatre Company performing "The Grapes of Wrath" in 1988.

" 'Just Say No' is about sexual hypocrisy and how the people who make the rules that all of us, be we gay or straight but particularly be we gay, have to live by and how they don't live by those rules themselves," Mr. Kramer said. "The play is another way of fighting back against a world that I think has intentionally let people—first gay people and now people who are unfortunate enough to be drug-addicted—die."

Mr. Kramer has tentative plans to take a sabbatical from New York to write a novel about the AIDS epidemic.

"It will have a cast of thousands," he said, "and I'm not just talking about people who have died in the gay community but every incompetent, second-rate person who has helped perpetuate this disaster, from the President on down." ■

OCTOBER 23, 1988

Steppenwolf Plays Together, Stays Together

Benedict Nightingale

CHICAGO—It's the sort of story that, written by any of a score of modern dramatists, would end ironically. Those glittering-prizes would turn out to be gilded lead. Conspicuous success would actually be moral defeat.

After all, consider the facts. A group of idealistic young people, most of them just graduated from a not-hugely-distinguished college, form a theater company called Steppenwolf, start performing plays in the basement of a Catholic school in a Chicago suburb. They flourish and they grow. They transfer productions to New York and win a Tony award for regional excellence. Individuals within the troupe are lured west to Tinseltown and east to Glitterville. One becomes an international star, and others begin to get comparably famous. What hope is there that the company will hold together? More specifically, what future for Steppenwolf?

Part of the answer is "The Grapes of Wrath," which is currently to be found, not in a New York theater or on a Hollywood film set, but in a smallish playhouse a few yards from one of North Chicago's more desolate ghettos. The production is Steppenwolf's largest, most ambitious project to date, and one of its most rapturously reviewed. A company member, Frank Galati, adapted the play from the Steinbeck novel and directed it. Seven of the company's members are in the cast, including three who have been with Steppenwolf from the start. Gary Sinise, one of Steppenwolf's founders, has returned from directing the movie "Miles From Home" to play the gritty young hero, Tom Joad. It doesn't sound altogether like a troupe in disarray.

So far, so good, but the company numbers 21 these days, which means that most of its members are not in "Grapes." Indeed, fully half of them are no longer permanently residents in Chicago. Where's John

(cont'd. next page)

(continued from previous page)

Malkovich, star of "The Killing Fields" and of much else? Where are Joan Allen and Laurie Metcalf and John Mahoney? Where are the others?

The fact is that 18 of the 21 company members acted or directed for Steppenwolf in Chicago last season, among them Ms. Allen and Mr. Malkovich, the two leading performers in the New York production of Lanford Wilson's "Burn This." Ms. Metcalf was on its stage, too, in a production of John Olive's "Killers" that did not move to New York.

Even skeptical observers would have to admit that the company has held together when others would have fallen apart. Steppenwolf is, its members will tell you, a "family," in some cases literally so. Mr. Sinise, for example, is married to Moira Harris, another original member of the company. Rondi Reed, an actress and director, is the wife of Stephen Eich, Steppenwolf's managing director. ■

JANUARY 8, 1989

ON BROADWAY, SPECTACLES RAISE THE STAKES

Mervyn Rothstein

"The Phantom of the Opera," Andrew Lloyd Webber's $8 million megamusical, has been a consistent sellout since its opening last January, taking in more than $28 million at the box office. But it is not expected to reimburse its investors fully until the end of April—more than 15 months into its run.

"Starlight Express," another Lloyd Webber megamusical, has still not recouped its investment (of more than $8 million) 22 months after its March 1987 opening, even though it has taken in more than $42 million at the box office.

Andrew Lloyd Webber (right) with actress/wife Sarah Brightman and actor Michael Crawford, during rehearsal for Webber musical "The Phantom of the Opera."

The era of the multimillion-dollar megamusical is changing the way Broadway musicals are produced, and creating potential problems for their future, producers and theater owners say. The high costs of opening a musical—and equally important, of keeping it, and its special effects and elaborate sets, running—mean that investors very often have to wait an increasingly long time to get their money back and to realize a reasonable profit.

"When 'My Fair Lady' opened more than 30 years ago, it recouped its investment in 25 weeks," said Rocco Landesman, the head of Jujamcyn Theaters. "That doesn't happen now."

John Breglio, a theater lawyer involved in many Broadway shows, said the problems of the musical theater begin with the skyrocketing costs of the musicals. "What's happened," he said, "is that production costs, which we all assumed just a few years ago for a major musical hovered around $5 million, have often swelled and surged to $7 million or $8 million."

"Inflation plays a part," Mr. Breglio said. "But there is also the public's demand and expectations of what a musical is. It started with 'Cats'—the British influence, the megamusical—and continued with 'Starlight,' and 'Phantom,' and perhaps 'Les Miserables.' The public is demanding so much more in terms of production value, and giving them that kind of spectacle has added a whole new level of costs.

"You never had this before," he added. "Up until the last several years, the expectation in the musical theater was 'music, book, lyrics.' Now it's 'music, book, lyrics, spectacle.'"

Mr. Landesman said that "a big factor in all this is the addiction of Broadway theater owners to spectacle."

"The Broadway theatergoer has also become addicted to getting his $50 worth," he said—$50 is the current top ticket price for most musicals. "The Broadway musical is increasingly becoming a special event, and if you want to go to a Broadway musical once or twice a year you want to see your $50 on stage in a palpable way." ■

JANUARY 4, 1980

THE POP LIFE 'London Calling' helps the Clash live up to billing

John Rockwell

The Clash perform on stage at Hammersmith Palais on June 16, 1980, in London.

Although it's only been available as an import for a couple of weeks and won't be released domestically for a couple of weeks more, the Clash's "London Calling" still counts symbolically as the first important rock album of the 1980's. This is a two-disk ser that justifies its length, and the first Clash album that fully explains the acclaim that the band's admirers have been heaping upon it all along.

That praise has indeed been extreme; for many serious rock critics the Clash is the best rock band in the world. To this listener, the Clash's first album (its second album released in this country, oddly enough) was muddily produced but full of fine, fervent songs. But the band's live performances seemed more hectically energetic than effective; if you weren't swept along by the energy they could sound emptily raucous. The second album (the first released here) was slicker in production but less interesting as music. And so it stood, until "London Calling."

This is an album that captures all the Clash's primal energy, combines it with a brilliant production job by Guy Stevens and reveals depths of invention and creativity barely suggested by the band's previous work.

The songs are full of ingenious touches, as are the arrangements with their pervasive brass parts. Yet the directness and passion of the band are never subverted.

As with all the Clash's music, the themes are political, either directly or indirectly. They're direct in songs that call the audience specifically to battle; more often they're more implicit, as with descriptions of London life that make one realize all that's gone wrong with the English ideals of fairness and opportunity. What one doesn't have here are the themes that normally make for success in the United States—sex and love. But the music is so superior, capturing all the diversity of present-day London underclass life, and the Clash—with material like this to perform—can be such a passionately convincing performing band that it will be very surprising if Epic Records can't sell them to a mass American audience. "London Calling" may just be that increasingly rare phenomenom, an album prized for its seriousness even as it reaches out to the millions. ■

music

APRIL 13, 1980

The Future Is Digital

Allan Korinn

An early model of CD player.

On a spring day, a group of audio experts and record producers gathered in a suite at New York's Plaza Hotel and waited for what promised to be a glimpse of the future. Their hosts were representatives of N.V. Philips, the large Dutch electronics firm that had developed the cassette tape format. The Philips creation about to be unveiled was a new kind of audio component

(cont'd. next page)

(*continued from previous page*)
designed to render all conventional LP-disks obsolete by the early 1990's.

Encased in a sleek, brushed-chrome box about the size and shape of a portable cassette deck, the Philips miracle machine plays a four-and-one-half inch vinyl disk that is as different from today's LP as the LP is from Thomas Edison's first wax cylinder. Called Compact Discs (CD for short) and expected to enter the market by 1983, they play an hour per side and are virtually indestructible. You can drop them, step on them, but when you slip them into the CD player, they will still sound good as new. They will sound better, in fact, than the most meticulously cared-for-LP.

As for music reproduction, the CD boasts a dynamic range far greater than is possible on an LP. Treble instruments sound brighter, and basses more full-bodied. Stereo separation is better, too.

All one has to do is buy a new player, which will probably be priced at about $500, and replace what may be an extensive, expensive, record library. ■

MAY 2, 1980

THE POP LIFE: The Pretenders

John Rockwell

The Pretenders, who will make their New York Debut tomorrow night at the Palladium, on 14th Street, near Third Avenue, have aroused a considerable amount of interest for a new rock band. There would seem to be two basic reasons for that, apart from rock's constant need to renew itself with trendy novelties.

First, there is still a disturbing gulf between the rock intelligentsia's favorites and the commercial mainstream in the United States. Acts like Blondie, Talking Heads, Elvis Costello and the Clash have begun to close that gulf, by winning radio air play and sales. But there is still plenty of room for new bands that combine the hip and the marketable. With the success of their single "Brass in Pocket," and the warm audience response and reviews they've been winning around the country, the Pretenders seem to have got the knack, too, so to speak.

Second, there is the figure of Chrissie Hynde, whose band this is; in other words, she founded it, writes its songs, is the lead singer and plays guitar. On this tour she has been winning reviews that suggest that she is this year's rock female archetype. Rock critics keep searching for ever-stronger female rock performers; the days of vulnerable suffering as something to be exploited are fading.

Miss Hynde, who is 28 years old, comes from Akron, Ohio. She left for London in early 1973, after three years at Kent State University, and has been based in London ever since. She lived happily through the height of the punk scene in 1977–78, but only formed the Pretenders a year and a half ago. The band is what she calls a "bright, accessible pop sound," especially in its singles. ■

Chrissie Hynde on stage during a Pretenders concert.

MAY 22, 1981

With Pride And Music, Jamaicans Bury Bob Marley

Jo Thomas

KINGSTON, Jamaica, May 21—It is not that he changed the landscape—the ghetto where he grew up is still scarred by violence—but he turned the despised dialect of that place into songs that transformed the way people saw themselves. For this, Jamaicans by the thousands came out today to bid farewell to Bob Marley, the king of reggae.

Mr. Marley died of cancer at the age of 36 at Cedars of Lebanon Hospital in Miami on May 11. He was on his way home to Jamaica to receive one of his nation's highest awards, the Order of Merit.

Instead, he was brought home to Kingston for a state funeral in a gold coffin draped in the bright colors of both Jamaica and Ethiopia, to be honored with speeches and hymns and the sounds of drums and bells, guitars and saxophones. Six thousand people, many dressed in white, jammed into the National Arena for today's services, which were conducted by Abunda Yesehaq, Archbishop of the Ethiopian Orthodox Church in the Western Hemisphere.

The services were broadcast to hundreds of others who waited outside. "I feel moaning till I can't stand it no more," said Billy Boyle, 20 years old. "I know him from down in the ghetto. He know his destiny. He live his destiny. He showed black people truth and light."

Mr. Marley was a member of the Rastafarians, a Jamaican cult that believes that blacks are descended from the tribes of Israel and are destined some day to return to Africa. He wore his long hair in the locks favored by the Rastafarians and believed in nature, simplicity, peace and marijuana.

"As an orator, he wasn't much," conceded Faith Webley, one of the thousands who went to the arena to pay him homage. "But his music said it all."

His songs spoke of poverty, justice, oppression, and cried out for dignity and hope. There was something in his songs, his fans said, that could make each listener feel worthwhile and unique.

"We were living the situation he was talking about," said Petronila Mutenda, 25, a student from Zimbabwe, where Mr. Marley was so admired he was invited by the newly elected Patriotic Front Government to perform at the independence celebrations in 1980. "He was not against whites, but he wanted the other race to realize they are human beings and mustn't feel inferior."

"There is no other person take his place," said Devon Douglas, a salesman at Mighty Cloud Records, which manages to blast the music of reggae over the din of traffic of the Halfway Tree crossroads. "I don't know for coming time—but not for now." ■

APRIL 7, 1982

THE POP LIFE: Joan Jett and The Go-Go's

Stephen Holden

Joan Jett

Pop history was made recently when the Go-Go's "Beauty and the Beat" became the first No. 1 album ever by a band of women who write their own songs and play their own instruments. Founded in Los Angeles four years ago by the lead vocalist Belinda Carlisle and the rhythm guitarist Jane Wiedlin, the quintet recorded their debut album last spring, and it took more than six months to climb to No. 1, spurred by the success of the hit single "Our Lips Are Sealed." Now, with another single, "We Got the Beat," near the top, and album sales approaching two million, the Go-Go's are the hottest new act in rock-and-roll.

Another very hot new act, Joan Jett, is also a veteran of the underground rock scene in Los Angeles, having played guitar and sung with the Runaways, one of the first all-female hard-rock bands. Since the Runaways broke up Miss Jett has made two albums, the second of which, "I Love Rock 'n Roll," has caught fire. Miss Jett's current band, the Blackhearts, consists of three men plus herself on guitar. Along with original songs, their material includes the Dave Clark Five hit, "Bits and Pieces," Tommy James's "Crimson and Clover" and the Christmas standard "Little Drummer Boy."

The success of the Go-Go's and Joan Jett signals not only a generational turnover in rock, but the strengthening of women's role in rock. Olivia Newton-John, Stevie Nicks, and the woman-led sextet Quarterflash, from Portland, Ore., also have albums high on the charts.

Both the Go-Go's and Joan Jett make simple, aggressive rock-and-roll that doesn't go out of its way to imitate the macho

(cont'd. next page)

(continued from previous page)

posturing of most male hard-rock acts. But in no way could their music be described as passive. Both offer a striking contrast to Linda Ronstadt and Joni Mitchell, the most popular Los Angeles-based female rock singers of the 1970's. Though Miss Ronstadt eventually adopted a tougher stance with her wave album "Mad Love," her most characteristic performances were sad-hearted romantic ballads arranged and produced with a high-tech polish. Joni Mitchell's songs obsessively explored the conflicts between career and love, sexual freedom and monogamy with a brooding down-hearted intensity.

The Go-Go's songs, written mostly by Jane Wiedlin with the lead guitarist Charlotte Caffey, have a buoyant thread of humor, and the coy, kittenish quality of the group vocals suggests a parody of traditional feline wiles rather than the real thing. The humor is underscored by album art that pictures the group in cold-cream masks and bubble baths. The song in their album that most perfectly captures the Go-Go mixture of rock-and-roll enthusiasm and hip irony is a blithe, double-edged song about Los Angeles called "This Town." "This town is our town/ It is so glamorous/ Bet you'd live here if you could and be one of us," goes the chorus.

Joan Jett's brand of rock is heavier than the Go-Go's. But in its calculated simplicity, it too owes much to late 60's bubble-gum music. And indeed, Miss Jett's producers, Kenny Laguna and Ritchie Cordell, helped write and produce hits for the Ohio Express, 1910 Fruit Gum Company, and Tommy James. Miss Jett has a tough, deep voice, devoid of blues and soul inflections, that takes on a husky edge when she sings out. But she doesn't push that edge to its breaking point the way Janis Joplin and her imitators have done. Instead of swaggering and strutting, Miss Jett projects a tough, unblinking directness that's altogether devoid of affectation and sentimentality.

The title song and No. 1 hit from her second album, "I Love Rock 'n Roll" suggests a new sexual equation in 80's rock. The singer picks up a 17-year-old boy after seeing him play her favorite song on the juke box. The connection is direct and simple with no fantasizing and game-playing. Romance is nice, but nothing to die over.

Is the vogue for hip bubble-gum rock by women a long lasting trend? Or will it go the way of "power pop" after the success of the Knack prompted the record industry to invest millions in a trend that didn't pan out? One clue lies in the fact that neither the Go-Go's nor Joan Jett were heavily promoted by their record companies until after both had achieved some grass-roots acceptance. The Joan Jett album, in fact, was rejected by 23 record companies until Boardwalk picked it up. The Knack, on the other hand, started out as a highpowered record-company hype.

FEBRUARY 13, 1983

FREE JAZZ COMES UNDER FIRE

Robert Palmer

Jazz entered its free-form phase at the beginning of the 1960's, and Charles Mingus, Ornette Coleman and Lennie Tristano were experimenting with free-form improvising as early as 1949–50. But in much jazz literature, free-form jazz is still called "new jazz" or "new music."

Until recently, resistance to free jazz within the jazz community came mostly from the be-bop players, jazz's first-generation modernists, and from more traditionally-minded musicians and critics. But during the past several years, a new traditionalism has been sweeping through the jazz ranks. Like the "moldy fig" traditional jazz fans of the 1940's, today's traditionalists dismiss as pretentious junk any modern jazz in which they fail to discern the cry of the blues and the rhythmic momentum called "swing."

The innovations of young jazz musicians have often met with resistance. But whenever a revolutionary movement within the music attracted enough talented young players and proved itself by enduring for a decade or so, it gained acceptance, eventually becoming the music's dominant orthodoxy. By the late 1950's, this had happened to be-bop or modern jazz, still the most musically demanding of all jazz styles because of the harmonic sophistication and technical expertise it requires. For the next two decades or so, bright young musicians who were unwilling or unable to master be-bop's intricacies simply convinced themselves that it was out of date. But most of these musicians were equally put off by avant-garde jazz, which seemed to them to be chaotic or formless. So a distressingly large number of talented young players avoided both be-bop and free jazz and went into more commercial areas such as jazz-rock.

Critics and fans who treasured the jazz tradition were delighted when the situation began to change, around the end of the 1970's. A new generation of young jazzmen, some of them the sons of be-bop modernists, began making vital new music that had plenty of good old-fashioned swing. This was indeed a welcome development. But soon, the neo-traditionalist critics and fans began dividing the younger musicians into two camps, those who were playing "real" jazz and could be considered "in the tradition" and those who were more heavily influenced by avant-garde classical music from the European tradition and were therefore decadent or inauthentic. This new traditionalism has gained wide currency, and the unfortunate result is that the jazz avant-garde now seems more isolated from the mainstream than ever, despite 20 years of solid artistic achievement.

Musical movements and styles sometimes lose their direction and punch when confronted with this kind of resistance, but sometimes the pressure helps weed out the poseurs and the lazy thinkers from the dedicated players with something important to say. And the best of the more recent recordings from the jazz avant-garde suggest that a little isolation may actually benefit the music in the long run—if the best avant-garde players don't starve first. ■

JUNE 19, 1983

A TRUMPETER AT HOME WITH JAZZ AND THE CLASSICS

Jon Pareles

The 21-year-old trumpeter Wynton Marsalis is running out of worlds to conquer. While still in his teens, he came to national attention playing with Art Blakey and the Jazz Messengers. He soon became one of a handful of mainstream jazz musicians with a major-label (CBS) recording contract, and last year his debut LP as a leader sold 100,000 copies, an extraordinary figure for an album that used no electric instruments. He also won the annual Down Beat jazz poll as Artist of the Year.

Meanwhile, Mr. Marsalis has performed—and held his own—with jazz figures twice his age, including the saxophonist Sonny Rollins and three veterans of the forward-looking Miles Davis group of the 1960's—the pianist Herbie Hancock, the bassist Ron Carter and the drummer Tony Williams. He has toured and recorded with the group, which now calls itself V.S.O.P. or the Herbie Hancock Quartet, and is scheduled to appear with them next Sunday on a Kool Jazz Festival double bill with Mr. Davis's latest band.

Mr. Marsalis's latest coup is the simultaneous release this week of two very different albums. "Think of One" is his second album leading a jazz quintet and marks the recorded debut of his working band. Meanwhile, Mr. Marsalis has made an album of classical trumpet concertos—by Haydn, Hummel and Leopold Mozart, as standard as standard repertory gets—with Raymond Leppard briskly conducting the National Philharmonic Orchestra. Can one musician really handle two such dissimilar traditions? In Mr. Marsalis's case, the answer is yes. He has proven his jazz credentials in clubs and concerts all over the world; he has also studied classical trumpet and played with the New Orleans Philharmonic. Mr. Marsalis is no dilettante; he plays the Haydn and Hummel concertos every bit as precisely—and distinctively—as he plays his own compositions.

Mr. Marsalis's efforts as a bandleader and composer hark back to the music his

Wynton Marsalis playing with Dizzie Gillepse in the background.

current V.S.O.P. cohorts and their contemporaries were making in the 1960's. It wasn't free jazz, but jazz with a dizzying panoply of rules and improvisational possibilities. At its core were some of the most harmonically complex tunes in jazz, drawing not only on the traditions of Duke Ellington and Thelonious Monk but on Eastern modal scales and the whole-tone harmonies of Debussy and Ravel; as one kind of harmony melted into another, the tunes seemed to turn themselves inside out. With Mr. Davis, and on innumerable Blue Note Records sessions in the 1960's, musicians made these labyrinthine tunes swing—and swing hard—even when they were played at whirlwind tempos. ■

JUNE 26, 1983

THE POLICE FUSE AVANT-GARDE AND THE COMMERCIAL

Robert Palmer

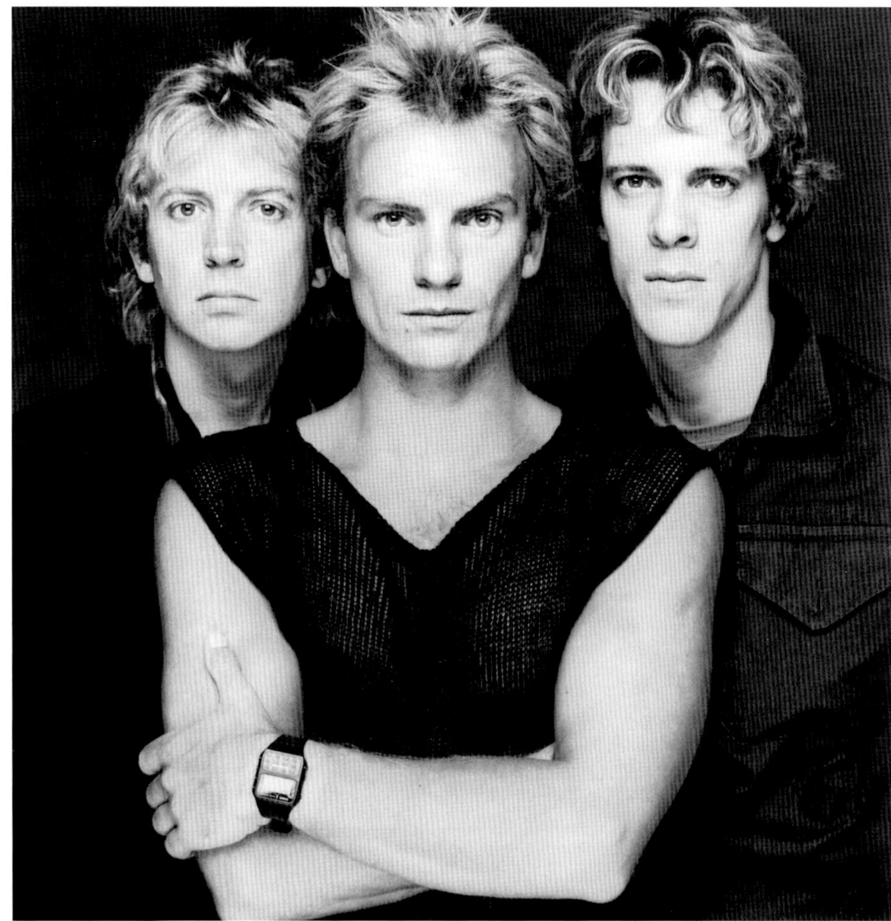

The Police, from left to right, Andy Summers, Sting and Stewart Copeland.

The Police, who gave their first New York performance at CBGB on the Bowery in the late 1970's and last performed here a year ago as headliners at Madison Square Garden, will be back again on Aug. 18—at Shea Stadium. This British trio has been nothing if not upwardly mobile, and its rise to the top has been rapid, especially for a time when rock economics have been closer to bust than to boom.

The Police have worked hard for their success, but their career strategy has been utterly unconventional. Their music, once a distinctive but constricting blend of reggae rhythms, jazzy harmonies, and exceptional pop songwriting facility, has broadened and deepened. And on their exceptional new album, "Synchronicity" (A&M), they have brought all the aspects of their singular pop art into focus. This is an innovative album, even if one compares it to the work of rock's much more self-consciously arty experimental fringe. And it is already one of the year's biggest popular successes, having spawned a hit single ("Every Breath You Take") and begun zipping up the album charts upon its release.

It's an easy album to listen to, for on even a superficial level its arching melodies and unprecedented rhythmic variety are exhilarating. But it can't really be understood unless one understands a bit about the Police—who they are, where they came from, how they arrived at this fortuitous juncture of art and commerce.

To begin with, the Police—the bassist, singer and chief songwriter Sting, the guitarist Andy Summers, and the drummer Stewart Copeland—had confidence, and they had an astute manager, Ian Copeland, who wasn't afraid to gamble. The Police and Ian Copeland built a word-of-mouth reputation on the volatile English punk-rock scene of the mid-1970's and then signed with A&M records for virtually no cash advance against future royalties, thus breaking the first rule of rock-and-roll career-building—take the money and run. When their first single, "Roxanne," and their first album, "Regatta De Blanc," became hits, they began making money right away, for not only had they managed not to borrow against their future earnings, they had talked the record company into giving them an unusually high royalty rate for an unknown group.

On "Synchronicity," the Police have expanded their style in a multitude of directions, using as much of what they have learned as can sensibly be fitted on one record. And what comes out isn't a mishmash of borrowed ethnic rhythms and melodies, it's an organic, original sound.

Some critics have suspected the Police of being a 1960's progressive band—or, less charitably, a hippie band—in new wave clothing. But the Police have always insisted that the idea of a "new wave" in rock actually meant something. It meant refusing to spend more than you make, starting small and getting big gradually, avoiding the pitfalls of sudden success and artistic license that led to so many tragic early deaths and botched careers in the "oldwave" 1960's.

Sting, who wrote all but two of the songs on "Synchronicity," has a gift for turning melodic phrases that recalls Paul McCartney, but the intensity and acerbity of his latest songs is more reminiscent of John Lennon. "Synchronicity" is especially welcome because it has more bite, more juice, than any previous Police LP. Transformations of this sort may never be adequately explained, but both Sting and Andy Summers endured painful and drawn-out divorces during the months when "Synchronicity" was being written and recorded, and one way of looking at the album is as an exploration of the lacerated self-awareness a wrenching emotional experience that a protracted divorce can bring. But however one choses to explain it, this is one pop album nobody should miss. ■

NOVEMBER 20, 1983

POP MUSIC SURGES ALONG NEW AND UNEXPECTED PATHS

Stephen Holden

As the rock generation approaches middle age, it has become the pop cultural establishment. The old intergenerational battles that pitted rock hipness against pop squareness—the Beatles and the Rolling Stones against Frank Sinatra—have receded into the past.

After a long period in which pop was so rigidly formatted on the radio that one had to switch stations in order to hear different musical styles, the barriers separating sounds have begun to crumble. More important, the artists themselves have begun to push across the lines dividing records from other popular art forms.

Along with records, the pop marketplace has begun to be flooded with video music software, much of it rock concert footage. The best-selling full-length musical video program to date has been "The Compleat Beatles," with sales of over 65,000 video cassettes and video disks. But the music industry will be closely watching the sales performance of Michael Jackson's hour-long video program, "The Making of the Thriller Video," which hits the marketplace Dec. 14.

The program, which cost more than a million dollars to produce, and features a 14-minute version of the title song from his "Thriller" album, will retail for $29.95. The centerpiece was directed by John Landis, one of the first big-name movie directors to enter the music video field.

But even more heartening than the fact that pop music has entered a growth cycle is the fact that many of the rock generation's old guard—musicians who achieved prominence between 1965 and 1975—are reaching outside the world of pop records into video, theater, film, performance art and concert music.

At 37, Linda Ronstadt is one of the most audacious pop stars to pursue non mainstream projects. Three weeks ago, Elektra-Asylum Records shipped its millionth copy of "What's New," an album of prerock standards sung by Miss Ronstadt with the Nelson Riddle Orchestra. The success of the album, which was released in early September, has taken the record industry by surprise.

Sales of Miss Ronstadt's albums had slipped from a peak of three million for "Simple Dreams," in 1977, to around 800,000 for her last rock record, "Get Closer."

Record industry executives agree that "What's New" benefited from a broadcasting climate that has been loosened up by the rapid ascendancy of music video. MTV, the 24-hour Warner Amex cable channel that now reaches more than 16 million homes, led the way. "In its importance, the rock video clip is comparable to the development of the 45 r.p.m. single," Bob Krasnow, the chairman of Elektra-Asylum Records, said. "Linda's HBO/Cinemax video program, which featured four songs from the album and an interview, was crucial in exposing the record."

Along with the impact of music video, the opening up of radio has had a dramatic effect on record sales. Michael Jackson's album "Thriller" has sold close to 10 million copies in the United States. That figure may be double what the record would have sold in the more racially segregated pop radio climate of two years ago. Other impressive sales performances this year include the Police's "Synchronicity" (four million), Def Leppard's "Pyromania" (five million), the "Flashdance" soundtrack (over four and a half million), and Men at Work's "Business as Usual" (over four and a half million). By comparison, last year's two best-selling pop albums—John Cougar's "American Fool" and "Asia"—each sold under three million. ■

JANUARY 14, 1984

MICHAEL JACKSON AT 25: A MUSICAL PHENOMENON

Jon Pareles

In the world of pop music, there is Michael Jackson and there is everybody else.

Earlier this week the singer-dancer-songwriter received 12 nominations for Grammy awards, the record industry's equivalents of Hollywood's Oscars. No one has ever received so many nominations, a reflection of the popularity of a performer who has stirred the kind of worldwide enthusiasm that recalls the Beatlemania of the 1960's.

Michael Jackson has been doing more than just selling records, however. While his latest album, "Thriller," was selling better than any long-playing record ever made by a single performer, he also was breaking through the racially segregated programming policies of many radio and television stations. And although he has been singing hits since the 1960's, when he was the child star of the Jackson Five, he has become a pioneering entertainer in the new technology of the music video cassette.

"Michael Jackson is mass culture, not pop culture—he appeals to everybody," said Charlie Kendall, program director of the New York rock radio station WNEW-FM. "No one can deny that he's got a tremendous voice and plenty of style, and that he can dance like a demon. He appeals to all ages and he appeals to every kind of pop listener. This kind of performer comes once in a generation."

Over the last year, Mr. Jackson's songs have defined dance music. The arrangements on the "Thriller" album mesh his piping voice with a muscular blend of real and electronic sounds, in rhythms that can't be categorized as rock or funk or disco.

"Thriller" is now played on rock radio stations that cater largely to young white listeners as well as on urban dance-music stations that appeal largely to blacks. Before "Thriller," few entertainers were able to cross that subtle color line. A similar crossover has taken place

(cont'd. next page)

(continued from previous page)
on cable television, where Mr. Jackson's video clips are shown on programs that rarely offer black performers.

Since its release just over a year ago, the "Thriller" album has sold 20 million copies worldwide; it is now in its 25th week as No. 1 on Billboard's chart of best-selling LP's. Meanwhile, Mr. Jackson's singles have been in the top 10 since November 1982, when "The Girl Is Mine," a duet with the former Beatle Paul McCartney, was released in advance of the "Thriller" album.

Five other singles from "Thriller" have also reached the top 10—an unparalleled number for anything other than a greatest-hits album. (America's current No. 1 single, in fact, is "Say Say Say," a duet by Mr. Jackson and Mr. McCartney that appears on Mr. McCartney's album "Pipes of Peace.")

A major factor in these record sales is Mr. Jackson's command of video. He is one of the few musicians at ease in rock video clips, song-length films that simultaneously promote and reshape a hit single and that have had a profound effect on mass entertainment.

Mr. Jackson also is one of the few pop performers who finances and owns his promotional video clips. These clips have not only been popular with television viewers, they have also become an industry in themselves.

"Making the Thriller Video," an hourlong documentary of Mr. Jackson rehearsing and acting in his "Thriller" short, was released as a home video cassette on Dec. 14 by Vestron Video, with a list price of $29.95. Its initial order—more than 100,000 copies—was the largest registered for a video cassette that had not been previously released as a movie.

One reason Mr. Jackson's videos are so popular is Mr. Jackson's tautly controlled dancing, which mixes moves from break-dancers and such entertainers as James Brown with earlier popular dance styles.

As a top song-and-dance man, Mr. Jackson draws large audiences to live concerts. A coming world tour by Mr. Jackson with the Jacksons (formerly the Jackson Five) is shaping up as one of the most profitable entertainment events in history. Pepsi-Cola will pay the Jacksons at least $5 million to become the sponsor of the tour, which will come to New York City in the summer.

Yet Mr. Jackson does not fit the rebellious image of the typical pop star. Indeed, he projects a personality of wide-eyed, vaguely androgynous innocence. He is a Jehovah's Witness who lives with his mother and who is close to his family; his group, the Jacksons, includes four brothers and is supervised by his father.

Michael Jackson, who has been in show business for 20 of his 25 years, never talks to the press unless he is in a carefully controlled public relations situation. The reclusive singer keeps such pets as a boa constrictor and a llama, and a recent visitor to the Jackson family's home in Encino, Calif., saw a working popcorn stand and hot-dog cart in the yard, where outdoor speakers played themes from Walt Disney movies.

"I think he's really Peter Pan," said Mr. Peters. "He is this constant dichotomy of man and child. He can run corporations and tell record companies what he wants, and then he can sit in a trailer and play Hearts for hours with a friend who is 12 years old. He loves fantasy, and when he writes about real life it's a role for him, a fantasy—he sees it from his bubble."

APRIL 2, 1984

MARVIN GAYE IS SHOT AND KILLED; POP SINGER'S FATHER FACES CHARGE

Alberta Gaye with family during the funeral service for Marvin Gaye in 1984.

LOS ANGELES, April 1—Marvin Gaye, who blended the soul music of the urban scene with the beat of the old- time gospel singer and became an influential force in pop music, was shot to death today.

The singer, who would have been 45 years old Monday, died of bullet wounds in his chest at 1:01 this afternoon at the California Hospital Medical Center. Police officials booked his father, the Rev. Marvin Gaye Sr., 70, an Apostolic minister, for investigation of murder. The elder Mr. Gaye was being held without bail.

Lieut. Bob Martin of the Los Angeles Police Department said the singer was in his father's home about 12:30 P.M. when the men "became involved in a verbal dispute that led to a physical altercation, pushing and shoving."

Subsequently, Lieutenant Martin asserted, the singer's father got a pistol that was in his home and fired several shots at his son.

Lieutenant Martin said he did not know why an argument might have occurred, but said there were indications that there had been "bad blood" between the father and son recently.

The singer, who was born in Washington on April 2, 1939, played the organ in church as a child. He later joined the generation of black performers including Diana Ross and Gladys Knight and the Pips who, in the 1960's and 1970's, skyrocketed to fame out of Detroit under the Motown label.

Mr. Gaye had increased the pace of his performing and recording in this country over the past year after spending an extended period of time in Europe. In 1981, CBS Records tracked him down in Europe and bought his Motown contract for a reported $2 million. While Mr. Gaye started recording in Belgium, legal advisers at home made arrangements to clear up his debts in the United States.

Mr. Gaye gained renewed fame for several sexually explicit hits, including "Let's Get It On," and "Sexual Healing," which won him two Grammy awards last year.

At his best, critics said, Mr. Gaye combined the soulful directness of gospel music, the sweetness of soft-soul and pop, and the vocal musicianship of a jazz singer. Among the singers who have said to have been influenced by Mr. Gaye was Michael Jackson.

Mr. Gaye said last year that he had always resented being categorized. He said that while the singers Ray Charles and James Brown had been early inspirations of his, he also enjoyed the work of Peggy Lee and Barbra Streisand.

"I don't feel I have to conform to any particular expectations," he said. "But I would like for my music to raise people's consciousness, rather than lower it, to give people hope."

Friends said Mr. Gaye had been working on a new album. ■

SEPTEMBER 11, 1984

THE JULIO IGLESIAS PHENOMENON AND POP'S FUTURE

Stephen Holden

The instant acceptance of the first English-language album by Julio Iglesias, the Spanish pop singer, is a positive sign of the continuing internationalization of American pop. Just five days after its release, the album, "1100 Bel Air Place," topped the million mark in sales. On Billboard's pop album chart, the record leaped to No. 8 in its third week, and five of the singer's earlier Spanish-language records have also entered Billboard's album chart. Mr. Iglesias's weeklong Radio City Music Hall engagement, which ends tomorrow, sold more than a million dollars worth of tickets in 15 hours.

Mr. Iglesias's American conquest is a combined triumph of talent, marketing and timing. The main barrier to his success in this country was language. The United States, while accepting the occasional foreign-language hit ("Volare," "Dominique," etc.), has traditionally demanded that its pop stars demonstrate a confident idiomatic command of English.

Rock has been more open to internationalization for some time, as witnessed by the music's embrace of Jamaican reggae and the popularity of such groups as the Police, who espouse a "One World" political and cultural philosophy.

Mr. Iglesias, the traditional Latin Lover incarnate, represents the conservative wing of this movement by bringing to American pop an Old World formality. Although he records successfully in several European languages, he still sings and speaks English with a strong Spanish accent.

Mr. Iglesias's wholesale acceptance by a mature, culturally conservative audience is proof that both our linguistic provincialism and our need to sound musically "American" are crumbling.

Singer Julio Iglesias performing.

(cont'd. next page)

(continued from previous page)

"1100 Bel Air Place" was originally conceived as a sharp break from that tradition. The American producer Richard Perry was brought in to make a Los Angeles pop-funk album, but he ended up playing a subsidiary role to Mr. Iglesias's longtime producer, Ramon Arcusa. The result is an album that sounds only slightly more contemporary than the many records the singer has recorded in Spanish. The singer doesn't "interpret" lyrics so much as sustain a mood of exalted passion in a voice deified in twinkling, echoey arrangements; Mr. Iglesias sounds as though he comes directly from heaven.

But there's a powerful macho component in this hearts-and-flowers world. Underneath his sweetness, Mr. Iglesias projects the coiled muscular control of a world-class athlete. He treats crooning as a competitive solo sport involving a precise balance between extremes of tension and courtly smoothness. In doing so, he has made the Latin lover a new symbol of manliness in an age of androgynous pop stars. ■

JANUARY 6, 1985

MADONNA'S SIREN SONG

Stephen Holden

No phenomenon illustrates more pointedly how pop music history seems to run in cycles than the overnight success of the 24-year-old pop siren known as Madonna. The month before Christmas, Madonna's second album, "Like a Virgin," sold more than two million copies. Teenagers were lining up in stores to purchase the album the way their parents had lined up to buy the Beatles records in the late 60's. And the title song, a mildly titillating dance-rock ditty about how true love can make a girl feel "shiny and new, like a virgin," is one of the fastest-selling singles in the history of Warner Bros. Records.

The singer, who was born Madonna Louise Ciccione in Bay City, Michigan, and who now lives in New York, has already become a symbol of the 50's-in-the-80's sensibility that is swamping contemporary pop culture. With a tough-cookie voice that's both coy and streetwise, Madonna's singing harks back to the rock-and-roll "girl-group" tradition that preceded the Beatles. But where girl groups, from the Shirelles to the Ronettes, worshipfully extolled their boyfriends' cars, haircuts and rebel poses, Madonna's point of view is decidedly more self-interested. In matters of love, she is a comparison shopper with a shrewd sense of her own market value.

The words "shiny and new" describe not only the way the love-smitten singer feels in the title song but the sound of the album, which was handsomely produced by Nile Rodgers, one of the masterminds of the late 70's disco group Chic. Mr. Rodgers has adapted some of the elements of Chic's sound—a scrubby guitar, glistening electric keyboards and light, strutting dance-pop rhythms—to enshrine Madonna's personality. Among other idioms, the songs gloss Philadelphia soul ("Love Don't Live Here Anymore"), orchestrated doowop ("Shoo-Bee-Doo"), frilly pop-soul ("Dress You Up," "Angel"), and pop-reggae ("Material Girl"). The dance-floor fantasy, "Pretender," is as elegant a piece of disco fluff as Chic at its airiest. The glittering unfussy arrangements are spun around Madonna's kewpie-doll voice like swirls of cotton candy with a skill that makes "Like a Virgin" this year's definitive model of danceable urban teen-pop.

Madonna at the 1984 MTV Awards

Madonna is the brassiest star to emerge so far among the new breed of singing starlets that have been spawned by music-video. Wrinkling her pretty doll face into a provocative pout and exposing her bare midriff, she sometimes suggests a contemporary equivalent of blonde bombshells like Marilyn Monroe, Mamie Van Doren and Jayne Mansfield. Born out of punk and disco

(cont'd. next page)

(continued from previous page)

in the late 70's, the anti-intellectual, artifice-flaunting female pop traditon that Madonna represents found its first heroine in the sullen punk-rocker Debbie Harry of Blondie. Since then, more and more post-new wave pop stars have followed Miss Harry's example and rejected artistic goals for deadpan ironic attitudinizing. The new generation of MTV-bred pop stars have happily traded in their complicated real selves to become preening music-video products with self-christened brand names like Billy Idol, Prince, Duran Duran, Wham and Madonna. They are real- life cartoon figures who, instead of dealing in musical literature, find it easier to traffic in video iconography. Madonna, who has rarely performed in concert, is the best evidence yet that a strong live act is no longer a prequisite to pop stardom. A telegenic image is far more important.

Eventually, of course, the cycle will swing back. A younger generation will reject the selfishness and superficiality of the "Material Girl," with her mirror, her schemes and her money, and demand something more substantial. But the pendulum can't be forced into reverse. Until it swings of its own accord, Madonna, the hottest female star in pop, will stand as a very revealing sign of the times.

JULY 22, 1984

PRINCE CREATES A WINNER WITH 'PURPLE RAIN'

Robert Palmer

Prince performing in 1985.

While the Jacksons and Bruce Springsteen were busy last spring, putting finishing touches on their new albums and arranging summer tours, the Minneapolis rocker known as Prince was making a few arrangements of his own. Just when the Jacksons' tour was beginning, and attracting near-saturation media attention, Prince's new single, "When Doves Cry," went straight to Number One on the pop charts. And while the Jacksons and Springsteen albums, fueled by their summer shows, will certainly be big sellers, Prince may well top them both. His new album, "Purple Rain" (Warner Bros.), sold approximately 1.5 million copies its first week in the stores and is presently giving the Jacksons and Springsteen albums a run for their money. And while Prince has not announced a summer tour, his first film, also called "Purple Rain," has received some exceptional advance reviews and will open in more than 700 theaters, including four in Manhattan, on Friday.

"Purple Rain" is not just another Prince album. It is musically and emotionally tougher and considerably more personal than his last album, "1999," released two years ago, or any of his earlier disks. Prince's personality shines through more brightly than ever, but it's something of a new Prince we're seeing.

The hard-hitting lyrics give his "Purple Rain" album a highly charged text to work from, and the music feels equally intense and equally liberated, the best of Prince's career.

In solitude, even the work of a prodigally gifted, self-made genius must eventually become constricted. On "Purple Rain," the band's contributions do make the music sound more alive and more sensual. There are dazzling musical moments—the synthesizers and guitars that rave and rage at each other, yet remain almost frighteningly controlled in "Let's Go Crazy," or the strutting, almost-scat vocalizing on "The Beautiful One." "Darling Nikki" features some of the most unrestrained piano-thumping and leather-lunged screaming since Little Richard. The album's closer, the cathartic "Purple Rain," sets a gospel rap and jazz borrowings into the framework of a country-rock ballad, decorated with Nashville-style, Floyd Cramer-like piano arpeggios.

For the first time, Prince has stepped beyond the image he so obsessively constructed for himself on earlier records, and the result is exhilarating. What the film critics will make of all this remains to be seen, but the album "Purple Rain" is a winner, creatively and commercially. It may lack the Jacksons' multiformat sophistication and Bruce Springsteen's single-minded vision of America's hopes and failures, but this listener suspects that long after this summer's hits are forgotten, and the Jacksons and Springsteen albums are packed away, "Purple Rain" will still be remembered, and played, as an enduring rock classic. ■

FEBRUARY 27, 1985

ARTISTS JOIN IN EFFORT FOR FAMINE RELIEF

Stephen Holden

On March 11, Columbia Records will release "We Are the World," a new song written by Lionel Richie and Michael Jackson and performed by a chorus of 45 pop stars calling themselves USA for Africa (United Support of Artists for Africa). Roughly 90 percent of the proceeds from the single and an album to be released April 1, as well as a full-length video and related merchandising, will be donated to African famine relief. Another 10 percent will go to fight homelessness and malnutrition in the United States.

"We Are the World" is an American response to "Do They Know It's Christmas?," the single that was recorded late last year in London by Band Aid, a group of British rock stars. The record became the most successful single in British history, selling 3.5 million copies in Britain and 2.5 million in the United States and raising $9.2 million.

"We Are the World" originated last December with a telephone call from Harry Belafonte to Ken Kragen, the manager of Lionel Richie, Kenny Rogers and other top pop acts. "If Jews were starving in Israel, American Jews would have raised millions," said Mr. Belafonte, whose idea it was to organize a black superstar benefit concert.

Mr. Kragen contacted Mr. Richie, who in turn contacted Michael Jackson and the producer Quincy Jones. Mr. Richie and Mr. Jackson spent four days writing the song, and on Jan. 22 Mr. Jones and a group of top Los Angeles studio musicians recorded the rhythm and instrumental tracks and also made a demo with Mr. Jackson and Mr. Richie that was sent to all the artists involved.

What had begun as a supersession of black singers expanded after Bruce Springsteen agreed to become involved. Some of the stars who ended up donating their talents were Bob Dylan, Stevie Wonder, Willie Nelson, Diana Ross, Tina Turner, Ray Charles, Billy Joel, Cyndi Lauper, Huey Lewis, Paul Simon and Dionne Warwick. The vocals were recorded on Jan. 28 in a marathon 10-hour recording session at A & M Recording Studios in Los Angeles. ■

MAY 5, 1985

WHAT THE CHARTS SAY ABOUT THE HEALTH OF POP MUSIC

Stephen Holden

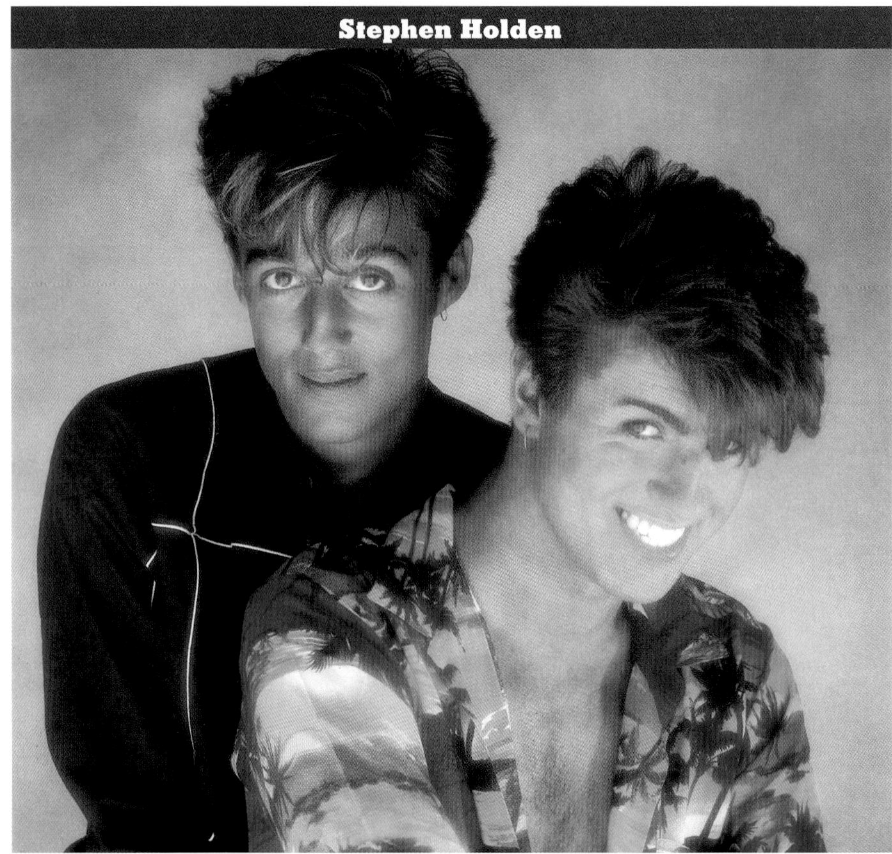

George Michael and Andrew Ridgeley of Wham!

Pop music is in the throes of a new boom cycle, both economically and artistically.

The robust health of the record industry, which was seriously ailing just three years ago, is symbolized by USA For Africa, one of the most spectacular displays of charity in show business history. "We Are the World," the "supersingle" for African famine relief, has already sold 5.5 million copies and remains first on Billboard's pop singles chart.

The "We Are the World" album, which was released just over a month ago and now tops Billboard's album chart, is fast approaching the four million mark in sales. Besides the title tune, the album includes eight cuts donated by individual acts. By far the most impressive are a version of Jimmy Cliff's "Trapped," recorded live in concert last August by Bruce Springsteen and the E Street Band, and Tina Turner's "Total Control," a rock ballad written by Martha Davis and Jeff Jourard of the Motels.

As it happens, Mr. Springsteen and Miss Turner also have albums in Billboard's Top 10 that attest to the artistic maturity of the best 80's rock. Both records are nearly a year old, yet they continue to spawn hit after hit. Mr. Springsteen's "Born in the U.S.A." employs a traditional rock and roll vocabulary, modernized with jagged jackhammer rhythms and flavored with synthesizer. His songs, mostly despairing dramatic monologues by blue-collar workers who have lost touch with the American dream, portray the dissolution of hope and community experienced by working-class America in a postindustrial age. Miss Turner's "Private Dancer" expresses much the same spirit of embattled self-sufficiency in songs that blend American rock and soul with a moody synthesizer music. Mr. Springsteen and Miss Turner emerge on these albums as heroic popular symbols of resilience and passion.

The coalescence of a new pop establishment was largely achieved by MTV. By bringing 24-hour pop, including a "We Are the World" promotional blitz, into millions of homes, MTV has given pop music a national center of consciousness. The latest demonstration of MTV's extraordinary power has been its impact on heavy metal rock.

"We Are the World" underscores the fundamental role of black music in American pop. Four of the top five stars of American pop—Michael Jackson, Prince, Lionel Richie and Stevie Wonder—are black, as is pop music's most successful and admired producer, Quincy Jones. Addressing the National Association of Record Manufacturers last month, Mr. Jones called for the dissolution of the demographic categories of music—pop, black, country, etc.—enthusiastically proclaiming that "the music is truly color-blind now."

Further examination of last week's album chart in Billboard bears out Mr. Jones's contention. Even mainstream English pop is thoroughly infused with American pop-soul and funk influences. The enigmatic art-rock songs on Phil Collins's "No Jacket Required" (second place) are grounded in contemporary black dance grooves inspired by Prince and Motown. Motown, the early-60's girl-group productions of Phil Spector, and the blue-eyed soul of the Bee Gees are also primary influences on Wham!, the British pop duo whose album, "Make It Big," was 10 in Billboard. The duo's simple, bouncy synthesizer pop, composed and produced by the 22-year-old teenage heartthrob George Michael, is the 1980's equivalent of the clean-cut pop of 25 years ago by the likes of Cliff Richard and Paul Anka. Madonna, with her teenage magazine sex appeal and tough-cookie singing style, is the female American equivalent of Wham!

The success of so many serious mainstream albums suggests a large and still-growing mass audience for popular music that is quite discriminating in its tastes. With "We Are the World" setting the pace, mid-80's pop is a diverse grab bag of compassionate exhortation, pungent social commentary and pure fun. ■

JULY 12, 1985

'LIVE AID' CONCERT IS AIMING FOR THE SKY

Esther B. Fein

The Live Aid concert at Wembley Stadium in London on June 13, 1985.

In technical terms, it can be measured in superlatives: the largest potential television audience, the biggest intercontinental satellite hookup, the grandest stage, the most impressive list of rock-and-roll performers.

But in human terms, according to the producers, promoters, technicians and performers for tomorrow's Live Aid concert—an event that is being staged in London and Philadelphia, supplemented with footage from seven other concerts around the world and simultaneously broadcast on radio and television to more than 150 countries—it comes down to the possibility of raising, in one day, more than $50 million for the hungry and the homeless in the famished regions of Africa.

"The logistics of this thing are staggering," said Bob Geldof, the Irish rock musician and coordinator of the event, who first organized Band-Aid, an all-star ensemble of British performers that produced a record to raise funds for famine relief. "But we tend to forget, in and amongst all the hoopla, what this is all about, and that is that this should be able to raise a lot of money to feed a lot of people."

The main sites for the benefit are Wembley Stadium in London and John F. Kennedy Stadium in Philadelphia—where such stars as Tina Turner, Mick Jagger, Paul McCartney, David Bowie, the Cars, the Who, Tom Petty and Bob Dylan will donate their performances. But the television extravaganza, according to organizers, will include the first live broadcast of a rock-and-roll performance from the Soviet Union and will be seen by perhaps 1.9 billion viewers when the 17 hours of concert and appeals ends at midnight Saturday.

SEPTEMBER 29, 1985

'New Age' Music Just Keeps Oozing Along

Jon Pareles

It's soft and sweet, smooth and unassuming. It turns up at better restaurants all around town. It's not the latest recipe for creme caramel—it's "new age" music, a creditable idea gone awry. Or so it would seem with the latest of new age record releases.

"New age" is the current catchall term for music that draws on non-Western, or nonclassical, traditions from a 20th-century standpoint. The idea, a good one, is to preserve or rediscover older methods without pretending that we live in primitive times.

Typically, new age pieces use modal and microtone-inflected melody lines, open-ended improvisations, ancient or non-Western instruments and, especially, repetition. Meanwhile, the music is produced with the latest in studio technology. A typical new age recording is packaged with copious technical data; one new company, Private Music, releases its digitally recorded efforts only on chromium tape and compact disks.

The fusion of new and old, Western and non-Western techniques has produced extraordinary music, from Steve Reich's "Drumming" to Jon Hassell's "Fourth World Music" to John McLaughlin's first Mahavishnu Orchestra albums. The efforts of the pioneering minimalists—whose impulses were always pan-global as well as reductionist—garnered respect for procedures that other modern composers had lost in a rush toward complexity. Lately, however, serious, rigorous minimalist music has been thrown into the new age record bins, where it is outnumbered by more amorphous efforts.

Consider Patrick O'Hearn's "Ancient Dreams" (Private Music). Like most new age recordings, it lets every sound bask in soothing reverberation; the leader in new age music, Windham Hill Records, engineers majestic-sounding solo piano and guitar albums, and other companies try to do the same with electronic instruments.

There is folksy new age music—Windham Hill's corner of the market—and high-tech new age music, like that of the synthesizer group Tangerine Dream.

Sanford Ponder's "Etosha—Private Music from the Land of Dry Water" (Private Music) uses natural sounds—water splashing, birds calling—both au naturel and as material for a digital synthesizer's keyboard tones in busy counterpoint.

Like Mr. O'Hearn, both succeed in deflecting attention from where the music is going to how neatly it is arranged. Actually, that seems to be the idea. New age music shows up at restaurants because it doesn't distract anyone from the food; it's just there, oozing along. ■

OBITUARY

JUNE 14, 1986

BENNY GOODMAN, KING OF SWING, IS DEAD

John S. Wilson

Benny Goodman performing in 1980.

Benny Goodman, the King of Swing whose clarinet led a generation of music fans into the Big Band era in the 1930's, died yesterday afternoon at his Manhattan apartment, apparently of a heart attack. He was 77 years old.

The death of the man who brought jazz to Carnegie Hall and enthralled millions with renditions of "Sweet Georgia Brown" and "Stompin' at the Savoy" brought expressions of grief and loss from his colleagues.

Lionel Hampton, the vibraphonist, recalled that Mr. Goodman was the first major music figure to put black and white musicians together on stage in the 1930's.

"The most important thing that Benny Goodman did," he said, "was to put Teddy Wilson and me in the quartet. It was instant integration. Black people didn't mix with whites then. Benny introduced us as Mr. Lionel Hampton and Mr. Teddy Wilson. He opened the door for Jackie Robinson. He gave music character and style."

The tall, apple-cheeked bandleader with the horn-rimmed glasses had had a pacemaker implanted in 1984, but he had been active and about town in recent months, and had appeared to be in good health yesterday morning, according to Lloyd Rauch, his personal assistant.

Mr. Goodman became the King of Swing the night of Aug. 21, 1935, at the Palomar Ballroom in Hollywood. In the following years, he drew throngs to nightclubs and theaters and introduced jazz to Carnegie Hall, toured the world as a representative of a distinctive American culture, was instrumental in breaking the barrier that had kept white and black musical groups separate and developed a band that was a training ground for many other band leaders, including Harry James, Gene Krupa, Lionel Hampton and Teddy Wilson.

"Benny was a phenomenon," Willard Alexander, a booking agent, once said. "He was not really the biggest band of the swing era. Glenn Miller was. But Benny was the biggest new thing in this type of presentation. He was even different physically, contrary to what everybody expected in a band leader. No glamour. No sex appeal. But a well-grounded musician." ■

MAY 10, 1987

PUBLIC ENEMY'S ALBUM

Jon Pareles

"Uh-oh, Chuck, they out to get us!" are the first words on the debut album by Public Enemy, "Yo! Bum Rush the Show" (Def Jam/Columbia)—the grittiest rap album so far this year and one of rap's fastest sellers. "Us" refers to Chuck D (whose last name is Ridenhour) and Flavor-Flav (William Drayton), Public Enemy's songwriters and rappers. While they don't usually get preachy about it, they make it clear that they're also speaking for an embattled black underclass, shown as targets on the album's cover and innersleeve. With Bernhard Goetz currently on trial for shooting four young black men in the subway, and with the Howard Beach racial incident still in the air, Public Enemy can't help being topical.

Public Enemy got started at Adelphi University on Long Island, where Mr. D began rapping on the college radio station while earning a degree in design. The group did its rap homework well, because Public Enemy builds on some of the best ideas of earlier rappers: the dry-eyed storytelling of Grandmaster Flash (and Melle Mel's) "Message," the shouted, half-speed declamation of Run-D.M.C. and the stark but multilayered production style of two fellow-Def Jam acts, L. L. Cool J. and the Beastie Boys.

Like other recent rap albums, "Yo! Bum Rush the Show" is audio theater with a dance beat. Public Enemy has a distinctive play of personalities: Mr. D raps in a booming radio voice and stylized syncopations, while his less professional-sounding sidekick, Flavor-Flav, eggs him on like a representative of the audience (or like a rap version of Ed McMahon).

Public Enemy relies on some of rap's usual gambits—boasting in wild free associations about Mr. D's verbal prowess, celebrating a brand-name possession (an Oldsmobile 98 in "You're Gonna Get Yours"), putting down a snooty woman. Yet where the Beastie Boys dispense bratty adolescent fantasies and Run-D.M.C. generally sticks to self-praise, Public Enemy sometimes draws sociopolitical lessons. ■

The rap group Public Enemy in 1988.

Whitney Houston

OCTOBER 29, 1985

WHITNEY HOUSTON IN CARNEGIE HALL DEBUT

Stephen Holden

The essence of Whitney Houston, the dazzlingly talented 22-year-old pop-soul singer whose first album has sold double platinum (two million copies), might be summed up in two lines from one of her signature songs, "The Greatest Love of All": "No matter what they take from me, they can't take away my dignity."

"The Greatest Love of All," which Miss Houston used to open her show last night, set the tone of a concert in which the singer, who looks and acts considerably

(cont'd. next page)

(continued from previous page)

more mature than her years, offered a potent yet refined mixture of pop, soul, and funk, accompanied by a five-piece band and three backup vocalists.

The daughter of the pop-gospel singer Cissy Houston and the first cousin of Dionne Warwick, Whitney Houston has a voice that is smaller, clearer and higher than those of her distinguished relatives. Where the timbres of most soul singers contain strong earth tones, Miss Houston's voice is ringing and bell-like most of the time. But behind the delicacy and reserve lurks a ferocious power that she can unleash with a sudden, almost blinding force.

At last night's concert, Miss Houston's moment of truth came late in the evening, with a searing, incandescent rendition of "I Am Changing" from the musical "Dreamgirls" that drew a standing ovation from an audience that included Eddie Murphy, Mayor Koch, Melba Moore, Nick Ashford and Valerie Simpson. For the first two-thirds of the show, Miss Houston had revealed herself to be a superb, though somewhat shy pop-soul technician in the sweetly glamorous mode of Diana Ross. By the end of the concert, Miss Houston demonstrated the potential for greatness. ■

NOVEMBER 2, 1986

ROCK-SOUL STARS OF THE 60'S HAVE A STRATEGY FOR THE 80'S

Jon Pareles

Aretha Franklin and Tina Turner, two definitive rock-soul singers of the 1960's, are still hit-making contenders in the 1980's. Ms. Turner's new album, "Break Every Rule" (Capitol album), follows up on the blockbuster, multimillion-selling "Private Dancer," released in 1984. Meanwhile, the new "Aretha," (Arista) catches Ms. Franklin on one of her career's periodic upswings, sparked by the 1985 album "Who's Zoomin' Who."

Both albums have a lot to do with the way the singers—and the people plotting their careers—have decided to use the past. In fact, "Break Every Rule" was released concurrently with "I, Tina," the singer's harrowing, tell-all biography co-written with Kurt Loder, senior editor of Rolling Stone.

With sales of nearly 5 million copies, "Private Dancer" established Ms. Turner, now 46 years old, as a solo hit maker and a resurgent sex symbol. It also established a strategy (and a sales benchmark) for a mature, gospel-charged, black singer to reach the largest possible audience.

Part of the strategy was musical. Like such best-selling early-1980's albums as Michael Jackson's "Thriller" and Cyndi Lauper's "She's So Unusual," "Private Dancer" had something for nearly every pop radio format, from ballad to hard-rock. But Ms. Turner and her producers also drew on the singer's own story. After 15 years as the hard-working, hip-shimmying, microphone-caressing lead singer for the the Ike and Tina Turner Revue, Ms. Turner had walked out on her abusive husband in 1975 and started again on her own.

In the meantime, along came another multimillion-selling singer's showcase, Whitney Houston's debut album. Unlike "Private Dancer," however, "Whitney Houston" sidestepped rock in favor of pop, and as far as the public was concerned, Ms. Houston had no past—just a glorious voice dispensing friendly, upwardly mobile sentiments against a plush backdrop. "Private Dancer" and "Whitney Houston" have raised the stakes (and probably the recording budgets) for black pop singers; best-selling albums by Patti LaBelle and Anita Baker, not to mention Aretha Franklin's "Who's Zoomin' Who," profited by their examples.

Since she signed with Arista Records, Aretha Franklin has veered between trying to be streetwise (and tossing off up-to-the-minute slang) and acting as a seminostalgic, 1960's-vintage grande dame. On "Who's Zoomin' Who," she sang some peppy, generic love-and-lust lyrics over a beat vaguely reminiscent of her 1960's songs; the video clip for "Freeway of Love" shows her driving off in a car with the license plate "RESPECT," recalling her 1967 hit. She also had a lyric about "surviving," a la Turner, in "Another Night" and a noncontroversial feminist tract, "Sisters Are Doin' It for Themselves," with another 1960's beat.

Tina Turner performing in 1987.

U2 MAKES A BID FOR 'GREAT BAND' STATUS

U2 in 1984.

John Rockwell

The members of U2, the Irish rock band—Bono Vox, also known as Paul Hewson, the singer; Dave (the Edge) Evans, the guitarist; Adam Clayton, the bass player; and Larry Mullen Jr., the drummer—are in their mid-20's. Even before their first album, "Boy," in 1981, they had a strong cult and critical following in Britain, and through extensive touring they have developed a critical and now popular following in this country as well.

Their 1983 album, "War," marked their emergence into serious contention for "great band" status. Now they have released their fifth studio album (not counting a couple of partly live, 12-inch mini-albums). It's called "The Joshua Tree" (Island), and in conjunction with a yearlong world tour (due into New York in mid-May), it's designed to achieve megastatus for this band at last. Robert Hilburn of The Los Angeles Times wrote earlier this month: "U2 is what the Rolling Stones ceased being years ago—the greatest rock 'n' roll band in the world."

The group won its fans because at a time of punk anarchy, fashion overkill and synth-pop triviality, this was a band that stuck to singer-guitar-bass-drum basics. And solid basics, to boot: Bono was a powerful singer, the Edge played guitar that was both imaginative and soulful, and Mr. Clayton and Mr. Mullen made for a propulsive rhythm section.

In addition, Bono's lyrics—the music is by the band as a whole—addressed sensitive and interesting themes in a way that was, if not truly poetic, at least evocative and challenging.

In "War," they addressed the political tensions in Northern Ireland—they're from Dublin, and Bono has a Catholic father and a Protestant mother—with real intensity, especially in their anthem, "Sunday Bloody Sunday." This sort of sentiment, which the band was wise enough to broaden to include condemnations of all sorts of hatred and strife, not just the Irish variant, appealed to the kind of idealistic young person who also admired Bruce Springsteen's social consciousness. And like Mr. Springsteen, U2 gives a superb live show, easily evoking the sound of their studio records but surpassing those records with rhapsodic extensions of their songs, featuring Bono's impassioned, athletic leapings about the stage and guitar-playing by the Edge that rarely oversteps the bounds of expression into empty virtuosity. No wonder two live mini-albums have been released.

The title of "The Joshua Tree" is not the only biblical image on this album, but this is not by any means a hectoring Christian album. Song subjects range from commentary on America's wealth and hypocrisy to heroin addiction, romantic despair, the loss of a friend, political and economic oppression and totalitarian brutality.

Musically, the band stretches its range here in two ways. One is the inclusion of musical idioms never so overtly explored

(cont'd. next page)

(continued from previous page)
before on a U2 record, especially the gospel chorus of "One Tree Hill" and the country blues guitar and harmonica of "Running to Stand Still" and "Trip Through Your Wires."

Once upon a time, rock-and-roll was cheerful music, meant to galvanize teenagers into dancing or worse. "The Joshua Tree" puts U2 squarely into the camp of what Jon Pareles last week called "mope rock." This is not to discount U2's aspirations to rock greatness, nor to deny any possibility of commercial success for this new album, nor certainly to doubt that U2 won't perform terrific live concerts during its 1987 tour. Quite the reverse, actually. We know this is a wonderful live band, and the haunting songs on "The Joshua Tree" should be ideal for the toughening and expansion that concert arrangements can bring to studio material. ■

JUNE 21, 1987

The New Jazz Era Claims Its Audience

Robert Palmer

Jazz is back, they say. Not so long ago, jazz musicians were rarely seen on television or in national magazines, jazz records were either small-label affairs or imports from Europe and Japan, jazz radio was something of a contradiction in terms, and even watered-down jazz-pop hybrids were hiding behind the rubric "fusion." Now they—the trend-spotters, the arbiters of au courant—have declared that jazz is back. But the music hasn't simply become stylish; it has been integrating itself into the larger culture. Jazz is showing signs of an unprecedented resilience, a determination to hold onto hard-won gains.

The lineup of the 1987 JVC Jazz Festival, which opened this weekend, reflects the music's resurgence. Musicians whose innovations have set new agendas for jazz are making statements—Ornette Coleman with a combined program featuring his original quartet and his electric band, the Modern Jazz Quartet with a presentation of new works for quartet and orchestra by its pianist, John Lewis. Pioneering modernists such as Dizzy Gillespie and Hank Jones are being presented in retrospectives, and the young turks, from Wynton and Branford Marsalis to less ballyhooed but equally significant players such as the trombonist Craig Harris, are out in force.

The festival's renewed vitality is only one of the signs that jazz has arrived. Major corporations, foundations, city and state governments and arts organizations are sponsoring jazz events and funding projects by jazz artists. CBS, RCA, MCA and the other major record labels were largely ignoring jazz 10 years ago; now they are competing for new and established jazz talent and flooding the record stores with reissues of classic jazz performances on albums, CD's and cassettes. Several of this year's festival events have been sponsored by major record labels, something that happened rarely in earlier years.

Jazz boosters used to dream of the elusive crossover that would introduce the music to a broad popular audience. That crossover is now reality, as today's pop stars show unprecedented jazz consciousness. Sting, formerly the singer-bassist and principal lyricist for the Police, has been working with a band of young jazz stars, including the saxophonist Branford Marsalis, and making guest appearances with Gil Evans's big band. Charlie Watts, drummer for the Rolling Stones, is returning to New York City for the second time this year at the helm of a British jazz orchestra, which will play "Stompin' at the Savoy," "Lester Leaps In" and other big-band evergreens next week at the festival.

The singer-songwriter Tom Waits and the Lounge Lizards' leader and saxophonist, John Lurie, stars of the cult film "Down by Law," are popularizing a kind of fractured, film-noir be-bop. Open-minded young musicians are hard at work obliterating generic boundaries; the guitarist Pat Metheny, for example, collaborated with David Bowie on a film soundtrack, then recorded with the creative mainspring of the jazz avant-garde, Ornette Coleman.

Another new phenomenon, the jazz-classical crossover, may prove even more significant. Wynton Marsalis, the young trumpet star, is making swinging, straight-ahead jazz albums for Columbia, and albums of classical music, from Baroque to Romantic to 19th-century Americana, for CBS Masterworks. He has been winning Grammy awards in both categories. Nonesuch Records and other adventurous classical-music labels have been recording, and successfully marketing, jazz-rooted artists such as John Zorn and the World Saxophone Quartet, whose exploratory bent limited their appeal among mainstream jazz fans.

Who is listening to this music—buying the records and CD's, attending the concerts, supporting the jazz clubs? "It's a young audience, mostly college-age, and getting younger," says George Wein, the originator and producer of the Newport Jazz Festival, now called the JVC Festival in honor of its sponsor, the Japanese electronics manufacturer. "They aren't terribly knowledgeable in terms of the music's past, its roots. They seem to accept the way the music is today as a given; music that's very familiar to someone like me seems fresh to them. But they're a good audience, with a lot of enthusiasm." ■

Sax player John Lurie of the Lounge Lizards performing in 1981.

IT'S OFFICIAL: RAP MUSIC IS IN THE MAINSTREAM

Peter Watrous

Rap, the music that began in the nation's black urban ghettoes, enters the mainstream commercial music world in earnest this morning when 1,250,000 copies of Run-D.M.C.'s new album "Tougher Than Leather" go on sale.

If "Tougher Than Leather" succeeds, it will serve as evidence of how a distinct new black youth culture is influencing young Americans regardless of color.

"We expect to sell at least 4 million to 5 million copies of 'Tougher Than Leather,'" said Steve Plotnicki, vice president of Profile Records. "Rap now has a much broader audience. The music has crossed over to new radio formats—for which Run-D.M.C. is responsible. White kids are buying more and more of it. There is wider acceptance at retail: it's now retailed as well as any artists you can think of, whether its Bruce Springsteen or Prince or Madonna. Before 'Raising Hell,' there were some holdouts in terms of large national accounts who didn't want to load up a K-Mart with Run-D.M.C. Now they're all going full blast. We've heard that some accounts have taken about as many as they did of the Michael Jackson record."

Until recently, many radio stations refused to play rap and many record stores did not stock it. Rap was considered music by and for an audience of young urban blacks and thus of limited appeal. But fueled by such groups as Run-D.M.C. and by Whodini and Dana Dane, it has been growing in popularity in all areas of the country and with all manner of audiences.

"Tougher than Leather" is the group's fourth album. As in the rest of rap, the tempos on the record are faster than they might have been two years ago. The group is trying more sampling and scratching—snippits of other records thrown in to color and texture the sound of a song. Mr. Simmons and Mr. McDaniels rap in unison, and trade smoking lead vocals. There are three rockish songs, no endorsements ("Raising Hell" had one song called "My Adidas") and more use of live musicians.

"The record's about variety," said Mr. McDaniels. "We wanted to prove that all rap doesn't sound alike. We have everything from live piano to rock guitar to New Orleans ragtime horns. And it's intense, hard-core rap—everybody was saying we'd go soft, so we came at them with the hardest thing possible." ■

Darryl "DMC" McDaniels, Joseph "DJ Run" Simmons and Jason "Jam Master Jay" Mizell of the rap group Run-D.M.C. in 1986.

DECEMBER 28, 1988

CD'S: TOO MUCH OF A GOOD THING?

Allan Kozinn

When the Compact Disk was introduced to the American market in April 1983, its inventors—the Sony and Philips corporations—predicted that it would render the long-playing record extinct within a decade. The LP may not take that long to die.

In the first half of this year, CD's in all categories of music outsold LP's for the first time, according to the Record Industry Association of America. The current Schwann record catalogue lists more than 20,000 CD titles of all kinds, and retailers around the country are clearing out their LP bins to accommodate the explosion of CD's.

But there are some in the record industry who fear that CD's have proliferated too quickly: that after five years of a CD drought, when consumers had few titles to choose from, the market is becoming flooded. What makes the record industry particularly nervous is that according to the Electronics Industry Association, only 15 to 20 percent of American households have CD players, and after five years of steady growth, player sales seem to have hit a plateau.

Record companies say the vigor with which they have been issuing both new titles and back catalogue on CD should attract those consumers who have not changed to the new format. But given the cost of CD's—$9 to the retailer, $15 to the consumer for a full-price recording—the quick expansion of the catalogue has led many retailers to be more selective in their ordering. As a result, even the largest chains are no longer able to offer consumers the kind of full-line service they offered at the height of the LP era. And even selective ordering has not kept slower-selling CD's from cluttering the bins.

A "CD glut," as many industry executives openly call it, has already hit the classical-music market, where current recordings of standard-repertory works are now forced to compete for consumers' attention with dozens of earlier versions, including legendary performances reissued on budget-priced CD's.

Signs of a glut are particularly apparent in classical music, which accounts for only 4 percent of the American record market, according to the Record Industry Association of America. But an East Coast regional manager for the Tower Records national retail chain—which has long prided itself on carrying full lines in all genres—says that 25 percent of the chain's sales are of classical music. And industry observers point out that CD sales trends have emerged in classics a year or two before other kinds of music.

"What often happens in any industry," said Joseph F. Dash, vice president and general manager of CBS Masterworks, "is that when you have an undercapacity, people overreact without thinking about the big picture. So we all began issuing on CD some of the wonderful performances we had in our back catalogues. And suddenly, what was a dearth has become an overabundance."

Alison Ames, vice president in charge of Deutsche Grammophon's American operations, said the seeds of the glut were planted in 1985, when labels that had been slow to enter the CD market came streaming in.

"There was a time when we and the other Polygram labels, London and Philips, each had catalogues of 300 to 400 CD's and Angel had 20," Ms. Ames said. "Then, in a single month, Angel issued 60 disks. To me, that was the beginning of the CD glut. It meant that the classical dealer had a choice of putting all his eggs in one basket that month or spreading his budget around more thinly."

Michael Emmerson, president of BMG Classics, which owns RCA, said: "I don't think the problem is the glut itself but rather the fact that we have not done enough to persuade the other 80 to 85 percent of the American public that the CD is accessible, reasonably priced and here to stay." ■

MARCH 19, 1989

Madonna Re-Creates Herself—Again

Stephen Holden

In "Like a Prayer," the music-video and title song of an album that represents Madonna's convincing bid for recognition as a serious rock artist, the 30-year-old star has never looked more beautiful or sung with more feeling. The songs, which deal directly and very emotionally with her failed marriage to the actor Sean Penn, her family, and her Catholic girlhood, transcend the brassy dance-pop of her three previous records to reveal Madonna as a vulnerable human being.

With its images of interracial love, religious ecstasy, stigmata and burning crosses carried forward by lush Caribbean-flavored pop-gospel music, "Like a Prayer" surpasses Madonna's earlier music videos in its heady swirl of sacred and profane images. It is titillating, heart-tugging and funny all at once.

Madonna, speaking by telephone from Los Angeles last week, shrugged off the controversy surrounding the video, which has been denounced as offensive by the American Family Association and has led Pepsi-Cola, which paid her more than $5 million to use the song in a TV commercial, to ask that it be withdrawn from MTV. The company's request was denied.

"Art should be controversial, and that's all there is to it," Madonna declared, reiterating the philosophy behind many of her videos.

Since becoming an international star just over four years ago, Madonna Louise Veronica Ciccone from Detroit has shown a genius for stirring up just enough controversy to advance her career without tipping the balance of public opinion against her. Indeed, the seeds of controversy are embodied in her very name. That name, she said, has always made her feel special.

Pictures of Madonna, in a photogenic swoon with eyes half closed, have become as ubiquitous as the faces of Elvis Presley, Marilyn Monroe and the Beatles. But Madonna—far more than the idols of the 50's

discs

and 60's—has exercised an impresario's shrewd managerial control over her image. Steeped in pop-culture iconography, she has manipulated the persona of the good-bad girl in music videos, concerts and endless photographs in a way that has made her self-invention a kind of ongoing performance, and has made her one of the 10 highest-paid entertainers of the late 1980's, having earned, according to Forbes magazine, more than $20 million in each of the last three years.

"What I do is total commercialism, but it's also art," said Madonna. "I like the challenge of doing both, of somehow making art that is accessible and making commerce something artistic."

The idea of integrating one's image into one's act, whatever that act may be, is as old as the profession of press agentry. But Madonna brings to it a knowingness and an inspired spontaneity that could only have come in an age when the abundance of media allows any American with a talent for self-promotion the possibility of at least a few minutes of air time.

Initially, the persona Madonna presented was a saucy post-teenage rebel togged out in lingerie, baring her midriff and adorning herself with crucifixes. The flap she kicked up in 1984 with "Like a Virgin," in which she flouncingly mocked the traditionally chaste stereotype of a blushing bride while also affirming the value of true love, was comparable to John Lennon's offhand remark that the Beatles were more popular than Jesus. In "Material Girl," a joke that went over many heads, Madonna drily satirized Reagan-era materialism by parodying a shallow glitzy gold digger.

Those who didn't get the joke confused Madonna with the material girl, and for them she became a cultural symptom, a brazenly opportunistic performer substituting exhibitionism for talent. Playing a gum-chewing, leather-jacketed blue-collar Juliet in the music-video for "Papa Don't Preach," in 1986, the star appeared to encourage teenage pregnancy. And in the music-video for "Open Your Heart" that same year she portrayed a seductive peep-show siren observed by a young adolescent boy.

As her star ascended, Madonna's urban-rebel pose has softened and matured into a more sleekly glamorous and aerobicized look without losing its hard-edged sensual provocation. Her music also metamorphosed from simple blaring dance pop to the somewhat sweeter post-Motown valentines of "True Blue" to the rich, fully rounded pop of "Like a Prayer."

If the album has one song in which Madonna expresses a 30-year-old's view of life unshadowed by rebellion and lingering lapsed Catholic pain, it is "Express Yourself," in which she repudiates the philosophy of "Material Girl" and advises women not to settle for a less-than-wonderful relationship. "You don't need diamond rings or 18 carat gold / Fancy cars that go very fast you know they never last," she proclaims.

"The message of the song is that people should always say what it is they want." ■

DECEMBER 28, 1980

THE BEST CAME FROM DIRECTORS WITH STRONG VISIONS

Vincent Canby

This year's best films define no special trends except that, with one exception, each is the work of a single strong director with a particular vision of the world, which is as it should be. The exception? Read further. The 10 best films of 1980, listed in alphabetical order, are:

"Airplane!" This marvelous, full-bodied, nut-packed parody, having been directed by three people, is the exception to the above statement. Jim Abrahams, David Zucker and Jerry Zucker not only wrote the screenplay together, they then directed it in some sort of magical collaboration. However they did it, "Airplane!" is the most thoroughly satisfying movie spoof since Mel Brooks's "Young Frankenstein."

"Dressed to Kill." Brian De Palma, whose professional personality had previously been split between his surreal comedies ("Hi, Mom") and suspense-thrillers in the Hitchcockian mode ("Obsession," "The Fury"), got both sides together in this superior comedy mystery about, of all things, a split personality.

"Every Man for Himself." Jean-Luc Godard, the enfant terrible of world cinema in the 60's, is now in his 40's and no less the restless genius he was 20 years ago. "Every Man for Himself" is a series of dramatized essays on contemporary life and on narrative cinema, set in a middle-sized Swiss city and having principally to do with three young adults.

"Melvin and Howard." The real-life story of Melvin Dummar, the gas station attendant who gained brief fame as a possible heir to Howard Hughes, is a nearly perfect comedy for the 1980's, when all of our most treasured beliefs suddenly seem open to question. It's also nearly perfect material for director Jonathan Demme.

Robert De Niro as boxer Jake La Motta in a scene from "Raging Bull," directed by Martin Scorsese, 1980.

"Mon Oncle d'Amerique." French director Alain Resnais new film, "Mon Oncle d'Amerique," which is one of his best, reflects his interests in the work of Dr. Henri Laborit, the medical doctor and behavioral scientist who is convinced that unless mankind quickly learns how to understand its nervous system, the race may be over sooner than anyone realizes.

"Ordinary People." The screen adaptation of Judith Guest's novel, written by Alvin Sargent and directed by Robert Redford, is this year's "Kramer vs. Kramer," a small, precisely observed portrait of a particular kind of middle-class American life.

"Raging Bull." The source material for Martin Scorsese's "Raging Bull" is the life and hard times of Jake La Motta, the Bronx-bred boxer who fought his way to the middleweight championship in 1948 and just as aggressively went on to lose everything he'd won. As written by Paul Schrader and Mardik Martin, directed by Mr. Scorsese and acted by Robert De Niro in the central role, the film is less a biography than a meditation upon the human condition, on the struggle to make order out of primal chaos. This is Mr. Scorsese's best, most ambitious film.

"Stardust Memories." Woody Allen wants very much to be taken seriously, and at no time is he more serious than when he's being slyly funny, usually at his own expense, as he shows in this latest, most stylish of his comedies. Mr. Allen's command of his talent has never been more evident, nor his generosity to his fellow players, including Marie-Christine Barrault, Charlotte Rampling and Jessica Harper.

"The Third Generation." Rainer Werner Fassbinder, the most brilliant talent to come on the cinema scene since Jean-Luc Godard, doesn't make individual movies. Though the subject matter varies from picture to picture, each succeeding film is a continuing record of the director's preoccupations with the state of the world he inhabits. As this particular film shows, he sometimes changes his mind. "The Third Generation" is a dark, bitter comedy about a bunch of middle class German revolutionaries Mr. Fassbinder now finds as dangerous as they are ridiculous. The movie is startling in its images (Mr. Fassbinder was the cameraman as well as the writer and director), and it's funny, if you can divorce the actions of the characters from the consequences, which are horrendous. The cast includes such Fassbinder regulars as Hanna Schygulla, Volker Spengler, Harry Baer and Margit Carstensen, plus Bulle Ogier and Eddie Constantine.

"Wise Blood." John Huston's 33rd film, based on the classic novel by Flannery O'Connor as adapted by Benedict Fitzgerald, is one of the master's most exuberant works, as crazy as "Beat the Devil" and far more haunting. It's John Huston at the top of his form. ■

"They called me an animal. I'm not an animal."

JANUARY 18, 1981

WHY HOLLYWOOD BREEDS SELF-INDULGENCE

Hans Koning

Dan Aykroyd and John Belushi stared in "The Blues Brothers" in 1980.

In the movie industry, 1980 is likely to be remembered as the year of the gold-plated dud. From Steven Spielberg's "1941" to John Landis's "The Blues Brothers" to the most resounding flop in recent memory, Michael Cimino's "Heaven's Gate," Hollywood turned out a series of films afflicted with what might best be described as terminal bloat. Directors with one or two successes behind them were encouraged to spend millions and then more millions.

(cont'd. next page)

(continued from previous page)
Studio production chiefs seemed to have lost all sense of artistic and financial control.

Mr. Cimino's $36 million "Heaven's Gate" was an "unqualified disaster" in the estimation of Vincent Canby. Mr. Spielberg's $40 million "1941" was described by Mr. Canby as "about as much fun as a 40-pound wristwatch." Mr. Landis's $30 million "The Blues Brothers" was condemned by Janet Maslin for its "hollowness." These may be extreme examples, but they do not exhaust the list.

Many relatively successful films were marred by their directors' self-indulgence, too. Most critics enjoyed "The Coal Miner's Daughter" but found it much too long; others enjoyed "Just Tell Me What You Want" but found it meandering; and "All That Jazz," for all its sparkle, wallowed in the unnecessary. What, for example, was an excruciatingly gory open-heart operation doing in the middle of a musical? By contrast, critics were lavish in their praise for the economical story-telling of "Kramer vs. Kramer."

Last year's notable failures, with their super-inflated budgets, seemed to stir extraordinary concern about how and why they went wrong. The major studios are, in fact, echoing with self-doubt and talk of retrenchment.

Moviemakers offer a variety of explanations for the outbreak of self-indulgence. These include the need to attract audiences with blockbuster films that outdo anything available on television, the ascendancy of "accountants" in the ranks of Hollywood producers, the decline of the old studio system, and the bowing to the "auteurist" director-as-demigod approach to filmmaking.

But why the push for blockbusters in the first place? It seems that today many movies must be either sensational or nothing at all. In the old pre-television days, a habitual movie-going public used to queue up at the box office every Saturday night almost regardless of the attraction; today the theaters are empty unless something genuinely out of the ordinary packs in an audience. When a movie connects, however, it scores as never before. Films such as "Star Wars" generate profits reckoned in the hundreds of millions. For this reason a production cost of $30 million becomes less unthinkable today than at an earlier time. And a director believed capable of creating such a profit gusher becomes a person of awesome power. ■

MARCH 30, 1982

'CHARIOTS OF FIRE,' KATHERINE HEPBURN AND HENRY FONDA WIN TOP OSCARS

Aljean Harmetz

Actress Katharine Hepburn and co-star Henry Fonda during filming of movie "On Golden Pond."

HOLLYWOOD, March 29—On a night with more upsets than any Academy Awards in recent years, "Chariots of Fire" was the unexpected winner as best picture, and Katharine Hepburn took an unprecedented and unexpected fourth Oscar as actress for her portrayal of Henry Fonda's wife in "On Golden Pond." Until tonight Miss Hepburn had been tied with Walter Brennan and Ingrid Bergman, with three acting awards each.

As had been widely expected, Henry Fonda won his first Academy Award as actor for his portrayal of a man raging at the approach of his 80th birthday and the spectre of his death. In the way life has of imitating art, Mr. Fonda has been critically ill with heart trouble during the last year and was unable to be at the ceremony. His daughter Jane, whose company produced the film, accepted the award.

Surprisingly, in his almost 50-year movie career, Mr. Fonda had been nominated only once before, for "The Grapes of Wrath" (1940).

"Oh dad I'm so happy and proud for you," Miss Fonda said in accepting, she added that she was sure her father had reacted to the award by saying, " 'Ain't I lucky!'—as though luck had anything to do with it."

Miss Hepburn was not at the Los Angeles Music Center tonight to pick up her golden statuette, just as she was not at the previous awards ceremonies when she won

ain't I lucky...

for "Morning Glory" (1932–33), "Guess Who's Coming to Dinner" (1967) and "The Lion in Winter" (1968).

"Chariots of Fire," an inexpensive British film about two runners in the 1924 Olympic Games who competed for very different reasons, also won for original screenplay, costumes and original score.

"Raiders of the Lost Ark" also took four awards, for sound, visual effects, art direction and editing. "Reds," Warren Beatty's complex epic about the journalist John Reed and American socialism, won Mr. Beatty the award for directing. ■

EXPLORING INNER AND OUTER SPACE WITH STEVEN SPIELBERG

Vincent Canby

"Children's literature in America," says "The Oxford Companion to American Literature," "first consisted of aids to piety, seemingly addressed to miniature adults." Among the earliest such works, the companion cites John Cotton's "Milk for Babes, Drawn out of the Breasts of Both Testaments," published in 1633.

American babes have come a long way since. Our children's literature now embraces everything from the Uncle Remus stories to Mark Twain, Louisa May Alcott, E.B. White, Nancy Drew, same sex manuals, comic books and, this century's crowning contribution, motion pictures, especially the work of Walt Disney. Now add the work of Steven Spielberg, currently represented by two new films, each of which is an extension of a popular children's form, though neither is an aid to piety or seeks an audience of miniature adults.

The films are "Poltergeist," which was produced by Mr. Spielberg, directed by Tobe Hooper and is one of the few really satisfactory haunted-house movies I've ever seen, and "E.T. the Extra-Terrestrial," directed by Mr. Spielberg, a sweet-natured fantasy with all sorts of connections to earlier children's literature including "Peter Pan," "The Wizard of Oz," "Lassie," "Flubber," Mr. Spielberg's own "Close Encounters of the Third Kind," "Star Wars" and "The Empire Strikes Back."

As good as both films are, their simultaneous release may not be a wise decision, even if, as now seems possible, they succeed in cornering a large portion of this summer's movie business between them. "Poltergeist" and "E.T." are enough alike to invite comparisons but just different enough that anyone who is charmed by one will probably be disappointed by the other.

What they do give us, however, is the opportunity to consider the concerns and methods of a very particular talent as demonstrated in two separate films seen side by side. In this day and age, when most filmmakers take three or four years on each project, this kind of opportunity doesn't come along very often. Since 1977, when "Close Encounters" was released, Mr. Spielberg has made four films, "1941," "Raiders of the Lost Ark," "Poltergeist" and "E.T."

The most immediate conclusion: Steven Spielberg has become his own filmmaker, even when working through an

(cont'd. next page)

Steven Spielberg (left) directs American actor Henry Thomas in a scene on the set of his film, "E.T. the Extra-Terrestrial."

(continued from previous page)

associate, as he did with Mr. Hooper on "Poltergeist." If he were a playwright or a novelist, one would say that he had found his own voice, but because a filmmaker deals in images and sounds as well as words, I'm not sure what the movie equivalent would be.

Of the two new films, "E.T." is the more conventional. At heart it is an updated version of that old Hollywood standby, the boy-and-his-dog picture, but with a small, frightened creature from outer space instead of a dog. This fellow, E.T., a piece of walking-talking sculpture created by Carlo Rambaldi, looks like a chubby, distant cousin of the creatures in "Close Encounters." He's about three-feet tall with bulgy forehead and eyes, spindly arms, dachshund legs—just two, duck feet, a stratospheric intelligence and, when walking, the wobbliness of a wind-up toy manufactured in Taiwan.

"E.T." is one of the shrewdest non-Disney, Disney-type pictures ever made. It's a funny, clever variation on a Hollywood formula film, made by adults working to come up with an adventure that will satisfy the yearnings of children, at least as those yearnings are perceived by adults. The perceptions are not far off the mark.

"E.T." seems to have been photographed mostly at the eye-level of the children—though this may only be an impression—so that it implicates the audience in everything the children and E.T. do. However, because there are no real villains in the piece, the result is not a "them" (adults) against "us" (children) situation. It's a simple reflection of a world in which children can be in control.

Quite different, and possibly more risky, is "Poltergeist," which is a child's nightmare cast in the form of a movie. It's a tale of ghosts and goblins and creepy, slimy, unspeakable things, the sort of narrative one child might make up for the heart-pounding delectation of his friends.

The Freeling family—Mom and Dad, daughter Dana in her mid-teens, son Robbie, who's somewhat younger, and Carol Anne, who is 10—live a representatively ordinary existence in a house that may well be on the other side of the same real estate development where E.T. is being hidden by Elliot and his family.

"Poltergeist," rated PG, is not a film to be seen by very small children with sleeping problems. Slightly older kids will probably find it less shocking than their parents do. "Poltergeist" is more deliciously spooky than seriously frightening because Mr. Spielberg is so obviously in touch with the child's imagination. This is the haunted house film that he—and we—always wanted to see as kids but never did.

At their best, both "E.T." and "Poltergeist" demonstrate a feeling for children's fantasies that is most unusual in American films. They meet kids on their own turf. They don't look down on them or pat them on the head or flatter them by making them behave like the miniature adults in the old Our Gang comedies. ■

OBITUARY

AUGUST 31, 1982

INGRID BERGMAN, WINNER OF 3 OSCARS, IS DEAD

Murray Schumach

Ingrid Bergman, the three-time Academy Award-winning actress who exemplified wholesome beauty and nobility to countless moviegoers, died of cancer Sunday at her home in London on her 67th birthday.

Miss Bergman had been ill for eight years. Despite this, she played two of her most demanding roles in this period, a concert pianist in Ingmar Bergman's "Autumn Sonata" and Golda Meir, the Israeli Prime Minister in "A Woman Called Golda," her last role.

Miss Bergman said in an interview earlier this year that she was determined not to let her illness prevent her from enjoying the remainder of her life.

Incandescent, the critics called Ingrid Bergman. Or radiant. Or luminous. They said her performances were sincere, natural. Sometimes a single adjective was not enough. One enraptured writer saw her as "a breeze whipping over a Scandinavian peak."

In temperament, Miss Bergman was different from most Hollywood superstars. She did not indulge in tantrums or engage in harangues with directors. If she had a question about a script, she asked it without fuss. She could be counted on to be letter perfect in her lines before she faced the camera. And during the intervals between scenes, her relaxing smile and hearty laugh were as unaffected as her low-heeled shoes, long walking stride and minimal makeup.

Yet this even-tempered and successful actress, who was apparently happily married, became involved in a scandal that rocked the movie industry, forced her to stay out of the United States for seven years and made her life as tempestuous as many of her roles. In a sense, she became a barometer of changing moral values in the United States.

In 1949 she fell in love with Roberto Rossellini, the Italian film director, and had a child by him before she could obtain a divorce from her husband, Dr. Peter Lindstrom, and marry the director.

Before the scandal, millions of Americans had been moved by her performances in such box-office successes as "Intermezzo," "For Whom the Bell Tolls," "Gaslight," "Spellbound," "The Bells of St. Mary's," "Notorious" and "Casablanca," roles that had made her, somewhat to her annoyance, a symbol of moral perfection.

"I cannot understand," she said, long before the scandal, "why people think I'm pure and full of nobleness. Every human being has shades of bad and good."

Suddenly, in 1949, the American public that had elevated her to the point of idolatry cast her down, vilified her and boycotted her films. She was even condemned on the floor of the United States Senate.

Then, seven years after she had fallen from grace in this country, she returned to gather new acclaim and honors for her acting, and she never again suffered any noticeable loss of favor as an actress or as a person. But she spent nearly all of her remaining working life in Europe, sometimes for American movie companies. ■

APRIL 12, 1983

'GANDHI' IS WINNER OF EIGHT ACADEMY AWARDS

Aljean Harmetz

HOLLYWOOD—In an evening devoid of surprises, "E.T. The Extra-Terrestrial" won most of the minor Academy Awards, and "Gandhi" won most of the major ones, including best picture, actor, director and screenplay.

Sir Richard Attenborough had spent 20 years struggling to finance and produce a screen biography of the father of modern India. At the 55th annual Academy Awards tonight, he was awarded an Oscar as director for the result. On the verge of tears, Sir Richard raised his Oscar to his fellow nominees and said, "I am honored to be in their company." A few moments later, when he returned to pick up his Oscar as producer of the best picture, he said, "The person whom you really honored was Mahatma Gandhi himself" and "his plea to all of us to live in peace."

In all, "Gandhi" won eight awards, from art direction, costume, cinematography and film editing to Ben Kingsley's award as best actor.

For her portrayal in "Sophie's Choice" of a concentration camp survivor who cannot live with her memories, Meryl Streep won the award for best actress. Miss Streep—radiant, tearful and six months pregnant—thanked dozens of people, including, individually, most of the members of the movie's crew. ■

DECEMBER 2, 1984

SHORT ON TALK, BIG AT THE BOX OFFICE

Janet Maslin

Chuck Norris, Arnold Schwarzenegger, Charles Bronson: not everyone's idea of perfect party guests but nonetheless deserving of attention and even respect, since together they control such a formidable

(cont'd. next page)

Poster for "The Terminator," 1984.

(continued from previous page)
share of the movie market. Only last week, Mr. Norris's "Missing in Action" and Mr. Schwarzenegger's "Terminator" were being advertised as the nation's "New no. 1 hit!" and "The N1 movie in the U.S.A.," respectively. And "The Evil That Men Do," the latest from Mr. Bronson, made a comparable splash several months earlier.

The success of this triumvirate is greeted in some quarters by indifference, even scorn. For all the many filmgoers who would not, even at gunpoint, watch a Bronson or a Schwarzenegger epic, there are even greater numbers who could not pick out Mr. Norris from a lineup of fortyish blond tennis pros. Surely Mr. Norris, who spent many years as a karate instructor (and enjoyed a reign as world karate champion) before launching his film career, is the most underrecognized movie star in America, if not the most underrated.

Empirical evidence, in the form of millions of ticket-buying patrons, tells us that Mr. Norris unquestionably has his appeal. But explaining that appeal isn't easy. Certainly much of it is nonverbal, as is Mr. Bronson's and Mr. Schwarzenegger's.

What the Messrs. Norris, Schwarzenegger and Bronson offer audiences is the opportunity for utterly uncomplicated visceral response, often to political-sounding issues. It is no accident that "Missing in Action" concerns itself with prisoners of war in Vietnam, or "The Terminator" with a nuclear holocaust or "The Evil That Men Do" with human rights violations.

Unlike "Uncommon Valor," another vehement action film about a scheme to rescue missing American soldiers, "Missing in Action" wastes neither time nor words on veterans' complex feelings about Vietnam, or the war's effects on their families. Instead, it begins as an unabashed shoot-'em-up, with Mr. Norris, as an Army colonel, blasting his way through the jungle. Most of his men disappear during the battle, after which the colonel is seen back home, brooding about their fate. A little later, he embarks on his own private rescue mission and returns to Vietnam. The rest of the film is distinguished by its vigorous action sequences, its unequivocal depiction of the Vietnamese as shifty-eyed villains, and an ending in which Mr. Norris's bravado is allowed to show up the weak-kneed foreign policy of the United States Government.

Presumptuous and overbearing as this may sound, it doesn't play that way; in fact, the bashfulness with which Mr. Norris approaches such issues is a large part of his charm. Only with the greatest reluctance does he hurt anyone, albeit also with the greatest finesse. His singlemindedness is so great that he makes a point of not noticing the nude barroom dancers who, in a movie like this, constitute an obligatory bit of atmosphere. And when a female co-star, enlisted in a plot to fool Vietnamese officials by pretending to be in bed with Mr. Norris, tries to pique his genuine interest in such activities, Mr. Norris stares blankly into space. Audiences seem to love his imperviousness even more than his righteous rage.

Of course, no one's self-sufficiency can match Mr. Schwarzenegger's in "The Terminator," which casts him as a post-holocaust robot capable of repairing his own physical equipment. Mr. Schwarzenegger, in preferring the villainous title role to the leading man's heroic part originally offered him, opted for a much steelier character than the grunting lunkheads he had previously played. The change is strategic, since it presents Mr. Schwarzenegger as a figure of pure menace rather than one meant to invite understanding or sympathy. In addition to its lively and intricate plot, which has the Terminator returning from the year 2029 as a hit-man making a mysterious effort to change the future, the film owes much of its success to the star's sheer inexorability. Mr. Schwarzenegger's relentlessness here is matched only by his cautionary import as a harbinger of what a post-nuclear future might bring.

It's true that both Mr. Norris and Mr. Schwarzenegger have a long way to go before they graduate from the ranks of exploitation films to anything above-ground. But both "Missing in Action" and "The Terminator" are significant improvements over what, in each star's career, has come before. Mr. Schwarzenegger may be ready to treat his own hulking strangeness as his most marketable asset, instead of an obstacle to roles that revolve around sex appeal. And Mr. Norris, such a quiet firebrand and so sheepishly sincere, has moved well beyond the all-karate crowd. ■

JUNE 28, 1984

NEW CAUTIONARY FILM RATING READIED FOR PARENTS

Leslie Bennetts

The motion picture industry has designed a new movie rating, a category between the current ratings of PG and R, to warn parents to exercise special caution in allowing children under the age of 13 to attend certain movies. The new rating, known as PG-13, will go into effect on Sunday.

Unlike the current R rating, which is aimed at prohibiting children under the age of 17 from attending a movie unless accompanied by a parent or adult guardian, the PG-13 rating is advisory rather than restrictive. The description to be used on advertisements and other promotional material states: "Parents are strongly cautioned to give special guidance for attendance of children under 13. Some material may be inappropriate for young children."

The criteria used to judge such inappropriateness will include "violence, sensuality, language, theme—such as incest—drugs, suicide, any number of things," said Jack Valenti, president of the Motion Picture Association of America, which represents the large movie studios.

The new rating is the industry's response to a growing clamor from parents and others concerned about what they see as the inadequacy of existing categories of movie ratings. Many critics of the rating system have objected to the PG rating of such recent movies as "Indiana Jones and the Temple of Doom" and "Gremlins," protesting that the levels of violence depicted make the PG description misleading.

OBITUARY

AUGUST 6, 1984

RICHARD BURTON, 58, IS DEAD; Rakish Stage and Screen Star

Maureen Dowd

Elizabeth Taylor and Richard Burton in 1983.

Richard Burton, a Welsh coal miner's son whose celebrity was defined as much by his rakish personal life as his remarkable acting skills, died of a cerebral hemorrhage yesterday in Switzerland. He was 58 years old.

The death stunned the actor's family and friends, who reported that he had been looking tan and healthy and feeling sanguine about his busy work schedule.

One of Britain's greatest Shakespearean stage actors by the age of 27, Mr. Burton offered rugged good looks, a magnetic stage presence and an incomparable voice, as John McPhee once wrote in Time magazine, "with a tympanic resonance so rich and overpowering that it could give an air of verse to a recipe for stewed hare." Even Mr. Burton himself was wont to refer to "the Burton voice."

He was remembered by friends as "a monstrous perfectionist" and a "troubled spirit."

He made more than 40 movies, ranging from such classics as "Who's Afraid of Virginia Woolf," "The Spy Who Came in From the Cold," and "Becket" to multimillion-dollar blockbusters like "Cleopatra" to a string of forgotten failures. He was nominated for seven Academy Awards.

a troubled spirit

Elizabeth Taylor, who was married to Mr. Burton twice and worked often with him in films and plays, was told the news in California, where she was staying with their adopted daughter, Maria Burton, age 23.

"They are extremely, extremely upset," said Miss Taylor's spokeswoman, Chen Sam, weeping.

Many in his profession felt that his tragedy was that he was one of the finest young actors of his generation who squandered his energy on second-rate films, five marriages and legendary bouts with the bottle. ■

OBITUARY

OCTOBER 22, 1984

FRANCOIS TRUFFAUT, NEW WAVE DIRECTOR, DIES

Eric Pace

Francois Truffaut, the exuberant film director whose depictions of children, women and romantic obsessions helped make him a leader of the New Wave group of French movie makers, died yesterday. He was 52 years old.

Widely considered to be the New Wave's most respected member, Mr. Truffaut was one of the most important film directors of the 20th century. Vincent Canby of The New York Times, writing in 1981, called him "one of the most continuously surprising and accomplished directors of his day."

Mr. Truffaut's romantic comedy "Day for Night" (1973) won an Academy Award for best foreign film of the year. His other noteworthy movies included his first full-length feature, "The 400 Blows" (1959), "Shoot the Piano Player" (1960), "Jules and Jim" (1961), "Stolen Kisses" (1968), "The Wild Child" (1970), "The Story of Adele H." (1975) and "Small Change" (1976).

Mr. Truffaut displayed many strengths in the score of feature films that he made at the rate of almost one a year.

His admirers had particular praise for his screen depictions of children, obsessed men, and women driven by strong passions. A writer for The Times noted Mr. Truffaut's interest in "the extremities of romantic agony."

Mr. Truffaut once said that Europeans, unlike Americans, were leery of making movies about the achieving of grand goals.

"We don't make pictures about taking 5,000 steers across the country," he said. "So what do I do? I take sentiments to the end instead of enterprises"—as in "The Woman Next Door" (1981), which was about adulterous passion.

The emotion that Mr. Truffaut conjured with most was love—in many forms. One particularly memorable treatment was in "Shoot the Piano Player" with Charles Aznavour.

"There is more truth in the bedroom," Mr. Truffaut once said by way of explanation, "than in the office or the board room." ■

JULY 8, 1985

THE SEQUEL BECOMES THE NEW BANKABLE FILM STAR

Aljean Harmetz

HOLLYWOOD, July 7—At last Hollywood has found a star who won't throw tantrums, demand a higher salary or insist on first-class airplane tickets home from location every weekend.

"We used to have bankable actors," said Steve Randall, marketing vice president at Tri-Star. "Now the most bankable thing going is the sequel to a successful movie. Once a movie is successful, the concept of the movie itself becomes a star."

Of the top 10 box-office movies of 1984, nine are already being mined for sequels. There will definitely be "Ghostbusters II," a third movie starring Harrison Ford as the archeologist hero of "Indiana Jones," "The Karate Kid II," and "Star Trek IV." "Police Academy II" has already been made and sent to its fate in theaters. Despite poor reviews, the movie did well enough so that there will probably be a "Police Academy III." "Jewel of the Nile," the sequel to "Romancing the Stone," is now in production on exotic locations along the Mediterranean. "Sudden Impact" was the fourth movie in Clint Eastwood's "Dirty Harry" series and there is bound to be a fifth. And sequels to "Gremlins," No. 3 on the 1984 list, and "Beverly Hills Cop," No. 4, are seriously being discussed.

The only movie resistant to a sequel is the Academy Award-winning best movie of 1983, "Terms of Endearment." The fifth most successful film of 1984, "Terms" was a serious movie that ended with the death of a major character.

Hollywood has always made sequels. What is new is the cost and box-office potential of sequels and the intensity with which Hollywood is spewing them out.

Hollywood really became aware of the box-office potential of sequels with George Lucas's "Star Wars" trilogy and Sylvester Stallone's "Rocky" movies. Suddenly the returns for characters audiences wanted to see again were astronomical. "Rocky" grossed $117 million in 1976. "Rocky III" grossed $123 million in 1982. The 1978 "Star Wars" has sold nearly $400 million worth of tickets.

Harold Ramis, Dan Aykroyd, and Bill Murray in a scene from the film "Ghostbusters," 1984.

"The Empire Strikes Back" grossed $280 million. "The Return of the Jedi," the last movie in Mr. Lucas's trilogy, zoomed past its predecessor to gross $330 million.

"If something works at the box-office, now you make the sequel much faster," said Alan Ladd Jr., president of the MGM/UA Entertainment Company, where "Poltergeist II" is currently in production. "I guess people want to know what they're paying their $5 to see." ■

OBITUARY

OCTOBER 11, 1985

ORSON WELLES IS DEAD AT 70; Innovator of Film and Stage

Orson Welles, the Hollywood "boy wonder" who created the film classic "Citizen Kane," scared tens of thousands of Americans with a realistic radio report of a Martian invasion of New Jersey and changed the face of film and theater with his daring new ideas, died yesterday in Los Angeles, apparently of a heart attack. He was 70 years old and lived in Las Vegas, Nev.

Despite the feeling of many that his career—which evoked almost constant controversy over its 50 years—was one of largely unfulfilled promise, Welles eventually won the respect of his colleagues. He received the Lifetime Achievement Award of the American Film Institute in 1975, and last year the Directors Guild of America gave him its highest honor, the D. W. Griffith Award.

In film, his innovations in deep-focus technology and his use of theater esthetics—long takes without close-ups, making the viewer's eye search the screen as if it were a stage—created a new vocabulary for the cinema.

By age 24, he was already being described by the press as a has-been—a cliche that would dog him all his life. But at that very moment Welles was creating "Citizen Kane," generally considered one of the best motion pictures ever made. This scenario was repeated several times. His second film, "The Magnificent Ambersons," was poorly received, but is now also regarded as

OCTOBER 11, 1986

The All-American Guy Behind 'Blue Velvet'

Nan Robertson

David Lynch loves the description of his new film, "Blue Velvet," by one of his sound mixers: "It's like Norman Rockwell meets Hieronymus Bosch."

The movie—one of the most talked-and written-about of the year, seeming to divide audiences into those who love it and find it brilliant and bizarre, and those who hate it and find it sick and disgusting—has been drawing around-the-block lines in New York for the last three weeks.

It begins with Bobby Vinton's rendition of the 1950's tune "Blue Velvet" against scenes of an idyllic small American city with whiter-than-white picket fences and redder-than-red roses. It moves within minutes to a severed, ant-covered human ear lying in a field. And that's only the beginning.

The writer and director of "Blue Velvet," Mr. Lynch is as clean-cut and innocent-looking as the actor Kyle MacLachlan, the movie's hero, who follows the grisly clue of the ear into a nightmarish world of murder and sexual perversity.

Weirdness is a Lynch trademark, from his first full-length movie, a 1978 cult classic called "Eraserhead," through the haunting "Elephant Man" to "Dune," also starring Mr. MacLachlan.

Yet Mr. Lynch, the son of a research scientist specializing in tree diseases and growth for the Department of Agriculture, is the product of an all-American boyhood spent in small cities in Montana, Idaho and Washington State.

Lumberton, the town in the movie, "is sort of a thing from my past," he said. "It has an American feeling, a wholesome feeling, with a clumsy, comical side to it."

That is the Hieronymus Bosch part beneath the Norman Rockwell exterior of David Lynch. He is as fascinated by forbidden and unhealthy subjects as he is by the surface of sunny, cornball Lumberton—a mirror of what he called his "picture-perfect" boyhood homes.

Mr. Lynch, looking for a foreigner to play Dorothy because he "needed somebody for the part who would seem mysterious, lost and vulnerable," was introduced to Miss Rossellini, the daughter of Ingrid Bergman and Roberto Rossellini, by a mutual friend in a restaurant.

"You look strangely familiar," were the first words out of Mr. Lynch's mouth. "You could be Ingrid Bergman's daughter." The friend said, "You idiot—she is Ingrid Bergman's daughter!"

It could have been a line out of "Blue Velvet." ■

Isabella Rossellini and David Lynch attend the 59th Annual Academy Awards on March 30, 1987.

a classic, although the distributors re-edited it and Welles never liked the result. "Falstaff" and "Touch of Evil," two of his later films, were also changed by others before their release.

For his failure to realize his dreams, Welles blamed his critics and the financiers of Hollywood. Others blamed what they described as his erratic, egotistical, self-indulgent and self-destructive temperament. But in the end, few denied his genius.

He was a Falstaffian figure, 6 feet 2 inches tall, weighing well over 200 pounds, with a huge appetite for good food and drink and large cigars. Loud, brash, amusing and insufferable by turns, he made friends and enemies by the score.

Welles inspired harsh criticism, yet most people felt that even his most unsuccessful, most self-indulgent works all had some feature, some turn that was memorable. There were no dissenters when, at the dedication of a Theater Hall of Fame in New York in 1972, his name was among the first to be chosen.

AUGUST 6, 1986

Eating the Lotus of Movie Stardom

Benjamin J. Stein

Ben Stein

(cont'd. next page)

(continued from previous page)

Eating the Lotus Of Movie Stardom

LOS ANGELES—Imagine if you could take a pill that would make you cool. I don't mean cool in the sense of low temperature, but cool as in hip, with-it, admired, buffed out, radical.

You can. It's called having a featured part in a summer hit movie.

Eight months ago, by total chance, without ever having seen the inside of an acting school, without ever having read scripts or gone on a cattle call, I was given a part in "Ferris Bueller's Day Off."

By a stroke of luck, my part was built up on the day of the shooting, and the director and editor left me in the final cut. I played a teacher asking a group of torpid students if they had ever heard of the Great Depression. When no one answered, I would say, "Anyone? Anyone?" in a mournful cadence.

Now the movie is playing on about one thousand screens. It's brought in $60 million, and my life has changed, based upon no more than one hundred and fifty seconds on screen.

Example: At a malt shop in Van Nuys, a group of teenagers sitting at a table literally gasped when I walked in the door two nights ago. "Ohmigod," one Val said to the others. "That's the guy from 'Ferris Bueller.'"

"That's better anyway," he said. "Because you don't want to be recognized and have people like crash into you because they're staring so hard." "My thoughts exactly," I said. On a side street in Van Nuys, a carload of Mexican-American teenagers pulled up to me. First one looked, then looked again, then spoke in Spanish. Then the whole carload rolled down their windows, looked over and said, in unison, "Anyone? Anyone?" laughed hysterically, and zoomed away.

At Morton's, a hangout of the true powers in Hollywood, after the movie's first big weekend, the waiters stood in a circle and stared at me. Every one of them is a potential actor, going to classes, the whole bit. "God, you were great," the headwaiter said. "We were going to give this table to Paul Newman, but he's not coming in after all, so you have it. It's our actor's table." The phone has been ringing 10 times a day all summer. Studio heads call. Major agents call. My sister in Brooklyn called. My parents, who live in Washington, D.C., have seen the movie four times and always call to tell me how great I was.

All of this is for two and a half minutes on the screen, and I didn't have to change at all! No crash diets, no new clothes, no trips to Club Med, no drugs. I'm still the same brainoed-out nerd. But to the outside world, I'm a righteous dude, cooler than ZZ Top, just for standing in front of a klieg light. Who in his right mind would not do anything for this kind of miracle?

Anyone? Anyone?

"Oh, forget it," said another Val. "What would a big movie star be doing here?"

But I was there, heh, heh. I joined them at their table and gave one of them my autograph on her napkin. "I've seen it three times," she said. "You were so rad!" At Gelson's Supermarket in North Hollywood, a bag boy of about 17 stared at me as he stowed my diet pizza. "Are you a movie star?" he asked me shyly.

"Well, I have been in a movie," I said modestly.

"Oh, you're the guy in the movie, the one who says 'Anyone, anyone,' aren't you? You were so great. Could you sign my grocery bag?"

He insisted on taking my bags out to my new Toyota. "I gave the Porsche to charity," I said demurely.

Let's try this: No more defense program, O.K.? Instead, we'll put Gorbachev in a movie. No need to aid the contras, because we'll put Commandante Ortega in a comedy with Rodney Dangerfield. We won't need trade wars, because we'll co-star Nakasone with Rachel Ward.

Who would ever want to wage worldwide aggression, close newspapers, or dump computer chips, after seeing what life is all about—being in a movie? Who would ever want to do anything mean after having eaten the lotus of movie stardom?

Of course, some day the movie will stop playing and people will stop remembering that I was ever in it, or that I was ever cool. You know what? Frankly, my dear, I don't give a damn, because I'll think about that tomorrow. ■

MARCH 15, 1987

MARCHING TOWARD MATURITY

Janet Maslin

John Hughes is a man with few champions, and for good reason. His detractors would argue that he has made some of the most cavalier, sophomoric films in recent years, and they would be right. They could say that "Ferris Bueller's Day Off," for example, reaches a pinnacle of shameless pandering with its plot about a smug, self-congratulatory high school boy who decides to skip school by conning his witless parents into believing he is ill. This boy's idea of a meaningful gesture is encouraging a friend to wreck his father's Ferrari. His life is so privileged and unexamined that the thought of "Ferris Bueller's Day Off" being viewed as representative Americana by foreign audiences is frightening.

It could be noted that Mr. Hughes's "Weird Science" is almost as bad, and that even his Molly Ringwald trilogy—"Sixteen Candles," "The Breakfast Club," "Pretty in Pink"—treats teenage concerns like dating, fashion and popularity as if they were matters of state. And his critics could certainly say that Mr. Hughes, who is somewhere in his mid-30's, is too old for this sort of thing. They would be right about that, too.

But to concentrate on this is to ignore the more important facts about Mr. Hughes: that he burst onto the scene with the hilarious screenplay for one film ("National Lampoon's Vacation") and the potentially funny idea for another ("Mr. Mom"); that he has since carved out a significant section of the moviegoing public and made it his own, with five films grossing a reported $200 million in three years' time; that he is now ready to set his sights on an older audience.

What marks all of Mr. Hughes's films, first and foremost, is their lack of condescension to teenage characters and their real understanding of how these characters feel. Much of "Sixteen Candles," for example, seems to come directly from the heart of a lovestruck, sullen, deliriously adolescent girl (played by Miss

Anthony Michael Hall and Molly Ringwald browsing in a record shop during break in location shooting of "The Breakfast Club."

Ringwald). Mr. Hughes understands this girl's every thought. He knows that her reaction, for example, to the sight of visiting grandparents setting up shop in her bedroom would be a fine blend of affection and horror, and that mood is captured perfectly in Miss Ringwald's aghast expression.

These nuances, the ones that launched Mr. Hughes's career, are distinctly tiny, which is what makes them so real. Most of the John Hughes adolescents care more about sex appeal than sex itself, and have no real money worries (even if they go to school with much wealthier peers). They care about high school status, about being liked and accepted and about the compromises that go into winning their friends' approval. These are things that have made Mr. Hughes's films fiercely engaging for adolescent viewers, especially American ones, and of very limited interest to anyone else.

Beneath the up-to-the-minute flourishes that help sell the film to Mr. Hughes's longstanding admirers, there lurks a sweet, familiar love story any audience might enjoy, a story whose resolution is every bit as charming as it is unreal. The result is something much less dependent on little details, and more involving on the basis of a plot that might work just as well if the characters were older. ■

AUGUST 30, 1987

VCR's Give Movies a Fresh Start

Vincent Can

This is written in praise of the video cassette recorder, even as one attempts to deal with the sad news of the imminent demise of the Regency Theater, Manhattan's foremost film repertory house. The Regency has been sold to a giant exhibition combine and is due to be closed next week, remodeled and turned into yet another first-run theater on Manhattan's gentrified Upper West Side.

The existence of the video cassette recorder certainly hasn't made things easier for repertory houses, but, in this case, I suspect that VCR's did less to undercut the old Regency than rising real estate values.

When it opened here last summer, Mike Nichols's "Heartburn," based on Nora Ephron's adaptation of her own comic roman a clef, received mostly feeble reviews. They generally agreed that "Heartburn" had its funny moments but that, basically, it was nothing to break your neck to see, much less write home about.

I was away at the time it arrived. When I returned to town, I somehow didn't get around to looking for it until it had disappeared from the neighborhood theater near me.

In another era, that might have been the end of "Heartburn," at least until it showed, briefly, on pay television, or on free television, sliced up like last week's newspaper, for use as filler between the award-winning commercials. This would have been the film's only hope. For all intents and purposes, "Heartburn" would have become a non-movie.

That, however, was in the old, pre-video cassette days. Today movies that haven't been smash hits in their theatrical engagements turn up less than a year later, in video rental shops, side by side with the latest masterpieces of John Avildsen, John Hughes and Joe Dante, and golden oldies by Michael Curtiz and Irving Rapper. On the shelf of the video shop, every movie is the same size. Every movie is equal. It's true that theatrical films do not look the same on the small screen as they do in theaters. At the moment, there's no way that a small screen can reproduce the clarity of the image seen on the big screen. Sound levels also may be off. But, just as often, the color values of a video cassette may be even better than those of a theatrical print caught near the end of a long first run.

Most important, however, is that films continue to exist after their initial release. They aren't sent away to air-conditioned vaults in North Dakota.

What I'm trying to say is that "Heartburn," which I rented 10 days ago, is an exceptionally good movie, an opinion possibly affected by my expectations (not great) in the same way that high expectations of first-run audiences may have led to disappointment. Whatever the reasons, the differences of opinion couldn't have been expressed 10 years ago. A year after its release, the film would be in limbo. There would have been no easy way to catch up with it. ■

FEBRUARY 16, 1988

If Willis Gets $5 Million, How Much for Redford?

Aljean Harmetz

20th Century-Fox has paid Bruce Willis $5 million to star in a movie. For Hollywood, the result is equivalent to an earthquake. The map of movie-star salaries must now be redrawn.

"This throws the business out of whack," said Alan Ladd Jr., chairman of Metro-Goldwyn-Mayer Pictures, a division of the MGM/UA Communications Company. Speaking of the money Fox offered Mr. Willis to star in "Die Hard," an action-adventure movie, Mr. Ladd said, "Like everybody else in town, I was stunned."

Hollywood has a definite hierarchy. An actor who has just starred in a big hit can move several places forward in the line for the feeding trough—perhaps from $3 million a picture to $4 million. But the last major realignment came in 1982 when Dustin Hoffman was paid approximately $5.5 million to star in "Tootsie." That huge jump from top salaries in the $2 million to $3 million range led to similar front-of-the-pack salaries for Warren Beatty and Robert Redford.

Mr. Willis, the star of the television series "Moonlighting," has been seen in one movie, the unmemorable "Blind Date," which was 31st in the ranking of successful movies of 1987. If he is paid $5 million, say distraught executives, what will Michael Douglas have to be paid for the next sequel to "Romancing the Stone"? What will $3 million stars who have proved their worth at the box office—including Tom Cruise and Michael J. Fox—have to be paid for their next movies? ■

JUNE 25, 1989

IN A NEW FILM, SPIKE LEE TRIES TO DO THE THING

Michael T. Kaufman

Even before "Do The Right Thing," opens on Friday, Spike Lee, its producer, director, writer and star, has already got what he expected most from the film: hot debate, heavy discussion and even denunciation from some who think he did the wrong thing.

The film, both funny and surrealistically sorrowful, has generated torrents of written and spoken commentary. Some who have seen it have warned that it might spark violence. Others have offered tributes, contending that Mr. Lee has dealt with a troubling issue—race relations—in an inspired, honest and troubling way.

The assessments will surely proliferate and clash further once the movie opens. But what is clear enough now is that Mr. Lee, a bold, 32-year-old Brooklyn native, has with this film ventured into an area of film making that has touched a raw nerve.

"Essentially what I hoped was that it would provoke everybody, white and black," said the iconoclastic film maker of the movie, which describes how, on the hottest day of the year, the often amusing foibles, prejudices and conflicting group allegiances of generally symbiotic neighbors in Brooklyn's Bedford-Stuyvesant escalate into a tragic killing of a black man by the police and the torching of a white-owned pizza parlor.

While the film maker was pleased by all the talk that has preceded the film, he was somewhat angered by articles published around the country suggesting that "Do The Right Thing" might inspire violence. "I knew I would take heat," he said, noting that he had absorbed much criticism, largely from blacks, for his treatment of color prejudices of light- and dark-skinned blacks in his second feature film, "School Daze." "I figured there would be a hundred times more this time," he said.

(cont'd. next page)

Movie poster for "Do The Right Thing."

JULY 17, 1989

25 Films to Become U.S. Treasures

Aljean Harmetz

American movies have been called many things. Now, 25 of them will officially be called treasures. The public will be warned when any of those classic films are significantly altered.

Under the National Film Preservation Act passed by Congress last year, representatives from 13 movie organizations are to meet at the University of California at Los Angeles on Wednesday to try to decide on the first 25 movies to be taken under the Government's wing.

In preliminary balloting, 57 movies were nominated by at least 2 of the 13 members of the National Film Preservation Board. The leader, a surprise, was the 1939 movie made from John Steinbeck's novel "The Grapes of Wrath." It had eight votes. "Casablanca" and "It's a Wonderful Life" had seven votes apiece. "The Best Years of Our Lives," "Citizen Kane" and "On the Waterfront" were nominated by six members.

The National Film Preservation Act of 1988 has a loud roar but no teeth. Angered by the computerized coloring of classic black-and-white films and the routine cutting of scenes in order to make movies fit a television time slot, the Directors Guild of America led a successful fight for a National Film Registry.

Among the other movies that ranked high in the preliminary balloting were "Gone With the Wind," "High Noon," "Mr. Smith Goes to Washington," "The Searchers" and "Snow White and the Seven Dwarfs" with five votes apiece.

Four votes each went to "The Apartment," "Doctor Strangelove," "The Godfather," "His Girl Friday," "The Maltese Falcon," "Rebel Without a Cause," "Sunset Boulevard," "To Kill a Mockingbird," "West Side Story" and "The Wizard of Oz." Four votes were also cast for one documentary, Robert Flaherty's "Nanook of the North," and for four silent films: King Vidor's "Crowd," Buster Keaton's "General," D. W. Griffith's "Intolerance" and Charlie Chaplin's "City Lights." Chaplin's "Modern Times," which has a sound and music track but no dialogue, also got four votes. ■

(continued from previous page)

"That's O.K. The only thing that really hurts are those articles that are saying that 'Do The Right Thing' is going to cause riots. I know black people better than those critics. They are not going to go crazy because of a film. Meanwhile, I know that all you can do is the best you can do, and I did not make this film to make people go crazy." Mr. Lee, whose film stars Danny Aiello, Ossie Davis, Ruby Dee, Richard Edson, Giancarlo Esposito and John Turturro, as well as the director himself, received very positive reviews in May at the Cannes film festival.

Mr. Lee said the idea for "Do The Right Thing" first germinated when he read news accounts of the 1986 incident in Howard Beach, Queens, where white youths attacked three black men, one of whom, Michael Griffith, was killed by a passing car as he sought to escape his tormentors. At the end of the credits for "Do The Right Thing," Mr. Lee includes a dedication to the family of Mr. Griffith and to the families of five other black New Yorkers who died in controversial circumstances.

. . . has touched a raw nerve

JULY 16, 1989

HOW ROCK IS CHANGING HOLLYWOOD'S TUNE

Stephen Holden

Jack Nicholson's fiendish Joker and Michael Keaton's Caped Crusader aren't the only forces that collide in the smash-hit movie "Batman." The film's noisy soundtrack presents a pitched battle between the two strains of music that have accompanied movies since the dawn of the sound era: one derived from high culture, the other from pop. The majority of the film's score is loud, post-Wagnerian action music composed by Danny Elfman. Sly, subterranean funk songs by Prince make up the rest.

For years many in the film industry have worried that the rise of the pop compilation might spell the demise of the traditional score. But it hasn't happened; nor is it likely to. Artistically, the late 80's are a very healthy period for movie music. Major directors like Martin Scorsese have the power to see their personal, offbeat musical visions reach fruition in their films.

And they are calling on the art-rock fringe. Besides Peter Gabriel's score for Mr. Scorsese's film "The Last Temptation of Christ," the last year has seen distinguished iconoclastic movie scores by Scott Johnson for "Patty Hearst" and Philip Glass for "The Thin Blue Line." Jonathan Demme's "Married to the Mob" used a peppy nontraditional score by David Byrne.

It wasn't until 1978, when the soundtrack for "Saturday Night Fever" became the best-selling album in history that movie producers and record executives recognized the full economic potential of cross-marketing movies with records.

From that moment, the race was on in the record industry to create blockbuster soundtrack albums for potential hit movies. The albums for "Urban Cowboy," "Flashdance," "Footloose," "Beverly Hills Cop," "The Big Chill," "Top Gun," "Cocktail," "Dirty Dancing" and "Beaches" are among the many soundtracks that have sold in the millions.

With the infusion of pop, rock and other elements of contemporary music, movies have become louder, just like the rest of the environment. Audiences who have grown up going to rock concerts, listening to rock radio and to MTV expect a relentless barrage of images and sounds. In the contemporary pop movie, the hits follow one another as quickly as the car chases and explosions in a James Bond movie. ■

FEBRUARY 15, 1980

DAN RATHER TO SUCCEED CRONKITE

Les Brown

Dan Rather in 1980.

CBS News announced yesterday that Walter Cronkite would voluntarily step down early next year as anchor of the country's most watched television newscast, "The CBS Evening News," and that he would be succeeded by a younger colleague, Dan Rather.

William A. Leonard, president of CBS News, said of Mr. Cronkite, who is 63 years old, had been asking for almost two years to be relieved of the "day-to-day grind" to concentrate on hard news and special-events assignments and to work on a new occasional series, "Universe."

Mr. Cronkite said of Mr. Rather, "I can't think of anyone in the entire business as well qualified to take over that job."

MAY 25, 1980

The TV News, Starring Ted Turner

Tony Schwartz

Ted Turner being interviewed at the CNN studio in Atlanta, 1980.

ATLANTA—The headquarters are in an enormous antebellum-style mansion on 22 acres adjacent to Georgia Tech University. They are equipped with a newsroom the size of a football field and $10 million in state-of-the-art technology. Barring last-minute hitches, the Cable News Network will go on the air next Sunday evening as the nation's only 24-hour-a-day, seven-day-a-week all-news network, broadcasting via satellite to more than two million cable television homes.

The Cable News Network represents a tremendous gamble. It could eventually evolve into a money machine, reaching tens of millions of homes at a fraction of what it costs to run a major network.

CNN is an audacious project, but scarcely the first one for 41-year-old Robert

E. "Ted" Turner. He is the yachtsman who came to prominence by winning the America's Cup race three years ago in Newport, R.I. He is also the owner of three Atlanta professional sports teams and of WTBS in Atlanta, an immensely profitable sports and entertainment "superstation" that was his first venture into cable broadcasting. Mr. Turner is equal parts an entrepreneur and an evangelist, and 24-hour news just happens to be his current crusade.

Although he is an utter novice at the news business, Mr. Turner is investing $40 million in CNN this year and even his brightest forecasts suggest that his network will continue losing money at least until 1982. The obstacles he faces are formidable. CNN will be attempting to offer six times the amount of news that each of the three networks provide at one fifth of the cost, and with a total staff about the size of a network Washington bureau.

In a sense, Mr. Turner faces a future analogous to that of the cable industry as a whole: The promise is enormous, but the territory is so uncharted, that the future is uncertain. The number of homes wired for cable has doubled since 1973 to more than 16 million today—about a fifth of all those with television. By 1990, half of the homes with television are expected to have cable. ■

AUGUST 21, 1980

WHERE CABLE TV STANDS AFTER F.C.C. DEREGULATION

Tony Schwartz

Although cable television has been around since the 1940's, it is only in the last several years that it has begun to emerge as a formidable competitor to broadcast television. Cable television is spreading at a fast pace and, increasingly, new systems are offering viewers a wide array of programming received from satellites, including commercial-free first-run movies, sporting events, a 24-hour news channel, and such specialty offerings as an all-children's network, and an all-Spanish-language network.

The cable boom is largely attributable to a series of decisions by the Federal Communications Commission, which has begun progressively repealing regulations that have limited the expansion and reach of cable. Four weeks ago the F.C.C. voted to repeal two of the last rules that had limited the variety of programs available on cable systems.

The following explains how the cable industry shapes up in the aftermath of the F.C.C. action.

Q. How widespread is cable television?

A. There are more than 4,200 cable systems throughout the United States, which reach approximately 17 million homes. By contrast, broadcast television reaches 75 million homes. The number of channels on cable systems varies widely, from less than a dozen on the oldest systems, to as many as 54 in some of the new systems under construction.

Q. What services does cable offer that attract subscribers?

A. At the start, the sole advantage of cable television was that it provided better reception than was generally possible with an antenna. But now, in addition, it offers a variety of programming alternatives. The most popular services are the pay networks such as Home Box Office (HBO) and Showtime, which feature commercial-free first-run movies and other entertainment specials available at a separate monthly cost to subscribers.

Q. What regulations must cable systems continue to observe?

A. First, they cannot show current network programs, such as "Dallas" or "60 Minutes," except on the network channels on which they are shown normally. Second, cable systems must also continue to black out local sporting events if the local broadcast station is also obliged to do so. Such blackouts take place in cases where the sporting event has not been sold out.

Q. Will the F.C.C. ruling be damaging to the broadcast industry?

A. The F.C.C. commissioners based their decision on a study that showed broadcast stations stood to lose less than 10 percent of their audience to cable as a result of the deregulation. Moreover, the F.C.C. argued that such losses to broadcasters should be more than offset by an increase in advertising revenues.

Broadcasters counter that the F.C.C. rulings are unfair both because they will no longer get the exclusivity they have paid for, and because cable systems pay much less for rebroadcasting programs than do broadcast stations, which buy programs directly from the syndicators. ■

NOVEMBER 23, 1980

DALLAS BROKE RATING RECORD, NETWORK SAYS

Paul L. Montgomery

A group portrait of the Ewing family from the U.S. television soap opera "Dallas," 1980.

(cont'd. next page)

(continued from previous page)

DALLAS BROKE RATING RECORD, NETWORK SAYS

The episode of the television series "Dallas" broadcast Friday night got the highest audience ratings ever for a regular series and will probably surpass the nationwide record for any entertainment program, the CBS network said yesterday.

A spokesman said the episode, coming after five months of ballyhoo and speculation about who shot the series' antihero, J.R. Ewing, apparently attracted about 82 million viewers in the United States.

According to the network, the "overnight" or preliminary ratings were 45.9 with a 65 percent share of the television audience in New York, 42.5 with a 68 percent share in Los Angeles and 54.8 with a 76 percent share in Chicago. The ratings figure reflects the percentage of televison sets in the metropolitan areas tuned to the program, as opposed to turned off or tuned to other stations; the share is the percentage of people watching television at that time who chose the program.

In "Dallas" it turned out that Mr. Ewing's sister-in-law and former mistress, Kristin Shephard, apparently had pulled the trigger, according to flashbacks through the eyes of Mr. Ewing's wife, Sue Ellen.

Miss Shephard was the cofavorite with Cliff Barnes, a business rival, in informal betting on the identity of the assailant; both had been listed at odds of 4-1, followed closely by Mrs. Ewing at 5-1. The New York Times switchboard got a number of calls Friday night, including some from England and South Africa, inquiring about the identity of the assailant. Many calls appeared to be from bettors. ■

who
shot
JR?

DECEMBER 7, 1980

Who's Behind The 'Nightline' Success Story?

John J. O'Connor

For years, the news departments of the three commercial networks have been struggling to expand their nightly half-hour editions, to offer viewers more than the "headline service" that is crammed into the about 22 minutes overseen currently by the Messrs. Cronkite, Chancellor and Reynolds. Affiliate stations, however, have been reluctant to turn over the networks more of their increasingly valuable local-programming time. The result has been an ostensible stalemate, with the network people now talking optimistically about the possibility of getting an extra 15 minutes in the not-so-distant future.

In fact, one network has already extended its news time—not in the early evening but, taking an imaginative leap, in the late evening. "ABC News Nightline" offers the viewer a legitimate choice at 11:30 P.M. NBC has Johnny Carson; CBS has an old movie or television rerun; ABD has Ted Koppell anchoring a news report that is usually connected with some event that happened that day. Much to the surprise of just about everybody, the news production is doing quite well in the crucial sector of audience ratings. When a big story is breaking, "Nightline" can knock Johnny Carson off his long-time top-rated perch.

"Nightline" began a little more than a year ago with the taking of American hostages in Iran. On Nov. 8, 1979, ABC News introduced a series of late-night news specials entitled "The Iran Crisis: America Held Hostage." Under the guidance of Jeff Gralnick, one of the more ambitious of ABC News younger vice presidents, and with Robert Siegenthaler as executive producer, the reports progressed from updates on the hostage situation to broader essays on United States-Iran relations and on the Islamic revolution. A 20-minute edition of "Nightline" was established as a permanent news program that, Monday through Thursday, would focus on one major story and would include reporting from correspondents in the field as well as live interviews with Mr. Koppel. It was that point that William E. Lord took over as executive producer.

Mr. Lord, still only in his 40's, has been working at ABC News for 19 years. He is enthusiastic about "Nightline's" present and future. In January, the program will be expanded to a half-hour. In April, it will pick up an extra evening, running Monday through Friday. ■

JANUARY 12, 1981

PREMIERE OF 'DYNASTY,' A SERIES ON AN OIL FAMILY

Tom Buckley

John Forsythe and Linda Evans

It's mighty low-grade crude that comes oozing out of the tube in "Dynasty," which will have a three-hour premiere showing from 8 to 11 P.M. tonight on ABC-TV.

An embarrassingly obvious knockoff of "Dallas," "Dynasty" deals with a ruthless petroleum baron, played by John Forsythe; his new wife, Linda Evans; his two children by a previous marriage, one of them a young woman in training to be Messalina and the other a young man who is revealed to be homosexual, and their assorted enemies, friends, lovers and employees.

Not one of these characters had a moment of believability in the endless opening installment. It begins with the seizure of the tycoon's holdings in the Middle East by troops who for some reason are wearing what look like American uniforms, goes on to his wedding and ends with his sabotaging of a promising exploratory well being drilled by a grizzled old wildcatter.

The action is supposed to be taking place in and around Denver, which has in fact become a center of the oil business in recent years, and there are establishing shots of the city skyline and Pikes Peak, but everything else looks as though it were filmed in the environs of Hollywood.

Written by Richard and Esther Shapiro, who are also credited as the creators of the series, the roles are so devoid of life and the situations of dramatic impact that it is hard to judge the performers fairly.

"Dynasty" is a production of Aaron Spelling, who, either alone or in collaboration with Leonard Goldberg, provided many of the shows that helped to propel ABC into first place in the Nielsen audience popularity ratings for several seasons. This ranking has been lost, at least for the time being, to CBS, the home of the often top-rated "Dallas." ■

NOVEMBER 10, 1981

LETTERMAN REPLACING SNYDER

Tony Schwartz

NBC announced yesterday that a one-hour entertainment show starring the comedian David Letterman would take over the slot occupied for eight years by the "Tomorrow" show starring Tom Snyder.

"The David Letterman Show," which is scheduled to begin Feb. 1, will run Monday through Thursday from 12:30 to 1:30 A.M., following the hourlong "Tonight" show starring Johnny Carson. It will originate in NBC's Rockefeller Center studios.

Mr. Snyder had been offered the opportunity to continue as host of "Tomorrow" from 1:30 to 2:30 A.M., following the Letterman show. But he told NBC yesterday that such an option was unacceptable.

For Mr. Letterman, the new show represents a second chance at NBC. Last summer he had an 18-week run with a 90-minute morning talk show. The show was widely praised and won an Emmy Award, but was canceled because of low ratings. Many critics contended that Mr. Letterman's fast-paced, off-the-wall comedy style was better suited to the ambience of late night—and its younger audience.

Mr. Carson's contract gives him approval over the show that follows his, and as part of the deal his production company will produce the new "David Letterman Show." ■

David Letterman, 1980.

OBITUARY

MARCH 6, 1982

JOHN BELUSHI, MANIC COMIC OF TV AND FILMS, DIES

Robert D. McFadden

John Belushi, the manic, rotund comedian whose outrageous antics and spastic impersonations on the "Saturday Night Live" television show propelled him to stardom in the 1970's, was found dead yesterday in a rented bungalow in Hollywood, where he had launched a film career in recent years.

The 33-year-old actor was found by his physical trainer, William Wallace, in a bedroom of a small house Mr. Belushi had rented at the Chateau Marmont Hotel, a famed hostelry on Sunset Boulevard favored by entertainers.

(cont'd. next page)

(continued from previous page)

The cause of death was not immediately determined, but there were no indications of foul play or drugs on the premises, the police said. A hotel security guard said Mr. Belushi may have choked to death on some food, but a heart attack was not ruled out by the police.

Mr. Belushi, whose bulging belly, rasping voice, wild eyes and lunatic portrayals of grunting Samurai warriors, antenna-quivering killer bees and greasy luncheonette hash-slingers made him a favorite of television audiences, was a member of NBC-TV's "Saturday Night Live" troupe from 1975 to 1979, when he left for Hollywood.

Since then, he had appeared in a number of films: "The National Lampoon's Animal House," "1941," "Old Boyfriends," "Continental Divide," and, most recently, "Neighbors."

Teamed with Dan Aykroyd, one of his old side-kicks from "Saturday Night Live," he also starred in "The Blues Brothers," a movie based on the dead-pan antics of a pair of white soul-singers.

Tribunes to Mr. Belushi were voiced last night by many of his former associates. "He was one of the most intrinsically funny men I have ever known," said Chevy Chase. "I count myself lucky to have known him. We will all miss him." ■

John Belushi in 1981.

APRIL 27, 1982

HOW 'HILL STREET' BROKE THE POLICE-SHOW MOLD

Tony Schwartz

In Los Angeles over the years, while he was working as a writer and producer on a string of police shows including "Columbo," "Richie Brockelman" and "Delvecchio," Steven Bochco would occasionally meet with policemen who had ambitions to write.

"They'd come in to pitch a story, and it would invariably be the worst idea imaginable," Mr. Bochco remembers. "They'd be trying to come up with something based on what they'd seen on television, and it would be completely unreal. Then we'd just sit back and talk about their lives, and these wonderful stories would come pouring out. Cops have extraordinary emotional lives."

It was with that in mind that Mr. Bochco and his partner, Michael Kozoll, were intrigued three years ago when Fred Silverman, then president of NBC, suggested a one-line concept for a series—a police show set in an inner-city precinct with an emphasis on the personal lives of its station-house characters.

The idea ultimately became "Hill Street Blues," arguably the best series on network television, certainly one of the most inventive and consistently absorbing, and now, after a disastrously poor start, a commercial hit, as well.

"We wanted 'Hill Street' to be a show about people who happen to be cops, as opposed to cops who, in some small corner of their lives, happen to be people," Mr. Bochco explained. "We had a strong belief in the cop as hero, not in the macho 'Kojak' sense, but in the sense of an individual performing a thankless task under extreme physical and emotional stress, with no reward to speak of—social, psychological or financial."

From that perspective, Mr. Bochco and Mr. Kozoll sat down to write a script that resisted every formula they had mastered over the years. They avoided a single heroic character in favor of an ensemble of richly variegated characters who were interesting as much for their flaws and quirks as for their virtues. Rather than a central story, they introduced many story lines in each show, few of which were resolved at the end of an episode, and almost never with the good-guy-triumphantly-prevails catharsis that viewers have been conditioned to expect from police shows.

The first script for "Hill Street" was completed in just two weeks, and nearly everyone who read it—including Mr. Silverman—felt it was very special. But when the show made its debut in the fall of 1980, the audience was not enthralled.

"For viewers, I think the experience of the first season was an absolute surprise," Mr. Bochco said. "We did the shows in groups of four, so that it took four hours to resolve a half-dozen stories. If you missed any of the four, you were out of luck. Within each episode, the action was hugely busy. Most television invites you to check it out while you're doing other things. This show was designed to grab you and make you pay attention. I think we were getting people angry. They tuned us out in droves."

But for those who stayed, the series had a cumulative effect. Its texture, complexity and sheer unexpectedness won rave reviews—and a slew of Emmy Awards. But it was not until last fall that "Hill Street" began to attract a large audience. One reason was that it began appearing regularly at 10 P.M. on Thursday each week; another may have been that the series received so much favorable attention that viewers decided to give it a longer look.

For all its style, the key to the strength of "Hill Street Blues" still rests with its characters. "Writing a wonderful character is everything," Mr. Bochco says. "I've always found that you can bust your back producing intricate plots, and then the audience will notice the tiny distinctive detail, the wonderful recognizable human moment that is so horrendously rare on television." Indeed those moments are what encourage viewers to care about the show's characters and to identify with the dilemmas they find themselves in. ■

MARCH 3, 1983

Finale of M*A*S*H Draws Record Number of Viewers

The final episode of "M*A*S*H" on CBS-TV on Monday night was the most-watched single program in television history, according to CBS research. The two-and-a-half hour program drew an estimated total audience of 125 million people.

Tom Freston, the Head of MTV, 1981.

MAY 8, 1983

TV ROCKS WITH MUSIC

Ed Levine

To a strong musical beat, melted cherry ice cream drips onto a woman sunning herself on a beach. A young man in a bathing suit sings about a woman who boards his yacht, her body painted orange, blue and green. Nearby, on an oceangoing raft, another man plays a saxophone.

Next on the television screen: An oil sheik emerges from a fastfood restaurant, munching a hamburger. A fatigue-clad rock band, surrounded by oil derricks, sings about "rockin' the casbah." An armadillo crosses a road. A rocket ship lands on the moon; an astronaut emerges to plant a flag bearing the initials MTV. Voiceover: "MTV, the world's first video-music channel."

The painted woman, the sheik and the others are characters in rock-video clips, brief, song-length blends of rock music and visual images—some with plots (known as "concept" videos), some nonlinear—that can be seen on MTV (Music Television), 24 hours a day, seven days a week. MTV, with a target audience between the ages of 12 and 34, is the advertising-supported, cable-television arm of Warner Amex Satellite Entertainment Corporation, a joint venture of Warner Communications and the American Express Company. Started at a cost of more than $20 million in August 1981, a time when the record business was in trouble, MTV's game plan was formulated by Bob Pittman, WASEC's executive vice president, and John A. Lack, a former WASEC executive vice president. "The radio stations weren't playing new artists," Lack remembers, "so record companies needed new ways to promote records. Cable television offered us the possibility of promoting music in stereo on television." MTV currently beams 300 videos a day through more than 1,500 cable systems into more than 12 million homes throughout the country.

With the exception of several hourlong documentaries or videotapes of rock concerts (video clips run approximately three minutes), MTV shows nothing but videos.

(cont'd. next page)

(continued from previous page)

The most popular ones, determined by audience research, are played four to five times a day. In between, there is patter and rock lore, taped a day in advance, by five video jockeys (VJ's), who work in four- to five-hour shifts. Several times an hour, they offer news morsels about rock musicians.

The troubled record industry, which underwrites most of the videos, sees them as the most promising marketing tool to come along in the 20 years since the proliferation of FM rock stations in the 1960's.

MTV has become, in the words of one record executive, "one of the most important tools in promoting and selling records." One need look no further than the experience of such groups as Men at Work, the Stray Cats and Adam Ant: After initial difficulty in gaining radio exposure, they won wide acceptance after their videos were seen on MTV. ■

NOVEMBER 29, 1983

NBC COMEDY 'CHEERS' TURNS INTO A SUCCESS

Peter Kerr

The cast of the TV series "Cheers" circa 1985.

The scene is a Boston bar, where the regulars hoot, back-slap and dissolve into giggles when somebody makes a joke about sex. Diane Chambers (Shelley Long), a former graduate student working as a waitress, once again is offended. She begins to lecture the customers in her most professorial tone.

DIANE: Ah yes, unlimited sex. The adult male version of owning a candy store. But once you've consumed as much sex as you want for as long as you want, what do you do then?

NORM (a regular): I'd help the poor.

So goes the dialogue in "Cheers," a half-hour NBC television comedy that is one of the network's few success stories this season. After months of dismally low ratings last year, the show has managed this season to gather a respectable audience. And it has done so, critics say, with good acting and witty writing, the type of quality programming that Grant Tinker, the president of NBC, has said he wants on the network.

The show was a particular point of pride for NBC executives this fall when it won five Emmy Awards, including the categories for outstanding comedy, for writing and for direction. Miss Long received the award for outstanding actress in a comedy series for her portrayal of Diane.

" 'Cheers' is a very important comedy for us," said Brandon Tartikoff, the president of the NBC entertainment division. "It is classy, sophisticated and for adults. We never for a second doubted that we would renew it for this year."

Another point of pride for NBC is that the dialogue on the show at times reaches a sophistication that is rare on network television. Jokes have included references to Shakespeare, John Donne and Spinoza. Among other affectations, Diane has the unfortunate habit of dropping phrases in French.

The show was created and developed by three men who have had considerable experience with award-winning television programs, such as "M*A*S*H" and "Taxi"—two brothers, Glen and Les Charles, and James Burrows, who directs the program.

Throughout the program's development, Glen Charles said, the creators attempted to draw ideas for the set, the characters and the dialogue from reality. Glen Charles traveled to Boston to find a bar that could be used as a model for the set. They settled on an establishment named The Bull & Finch. In the program, it took the name "Cheers."

Rhea Perlman, the actress in "Cheers" who plays a tiny, sharp-tongued waitress named Carla Tortelli, was sent to The Bull & Finch to watch the bar in operation. The character of Norm, a bloated, unemployed accountant on a regimen of one beer every half hour, is based on a real character Les Charles said he encountered when he worked as a bartender in college.

The three creators of the show also visited bars around Los Angeles, picking up bits of conversation that would later be used in the show. "Cheers" dialogue that was taken from real bars, included a discussion of which is "the sweatiest movie ever made," and what is the best flavor of canned soup.

NOVEMBER 18, 1984

COSBY PUTS HIS STAMP ON A TV HIT

Sally Bedell Smith

Bill Cosby filming a scene of "The Cosby Show."

"The Cosby Show," appearing each Thursday at 8 P.M., is this season's prime-time phenomenon. A gently funny view of an upper middle-class couple—the husband is a gynecologist, the wife an attorney—and their five children, it is the most popular new series introduced this fall, and it has achieved near-unanimous critical praise. Each week it is seen by an average of 38.3 million people—roughly one-third the viewing audience, and it consistently ranks among the 10 most popular programs. The show's success has helped propel NBC from third to second place in the prime-time ratings.

But "The Cosby Show" is not just another family comedy. Unlike most such series, where contrived plots and rat-a-tat one-liners prevail, the Cosby series attempts to echo reality. It is filled with small moments that prompt chuckles of recognition in the viewer. The family is loving, but there is an edge as well: The children squabble, and the parents get exasperated.

The Cosby show is also different because its family, the Huxtables, is black. Television has had successful comedies based on a variety of black caricatures—maids, butlers and jive-talking ghetto youngsters—but the Cosby show breaks through the stereotypes to portray another view of the black family: intact, successful, sensible and funny without the self-deprecation of such series as "The Jeffersons."

"Some people have said our show is about a white family in blackface," says Bill Cosby. "What does that mean? Does it mean only white people have a lock on living together in a home where the father is a doctor and the mother is a lawyer and the children are constantly being told to study by their parents?"

"This show gives the other side of the black experience. There are a lot of black middle-class families like this one," says Dr. Alvin Poussaint, a prominent black psychiatrist and professor at Harvard University who was hired by Mr. Cosby to evaluate scripts for the show.

A man with strong views as well as a keen sense of comedy, the 47-year- old Mr. Cosby is in large measure responsible for the success of his new show—which at his insistence is taped in Brooklyn rather than Hollywood because he lives in the East and did not want to uproot his family. In front of the camera, he works the magic of the veteran stand-up comic—the dumbstruck stare, the wicked cackle, the refreshingly personalized comedic riffs.

"This show is saying things that go on in an awful lot of homes across the U.S.," says Mr. Cosby, relaxing between rehearsals in his pale-gray dressing room, the walls lined with photographs of his family, jazz musicians and basketball players. "It probably works now because the children love the parents, the parents love each other, yet they still have problems," he continues. "As a kid, I never really enjoyed 'Leave It to Beaver.' There were some good stories, but everything was so placid. The more I did my monologues, the more I found that people have been—not in a serious way, mind you—repressing how they felt about children and themselves. They were beginning to think they were the only ones with the problems of kids not studying or going out and borrowing the car without a license." ■

JANUARY 3, 1985

'MIAMI VICE': ACTION TV WITH SOME NEW TWISTS

Sally Bedell Smith

On the surface, it has all the familiar elements of the standard action program: a pair of undercover detectives, one black, one white, in pursuit of drug dealers in an exotic locale. But "Miami Vice," NBC's police series on Friday nights at 10 P.M., has become the most talked-about dramatic series in the television industry since "Hill Street Blues."

Through its use of music, cinematography, fashion and settings—it is filmed entirely in and around Miami—"Miami Vice" has created a new hybrid for television, the music-video police program. Moreover, unlike most television programs, which tend to lag behind the culture in their look and point of view, "Miami Vice" is aggressively contemporary—with locations in such celebrated post- modern homes as the sleek, flamingo- pink Spear House, and the Italian designer clothes worn by the two stars, Don Johnson, who plays the raspy-voiced Sonny Crockett, and Philip Michael Thomas, who plays Ricardo Tubbs, an ex-New Yorker who wears a small diamond in his left earlobe.

"There is a buzz out there about the show," said Jeff Sagansky, senior vice president for series programs at NBC, "and our surveys show real intense loyalty to the show. The audience that watches it loves it. So far, the audience isn't big enough to

(cont'd. next page)

(continued from previous page)

make a hit, but once the drums get going, we think it will be a hit."

The most striking aspect of "Miami Vice" is its use of music. In most television programs music is employed to emphasize the action on the screen, to highlight tension, for example, or underscore sadness. But "Miami Vice" takes rock-and-roll selections by popular performers, such as the Rolling Stones and Phil Collins, as well as more obscure works by Jamaican Rastafarian reggae groups, and combines them with closely edited film montages to create music videos similar to those shown on MTV Music Television, the round-the-clock rock-music cable channel.

The visual style of "Miami Vice" is as crucial as its sound, according to the producers, and as important in creating the program's distinctiveness. "In the way it is shot, where it is shot, the kind of people it has, 'Miami Vice' conveys a dreamlike quality, yet a certain humanity," said Brandon Tartikoff, president of NBC Entertainment.

The program's directors, who have included Paul Michael Glaser and David Soul, formerly stars of "Starsky and Hutch," also have a mandate to use camera techniques unsual for television to come up with striking images—a stark shot of a hand against a white door, or a polo ball amid horses' hooves, a distant view of a drug dealer doing business from a table on his wide back lawn against a backdrop of cerulean sky, and jarring scenes of violence like the one in a recent episode in which Crockett shot a villain in the forehead after saying, "Maybe you won't even twitch." ■

"Miami Vice" stars Don Johnson and Philip Michael Thomas in 1985.

JANUARY 6, 1985

WHO'S WATCHING TV? IT'S GETTING HARD TO TELL

Sally Bedell Smith

After years of submitting passively to the tyranny of television programmers, viewers are taking charge. With the video-cassette recorder—now in nearly 20 percent of American homes—viewers can tape programs off the air to watch later, they can use their fast-forward button to "zap" or whiz past commercials when they play back programs, or they can ignore the evening's television schedule entirely and play a movie rented from a local video store. And using hand-held channel selectors—now available with one-third of all new television sets sold—viewers can hopscotch around the dial, deftly avoiding commercials that may intrude on their enjoyment.

All this unpredictable behavior is placing great pressure on the ratings that for nearly four decades have been the yardstick for measuring the size and composition of the television audience and whose daily accounting determines which television shows live and die.

"There is no question that the new electronic media are rendering a lot of the traditional ways we measure audiences old-fashioned and basically unsatisfactory for advertisers," says David Braun, director of media services at General Foods Corporation, which spends $243 million a year on television advertising in such programs as "The Cosby Show," "Remington Steele" and "Family Ties."

Indeed, advertisers are worried that viewers are using the new technologies to avoid watching their commercials and that television networks and stations may be overcharging for advertising time. As a consequence, new approaches are being sought, principally by advertisers, that could produce different and more sophisticated insights into how viewers watch television.

"It's possible that we may see more changes in the ratings in the next five years than we have seen in the previous 20," says John Dimling of the Electronic Media Rating Council. But more finely tuned knowledge of the audience could alter television fare as well. Programs with smaller but more attentive and loyal audiences could be shown by the networks rather than mass-appeal programs whose audiences are easily distracted. Or shows could be aimed at more clearly defined groups based on interests and habits as well as age and income. And commercials could change as well, perhaps by being shortened and incorporated into a program's dialogue and story line to avoid zapping. ■

OCTOBER 11, 1985

PLAN FOR A FOX NETWORK INTRIGUES TV INDUSTRY

Peter W. Kaplan

The television industry yesterday was by turns intrigued, skeptical and sympathetic to the announcement that Rupert Murdoch would attempt to start a television network of affiliated stations. Many industry insiders said that while they believed he faced a difficult challenge he stood a reasonably good chance of succeeding.

Mr. Murdoch announced Wednesday that he would consolidate his recently purchased 20th Century-Fox Film Corporation with the six Metromedia Inc. television stations he has agreed to buy.

Television executives—many of whom would not agree to be quoted by name—said that an advertising market existed to support another network but that the effort of collecting and compensating stations for their participation would, in the words of one, be "extraordinary."

Although some network executives said they didn't see why Mr. Murdoch would want to start another television system—"I bet Fox can make more money syndicating than they can starting another television network," said one—others admired the effort.

"You have tremendous obstacles in starting a network," said one senior television network executive who asked not to be identified. "You have program development, you have an infrastructure to collect, you have to gather the news, the equipment involved is expensive, you have thousands of employees. It's a big deal. The three networks pay more than $100 million each to their affiliates. That's pretty formidable." ■

NOVEMBER 22, 1987

Jay Leno, Common-Sense Comedian

Elvis Mitchell

Jay Leno during a stand up routine in 1989.

"Don't you just love it?" says the comedian Jay Leno, beginning another of those hard-nosed, common-sense riffs that sound as effortless as a cool bop solo. "I had Donna Mills on 'The Tonight Show' with me and she says [launching into a coquettish voice], 'I was just voted one of the 10 sexiest women in America, and I don't know what that means.' Doesn't know what it means? I said to her, 'Take a guess. What do you think it means? Duh. . .' Give me a break. It means the publicist that she hired to get her name out there is doing his job." Mr. Leno stops and chuckles at the "Knots Landing" star's corny false modesty.

It's his willful demystification of show business, politics and popular culture that has pushed the 37-year-old comedian from Boston into the spotlight after many years of carrying his own bags from one city to another on the Lonely Guy Comedy Club Circuit. His low-pressure stand-up gained a higher profile through countless appearances on "Late Night With David Letterman." That late-night audience included Johnny Carson, who last year named Mr. Leno one of two permanent rotating "Tonight Show" guest hosts, along with Gary Shandling. He's also done several cable and late-night comedy specials and is a favorite guest at televised awards ceremonies. Mr. Leno's broad-based intelligence—he seems interested in almost everything under the sun, like Johnny Carson but with a sunnier disposition—contrasts rather well with Mr. Shandling's neurotic, city-boy self-obsession.

Mr. Leno's Irish-Italian heritage may be responsible for the seemingly contradictory elements of his presence: burliness and gentleness. His oversized jawline and friendly blue eyes make him look both vivid and likable, a perfect package for his Everyman's one-upmanship.

Mr. Leno may have achieved nighttime success by virtue of his work on "The Tonight Show" and "Late Night," but he's by no means an overnight success. He began doing stand-up in the early 1970's after graduating from Emerson College in Boston, and one of his contemporaries on that scene in those scrimp-and-hustle days was a shaggy Hoosier fresh from the heartland named David Letterman. The two became friends in the trenches.

Mr. Leno chooses not to romanticize what he does, saying that he finds it easier to host "The Tonight Show" than to be a guest, because the pressure is far less wearing.

"I really like hosting, because it's the only job in show business that meant anything to me. By that, I mean it's a job that was there when I started in show business and it's still there; it's like stepping into a long-running play." ■

DECEMBER 6, 1987

FAREWELL TO WIT, HELLO VULGARITY

John J. O'Connor

The cast of the television series "Married With Children."

Commercial television entertainment is tumbling into a Vulgarity Sweepstakes. Today's viewers will find language and situations on their weekly series that would never have got past the "program practices" guards just five years ago. One major reason for the change is the expanding presence of cable television, where more permissive rules about content allow operators to carry uncensored theatrical-release films and stand-up comedy acts that revel in aggressive coarseness. According to some current standards, this has something to do with being "adult."

Pouting openly about the unfairness of it all, commercial broadcasters have been inching forward into previously forbidden territories. Sexual allusions are more explicit. Love scenes are more graphic. Language is, as broadcast executives like to say, more colorful. In many respects, the

(cont'd. next page)

(continued from previous page)
changes are refreshing, welcome doses of reality to counteract the vapid days of "Father Knows Best" and Mom worrying about burning the roast when the boss has been invited to dinner. "The Cosby Show" has cleverly updated those old scenarios.

But the accelerating impulse toward being crude or outrageous—would-be sophisticates talk about being "gloriously trashy"—can be found in all corners of the schedule, from the highly acclaimed network creations of Steve Bochco and Terry Louise Fisher, "L.A. Law" and "Hooperman," to a kind of nadir in the Fox Broadcasting Company's "Married . . . With Children" and "Women in Prison."

The Bochco-Fisher team has been ingenious enough to have its contortions mistaken for wit. Earlier on in the run of "L.A. Law" there was, for instance, the phenomenon of the Venus butterfly, a secret sexual calisthenic discovered by the Michael Tuckner character and then used to seduce and conquer Jill Eikenberry. The staff was so proud of this advance in adult programming that they cutely mentioned the Venus butterfly while accepting their Emmy awards this year.

And then, taking a giant leap, there is Rupert Murdoch's Fox Broadcasting outfit, evidently determined to win the hearts of blue-collar workers and very young audiences as it slowly struggles to build to a full prime-time schedule. Swooping bravely into the blatantly crude, there is "Married . . . With Children."

Created by Ron Leavitt and Michael G. Moye, "Married . . . With Children" features Katey Sagal and Ed O'Neill as Peggy and Al Bundy of suburban Chicago. He is a salesman in a shoe store, she a bored housewife with an aversion to cleaning and cooking. Their two whiny children are props, not even bothering to appear in some episodes. After 15 years of marriage, Peggy and Al spend most of their time insulting each other. She is especially pointed on his sexual prowess or the lack of it. The weekly regulars also include their neighbors, Marcy and Steve (Amanda Bearse and David Garrison), young marrieds discovering that they may be the Bundys of tomorrow. Some typical story lines plucked from press releases: "Steve moves in with the Bundys and becomes the housewife of Al's dreams"; "Marcy loses her wedding ring down the pants of Zorro the Great, a male exotic dancer."

There is, apparently, a lofty purpose to the existence of the boorish, loud-mouth Bundys. Mr. Moye explains: "Other shows deal with families where Dad has a great job and Mom wears tasteful and expensive clothing. How about families where Dad is in a go-nowhere job, Mom sits home all day and the kids are constantly looking for money? We're now addressing a totally different type of family unit—one many people can truly identify with." Apparently, Mr. Moye never heard of "All in the Family" or even "The Life of Riley." In any event, "Married . . . With Children" delivers its reality with unflagging gusto. Here, with a vengeance, is marriage with the wife as bimbo and the husband as determined chauvinist. According to Mr. Moye, "Al says what we believe a lot of men in his position would like to say to their wives and children." Needless to say, the humor has limits. As Peggy, in her best Eve Arden manner, confides to her daughter, "Your dad will always be your dad—until I can't take it anymore and hop on a freight train."

As far as permissiveness goes, the audience is likely to see more rather than less, until the industry discovers that being coarse and outrageous has nothing to do with quality or wit. Oddly enough, such dopily quaint series as "Father Knows Best" and "Leave It to Beaver" are currently being revived in syndication—and often on cable, no less—with considerable success. Perhaps reaction to the Vulgarity Sweepstakes is already beginning to simmer. ■

FEBRUARY 1, 1988

Donahue vs. Winfrey: A Clash of Talk Titans

Nan Robertson

The reports of Phil Donahue's death at the hands of Oprah Winfrey have been grossly exaggerated.

Mark Twain's famous riposte to a premature obituary was mentioned spontaneously on two occasions by television analysts interviewed recently about the Donahue-Winfrey phenomenon. Is the sexy, sassy, 34-year-old black woman really beating the socks off the salty, energetic, 52-year-old Irishman who has taken on every topic from Chubby Checker to Chernobyl?

Mr. Donahue had been around and mostly on top five days a week for 20 years as host of the issue-oriented talk show that David Halberstam called "the most important graduate school in America," informing a huge audience about changes in society and modern mores. Then Ms. Winfrey, who had earned a 1986 Academy Award nomination for her spectacular screen debut in "The Color Purple," went up like a rocket on national television in September 1986, with essentially the same format as Mr. Donahue. Five months later her talk show became the third highest-rated series in syndication.

The fact is, when the old pro and the new kid on the block are broadcast at the same hour, which they are in only nine cities out of a total of hundreds, Ms. Winfrey tends to win. She beats Mr. Donahue in the biggest markets of all—New York and Los Angeles—although Mr. Donahue said in an interview the other day that "on KNBC in L.A., we've gained on, tied and in many cases overtaken Oprah in recent weeks."

Sometimes the numbers game of ratings in television seems like voodoo economics, but to take one authority—the November 1987 Nielsen Cassandra ranking of syndicated programs—Mr. Donahue is aired daily in a total of 187 cities across the United States, appearing on 149 in the morning and 38 in the late afternoon. Ms. Winfrey is broadcast in 192 cities, 168 in the afternoon and 24 in the morning.

"Donahue is King of the Morning and Oprah is Queen of the Afternoon" is the message that Katz Television Group officials will convey to 8,000 television programmers and syndicators at their convention in Houston on Feb. 25.

"We have identified only two hits this year in the talk-show category," said John von Soosten, the Katz Television Group's vice president for programming. "Oprah Winfrey and Phil Donahue." He added: "Phil is not slipping, not fading. He's really at a peak level. Oprah came on like a steamroller but he is not showing any attrition—he's pulling better than he did a couple of years ago. As for Oprah, there's no denying she does blockbuster numbers around the country." ■

APRIL 17, 1988

FORGET MURDER AND CAR CHASES: NOT IT'S 'SLICE OF LIFE' SHOWS

Ella Taylor

Is the television plot dead? In the emerging strain of slice-of-life "dramedies" currently favored by the networks, nothing (in the dramatic sense) seems to happen anymore. ABC's "thirtysomething" offers us life style writ large; a group of friends, their lives vaguely defined by a prior decade that could be the 60's or the 70's, kvetch their way through the business of middle-class life in the 1980's. NBC's "Days of and Nights of Molly Dodd" meanders through the hair-raisingly unstructured world of a New York City woman in her mid-30's, anchored by neither marriage nor career. And Kevin, the 32-year-old narrator of "The Wonder Years" (whose ratings are buoying the flagging fortunes of ABC), recalls the feel of the summer of 1968 when, as a chubby suburban adolescent, he struggled to be cool, got his first taste of death when the neighborhood's teenage hero was killed in Vietnam and achieved his first fumbling kiss.

In series like these, there are no murders, no car chases, no heroism or villainy. Even death and disease, the stock pegs on which prime-time plots are hung, are played in a low register, woven into the fabric of daily routine. The story lines become precisely the hum of ordinary lives as well as the ideas that guide people making small-scaled moral choices and struggling to absorb bewilding changes in the received meanings of family, work and love.

What might be called "video verite" has its immediate roots in the hip early-80's dramas designed for that huge, infinitely elastic demographic category we breezily called youth. These dramas-cum-prime-time-soaps, such as "Hill Street Blues," "St. Elsewhere" and "Cagney & Lacey," have story lines that play second fiddle to the mesh of relationships involving a sizable ensemble of characters.

In some of the newest series, though, the attention to detail takes over and becomes the show's essential project, creating a world so self-absorbed, so hermetically sealed, that its connection to public life is severed altogether, or reduced to a trite shorthand of pop-cultural icons—songs, movie titles, political events—that casually cue us into time, place and generation and then shrink back into the politics of the personal.

"Thirtysomething," for example, has begun to echo one of the more troubling difficulties of some contemporary fiction, the displacement of bolder ethical and political concerns by a flimsy and distracting social psychology, in which people worry ceaselessly, not about whether they've done right but whether they're thinking or acting appropriately. There's nothing crude about this gorgeously accomplished show; its production values—the discreet amber lighting, the introspective banter and waggish dream sequences—are immaculate, and in series television, when sets typically look like sets, that's refreshing. It also, mercifully, avoids hurling Social Issues at us in textbook features carved boldly into the dialogue, the way most TV movies do.

The cast of "thirtysomething" in 1987.

Far from being yuppies, the "thirtysomethings" are a middle-income, assiduously unpretentious peer group, a vaguely countercultural family whose members exchange great lines from "Now, Voyager," cook impromptu meals together or eat pizza en groupe on the living room carpet. The mood is anxious and febrile; there's a good deal of worried interior thought and fantasy played out in dream sequences and voice-overs, charmingly neurotic litanies about mortgages, relationships, marriage, children, careers, jealousy.

And by the end of each weekly dose of "thirtysomething," somebody is learning the mature, the "socially skilled" way to handle a controlling mother, a marital collapse or a father dying of cancer. As the season wears on, "thirtysomething" has become so engrossed in its own claustrophobic detail, it seems to be creating an airless prison in which no one, neither characters nor viewers, can transcend the petty confines of their own lives. And it's so quietly civilized, so cool and poised, that it becomes a thinking person's Hallmark card, full of "appropriate" sentiments.

OCTOBER 16, 1988

ROSEANNE: June Cleaver Without Pearls

Joy Horowitz

On "Roseanne," Roseanne Barr plays a mother named Roseanne who works in a Midwestern plastics factory. If Ms. Barr has her way, she will transform the legacy of television moms from wimpy wives to spiky matriarchs. Lucy Ricardo may have begged Ricky for a weekly allowance. June Cleaver may have worn pearls and an apron when Wally and the Beav came home for cookies and milk. And Edith Bunker may have tried her best to hush up Archie's bigotry. But when Roseanne comes home from work, the darker side of domestic life erupts in full force.

Unlike most television moms, Roseanne is flawed. For one thing, you know she has stretch marks, not cover-girl looks, like Alyce Keaton on "Family Ties" or Kate and Allie. A beatific Claire Huxtable comes home from the law firm with briefcase in hand to a picture-perfect house. Roseanne, looking haggard in her sweatshirt and blue jeans, returns home from the factory, lugging an armload of groceries to a pigsty of a kitchen. In short, she is real. And smart. And self-confident. And sexual. And not so wonderful to her kids all the time. Roseanne says what most of us think but repress. She is a true TV anomaly.

What "Roseanne" will not be, says its 35-year-old star, is a show about people who are perfect or who solve problems in 22 minutes -

"I want to do real revolutionary TV," she was saying the other morning, sitting in her dressing room next to Stage Two on the MTM lot in the San Fernando Valley.

"I want to do a show for the 90's. I want to do a show that reflects how people really live. Telling the truth at any point in time is really revolutionary. I want this show to tell the horrible truth rather than parody the truth. When you tell the truth you don't insult the audience's intelligence. I want people to watch it and go, 'Wow, that happens to me.' I want them to feel healed. I want them to feel happy. I want them to feel like, at least, there's a real woman-mother on TV." ■

OBITUARY

APRIL 27, 1989

LUCILLE BALL, Spirited Doyenne Of TV Comedies, Dies at 77

Peter B. Flint

Lucille Ball, the irrepressible queen of television comedy for nearly a quarter-century, died yesterday at Cedars-Sinai Medical Center in Los Angeles a week after undergoing heart surgery there. She was 77 years old.

Miss Ball, noted for impeccable timing, deft pantomime and an endearing talent for making the outrageous believable, was a Hollywood legend: a contract player at RKO in the 1930's and 40's who later bought the studio with Desi Arnaz, her first husband.

She made her last public appearance four weeks ago at the Academy Awards ceremonies, when she and Bob Hope introduced a production number.

The elastic-faced, husky-voiced comedian was a national institution from 1951 to 1974 in three series and many specials on television that centered on her "Lucy" character. The first series, "I Love Lucy," was for six years the most successful comedy series on television, never ranking lower than third. The series, on CBS, chronicled the life of Lucy and Ricky Ricardo, a Cuban band leader played by Mr. Arnaz, who was Miss Ball's husband on and off screen for nearly 20 years.

The Ricardos were the best-known, best-loved couple in America, and the first "Lucy" series is still in syndication in more than 80 countries, at times with six episodes a day in a single area.

Analyzing the reasons, Miss Ball explained why her inspired exaggeration of an average middle-class housewife was credible: "I believe it all the way. I do what I do with all my strength and heart."

"Lucille Ball will always be the first lady of CBS," William S. Paley, the chairman of the network, said yesterday in a tribute issued by his office. "Lucy's extraordinary ability to light up the screen and brighten our lives is a legacy that will last forever."

Miss Ball was also an astute business executive. From 1962 to 1967, she headed Desilu Productions, one of the biggest and most successful television production companies. Also, starting in 1968, she and her second husband, Gary Morton, a former nightclub comic, headed Lucille Ball Productions.

She bought Mr. Arnaz's share of Desilu Productions in 1962 with a $3 million bank loan, and she sold the company to Gulf and Western Industries in 1967 for $17 million. Her share totaled $10 million.

Discussing how she became an executive, Miss Ball said: "My ability comes from fairness and a knowledge of people. I ran my studio like I run my home, with understanding of people. We touch in our house. I tell my children, 'There's so little time.'" ■

Lucille Ball with Bob Hope at the taping of the Bob Hope special "The Women I Love: Beautiful, But Funny" in 1982.

Sports

International politics cast a dark shadow over sports in the 1980's. The United States, responding to the Soviet invasion of Afghanistan in 1979, called for an international boycott of the Summer Olympics in Moscow. Most of its allies fell in line, turning the 1980 Olympic Games into an intramural competition dominated by athletes from the Soviet Union and East Germany. In past Olympics, superpower rivalry had made the games a kind of proxy war, heightening their drama. This time, the crackling tension of West versus East was missing, and the games fell flat.

It was all the more disappointing after the unforgettable hockey finals of the winter games in Lake Placid, where the underdog Americans pulled off the "miracle on ice," defeating a seemingly invincible Soviet team and providing one of the decade's greatest sports moments.

USA's Neal Broten shoots against Russia's goalie during the 1980 Winter Olympics in Lake Placid.

There were others. In basketball, Kareem Abdul-Jabbar, playing for the Los Angeles Lakers against the Utah Jazz in 1984, sank one of his patented sky hooks for a career total of 31,420 points, breaking Wilt Chamberlain's record. A year later, Pete Rose of the Cincinnati Reds singled to left center field off San Diego Padres pitcher Eric Show and notched his 4,192nd career hit, breaking a seemingly unreachable mark set by Ty Cobb nearly 60 years earlier. In football, Walter Payton of the Chicago Bears broke Jim Brown's lifetime rushing record.

Although the Soviet Union retaliated by boycotting the 1984 Summer Olympics in Los Angeles, the Olympic Games continued to enthrall with dazzling performances by athletes who competed in sports well outside the mainstream. The Summer Games in Los Angeles and in Seoul four years later created a slew of stars overnight. Mary Lou Retton's precision and power dominated women's gymnastics. Carl Lewis put on a spectacular show in Los Angeles, equaling Jesse Owens's record of four gold medals, as he won the 100-meter and 200-meter events and the long jump, and anchored the winning 4x100-meter relay. Greg Louganis, the picture of perfection in diving, won two gold medals at both the L.A. and Seoul games.

It was a golden age for tennis. The decade started with a grueling marathon victory by Bjorn Borg over John McEnroe to win his fifth consecutive Wimbledon title. When Borg unexpectedly retired at the age of 26, in January 1983, he left

The Opening Ceremony at the 1984 Los Angeles Olympics.

the stage open for McEnroe, ranked first in the world from 1981 through 1984, to fight it out with Jimmy Connors in a sizzling rivalry that mesmerized fans. Both yielded to the style of power tennis introduced by the Czech player Ivan Lendl.

Bjorn Borg and John McEnroe at Wimbledon in 1981.

Women's tennis had its own superstars led by Martina Navratilova, another Czech, who seemed to own women's tennis in the first half of the decade. From 1982 through 1984 she lost only six singles matches, and at one point maintained a winning streak of 74 matches, a record. It was not until the arrival of Steffi Graf that her iron grip on the number-one ranking was broken.

Players' strikes plagued professional baseball and football. Baseball owners were repeatedly fined for collusion. Fans groused that the players, in the new era of free agency, were overpaid.

Allegiances shifted. For the first time, baseball could no longer claim to be America's pastime, as football became the country's most popular sport. One reason was the brilliant play of the San Francisco 49ers, led by quarterback Joe Montana, whose come-from-behind victories electrified fans. Exploiting an innovative passing game developed by Bill Walsh, the head coach, Montana steered the team to three Super Bowl victories in the 1980's. A championship finish in 1989 resulted in a fourth Super Bowl win the following year.

49ers quarterback Joe Montana (left) and backup quarterback Steve Young (center) with their coach, Bill Walsh, in 1987.

Old warriors fought on. Jack Nicklaus won his sixth Masters. Bernard Hinault took his fifth Tour de France in 1985. One year later, the unthinkable happened: Greg LeMond, an American despite the last name, pedaled his way to victory in the tour, becoming the first non-European to win the race since it was first held in 1903.

It was a great 10 years for sports. All of them.

FEBRUARY 23, 1980

U.S. DEFEATS SOVIET SQUAD IN OLYMPIC HOCKEY BY 4-3

Gerald Eskenazi

LAKE PLACID, N.Y., FEB. 22—In one of the most startling and dramatic upsets in Olympic history, the underdog United States hockey team, composed in great part of collegians, defeated the defending champion Soviet Squad by 4-3.

The victory brought a congratulatory phone call to the dressing room from President Carter and set off fireworks over this tiny Adirondack village. The triumph also put the Americans in a commanding position to take the gold medal in the XIII Olympic Winter Games, which will end Sunday.

The American goal that broke the 3-3 tie tonight was scored midway through the final period by a player who typifies the make up of the American team. His name is Mike Eruzione, he is from Winthrop, Mass., he is the American team's captain and he was plucked from the obscurity of the Toledo Blades of the International League. His opponents tonight included world-renowned starts, some of them performing in the Olympics for the third time.

The Soviet team has captured the previous four Olympic hockey tournaments, going back to 1964, and five of the last six. The only club to defeat then since 1956 was the United States team of 1960, which won the gold medal at Squaw Valley, Calif.

Few victories in American Olympic play have provoked reaction comparable to tonight's decision at the red-seated, smallish Olympic Field House. At the final buzzer, after the fans had chanted the seconds away, fathers and mothers and friends of the United States players dashed onto the ice, hugging anyone they could find in red, white and blue uniforms. ■

The US hockey team celebrates their "Miracle on Ice" victory over the USSR in 1980.

FEBRUARY 25, 1980

U.S. Hockey Squad Captures Gold Medal

Gerald Eskenazi

LAKE PLACID, N.Y., FEB. 24—The come-from-behind United States hockey team performed the improbable today. Amid flagwaving, foot-stomping and patriotic singing at the Olympic Field House, the Americans defeated Finland, 4-2, and won the gold medal at the XIII Olympic Winter Games. ■

JULY 6, 1980

BORG CAPTURES FIFTH WIMBLEDON

BEATS MCENROE IN FOUR-HOUR, 5-SET STRUGGLE

Neil Amdur

Bjorn Borg posted a five-set victory over John McEnroe today that not only gave the Swede his fifth consecutive Wimbledon singles title but also gave tennis followers something to cherish long after both players have left the sport.

Like well-conditioned fighters, they traded shots for 3 hours 53 minutes on the center court of the All England Lawn Tennis and Croquet Club. The top-seeded Borg won, 1-6, 7-5, 6-3, 6-7, 8-6, only after the determined second-seeded McEnroe had saved 7 match points in the fourth set, including 5 in a dramatic 34-point tiebreaker that will stand by itself as a patch of excellence in the game's history.

(cont'd. next page)

"Electrifying," said Fred Stolle, a former Australian great, of the tiebreaker that the 21-year-old McEnroe finally won, 18 points to 16, to deadlock the match, after Borg had earlier lost 2 match points on serve at 5-4, 40-15.

"For sure, it is the best match I have ever played at Wimbledon," said the 24-year-old Borg, who now has won a record 35 singles matches in a row here, including five-set finals from Jimmy Connors in 1977 and Roscoe Tanner last year. Connors and Tanner, like McEnroe, are left-handers.

This one was more a struggle of indomitable wills that would not buckle, even under the normally strenuous circumstances of a championship final. Heightening the drama were the contrasting playing styles and personalities of the participants—Borg, the stolid, silent man of movement, and McEnroe, the brash, aggressive serve-and-volleyer, dubbed by one Fleet Street tabloid as "Mr. Volcano" for his outbursts during yesterday's stormy four-set triumph over Connors in the semifinals.

Borg collected $50,000 and made his score 82 victories in his last 84 singles matches since last year's Wimbledon final. His only losses have been to Tanner at the United States Open, which McEnroe won last September, and to Guillermo Vilas in the recent Nations Cup.

His goal, he says, is to leave the sport as No. 1 of all time. He already has achieved that distinction at Wimbledon. The records show that H. Laure Doherty won five titles between 1902 and 1906 and William Renshaw took six from 1881 to 1886. But those crowns were won during an era when defending champions played fewer matches. ■

AUGUST 4, 1980

Absence of U.S. Dimmed Games

Neil Amdur

The Opening ceremonies of the 1980 Summer Olympic Games in Moscow, Russia.

MOSCOW, Aug. 3—After the commotion over world records and gold medals have been digested, the XXII Olympic Summer Games will be remembered primarily for the efficient hospitality of the hosts and for the invited guests who failed to appear.

The Summer Games were in contrast to the Winter Games in Lake Placid, N.Y., where stumbling inefficiency occurred in most everything from routing buses to selling tickets. But if the abundance of manpower and machinery achieved technical brilliance, a hollow atmosphere existed throughout this fortnight. Security was so intense that almost all athletes were denied the joy of victory laps or spontaneous celebrations. The official explanation was that such exercises only tended to "provoke" spectators. In reality, allowing athletes to express their emotions might have encouraged Soviet spectators to take a more objective look at some of the foreign gold medalists and their performances.

The whistling that accompanied last Wednesday's pole vault competition, when Wladyslaw Kozakiewicz of Poland set a world record, may have been the worse display of sportsmanship in Olympic track and field history. It was not an isolated example: Soviet crowds, perhaps spoiled by their country's harvest of 80 gold medals, booed their soccer and basketball teams.

The boycott by the United States, West Germany, Japan, China, Canada, Kenya, and about 50 other nations had its effect. The all-white Zimbabwe women's field hockey team, not even among the world's top 10 won a gold medal, the first ever for the country. The East Germany took 11 pf the 14 rowing events. Judo without Japan was like New York without Bloomingdales. Horses fell so frequently during the equestrian exercises that stumbling seemed part of the program.

The Russians also may have allowed greed to tarnish an otherwise shining technical hour. Charges of officiating bias in diving, gymnastics, and track and field were as embarrassing for the various international organizers as they were for the various international federations that seemed only to willing to look the other way.

How this situation will be resolved will be an interesting question of whether the Russians and their friends decide to accept invitation to the barbecue in Los Angeles or stay home. ■

NOVEMBER 27, 1980

PREFIGHT FOOD SPREE AND LEONARD'S STYLE TOO MUCH FOR DURAN

Neil Amdur

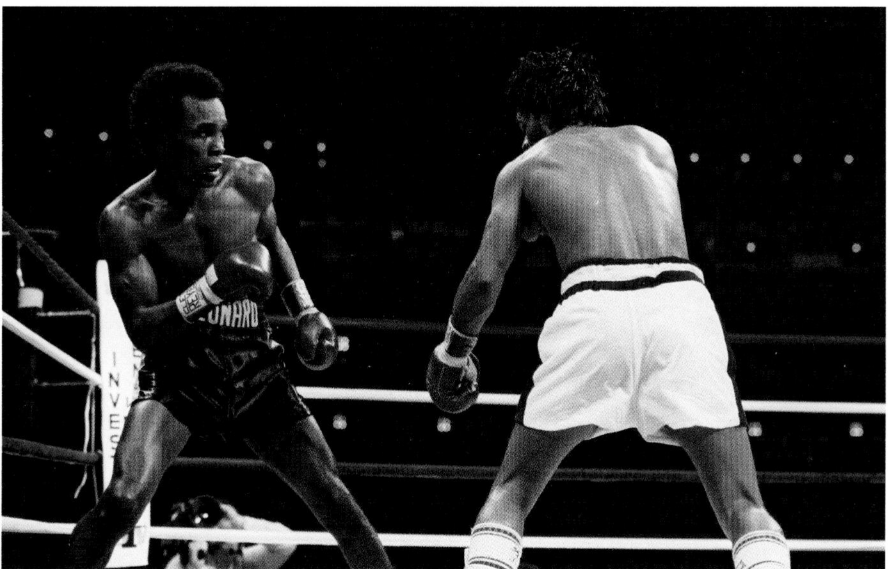

Sugar Ray Leonard (left) fighting Roberto Duran (right) during at the Super Dome in New Orleans, Louisiana, in 1980.

A change in Roberto Duran's eating habits, combined with a tactical shift in Sugar Ray Leonard's fighting style, was an apparent ingredient in Leonard's stunning victory for the World Boxing Council's welterweight championship last night.

Duran's eating spree began shortly after yesterday's noon weigh-in. Duran weighed 146 pounds, one pound under the limit. He had not eaten, his camp said, since Monday morning, when he was still overweight at 148 pounds after a steak for breakfast.

After the weigh-in, Duran finished a small thermos of hot beef broth and ate several oranges while still at the Superdome. Later, at a restaurant, he consumed almost all of two 16-ounce steaks, more oranges and close to three glasses of orange juice during a mid-afternoon meal, according to Freddie Brown, his co-trainer, and Luis Henriquez, a friend.

The fight was scheduled for 9 P.M., local time. At 5:30, said Ray Arcel, his other co-trainer, Duran ate a "small steak" in the hotel coffee shop, along with a cup of tea.

"He ate too much yesterday," Dr. Nunez said. "After three months of having been on a strict ration, he couldn't contain himself any longer."

According to Dr. Nunez, Duran began cramping in the fifth round of the fight. By the seventh round, as Leonard taunted the champion, Duran had become nauseated, the doctor said.

"In the eighth round, he said he felt like he was going to throw up and faint on the floor," Dr. Nunez related. "That is why he stopped."

The ending marked only Duran's second loss in 74 professional fights and the first time he had ever been stopped. It also, he said, marked the end of a pro career spanning 14 years. "I've gotten tired of the sport," he said immediately after the fight. "I feel it's time for me to retire."

Leonard, sitting today with his son, Ray Jr., and wife, Juanita, appeared fresh and unmarked. "I mesmerized Duran," said Leonard, whose next fight may not be until the summer of 1981, perhaps against Thomas Hearns, the unbeaten welterweight champion of the World Boxing Association. "I bewildered Duran. I made Duran lose his composure. He was completely upset." ■

AUGUST 14, 1983

Carl Lewis Emerges: The Best At All He Does

Neil Amdur

Carl Lewis crouched in the starting blocks and positioned himself for the most important race of his career. Mind and body were ready, but Lewis's concentration was suddenly shattered by a bee who decided to take up space in Lewis's lane moments before the 100-meter dash final at the first world track and field championships.

Lewis flicked at the bee but then realized that he had lost his focus. Twice earlier in the year, he had allowed himself to become distracted at the start of sprint races and performed poorly. This time, at the risk of being called for a false start, Lewis calmly stood up in the blocks. Minutes later, after stumbling slightly between his second and third stride, he powered to a gold medal in the 100, only to be greeted again at the finish line by another bee.

The same bee? "I hope not," Lewis said, several days later. "I thought I was faster than that."

Lewis is fast, but speed is only one of the attributes that helped the 22-year-old Willingboro, N.J., athlete win three gold medals and emerge as the most talked-about competitor at this international championship.

Not since Jesse Owens won four gold medals at the Berlin Olympics in 1936 has any American track and field athlete shown such versatility. "King Carl," European periodicals proclaimed this week after Lewis's three golds. Once finding the comparisons to Owens "difficult," Lewis now says, in response to such overworked questions, "I don't think it's exaggerated because everything that's happened has happened positively."

Thinking positively keeps Lewis a psychological stride or two ahead of opponents. "I'm not afraid of anybody," he said after his arrival. "The only thing I'm afraid of is that I'm not going to be the perfect athlete one day."

Because he is so visible, what Lewis says and how he acts draws increasing scrutiny

(cont'd. next page)

(continued from previous page)

from the news media and rivals. How many times he looks around in a 100—he did so eight different times in the first three rounds, none in the final—becomes as much a part of the competition as John McEnroe questioning linesmen or Billy Martin baiting umpires. Lewis was criticized by some competitors for slowing and failing to dip down and lunge at the finish line of the 200 during The Athletics Congress national championships in June when he might easily have broken the world record. His time, 19.75 seconds, was an American record. By slowing down, some say, Lewis may be showing up the competitors he defeats.

"I've talked to a lot of people and the words they used were lack of sportsmanship," said Edwin Moses, the 1976 Olympic champion and world record-holder in the 400 meter hurdles, who, unlike Lewis, prefers a more scientific attitude. "Everybody knows he's a big winner, and nobody envies him or anything like that. But for some people, it's a little too much."

"To each his own," says Leo Williams, a world class high jumper who considers Lewis a close friend. "I don't think Carl's intention was to make the field look bad. He said it was the joy of winning, and I believe just that. He's sharing it. You can bet that if I jump 2.40 meters, I'm going to act the clown." The world record is 2.37 meters, or 7-9 1/4 feet, an inch and a quarter lower.

Lewis works. Between the T.A.C. meet and this event, Lewis was clearly more interested in training than traveling around Europe picking up competition dollars, which are available to athletes through revised rules on amateur eligibility. After his arrival, when journalists wondered whether one 200-meter race since the national championships in June was sufficient preparation, Lewis said, "I'm confident in my ability, I'm confident in my technique and I'm confident in my coaching." ■

USA's Carl Lewis (left) celebrates as he crosses the line to win the gold medal at the 1983 World Athletics Championships.

OBITUARY

APRIL 13, 1981

Joe Louis, 66, Heavyweight King, Is Dead

Deane McGowen

Joe Louis, who held the heavyweight boxing championship of the world for almost 12 years and the affection of the American public for most of his adult life, died yesterday of cardiac arrest in Las Vegas, Nev. He was 66 years old.

Slow of foot but redeemingly fast of hands, Joe Louis dominated heavyweight boxing from 1937 to 1948. As world champion he defended his title 25 times, facing all challengers and fighting the best that the countries of the world could offer. In the opinion of many boxing experts, the plain, simple, unobtrusive Brown Bomber—as he was known—with his crushing left jab and hook, was probably the best heavyweight fighter of all time.

The 6-foot-1 1/2-inch, 197-pound Louis won his title June 22, 1937, in Chicago, by knocking out James J. Braddock in eight rounds, thus becoming the first black heavyweight champion since Jack Johnson, who had reigned earlier in the century. Before Louis retired undefeated as champion on March 1, 1949, his last title defense had been against Jersey Joe Walcott. Louis knocked him out on June 25, 1948, in New York.

Of the 25 title defenses, only three went the full 15 rounds. Tony Galento, for example, survived four rounds in 1939, and Buddy Baer managed one round in 1942.

Excluding exhibitions, Louis won 68 professional fights and lost only three. He scored 54 knockouts, including five in the first round.

The most spectacular victim of Louis's robust punches was Max Schmeling, the German fighter who was personally hailed by Adolf Hitler as a paragon of Teutonic manhood. Schmeling, who had knocked out Louis in 12 rounds in 1936, was given a return bout on June 22, 1938, in Yankee Stadium. He was knocked out in 2 minutes 4 seconds of the first round.

Since 1977, Mr. Louis had been confined to a wheelchair following surgery to correct an aortic aneurysm. His health over the last decade had been poor, beset with heart problems, emotional disorders and strokes.' ■

MARCH 4, 1984

MARY LOU RETTON: POWER AND FINESSE

Robert McG. Thomas Jr.

From the tiny gold earrings in her pierced ears to the soles of her size-3 saddle shoes, 16-year-old Mary Lou Retton would seem to be a typical American teenager—a study in girlish giggles who snuggles a dogged-eared stuffed lamb, dotes on rock music and has a crush on a movie star.

Things, however, are not always what they seem.

For one thing, Miss Retton is an all-A student who is fastidious about picking up her clothes, conscientious about her household chores and never has to be reminded to do homework.

For another, she is the nation's leading female gymnast—a diminutive dynamo of such explosive power and delicate finesse that she is considered a very strong candidate to become the first American woman to win an Olympic medal in gymnastics.

"Her vault is unbeatable—she is the best in the world," said Bela Karolyi, the longtime coach of the Rumanian national team, who ranks Miss Retton with his former star pupil, Nadia Comaneci, who won three gold medals at the 1976 Montreal Olympics.

Karolyi, who defected to the United States in 1981 and has been working with Miss Retton for the last 14 months at his school in Houston, also considers her barely beatable in the floor exercises and so good on the uneven bars and the balance beam that she could easily win the all-round Olympic championship this summer in Los Angeles.

Unlike the cool and calculating Miss Comaneci, Miss Retton is an ebullient, high-spirited competitor who radiates such sheer joy in her performances that like Miss Comaneci and Olga Korbut before her she seems ready-made to become a star in Los Angeles, according to Don Peters, the coach of the women's Olympic team.

"She's fantastic," said Sylvia Cazacu, a former Rumanian coach who now works at the Manhattan Gymnastic Center on East 73d Street, where Miss Retton worked out last week. She warmed up with a couple of back flips in the tuck position, then added a twist for good measure.

In her next effort, she sprinted to the center of the mat and bounded into the air for another double-back flip, this time leaving her body extended, propellerlike, in the full layout position as she spun twice before landing on her feet—something no other woman in the world can do, according to Karolyi.

"Oh, wow," said Miss Cazacu. "Wow." ■

Mary Lou Retton performs her routine on the balance beam during the 1984 Olympics.

Kareem Abdul-Jabbar in 1984.

APRIL 6, 1984

ABDUL-JABBAR SETS N.B.A. RECORD

Roy S. Johnson

LAS VEGAS, Nev., April 5—After almost 15 splendid seasons, Kareem Abdul-Jabbar tonight achieved the most important feat of his career in a fitting manner. With a 12-foot sky hook fired over a helpless defender from the right baseline, the Laker center became professional basketball's leading career scorer.

The basket, which came with 8 minutes 53 seconds to play against the Utah Jazz at the Thomas and Mack Arena, gave Abdul-Jabbar 22 points in the game—and 31,421 for his career. That total eclipsed the 31,419 points scored by Wilt Chamberlain, who retired from the Lakers after the 1972-73 season.

The Lakers won, 129-115, before 18,389 fans. The crowd was the largest for the Jazz since the team moved west from New Orleans for the 1979-80 season.

Amid the ensuing swarm of photographers and well- wishers on the floor, the National Basketball Association commissioner, David Stern, told the crowd: "N.B.A. players are the greatest in the world. And Kareem, you are the greatest."

Cradling the game ball, Abdul-Jabbar took the microphone and said: "It's hard to say anything after all is said and done."

He went on to thank his parents, who were here from New York, the remainder of his family, and the fans. He closed with an Islamic saying, which he translated. "It means God bless you and keep all of you."

Purists may argue that Abdul-Jabbar attained the record in 15 seasons rather than the 14 in which Chamberlain did it. Or that he needed 1,166 games, 121 more than Chamberlain played. But Chamberlain also played 47,859 minutes, while Abdul-Jabbar has played only 45,625. ■

MAY 15, 1984

OLYMPICS DECISION FINAL, SOVIET SAYS

Serge Schmemann

MOSCOW, May 14—The top Soviet sports official said today that the decision not to participate in the Los Angeles Olympic Games was final.

The official, Marat V. Gramov, head of the State Committee for Physical Culture and Sports, spoke at a news conference six days after Moscow announced its decision not to participate. He said the decision was made after it was concluded that the United States "cannot be expected to insure any radical change toward making the Games a festival of peace and friendship, secure for athletes."

Mr. Gramov's statement effectively ended speculation that the Soviet Union might reconsider its boycott, which has been joined by East Germany, Bulgaria, Czechoslovakia, Vietnam, Laos, Mongolia and Afghanistan and is likely to include other Moscow allies.

Following the trend of the Soviet press, Mr. Gramov placed the major blame on President Reagan.

"Our nonparticipation is on the conscience of the Reagan Administration," Mr. Gramov said, "which in the entire period of preparations for the Games did everything possible to thwart our participation."

He insisted that what he called Soviet nonparticipation was not a boycott, and thus was not comparable to the American-led boycott of the 1980 Olympics in Moscow after Soviet intervention in Afghanistan.

"Some Western press media describe the decision of the Soviet National Olympic Committee as a boycott," he said. "This is absolutely untrue. Every National Olympic Committee has the right to decide whether it will attend the Games."

Mr. Gramov did not say whether Soviet officials would attend the opening ceremonies or whether the Soviet flag would be flown.

He said the Soviet Union had no plans to organize "alternative" or "parallel" games while Olympics were being held in Los Angeles.

"This is something invented by the Americans," he said. ■

JUNE 10, 1984

MISS NAVRATILOVA MAKES IT A SLAM

E.J. Dionne

PARIS, June 9—Martina Navratilova overwhelmed Chris Evert Lloyd for the 11th straight time today, winning the French Open final in 63 minutes, 6-3, 6-1. In doing so, Miss Navratilova earned a bonus of $1 million and a somewhat grudging recognition as the third woman to capture the four Grand Slam events in tennis.

Miss Navratilova took control in the fourth game, as she caught Mrs. Lloyd out of position, particularly by using the drop shot, and forced her to scramble.

Mrs. Lloyd, the longtime world's No. 1 player until displaced by Miss Navratilova, paid tribute to her conqueror, saying:

"I couldn't find any weaknesses. I couldn't anticipate the drop shots, I couldn't read her. She took advantage of making me run forward, and I wasn't quick enough. She is playing the best she has ever played. I don't know how much better she can get."

Miss Navratilova, who was born in Czechoslovakia and is now an American citizen, completed her consecutive sweep of the Big Four titles—Wimbledon, the United States, Australian and the French.

Miss Navratilova seems likely to dominate the circuit for some time. Asked whether having one overwhelming favorite would be bad for women's tennis, she replied:

"I don't think I need to play worse for women's tennis to catch up with me. It will raise the level of play for the others. People will come out to see if I'm as good as I'm supposed to be."

Martina Navratilova holds up her trophy after winning the French Open in 1984.

OCTOBER 8, 1984

Payton Breaks Brown's Record

Michael Janofsky

CHICAGO, Oct. 7—The moment finally came on the second play from scrimmage in the third quarter today. Jim McMahon, the Chicago Bears' quarterback, called "Toss 28 Weak," a pitchout for Walter Payton and a play the Bears have run countless times before.

Only this time there was something special about it.

This time, Payton ran the pitchout to his left behind the fullback Matt Suhey and the left guard Mark Bortz for a 6-yard gain and a place in history. The yards moved him him past Jim Brown to become the National Football League's career leading rusher.

Brown, who gained 12,312 yards from 1957 through 1965 with the Cleveland

Browns, had led Payton by 66 before today. Payton's run lifted him past Brown by 5 yards, and he finished the game, a 20-7 victory over the New Orleans Saints, with 154, for a career total of 12,400 and 775 this season, the best start in his career.

Payton's performance set another record. He ran for 100 yards or more for the 59th time; until today, he and Brown had shared the record at 58.

Payton said he felt "relieved" that the chase was finally over. After speaking by telephone for several minutes to President Reagan, who offered his congratulations from aboard Air Force One, flying him to Louisville for tonight's debate with Walter F. Mondale, Payton decribed how the chase had begun to bother him.

"For the past three weeks, I have tried to conceal it, but there has been a lot of pressure," he said. "It's been really hard to deal with; I'm glad I don't have to do this every week. There was a lot of pressure, and if you don't know how to deal with it, you can go astray." ■

NOVEMBER 24, 1984

FLUTIE'S PASS ON LAST PLAY OVERCOMES MIAMI BY 47-45

Gerald Eskenazi

Doug Flutie and his teammate celebrating their Boston College's victory over Miami.

MIAMI, Nov. 23—Doug Flutie enhanced his legend today with a last-play touchdown pass that soared 64 yards, just out of reach of three defenders at the goal-line and into the hands of Gerard Phelan to give Boston College a 47-45 victory over Miami.

The pass, credited as a 48-yard play, found its way to Phelan, Flutie's roommate. Phelan somehow extracted it out of the evening mist—just as he had countless times in fantasy when the two talked about such a play in their dormitory room.

It was the last spectacular play of a spectacular game, contested on a wet day before a crowd of 30,235 in the Orange Bowl and a national television audience. The matchup was made special by the confrontation between two of college football's most glamorous and appealing quarterbacks—Bernie Kosar, the Miami sophomore, and Flutie, the daring senior scrambler who today became the first collegian to pass for more than 10,000 yards in a career.

Despite his years of heroics, which will wind up with a Cotton Bowl appearance New Year's Day, today's final challenge appeared to be asking a bit much of Flutie. Only 28 seconds remained when Boston College took over on its 20-yard line with Miami holding a 45-41 lead, fashioned on Melvin Bratton's fourth touchdown.

Only 6 seconds remained when Flutie took the final snap on the Miami 48.

In the huddle, Flutie called the "Flood Tip" play. In theory, there would be two other wide receivers besides Phelan in the end zone. Phelan's job was to tip the ball to them.

Flutie scrambled back, all the way to his 37, and then, under pressure, went to his right. Twice this season he had passed for touchdowns with no time left, but that was at halftime. This was for the game and a victory against the defending national champion.

(cont'd. next page)

(continued from previous page)

Phelan, one of several receivers lined up right of center, was 1 yard past the goal line when the ball arrived. In front of him, three defenders tumbled over one another, attempting to get to the ball. But the other receivers were not nearby. So Phelan caught the ball himself.

"He threw it a long, long way," Phelan said. "I didn't think he could throw the ball that far."

"He and I are roommates," said Flutie, the leading candidate for this season's Heisman Trophy, and we talk all the time about plays like this.

"I honestly believe when we ran that play we had a legitimate chance. I'm not saying that I anticipated it happening, but I'm saying we had a chance and that's all I ask for."

It has seemed to be all he ever needed, and some of the Miami sensed it.

One of their linebackers, George Mira Jr.—whose father is the former Miami quarterback—recalled thinking, "I had a funny feeling they were going to catch it." ■

JULY 8, 1985

17-YEAR-OLD CHAMPION: BORIS BECKER

WIMBLEDON, England, July 7—Within the span of two weeks, the 17-year-old West German Boris Becker has made history in the most famous tennis tournament in the world. Today, Becker became the youngest champion in the history of the men's singles at Wimbledon, defeating Kevin Curren, 6-3, 6-7, 7-6, 6-4.

Playing on the most hallowed stage of tennis, Becker fit easily into his starring role here, enchanting the crowd with a booming serve and lively court acrobatics. He displayed poise in an arena that has shaken many older, more experienced players. And his zest for the game was evident as he pumped his fists or waved to the crowd; indeed, his father said that his son enjoyed tennis so much that back in his hometown of Leimen he played anyone.

Boris Becker was born on Nov. 22, 1967, in Leimen, a town a few miles south of Heidelberg in southwestern West Germany. He is the son of Karl Heinz and Elvira Becker. His father is an architect who built the tennis club where Becker learned to play as a child. At the club tonight, more than 100 people gathered to celebrate what had become a day of national pride.

"I'm the first German, and I think that will change tennis in Germany," the younger Becker said after his victory. "They never had an idol, and now maybe they have one."

Some residents in the town of 17,000 fired pistols in the air and hundreds of people took to the streets at 6:28 P.M., West German time, when Becker's service winner closed out the match against Curren. "Boris Becker is now our prominent citizen," said Mayor Kurt Weber of Leimen.

Becker's popularity crossed the boundaries of his hometown as an estimated 20 million West Germans watched the match on television. One of the interested spectators was West German Chancellor Helmut Kohl who sent a congratulatory telegram to the teenage sensation.

French Bernard Hinault, winner for the fifth time of the 72nd Tour de France cycling race in 1985.

JULY 22, 1985

HINAULT WINNER AGAIN

Samuel Abt

PARIS, July 21—As nearly half a million of his fellow Frenchmen cheered, Bernard Hinault won the Tour de France bicycle race today for the fifth and, he insists, probably the last time.

His victory, after a three-week, 4,000-kilometer (2,500-mile) clockwise ride round the country equaled the record number of five set by two of the greatest champions, Jacques Anquetil and Eddy Merckx.

Anquetil, a Frenchman, won in 1957, 1961, 1962, 1963 and 1964. Merckx, a Belgian, was first in 1969, '70, '71, '72 and '74. His retirement ushered in the era of Hinault, who won in 1978, '79, '81 and '82 Now Hinault is approaching his 31st birthday and planning to retire after one more season. His last year, he says, will be put at the service of his Vie Claire teammate and heir apparent, Greg LeMond, an American.

Hinault was radiant when he reached the victory podium while his supporters chanted his name and a military band broke into "La Marseillaise." His face bore few of the signs of fatigue and injury that have marked him since he crashed in a sprint and broke his nose July 13.

And, except for a long scar on the side of his right knee, his legs showed no sign of the surgery that kept him out of the 1983 tour and limited his power in 1984. "I have something to prove," he has been saying since his second-place finish in the last tour to Laurent Fignon, who missed the race this year because of similar surgery for tendinitis.

At the start of the season Hinault set his team goals: victory in the Tour of Italy, the Tour de France and the world championships. He accomplished the first two and leaves for the United States at the end of July to ride in the Coors Classic in preparation for the world championship in Italy Sept. 1.

"After that," Hinault said, "I am at Greg's service." ■

"I congratulate you," Chancellor Kohl wrote. "We are proud that you are not only the youngest Wimbledon winner but also the first German. I followed the suspenseful match on television and kept my fingers crossed. I wish you all good fortune and many more sporting successes."

Like many European youngsters, Becker grew up playing soccer, which helped him develop the footwork that is such an important part of tennis. He is 6 feet 2 inches tall and 175 pounds, with thighs like tree trunks and a bullying style on the tennis court. He reportedly likes basketball to help condition his legs for quickness and power.

According to his father, he started playing tennis competitively at age 8, and by 11 he was playing in an area league, but in the adult divisions. When he was 12, Becker decided to concentrate on tennis.

His tennis idol, he said last week, is Bjorn Borg, the retired Swedish star who won five consecutive Wimbledon titles beginning in 1976. But he also draws some inspiration from John McEnroe, a total opposite of the stoic Borg. Becker has defended McEnroe's brash style and, in a recent interview in a West German magazine, he said McEnroe "has a hard life" because "people come to see if he does something. If he wins normally, then they're disappointed."

Becker played only a few tournaments on the men's grand-prix tour last year. He had to win three qualifying matches to enter the main draw at Wimbledon. He advanced to the third round before his ankle was twisted during a match and tendons were torn. He left the court in a wheelchair.

Even as he was recuperating, Becker toyed with his racquet, eager to practice. In January this year, he joined the tour full-time and gradually began to move up in the rankings. At the Italian Open in Rome last May, he advanced to the semifinals.

Then the week before Wimbledon, he won his first tournament at the Queen's Club in London. He entered Wimbledon ranked 20th in the world, and British fans made him a long-shot favorite.

Becker endeared himself to them with a boyish smile that shone under his reddish-blond hair and self-effacing humor that belied his aggressive game. Although opponents gave him little chance to win the championship, Becker smiled shyly and said, "Maybe it will be me." ■

Pete Rose collects hit number 4,192.

SEPTEMBER 12, 1985

PETE ROSE: BASEBALL'S BOUTONNIERE

Dave Anderson

CINCINNATI—With a line single in the first inning last night, baseball pinned a Rose named Pete on its lapel just when it needed something to celebrate.

Swinging left-handed with a new black bat and determined not to "go after any bad pitches," as he had Tuesday night, 44-year-old Pete Rose lashed a 2-and-1 slider from Eric Show of the San Diego Padres for the 4,192d hit of his 23d major league season. When the ball landed in left-center field on the green artificial turf of Riverfront Stadium, the Cincinnati Reds' manager and first baseman surpassed Ty Cobb's record that had endured since 1928 as one of baseball's monuments. In the seventh inning of the Reds' 2-0 victory, Pete Rose drilled a triple into the left-field corner for his 4,193d hit. He also walked in the third and scored both runs.

"In runs," he would say later with a smile, "that gets me two closer to Cobb."

The single, which occurred at 8:01 P.M. (Eastern Daylight Time), set off fireworks and a seven-minute standing ovation from 47,237 spectators in appreciation for what Pete Rose has meant to baseball. And also, in a way, for what baseball has meant to Pete Rose.

After taking a big turn at first base with his usual hustle, Pete Rose returned there as Tommy Helms, the Reds' first-base coach, greeted him with a hug. In a rush, the Reds' dugout emptied, the other players and the coaches hurrying to congratulate him, as did several Padre players. With them was 15-year-old Petey Rose, wearing a Reds uniform with his father's No. 14 on the back. After having been carried upon his teammates' shoulders, Pete Rose later could be seen wiping his eyes at the ovation.

"The only other time I remember crying was when my father died," he would say later. "I looked up tonight and saw him up there and right behind him I saw Ty Cobb—regardless of what you think, Ty is up there. But he was sitting behind my father who was in a front-row box."

(cont'd. next page)

(continued from previous page)

When the other Reds retreated to the dugout, Pete Rose stood alone at first base, just as he now stood alone in total hits. But it was a new first base. The dusty bag he had stepped upon for the record hit had been removed for posterity. Now he was waving his red cap to the fans to whom he relates so well. As a youngster growing up here, he had been one of them, rooting for the Reds at old Crosley Field.

As the applause and the chant of "Pete, Pete" continued, he walked a few feet into foul territory to hug Marge Schott, the Reds' owner.

Moments later, after emerging from a gate in the right-center-field wall, a red Corvette was driven to a stop near him—a gift from Chevrolet as a memento of the occasion. The message board diplayed the red Corvette's Ohio license number:

"PR 4192"

As always, Pete Rose was strictly baseball. In a home-plate ceremony after the game, he wore a white baseball cap with a red commemorative logo marking his historic hit, then he spoke with President Ronald Reagan in a telephone conversation piped over the stadium's public address system.

"Thank you for taking time out of your busy schedule to call," Pete Rose said. "You missed a good ballgame tonight."

When what was described as a "Rose red" Corvette was driven onto the field again, Pete Rose suggested, "Let's call it Cincinnati Reds' red." And when Marge Schott presented him with a silver punch bowl set that included several silver cups, he looked toward his wife, Carol, who was with their 11-month-old son, Tyler.

"I'm sure my wife," he said, smiling, "will enjoy polishing that once a week."

At a time when baseball's image as the national pastime was being battered by the testimony of several players at the Pittsburgh drug trial, Pete Rose had people talking about one of baseball's basic appeals—a current player's ascent above what had once been considered an old-timer's unassailable record. Asked about the national interest in his record hit, Pete Rose nodded.

"It proves that baseball is still America's No. 1 pastime," he said Tuesday. "It's the nation's oldest game, it's a very statistical game. People know baseball memorabilia and trivia and statistics." ■

NOVEMBER 10, 1985

KASPAROV, 22, DEFEATS KARPOV FOR CHESS TITLE

Serge Schmemann

MOSCOW, Nov. 9—Gary Kasparov wrested the world chess crown from Anatoly Karpov today with a stunning victory in the last game of their 14-month struggle, becoming at 22 the youngest champion in the history of the game.

Caught in an unexpected trap, Mr. Karpov, 34 years old, resigned the game and his title after 43 moves, making way for a maverick player who has electrified the chess world in his meteoric rise.

It was a game that proved a fitting finale to a grueling duel that matched any previous championship in tension, controversy and excitement.

Needing a victory to retain the title he has held for 10 years, Mr. Karpov, playing white, plunged into an aggressive king-side assault. Mr. Kasparov, leading the match, 12 points to 11, and needing only a draw to seal his victory, fashioned a Sicilian defense into a firm defensive line and seemed intent on hunkering behind it for the duration.

But the champion maintained the pressure, and suddenly Mr. Kasparov, perhaps sensing that a static defense was turning dangerous, shifted to the daring style that is his trademark.

With the clock approaching the two-and-a-half-hour limit each player has for the first 40 moves, he shifted his rooks into an offensive stance and boldly sacrificed a pawn. Then, after he advanced another pawn to be sacrificed, Mr. Karpov seemed to falter, and suddenly Mr. Kasparov had the champion in a lethal vise.

A muffled roar gathered in the crowd as Mr. Karpov tried to wriggle free. Mr. Kasparov leaned back in his chair and flashed a smile at his mother, Klara, sitting in the third row of the Tchaikovsky Concert Hall where she has been throughout the match.

Finally, Mr. Karpov offered his hand, and the capacity crowd of more than 1,000 erupted in cheers. Mr. Kasparov threw his hands over his head to shouts of "Gary! Gary!" Mrs. Kasparov, now with a bouquet of white carnations in her hand, hugged anyone who drew near.

The celebration continued in the lobby, where dark-haired Azerbaijanis from Mr. Kasparov's native republic danced and posed for pictures with posters of their hero while sedate Karpov fans filed quietly out. More people crowded around police lines outside hoping for a glimpse of the new champion.

Since assuming the title that Bobby Fischer refused to defend in 1975, Mr. Karpov had been the model Soviet champion. An ethnic Russian, he fulfilled the civic functions asked of him in the Young Communist League and in the World Peace Committee. In his two defenses of the title, in 1978 and 1981, he salvaged Soviet honor by defeating Viktor Korchnoi, a defector.

Mr. Kasparov, by contrast, was a brash young outsider, a native of Baku in Azerbaijan, the son of a Jewish father and an Armenian mother. His father, Kim Veinshtein, died when the boy was 7, and his mother Russified her maiden name from Kasparyan to Kasparov, which the son then adopted.

The game today, with its bold sacrifices and its last-minute turnaround, was typical of Mr. Kasparov's style. Chess fans, who are legion in the Soviet Union, find his approach more exciting than Mr. Karpov's technical mastery, and Mr. Kasparov is perceived to be as outspoken and daring as Mr. Karpov is considered orthodox and tame.

The contrast may not be so stark. Mr. Kasparov is also a party member, and although Mr. Karpov's political support in the Kremlin may have waned with the death of Leonid I. Brezhnev in 1982, Mr. Kasparov seems to have the backing of powerful Transcaucasians on the Politburo like Geidar A. Aliyev, a First Deputy Prime Minister, and Eduard A. Shevardnadze, the Foreign Minister.

Yet the jubilation that followed Mr. Kasparov's victory showed that, whatever the ingredients, he is an enormously popular champion.

APRIL 14, 1986

NICKLAUS WINS SIXTH MASTERS

Gordon S. White Jr.

AUGUSTA, Ga., April 13—Jack Nicklaus, who was four shots off the lead with four holes left, got an eagle and two birdies in those closing holes to win the Masters Tournament for a record sixth time today with a stunning 7-under-par 65.

He beat Greg Norman and Tom Kite by a single shot in what may become the most memorable of the 50 Masters played so far.

The 46-year-old Nicklaus, who was in his prime in the 1960's and 1970's, became the oldest man ever to win a Masters. He increased his record to 20 major tournament victories, including 18 in professional golf. No other golfer has come close to that number of major victories.

It was a classic golf charge from behind by Nicklaus, who got six birdies and the eagle at No. 15 in his last 10 holes to win with a final total of 9-under-par 279.

"This may be as fine a round of golf as I ever played, particularly those last 10 holes," Nicklaus said. "I haven't been this happy in six years." ■

Jack Nicklaus celebrates a birdie during the US Masters Golf Tournament in 1986.

JULY 28, 1986

IN PARIS, AN AMERICAN WINS TOUR DE FRANCE

Samuel Abt

American Greg LeMond poses with his trophy in Paris after winning the 1986 Tour de France.

PARIS, July 27—Greg LeMond won the big one today: the Tour de France. The Tour is the world's most important bicycle race, and LeMond became the first American—the first non-European—to win it since it was first held in 1903.

The 25-year-old LeMond, who lives in Sacramento, Calif. in the off season, cruised across the final finish line on the Champs-Elysees as the overall winner after racing 2,500 miles over a course that included stretches of the Alps and the Pyrenees.

He finished the race, which began July 4, in the total elapsed time of 110 hours 35 minutes 19 seconds, 3 minutes 10 seconds faster than Bernard Hinault, a French teammate on the Vie Claire team.

"Wonderful, it feels just wonderful," LeMond said at the finish. "I was nervous, but everything went perfectly today."

(cont'd. next page)

(continued from previous page)

LeMond had been virtually certain of victory since Thursday, when Hinault, his longtime friend and mentor and this year his principal rival, called off a series of physical and psychological challenges he had been making in an attempt to gain a sixth, record-setting, Tour triumph.

LeMond, who has ridden for French teams since 1980 and is well known in Europe, relished the acclaim he received himself, even if he usually played second fiddle to Hinault with the news media.

"The race was fantastic and to win you've got to be one of the great champions," he said today on the victory podium. ■

MARCH 8, 1987

TYSON UNIFIES W.B.C.-W.B.A. TITLES

Phil Berger

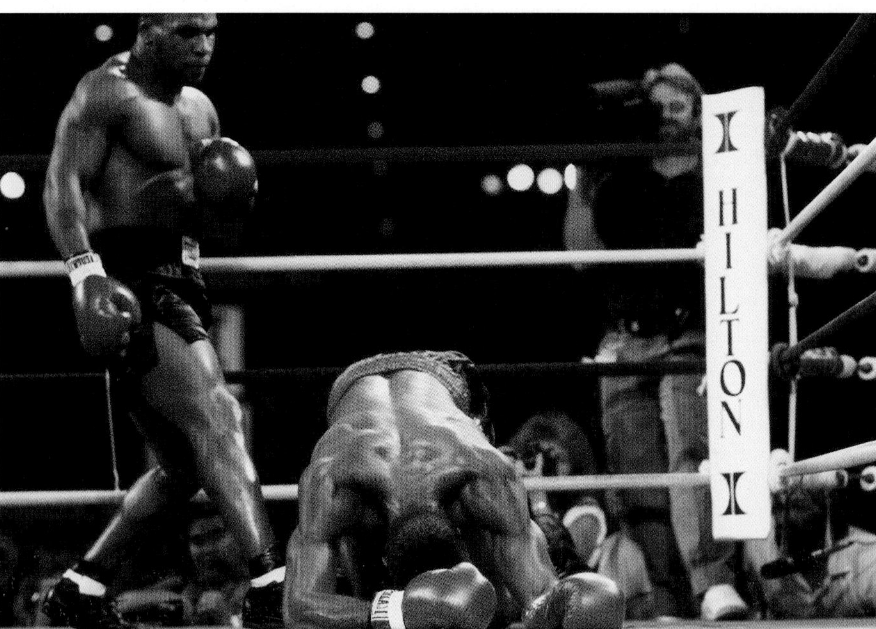

Mike Tyson watches his opponent attempt to get up during a boxing match at the Hilton in Las Vegas, Nevada.

LAS VEGAS, Nev., March 7—James (Bonecrusher) Smith's chin was good, but his grip was even better. He held and held Mike Tyson and turned the advertised bout between heavyweight champion sluggers into a dreary charade of a fight.

What fight there was, Tyson won, and convincingly, as he took a unanimous 12-round decision from Smith and unified the World Boxing Council's heavyweight title, which he already held, with the World Boxing Association title.

Tyson now has a 29-0 record, with 26 knockouts. Smith is 19-6, with 14 knockouts.

From early on, it was clear that Tyson was too big a puncher for Smith. And it was most clear to Smith, the 33-year-old fighter from Lillington, N. C. Smith abandoned any notion of winning the bout, and fought merely to survive, squeezing Tyson to his body every time the 20-year-old slugger from Catskill, N.Y., came forward winging punches aimed to end the fight quickly.

"He's hard to hit," Smith said afterward. "He caught me early. He's very quick. Quicker than I thought he was."

"I thought he was in there to win," Tyson said. "He wasn't fighting. He didn't want to expose himself and put himself on the line. And I've got to suffer for it from the critics." The crowd frequently booed Smith for his tactics, and Mills Lane deducted a point from Smith in rounds 2 and 8 for excessive holding.

The winner of the Tyson-Smith bout was to have fought in May against Michael Spinks, who was the International Boxing Federation champion until that organization vacated his title after Spinks refused to fight the I.B.F.'s mandatory challenger, Tony Tucker. Spinks decided to leave the Home Box Office unification series to fight Gerry Cooney, but that bout was enjoined recently by the courts. Spinks's promoter, Butch Lewis, will be in court on Monday attempting to have the injunction overturned.

Meanwhile, the I.B.F. has ordered Tucker, its No. 1-ranked boxer, to fight James (Buster) Douglas, who is rated No. 2.

That would leave H.B.O. with a gap in its unification series and Tyson with time on his hands. The expectation was that neither H.B.O. nor Tyson would wait for the I.B.F. title picture to be clarified and would look elsewhere for a next bout.

As the champion of both the W.B.A. and W.B.C., Tyson would have mandatory challenges of those governing bodies to meet. If an I.B.F. title bout is not scheduled in the near future, one option for the new champion would be to satisfy his mandatory obligations by fighting either the W.B.C.'s mandatory challenger, Pinklon Thomas, or the W.B.A.'s mandatory challenger, Biggs, probably in Las Vegas no later than June. ■

OCTOBER 25, 1987

THE POWERFUL ALLURE OF MIKE TYSON

Joyce Carol Oates

It is the boxing match with the distinct premise as its axis that is likely to be the most profound, and in our time the boxer whose matches are most consistently fueled by such interior (if rarely articulated) logic is Mike Tyson, the youngest "undisputed" world heavyweight champion in history.

The premise underlying Tyson's first title match, for instance, with the World Boxing Council titleholder Trevor Berbick in November 1986, which Tyson won in six brilliantly executed minutes, was that a boxer of such extreme youth (Tyson was 20 at the time, and fighting in a division in which boxers customarily mature late), who had never fought any opponent approaching Berbick's quality, could nonetheless impose his will upon the older boxer: thus Tyson was a "challenger" in more than the usual sense of the word.

The premise underlying his title defense in Atlantic City nine days ago was something along the lines of: the 26-year-old challenger Tyrell Biggs, an Olympic gold medalist in the superheavyweight division in 1984, deserved to be punished for having enjoyed a smoother and more triumphant career as an amateur than Mike Tyson; and deserved to be punished particularly badly because, in Tyson's words, "He didn't show me any respect." (Tyson said, post-fight, that he could have knocked out Biggs in the third round but chose to knock him out slowly "so that he would remember it for a long time. I wanted to hurt him real bad.") As with the young, pre-champion Dempsey, there is the unsettling air about Tyson, with his impassive death's-head face, his unwavering stare, and his refusal to glamorize himself in the ring—no robe, no socks, only the signature black trunks and shoes—that the violence he unleashes against his opponents is somehow just; that some hurt, some wound, some insult in his past, personal or ancestral, will be redressed in the ring; some mysterious imbalance righted. The single-mindedness of his ring style works to suggest that his grievance has the force of a natural catastrophe. That old trope, "the wrath of God," comes to mind.

Tyson has said that he doesn't think in the ring but acts intuitively; like his great predecessor Joe Louis, he gives the chilling impression of being a machine for hitting, and in this most rococo of his fights a machine for rapid and repeated extra-legal maneuvers—low blows, using his elbows, hitting after the bell.

I wanted to hurt him real bad

These fights do linger in the mind, sometimes obsessively, like nightmare images one can't quite expel, but the actual experience of the fight, in the arena, is a confused, jolting, and sometimes semi-hysterical one. The reason is primary, or you might say primitive: either Tyson is hitting his man, or he is preparing to hit his man, and if nothing nasty happens within the next few seconds it will not be for Tyson's not trying. In the average boxing match, contrary to critics' charges of "barbarism," "brutality," et al., nothing much happens, as boxing aficionados affably accept, but in Tyson fights (with one obvious exception—last March's title fight with Bonecrusher Smith) everything can happen, and sometimes does.

Thus individuals in the audience behave oddly, and involuntarily—there was even a scuffle or an actual fight at the rear of the Convention Hall during the third or fourth round, a matter of some confused alarm until security guards broke it up. Some women hid their faces, some men emitted not the stylized cries of "Hit him!" or even "Kill him!" but parrot-like shrieks that seemed to be torn from them—perhaps the "woman-like" shrieks Tyson amusingly described coming from Biggs when he was hit.

When the fight was over people remained for some minutes in their seats as if spellbound or dazed, like Biggs; or exhausted—the 20 minutes of action had seemed rather more like 20 hours.

The fight being over, the "real" world floods back, and the powerful appeal of Mike Tyson, as of his great predecessors, is that, in however artificial and delimited a context, a human being, one of us, reduced to the essence of physical strength, skill, and ingenuity, has control of his fate—if this control can manifest itself merely in the battering of another human being into absolute submission. This is not all that boxing is, but it is boxing's secret premise: life is hard in the ring, but, there, you only get what you deserve. ■

Wrigley Field in Chicago, Ill.

AUGUST 9, 1988

THE GLOW IN WRIGLEY FIELD

Ira Berkow

Wrigley Field was lit up like an old drunk.

With it came the giddiness of the moment—the imbibing of this novelty—along with the melancholy of what was and will never be again.

Last night at 6:09 Chicago time, 540 floodlights were turned on in the old ball park and the whole historic place glowed.

With one flick of the switch in the Chicago summer dusk the Cubs suddenly were no longer the only team in the major leagues to play only day games. Now there were none. Or were there? For a long time there was a segment of the population that said night baseball was against nature.

This was a good joke, and the atmosphere for the first night game in The Friendly Confines was primarily celebratory.

It was party time, from old stars like Ernie Banks and Billy Williams throwing out the first balls, to the brass section from the Chicago Symphony Orchestra doing their thing, to bunting on the walls and facades

(cont'd. next page)

(continued from previous page)
of the park as if it were a championship or all-star game.

Then the game began, and the first batter for the Phillies, Phil Bradley, slammed a home run over the left-field bleachers. Take that Cubs, and your night-game pretensions.

It was a lovely evening, though a little warm—that is, 91 degrees.

That was only nature's first indication that someone upstairs was out of sorts.

The Cubs took the lead, 3-1 in the third, and shortly after there was a dust storm that halted play briefly.

Then there was thunder, and then lightning, which brought oohs from the standing-room-only crowd of more than 40,000.

In the bottom of the fourth came rain—a sudden downpour—and the fans in the box seats and the players and umpires ran for shelter.

"Next," someone said, "there will be a plague of locusts."

As he said it, another bolt of lightning lit the night sky.

Would they ever finish the game? Would they ever complete a night game in Wrigley Field? Not on this night.

The next-to-last major league team before the Cubs to institute lights was the Tigers in then Briggs Stadium, 40 years ago.

Like many, Ray Meyer, the former DePaul basketball coach here, said, "I never thought I'd live to see the day when Wrigley Field had lights."

Some say that big-league baseball will never be quite the same again, with lights in Wrigley Field. Fact is, little remains the same.

Dinosaurs came and went, men's plumed hats came and went, and even Hula Hoops came and went. ■

OCTOBER 01, 1988

THE SEOUL OLYMPICS;
A PLEA: SAY IT AIN'T SO, BEN

John F. Burns

A crowd gathered outside Ben Johnson's house today as it has every day since the athlete returned from Seoul, South Korea, on Tuesday. Many of those gathered here are sustained by the hope that Canada's fallen athletic idol will somehow explain his drug-testing disaster in Seoul in a way that will make it possible for the nation to believe in him again.

A week after the 26-year-old Jamaican-born speedster captured the hearts of the people of his adopted country by outsprinting Carl Lewis in a 100-meter race that was one of the most ballyhooed matchups in track history, he emerged briefly from his home to wash his Ferrari. But he continued to maintain silence about the events that led to his being stripped of his gold medal and of the world record of 9.79 seconds he set in the Olympic race.

For the first time since the announcement of Johnson's disqualification, the country awoke today to the possibility that some details may emerge. Late on Thursday evening, an attorney for the Johnson family announced that the athlete would put his version of the Seoul debacle directly to Canadians and not through the medium of a paid interview in Stern, a West German magazine that claimed to have an exclusive contract for Johnson's story with his American business agent, Larry Heidebrecht.

The implication was that Johnson would present himself as an unknowing, or at least reluctant, participant in the events that led to the Olympic laboratory finding traces of the banned steroid stanozolol in the urine specimen taken from him after the 100-meter final.

Since his disqualification, many in Canada who know him have maintained that Johnson would not have been able to manage a drug-taking scheme on his own, and might not have known if others had been administering a drug to him. George van Zeyl, a coach with the Mazda Optimists Club, for which Johnson ran, said that he was told by people in touch with Johnson that the athlete would say that somebody with a financial interest in his success, but not Dr. George M. Astaphan, Johnson's doctor, had been administering steroids without his knowledge.

No matter what Johnson says, it seems clear that the shock waves set off by his downfall cannot be contained without a major shake-up in Canadian track and field. The Government has hinted that the investigation it announced earlier this week may be increased to a judicial inquiry, with power to question witnesses under oath.

A primary focus of the investigation is likely to be why the Sports Ministry, the Canadian Track and Field Association and Canadian Olympic officials ignored the repeated warnings they are said to have received that steroid abuse was widespread. ■

SEPTEMBER 28, 1988

THE SEOUL OLYMPICS: DIVING; LOUGANIS AT BEST IN TEST OF WILL

Peter Alfano

These Olympics tested his courage and, ultimately, his will to succeed. At the age of 28, 12 years after he made his first splash in diving—winning a silver medal in Montreal—Greg Louganis today gave what was probably the finest performance of his career in Seoul, overcoming adversity and his heir apparent, to earn a place among the great champions of the Summer Games.

It would have been easy for Louganis to settle for something less, especially after he struck his head on the springboard in a qualifying round last week, suffering a cut that required five stitches to close. Not only did he dive two more times that night to qualify, but he came back the following day to win the gold medal.

Then today, when it looked as if he would have to settle for the silver in what is probably his last Olympics, Louganis stood on the 10-meter platform in a familiar pose, rubbing his face, deep in concentration, knowing he would need a near-perfect score on his final dive to overtake Xiong Ni, a 14-year-old wisp from China.

He chose a reverse three and one-half somersault, considered the most difficult dive in the sport. "I knew I was trailing going into the last dive," Louganis said. "I knew I had a 3.4 degree of difficulty and he had a 3.2, so I had a slight advantage."

His execution appeared flawless, Louganis piercing the water like a dart. When he is pleased with a dive, he bobs to the surface with a smile, but this time he emerged with an expression of doubt. When the scores were posted, the spectators burst into applause and Louganis, tears running down his face, ran to embrace Ron O'Brien, the United States diving coach.

"That was probably the biggest dive of his career," O'Brien said. "To hit it like that, under those circumstances, certainly proved that he was a champion."

Louganis received 86.70 points to finish with a total of 638.61, only 1.14 ahead of Xiong. It enabled him to become the first male to win a pair of gold medals in diving in consecutive Olympics.

Louganis said he would dive again, but probably not at this level. It is time to move on, his gold medal today the perfect exit line. "I'm looking forward to pursuing my career as an actor," he said. "I don't think it will be my last competition, but it may be my last world-class competition."

Greg Louganis of the U.S. bangs his head against the board after mistiming his dive during the 1988 Seoul Olympic Games.

OBITUARY

APRIL 13, 1989

SUGAR RAY ROBINSON, BOXING'S 'BEST,' IS DEAD

Dave Anderson

Sugar Ray Robinson, the five-time world middleweight champion who was considered by many boxing experts to have been the best fighter in history, died yesterday in Culver City, Calif. He was 67 years old.

Robinson, who died at Brotman Medical Center shortly after having been admitted, was suffering from Alzheimer's disease and diabetes.

With his boxing artistry and knockout power in either fist, Robinson, who had also been the world welterweight champion, inspired the description "pound for pound, the best," a phrase designed to transcend the various weight divisions.

"I agree with those who say Sugar Ray Robinson was the greatest," said Don Dunphy, the longtime ringside broadcaster. "He's my choice for number one."

Ali, who described himself as the Greatest, acknowledged that Robinson's "matador" style had been his inspiration in dethroning Sonny Liston as the heavyweight champion in 1964. Ali, then known as Cassius Clay, had asked Robinson to be his manager.

"You are the king, the master, my idol," Ali was fond of saying to Robinson.

Over a quarter of a century, from 1940 to 1965, Robinson recorded 175 victories against 19 losses. Five of those losses occurred in the last six months of his career, after he turned 44 years old. He registered 110 knockouts, but he was never knocked out and he was stopped only once.

Robinson was undefeated in his first 40 bouts, with 29 knockouts. He lost a 10-round decision to Jake LaMotta in 1943, then extended his record to 128-1-2, with 84 knockouts, while ruling the welterweight division and later the middleweight division.

He earned the 160-pound middleweight title in 1951, stopping LaMotta in the 13th round. Five months later he lost the title for the first time, on a 15-round decision, to Randy Turpin in London. Two months later, at the Polo Grounds, he regained the title from Turpin in a desperate and dramatic 10th-round knockout although he was bleeding from a cut above the left eye.

At his peak, Robinson was as flashy out of the ring as he was in it. He owned a nightclub in Harlem called Sugar Ray's, and also a dry-cleaning shop, a lingerie shop and a barber shop. He drove a flamingo-pink Cadillac convertible. On his boxing tours of Europe, his entourage included his valet, his barber, who doubled as his golf pro, several members of his family and George Gainford, his trainer throughout his career.

After his boxing career ended, Robinson moved to Los Angeles, where he lived comfortably but simply with his wife, Millie. He is survived by her; a son from an earlier marriage, Ray Jr.; two stepchildren, Ramona Lewis and Butch Robinson; four grandchildren, and a sister, Evelyn Nelson of New York.

Robinson's given name was Walker Smith Jr. He was born in Detroit on May 3, 1921. He moved with his family to New York, where he grew up in Harlem. As a teenage amateur boxer representing the Salem-Crescent gym, he borrowed the Amateur Athletic Union card of another Harlem youngster named Ray Robinson. Once his Sugar Ray nickname stuck, he never used his real name.

"Sugar Ray Robinson had a nice ring to it," he once said. "Sugar Walker Smith wouldn't have been the same."

Supporters being crushed against the barrier as disaster strikes at the Hillsborough Stadium.

APRIL 17, 1989

After 93 Die, British Again Anguish Over Soccer

Steve Lohr

At the entrance to the Hillsborough soccer stadium, where at least 93 fans died and roughly 200 were injured in a crush on Saturday, a steady trickle of mourners came today, bowing their heads in silence and placing small floral tributes to the victims at the blue wrought-iron gate.

The card on one bouquet read: "Soccer lovers of the world unite. Live in peace."

For the troubled sport of British soccer,

with its international reputation for hooliganism and crowd disturbances, the wish for tranquility would seem to be a forlorn hope.

As Prime Minister Margaret Thatcher came to Sheffield today, announcing a full investigation and donating $850,000 of Government money to a relief fund for the victims, there is uncertainty about precisely what actions precipitated the tragedy and how it might have been prevented.

The incident occurred just after the start of a Football Association playoff match between Liverpool and Nottingham Forest when Liverpool fans surged forward in overcrowded stands. The victims were crushed and suffocated in the penned-in standing area, or "terraces."

One grim paradox of the disaster is that the fortified walls and high steel-frame fencing in the terraces, intended to control hooliganism, were a major reason that fans could not escape from the penned-in area and were crushed to death when the crowd surged forward.

In a sense, the overcrowding problem started well before the match. The Nottingham Forest side was allocated 6,000 more tickets than Liverpool, even though the average number of Liverpool fans at their games was more than twice the average gate for Nottingham Forest. The police say Liverpool was given fewer tickets in the interests of traffic and crowd control.

Even though all the 54,000 tickets for the playoff game at the neutral Sheffield stadium were sold in advance, large numbers of Liverpool fans apparently showed up at the game without tickets but hoped to gain entry, a Sheffield police officer said. Because fans do not have designated places in the standing-room terraces, it is possible to squeeze in extra spectators.

A situation of that type, a police officer at the stadium said, apparently got out of hand on Saturday. Peter Wright, Chief Police Constable for South Yorkshire, said that faced with a dangerous overcrowding problem outside the turnstiles, the police decided to let people go in just before the start of the match. Then, witnesses said, the crowd surged forward into the terrace area.

It is the standing-room terrace, a tradition at British soccer stadiums for more than a century, and still preferred by many fans, that is likely to get the closest scrutiny in the aftermath of the Sheffield disaster. "We will have to look at the future of terraces," Prime Minister Margaret Thatcher said. ■

MAY 22, 1989

LOPEZ BRINGS HOME THIRD L.P.G.A. TITLE

Gordon S. White Jr.

Nancy Lopez, who said she has always felt comfortable on the Grizzly Course here in Mason, Ohio, birdied five of the last eight holes today as she came from two shots back after 10 holes to win the L.P.G.A. Championship for the third time on this course. She beat Ayako Okamoto of Japan by three strokes.

Lopez, 32 years old, chipped into the cup at the 11th hole for birdie 3 and sank a 20-foot birdie putt on No. 12 to get in front. Then she stayed there and increased her lead with birdies at 14, 17 and 18 for a six-under-par 66 to defeat Okamoto, who has come close in this tournament six times but has never won a major event.

"This victory was sweet and special," Lopez said after achieving her 40th career victory, her third in a major and her first triumph in 12 months.

Lopez, the 11th and most recent member of the Ladies Professional Golf Association Hall of Fame, was described by Okamoto as "the best woman golfer under the skies" after the triumph ended a bit of recent frustration for the champion. Lopez had played in nine events on the tour this year before this event and had finished third three times and second twice.

MAY 25, 1989

How Abbott Has Changed Baseball

Dave Anderson

Almost weekly, another photographer from another magazine will descend on Jim Abbott and ask the same question: What do you do at home?

"Not much," the California Angels' rookie pitcher invariably answers. "I get up, run a couple of errands and come to the yard. I play baseball." With one hand. By now, the 21-year-old left-hander has proved to be a capable pitcher: before last night's start against the Yankees, he had a 3-3 record with a 3.56 earned-run average. And when he returned to his Flint, Mich., home he proved that he hasn't let all his headlines inflate him.

"Nothing's changed," his father said at the time. "He came in the back door and went straight to the cupboards."

Jim Abbott may not have changed, but baseball has. For the better.

In the three months since Abbott reported to spring training as a nonroster player expected to go to a Class AA farm, this 6-foot-3-inch, 200-pound athlete has received thousands of fan letters, many from youngsters also born with only one hand. One letter was from a teenage catcher with only one leg, others from people with various physical handicaps.

His teammates don't dare alibi their baseball mistakes when a rookie who in a split-second switches his glove from the stump of his right hand to his left hand can outpitch Roger Clemens, the two-time Cy Young Award winner, striking out four in four-hit, 5-0 shutout of the Boston Red Sox.

After that shutout, some of Abbott's teammates created a white carpet of towels leading to his locker. But perhaps the most emotional moment of Jim Abbott's career occurred April 24 when he was credited with his first major league victory, pitching a four-hitter through six innings in a 3-2 triumph over the Baltimore Orioles. When he got on the phone later that night with his parents, Mike and Cathy, and his 17-year-old brother, Chad, at their Flint home, he didn't shout or brag. Instead, his voice was soft, almost subdued. "I won," he said.

More than a game. ■

AUGUST 25, 1989

THE PETE ROSE CASE

Fans Are Puzzled and Dismayed

They were glad it was over, but they weren't sure exactly how it ended. They voiced strong opinions, then asked for clarifications on the ruling. They read newspapers and listened to morning radio reports, but they still couldn't figure out just what had happened to Pete Rose.

New York sports fans, knowledgeable and direct as they are, were in a state of confusion yesterday. When Rose, the manager of the Cincinnati Reds, was permanently banned from baseball yesterday morning by Commissioner A. Bartlett Giamatti, the six-month investigation into Rose's betting had reached a conclusion, but questions remained.

How could Rose be banned for life but be allowed the opportunity to apply for reinstatement after a year? How could Rose accept such a suspension and continue to deny that he ever bet on baseball?

The issue that drew the most direct responses was whether Rose, baseball's career leader in hits with 4,256, should be voted into the Hall of Fame. Those who said Rose belonged in the Hall of Fame thought that the only criteria for induction should be performance on the field. Those who said Rose didn't belong thought that Hall of Fame candidates should also be judged by their personal character and actions off the field.

"What Rose did off the field should have nothing to do with the Hall of Fame," said Anthony Rogers, a 24-year-old resident of Brooklyn. "The man got more than 4,000 hits, and no one can take that away from him. There's no question he belongs in the hall."

"His recent actions have overshadowed his playing career," said Richard Rosman, a 28-year-old resident of Manhattan. "I don't think he should ever be allowed in the Hall of Fame. He has showed disregard for the game."

Although fans expressed relief that the Rose case had been resolved before the start of the playoffs, they expressed sadness as well. Hector Delgado, a 31-year-old Manhattan street vendor who wears an Oakland Athletics cap, said he felt sorry for Rose.

"I wish I could tell him that he should have never gambled," Delgado said. "It's too bad. Look what he had done for the game. Just look at what he had done."

Quarterback Joe Montana played for the 49ers from 1979-92.

DECEMBER 17, 1989

JOE MONTANA: STATE OF THE ART

Irvin Muchnick

In the most violent of team sports, Joe Montana is the maestro of guile and finesse. Putting his body on the line, maintaining clear vision of the entire field, throwing accurately on the run and manufacturing big plays in the game's final, hyperventilating moments—these are among the qualities that make him the essential quarterback of his era.

And, arguably, of any era. According to the National Football League's complex statistical formula for quarterbacks—which considers factors such as completion percentage, yards gained per pass, touchdown passes and interceptions—he is the highest-rated player ever at that position. He is also one of the most successful. Today, as the 49ers face the Buffalo Bills in the penultimate game of the regular season, they are virtually assured of their eighth playoff appearance in 11 seasons with Montana calling the signals. During that time, they have won three of four National Football Conference championship games. In the 49ers three Super Bowl victories, Montana was twice—in 1982 and 1985—named Most Valuable Player, and in last January's contest he engineered a dramatic victory over the Cincinnati Bengals in the 49ers' final game under Coach Bill Walsh, Montana's mentor and the mastermind of their state-of-the-art offense.

That triumph not only validated San Francisco's claim to the title "Team of the Decade," but also completed a heroic personal arc for Montana, whose career was threatened in 1986 by major surgery for a ruptured disk in his back.

At the age of 33, Montana has elevated his uncanny flair for eking out last-minute victory to a level unseen since Roger Staubach stopped practicing alchemy for the Dallas Cowboys 10 years ago. It's a mysterious trait, not a function of size or speed or

The Olympic flame continues to burn during the closing ceremony of the 1988 Summer Olympics held in Seoul in South Korea.

strength. Most experts agree that Denver's John Elway can heave a football farther and harder than Montana, Miami's Dan Marino can release it more quickly and that Philadelphia's Randall Cunningham is a better runner. "But when you talk about putting it all together—throwing, faking, leadership, running the two-minute offense—there's still no one who touches Joe," says Joe Theismann, the former Washington Redskins quarterback who himself played in two Super Bowls, echoing the consensus. "He's the quarterback of the 80's."

Montana's secret, football technicians say, is a complement of quarterback-specific meta-skills involving his feet, his eyes and the catchall characteristic known as "instinct." Of course, the assessment of the experts is mostly retrospective: Montana wasn't selected until the third round of the 1979 N.F.L. draft. Though a string of glorious comeback victories for Notre Dame hinted at his potential, his college career was erratic and injury-plagued. He was never named to an all-America team. Moreover, Montana had to overcome the conventional wisdom of those days that the prototypical pro quarterback stood 6 feet 4 and featured a high release point on his throw, the better to clear the arms of tall defensive linemen. This year, Montana has enjoyed what, in many respects, is his finest season. Even as he creeps higher on the actuarial tables for his profession, he has kept his quarterback rating well over 100—at times 20 points higher than his closest competitor—and his touchdown passes-to-interceptions ratio at an astonishing five-to-one.

Amazingly, Montana is at the top of his game despite an increasingly evident fragility. He returned from the 1986 back surgery after missing only eight games, but sustained a concussion in a playoff loss two months later on a bruising tackle by Jim Burt of the Giants, ironically a 49er teammate this season. When, the next year, San Francisco was again eliminated in the opening round of the postseason tournament, and the team struggled through a shaky first two-thirds of its 1988 schedule, Montana, who was bothered by nagging injuries, actually lost his starting job to Steve Young. But this year, even though Montana has missed two full games and parts of several others, there's no doubt as to who's No. 1. ■

DECEMBER 31, 1989

THE 80'S:
An Improbable Decade in Sports

Dave Anderson

With the calendar approaching 1990, it's fashionable to assess what has happened since the calendar was turned to 1980, a decade in sports when money got bigger but not necessarily better, when "drug rehab" and "Olympic boycott" entered our vocabulary. It's also fashionable to assess "the best" of the decade. Such as the best athlete. And the obvious nominees are five whose success spanned the decade: Joe Montana, Wayne Gretzky, Earvin (Magic) Johnson, Larry Bird, Martina Navratilova. All winners, all artistes on their personal stages.

When the calendar turned into 1980, surely nobody expected that:

The United States Olympic hockey team would win the gold medal at Lake Placid by upsetting the Soviets.

Bo Jackson would hit 32 homers as an outfielder for the Kansas City Royals and rush for 950 yards as a running back for the Los Angeles Raiders—in the same year.

Two fillies, Genuine Risk in 1980 and Winning Colors in 1988, would win the Kentucky Derby.

The Mets would win the 1986 World Series after a three-run 10th-inning rally in the sixth game, which ended with Mookie Wilson's gentle grounder bouncing between the legs of Bill Buckner, the Red Sox first baseman.

Columbia would lose 44 consecutive football games.

The Giants would win Super Bowl XXI with Phil Simms completing 22 of 25 passes.

Jack Nicklaus would win the Masters at age 46.

Many sports fans would be wondering about the outcome of yachting's America's Cup and golf's Ryder Cup.

The Edmonton Oilers would trade Wayne Gretzky.

Muhammad Ali, once the liveliest mouth in sports, would be mumbling his words because of an illness diagnosed as Parkinson's syndrome.

(cont'd. next page)

(continued from previous page)

Ali's eventual successor as heavyweight champion, Mike Tyson, would find his toughest opponent to be an actress who's now his former wife.

Bill Shoemaker would ride a Kentucky Derby winner at age 54.

The Raiders would move from Oakland to Los Angeles (and would consider returning to Oakland), and the Colts would move from Baltimore to Indianapolis.

The Yankees would not win another World Series.

The most popular competitor at the 1988 Winter Olympics in Calgary would be a ski-jumper whose nickname was more impressive than his skill, Eddie the Eagle.

Dan Marino would throw for 48 touchdowns in one season.

The Baltimore Orioles would open the 1988 season with 21 consecutive losses and duel the Toronto Blue Jays for the American League East title to the final weekend the next season.

Michael Jordan would play basketball in midair.

The National Hockey League would postpone a Stanley Cup playoff game because the Boston Garden lights went out.

Southern Methodist would be prohibited from playing football.

Roberto Duran would outpunch Sugar Ray Leonard in Montreal, walk away muttering "no mas" in their New Orleans rematch, and nine years later in their Las Vegas rubber match walk away with more than $7 million while muttering to himself.

The World Series would be interrupted by an earthquake.

Orel Hershiser would pitch 59 consecutive scoreless innings.

Greg Louganis would win an Olympic gold medal at Seoul even though he bloodied his head on the diving board.

The Knicks would win Patrick Ewing in a lottery.

Pine tar on George Brett's bat would create an uproar that had a Royals-Yankees game being completed a month later.

The Islanders would win four consecutive Stanley Cups.

A 17-year-old, Boris Becker, would win Wimbledon.

U.C.L.A. would not win a college basketball title.

Another new pro football venture, the United States Football League, would schedule its games in the spring, file an antitrust suit against the N.F.L., hear the N.F.L. ruled a monopoly, and be awarded $3 in trebled damages.

Eric Heiden would win five speed-skating gold medals at Lake Placid.

The Mets would discover a pitcher, Dwight Gooden, who would produce a 24-4 record and a 1.53 earned-run average at age 20.

Edwin Moses would win 122 consecutive races in the 400-meter hurdles.

The Chicago Bears would win Super Bowl XX with a "Refrigerator" on defense and occasionally at fullback.

And a kid born without a right hand would establish himself as a starting pitcher in the big leagues. ■

Index

Illustrations are in **BOLD**